Island Adventures

Island Adventures

The Hawaiian Mission of Francis A. Hammond 1851–1865

John J. Hammond

Signature Books | Salt Lake City | 2016

To my wife Pamela and my daughter
Jennifer and sons Mark and Greg

 Island Adventures was printed on acid-free paper. It was composed, printed, and bound in the United States of America.

For more information, consult www.signaturebooks.com.
Interior design by Jason Francis, including maps.
Jacket design by Ron Stucki.

20 19 18 17 16 5 4 3 2 1

LIBRARY OF CONGRESS CATALOGING-IN-PUBLICATION DATA

Names: Hammond, John J., author.

Title: Island adventures : the Hawaiian mission of Francis A. Hammond, 1851-1865 / John J. Hammond.

Description: Salt Lake City : Signature Books, 2016. | Includes bibliographical references and index.

Identifiers: LCCN 2016003641 | ISBN 9781560852421

Subjects: LCSH: Hammond, Francis Asbury, 1822–1900. | Mormon missionaries—Hawaii—Biography. | Church of Jesus Christ of Latter-day Saints. Hawaii Mission—Biography. | Mormons—Hawaii—History—19th century.

Classification: LCC BX8695.H27 H36 2016 | DDC 266/.93092—dc23 LC record available at http://lccn.loc.gov/2016003641

Contents

preface ix

1 Whaling 1
2 Conversion 18
3 The Hawaiians 31
4 The Protestant Missionaries 40
5 The Gold Missionaries 47
6 Penniless 68
7 Almost Hell 77
8 Translating Books 87
9 Trouble in Paradise 98
10 The Shoemaker Priest 109
11 New Brethren 123
12 Dramatic Success on O'ahu 134
13 Smallpox 141
14 Violating the Quarantine 150
15 Rationalizing Death 157
16 The Gathering 167
17 The Haleakala Excursion 175
18 Removing from Babylon 184
19 President Lewis becomes a Tinsmith 197
20 Pressuring the Moloka'i Mormons 206

maps 213

21 Death's Door 219
22 Preaching at the Hospital 231
23 Bidding Farewell 240
24 The Ship Fiasco 254
25 Moses to This People. 263

26 Getting Oxen to Lana'i 271
27 Nine New Elders 280
28 Jurisdiction over "Zion Two" 289
29 Problematic Authority 298
30 Mad Dash for Home 305
31 Keeler Left Behind Again 315
32 A Star-Crossed Sloop 327
33 Hammond Takes Charge 336
34 The Faltering Lana'i Experiment 346
35 The 1855 Conference 352
36 Struggling to Get Fitted Out 360
37 Sailing the *Lanai* 369
38 Apostasy at San Bernardino 383
39 Return to Utah .396
40 Closing the Mission 405
41 The Walter Murray Gibson Fiasco 415
42 A Triumphant Return 427
43 The Laie Plantation 433
44 An All-Night Struggle 445
45 Missionaries and Families Arrive 457

afterword 467
bibliography 476
index 490

"I now pray God my Heavenly Father to preserve this book yea even that my children's children down to the latest generation may have the privelege of reading this my history ... I dedicate this Book unto thee, praying thee, O Lord, to preserve it that it be not distroyed by accident or design, that my children's children even down to the latest generation may have the privilege of reading the history of their Father. Grant O Lord that I may never have to record one single unrighteous act against myself, but that I may have thy Holy Spirit to be and abide with me continualy to preserve me from the snares of Satan."

—Francis A. Hammond Journal,
Honolulu, July 27, 1854

Preface

It is hard to imagine today what a shock it was for New England sailors and missionaries to see the Sandwich Islands (Hawaii) for the first time: the flora and fauna was different, the food unrecognizable, the customs and language incomprehensible. For Mormon missionaries like my ancestor Francis (Frank) A. Hammond (1822-1900), who was among the first Latter-day Saints to visit the islands, it was an extreme exercise in faith. They had little funds; there was no support system in case they were without food or lodging; the mission existed in name only and had no assets. For the first wave of ten missionaries who arrived about eight months before Hammond, there were not even any prior converts. Consequently, many of the missionaries could not cope and soon left the islands.

The more I learned about my ancestor, the more impressed I was that he was able to survive and thrive while many others were giving up and going home. Who was this individual, and what motivated him? I learned that as a former whaler—who had lived on Maui for three years during the 1840s before he became a Mormon himself—had a set of experiences and talents that other missionaries lacked. This, however, was a mixed blessing because the same attributes that gave him strength ensured that he would be seen as an outsider among the LDS missionaries, having converted and lived in Utah for only about two years.

Although this is a study of one individual (Frank), including his interactions with his missionary wife Mary Jane Dilworth Hammond (1831-1877), the native converts, fellow missionaries, and non-Mormons on Maui, the information is significant, not only as a case study in human nature, but as a valuable account of the first fifteen years of the Hawaiian mission, drawn from the journals and other records of about a dozen individuals, one of them a non-Mormon Protestant opponent. It vividly shows the clash of cultures, unexpected turns of events, moments of spiritual ecstasy, extremely bad behavior, divided loyalties, pettiness, grandiosity, stubbornness, selflessness, backwardness, enlightenment, and everything else that went into establishing a Mormon foothold in Hawaii. It sheds a welcome light on a time and place we otherwise struggle to comprehend.

In his recent insightful analysis of ancient Greece, Thomas Cahill emphasized the unique character of each civilization and age, which is as true of our own as it is of those buried in the dim recesses of time. "Like fish who do not know they swim in water, we are seldom aware of the times through which we move, how strange and singular they are. But when we approach another age, its alienness stands out for us, almost as if that were its most obvious quality; and the sense of being on alien ground grows with the antiquity of the age we are considering."[1] This was the view of French historian Fustel de Coulanges in his classic 1864 study of religion in the ancient world, as he attempted "to see in a clear light the radical and essential differences which at all times distinguished these ancient peoples from modern societies." Their vast heritage to western civilization makes it difficult to consider them as foreign nations and "leads us to believe we resemble them," so that "it is almost always ourselves that we see in them. Hence spring many errors ... To understand the truth about the Greeks and Romans, it is wise to study them without thinking of ourselves, as if they were entirely foreign to us."[2]

Of course the worldview of Frank Hammond is not as distant from our perspective as the belief systems of the ancient western world, but the Polynesian world of the mid-nineteenth century was even more remote from our modern existence, and in many respects Hammond's early Mormon worldview was equally alien—radically

1. Cahill, *Sailing the Wine Dark Sea*, 5.

2. Fustel de Coulanges, *Ancient City*, 11-12.

different not only from current American attitudes but also from the perspective of contemporary Latter-day Saints. Nineteenth-century Mormonism—with its belief in polygamy, the doctrine of Blood Atonement, the imminence of an apocalyptic millennium, glossolalia (speaking in tongues), faith-healing, frequent rebaptisms for health purposes, and a host of other characteristics—is far removed indeed from mainstream twenty-first-century LDS Church members' expectations. "The Mormonism now so successful in Hawaii and the Tuamotu," Furnas wryly noted in 1948, "is hardly anything that [Mormon apostle] Parley P. Pratt would recognize."[3]

There is no better way to understand this radical difference than to immerse oneself in the writings of committed mid-nineteenth-century Mormons who wanted to come to terms with the very different Polynesian society, an exercise that allows us to see both these worlds through their eyes. As Cahill puts it, "the historian's task should be to raise the dead to life." By looking carefully at journals, letters, and other pieces of the historical puzzle, we can "begin to see and hear and love what living men and women once saw and heard and loved, till from these scraps and fragments living men and women begin to emerge and move and live again."[4] And when one is a direct descendant of those brought back to life in this fashion, the exercise becomes even more compelling.[5]

The late Arrell Morgan Gibson characterized the Pacific Basin as "America's Last Frontier,"[6] and in truth the American whalers, traders, and Christian missionaries who fundamentally changed life in the Sandwich Islands were continuing, beyond the west coast, the "westward movement" of expansionist, Manifest Destiny, America. An important part of that movement was the attempt to Christianize the so-called heathen peoples on the part of, for instance, the Protestant American Board of Commissioners for Foreign Missions

3. Furnas, *Anatomy of Paradise*, 279.

4. Cahill, *Sailing the Wine Dark Sea*, 7-8.

5. F. A. Hammond Sr. was my great-great-grandfather, and his second son, Samuel Smith Hammond Sr.—born at Lahaina, Maui, in April 1853—was my great-grandfather.

6. Gibson, *Yankees in Paradise*. Gibson identified several areas of American frontier ambition: maritime and whaling, mining, missionary, agrarian, and military.

(ABCFM), which sent Hiram and Sybil Bingham to Hawaii in 1820 and then sponsored Marcus and Narcissa Whitman to the Nez Pierce Indians in Idaho and Oregon fifteen years later.[7] The Mormons who arrived in Hawaii in late 1850, fresh from the goldfields of northern California and Great Salt Lake City, were a part of that national westward movement into the Pacific, just as they had been prominent in the American expansion into the Rocky Mountains.

Frank Hammond was a colorful and important figure in the western saga, especially the part that has to do with the Sandwich Islands and the Later-day Saint/Mormon Church.[8] During two extended periods of his life, he kept a daily journal. Eight books cover the years 1852-57 and a ninth the years 1864-66, during which he served two missions to the Sandwich Islands. Thirty-four books cover the years 1883-1900 when he presided over the LDS San Juan Stake (diocese), with branches and wards throughout southeastern Utah, southwestern Colorado, and northwestern New Mexico—the Four Corners Area.[9]

Called with him to serve as a missionary in Hawaii during the 1850s was his first wife, Mary Jane.[10] She kept a journal for about two years during their mission, from the spring of 1853 to the spring of 1855 (between the births of her second and third sons), and it provides the rare opportunity to hear a woman's view from that patriarchal age.[11] Frank was a prolific letter writer as well, and many other

7. Ibid., ix-x.

8. There is no comprehensive and detailed biography of F. A. Hammond. The best single work is Nathan W. Adamson Jr's relatively brief and privately published *Francis Asbury Hammond: Pioneer and Missionary*.

9. The nine Hawaiian Mission journals are in the archives of the LDS Church History Library in Salt Lake City and are labeled 1-9. Hammond wrote in journal 38 on October 5, 1898: "Took my Journals to [the LDS] historians Office for reference concerning Sandwich Islands Mission." Eleven of the San Juan Stake Journals, all from the period 1883-93, are also in the LDS archives, but the remaining twenty-three are at the BYU library in Provo. Between 2003 and 2007 I completed the first and only typescript of all forty-three journals, then donated the typescripts of the first nine (Hawaiian Mission journals) to a number of library archives. Eventually I will place the remaining thirty-four in public repositories as well.

10. My great-great-grandmother.

11. The original is in the BYU library in Provo.

individuals whose lives intersected with his kept journals and wrote letters. Many of the journals and letters have survived, bequeathing us a virtual treasure trove of historical documents covering this early period of the Mormon Hawaiian Mission.

Frank made his first journal entry we know about on February 4, 1852, but actually this was his second rather than first missionary journal. He and Mary Jane left Great Salt Lake City on March 15, 1851, and arrived at Lahaina, Maui, on August 20, and apparently Frank began keeping a journal either when he left Salt Lake City or when he arrived on Maui. Unfortunately, that journal is not extant. The third, fourth, and fifth journals in this series begin with the words (in his handwriting) "Book 4th," "Book 5th," and "Book 6th," respectively, confirming that the earliest surviving book is the second in the series and a "Book 1st" has been lost. If entries in the missing first book began when the Hammonds left Salt Lake City, it covered approximately the first eleven months of their mission; if these entries began when they arrived on Maui, it covered approximately six months.

Frank made daily journal entries as regularly as clockwork, many of them lengthy. In addition to documenting routine events, he wrote about his beliefs, feelings, dreams, hopes, and frustrations, both about other missionaries and regarding his dealings with many non-Mormons. Using his journal as the central focus of this story, and supplementing it with selections from his and others' letters and diaries, I found it possible to compose an interesting narrative of his life as he saw it, tempered by how others saw it.

As for the Hawaiian mission itself, after initial breath-taking successes between 1851 and 1854, a period of decline set in, culminating in 1858 when the church called all its missionaries home to Utah, with no assurance they would ever return to Hawaii. Few contemporary Mormons know about this decline and mission closure, as church leaders and historians have tended to focus on the early successes, gloss over the decline and closure, and blame the Hawaiian Mormons, the Hawaiian people generally, and the adventurer Walter Murray Gibson, for the reduced state of Mormonism in Hawaii by 1864, when the mission was re-opened under Frank Hammond's direction.

One of the most important missionaries during the first three and one half years of the mission was the young George Q. Cannon, whom Frank describes as unusually competent in the language and impressive as a speaker. He later became an apostle and a counselor in the church presidency. After years of denying access to the three Cannon Hawaiian Mission journals, the LDS Church published them in 2014, along with the following caveat by editor Richard W. Turley Jr.

> Preparing the journals of Church leaders for publication poses serious ethical challenges. The work of these leaders, by its very nature, involves them in many matters that are sacred, private, or confidential. Matters of great sacredness deserve reverence. Divulging some kinds of information may violate principles of privacy. And persons who confess to religious leaders or communicate other information in a confidential setting expect that leaders will maintain their confidences.
>
> In publishing George Q. Cannon's journals, we in the Church History Department seek to honor these principles while also making as much information as possible available to the public and clearly indicating any omissions with ellipses or notes.[12]

In other words, the published version of Cannon's diaries was expurgated to remove portions that were the most controversial. On one hand, one could say this is a fair compromise. In fact, those of us who had hoped for access to the diaries over the years were pleased to see anything at all. On the other hand, I disagree that documents created 150 years ago require that kind of scrutiny and censorship. As this book was being prepared, the Church History Library posted scans of Frank Hammond's diaries on its website, again with redactions for portions that someone deemed to be too sensitive but which I would argue are essential to understanding the history of the Hawaiian mission. Since I prepared my typescript prior to the recent scanning and redacting, readers of this book may find some benefit from that added information.

For the sake of space, I have dispensed with footnote citations

---

12. Orton, *Journals of George Q. Cannon*. Part of a series, the general editors are Adrian W. Cannon and Richard E. Turley Jr.

to Hammond's journals except in the case of extended quotations. Since I have relied heavily on the journals, the repetition of that source would be distracting. Everything else is sourced, so short quotations and information not explicitly documented can be assumed to come from Frank's journals. Where I occasionally cite the Journal History, it is the daily scrapbook of Mormon history compiled by the Church Historian's Office. Readers may consult the bibliography at the end of this volume for that and other sources which are referenced in abbreviated form at the bottom of each page throughout the book. In quotations from journals and other manuscript sources, I have kept the original spelling and wording as much as possible. For Hawaiian words, I have included the diacritical mark in the names of islands (Hawai'i) but not in the name of the state (Hawaii), towns, people, food, clothing, or other native words.

By the time I completed my typescript of Hammond's nine Hawaiian mission journals, it ran to more than 1,200 pages, so of course this work had to omit a wealth of interesting material. Readers can peruse the entire typescript, if they wish, at the repositories where I have donated it: the libraries of Brigham Young University in Laie and Provo, the LDS Church History Library in Salt Lake City, the Maui Historical Society in Wailuku (Maui), the Marriott Library at the University of Utah, and the Utah State Historical Society Library.

Many thanks to my wife for putting up with all those hours (really years) in my basement study working on this project, and for her suggestions, based on her expertise as a writer. Thanks also to Ronald Watt, who was the first person I encountered on my initial visit to the LDS archives. Though he is now retired, he was a professional colleague at Southern Utah State College for the year 1966–67. I am indebted to archivist and historian David Whittaker, also now retired, who at the time was a professor of history and director of Special Collections at BYU's Harold B. Lee Library in Provo. He had the library workers copy for me all the materials in the F. A. Hammond Collection and the handwritten journals of other 1850s Hawaiian missionaries. Archivists at the University of Utah Marriott Library were equally helpful, as was the staff of the Utah State

Historical Society. And I owe much to the friendly people at the Maui Historical Society in Wailuku, who made me aware of the letters and mission reports of the Reverend Dwight Baldwin, who was Frank Hammond's nemesis in Lahaina.

There are two individuals whose help was so indispensable, I need to mention them by name: the historian Will Bagley, who first suggested I publish a book on my ancestor's journal and edited an earlier version of it. And then there is my good friend Michael Marquardt, who when I met him on my first visit to the LDS Church History Library introduced me to Will Bagley and the sophisticated field of Mormon studies. He has on numerous occasions provided me with crucial information from his extensive personal research, for which I am grateful, especially since I live in Ohio, far away from the Utah archives. And lastly, I appreciate the people at Signature Books for believing in this work, and in particular the editorial work of Ron Priddis and Devery Anderson, and Jason Francis for his help with the photographs and map design.

CHAPTER 1

Whaling

Before the season was near over, we came in contact with a "Tiphoon," a dreadful storm of wind, that came from the Japanese Islands or coast; by this storm we were driven off the whaling ground and came near loosing our ship. During the gale, fore part of it, I was employed in stowing down oil in the lower hole [hold] when a barrell of flour, from between decks, fetched away and struck me in the small of the back, which nearly killed me instantly.

—*Frank Hammond to David Edwards, June 14, 1889*

On the first day of November 1822, Francis Asbury Hammond was born on the south shore of Long Island in Patchogue, now part of Brookhaven, in the same general vicinity where his great-great-grandfather, the Reverend Noah Hammond, had presided over a Baptist church in the 1740s.[1] Frank's father, Samuel (1790–1875), was a shoe and harness maker, as was his son in due time, and active in the local Methodist Episcopal Church as a class leader, steward, and trustee. He named his son after Bishop Francis Asbury (1745–1816) of the American Methodist Church, who had great influence over frontier America by setting up circuit riders to reach people in rural areas.[2]

What was unconventional about Hammond's parents, Frank noted, was that his father was more outwardly religious than his

---

1. The Baptist church was in Coram, now also a neighborhood in Brookhaven. For more information, see my *Family and Mormon Church Roots*, 163–92, the first of several volumes in a series titled *Quest for the New Jerusalem: A Mormon Generational Saga*.

2. Frank's younger brother, John Fletcher Hammond (1830–1850), was named after another Methodist bishop. See Hammond journal, Mar. 23, 1890, Lee Library.

mother, Charity (1792–1867), who "never made an open profession of releigon, but [was] a moddle mother and a faithful wife" and "taught her children to pray, and to be honest, temporate, virtuous and chaste in all things." She was nevertheless "a very industrious woman of excellent capacity for business, a good manager in all her household duties."[3]

Around 1837 when the fifteen-year-old Frank was "overcome" by "a desire to see the world," he ran away from his apprenticeship as a shoemaker about thirty miles from home and landed in New York City. This resulted in "suffering much at times with hunger [and] often times weeping and regretting I had left my home and friends" even though he found work off and on along the waterfront. He left New York for Boston and tried working in the "groceries and provisions business," but eventually the prodigal returned home, where he was received "kindly" by his parents. For the next two summers he worked as a cabin boy on ships moving goods up and down the coast, and during the winter months attended school and worked in his father's shop.[4]

In early 1840 the tall and fit seventeen-year-old Hammond[5] shipped out of the port of New London, Connecticut, as an "able seaman" on the whaleship barque[6] *White Oak,* accompanied by the smaller brig *Summerset,* to the South Atlantic in search of whales and seals between the Falkland Islands and Argentina. Most ships out of New London at the time were noted for their strict temperance onboard, although despite the added safety and appearance of sobriety among the crew, the men had a propensity to binge-drink when they docked at ports of call.[7]

---

3. Hammond to David Edwards, June 14, 1889. Edwards was Frank's first cousin and lived on Long Island.

4. Ibid.

5. He would grow to be two inches over six feet and was said to have broad shoulders, and whaleship captains wanted large powerful men.

6. A barque was one of the largest ships of the day, with two or three square-rigged masts (sails aligned perpendicular to the ship) and a latin-rigged foremast (sails aligned parallel to the ship).

7. Francis Allyn Olmsted wrote that "out of the thirty or forty whaling vessels belonging to the port of New London" at the time, "almost all are navigated upon

The *White Oak's* Captain Daniel Fitch and *Summerset's* Captain William Beck were "cruel to the men[,] treating them at times in such a manner that they broke out into open mutiny."[8] Strange but true, on one occasion the chief mate and steward stole whatever was not tied down (chronometer, small arms, munitions, and spices) and tried to escape in a longboat "on the Spanish coast." When they were captured and returned in chains, Hammond was given a promotion in rank from "able seaman" to "steward" and put in charge of them.[9] When they landed in Rio de Janeiro, he and two other guards took the mutineers to the US consulate, and from there to Richmond, Virginia, on the US Navy sloop (one mast) *Decatur*. Hammond and the other guards ended up being questioned in court, where they must have expressed some sympathy for the prisoners because the wayward sailors were acquitted in May 1842. Hammond returned to New London to collect his "lay" of $150, a percentage of the ship's profits, which he called "a genuine swindle on the part of the captains."[10]

After spending about a year back home nn Long Island, the now veteran whaler, still only twenty years old, shipped out of Sag Harbor on the *Thames* on July 7, 1843.[11] Waving goodbye to his family, he was unaware—indeed, he could not even fathom—that twenty-six years would pass before he would see his loved ones again. He was the ship's boatswain (pronounced *bose-un*), in charge of the deck crew, ropes, and rigging (sails). He received a higher percentage of the profits and would have commanded one of the whaleboats, the smaller

temperance principles" (Olmsted, *Incidents of a Whaling Voyage*, ix–xiii, 12–13). However, the Reverend Daniel Wheeler of the London Missionary Society added that the crews were "lamentably, in many instances, notorious for drinking to excess" when on land (qtd. in Dodge, *Islands and Empires*, 74–75; see also Furnas, *Anatomy of Paradise*, 144n36).

8. Hammond to Edwards, June 14, 1889. The two captains are identified further in *United States Commission of Fish and Fisheries*, 378.

9. Jenson, *Biographical Encyclopedia*, 1:351; Hammond to Edwards, June 14, 1889.

10. Hammond to Edwards, June 14, 1889.

11. This was the second ship of the same name docked at Sag Harbor. The original, built in 1818, was condemned and scuttled in 1838, and the new *Thames* sailed the next year. See "Thames Keel and Shipbuilding," *Mystic Seaport;* "Voyages of Thames II (Ship)," *National Maritime Museum*.

vessels that had oars and one or two short sails and were latched onto the side of the ship. It was in the boats that the crew, wielding harpoons and lances, chased whales when they were located and hauled them back to the ship.[12]

In 2010 the Sag Harbor Whaling Museum furnished me with a typescript of the diary they have in their possession from another *Thames* crewman, the twenty-four-year-old cooper (barrel maker) George G. Smith. Since Hammond was not yet keeping a journal and wrote his recollections long afterward, Smith's journal provides useful additional information about the crew's experiences in 1843–44.[13] The young man's first journal entry on July 7, 1843, recorded how they "left our native home for A Long Voyage with heavy hearts. At 10 O clock weighed Anchor from Gardiners Bay," he wrote, and at 2:30 p.m. they passed Montauk Point. By 5:00 "our native land was out of sight," and he asked "kind Providence [to] protect us in all our wanderings." Two days later he mournfully thought of "those we Left behind us. Never felt so bad in all the days of my life. Homesick in every sence of the word and wished myself back again." He had married about six months before the voyage, so he had even more reason to be melancholy than the younger Frank, who himself would have been depressed had he known that by the time he returned home his mother had died.

About three months after the *Thames* departed, four Mormon men—Benjamin F. Grouard, Knowlton Hanks, Addison Pratt, and Noah Rogers—sailed for the Society Islands (French Polynesia) from New Bedford, Massachusetts, and followed the same initial route across the Atlantic Ocean and around Africa. It was the first Latter-day Saint mission to Polynesia, reported on a year later in a Mormon newspaper published in Nauvoo, Illinois, that drew from Rogers's journal:

> By counsel of Br[igham] Young, Br. [Addison] Pratt went to N[ew] Bedford, to procure a passage, which he did for $100 each, in the ship

12. Creighton, *Rites and Passages*, 29–30.
13. The details in this chapter, unless otherwise noted, come from Smith's diary.

> *Timoleon*, Capt. Plasket. The brethren in Salem and Boston contributed liberally, as did also the brethren in New Bedford, particularly Br. [Philip B.] Lewis, who with a liberality becoming a saint, gave us $300. After paying our passage we had 80 dollars left for contingent expenses ... on the 9th October, we embarked for the Pacific Ocean ... Br Hanks was quite feeble when we embarked ... [and] continued to fail until the 3d of November, when he departed this life without a struggle ... The Captain and officers were not willing to keep the body until we could make the Cape Verde Islands [off West Africa], consequently we were obliged to bury our brother in the deep blue sea.[14]

Perhaps because of his generosity in donating to the Polynesian mission, Philip Lewis would be appointed in 1851 as president of the Sandwich Islands Mission, or Hawaii. Rogers, Grouard, and Pratt reached Tahiti in the spring but had trouble with the French colonial government and continued on to other islands, where they met with success.

The *Thames*, unlike the *Timoleon*, stopped on July 28 in the Azores so Captain Jeremiah Hedges could go "on shore to engage our vegetables," and as the ship shuttled "back and forth between the islands of Pico and Fayoll," they invited the crew of the whaleship *Anne* to "a gam," a social event involving two or more whale ships. It was more than a month before they actually saw a sperm whale, and then they encountered some "hard luck" when after striking it, the whale escaped with the "lines [and] irons [harpoons] of two boats." On October 4 they spotted a "right whale" and "lowered [the boats] and chased but without success." Right whales were filter-feeding whales which, as one source explained, were so called because they were

> "the right whales" to hunt, because they float[ed] when killed and because they yield[ed] enormous quantities of oil and of baleen, or whalebone, the substance forming the fringed, triangular plates that hang from the roof of the whale's mouth and serve as a filter for plankton. It commanded such a high price in the 19th cent[ury for corset stays] that baleen whales ... were nearly exterminated by hunting.[15]

---

14. *Times and Seasons*, Jan. 1, 1845, 1085–87.
15. *Columbia Encyclopedia*, 2325.

Hammond explained in his reminiscences that they "rounded the Cape of Good Hope ... [and] took in water at the Cape and sent Capt. Hedges home sick, when Chief mate [James] Bishop became our captain."[16] Smith said the American consul was the one who placed Bishop in command and that when they pulled anchor at Cape Town "and stood out to sea," they left "Jeremiah B. Corey behind as he could not be found on shore."

They soon harpooned a sperm whale in the Indian Ocean, Hammond remembered.[17] Although his memory was true, the men took in some right whales before their first sperm whale. Along the way, around the southern coast of Australia, Tasmania, and New Zealand, then up to the north Pacific, they competed with other New England whaleships that were following the same course. The New Zealand region was a particularly popular whaling ground.

On November 9, Smith wrote that he "saw 15 or 16 Right whales[,] lowered the boats and chased several times[,] [and] at sun down fastened to and killed one. Took him along side [at] 10 P.M." and cut the whale into 18-inch-wide slabs of blubber the next day, boiling or "rendering" it in huge iron pots. As the cooper, Smith's task was to maintain the casks that held the whale oil.[18] On November 13, Smith was "engaged in stowing down" forty-five barrels of oil of the ship's first whale. The next day they "cleaned the head of Bone," meaning they harvested the baleen, and saw another whale, at which they "lowered our boats[,] fastened and killed him[,] took [him] along side[,] and cut him in." The following morning at daylight they "commenced boiling out our whale" but were disappointed because it "prove[d] to be a very poor one" in oil quantity.

As Hammond claimed in a recollection, they saw sperm whales occasionally. At 6:00 on the morning of November 29, Smith reported that they saw several of them and "lowered our boats[,] fastened to one[,] and killed him," although in doing so the second mate's boat capsized. Fortunately the crew was rescued. They brought

16. Hammond, "Life Sketch."

17. Hammond to Edwards, June 24, 1889.

18. Creighton, *Rites & Passages*, 29.

the whale alongside the ship and worked on it until 9:00 that night, but regrettably they had to "let his head go. Could not save it," Smith wrote. This would have been especially disappointing because the head contained material ("spermaceti") for making superior candles and unguents and ivory teeth for scrimshawed items. In fact, nothing was wasted; they even saved highly profitable undigested fecal matter ("ambergris"), used as a spice to flavor Near Eastern wine and as an aphrodisiac in China.

Early on December 1, they had no sooner finished boiling the blubber than they saw two more right whales. Taking one "along side," the weather proved "too rough to cut him," so they waited a day until heavy gales convinced them to cut the animal loose. At the far southern latitudes between forty and forty-four degrees, the weather was predictably stormy and cold, even in the summer.

Smith noted wistfully on December 11 that it was his first wedding anniversary. Hammond later reported that he left a childhood sweetheart at home but they had not yet married. Traveling now in company with the whaleship *Washington* from Sag Harbor, both ships took right whales on December 19. Starting the boiling process at 8:00 the next morning, the crew of the *Thames* killed another whale two hours later and brought it alongside. Rough weather prevented them from cutting up the second whale and bringing the blubber on board, so they had to be content with taking enough for twenty barrels of oil before letting the remainder of the carcass go. Smith estimated that they lost 160 pounds of oil that day to the weather.

On Christmas Eve, Smith stowed ninety-five barrels in the hold. Whether they did anything to celebrate the holiday, he did not say. Three days later they were "engaged in cleaning bone," or baleen, when "Elijah Simons had the misfortune to get 3 of his finger[s] cut almost off." Between the pitching ship and oily deck, injuries were common among knife-wielding men cutting blubber into manageable slices.

The ship moved down to latitude 47.25 on New Year's Day to pass below Tasmania, and when they were at 156.30 east longitude, off the east side of Australia, they ate a dinner of mincemeat pie and plum duff (fruit cake), which was a pleasure for the crew, whose diet was typically poor. As the *Thames* sailed farther south, it constantly gamed with other ships, all the while competing for the same prizes. The crew harpooned a whale on January 5 and lost it. Two days later, they found compensation in a whale that was so large it took two weeks to cut and boil. The "renderings" of blubber continued into the evenings, as the ghostly fires and lamps illuminated men covered with blood, black soot, and whale oil. Some of them experienced nightmares.[19]

The next stop on their long voyage was the Pitcairn group of islands. They arrived there on January 27 in company with the "Ship Genl Williams." As Hammond explained, the islands had been "settled by mutineers of the Ship Bounty in 1791" and had since grown to "some 360 decendents ... by marriage with females from Tahite." They had become an "industrious, temporate, virtuous people, and [were] finely formed," he thought.[20] Smith recorded that the islands came into view when they were thirty-five miles away on February 13. This was the first land they had seen since leaving Cape Town. "Captain [Bishop] went ashore and engaged [the locals for] some sweet Potatoes. Got off two boatloads of them ... and on the remainder of the day ... had some of the male islanders on board of us. Population 116 nearly all of them Protestant christians." This was one of the whalers' favorite stops, so it is not surprising that the *Thames* had company. The next morning the New Bedford ship *Isaac Howland* arrived, and after that the *Cherokee*. The captain of the *Thames* was on shore procuring "cocoanuts [and] melong [melon]."

After eight more days at sea, Smith saw the *Cherokee* again as they neared the Marquesas Islands, and then there followed a day that seemed like it was right out of Herman Melville's *Moby Dick*. Smith wrote that "at 8 AM [we] saw a Large number of Sperm Whales[,] chased them a long while[, and] at last fastened to two of them. One took the line[,] the Other upset the boat[,] so [we] lost him [and the] Line[,] and in all lost 2 lines 4 irons and 2 lances [spears]. Very

19. See, e.g., Creighton, *Rites and Passages*,

20. Hammond to Edwards, June 14, 1889.

hard luck [but] all got on board safe, myself lost a wool hat and handkerchief."

Melville's biographer Laurie Robertson-Lorant explained that whaleships were "built for toughness and utility, not speed," and that "when the crew was out hunting whales from longboats, the ship could be handled by a skeleton crew comprising the cooper, the cook, and the cabin boy, the only three men who did not join the chase."[21] It appears, however, that on the *Thames* the cooper joined in because he mentioned on two different occasions being on a boat that capsized. The captain and his officers ("mates") each took charge of a boat. As a bos'n/boatsteerer, Hammond would have been responsible for one of the boats and would have handled the rudder.

After the *Thames* crossed the equator on March 5–6, it was only another two weeks to the Sandwich Islands, which they reached on March 19.[22] "At 6 P M [Smith] saw the island of Mowee [Maui] Right ahead distant 35 miles." They anchored at Lahaina the next day, along with thirty-three other whaleships, most of them from America. The crew typically went ashore in the boats and returned each night to their ships. While anchored beyond the docks, the wharf being too limited to accommodate the huge traffic, the big ships were supplied by flat-bottomed scows or lighters from the town. Unknown to Hammond, this port would become his residence for about eight years in the 1840s and 1850s; but for now, he joined the rest of the crew in taking a few days off and enjoying the feasting and lounging on shore. "We found the natives very kind and hospitable," Hammond wrote, "a generous hearted race, many of them had been converted, nom[i]n[al]ly at least, from heathenism to a belief in christianity, through the labors of American pro[te]stant Missionaries."[23]

After loading the ship with fresh water, vegetables, and even live

21. *Melville: A Biography*, 94.

22. Hammond later claimed that when they reached the Sandwich Islands they stopped first at the "Big Island," or Hawai'i, at the place on the east coast where Captain Cook was killed. From there they went to Lahaina to "recruit" the ship. If Smith's diary is correct, Hammond's recollections are in error. Smith does not mention stopping at Hawai'i in the spring of 1844. See Hammond to Edwards, June 14, 1889.

23. Hammond to Edwards, June 14, 1889.

goats, at midnight on April 3 they "took [up] our anchors [and] set sail," heading "out to sea in company with the Huron of Sag Harbour and 3 other ships." The *Thames* was headed for the Kamchatka Peninsula off the Siberian coast northeast of Japan. Smith noted that on May 3, while unsuccessfully chasing whales, the ship's dog "got his leg broke. [We] killed him and threw him overboard," he wrote. They chased some right whales, but the animals were "to[o] cunning for us." They killed one on May 8 but it sank before they could take it in. A week later they were successful; it took them four days to process 100 barrels of oil from the kill.

After catching and boiling another whale, the crew went aboard the *Peruvian* on June 8 and heard, for the first time, rumors that their former captain Jeremiah Hedges had died. It proved to be as untrue as it was persistent.[24] On about June 11, the ship arrived at the southern tip of the Russian peninsula and chased whales that were so "wild [they] could not get hold" of them. On the morning of June 14 they followed several more whales, put out their boats, and soon had "both quarter boats fastened to a whale apiece." Unfortunately, one boat "got stove[d] [side crushed in] bad[, the] men chilled most through. Before we got them on boar[d,] one of the lines parted and [the] whale Got clear." Thick fog came in, forcing them to "hasten to the ship. Put a new boat on the craines and commenced repairing the stoven one."

It was extremely cold in the Sea of Okhotsk, with added danger since the men did not wear life preservers. A particularly frightening aspect of the experience was that sharks were attracted to whale blood, which is why the butchering process had to be speedy. Men worked on platforms above the whales, often with sharks thrashing around in the water below in feeding frenzies.

Fog was a constant problem. With low visibility it was hard to find the whales, kill them, and then find their way (with or without the creatures) back to the mother ship. They lost one whale on June 20 because the harpoon broke and the fog forced them "to leave him"

24. He would not die for another thirty-six years. Louis T. Vail, Grave Stone Inscriptions from Oakland Cemetery, Sag Harbor, L.I.," dunhamwilcox.net.

A nineteenth century barque with four whaleboats.

Courtesy Library of Congress.

so they could get back to the ship. The next morning after the fog lifted, they killed one of twelve whales they could see, but that one sunk too, and returning fog forced them back to the ship. On June 26 they had success and extracted seventy-five barrels of oil. "Saw from 6 to 8 right whales through the day. Saw one dead whale," Smith wrote. The *Thames* was east of the southern tip of Kamchatka.

A conflict broke out on June 26 between the ship's captain and steward, the latter consigned to the ship's forecastle with the plebeian seamen. On July 1 the crew grew depressed after "one right whale came up close to the ship" and they heard "other whales blowing" but the fog was too thick to give chase. By July 3 it was so "thick and foggy" that their "prospects appear[ed] dark." It was "quite a dreary fou[r]th of July with us." Two days later, a year to the day since the *Thames* left Long Island, the crew celebrated 110 barrels of oil from their latest catch.

There was a serious accident on July 18 when they lowered a boat and a whale struck it, probably with its tail, or fluke: "We found the water very cold [but] all of us [were] saved with difficulty. The whale got away from us. Hoisted in our stoven boat at 6 o clock." It appears that again, Smith was with Captain Bishop in the whaleboat that capsized.

By August 2 there were several other whaleships in the area: the *Swift*, the *India*, both of New Bedford; and the barque *Connecticut* of New London, hunting "bowhead whales," among others. Hammond wrote that he "witness[ed] one fatal accident while on the whaling ground. I saw an negro killed by a whale." While "st[al]king the boat," the whale "pulled the midship oar, cutting the boat [in two] and driving [the sailor] through the bottom into the sea; we never saw him after wards."[25] Smith added details about this happening on August 17 as a result of "Mr Isham[,] the first mates Boat steerer[,] dart[ing] a whale." When "the whale struck the boat [and] cut her into amidships," it "killed a colored man by the name of Charles Conklin instantly and he sunk to rise no more. Also hurt another man David Petty some considerably. [We] picked up the pieces of the boat and Brought them on board ... and put a new boat on the craines." From Smith's perspective, this was "surely an awful visitation of Providence and a warning for all us on board to be also ready" for death at any time.

Despite this casualty, the crew chased whales again the next day, competing with eight other ships in the area. On August 22 they "fastened to one but the iron soon drawed [out and] he got away from us." Over the next three weeks, with the Kamchatka Peninsula in sight, they were constantly gaming with the *Bayward* and *Tuscarora* until the three turned toward Maui for the winter and provisions. Without the benefit of modern weather forecasting, the captains did not know they were heading into a typhoon. On October 1, Smith reported that the "wind shifted ... and increased very fast ... the wind blowing a severe Gale ... the Tuscarora in company a heavy sea on all day." The next day there was "a severe Gale ... with some hard squalls and rain ... [a] heavy

25. Hammond to Edwards, June 14, 1889.

sea sweeping the deck of everything moveable and damaging one boat some." With the *Tuscarora* still "in company," on October 5 the *Thames* found itself off the northern tip of the main Japanese island of Honshu when it experienced the worst of the storm:

> Kept the ship off [sails] before the wind under the main top sail only. Blowing tremenduously till 5 P M then begun to lull some ... At 10 set the foresail. So ends this day. <u>I never saw the wind blow so hard before</u> ... [The next day we continued on] under all sail[s,] the Tuscarora in company ... Latt 39.00 [north,] Long[itude] 166.34 West.[26]

What Smith failed to mention was that in the middle of the typhoon, the bos'n Frank Hammond suffered a broken back and was afterward lying injured in his bunk. Hammond emphasized the seriousness of it to his non-Mormon cousin:

> We came in contact with a "Tiphoon," a dreadful storm of wind, that came from the Japanese Islands or coast; by this storm we were driven off the whaling ground and came near loosing our ship. During the gale, fore part of it, I was employed in stowing down oil in the lower hole [hold] when a barrell of flour, from between decks, fetched away and struck me in the small of the back, which nearly killed me instantly; I was hoisted up onto the main deck and carried down into my state room, and placed carefuly in my berth, where I lay for som[e] six weeks. A young man, a towny of mine, Jonas Wicks,[27] was detailed to wait on me; I suffered greatly till we arrived back to the sandwich Islands in the succe[e]ding fall of the year.[28]

"When I bade good-by to my shipmates," Hammond wrote elsewhere, "it was their firm belief that they would never see me again alive; in fact I had but little hopes of recovery myself."[29] He reiterated this in a third account, in which he divulged that "the captain and my fellow-officers thought I was a first rate candidate

26. Underlining original to Smith's journal.

27. Wicks was from Patchogue, and Hammond would later visit him there a number of times and correspond with him into the 1890s.

28. Hammond to Edwards, June 14, 1889.

29. Hammond, "Early Days," 353.

for the graveyard."[30] It is curious that Smith did not mention this, and one might explain this by the fact that, as the cooper, he was responsible for the accident. One of his primary tasks was securing the ten-barrel-capacity oil casks in the hold and making sure they were properly tied down. Evidently, during the typhoon some of the casks came loose. Hammond was tying them down when a barrel of flour, also Smith's responsibility, came loose and rolled into the hold, striking Hammond in the back. If the case were tried in court, Smith probably would have been found liable for Hammond's injury.[31]

On November 4 the *Thames* anchored at Lahaina for two weeks, sailing out on the nineteenth without Hammond, who was left with half his pay and the expectation that he would not live long. "At sunrise [we] took our Anchor [up] and stood to sea," was all Smith wrote, saying nothing of their abandonment of Hammond. The *Thames* spent three months visiting the islands of O'ahu and Hawai'i before returning to Lahaina on February 23, 1845, at which time Smith attended services at the "bethel church" in Lahaina and saw "John Winchester [whom he] found [was] married to a Kanaka [Hawaiian] wom[a]n."[32] Hammond was also attending the Bethel church during this period, and was acquainted with Winchester, a onetime whaler whom Hammond would later convert to Mormonism.

Smith only mentioned Hammond in passing on February 26:

> This day pleasant at anchor. Got off a raft of water [for the ship and] dischar[g]ed Elias Jones Boat steerer and James Lugar seaman. Both sick. Discharged Frances Hammond formerly boat steerer. Got off 53 bbls [barrels] of meat and ... Casks in Sto[c]ks. Bought from Mr Peek merchant. I was offered 75 dollars per month to [become] Cooper of the Ship Phe[o]nix of New Bedford but I could not get discharged from the Thames so could not go.

There was a "seaman's hospital" for sick sailors at Lahaina, financed by the US government, where Jones and Lugar were presumably left.

30. Jenson, *Latter-day Saint Biographical Encyclopedia*, 1:351–53.

31. Historian Will Bagley suggested this possibility to me by email, Aug. 20, 2010.

32. Emphasis in original.

However, notice that Smith did not say that Hammond was sick or even injured. In addition, instead of referring to him as the current boat steerer, he said Hammond was "formerly" engaged in that profession, implying a previous discharge. If one can read between the lines, it seems that Smith confirmed Hammond's account. After being put ashore, Hammond later wrote:

> I rented a small, native house and hired a native boy, Maikai, to take care of me. Here I lived on bananas, poi[,] and goat's milk. Strange to relate, in about sixty days I was able to get up and walk about, and soon after I was able to work. I then started in the business of shoemaking ... In a short time [I] had four or five journeymen shoemakers working for me, also several men boarding with me, while Maikai, my native boy, did the cooking."[33]

Hammond claimed he was up and walking sixty days after being put ashore, and was running his cobbler business by early January 1845, a month before the *Thames* returned to Maui. Since Lahaina was relatively small, everyone would have known of this miraculous recovery. Hammond also was involved in the activities of the local Protestant church, and he probably would have seen Smith there. Hammond was up and about but had no desire to return to the *Thames* and a whaler's life, even though during the 1850s he occasionally had dreams in which he saw himself as a ship captain.

During the three years Hammond spent on Maui from 1844 until 1847, he made friends and "learned enough of the native language to trade and traffic with the natives in a friendly way." The Hawaiians were his "principal customers," he said, while his business was augmented by the "foreign population, consisting of American missionaries, merchants, lawyers and doctors."[34] He became aware of Mormons when the *Brooklyn* arrived in Honolulu in June 1846, about 140 days out of New York and carrying 236 Mormon immigrants destined for Yerba Buena, soon to be renamed San Francisco. The historian Will Bagley found that "both Honolulu papers printed

33. Hammond, "In Early Days," 353.
34. Hammond, "In Early Years," 353.

accounts of the ship's voyage" based on records provided by the company's Mormon leader Samuel Brannan.[35]

The "pilgrims received a surprisingly cordial welcome from [the] Protestant minister and newspaper publisher Samuel C. Damon," Bagley continued, whose "sympathetic view of the emigrants" was communicated by Damon in his publication, *The Friend*:

> We feel ourselves in duty bound to give publicity to the testimony of Capt. [Abel] Richardson, master of the "Brooklyn" in regard to the general character of the emigrants as it has been developed during a long voyage round Cape Horn. Of their general behavior and character, he speaks in the most favorable manner. They have lived in peace together, and uniformly appeared to be quiet and orderly ... They have not lost sight of the means of promoting education and schools [when they arrive]. Capt. R[ichardson] informs us that during most of the passage they have maintained ... daily religious exercises, which still continue while lying in port.[36]

Hammond, however, later claimed that when he read about the *Brooklyn,* "little did I think at that time, that I would ever become associated with that people, for from all I had heard or read of the Mormons, I was led to believe they were about the worst people on earth."[37]

In September 1846 residents and seamen organized a Temperance Society and signed an abstinence pledge at the Lahaina Bethel Church. A committee consisting of "Messers. Jamison, Batts, Eggleston Lovel[,] and Hammond" was chosen to draft a constitution and bylaws.[38] Frank's involvement with the endeavor was consistent with his conservative religious life at that time. Although he rejected "orthodox Christianity," he said he believed in living "a just and upright life" and felt he "would be saved" if he did—even though he also

35. Bagley, *Scoundrel's Tale*, 143.

36. *Friend,* July 1, 1846, qtd. in Bagley, *Scoundrel's Tale*, 145. *The Friend* was published monthly by Damon (1815–85), chaplain of the Seaman's Friend Society at Honolulu; also *Sailor's Magazine*, Mar. 1848, 202. Abel W. Richardson (1798–1884) owned the *Brooklyn* and captained it. Hansen, "Voyage of the *Brooklyn*," 49n2; cf. Everett, "Ship Brooklyn."

37. Hammond, "In Early Days," 353–54. For the article, see "Arrival of the Brooklyn with Emigrants for California," *Polynesian*, June 27, 1844, in Bagley, *Scoundrel's Tale*, 142–43.

38. See D. D. Baldwin journal, Hawaii Mission Children's Society, Honolulu.

emphasized that he thought it would be just "as well [for him] outside as inside of any of the man-made churches."[39]

In the late summer of 1847, Hammond "was seized with a desire to leave the Islands and return to my home in Long Island ... and marry 'the girl I left behind me,'" as the shanty went,[40] and then "return and make my home with the people of Hawaii, as I had formed a great liking for the people and their delightful country." The girl he planned to marry (he would not) was Mary Smith. Other sailors in Hawaii were marrying native and "half-white" girls, but Hammond indicated in the 1850s that he was opposed to miscegenation,[41] and in speaking with the Reverend Forbes, Hammond was advised "to take passage round Cape Horn and land in the midst of good Christian society; 'for', says he, 'if you go home by way of California, you will find society there made up of Mexicans, Indians, a few renegade Americans and those poor, deluded Mormons that went there in the ship *Brooklyn*; of course, you would not wish to associate with them.'" Hammond responded, however, that "I had made up my mind to go home across the American continent, for the reason that it would give me a trip around the world, as I had doubled the East Cape [of] Good Hope [South Africa], in coming to the islands."[42] So he began planning to cross the continent west to east, a very dangerous proposition in the 1840s.

39. Hammond, "Early Days," 354. Cochran Forbes (1805–80), an 1831 graduate of Princeton Theological Seminary, was a missionary in the islands from 1833–45. When his wife became ill, he returned to the United States. At the time of his death, he was chaplain of the Presbyterian Hospital in Philadelphia. See Bliss, *Encyclopaedia of Missions* 1:375.

40. The lyrics are: "The dames of France are fond and free, / and Flemish lips are willing / ... but my heart goes back to Erin's Isle, / To the girl I left behind me."

41. Hammond, "Early Days," 354. See also Hammond to Edwards, June 14, 1889. Although they never married, Hammond visited Mary in January 1890 when she was "near seventy." Mormonism, he said, came between them in 1847 and "changed my whole history." See Hammond journal, Jan. 5, 1890.

42. Hammond, "Early Days," 354.

CHAPTER 2

Conversion

My business prospered ... and I was enabled to add considerable to the means I brought with me from the Sandwich Islands. During the winter I loaned to President Samuel Brannan some $500 which he invested in goods and fitted out a pack train and sent it into Lower California on a trading expedition among the Spaniards and Mexicans[1] ... He advised me to go into a partnership with him ... I told [him] ... I had agreed to start for Salt Lake [City] with a company in July and gather with the heads of the Church. He did all he could to dissuade me from my purpose ... He did not believe they could sustain themselves in the Rocky Mountains.

—*Hammond, "In Early Days," 395*

When Frank arrived at San Francisco on October 23, 1847, a substantial portion of the city's residents were Mormons, having either arrived on the *Brooklyn* or having been mustered out of the Mormon Battalion as veterans of the Mexican War. The battalion had marched from Iowa to southern California toward the end of the war.[2] When Hammond arrived, he jumped ashore from the ship's yawl boat, and the valet who transported his baggage to the local inn was William Corey, former sergeant in the Mormon Battalion. The boarding house was operated by *Brooklyn* immigrant William Glover, who had seven Battalion members staying with him on a long-term basis.[3]

1. Brannan sent William Glover south with $2000 in goods and told Brigham Young that if they made a profit, he would "fit [Glover] out immediately with more supplies" for Salt Lake City. Bagley, *Scoundrel's Tale*, 246.

2. For more on the Mexican War, see Howe, *What God Hath Wrought*, 744–91.

3. Hammond, "Early Days," 355; also Hammond to David Edwards, June 14, 1889. For more on the Mormon army, see Ricketts, *Mormon Battalion*.

Needless to say, Hammond was subjected to a heavy dose of Mormonism as he settled in and met Sam Brannan, who about a month earlier had returned from a meeting with Brigham Young in Wyoming. Brannan was the presiding elder on the West Coast and had tried to convince Young to bring the church headquarters to northern California.[4]

Hammond purchased the cook's galley from the *Brooklyn* and adapted it to a cobbler's shop with living quarters. He hired battalion members John White and O. F. Mead to work for him, and even at that, he found it difficult to keep up with the demand in that remote part of the world.[5] According to Hammond, the religious discussions at the inn that first night "lasted from early eve until the fowls commenced crowing for morning." His "faith in revealed religion," he wrote, "was at this time very weak indeed. I had for years doubted there being any church on earth that taught the Gospel as Jesus and His Apostles taught it." Admittedly, he had been

> led while in this state of mind to read infidel works, such as the works of Tom Paine, Voltaire, and others, who wrote with all the ingenuity of their souls to destroy faith in the Bible as a book revealed from the Lord, and indirectly at least to destroy faith in God. While I did not turn infidel entirely, I had lived for years as a sceptic concerning all forms of religion.

Though he may have flirted with the skeptical Deism of Paine and Voltaire, he later claimed he believed that God had "establish[ed] His Church and conferred the authority upon His apostles to preach His Gospel in power and demonstration of the Holy Spirit. I believed all this did occur as related in the New Testament."[6]

He countered Glover "with the doctrines of John Wesley, the

4. For Brannan's and Young's relationship, see Bagley, *Scoundrel's Tale*.

5. Hammond, "Early Days," 366.

6. Hammond, "Early Days," 365. Paine was the famous skeptic and author of *Common Sense* (1776), a catalyst for the American Revolution, while his *Age of Reason* (1794) enumerated the errors in the Bible. Voltaire's *Candide* (1759) was published anonymously but its authorship was pretty much an open secret, and it became one of the most influential books of the Enlightenment.

great founder of Methodism, free will and free grace, bringing all the scriptures I could think of, to prove that we did not need any further revelation, that the canon of scripture was full and complete." He thought Joseph Smith lacked credibility. "I could not stretch my mind to believe so much at once," he wrote of Smith's revelations. However, after reading apostle Parley P. Pratt's book, *Voice of Warning*, and talking at length with local Mormons, he became converted.

Two experiences in particular convinced him that it was right to believe in modern revelation. He had a dream in which "the Lord ... perfectly convinced me of the truth of the Bible."[7] Although he did not disclose the details of this dream, his remark implied that his faith had probably been shaken by the Enlightenment authors to a greater degree than he had admitted, and that he had a mystical side that was sensitive to spiritual communication. The other experience occurred after his conversion to Mormonism, when he was having second thoughts about the Book of Mormon, and prayed for an answer.

> Before the words were fairly uttered from my lips[,] a sheet or flame of fire commenced to descend upon me, not very warm at the first, but shock after shock succeeded till my whole frame seemed [it was] literally being consumed with fire ... This was heavenly fire, and filled me with joy unspeakable. My pen nor tongue cannot express the peace, joy and happiness that I experienced at this time ... This was as satisfactory to me as though an angel had appeared and told me the book was true.[8]

He was baptized in the San Francisco Bay by Elder Robert Petch on December 31, 1847. Petch had come to San Francisco with his wife and family on the *Brooklyn*. Hammond remembered that "Elder Samuel Brannan, ... president over all the [LDS] Churches on the Pacific Coast at that time," confirmed him a member of the church, although he also admitted that in writing his reminiscence after all those years, he was not certain he correctly remembered who had performed that ordinance.

7. Hammond, "Early Days," 365–67.

8. Ibid., 368.

Just a little over three weeks after Hammond's baptism, an event occurred on the south fork of the American River, about 130 miles from San Francisco, that transformed California and much of the world. On January 24, 1848, James Marshall (1810–85) showed some sparkling gold flakes to members of his construction crew who were building a sawmill for John Sutter, all of them Mormon Battalion veterans. One of the crew was Henry Bigler, who later served in the Hawaiian mission with Hammond. He is the one who recorded the discovery of gold in his diary, famously pinpointing the exact date.

After visiting the gold sites in April and confirming that the precious metal was indeed plentiful in the Sierra foothills, Brannan brought a sample of gold dust back to San Francisco and ran through the streets shouting the news of the discovery. Having worked as a printer, and having brought a printing press with him on the *Brooklyn*, with which he founded the city's first newspaper, the *California Star*, he used that medium to get word of the discovery to distant locations. That set off the stampede to the gold fields that attracted adventurers from around the world and left San Francisco a virtual ghost town.[9] Mormons were among the first to the hills, where they made spectacular early discoveries at Mormon Island, downstream from Sutter's Mill, and at Mormon Bar, Mormon Diggings, Mormon Gulch, and other sites.[10]

"I too caught the fever," Hammond admitted, and he outfitted himself with a pack train and arrived in Sacramento ten days after Brannan's announcement. In an incredible stroke of fortune, he "succeded in accumulating some $3000" in a short amount of time by working the sluice at Mormon Island.[11] What is even more remarkable is that Hammond, along with other Mormons in northern California, gave this up when Brigham Young called the church members home to Utah. In late June 1848, "I quit mining and divided the

9. Bagley, *Scoundrel's Tale*, 187–88; Holliday, *World Rushed In*, 32–35. Gibson documented in *Yankees in Paradise*, 216, that from 1848 to 1852 California's non-Indian population increased from under 8,000 to over 250,000.

10. Owens, *Gold Rush Saints*; Gibson, *Yankees in Paradise*, 211.

11. Hammond to Edwards, June 14, 1889.

results with my partners," Hammond wrote. Returning to San Francisco, he bought a government wagon drawn by four yoke of beautiful oxen, "filled the wagon with supplies," then headed east.

He joined a group of Mormons at Pleasant Valley, ten miles from what is now Placerville, and helped them build the first road over the Sierras on their way to Utah (a road followed later by the "forty-niners" going west). In the company were Addison Pratt, who had recently returned from a mission to Tahiti,[12] and Ephraim Green, who would later be with Hammond in Hawaii. While "blaz[ing] the trail," tragedy struck when three of the leaders, traveling ahead, were murdered in their sleep by Indians.[13]

Crossing what is now northern Nevada, the company reached Great Salt Lake City on September 6, and Hammond was unimpressed. "I remember thinking the name was much larger than the city." The settlement consisted at the time of three mud structures called North Fort, South Fort, and Middle Fort, with about ten acres apiece. The Saints were "located inside of these forts or enclosures, probably in round numbers not exceeding fifteen hundred souls," in a country "forbidding in appearance."[14] For Hammond, who had grown up on Long Island and had just left luxuriant Maui, the arid Great Basin must have been a shock.

One of the men who had been a cook on the *Brooklyn* gave Hammond a letter of introduction to Levi Riter, a wealthy convert from Philadelphia who had shipped freight on the *Brooklyn*. The Riters welcomed him with open arms and invited him to stay with them while he got his feet on the ground. Levi's wife was the older sister of Mary Jane Dilworth, a woman who would soon become Hammond's first wife.

Hammond was also introduced to apostle Parley P. Pratt. When the church leader was told that Hammond had lived in the Sandwich

12. Two of the first four missionaries to French Polynesia, Addison Pratt and Benjamin Grouard, were former whalers; Grouard stayed and married a native woman. Ellsworth, "First Mormon Missionary Women," 36.

13. See Bagley, *Road from El Dorado*; Hammond, "Early Days," 517.

14. Hammond, "Early Days," 519. He wrote in his journal on Sept. 6, 1897, that when he first arrived in the valley nearly fifty years earlier, it was "a solitary place, desert-looking and forbidding." On Sept. 6, 1899, he wrote that "it was desolate," the "whole country, dry and parched."

Above: Mary Jane Dilworth Hammond, and
below: Rebecca Dilworth Riter, her older sister.

Courtesy Daughters of Utah Pioneers.

Islands for three years, the apostle, according to Hammond's account, began talking about the biblical origin of the Polynesians, saying they were a remnant of the scattered House of Israel. If this is, in fact, what the apostle said, it would be a surprise because it preceded any other mention of the concept by a few years. In addition to that, Pratt failed to mention the doctrine in his 1852 pamphlet, *Proclamation! To the People of the Coasts and Islands of the Pacific.* The omission has led scholars to assume that an account, which had Addison Pratt telling Joseph Smith that "the native [man] of Hawaii was brother to the American Indian," was itself apocryphal. "Indeed, there is some evidence that [Addison] Pratt himself did not conceive his mission[s] as being necessarily to the Polynesians at all," an historian wrote, but rather to the "English" in the islands.[15] So it is possible that Hammond's memory was wrong, or that the idea was percolating in Mormon discussions but had not yet become concretized.

Of more immediate concern to Hammond was that apostle Pratt was a polygamist. "My poor soul, monogamic taught, fairly revolted at the idea," he wrote. "Thus was I sorely tried and tempted and my poor faith nearly shipwrecked." In discussions with his own future sister-in-law, Rebecca Riter, he tempered his judgment of polygamy.[16] Rebecca and Mary Jane, the two women from whom he was learning the expansive teachings of the church, had converted to Mormonism in Pennsylvania, along with their strong-willed, Quaker-born mother. Mary Jane was born at the end of July 1831, the eleventh child of Eliza and Caleb Dilworth. Of the eleven children, there were seven other girls and one boy living at the time of Mary Jane's birth. Caleb rejected Mormonism, so Eliza gathered up her children, including her married daughters and their families, and headed for the Mormon city of Nauvoo, Illinois, without him. She would never see her bereft husband again.

When the Dilworths arrived in Illinois, the church's forced

15. This was the opinion of Norman Douglas, then a student at Australian National University, in his 1974 article, "Sons of Lehi and the Seed of Cain," 94–97; cf. Ellsworth, *History of Louisa Barnes Pratt*, 147.

16. Hammond, "Early Days," 519–20.

expulsion was underway, so they simply kept going across Iowa Territory, pausing only long enough for fourteen-year-old Mary Jane to be baptized in the Mississippi River.[17] Arriving at the other side of the territory, Mary Jane set up a school for children in a small rock house at Winter Quarters, near present-day Omaha, and taught reading and writing through the winter of 1846–47. In doing so, she attracted the attention and praise of Brigham Young.[18]

In the summer of 1847, the family left Winter Quarters in Daniel Spencer's company. Once again Mary Jane caught Brigham Young's attention, this time near Grand Island, Nebraska, where she was holding makeshift daily classes while crossing the prairie. Young apparently encouraged her to found a school in the Salt Lake Valley when she arrived there, laying his hands on her head and giving her a blessing to do so. Following his instructions, she established school in a tent at the mud fort at what is now Pioneer Park. Several months later she moved the school to a log enclosure constructed by William Bringhurst, her sister Ann's husband. She continued to teach until shortly after her marriage to Frank Hammond.[19]

The twenty-six-year-old whaler/cobbler and seventeen-year-old school teacher wed on November 17, 1848, under the authority of apostle Heber C. Kimball, who married them civilly, or as Mormons termed it, "for time," rather than eternity.[20] "My goods having arrived," Hammond recalled, "I bought a log house of Brother Horace Alexander, located just north of the east gate of the South Fort, and commenced shoemaking again, with Brothers John White and O[rlando] Mead [again] working for me."[21] The newlyweds spent the winter in a rude cabin with what Frank described as a flat leaky roof. It was a desperate time, as the "crops were destroyed by grasshoppers,

17. Adamson, *Francis Asbury Hammond*, 27–28.

18. Whitney, *History of Utah*, 326.

19. Adamson, *Francis Asbury Hammond*, 27–28. There is a monument recognizing her as the first school teacher in Utah in Huntsville, where she lived and taught during the 1860s and 1870s.

20. Ibid., 29. An ideal LDS marriage is performed in a temple for "time and all eternity," but no temple had yet been built in Utah.

21. Hammond, "Early Days," 520.

also drouth [drought], [and] … we were at times obliged to subsist on roots, rawhide soup, bran bread, &c."[22]

In the spring the Hammonds moved onto a farm near Big Cottonwood Canyon, and on September 15, 1850, Mary Jane gave birth to Francis Jr. The boy was only six months old when Frank and Mary were called to serve a mission together to the Sandwich Islands, no doubt because Frank had lived on Maui and knew the native language. On March 3, 1851, in preparation, they received their temple endowments, probably on the second floor of the Council House or city hall. The endowment is a secret, private ceremony that involves disrobing and being ritually washed, anointed with olive oil to be a future celestial ruler, the donning of ceremonial clothing, the swearing of oaths promising not to reveal the endowment ceremony, fidelity to God, fairness toward all people, and marriage for all eternity.

Taking Frankey with them and leaving their farm in the care of Harriet and David Brinton, Mary Jane's sister and brother-in-law, the Hammonds left Salt Lake City on March 16 in a company of 155 wagons. The staging ground for the trip was a place called Peteetneet (now Payson), south of Fort Utah (now Provo). With them were some other couples on their way to Hawaii, including William and Patty Perkins and John and Elvira Woodbury.[23] John Woodbury kept an extensive missionary journal, which he began on March 13 with the following entry:

> I took leave of Father, Mother, Brothers, sisters & many kind friends & started on the mission to whitch I had been appointed to the Pacific Islands. Started with ox team and wagon. Travelled in company with Wm J. Perkins [to] Peteetnete where we camped & waited for the company to all get together & organize. Here we met with Elder Parley P. Pratt who had been appointed President of the Pacific Mission, and quite a number of others going on a mission to the Islands,

---

22. Adamson, *Francis Asbury Hammond*, 29; Hammond to Edwards, June 14, 1889.

23. Although Addison Pratt had been away from his family for over five years while he and brother-in-law Jonathan Crosby were in the Society Islands (Tahiti), they were immediately sent back again, and their wives prevailed on Young to let them and their children accompany the men. He consented, establishing a brief precedent for future missionaries to the islands. See Ellsworth, "First Mormon Missionary Women."

> Australia & South America, and a large company going to form a colony in Southern California. We were Here met by Pres[iden]ts [Brigham] Young and [Heber C.] Kimball who came out to Assist in organizeing the company & to give the necessary counsel, instructions &c.[24]

In fact, a general call had gone out for anyone willing to help colonize southern California, but Young was so incensed by the throngs who showed up, eager to leave Utah, that he famously declined to address the group before they left.[25]

They moved south, in any case, and arrived at Red Creek (now Parowan) on April 11, where Philip Lewis and his wife Jane joined them.[26] Lewis was a tinsmith, originally from Massachusetts, who in Nauvoo had been appointed to the Council of Fifty, the group that ran Joseph Smith's campaign for the US presidency and sponsored the early church exploration of the West. Lewis also had done metal work on the Nauvoo temple.[27] Although he married in Nauvoo, his first wife, Maria, died in 1846 and he married Jane Amanda Stevens at Winter Quarters in 1848. After arriving in Utah, they were sent to southern Utah as part of the mission to start an iron industry. Jane gave birth to two sons in 1849, but one of them had died.[28]

The trip to California was hazardous, as the wagons were repeatedly attacked by Indians, and the temperature was so high in the desert that they had to travel at night. Pratt observed that everyone "walked on foot," including the "women and children, young and old," and it was "the hardest time I ever saw."[29] On May 28 they

24. Woodbury journal, Mar. 13, 1851.

25. Lyman, "Rise and Decline," 53.

26. Woodbury journal, Apr. 16, 1851; Pratt journal, qtd. in Journal History, Apr. 11, 1851. Lewis funded the transportation of the first four missionaries to the Society Islands. Ellsworth, *Journals of Addison Pratt*, 121

27. The Council of Fifty also crowned Joseph Smith king over God's earthly kingdom in a secret ceremony. See Rogers, *Council of Fifty*; Quinn, *Mormon Hierarchy: Origins*, 105–64, 521–31. Smith had tried to establish a theocracy in Missouri in 1838, which is one of the reasons the Mormons were expelled from that state. See Hammond, *Mormon Expulsion from Missouri*.

28. See Lewis journal.

29. Pratt journal, qtd. in Journal History, May 22, 1851.

Parley Parker Pratt

Courtesy Daughters of Utah Pioneers.

John Stillman Woodbury

Courtesy Daughters of Utah Pioneers.

Brigham Young

Courtesy Utah State Historical Society.

Henry William Bigler

Courtesy Daughters of Utah Pioneers.

arrived at the Mohave River, halfway between today's Las Vegas and Los Angeles, "in an exhausted condition." It took them another three weeks to make it to the coast, and then the Lewises' surviving one-year-old son, William, died. One can only imagine the heartbreak and conflicted feelings the parents must have had.

Prior to boarding the *Ohio* steamer in San Pedro on July 5, the missionaries sold their wagons and animals. According to Lewis, they "hired a house" in San Francisco "and all of us moved into [it,] where we tarried for about 2 weeks." To this point the Lewises and Woodburys had been assigned to the Society Islands Mission, not the Sandwich Islands, but according to Lewis,

> just at this moment Bro Clark & Tompkins with his family arrived having been obliged to leave the Society Isles in consequence of the arbitrary acts of the French Governor in not permiting them to receive any assistance from the natives, and forbiding them speaking against the Catholic religion. This inteligence altered the whole face of affairs, and Bro. Pratt changed his mind and set Bro Woodbury and myself apart for a mission to the Sandwich Isles and Bro Pratt ordained me to the Presidency contrary to my expectations and very much to my surprise for I felt my insufficiency and wished that some one could have been appointed better qualified to fill the station but as I was the oldest member of the mission it properly belonged to me so I made no objection.[30]

On July 24 the Hammonds, Lewises, and John Woodbury took passage on the schooner *Eagle* for the islands. William and Patty Perkins could not afford the fare at this time and remained behind, along with Elvira Woodbury, who was ill. The five travelers reached Lahaina, Maui, on August 10, and the next day Lewis "sent Bro Hammond on shore to hunt up the Brethren, but could only learn that one of them was in Town the day before, but had left again." There were five missionaries on the islands who had been there since December. After another day went by, Lewis and Hammond gave up waiting. "Both went on shore, hired a house, [and] moved our things

30. Lewis journal, introduction, 3.

into it the same day." They sent someone to find Elders George Q. Cannon and James Keeler, who were laboring on Maui, to tell them of their arrival.

Lewis and Hammond traveled to Honolulu and found Elders Henry William Bigler and James Farrer. The four elders then returned to Lahina on August 19; the next day they received a visit from Cannon and Keeler, bringing all the missionaries together except for James Hawkins who was out of contact on the big island of Hawai'i.[31]

31. Lewis to Pratt, Sept. 1, 1851.

CHAPTER 3

The Hawaiians

About three miles from [Honolulu] we came to a place where the natives had a hula (dance) and ... Br. Reddin [Reddick Allred] proposed that we go in, as it is remarked as a grand exhibition. [Br.] Lelile had Said it was a wicked practice, that it led to illicit intercourse with the opposite sex ... [Two men] would beat their drumbs and Sing their mele a kind of h[y]m [or] Song suited to the ocasion. In front of them was three girls about the age of fifteen; their dresses extended a little below the knee. Their legs and feet wer[e] bare, and on the calf of each leg was a wreath of banana leaves, and a Kapa bound loosely around their waist and extending down to the knee. Their steps wer[e] very regular and gentle. Their hands wer[e] continually in motion, and each made the same gestures with the greatest exactness; every mustle and part of the body was in motion, & nothing unbecoming or immodest could be detected, except the motion of the hips, whitch I will not attempt to describe in my book. The whole affair was managed with the greatest civility immaginable.

—John Woodbury journal, Aug. 11, 1854[1]

On their arrival in Hawaii in December 1850, the first ten Mormon missionaries faced serious socio-cultural challenges. Forced by their poverty to rely upon the natives in their rural villages for food and lodging, the six waves of elders who arrived in the islands between 1850 and 1857 had a very difficult time coping with the alien culture. The exotic food, the lice, ticks, dogs, and pigs in the native cottages, and above all the nudity and sexual promiscuity, was too much for many

1. Woodbury says nothing about what the girls wore above their waists, which was probably nothing beyond a flower lei. See Bartholomew, *Maui Remembers*, 33. Ephraim Green also was in attendance, and possibly James Keeler.

missionaries to handle, and those who stayed devoted much of their energy to changing the culture and life style of their native converts.

The Hawaiians, as historian Ralph Kuykendall has explained, belong to the larger Polynesian family that is spread out across the Pacific Ocean, most closely connected to the people of the Cook Islands, the Maori of New Zealand, Marquesans, Samoans, Tahitians, and Tongans. Their initial ancestors came from the Marquesas and Tahiti on a seaway that was traveled back and forth until about 700 years ago. The way was "well known and was used by numerous [Polynesian] voyagers."[2] After the first settlements were established in about the eighth century CE, contact from Tahiti continued as late as the thirteenth century. Then mysteriously, the trans-Pacific voyages ended and the Hawaiians were left isolated for centuries until the British captain James Cook (1728–79) arrived in the late eighteenth century.[3]

The intrepid first Polynesians to Hawaii found insufficient food sources there and were forced to return to Tahiti and bring back starters for cultivatable crops. "These colonizers had not found agricultural richness on Maui," according to historian Gail Bartholomew.[4] They "encountered jungled valleys thick with hau"[5] and found they "needed to import what we now consider Hawaiian staples—taro, breadfruit, sweet potato, banana, coconut, pigs, dogs, chickens, ti,[6] and wauke[7] for making cloth." Needless to say, the colonizers were excellent sailors and shipbuilders, carrying out the settlement of islands 2,600 miles away.[8]

Richard Henry Dana and other sailors commented on the skill of nineteenth-century Sandwich Islanders in getting a boat across the difficult surf in Santa Barbara on the California coast. Referring to them as water-dogs, Dana said they were instinctual with boats,

2. Kuykendall, *Hawaiian Kingdom*, 3.

3. Daws, *Shoal of Time*, xii–xiii.

4. Bartholomew, *Maui Remembers*, 2.

5. Hau is the hardy hibiscus tree. Its wood was used in constructing canoes and its bark was braided into rope. Its leaves could be boiled for tea, but one could not subsist on it.

6. The leaves of the ti (palm lily) were used for thatching roofs and fashioning hula skirts.

7. The leaves of the wauke (paper mulberry bush) were used in producing tapa cloth.

8. See, for example, Bergreen, *Edge of the World*, 229–31.

were "good hands in the surf," and were "the most interesting, intelligent, and kind-hearted people that I ever fell in with." He would have "trusted my life and all I had in the hands of any one of these people," he wrote.[9]

When the first contact between Europeans and Hawaiians occurred in January 1778, it was through the arrival of the explorer James Cook, in command of *Discovery* and *Resolution*. He named the islands after his patron, Lord John Montagu, Earl of Sandwich.[10] On their arrival at the southern coast of Kaua'i, the natives "thronged off to the Ship with hogs and Women," the captain wrote. "It was not possible to keep the latter out of the Ship and no Women I ever met with were more ready to bestow their favors. Indeed it appeared to me that they came with no other view," Cook continued. Once the sailors were ashore, the women became even more demanding. Thomas Edgar wrote that the women, bare breasted and wearing only grass skirts, "used all their arts to entice [the sailors] into their Houses & even went so far as to endeavour to draw them in by force."[11]

When English ships under the command of explorer Samuel Wallis (1728–95) reached Tahiti in mid-1767, the sailors received the same reception by nude native Polynesian women, and this was equally true for French sailors under Louis Antoine de Bougainville (1729–1811) when his ships landed at Tahiti a few months later in April 1768.[12] The Englishmen under Cook were amazed to see how comfortable the women were in the ocean. Cook said the women jumped out of canoes with babies at their breasts and maneuvered through surf "so high that they could not land in the canoes ... and without endangering their little ones, sw[a]m to the shore."[13]

Cook left the islands and sailed north to the Arctic Sea, then returned and, to his chagrin found that venereal disease his men had initiated among the natives on Kaua'i had spread all the way to the

9. Dana, *Two Years Before the Mast*, 46–50, 67, 117–18. See also Gibson, *Yankees in Paradise*, 121–22.

10. Sandwich was a port town on the English channel.

11. Qtd. in Daws, *Shoal of Time*, 5–6.

12. Daws, *Dream of Islands*, 1–3.

13. Qtd. in Judd, *Hawaii*, 31.

A Hawaiian woman in a tapa cloth skirt.

Courtesy Hawaii State Archives.

"Big Island." After a series of additional social and political blunders, Cook and several of his men met their fates at Kealakekua Bay on the west coast of the big island.[14] As more Europeans arrived, the islanders received them as warmly as they initially had Cook and his crew, and not only tolerated the infiltration of foreign people and ideas, they seemed to welcome the cross-cultural exchanges.[15] Although we now think of the Hawaiians at the time as unified, there were four separate kingdoms when Cook arrived, ruled by chiefs (*alii*, including nobles) and priests (*kahunas*). As free and unstructured as the society looked, it was in fact an authoritarian system, where the chiefs' decrees were considered "absolute, and capital punishment for even small misdeeds was not unusual," as historian Lanier Britsch writes. "Tight restrictions, *kapus* or taboos, were placed on personal relationships (for instance, common men could not interact freely with *alii*); on eating habits (only certain foods could be eaten by women and commoners); and on land and water use."[16]

Nineteenth-century native historian David Malo explained what life was like for the natives before the foreigners arrived, stressing the rigidity and hierarchical nature of the social system.

> The condition of the common people was that of subjection to the chiefs, compelled to do their heavy tasks, burdened and oppressed, some even to death. The life of the people was one of patient endurance, or yielding to the chiefs to purchase their favor ...
>
> If the people were slack in doing the chief's work they were expelled from their lands, or even put to death ... The people held the chiefs in great dread and looked upon them as gods.
>
> Only a small portion of the kings and chiefs ruled with kindness; the large majority simply lorded it over the people.
>
> It was from the common people, however, that the chiefs received their food and their apparel ... [and] also their houses and many other things.[17]

14. Thomas, *Cook*; Daws, *Shoal of Time*, 11–28. In his journal in the 1850s Hammond lamented the ravages of venereal diseases, which were passed from the infected mothers to their children.

15. Furnas, *Anatomy of Paradise*, 119.

16. Britsch, *Moramona*, 8.

17. Malo, *Hawaiian Antiquities*, 87.

The restored Ahuena temple.

The religion was polytheistic. Temples of lava rock were fronted by large statues of gods and goddesses that were mostly personifications of nature. There were three main gods representing light and life (Kane), the harvest (Lono), and war (Ku), as well as lesser gods to oversee volcanoes (Pele), sports (Akua Paani), and aspects of everyday life.[18] There was little agreement on which gods to devote primary attention. The chiefs emphasized different ancestral deities, while common men worshipped male deities and women bowed to female ones, or natives worshipped gods presiding over their occupations.[19]

The fact that the royal families were thought to have descended from deities was important because if anyone questioned a chief's authority, the chief could point to a preserved genealogy that extended back to the gods. This was something that outsiders could not grasp, since the chiefs appeared to be ruling as political governors or mayors. Anthropologist Nicholas Thomas explains that the chiefs actually

> had more to do with religion than government; they stood for gods, they conquered and made demands like gods, they received sacrifices and tribute, and in return ensured fertility and abundance. Their largesse,

18. Gibson, *Yankees in Paradise*, 36–37.

19. Malo, *Hawaiian Antiquities*, 112.

> their trappings, their appearances, and their performances were phenomena on the most spectacular scale that Islanders knew; chiefs had, in liv[ing] and visible form, the look and the substance of divinity.

This is what Captain Cook and his crew failed to grasp when women offered themselves to them. The Hawaiians thought Cook was the high God Lono and his crew the divine court.[20]

Another interesting aspect of their theology was that they lacked a supernatural origin for evil, the concept that bad deeds were the result of temptation from a powerful devil, or Satan. To them, sexual desire, for instance, was something to be controlled by edict, not by spiritual influence.[21] Joseph Furnas emphasized that "these people were neither high-minded free lovers nor rabbits ... The Islander was nowhere promiscuous." They were governed by *tabus* that limited their sexual behavior. The "early white observer, unaware of such complications and given wide privileges himself, made unholy errors in describing what he thought he saw." Prostitution was allowed, for instance, within certain constraints, but this did not mean that Hawaiians were libertine.[22]

Nor were they pacifists. Their enthusiasm for trade included a desire to obtain rifles with which to better obliterate their native enemies. In exchange for arms, they sold the foreigners aromatic sandalwood, hogs, and other commodities that were plentiful in their communities. Some traders "sold guns to as many factions as they could find and then encouraged them to fight," and the islanders were not instinctually opposed to the idea.[23]

Captain George Vancouver commanded an official British expedition that made three trips to Hawaii in 1792–94, and he came to detect "the superior position of [Chief] Kamehameha," after which he was "assiduous in cultivating his friendship." Kamehameha was a

20. Thomas, *Cook*, 381; also Dodge, *Islands and Empires*, 39; Furnas, *Anatomy of Paradise*, 110–11.

21. Messadie, *History of the Devil*, 27–28, 34. Mark Twain wrote, "How sad it is to think of the millions who have gone to their graves in this beautiful island and never knew there was a hell." Qtd. in Furnas, *Anatomy of Paradise*, 125.

22. Furnas, *Anatomy of Paradise*, 88–98, 106.

23. Daws, *Shoal of Time*, 32–34.

valuable business partner because of his interest in western products. He allowed the introduction of cattle to the islands, and before long Hawaiians could be seen following herds "through dust clouds to the branding corral" like the cowboys of the American West.[24] Under Kamehameha, foreigners were allowed to import guava, lemon, mango, orange, and famously the pineapple and sugar cane, none of which were indigenous.[25]

The forward-looking chief unified the islands in about 1810 after amassing large caches of arms and engaging in both trade and piracy. Kamehameha's foreign military advisors became acclimated by learning the native language and marrying native women, and they became important figures in Hawaiian politics and society. The foreign population grew as more and more sailors liked what they found in the islands and jumped ship. The natives started drinking alcoholic beverages (rum, beer, etc.) and smoking tobacco. Their easy acquisition of vices notwithstanding, they were extremely industrious. Outsiders commented on the amount of "labor that went into the irrigated taro plantations," for instance, "and Archibald Campbell, who lived on O'ahu for a year in 1809–1810, thought Hawaiians worked harder than any people he had ever seen," Furnas wrote.[26] The Hawaiians were also quick learners. When Kamehameha invaded Waikiki, O'ahu, with a force of 1,200 canoes in 1795 and established his capital there—unifying Hawaii—he set up a European-style blacksmith shop run entirely by native people.

Kamehameha was succeeded by his twenty-two-year-old son Liholiho, who became Kamehameha II in 1819. The young king inherited a world in turmoil, the result of the Hawaiians for years having watched foreigners among them "ignore the taboos with no ill effect."[27] Women in particular were chafing under the *kapu* system, which they considered outdated. The deceased king's favorite wife,

24. Kuykendall, *Hawaiian Kingdom*, 39–40; Judd, *Hawaii*, 105.

25. Foreigners also brought in (intentionally) bees, coffee, eucalyptus trees, goats, prickly pears, and sheep, as well as (unintentionally) cockroaches, fleas, mongooses, mosquitos, rats, scorpions, and toads. Furnas, *Anatomy of Paradise*, 112–13, 121.

26. Ibid., 123; Daws, *Shoal of Time*, 46–49; Kuykendall, *Hawaiian Kingdom*, 29–30.

27. Dodge, *Islands and Empires*, 119.

Kaahumanu (he had twenty-one), assumed the title *kuhina nui* (executive officer) while her son was still young and became the center of political affairs. Her "imposing presence gave her words irresistible force," according to one historian.[28]

Her most notable achievement was to convene a public feast for women and invite her stepson, Liholiho, to attend, thereby breaking a major taboo against men and women eating together. Following his step-mother's advice, he also took the iconoclasm another step by ordering the literal defacing of statues of native deities. Furnas explained that "he sent messengers to all districts of Hawai'i and to the leeward islands, ordering the [temples] desecrated and the images of the gods overthrown." There was an immediate backlash from conservatives, who organized an armed resistance. When the king's forces overthrew the malcontents in December 1819, the lesser chiefs grudgingly acquiesced and the "commoners, as usual, followed where their ali'is led" them. The people generally "did not abandon their old faith completely," however.[29] Mormon missionaries John Woodbury and Ephraim Green found that on Moloka'i in the early 1850s, the natives were afraid the *kahunas* would "pray them to death" if they embraced Mormonism.

Traditional beliefs thwarted *haole* (white) proselytizing at every turn, but on the other hand, "nowhere else in the South Seas did the framework of tradition collapse under a self-administered kick before missionaries arrived."[30] It was lucky for the Protestants who appeared after 1819 and found that the taboos had been broken and that people in the major cities were free to pursue beliefs of their own choosing. To missionaries who were nervous about encountering a fate similar to that of Cook's, it was like a welcome mat had been set out for them, many of the natives suddenly open to new religious beliefs.

28. Daws, *Shoal of Time*, 55, 59.

29. Ibid., 56–57, 59; also Kuykendall, *Hawaiian Kingdom*, 66–67, Dodge, *Islands and Empires*, 120.

30. Furnas, *Anatomy of Paradise*, 164, 127.

CHAPTER 4

The Protestant Missionaries

The appearance of destitution, degradation, and barbarism, among the chattering, and almost naked savages, whose heads and feet, and much of their sunburnt swarthy skins, were bare, was appalling. Some of our number, with gushing tears, turned away from the Spectacle. Others, with firmer nerve, continued their gaze, but were ready to exclaim, "Can these be human beings! ... Can we throw ourselves upon these rude shores, and Take up our abode, for life, among such a people, for the purpose of training them for Heaven?

—Hiram Bingham, 1820

When the first Christian missionaries and their families went ashore from the chartered brig *Thaddeus* on the island of Hawai'i in 1820, the traditional religious beliefs had just been repudiated by Hawaiian leaders. The evangelists, on hearing this astonishing news, praised God for clearing the way for them. The missionaries "could not have selected a more propitious time to launch their endeavors," a researcher concluded. Sent out by the American Board of Commissioners for Foreign Missions, the party of Congregationalists and Presbyterians was led by two young ministers, Hiram Bingham and Asa Thurston, with two schoolteachers, a physician, a printer, and a farmer. They brought with them three young Hawaiians who had been attending a mission school in Connecticut.[1] The missionaries were young and had recently married because the board would only send married men on foreign assignments.

When the puritanical missionaries came ashore, they were

1. Dodge, *Islands and Empires*, 118–19; Gibson, *Yankees in Paradise*, 268–70.

unprepared for the scene that presented itself to them. Bingham, the unofficial leader, penned the above horror-stricken observations. For him, Hawaii was "not an earthly paradise where noble savages dwelled, but a dark and ruined land whose people were filled with 'unrighteousness, fornication, wickedness, murder, debate, deceit, malignity ... [and full of] back-biters, haters of God, [the] despiteful, proud, boasters, inventors of evil things, [who were] disobedient to parents, without natural affection, implacable, unmerciful.'"[2]

The social and theological gulf between the Hawaiians and the missionaries was enormous. The latter were contemptuous of the easy Polynesian lifestyle, which was oriented toward self-sufficiency rather than commercial wealth. The sexual norms and practices of the natives included both polygamy and polyandry (a woman having several husbands. There was public nakedness and "lewd dancing," their description of the hula; incest involving royal brother-sister marriages; abortion and infanticide; and homosexuality.[3]

The young Prince Liholiho was highly erratic, drank too much liquor, and could not be persuaded to study religion, traits that were perpetuated in many of his successors. But after the missionaries won over a number of lesser Hawaiian leaders (*alii*), they gained influence over native life.[4] Once a local chief was converted, the missionaries persuaded him to issue edicts having to do with proper Sabbath observance, sexual conduct, abstinence from dancing the hula, playing native games, and gambling. Historian Arrell Gibson found it "ironic that the Hawaiian leaders in effect exchanged one set of personal restraints, the kapus, for another set even more repressive to personal expression, called blue laws and applied by New England Puritan missionaries. These later [Christian] taboos were also claimed to be prescribed by the deity."[5]

The Caucasian expatriates in the islands were not pleased to

2. Daws, *Shoal of Time*, 64.

3. Gibson, *Yankees in Paradise*, 3; Morris, "Same-Sex Friendships in Hawaiian Lore," 71–102.

4. Kuykendall, *Hawaiian Kingdom*, 104.

5. Gibson, *Yankees in Paradise*, 279, 272–73.

have missionaries from New England meddling with native ways and imposing Calvinistic restraints on the former sailors' lifestyles. In fact, British and American diplomatic personnel were equally unsupportive of the missionary efforts, as were the officers of commercial vessels and military warships. The missionary compounds were attacked in the 1820s–30s by angry whalers and sailors who abhorred the new puritanical ordinances.

It had gone differently in Tahiti, although the ultimate effect was the same, as the French imposed Catholicism on the native population by force rather than persuasion. Looking to extend their influence, French priests arrived in Honolulu in July 1827 and began proselytizing. However, they had no sooner made converts than the Protestant missionaries intervened to have them banished, their converts jailed.[6] By such means, Protestantism increased its influence in Hawaii so that, by the late 1830s, a majority of the natives considered themselves Protestants, and thousands of them attended church regularly. In 1838 there were about ninety missionaries in the islands working out of seventeen missionary offices.[7]

There were aspects of Christianity the native people were drawn to in addition to the theology. They liked to dress in European clothes for church, "though admittedly they liked undressing afterwards too," Daws dryly noted. To the amazement of the missionaries, they enjoyed memorizing long passages of scripture and sitting through sermons, "the longer the better, so it seemed." Because of the cultural divide, the missionaries were reluctant to baptize the natives. Even though "one out of every two Hawaiians attended church," an observer explained, "not one in a hundred had been granted the privilege of communion with Christ."[8] It is nevertheless remarkable that in a few decades, the Sandwich Islands had essentially become a Christian nation.

By the time of the arrival of Mormon elders in 1850, the Protestants had already decided to close down their Hawaiian mission,

6. Daws, *Shoal of Time*, 77–79, 86–90; Gibson, *Yankees in Paradise*, 280–82; Dodge, *Islands and Empires*, 82–83

7. See *Missionary Album* for 1937 and 1969.

8. Daws, *Shoal of Time*, 97–98.

feeling that their work was done, the majority of islanders converted.[9] That year saw the formation of the Hawaiian Missionary Society at Honolulu to launch endeavors to Micronesia and the Caroline Islands near New Guinea.[10]

In the late 1830s, the Hawaiian government adopted a constitutional democratic monarchy in the wake of a blockade of the Honolulu harbor in 1839 by the French frigate *L'Artémise*. Captain Cyrille Laplace had threatened to bombard the city unless the king released the imprisoned Catholics. Kauikeaouli and his advisers negotiated a treaty of "commerce and friendship" that guaranteed religious freedom and the future sale of French wines and brandies on the islands.[11] The religious freedom benefitted not only the Catholics but other future proselytizers as well, including the Mormons. The Hawaiians continued along a path of reform in 1840 by drawing up a constitution establishing a representative government with a national legislature.

During the three years Frank Hammond was on Maui (1845–47), the legislature in Honolulu created an independent judiciary, cabinet, and civil service, and passed a law allowing foreigners to buy and sell land. In 1852 suffrage was extended to all males, whether Hawaiian or naturalized immigrants, for elections involving representatives in the lower house of parliament. These reforms were guided by the Protestant missionaries Richard Armstrong and Gerrit Judd, both of whom renounced their US citizenship to become Hawaiian citizens. However, they remained "ardent Americanists and formulated foreign policy that sought to exclude official French, Russian, and British influence from the government."[12]

The king also had native Hawaiians among his advisers, most of them graduates of the Lahaina-luna Seminary on Maui. But Hiram Bingham became so influential he was referred to as "King Hiram" along the Honolulu waterfront, and Gerrit Judd was considered

9. Madsen, "Mormon Missionary Wives in Polynesia," 143–44.
10. Dodge, *Islands and Empires*, 124.
11. Daws, *Shoal of Time*, 77–79, 103.
12. Gibson, *Yankees in Paradise*, 278–79.

a shadow dictator. When Hammond arrived, there were fourteen white men serving in cabinet positions, many of them former missionaries, and by 1851 there were forty-eight foreign advisors, including twenty-five Americans.[13]

In addition to political expertise and technological sophistication, the foreigners unwittingly infected the natives with devastating diseases for which they had no natural immunity. As a result, the population dwindled from 300,000 in the 1770s to only 51,000 by 1872.[14] The Hawaiians suffered more than just physical demise through contact with foreigners, according to BYU historian Lanier Britsch. They showed the effects of "moral, and especially psychological destruction. Ships, guns, and elaborate tools of iron and steel convinced the Hawaiians that their way of life was inferior to that found elsewhere. The immediate result was a sort of national shock as well as a sense of defeat."[15] Furnas was more explicit in blaming the missionaries. "Whether Catholic or Protestant," he wrote, they were "most uncivilized" in their condescension and exploitation. The "South Seas missions [were] a failure from any general point of view," even though the missionaries "deserve fragmentary credit in some respects" for, among other accomplishments, introducing a written language and literacy.[16]

In defense of his grandfather, who evolved from missionary to government advisor, Gerrit Judd IV suggested that "long before the first missionaries reached Hawaii in 1820, the Hawaiian people were well on their way to destruction as a result of forty-two years of contact with the pre-missionary foreigners." Among other factors he cited was the decline from 300,000 to 135,000 inhabitants before the arrival of the missionaries, which had already weakened Hawaiian institutions and culture.[17] Commentator Ernest Dodge found that too much "fun has been poked at the missionaries," even if they

13. The other advisors included twenty-one Brits, one Frenchman, and one German. Judd, Hawaii, 60, 70; Furnas, *Anatomy of Paradise*, 145.

14. Gibson, *Yankees in Paradise*, 255.

15. Britsch, *Moramona*, 9.

16. Furnas, *Anatomy of Paradise*, 290, 296.

17. Judd, *Hawaii*, 39.

deserve it for their "bigotry, their Mother Hubbards[18] for the girls, [and] their inflexible moral attitudes." These were "minor peculiarities compared with their achievements," in his estimation.[19]

For instance, the missionaries established excellent schools. "By 1829 at least forty-five thousand Hawaiians were receiving instruction in over seven hundred schools," and by 1832 more than half the adult population could read the native language, which the missionaries had begun writing down in the 1820s. In 1840 the government passed a law that required common schools in every area, and by 1850 some schools were led by Hawaiians. The missionaries completed the translation of the New Testament in Hawaiian in 1832 and the Old Testament in 1839.[20] By 1842, textbooks, tracts, and two newspapers were being printed in the native language. Britsch points out that "the literacy of the Hawaiians and the availability of the scriptures facilitated the work of the Latter-day Saints when they arrived."[21]

In similar fashion, it could be argued that the missionaries from the London Missionary Society eased the way for the first three Mormons to Tahiti. Thirty LMS missionaries arrived in the Society Islands in 1797. By 1802 the missionaries were preaching sermons in the native language, initiating both the Christianization and literacy of the region.[22] By comparison to the Tahitian missionaries, however, the Protestants in Hawaii were much better educated. The Tahitian Protestants were working-class artisans, while the ones in Hawaii were "graduates of good colleges and they had been trained in the tough intellectual atmosphere of New England Puritanism ... Their effect on education [in Hawaii] was massive and their influence on government critical."[23] The Mormon elders in Hawaii, like their

18. Mother Hubbards were blousy, full-length dresses similar to muumuus, but with high-neck collars to insure that every inch of skin was covered, a requirement for attendance at Protestant schools.

19. Dodge, *Islands and Empires*, 127.

20. Kuykendall, *Hawaiian Kingdom*, 105.

21. Britsch, *Moramona*, 11.

22. See Gibson, *Yankees in Paradise*, 267; Ellsworth, "New Wine and Old Bottles," 13–17; Perrin, "Seasons of Faith," 203.

23. Dodge, *Islands and Empires*, 88–101, 128. See also Furnas, *Anatomy of Paradise*, 267–71.

Protestant LMS counterparts in the Society Islands, were salt-of-the-earth craftsmen and farmers rather than intellectuals, and they were too few in number at first to significantly influence Hawaiian society and government. That would come later.

CHAPTER 5

The Gold Missionaries

I told them that I could not go home under existing circumstances, without feeling condemned ... It would sound badly for ten Elders to be sent out to the islands by Elder C[harles] C. Rich, one of the Twelve Apostles, to preach and to act as the Spirit and circumstances might dictate, and when we found there were not whites that would receive us, turn around and go home, and leave a whole nation to welter in ignorance, because he did not happen to tell us that we were to preach to them in their own tongue.

—*George Q. Cannon, My First Mission, 19*

As the Mormon pioneers were scratching out a permanent settlement in the Salt Lake Valley, aware that riches were flowing out of the ground in California, President Brigham Young dispatched missionaries to the gold fields in October 1849 with a strange calling—to prospect for the church. At least two of the missionaries were asked to do so for individual church leaders. Henry Bigler was called to work on behalf of the church's head patriarch John Smith, while James Keeler was to labor for Thomas Callister.[1] Uncle John Smith, the church founder's uncle, had arrived in Utah in a "destitute condition," so the directive was that he fit out Bigler for the gold fields, in return for which he would receive half of Bigler's earnings; the same for Keeler on Callister's behalf. Bigler made it clear in his journal that he was unhappy with this arrangement but complied with it.[2]

1. John Smith (1781–1854) was the father-in-law of Thomas Callister (1821–1880), a lower-ranking church leader.

2. See Landon, *Journals of George Q. Cannon*, 1:5–6n13.

Led by Apostles Parley P. Pratt and Charles C. Rich, and carrying themselves and their supplies on horses and mules, the missionaries left Great Salt Lake City on October 12, 1849, and traveled the southern route, crossing the Cajon Pass into California about December 9.[3] Moving north to the gold fields, many of them staked claims in a camp called Slap Jack Bar on the middle fork of the American River.[4]

Elder Rich visited these missionaries five months later on September 24, 1850, and proposed that they serve a mission to the Sandwich Islands during the winter. "This plan," historian Lanier Britsch wrote, "had much to recommend it, for the cost of living in California during the gold rush was high ... and no mining could be done in the winter months. Hence the idea ... was appealing."[5]

The next day eight men were selected, set apart, and given special blessings. William Farrer recorded on September 25 that "this morning a number of the brethren met to gather [together] when Bro Rich appointed the following to go on a mission to the Sandwich Islands, viz Tho[ma]s Whittle, Henry W. Bigler, James Keeler, John Dixon, George Cannon, Tho[ma]s Moriss, James Hawkins, and myself."[6] Hiram Clark and Hiram Blackwell, working in a nearby camp, were soon selected as well, and Clark, who had previously served two missions in England, was appointed mission president, probably because at fifty-four he was the oldest. They traveled to Sacramento to board a river steamboat to San Francisco, where the ten men found passage to the Sandwich Islands on the *Imaum of Muscat* on November 22. After a harrying experience getting out of the San Francisco Bay in the middle of a wind storm, they made it to the open sea and arrived at Honolulu on December 12.[7]

The native capital was a bustling town of about eleven thousand

---

3. Farrer journal, Oct. 12, 1849.

4. For an account of their activities during this period, see Landon, *Journals of George Q. Cannon*, 1:78–82.

5. Britsch, *Moramona*, 3; Furnas, *Anatomy of Paradise*, 156.

6. Farrer journal, Sept. 25, 1850.

7. Farrer journal, Sept. 25, 1850; also Britsch, *Moramona*, 4; Orton, *Journals of George Q. Cannon*, 2:18–22. Because the second volume of the Cannon journals will be cited so frequently, it will hereafter be abbreviated as *JGQC*.

George Q. Cannon

Courtesy Utah State Historical Society.

William Farrer

Courtesy Daughters of Utah Pioneers.

James Keeler

Courtesy Daughters of Utah Pioneers.

people and relatively few foreigners.[8] In the morning the elders hiked above town about two or three miles to a waterfall, bathed, climbed another thousand feet up a ridge, constructed an altar out of stones, sang, preached, and prayed. "Father Clark was mouth in prayer," wrote Keeler, after which Dixon spoke in tongues and "Brother Hawkins interpreted a part of it. He said that the Lord would bless us more than we had asked for or could ask for[, for] which I felt to rejoice mutch."[9]

Farrer reported that on December 15 the elders went to a popular chapel where there were "about seven or eight hundred people present mostly natives [and] one of the [Protestant] missionaries pr[e]ach[ing] to them in their native language."[10] Cannon recalled that until then they had thought their "time would be occupied in preaching to the whites," but realizing how small the white population was, and seeing the Protestant linguistic success, he and a few of the other elders decided to start learning Hawaiian.[11]

They also decided it would be best to fan out across the islands instead of remaining together. Clark chose O'ahu (Honolulu) for the mission headquarters, asked Whittle to be his assistant, and instructed Bigler, Cannon, Dixon, and Hawkins to draw lots to determine where they would work and who their companion would be.[12] However, no sooner had they done so than Clark changed his mind and decided he needed an extra elder in Honolulu, demonstrating the kind of indecision that would plague his brief administration. He directed Morris to stay at Honolulu and appointed his erstwhile companion, Elder Bigler, to forego Moloka'i in favor of joining Cannon and Keeler on Maui. Dixon and Farrer would go to Kaua'i and Hawkins and Blackwell would serve on Hawai'i.[13]

After Farrer loaned Hawkins ten dollars to get to the big island

8. "There were fewer than two thousand foreigners among the estimated eighty-four thousand residents of the Sandwich Islands in 1850." *JGQC*, xl.

9. Keeler journal, Dec. 13, 1850; also Farrer journal, Dec. 13, 1850; *JGQC*, 27–28.

10. Farrer journal, Dec. 15, 1850. See also *JGQC*, 30.

11. Cannon, *My First Mission*, 9.

12. Keeler journal, Dec. 14, 1850; also Cannon, *My First Mission*, 10.

13. Cannon, *My First Mission*, 11. See also Britsch, *Moramona*, 5.

of Hawai'i, Hawkins and Blackwell left immediately. On December 19, Keeler, Cannon, and Bigler sailed to Lahaina, Maui, and rented a one-room native house at a weekly rate of $4.00.[14] Cannon wrote that he "felt more feelings of despondency than I had done since I left home. I felt that there was a great trial and cross to go to a foreign nation and preach the gospel. There were but few whites here not as many as we had been led to expect." On Sunday three days later, the missionaries were permitted by the Rev. Townsend Taylor to preach at the Bethel Seaman's Chapel. "There were about thirty males and one female present," Cannon reported, apparently all white. After the three missionaries spoke, no one in attendance expressed any further interest in their message.[15]

They turned their attention to the language through Christmas, and had the quietest holiday Cannon had ever experienced.[16] He complained about the foreigners on Maui, saying the

> white men who go to the Sandwich Islands do not always behave themselves as they should ... They seemed to think that, because they were among the natives, they could abandon all decency. The natives are very close observers. They soon saw that we were not like many of the whites whom they had seen, and they began to take an interest in us. They readily helped us to pronounce and read their language.[17]

On January 13, 1851, Cannon found an older native woman named Nalimanui who allowed them to live with her for free. On Kaua'i, Dixon and Farrer spent three discouraging weeks, culminating in Farrer's confession that "this morning we thought it was best for one of us to go to Honolulu and see Bro[s] Clark & Whittle and see what was the best course for us to take[,] as the White people would not turn out to hear us & we could not make much progress in learning the native Lan[g]uage for want of some person to teach us." Farrer sailed to Honolulu, and President Clark told him "he did

14. Cannon, *My First Mission*, 11.

15. *JGQC*, 33, 38, with a note that the 1853 census showed a Maui population of 17,574, with only 244 foreigners (33n13).

16. *JGQC*, 38–39.

17. Cannon, *My First Mission*, 15; also *JGQC*, 40n35.

not think it was any use for those of the Brethren who were going home in the spring to stay any longer here than till they could get a suitable opportunity to get home." The mission president then wrote to Dixon, telling him to "come to this place the first opportunity."[18]

Four days later the president wrote to Brigham Young informing him that he had procured the Market House for preaching, free of charge, and "a few turned out the first time, but they discontinued and we gave up preaching; I am now trying to learn the language." He ended on a sour note, condemning the sexual practices of the native women. "They are guilty of all kinds of whoredoms and abominations and the more men the women can accommodate the greater they consider the honor," he said.[19]

When the elders at Lahaina heard that Whittle planned to return home, they also learned that Cannon was to be Clark's new assistant, something that did not sit well with Cannon. "This news," he wrote on January 23, "was rather unexpected [as] we had hoped that Bro. W[hittle] would have stayed longer. I felt very sorry to hear of his going as I thought he would do better to stay.—I was attached to this island [Maui] and had made calculations on it being the scene of my labors while I stayed & I was somewhat attached to the People."[20]

Even so, Cannon traveled to Honolulu in an upbeat mood, happy to have made some progress in learning the language. Bigler on Moloka'i and Keeler on Maui were also "in good spirits and felt as though there would be a great work on these Islands amongst the natives."[21] It was a surprise to Cannon to learn that Dixon and Farrer wanted to join Whittle in returning to California. In Cannon's mind, this was nothing less than desertion, and they would be "under [divine] condemnation" for it. "I told them that if I were to go home under

18. Farrer journal, Jan. 13, 18, 23, 1851.

19. Hiram Clark to Brigham Young, Jan. 27, 1851, qtd. in *JGQC*, 554–56. Ironically, as noted by Shaffer, "Hiram Clark," *Journal of Mormon History* 17, no. 1 (1991): 98, "in selecting Clark to preside over the mission, [Charles C.] Rich either did not know or chose to ignore allegations of moral impropriety made against Clark twice during his English missions."

20. Keeler journal, Jan. 23; Cannon, *My First Mission*, 19; *JGQC*, 46.

21. Farrer journal, Jan. 25, 1851.

existing circumstances the Lord in my opinion would hold me accountable for not doing my duty to this people and the people would be apt to rise up in judgment against me [in the next life] for not giving them the privilege of hearing the truth." Cannon believed the fact that he was making progress with the language was evidence of God's approbation. They had found housing at Lahaina and he had experienced "more of the spirit of the lord than I had ever enjoyed before."

Whittle and Dixon increased their determination to leave, but Farrer changed his mind. Whittle's feeling was that since Elder Rich had framed the mission as a seasonal endeavor, he "had given [them] the privilege of going home." In addition to that, he had experienced some inspired "dreams [that] led him to go home" rather than stay.[22] The two missionaries left on January 29 for Maui, looking for a schooner that would take them to San Francisco.[23] Dixon said he would "gladly take a mission to Europe ... but to labor [in Hawaii] he could not with any pleasure." Besides that, he said, he had remained a bachelor too long and wanted to get married.[24]

One of the reasons Whittle was leaving was because of his difficulties with President Clark, something he spoke to Hiram Blackwell about when Blackwell traveled to Maui and O'ahu to communicate his desire to leave. He left Hawkins behind on his own on Hawai'i while he consulted with the other missionaries.[25] It would "take one year to learn the language," Blackwell had decided, and besides that the people were "degraded."[26] On February 14 the elders in Lahaina heard by mail from Honolulu that Blackwell was going to join Whittle and Dixon. Five days later, when Clark visited Lahaina, he told Keeler he was going to go to the Marquesas Islands with a convert named Blake.

Instead of trying to impose discipline among the missionaries, Clark decided it was a good idea to expand the mission to include the Marquesas. The convert, Blake, was a printer and had typesetting

22. *JGQC*, 47–49.

23. Farrer journal, Jan. 25, 1851.

24. Cannon, *My First Mission*, 19–20.

25. Keeler journal, Jan. 23–24, 1851.

26. Farrer journal, Feb. 2, 1851. Cannon wrote almost exactly the same words in his journal that day concerning Blackwell's reasons for leaving the mission. See *JGQC*, 51.

materials for producing church pamphlets, so Clark thought this would enable them to reach whites in the islands.[27] But he said the other missionaries could follow him to the Marquesas Islands or stay where they were. The missionaries at Lahaina were secretly pleased to see Clark go. Keeler wrote that

> we have had very bad feelings since Father Clark came here. His conduct did not please us attall as we thought that he made to[o] free with the women in asking them foolish questions about their legs and about the stripes [tattoos] on their legs[,] how far the stripes went up[,] if it went up to their crotch[,] and telling them that he had seen some that did[,] and [he] also wanted to measure one womans thy [thigh] to see how larg[e] it was and so forth, and also the spirit that he had did not agree with ours at all. Therefore this caused us to feel very bad all the time that he was here.[28]

Instead of going to the Marquesas Islands, Clark returned to Honolulu for three days and then sailed alone to Tahiti.[29] In March 1853 the second mission president, Philip Lewis, wrote to the First Presidency and explained that "when I arrived here I found 'Mormonism' in bad odor among the foreigners, in consequence of the unwise policy which was pursued by a certain individual who preceded me."[30] Clark left Honolulu for Tahiti and from there traveled to Mormon San Bernardino in California, where he committed suicide on January 10, 1854. The branch president reported that Clark had been "slightly insane and low spirited," and one day, his mind confused, he went into a field behind the house and cut his throat with a razor. His son was nearby and watched him die.[31]

In the meantime, Blackwell, Dixon, Morris, and Whittle boarded a ship for California. Keeler later wrote that there had been ten missionaries at first but the "degradation of the [native] people"

---

27. Farrer journal, Feb. 20–22, 1851; *JGQC*, 52.

28. Keeler journal, Feb. 23, 1851. Cf. Lyman, *Candid Insights*, 294–95.

29. Ibid., Apr. 9, 1851.

30. Lewis to First Presidency, Mar. 16, 1853, qtd. in Manuscript History of the Hawaiian Mission.

31. Lyman, *San Bernardino*, 97; also *JGQC*, 481.

compelled four of them to leave. "One half" of them, including the mission president, "left & went home[,] leaving the rest [of us] to work it out the best we could."[32] The charismatic twenty-four-year-old Cannon spoke to the other missionaries on Maui about what he saw was their need to re-energize their efforts to learn the language. Hawkins was still on his own on Hawai'i, making what linguistic progress he could.

Cannon had already been toughened by his life's experiences to that point. He was orphaned as a teenager after his mother died in mid-Atlantic, on their way to America, and his father died in Nauvoo, Illinois, a few years after their arrival. George was placed with a foster family—that of his uncle, Apostle John Taylor, editor of the *Times and Seasons*—and he was taught the printing trade.[33] In Hawaii the future newspaper editor and church apostle came into his own as someone who was willing to take a controversial position, stand up in the face of adversity, and persuade people to his way of seeing things.

In an April 17, 1851, letter from Lahaina, he wrote "that our mission would be a fruitless one if we confined ourselves wholly to the whites." He thought that the natives' state of "ignorance and darkness" was the missionaries' challenge. "Placed in the circumstances we have been [in]," they had been forced to rely on God, seeking "an elder's privilege to have revelations to a certain extent for himself."[34] He learned that on Whittle's return to Utah, his group was "ambushed by Indians, and he was killed." "I often asked myself," he later wrote, "after hearing of his death, would it not have been better for him if he remained? For if he had, I believe he would have still been living."[35] Returning to the islands in 1900, Cannon pointed out that the five elders who had left the mission had all died early, while the five who stayed continued on into old age. "His belief in

32. Keeler journal, Jan. 1, 1853.

33. See *JGQC*, xiii, xv. For a full biography, see also Bitton, *George Q. Cannon*.

34. Cannon to Joseph Cain and Arieh Brower, qtd. in *JGQC*, 559; also Cannon, *My First Mission*, 14.

35. Cannon, *My First Mission*, 20.

the judgment of Divine Providence" regarding their mission performance was "obvious," Britsch commented.[36]

Cannon claimed that the Hawaiian people were "descendants of Israel, as circumcision has been practiced among them until recently; and [they] also had places of refuge for the shedder of blood, with many other things practiced by the Israelites."[37] He attributed this insight to revelation; as Britsch put it, the doctrine of Polynesian descent from biblical people originated with Cannon, and "from this time on [he] and his associates began to preach [this to] the Hawaiian people," telling them they were "an offshoot branch of Israel through the posterity of Lehi, a Book of Mormon prophet."[38]

The impulse to bring Polynesians into the biblical fold came in the context of the church's successes in Canada and Britain and relative lack of success elsewhere. On April 8, 1855, President Brigham Young spoke in the old tabernacle in Salt Lake City[39] about "calling upon the Elders to go and gather up Israel," saying he "doubt[ed] whether another Gentile ever comes into this Church." Missionaries would be sent to so-called gentile regions ("China, Russia, England, California, [and] North [and] South America"), but the expectation was that the biblical diaspora was scattered throughout those areas and the missionaries would "gather out the Israelites, wherever they were mixed among the nations of the earth."

Young also claimed that when non-Israelites were converted to the Mormon gospel, God would transform their blood so it would be composed of the same biological components as those who were Israelites by descent. He cited Joseph Smith as his authority that when such people were converted, "the Gentile blood was actually cleansed out of their veins, and the blood of Jacob made to circulate in them; and the revolution and change in the system were so great that it

36. Britsch, *Moramona*, 17.

37. *JGQC*, 560–61; also Cannon, *My First Mission*, 45.

38. Britsch, *Moramona*, 15; cf. Petersen, *Polynesians Came from America*; Cheesman, *Early America and the Polynesians*. DNA, linguistic, archaeological, and cultural evidence, however, confirms that the Polynesians came from Melanesia, Indonesia, and the Philippines (Southerton, *Losing a Lost Tribe*).

39. *Journal of Discourses*, 2:268–69.

caused the beholder to think they were going into fits (convulsions). If any of the Gentiles will believe, we will lay our hands upon them that they may receive the Holy Ghost, and the Lord will make them of the house of Israel ... You understand who we [Mormons] are; we are of the House of Israel, of the royal seed, of the royal blood."

Since Polynesians were relatively dark-skinned, Cannon's (and the LDS Church's) decision to place them in the same racial category as mainland Native Americans was consequential. According to the Book of Mormon, anciently the Indians had been cursed by God with a dark skin because of sin, but they nevertheless were of Israelite descent. Had they been grouped with Africans, their lot in the LDS Church would have been worse, and in fact there probably would have been no Mormon missions to Polynesia. It is important to briefly explain how blacks, more particularly American negroes, had been viewed by the LDS Church since it was founded in 1830.

For someone who came from a northern state, Joseph Smith's view of people of African origin was particularly harsh, more in keeping with the interpretations of Southern ministers who read into the Bible what was not there in order to justify slavery. For instance, Smith considered dark skin to be a sign of divine displeasure, a "curse" that was God's doing and only God could remove. Nevertheless, Smith authorized the baptism and confirmation of free Negroes (and slaves who had their master's permission) into the church and even authorized the ordination to priesthood office of a few free blacks, albeit without altering his theological views.

When he visited Missouri in August 1831, it was his first visit to a slave state, and he reported in his *History of the Church* that the "first Sabbath after our arrival in Jackson county, Brother W. W. Phelps preached in the western county, over [near] the boundary of the United States [and Indian Territory] wherein were present specimens of all the families of the earth; Shem, Ham and Japheth [three sons of Noah]; several of the Lamanites or Indians representative of Shem; [and] quite a few ... number of negroes descendants of Ham."[40] Four years later Phelps wrote to Smith from Missouri outlining his views on race, in essence summarizing what Joseph Smith himself thought about the issue at the time.

> Is or is it not apparent ... that God [curses] ... people [who] fall away from his church, to be cursed in time, with a black skin? Was or was not Cain, being marked, obliged to inherit the curse? ... And if so, as Ham, ... by marrying out of the church, did or did he not, have a Canaanite wife, whereby some of the black seed was preserved through the flood, and his son, Canaan, ... [inherited] three curses: one from Cain for killing Abel; one from Ham for marrying a black wife, and one from Noah for ridiculing what God had respect for? Are or are not the [American] Indians a sample of marking with blackness for rebellion against God's holy word and holy order? And can we not observe in the countenances of almost all nations ... a dark, sallow hue, which tells the sons of God, without a line of history, that they have fallen or changed from the original beauty and grace of father Adam?[41]

Smith's approval of this reasoning is indicated by the fact that he had the letter published in the official LDS newspaper in Kirtland, Ohio, the *Messenger and Advocate*. One year later, after an abolitionist organization had formed in Kirtland, the paper ran long articles by Joseph Smith, his counselor Oliver Cowdery, and his secretary Warren Parrish condemning abolitionists and defending slavery as a divinely established institution. They cited the biblical "curse of Ham and Canaan" as justification for slavery. Joseph said that when the patriarch Noah cursed his son Ham and grandson Canaan, it was a "singular prophecy" and "wonderful occurrence." Parrish declared that "although political demagogues and religious fanatics, in their blind zeal, m[a]y bustle and rage, and compass sea and land with the pretention to meliorate the condition of Ham's descendants, yet God's curse pronounced by his servant Noah will remain upon them; and Canaan must dwell in the tents of Shem and be his servant until He [God], who pronounced it[,] shall order it otherwise. And all the

40. *History of the Church,* 1:190–91.

41. *LDS Messenger and Advocate,* Mar. 1835, 81–82; cf. Gen. 4:1–16; 9:18–28.

abolition societies that now are or ever will be, cannot cause one jot or tittle of the prophecy to fail. The curse that was pronounced on that people was by the spirit of prophecy."

According to Cowdery, the curse of the "fourth son of Ham" was retained by his descendants "to this day," and "when it will be removed we know not ... Where he now remains in bondage, remain he must till the hand of God interposes." He considered "the project of emancipation [to be] destructive to our government, and the notion of amalgamation [miscegenation] devilish! And insensible to feeling must be the heart, and low indeed must be the mind, that would consent for a moment, to see his fair daughter, his sister, or perhaps, his bosom companion, in the embrace of a NEGRO!"

Missionaries proselytizing in the South took copies of the 1836 *Messenger and Advocate* with them to prove that Mormons favored slavery.[42] Joseph Smith reaffirmed this position in a question-and-answer column in the LDS *Elder's Journal* in 1838, explaining that Mormons "do not believe in setting the Negroes free."[43] Furthermore, he published his book of Abraham in serialized form in the newspaper, later adopted as LDS scripture, connecting the curse of Ham and Canaan to denial of the priesthood.[44]

While visiting the capital of Illinois a year before his death, Joseph Smith engaged in conversation with apostles Orson Hyde and Willard Richards, as well as non-Mormons, and declared that negroes "come into the world slaves, mentally and physically. Change their situation with the white and they would be like them. They have souls and are subjects of salvation ... Had I any thing to do with the Negro I would confine them by strict Laws to their own Species [and] put them on a national Equalization."[45] When he ran for president of the United States the next year, Smith suggested that Congress "pay every man a reasonable price for his slaves out of the

42. See Bush, "Mormonism's Negro Doctrine," 15, 50n20.

43. "Answers to Sundry Questions," *Elders Journal*, May 1838, 29.

44. The Book of Abraham was published serially in the March and May 1842 issues of the LDS *Times and Seasons*; see Abr. 1:21–27.

45. *History of the Church*, 5:217–18.

surplus revenue arising from the sale of public lands ... Break off the shackles from the poor black man, and hire him to labor like other human beings; for 'an hour of virtuous liberty on earth is worth a whole eternity in bondage.'"[46]

His political platform may have sounded progressive, but he was simultaneously thinking of establishing a Mormon settlement in the Texas Republic, not yet a part of the United States, so Mormon converts from the South could take their slaves there. Furthermore, he said in a speech in Nauvoo on March 8, 1844, that the issue of whether Texas should be admitted to the Union should be answered with an emphatic yes, that "we should grasp all the territory we can" and "as soon as Texas was annexed, I would liberate the slaves in two or three States, indemnifying their owners, and send the negroes to Texas, and from Texas to Mexico, where all colors are alike. And if this was not sufficient, I would call upon Canada, and annex it."[47] Even if he were committed to this idea because he thought it would benefit blacks, rather than to compromise in some way for political expediency, he still personally regarded blacks as divinely cursed.

It is true, however, that some free blacks joined the Mormon Church in its first two decades. In fact, a precious few—for instance Elijah Able, baptized in 1831 and ordained to the priesthood with Joseph Smith's consent, and Q. Walker Lewis, who received the priesthood sometime before 1843—were not held back by the theology.[48] Scholars have debated whether or not these two documented ordinations are evidence of a policy shift. If so, the significance was lost on apostle Orson Hyde, soon after Joseph Smith's death in 1844, when he said that in a pre-mortal War in Heaven, spirits destined to inhabit earthly tabernacles took sides with God or Lucifer, and some remained neutral. According to Hyde's "hypothesis," the spirits who were neutral were allowed to be born into mortality with certain "handicaps" such as a black skin.

46. Qtd. in Taggart, *Mormonism's Negro Policy*, 65–67.

47. *History of the Church*, 6:244.

48. Manuscript History of the Church, A-1; Reeve, *Religion of a Different Color*, 117. Brigham Young, in a later reference to Lewis, said, "We [have] one of the best Elders[,] an African in Lowell [Massachusetts]." Stevenson, *For the Cause of Righteousness*, 15.

Hyde either heard such things from Joseph Smith or imagined them himself, but in either case the hypothesis became doctrine. Another apostle, Orson Pratt, published the speculation in a church newspaper, *The Seer*, in April 1853, and it instantly appealed to Mormons because it blamed Africans for their supposedly undesirable skin color and forced servitude due to their behavior in the spirit "pre-existence" rather than saying that they were being held responsible for something their ancestors did.[49] It was cited in an LDS First Presidency statement as late as December 1969; one First Presidency statement in 1949 called it the church's official position and "doctrine."[50]

Brigham Young hardened the policy with regard to blacks in 1847 by establishing for the first time as an explicit prohibition that any descendant of Cain would not be given the priesthood and would not be allowed entrance to the temple because "the curse remains on them." The curse gave "the children of Abel an opportunity to keep [their] place," segregated from African Americans.[51] In line with the church doctrine, the Utah territorial legislature passed an act "in Relation to Service" in 1852 that legalized slavery, and at least eighty slaves and thirty-three free blacks were in Utah Territory by 1850, some of whom were members of the church. None of them were ordained to priesthood office or allowed into the temples or Endowment House.[52]

In a speech to the Utah territorial legislature on January 5, 1852, Young was quoted in the notes of apostle Wilford Woodruff that "any man having one drop of the seed of Cane in him Cannot hold the

49. See William E. Berrett, "The [LDS] Church and the Negroid People," in Stewart, *Mormonism and the Negro*.

50. See Bush and Mauss, *Neither White Nor Black*, 221–24. However, "today the Church disavows the theories advanced in the past that black skin is a sign of divine disfavor or curse, or that it reflects unrighteous actions in a premortal life." "Race and Priesthood," www.lds.org.

51. Qtd. in Reeve, *Religion of a Different Color*, 147; see also Stevenson, *For the Cause of Righteousness*, 17.

52. Reeve, *Religion of a Different Color*, 143.

priesthood."[53] That became the policy of the church until it was reversed in 1978.[54] Then the church began proselytizing blacks for the first time.[55] American Indians were considered cursed as well, but it was always thought to be a less serious branding than the mark that bedeviled the descendants of Cain, Ham, and Canaan. In the Book of Mormon, and in the teachings of Joseph Smith and Brigham Young, Native Americans—because they were purportedly of Israelite descent—were promised that their skin color would turn "white and delightsome" as they accepted the Mormon gospel, to my knowledge a promise never given to those of African descent.[56] Thus when Cannon and the LDS Church in 1851 placed native Hawaiians and other Polynesians into the same racial category as mainland Indians, they were given a more advantageous position in the Mormon racial hierarchy. This was so even though some, like the Fijians, had very black skin and features closely resembling those of African Americans.[57]

Cannon commented about his Hawaiian converts that "many a time their faces would glisten and appear almost white under the influence of the Spirit."[58] On March 18, 1851, while traveling between Lahaina and Wailuku on the island of Maui, he met with native historian David Malo and noted in his journal that

53. The legislative scribe, George Watt, who recorded the speech in shorthand, overlooked that statement. Reeve, *Religion of a Different Color*, 159.

54. For more, see Hammond, Quest for the New Jerusalem series, *An Inaccessible Mormon Zion: Expulsion from Jackson County*, vol. 4, 341–46; *Crisis in Mormon Kirtland: A Temple and an Illegal Bank*, vol. 5, 193–229.

55. When I was a full-time missionary in northern California, 1961–63, we were told by our mission president to avoid African Americans, and if we encountered them at their door to invite them to attend church and disengage.

56. See 2 Ne. 5:21–23; 30:3-6.

57. The question of ordaining Fijians was posed to church president David O. McKay in 1954, and he ruled that they should not be barred from priesthood offices. Mormon sociologist Armand Mauss saw this as switching the burden of proof "so that anyone ... could be ordained unless the local church leaders provided evidence of a candidate's African ancestry." Prince and Wright, *David O. McKay*; Mauss, *All Abraham's Children*, 232.

58. Cannon, *My First Mission*, 44.

> I told him that the Lord had … revealed the record and origen of the American Indians &c. &c. I could not express my ideas very well [as] my language was considerably broken. When he learned how long I had been here he was considerably <surprised> at my progress in the language. He said I would soon get it. He said he wanted to talk with me [later] when I ~~was~~ got [able to] … I told him that I thought [Hawaiians] were descendants of Israel because they resembled them very much. He said … the same because they had observed the same [rituals]: … one was [that] … at ~~certain~~ certain seasons they kept apart from their women when they had their courses. These things made him think that they were of this race.[59]

As the missionaries continued to work on the language through the spring of 1851, they began to connect with significant people, some of whom would convert to the church. For instance, on March 8, while passing through Wailuku, Cannon met with Jonathan Napela and his wife, Kitty. Napela was a graduate of the Protestant Lahaina-luna Seminary, located on the slopes above Lahaina. He was also a successful businessman, farmer, and judge. He was friends with the Rev. Daniel Conde (1807–97), a Congregationalist missionary who had graduated from Union College in New York.[60] In order to better learn Hawaiian, Cannon was invited to board with the Napelas in exchange for teaching English to Jonathan. He also taught his host about Mormonism, which rankled the Reverend Conde. As the situation heated up, Conde "threatened [Napela] with removal from his judgeship and with being cut off from their church."[61]

One Sunday, Conde delivered a sermon in which he condemned Joseph Smith and his adherents, saying according to Cannon "there

---

59. *JGQC*, 64; Malo discussed these ideas in his *Hawaiian Antiquities*. Many other Americans in Honolulu at the time put Hawaiians into the same diminished category as blacks, referring to them as "niggers," and the fact that Mormons did not see them in that light was an appealing aspect of Mormonism for the Hawaiians. See Daws, *Shoal of Time*, 148–49; Maffly-Kipp, "Looking West," 129, 134; Furnas, *Anatomy of Paradise*, 157; Lineham, "Mormon Message," 213; also Douglas, "Sons of Lehi and the Seed of Cain," 90–104.

60. *JGQC*, 60; "Daniel & Andelucia Conde (Journal)," Digital Collection, *Hawaiian Mission Houses Historic Site & Archives*, online at www.missionhouses.org.

61. Cannon, *My First Mission*. Davis Bitton wrote about Cannon's prickly exchanges with Conde in "George Q. Cannon in Hawai'i," 179–81.

were three of these men living at Lahaina and that one of them came very frequently to Wailuko and stopped at the house of Napela ... they were like Mohamet." Unknown to Conde, Cannon was in the audience and could by then understand the language. When Cannon walked up to him, Conde's "face turned pale ... [and] he looked like a man who had been caught in a mean, low act." Cannon refuted Conde for half an hour in the presence of about a third of the congregation. Napela's family and friends found the reverend's attempt to publicly shame the Napelas "distasteful," and so the stunt seemed to backfire on the minister.[62]

According to Cannon, Conde took action against Napela for drinking alcohol, "associating with a man that had been expelled from the Church," and boarding a disreputable Mormon. Cannon offered to part ways with Napela rather than see his career as a judge jeopardized, but Napela refused to have him leave.[63]

The other LDS missionaries found inspiration in this development and doubled their efforts with the native people in villages outside of Lahaina and Honolulu. Farrer visited many small villages on O'ahu where little English was spoken, and like Cannon discovered that the people were willing to listen to him, and even provide him with food and lodging. In May a man named J. W. H. Kauwahi showed interest in Farrer's message, possibly because he had heard of Cannon's success with three fellow graduates of the Lahaina-luna school. "The report of what we were doing," Cannon later wrote, "went through all the islands. The natives frequently went from one island to another. They are a talkative, gossipy people, and exceedingly fond of telling news."[64] Meanwhile, on the island of Hawai'i, Hawkins, who was living with a white blacksmith, baptized fourteen people.[65]

Opposition to the Mormons continued. On Sunday, April 6, Cannon was introduced to the elderly Rev. Jonathan Green at church services.[66] Green invited Cannon to a nearby house to talk. Gradually

---

62. *JGQC*, 69–72n26; Cannon, *My First Mission*, 30–31.

63. *JGQC*, 73.

64. Cannon, *My First Mission*, 44.

65. *JGQC*, 82; Farrer journal, June 6, 1851.

66. Green was the founder of the Central Maui Female Seminary at Wailuku. An

Traditional grass huts varied in size and appearance depending on their use.

Courtesy Hawaii State Archives.

the discussion became heated, Green started pacing the room, then "seized his hat & sa[id] God curse you; and went out" to mount a horse and leave. Turning to the shocked natives standing nearby, he said: *Ae enemi keia*, meaning "yes, this is the enemy." A little over a week later, Cannon had another testy confrontation with the same reverend at a church service in Kula. "His prayers and whole sermon w[ere] directed at us," Cannon said, and "after he got through I got up and spoke a few minutes to the people." Green cut him off and "commenced a series of catechetical questions" he assumed Cannon would have trouble answering. Whether or not Cannon knew how to answer, he decided to withdraw to avoid a "law against disturbing public meetings." Green "warned his people" not to listen to the Mormons.[67]

Cannon had discovered something interesting about himself.

abolitionist, he had broken with his church sponsor to run the independent churches called Makawao Union and Po'okela. Bartholomew, *Maui Remembers*, 18, 22. See also *Missionary Album*, 104-105.

67. *JGQC*, 74–75, 85–86.

When he was confronted by a "nearly full house" of natives under the influence of an agitator, he was only emboldened to speak fearlessly. "From this time I commenced to labor in a more public manner among the people," he wrote, "speaking in their meeting houses as I could get opportunity, and doing all in my power to give them a knowledge of our principles. My speaking before Mr. Green had a good effect; the people saw that I preached the doctrines of the Bible, and that I was not afraid to meet the preachers."[68] On June 15, as Napela inched ever closer to baptism, the judge instructed some acquaintances to build a hut for the Mormons to preach in, making it the first semi-permanent LDS meeting place in the islands.[69]

On O'ahu, Elder Bigler's spirits were revived when his landlord in Honolulu, a native lawyer named Ioane W. E. Maikai, said he wanted to learn more about Mormonism. And more importantly, Farrer, working outside Honolulu in the native villages and learning the language, wrote that his host, J W K Kauwahi, said "he wanted me to baptize him[,] that he believed we had the truth, that he had done wrong but that it was his determination to forsake his evel [evil] and obey the commandments of the Lord. We went to the water & baptized him [and] this is the first I have baptized into the Kingdom on these islands." The next day Farrer received word from Bigler that more missionaries were arriving from Salt Lake City. The following day Bigler took Farrer to meet the second wave of elders; Farrer wrote that "on arriving at the wharf I was Saluted by [the new missionaries] Lewis & H[ammond] and although entire strangers to me except by sight we were glad to meet each other. We soon started for Lahaina."[70]

When the new elders first arrived at Lahaina on August 19, the elders on Maui—Cannon and Keeler—were not there, and Hammond sent a note to them by way of a native courier. When they arrived, Cannon wrote that they found "Bro. Lewis[, who] I am some little acquainted with, Bro. Hammond[, who] I know by sight but have no acquaintance with him, and Bro. Woodbury[, who] I may know but do not know by name." He knew Hammond had lived in the

68. Cannon, *My First Mission*, 32–33; also qtd. in *JGQC*, 86–87n2.

69. *JGQC*, 92.

70. Farrer journal, Aug. 17–19, 1851.

islands, converted in California, and married in Utah.[71] Cannon and Keeler had just organized Mormon branches at Honomanu, Keanae, Waianu, and Wailua, ordaining local male converts to take charge, indicating how dramatically things had progressed since the missionaries first arrived in the islands about eight months earlier.[72]

When Cannon left Wailuku because of the opposition of Rev. Conde, Jonathan Napela found him a place to stay with relatives and employees at Waiakoa, near Kula, where he had a potato-raising business. Arriving there on May 13, he soon wrote to Keeler at Lahaina of his success in the area, and Keeler joined him on June 17. Five days later they baptized "three young men and one woman," according to Cannon, although Keeler put the total at five. Stimulated by Cannon's success working alone, Keeler traveled to the coastal villages of Keanae and Wailua, on the north coast of East Maui, where despite his poor knowledge of the language, he had great success.

Cannon baptized a native man on July 6, and another, H. K. Kaleohano (a future Mormon stalwart), and three native women the next day. On the morning of July 23 Keeler arrived, begging Cannon to return with him to the Keanae area, which they reached that evening. Quickly joined there by Kaleohano and four others from the area of Waiakoa and Kula, they baptized thirty-nine people on July 24 and fourteen the next morning. That afternoon they traveled about one mile to Wailua, baptized thirty-five more, and back at Keanae on July 26 twelve more. Keeler claimed that between July 23 and July 28 they baptized one-hundred-twenty-nine new converts in the area.

By the time Cannon and Keeler arrived at Lahaina to meet the new missionaries from Utah, they had just organized Mormon branches at Honomanu, Keanae, Waianu, and Wailua, adding to the ones already at Kula and Waiakoa, and had ordained local male converts to take charge.[73] Things had progressed dramatically since the missionaries first arrived in the islands less than a year earlier.

---

71. Keeler journal, Aug. 16, 1851; *JGQC*, 115–16.

72. *JGQC*, 116.

73. Keeler journal, May 31–June 17, July 1–28, Aug 16, 1851; *JGQC*, 93–107, 116.

CHAPTER 6

Penniless

In the evening Bro Hammond and myself called on the Revd Mr Baldwin for the second time. He appeared very uneasy at our presence. We asked him if he would like to converse further on our doctrine. He said he did not really know as he had time and said he should like to have a sign. If he should see a miracle performed [he] would have to believe as a matter of course.

—Philip B. Lewis Journal, Sept. 9, 1851

When George Cannon and James Keeler arrived in Lahaina on August 20 to meet the five missionaries of the second wave and the two first-wave elders who had come from Honolulu, it was a joyous occasion to see not only the men but their wives, Mary Jane Hammond and Jane Lewis. "Sis. H[ammond] recognized me as soon as I came in the yard—she being an old acquaintance[,] a friend of my sister Anne's," Cannon wrote. The Hammonds, he said, had "a fine little boy about 11 months old" named Francis Jr. "It done me a great deal of good to look upon the faces of the brethren and sisters."[1]

Lewis proposed that the missionaries be re-baptized as a way of recommitting themselves to the work. Even though four of the veterans had carried out this purifying ritual recently, the next morning the entire group "went down to the sea and Brother Hammon[d] baptised Brother Lewis[,] then Brother Lewis baptised the wrest [rest]."[2] The new arrivals had letters from the mainland informing the missionaries that Hiram Clark had arrived in San Francisco from

1. Farrer journal, Aug. 20, 1851; *JGQC*, 117.

2. Keeler journal, Aug. 20–21, 1851; also *JGQC*, 120.

Tahiti, and that he and Hiram Blackwell had been busy "crying down [decrying] the Islands," predicting that the missionaries would soon have to abandon their proselytizing and "work to make a living."[3]

Apostle Parley P. Pratt advised President Lewis to keep the missionaries together until they had learned the language, but once in the country Lewis decided to disregard that advice and have them split up to cover more territory.[4] The more experienced missionaries felt protective of the newer ones. "I thought they would need the Spirit of the Lord to enable them to endure things that they might have to endure, while upon these lands," Cannon wrote.[5] One of the things he knew would be difficult for them was the widespread nudity among the native people, something Hammond would have been familiar with from his earlier sojourn on Maui.

When Mary Chipman Lawrence, wife of the captain of the whaleship *Addison*, stayed in a cottage at Lahaina for several days in 1856, she wrote that many of the natives "go without clothing; both sexes bathe in the water entirely naked, unabashed. As I am writing, two men are close by my door without an article of clothing."[6] When Mark Twain visited in 1866, he wrote that "to see a nude woman bathing at noonday" was "so common that the white residents pass carelessly by, and pay no more attention to it than if the rollicking wenches were so many cattle. Within the confines of even so populous a place as Honolulu, and in the very center of the sultry city of Lahaina, the women bathe [nude] in the brooks at all hours of the day."[7]

In a letter to Apostle Pratt a week later, Hammond indicated how impressed he was with Cannon. "Bro Cannon says he has baptized About 200 Natives over on East Maui about 50 to 80 miles from Here ... Br Cannon says they come to him before he is up to go

3. *JGQC*, 118–19. In Tahiti, it was newly required that visitors support themselves and not rely on natives (*JGQC*, 118n41).

4. Lewis journal, introduction, 4.

5. Letter from George Q. Cannon, Aug. 22, 1851, qtd. in Manuscript History of the Hawaiian Mission. See also *JGQC*, 117.

6. Garner, *Captain's Best Mate*, 25.

7. *Mark Twain's Letters*, 196.

[to] the water, 30 and 40 at a time. He says that when he is Preaching to them about the book of Mormon the tears will Flow down thire [their] cheeks like little children. He is very smart for so young a man and has more wisdom than some Elders as old again as he is."[8]

On Saturday the missionaries put up notices throughout town announcing an English-speaking meeting for the following day at the home of James Kipp, one of Hammond's old friends from the 1840s. Cannon wrote that there was "a tolerable attendance." Even though President Lewis was "laboring under a severe cold and did not feel like preaching," he "done very well considering that it was his first attempt before a congregation. After he had got thro' he gave the congregation the privilege of asking questions," at which a man who "appeared to have a little liquor in him" began berating Joseph Smith. The mission president's reaction was to dismiss the meeting until 4:00 that afternoon and suggest that Cannon "had better try and speak" instead of the mission president. Cannon agreed and found he was "blest with a good flow of the spirit" until the same man as before "broke in upon <me> in the middle of my discourse" and caused another disturbance. Cannon told him to "please wait until I got thro'." The man was quiet for a while, then started in again until Kipp and another man identified as Judge Parsons told him to be quiet or they would "dispose of him in a way that would be anything but agreeable," at which the man retreated. Hammond was asked to speak, and he enumerated "his reasons for joining the Church and also bore his testimony to the truth of the work." After the congregation sang a hymn, the service was adjourned. Cannon was pleased with it, writing that he thought the people in attendance felt the Holy Ghost even though the services were interrupted twice.[9]

In his letter to Pratt, Hammond praised Cannon's ability to handle hecklers and the simplicity of his message. Lewis, by contrast, Hammond noticed,

---

8. Hammond to Parley P. Pratt, Aug. 28, 1851. Hammond dated it 1852, but it clearly was written a year earlier.

9. *JGQC*, 122 (Aug. 23, 1851).

> likes to preach big things[,] such as I call the Mistreys [mysteries] of [the] Kingdom. He loves to talk and tell all he knows[,] which has been no good as I can see in No instance. He has given so much at a time that it has chocked [choked] them and they would not come again, but he will learn about that after a while ... [L]ast Sunday he preached to about 40 [and] ... an old fellow attacked him rather ruff and Brother Lewis [was] somewhat embarrassed [that] he could not hold his way with him. Then I proposed to Closed [close] the Meeting seeing thare was likely to be a row ... I do beleive that if We get into troubel it will be by preaching big things.[10]

Lewis confessed to his journal that he too thought he performed poorly on that occasion, writing that "I attempted to preach for the first time. I did not do as well as I could on account of being very much embarrassed[,] and in the afternoon I invited Bro Cannon to preach[,] which he did."[11] Hammond probably invited some of his old friends from his three years at Lahaina in the 1840s, and if Lewis failed to make an impression, it might account in part for Hammond's chagrin. Whatever the cause of it, this began a mutual animosity that would continue between them.

Hammond told Pratt that he arrived at Lahaina "nearly out of money" but had enough to rent "a good large house of a native[,] about as good as any house in the place[,] cool and comfortable," until he could bring in some money by making shoes. He thought the church was wrong to send couples or families to the islands. "They should be single men," he wrote, "for they can go among the natives and Not cost them a cent to live[,] whereas with a family you Must keep house." He was making plans for "starting a shoe shop." Otherwise, they would "be in rather a tight place pretty soon."[12] It seems that Pratt may have heeded Hammond's advice because Mormon leaders would not send any more married couples to the islands in the 1850s.

On August 21 Lewis asked Hammond to accompany him to visit

10. Hammond to Pratt, Aug. 28, 1851.

11. Lewis journal, 5.

12. Hammond to Pratt, Aug. 28, 1851.

the Rev. Dwight Baldwin and see if they could get permission to preach in Lahaina's Bethel church.[13] The elderly Baldwin, an 1821 graduate of Yale College and subsequent student at Harvard and Auburn Theological Seminary, had been on Maui for thirty-five years. At 135 lbs., he would have appeared delicate next to Hammond, who at six feet two inches would have towered over him.[14]

Hammond had known Baldwin previously on the island when he regularly attended services conducted by the minister, so he must have had mixed emotions approaching him now as a Mormon. According to Lewis, Rev. Baldwin mentioned their prior acquaintance, saying "that if Bro Hammond was of the same persuasion that he was when here before[,] he should not hesitate to let us have" use of the chapel. Usually the scheduling was done by the Rev. Taylor, who had gone to O'ahu to preach, but Baldwin remembered that his colleague had "allowed the Mormons to preach" in the Bethel church "on conditions that they should not ask for it again." Four days later on August 25, Hammond and Cannon visited Baldwin, and Cannon found the elderly minister to be polite but "non-committal," someone who would "weigh every word and if we got upon any thing that he did not consider tenable—he would contrive to waive the subject." Once again, they departed without resolving the question on the use of the church.[15]

In the meantime, the elders were given their assignments: Bigler, Farrer, and the Lewises were to go to O'ahu; Woodbury to Hawai'i; Keeler to Keanae (East Maui); and the Hammonds to Lahaina (West Maui); while Cannon would return to the Kula/Waiakoa area thirty-five miles from Lahaina. The Lewises stayed long enough in

---

13. Cannon said that Lewis's "feelings prompted him to stay in Lahaina," having taken note of the fact that "Bro. Hammond was an old resident" of the city. The president encouraged Hammond to sustain himself through his former trade as a shoe maker. *JGQC*, 120.

14. Bartholomew, *Maui Remembers*, 18, 21; Dwight Baldwin to Abbey, Lahaina, Jan. 2, 1854; *Missionary Album*, 36–37. He practiced medicine on the side, having studied but not graduated in medicine from Harvard, but was refused a medical license in Honolulu until 1859 when he received an honorary medical degree from Dartmouth.

15. Lewis journal, introduction, 5; *JGQC*, 123.

Lahaina to assist Hammond on September 6 in baptizing and confirming James Kipp.[16] Cannon found it difficult, after the comfort of being around people from home, to have to "return and mix with the Natives and conform to their manner of living again. But," he added to his journal in a confessional style, "I am laboring for a liberal master [God] who knows that my motives are pure." As Hammond walked his fellow missionary to his horse, Cannon found it difficult to say goodbye, admitting that he had "not felt the pangs of parting more severe ... since I left home."[17]

Lewis and Hammond went together one more time to see Baldwin on September 9. Unfortunately, their visit turned contentious, according to Lewis's description of it in a long and entertaining journal entry. The mission president and former whaler met the minister in the evening at his private residence a block from the wharf, a two-story frame house that has since been preserved as a museum. The minister "appeared very uneasy at our presence," Lewis recorded. When the missionaries "asked him if he would like to converse further on our doctrine," he said "he did not really know as he had time" and that "it was of no use" anyway since we believed in new "revelation in the last days and that precluded everything else." Lewis said he would "waive revelation and give him an opportunity to put my doctrine" to the test "by the Bible," but Baldwin said he "did not wish to have any further conversation with us, and that he considered us all deluded."

At that point Lewis "requested the privilege of bearing [his] testimony to him," then proceeded to do so without an answer, warning Baldwin "not to fight against [Mormonism] lest he be found fighting against God, for the man who did it should not prosper." In response, Baldwin "said as [Lewis] had been plain[,] he would be plain also." Lewis encouraged him, saying he should "not be afraid of wounding my feelings and to speak out what was in him, which he did by saying that Mormonism ... [was] a lie[, that] ... it [was] his duty to fight

16. Keeler journal, Aug. 22–25, 1851; Lewis journal, Sept. 6–7, 1851.

17. *JGQC*, 124–25.

Philip B. Lewis

Dwight Baldwin

against it and should do so."[18] Lewis's contentious exchange with Baldwin guaranteed that the future relationship between Baldwin and Hammond would be a prickly one.

As Lewis prepared to leave for Honolulu, he ordained James Kipp to the office of elder and called him to be a missionary companion to Elder Hammond, counseling them to make "foreigners" their priority and to tell the natives that if they looked into "the doctrine[,] someone would come shortly and preach to them in their native tounge," with the implication that Hammond—despite all his years on Maui—was not as fluent in the native language as he needed to be. The following day the Lewises left for Honolulu.[19]

In late September the local government tried to close down Mormon meetings in the Keanae/Wailua area on the other side of the island where Cannon was laboring.[20] Because of his ability with the language, Cannon decided to sail to O'ahu and ask for an audience with King Kamehameha III.[21] He borrowed a horse from a

18. Lewis journal, Sept. 9, 1851.

19. Ibid., Sept. 10–11.

20. The towns are two miles apart, about sixty miles east of Lahaina; it is another sixteen miles farther east to Hana.

21. Keeler journal, Sept. 20–26, 1851; *JGQC*, 130; also Cannon, *My First Mission*, 41.

new convert, Brother Kaleohano, and on September 26 "arrived at Lahaina a little before sundown ... Bro. Hammond and lady were living with Mr. Treat," he wrote, "Sister Hammond doing the cooking &c. for their board."[22] Treat was one of Frank's white friends from the 1840s.

The Hammonds were not destined to stay long with Treat because the man proved to be an alcoholic. Instead, they moved in with James Kipp and his wife, Kua Moo, a "half-white" (half native, half Caucasian) woman whom Hammond knew from his whaling days. The Kipps were already themselves renting from Antonio Silver, a wealthy Portuguese man. Hammond later wrote that "when first we landed[,] not having much left out of 700 dollars; I went to shoe-making for a little time, only about a month, then we found a home with an old acquaintance of mine [Kipp] who was honest enough to receive the truth and obey the same."[23] In a letter to Apostle Charles Rich, Hammond explained that his Portuguese acquaintance was interested in the church and was contemplating moving to Salt Lake City or to the Mormon settlement at San Bernardino, which Rich and another apostle, Amasa Lyman, were governing. Hammond told Rich that Silver had "kept me and my wife a good deal of the time since I have been here ... [H]e has a large number of cattle and houses and lands to dispose of first; when he comes [to San Bernardino] I will give him a letter of introduction to you and bro. Amas[a] [Lyman]."[24] Silver did not convert and leave the islands, but he continued to be a good friend and helpful with regard to the Hammonds.

On the evening of September 30, Hammond and Kipp came up with five dollars for Cannon's passage to Honolulu. These interisland voyages were difficult for Cannon because of his susceptibility

---

Kamehameha III (Kauikeaouli) was the younger brother of Kamehameha II (Liholiho).

22. *JGQC*, 131, 135; see also the Manuscript History of the Hawaiian Mission, Sept. 22, 1851, which evidently has the wrong date.

23. Hammond to Levi Ritter, Mar. 1, 1852; qtd. in Manuscript History of the Hawaiian Mission.

24. Hammond to Charles C. Rich, Nov. 25, 1851, qtd. in Manuscript History of the Hawaiian Mission.

to seasickness. "I was sick all evening and night [and] scarcely able to lift my head without vomiting," he complained. In Honolulu on October 1, he tracked down the mission president and his wife, Philip and Jane Lewis, where they were boarding with a couple named Maikai, and he stayed with them while he prepared to meet the king.[25]

Back on Maui, Frank was making periodic forays outside Lahaina to meet old acquaintances and practice the language with the natives in areas where they had not been as exposed to foreigners. Sometimes Mary Jane and Frankey went with him, and on October 18, Keeler joined him on a fifty-mile jaunt from Lahaina to the Keanae/Wailua area. They left early in the morning and managed to reach Makawao, thirty-five miles away, and spent the night with an hospitable native. The next morning they continued to the home of John Winchester and arrived at about breakfast time. He said he was happy to see them, and in fact, "we found him very anxious to hear the doctrine that we preached," Keeler wrote. Winchester had known Hammond when the former whaler had been left on Maui with a broken back. Leaving Winchester's home, the missionaries continued on another twenty-five miles to Keanae, where Cannon had been working, and "found that there was a good maney" converts to the church who had subsequently "backed out on the acount of the percicution [persecution]."[26] The missionaries realized they had their work cut out for them to stop the apostasy of recent converts.

25. *JGQC*, 132.

26. Keeler journal, Oct. 17–22, 1851.

CHAPTER 7

Almost Hell

We have baptized some six or seven foreigners, which is a hard stick for [the Protestants], they having never done the like upon the islands, after a thirty years' residence here; the natives look at it and wonder to see [the white men] come thirty or forty miles to get baptized, and [the converts] are smart and intelligent men; the natives tell the [Protestant] missionaries of it, and that makes [the Protestants] double their diligence to stop the progress of this "wild delusion;" but they have failed in every attempt, as yet.

—*Hammond to Charles C. Rich, Nov. 25, 1851*

When Cannon asked to see King Kamehameha III, he was shunted into a room with seventeen-year-old Prince Alexander Liholiho,[1] who reassured Cannon that the Mormons were legally protected and that officials at Keanae and Wailua "had no right whatever to interfere" with the missionaries.[2] Cannon returned to Lahaina and stayed with Brother Kipp and Hammond's wife, Mary Jane, until October 24, 1851. He brought news from O'ahu that Elder Farrer was making progress linguistically and beginning to baptize natives. In fact, by the end of the next month Farrer had baptized forty-seven people and organized congregations at Punaluu and Hakipuu. Bigler in Honolulu, by contrast, was still unable to speak much of the native language and was struggling as a result.[3]

1. Alexander (1834–63) would reign as Kamehameha IV from 1855–63, after which his brother Lot Kapuaiwa (1830–72), whom Cannon also met, would reign as Kamehameha V from 1863–72.

2. *JGQC*, 136.

3. Farrer journal, Oct. 16–21, Nov. 2, 23, 27, 1851; also *JGQC*, 141. Punaluu is on

When Cannon returned to his own field of labor again on November 13, Elders Hammond and Keeler were doing their best to prevent converts from defecting. Hammond was feeling discouraged and felt he had been away from his wife and child in Lahaina too long. Only the heavy rains kept him from leaving the other two missionaries on their own. Fate placed him two days later in the home of some wealthy converts where Cannon spoke with such "a good flow of the spirit" to the members of the branch, upbraiding them for "their unbelief," that things started to turn around.

The next day was Sunday, and again it rained all day, which resulted in another well-attended meeting. As Cannon spoke by "the spirit," the "congregation was melted down," he related. "In [the] afternoon I cut off several and confirmed three that had been baptized in the forenoon; afterwards attended to the feast of the Lord's supper." The members were encouraged by the good word Cannon brought from the royal family and were reassured by his presence. The decline in the area seemed to have been stemmed.[4]

Hammond's connections to the sailors he had known in the 1840s continued to pay rich dividends. At Keanae on November 20, he and Cannon, with James Kipp who had traveled from Lahaina, met with John Winchester and Albion Burnham about being baptized. Hammond did the honors the next day,[5] and Cannon expressed pleasure with this development: "I like the new brethren much, and feel as though they were old friends; they are both smart men."[6] Neither of the men's wives followed them into the church at that time.

In his November 25 letter to apostle Rich, Hammond explained that the "natives are anxious to hear us preach; they are sending for

---

the northeast side of the island, a few miles south of Laie, while Honolulu lies along the southern shore. Hakipuu was seventeen miles south of Punaluu.

4. *JGQC*, 137–39.

5. Keeler journal, Nov. 3–4, 1851.

6. Cannon to Bigler or Farrer, Dec. 1, 1851; *JGQC*, 140–42. Cannon thought this fulfilled a dream of "two pine chips" igniting a fire in his coal furnace, "chips" being the nickname for a ship's carpenter, Burnham's and Winchester's former occupation. This may have led biographer Davis Bitton to unjustifiably credit Cannon with their conversion. Bitton, "George Q. Cannon in Hawai'i," 182

us from all parts of the Islands, and all that we lack is a thorough knowledge of the native language." He talked of opposition from Protestants who were protecting their "influence of thirty years' standing." Calling them the "priests of Baal," Hammond claimed that they had become "rich" off of the natives, "with good houses and large tracts of land, ... plenty of cattle and horses, and every thing to make themselves comfortable." From his perspective, the ones who had become government advisers were the worst of all; they had "thrown aside their Bible for the Law Book." The Protestants had purportedly become even more opposed to Mormons when some white people had converted to Mormonism.[7]

After explaining that poor Elder Hawkins "has had a hard time, and suffered a great deal for the necessaries of life" on the island of Hawai'i, Hammond expressed personal satisfaction for himself. "I have got along well enough, and have been treated well by the natives," he summarized. "My wife is no detriment to me but a help; I get many favors [from people] that I should not get if she was not along." On November 30 the remaining missionary and two wives who had been detained in San Francisco—William Perkins and wife Patty and Elvira Woodbury—arrived on the schooner *Ayrshire Lass.* James Kipp invited them to stay with him in Lahaina, where Elvira almost immediately began teaching the native female converts how to sew clothing and began trying to learn the language.[8] The same day she and the others arrived, Hawkins sailed in from the big island, saying he had been lonely there, the work was unproductive, and he wanted to return home. The others persuaded him to stay, suggesting he join Elder Keeler in Wailua, where it might be easier for him to learn the language.[9]

On December 1, Cannon told Bigler and Farrer that he was frustrated at being unable to make new converts because he had to spend

7. Frank Hammond to Charles Rich, Nov. 25, 1851; qtd. in Manuscript History of the Hawaiian Mission.

8. *Deseret News*, Apr. 25, 1855; Elvira Woodbury journal, qtd. in Manuscript History of the Hawaiian Mission.

9. *JGQC*, 143.

so much time tending to recent ones.[10] Hawkins felt bad about not being able to help more in that regard and "reproached himself" for having found accommodations with a foreigner instead of with natives. Cannon recommended that from then on, all the missionaries should "forsake the English language in every possible way, thoughts, prayers, words, & etc." He and Hammond intended to use "the Native as our medium of communicating" from then on, he announced. Referring to the recent conversion of a few foreigners, he added that the "natives say there is something different about this [Mormon] doctrine," since it converted even white former sailors, men the Protestants had not been able to attract.[11]

On December 3, Hammond and Cannon stopped at Honuaula (not Honolulu) on the southwest shore of East Maui to see another friend of Hammond and reach out to native people. They met with lively opposition but still organized a branch and ordained two men to the offices of deacon and teacher before the week was out. They then traveled to Wailuku, a town Cannon had avoided because he left under compromised circumstances in the wake of opposition from the Rev. Daniel Conde. As they got closer to town, they decided to stop to pray—or rather, Hammond prayed while Cannon stood guard—before deciding where to stay. Cannon was unsure if he was still welcome at the Napelas' house. Deciding to trust their instincts and risk imposing on the Napela family, they went first to the house of Cannons' old friends and found Jonathan meeting with Samuel Kamakau, a member of Parliament (Cannon called him "the best orator and one of the smartest natives on the islands") and other prominent native men.

Napela gave the two missionaries a warm reception and asked them to speak, telling his Hawaiian friends "that if they had any objections[,] now was the time to make them [known, when the missionaries were] present and could defend [themselves], and <not> to

10. Farrer agreed that if you left a newly organized branch alone, like he had in Hakipuu, half the members would leave; you could work "in vain to get them to come back." He said they were "leaving about as fast as they came in." Farrer journal, Jan. 9, 19, 1852.

11. Cannon to Bigler or Farrer, Dec. 1, 1851; also JGQC, 572–74.

go behind [their] backs and talk about [them]. It was nearly daylight when we got through," Cannon enthused. The young missionary found he was "blessed with fluency, and the Lord enabled me to answer all their questions to their satisfaction."[12] The all-night session became a springboard for previously unimaginable success in Wailuku and throughout the islands, everything changing so dramatically that Conde was soon "almost deserted by his congregation ... I confess that to see him thus treated pleased me," Cannon wrote with contempt. Before two weeks were out, Cannon and Hammond had baptized enough people at Wailuku and the surrounding villages, seventy-one in all, to have to build several meeting houses.[13]

With the onset of the new year, the most significant baptism in Maui occurred on January 5 when Jonathan Napela was immersed by George Cannon, joined by three other native people and another native convert five days later. The missionaries ordained Napela and a man named William H. Uaua (Jonathan Napela's cousin) to the office of teacher in the Aaronic priesthood. Like Napela a graduate of the Lahaina-luna seminary and a lawyer, Uaua would become the church's best native orator. On the day they were ordained, the missionaries baptized another eleven natives. Jonathan was so important to the early success in the islands that a native convert worried about the complete collapse of the church if Napela left. "All the church would follow," the man predicted.[14]

Instead of reacting with joy at the news of what had transpired, President Lewis in Honolulu seethed over the fact that Hammond had left his post in Lahaina and engaged in unauthorized excursions with Elders Keeler and Cannon. Nor was the president happy to learn of these developments by letter from Hammond after the fact on December 19.[15] Hammond said he had sent "as many as eight letters" to Lewis that had gone unacknowledged, leaving him to wonder why the president was ignoring him.

12. *JGQC*, 143–45.

13. Cannon, *My First Mission*, 42–43; also in Manuscript History of the Hawaiian Mission.

14. JGQC, 146–50; Bitton, "George Q. Cannon in Hawai'i," 183.

15. Lewis journal, Dec. 19, 1851.

Jonathan Napela

On January 15 the two white converts, Winchester and Burnham, were ordained to the office of elder, as James Kipp recently had been. Clearly, the missionaries were reluctant to elevate native brethren to this high office, limiting them to lesser positions now associated with teenage boys in the LDS Church. The "higher priesthood," encompassing the offices of elder, seventy, and high priest, required a separate ordination to the Melchizedek Priesthood. The authority the natives were given came from the "lower priesthood" involving the offices of deacon, teacher, and priest, through separate ordination to the Aaronic Priesthood. Peter Lineham found that this was the practice in New Zealand when missionaries converted Maori people. "In the first sixty years of the Maori mission, only a tiny number of converts received ordination to the Melchizedek Priesthood."[16]

Mormon scholar Lanier Britsch's claim that Utah missionaries "treated the Hawaiian members as complete equals from the beginning" is wishful thinking, according to what the evidence indicates. Native priesthood holders, even if they were eventually ordained

16. *JGQC*, 152; Lineham, "The Mormon Message in Maori Culture," 214.

elders, were not thought to be on par with the white brethren and were left out of important decision-making meetings. "Like their Protestant counterparts, and Americans generally," BYU professor Carol Cornwall Madsen rightly observed, "Mormon missionaries disguised an implicit racism in their paternalistic benevolence and perceived their relationship with the [Polynesian] natives as parental even after conversion."[17]

The situation at Keanae continued to be problematic. The natives were displeased with the leadership of Elders Hawkins and Keeler and showed this by refusing to feed them. The missionaries left the members, Keeler wrote, "to their own distruction for we Concluded that we Could not live without Eating." When Cannon heard from the missionaries what had transpired, he could not think of a resolution except to wait and see what might develop.[18] He and the other missionaries joined Hammond at Waiehu, about twenty-five miles from Lahaina, on the north side of the island near Wailuku, where Hammond was preparing to baptize another foreigner, David Rice.[19] The elders held a council and elected Cannon as council president to discuss what they should do next, in particular whether they had the authority themselves to decide where their individual labors should be, independent of President Lewis's input. Cannon listened to Hawkins make a case that he ought to return to the island of Hawai'i with a companion. No resolution was reached until the next day when both Cannon and Hammond decided that the mission president held exclusive authority in making assignments.[20]

That was easier said than done, since President Lewis was not answering mail—at least not Hammond's mail—on the apparent assumption that silence would be understood to mean no. The problem for the missionaries was that the circumstances on Maui were constantly changing, and Hammond felt forced to interpret

17. Britsch, *Moramona*, 20; Madsen, "Mormon Missionary Wives in Nineteenth Century Polynesia," 160.

18. Keeler journal, Jan. 13–14, 1852: *JGQC*, 151–52.

19. *JGQC*, 146, 148.

20. Keeler journal, Jan. 19–22, 1852. Cannon says nothing about this in his journal entries for Jan. 21–22.

the president's silence as consent. He and his family left Lahaina on February 6, saying they were fed up with what he called "the hell of this island," Lahaina, convinced that the natives there had become irreparably corrupted by pleasure-seeking whalers.[21] The Hammonds preferred to work outside Lahaina, which also was more conducive to learning the language, and they took up quarters with the new convert, David Rice, in Waiehu.

Paradoxically, Lewis had told apostle Parley Pratt on September 1, before he even left Lahaina for Honolulu, that he was thinking of sending Woodbury to work with Hawkins on the big island. "Bro. Woodbury can do nothing here and will never get the language by staying here." In a postscript he explained that he himself intended to go out "among the natives, where the English language is not spoken[,] for if I do not I shall never get a knowledge of the language."[22] The president made good on his word for brief periods in small native villages on O'ahu and Kaua'i.

Because Cannon, the youngest of the missionaries, was the most advanced with the language, his accomplishment generated fanciful stories about how he was able to acquire it. Native church member William K. Wallace III claimed that Cannon spoke by the gift of tongues, that "in one night [Cannon] was given the understanding of the Hawaiian Language." Even Britsch maintained that "in only three weeks Cannon had begun to understand the language. Although he did not boast complete mastery, he could understand most of what was said, and speaking ability followed relatively quickly."[23] The myth originated in 1879 when Cannon himself explained in a reminiscence that a few weeks after his arrival, he felt "a peculiar sensation in my ears; I jumped to my feet, with my hands at the sides of my head, and exclaimed to Elders Bigler and Keeler ... that I believed I had received the gift of interpretation! And it was so. From

21. Hammond to Farrer, June 8, 1852.

22. Philip Lewis to Parley Pratt, Sept. 1, 1851.

23. Wallace III, *Church of Jesus Christ of Latter-day Saints in the Hawaiian Islands for 1850–1900: An Abridgement*, a presentation of the Laie Stake, Jan. 2000; Britsch, *Moramona*, 15.

that time forward I had but little, if any difficulty in understanding what the people said."[24]

While Cannon developed the ability to communicate faster than the others, in part because he was very young, it came about through hard work over several months of study with the Napelas. It was at least six months after his arrival before he began to preach to native congregations. That in itself was impressive, but he was not yet fluent at that time, as he himself admitted.[25] He wrote to apostle Pratt in late August 1851 that after being in the islands about nine months, the language had finally begun to make sense to him. He said he had begun to be "able to preach in it for upwards of two months."[26] If he was aided by natural ability or motivated by supernatural belief, his equivalent in Tahiti, Addison Pratt, admitted to Brigham Young that "what knowledge we have obtained of the language is by hard study, and not by the '*gift of tongues*.'"[27] The missionaries generally made progress according to their age. Cannon wrote to his aunt in Salt Lake City in March 1852 that "Bro. H[ammond] had acquired some knowledge of the language during a former residence here; but this has not been of as much benefit to him as he anticipated it would be, being wholly obtained by the ear." Hammond had devoted "little attention to the grammatical construction of the language," which he now had to learn, and "unlearn" much of what he thought he knew. Cannon said that Farrer had "begun to preach," but that Lewis and Bigler remained "backward" in their ability.[28]

Younger missionaries were able to learn the native language faster, Lewis recognized, as he explained to the First Presidency in

24. Cannon, *My First Mission*, 15–16; also *JGQC*, 46n45.

25. "New Wine and Old Bottles," 15; Cannon and Keeler to Bigler and Farrer, June 23, 1841, in *JGQC*, 561–63.

26. George Cannon to Parley P. Pratt, Aug. 25, 1851; *JGQC*, 569–70. Also qtd. in Turley, "Gathering Latter-day Saint History in the Pacific," 154. See the Cannon letter, Dec. 12, 1851, qtd. in Manuscript History of the Hawaiian Mission (and summary of the language situation at the end of 1851); Whittaker, "Placing the Keystone," 505.

27. Pratt to Young, in *Times and Seasons*, Nov. 1, 1845, 1019–22; "News From our Mission in the Pacific," *Millennial Star*, Jan. 1, 1846: 15; also qtd. in Ellsworth, "New Wine in Old Bottles," 15. Emphasis in original.

28. See Manuscript History of the Hawaiian Mission; also qtd. in JGQC, 577–80.

March 1853. Hawaiian "is a hard language for an adult foreigner to learn," he wrote. "In fact the [missionaries] have all acquired it in proportion to their ages. Bro. Cannon got it first, Bro. Farrer next and so on. Bro. Bigler[,] being the oldest of those who preceded me, has just begun to preach a little and myself being the oldest one in the lot may expect to come out at the tail end of the heap." Lewis wrote to Pratt that "since I have been here I have been studying the native language. I can read & translate it very well, and I speak it a little, and I think that in a little time I shall be able to preach to the people. It is a hard language for an adult person to learn[;] it is too much like learning 'old dogs new tricks' but by the help of the Lord I shall be able to conquer it."[29] He never did.

Cannon was twenty-three years old on his arrival in December 1850. Hammond was twenty-one when he began living on Maui in 1844. Farrer, who began speaking after about seven months, had turned twenty-nine in 1850. Hawkins was thirty-one, Keeler thirty-three, Bigler thirty-five, and Lewis forty-seven. Woodbury was twenty-five when he arrived in August 1851.[30] The age gap was the best predictor of language ability, which was the key to success in almost all other areas. Immediately after Cannon left the mission in the summer of 1854, Hammond observed in his journal that the missionaries always looked to Cannon as the real mission leader and that Lewis was something of a figurehead. Cannon's facility with the language and adaptation to the culture were both consonant with his age, while the mission president struggled with both the language and customs and quickly lost the confidence of the missionaries.

---

29. Lewis to Pratt, Mar. 19, 1853.

30. Similarly in the Society Islands in the 1840s, Benjamin Grouard was twenty-five and learned the language with relative ease. Addison Pratt was forty-two, although he had spent six months on O'ahu at age twenty, and learned fairly quickly. Noah Rogers was forty-seven and could not learn the Polynesian language, so he left the mission after one year.

CHAPTER 8

Translating Books

My place of residence was at Brother J. H. Napela's, Wailuku. He was an educated, intelligent Hawaiian, who thoroughly understood his own language, and could give me the exact meaning of words ... Probably but few in the nation were as well qualified as Brother Napela, to help me in this respect. He was a descendant of the old chiefs of the Island of Maui, in whose families the language was preserved and spoken in the greatest purity, and he had advantages which no other equally well educated man, at that time, possessed.

—*George Q. Cannon, My First Mission*

The oldest surviving journal of Frank Hammond opens with his family's move to Waiehu, about three miles from Wailuku, on February 6, 1852. He wrote: "This morning set out with my Wife and little one to Waiehu. Parted from our friends at Makawao [fifteen miles to the east] with heavy hearts. May the Lord bless them for their kindness to us. Arrived at Waiehu about 4 o.c[lock]. All well but very tired." David Rice had invited them to stay with him.[1] Hammond had baptized nine people in Makawao, including Judson Gaston and Marcus Baker, friends of Albion Burnham, David Rice, and John Winchester, which means that Hammond probably knew them at the time of his previous interlude on Maui in the 1840s.[2]

The fact that the mission president was not answering his letters was an ongoing concern to Hammond. He had nightmares of

1. Emphasis in original. Cannon mentioned the Hammonds' move that same day. *JGQC*, 155.

2. See the entries for these dates in the Manuscript History of the Hawaiian Mission.

"seeing Brother Lewis" and offering to shake his hand and the president refusing. In the wake of his conversions at Makawao, two other missionaries, Cannon and Keeler, decided to organize a branch there in the house of Burnham and Winchester. At the branch's first meeting, there was a good spirit, Cannon thought, and several men were ordained to leadership offices. Winchester was set apart to preside over the branch.[3]

Cannon lived with the Hammonds and Rice for a short time while he was preparing for an island-wide conference for the native membership. He and Hammond hiked through Iao Valley on February 20 looking for a location for an open-air gathering and liked what they saw. The valley was convenient to Wailuku and Waiehu and was known for its beauty. Below the moss-covered cliffs, they "pray[ed] before [the] Lord [and] felt his spirit to be with us in a good measure," Cannon wrote.

Nine days later at a worship service in Wailuku, Cannon was impressed by Hammond's sermon. "It was the first time that I ever sat and listened to one of the brethren speak in native," Cannon remarked.[4] However, about "15 or twenty minutes" into the sermon, Hammond began to lose confidence and became "confused," although not enough to temper Cannon's enthusiasm. Cannon rose and spoke to relieve Hammond, then invited Napela and Maiola to speak in succession, after which the elders baptized seven converts.

Hammond humbly assessed his own language skills to Levi Riter in early March, admitting that his previous "knowledge of the language" had "not avail[ed] me much, having not learned it properly," saying he had to learn it "over again." Nevertheless, he could "preach a little" and was otherwise doing "what I can."[5]

In Cannon's journal we read of how much he enjoyed the company of the Hammond family during his stay with them. In a letter published in the *Deseret News*, he stated publicly how much "their society has been a solace to me, as also to the rest of the brethren. Sister

3. *JGQC*, 157.

4. *JGQC*, 158. Cannon thought Keeler was making good progress, as well.

5. Hammond to Levi Riter, Mar. 1, 1852, *Deseret News*, July 24, 1852; also qtd. in Manuscript History of the Hawaiian Mission. Riter married Hammond's sister-in-law Rebecca.

H[ammond] will not, I think, be soon forgotten by us; for she has been truly sisterly."[6] "All the Elders who labored in that field have reason to remember their kindness to them," Cannon elaborated in his reminiscence, *My First Mission*. "Under their roof we always found a warm welcome ... [They] were constantly speaking the native language ... [and] conform[ing], to some extent at least, to [native] modes of eating." Mary Jane had "unvarying ... patience and cheerfulness in the midst of privation, and her unsparing labors in our behalf, to sew and do other work for us, which among such a people we had need to have done," was appreciated. In fact, he noticed that Mary Jane even milked the fifteen cows every morning that belonged to Rice.[7]

Cannon was translating the Book of Mormon into Hawaiian, having begun in late January. Finding he needed the help of Jonathan Napela, he moved back in with the Napelas in Wailuku, where he had been living (without a white companion) for much of the previous year. They finished the first draft there within a year; the final handwritten version was completed on Kaua'i in January 1854.[8] Cannon later explained that his "conversations which I had with the natives concerning the Book of Mormon and the origin of the red men, made them anxious to see it." The translation proceeded as follows:

> In the beginning, my method was to translate a few pages, and then, when opportunity offered, explain to Brother Napela the ideas, whether historical or doctrinal, in great fullness. By this means he would get a pretty thorough comprehension of the part I was translating. I would then read the translation to him, going carefully over every word and sentence, and learning from him the impression the language [I had] used conveyed to his mind. In this way I was able to correct any obscure expression which might be used, and secure the Hawaiian idiom ... At some times in revising the translation, I had other intelligent men present with Brother Napela.[9]

6. *Deseret News*, July 24, 1852, qtd. in Manuscript History of the Hawaiian Mission for Mar. 1, 1852. See also JGQC, 159.

7. Cannon, *My First Mission*, 43; also qtd. in Manuscript History of the Hawaiian Mission; *JGQC*, 169–70.

8. *JGQC*, 154; Britsch, *Moramona*, 25–26.

9. Cannon, *My First Mission*, 59–60.

On the morning of March 31, the Hammonds, Cannon, and Rice traveled to Makawao for a "conference of white Brethren," consisting of the "thriveing little branch" of about eighteen members with "4 Elders, 1 Teacher, 1 Priest, [and] 1 Deacon." The leadership of this congregation of mostly Anglos became the decision-making council for the whole island, and in 1852 their decisions would be communicated to the native branches at the Wailuku conference on April 6. Members there would be given the opportunity to ratify the decisions that came out of Makawao, and this would be the pattern going forward through the 1850s. Napela and a few other ranking natives were invited to be present in Makawao; President Lewis, too, was invited but declined because, he said, "poverty prevented him from attending." Elder Keeler came in from Kaupo, located on the east coast of Maui, where he had recently baptized thirty-two converts.

The leadership council was presided over by Cannon. "We had landed in our weakness a year and a little more ago upon the islands with a total ignorance of the language," he said, "and now there were hundreds rejoicing in the truth of the work &c." Next up was Hammond, who "spoke well and with power[,] as also Bro. Hawkins." David Rice was ordained an elder, and then Cannon "laid before the brethren the propriety of ordaining some of the Native brethren to the Aaronic priesthood." He reported that "the conference had [not] nor knew of any objection."[10] Interestingly, there was no thought of ordaining Napela or any other native brethren to the higher priesthood.

The afternoon session at Makawao was left open for spontaneous speaking, singing, and prayer so "the brethern" would have "the privelage of witnessing the manifestation of the spiret abundantly in prophesying &c &c. I never enjoyed myself so well in all my life, & it was so with all the brethren & sisters," Hammond wrote. "The Native Brethern, what few were there, were filled with the Spiret & propheside by the power of the Spiret." The meeting adjourned at around 5:00 p.m., followed later that evening by another prayer meeting involving "visions and prophesying" that lasted until midnight.

10. *JGQC*, 162–65.

These emotional gatherings played an important role in the spiritual life of the members and produced converts. Mary Burnham was so moved she told Mary Jane that if she stayed another day she would be baptized, and Mary agreed to do so. When they "went up" the next day "& took tea with Br. Gaston, ... Mrs. G[aston] also concluded to be baptized this evening with Mrs Burnham." "About sundown," Frank wrote, "we repared to the water ... Brother Hawkins offic[i]ated. Baptised t[wo] Ladyes[,] 1 white boy [William Henry,] & one native woman." Many of the converts lacked a full appreciation of what it meant to be a Mormon. For instance, the missionaries had not yet broached the topic of tithing. At Wailuku on April 5, the day before the mass gathering, "a few of the natives met, when we set the principle [of tithing] before them." Cannon reported that "they were ready to receive it with joy," so it was decided to present the principle to the full conference. When Cannon had concluded, Hammond spoke on the same topic.

The conference began the next day in a kukui [candlenut tree] grove in the Iao Valley. Cannon described it as "a beautiful place—a bold mountain stream rolling down at one side of the grove." Hammond and Cannon called those together who had met the night before to verify whether tithing should be mentioned to the general membership. Napela made a motion that Cannon "should lay it before the conference, that for his part he [Napela] felt to observe it &c. The vote was unanimous." Cannon was chosen as conference president; other men were selected to represent "the different branches [on Maui] which numbered in all 500 [members]." Several ordinations were proposed for the men present: "Bros. Napela and Uaua to [be ordained priests in] the Aaronic Priesthood, and the remainder [of native brethren] to the offices of teachers and deacons." Hammond, Hawkins, and Keeler then spoke on tithing, which "was carried unanimously." Mary Jane was present at the meeting and found it enjoyable.[11]

After the conference, Napela felt inspired to write to Brigham

11. *JGQC*, 166–69; also Hammond journal, Apr. 6, 1852.

Young in native Hawaiian to describe how he had been converted and how Cannon and Hammond had founded the Wailuku branch. He affirmed that the branch was "constantly increasing at this time; and it is very plain to us that this is the church of God." He closed by saying, "My desire is great to see you, ye Fathers of the gospel of Jesus Christ; and my thoughts are buoyant to go to your place, when the proper time arrives."[12] Presumably Cannon included a translation of the letter before it was sent to President Young.

In his journal Cannon paid tribute to Napela's performance at the valley conference. "I never heard him speak as powerfully before," he wrote, "and he bore the most powerful testimony of any native I had before heard."[13] Indeed, he was emerging to play a central role in the church's progress on Maui. On April 11, Cannon confirmed eight more converts, all of whom had been baptized by Napela and Uaua, and three days later Napela baptized another nine converts. On April 16, Cannon baptized and confirmed Uaua's wife.

In Honolulu on April 23 President Lewis baptized an important white convert, Edward Dennis, a wealthy tinsmith who would become an important benefactor to the church.[14] His native wife, Hakuole, would also become Mormon. Mary Jane Hammond was trying to learn the language during this time and was doing her best to follow in the footsteps of Elvira Woodbury in clothing the women, or in "teach[ing] the natives how to sew and make there [their] own cloth[e]s." This was a preoccupation of the wives of the missionaries, something they approached with thinly concealed urgency. As an example of the male missionaries' activities, Frank was spending his time, when not proselytizing, in translating Orson Pratt's pamphlet, *Remarkable Visions*, into Hawaiian.

It was understood that the main responsibility of the Utah women missionaries was to cook and sew for their husbands and other missionaries, as well as earn money to help sustain their family. "Working

12. Jonathan Napela to Brigham Young, Apr. 8, 1852, Journal History for Apr. 6; *JGQC*, 169.

13. *JGQC*, 172; also qtd. in Turley, "Gathering Latter-day Saint History," 148.

14. Lewis journal, Apr. 23, 1852. See also JGQC, 170, 175.

with her needle," Sister Lewis not only clothed the native women but contributed to the mission's financial needs because white people on the island were eager to pay for clothes.[15] The women's attempts to learn the language were less productive. Mary Jane Hammond wrote in her journal that after two years in Lahaina, "for the first time" she could "understand a little Native."[16] BYU professor Carol Cornwall Madsen concluded that the "missionary wives did not find a ministerial function in mission service until the latter part of the century."[17]

On May 1 Cannon wrote of several healings by the native brethren in the Wailuku area. One involved "the younger brother of one of the brethren … [who] was nearly dead … [but] so much restored that he was able to arise and go around and be baptised." Next a woman who "had been crawling for five years[,] not able to walk upright[,] … [was] commanded … in the name of Jesus Christ to arise and walk [and] she immediately stood up and walked and they afterwards baptised <her>." In another instance a woman asked to be cured of what appeared to be an edema. The missionaries "done according [to her request] and the swelling left her and she was baptised." When she attended a Sunday service soon thereafter and made a critical remark, "her swelling returned," Cannon smugly reported.[18] In performing healings, the members were responding to the missionaries' claim that the true church exhibited all the gifts of the spirit mentioned in the New Testament, including healing. Their confidence would be severely tested in 1853 when smallpox decimated O'ahu and East Maui.

Beginning May 20 Napela became Hammond's traveling companion for eight days, visiting Keanae, where members had stopped feeding the missionaries. As part of their efforts, the missionaries rebaptized all the existing members. Napela was rebaptized first, and while he "commenced to baptise the brethren over again," Hammond "stood on the shore and confermed them as the[y] came out

15. Manuscript History of the Hawaiian Mission, Oct 27, Nov. 30, 1851.
16. Mary Jane Dilworth Hammond journal, June 26, 1853.
17. Madsen, "Mormon Missionary Wives," 142, 146.
18. *JGQC*, 172–74.

of the water." Hammond emphasized what "great assistance" Napela had been with the native members, "in building them up again. The Lords hand had been heavy upon them ever since they had turned away & refused to [feed] the Servants of the Lord." In a June 8 letter to Farrer, he again stressed how indispensable Napela was, along with other native men. "Brother Hawkins thinks of takeing [Brother H. K.] Kaleohano with him all the time, that is to travel with him. Brother Keeler wants one to go with him also."[19]

On June 9, Hammond finally received a letter from President Lewis after eight months of silence. Hammond had pressed the issue by sending his letter in care of Elder Farrer, asking the missionary to "give my love to Brother & Sister Lewis. Pleas[e] ask Brother Lewis whether he has ever received any letters from me[,] for I have written as many as 8 and I never received a scrap in return." The president responded with a biting sidebar, Hammond wrote in his journal, claiming that "if he had not received my [recent] letter, he [w]ould have forgot[t]en there was such a man in existence." Hammond wrote that if the president had forgotten him, he had not forgotten the president and "remember[ed] him in my pray[e]rs."

On June 10 several of the missionaries and wives returned to Makawao and got up early "with the intention of going to Kula on a strawberry frolic. Bro. Gaston took a cart in which the Sisters rode," Cannon wrote.[20] The result, Hammond noted, was that "Mrs H[ammond] has a large b[oil] under one of her arms [and is] very sore from the affects of the ride on a Spanish saddle." However, they "picked as much fruit as they could carry and soon were eating "strawbury pudding[,] Strawbury Sauce[,] Strawburys & Milk[,] and every other way that we could think."

Several missionaries were asked to travel to the nearby island of Moloka'i, only fifteen miles to the northwest of Maui, to see what could be done. John and Elvira Woodbury traveled there from the big island, where they had been laboring, and connected with the Perkinses, who had crossed the windy channel in a whaleboat on

19. Hammond to Farrer, June 8, 1852.

20. *JGQC*, 180.

June 16, accompanied by Cannon and Hammond. On June 24 the missionaries held a church service at which "Brother Woodbury spoke in tounges." Wanting to contribute to the spiritual outpouring, Hammond said he "had the interpratation but did not give it[,] not being acquainted with the o[r]der of the gifts at that time," as Cannon explained it. "Br. W[oodbury] gave a part of it. It was in relation to the nature of these islands." Whenever anyone spoke in tongues, it was usually Woodbury, and Hammond was often the one who tried to give an interpretation.

Meanwhile on O'ahu in late June, Farrer learned from Elder Bigler that he had baptized a Swedish man, Gustaf Linn (or Lynn), another foreigner who would prove to be invaluable to the missionary efforts. Farrer heard by letter from Hammond that "Bro Uaua had also been over to Moloka'i ... & that he had baptized there about 30 persons."[21]

The Hammonds were back in Wailuku the next month. While attending a council meeting, Frank became ill and felt "cold and chilly," and Cannon came down with something the next day.[22] Before long, everyone in the area had the "fever that is raging in Lahaina."[23] Brother Gaston gave Hammond a blessing. After going "to bed with a high fever," Hammond "slept tolerably well" but "had some frightful dreams &c &c." He said that when he was conscious, "Mary [Jane] laid on hands" with the intent to heal him. This is a significant entry in Hammond's journal for two reasons. First, it was the first time he referred to his wife by her first name, and second, it documented an instance of a woman ministering to a man in what is now considered an exclusively priesthood function. A comparable incident occurred in the Society Islands in 1852 when Louisa Barnes Pratt, wife of Addison Pratt, "prayed and laid my hands on the sick [native] woman. I told her she should be better in the morning and so it proved ... Consecrated oil which we brought with us from [Utah] has been ... blessed to their use often, all on account of the faith they have in it."[24]

21. Farrer journal, June 29–30, 1852.

22. JGQC, 184.

23. Keeler journal, July 22, 1852.

24. Ellsworth, "First Mormon Missionary Women," 40; see also Newell, "Gift Given,"

In Cannon's journal for July 15, there is a heavily censored entry that tells of two of the brethren having "indulged in a wrong spirit," for which one of them was "suspended," at which the other "justified him and condemned Bro. Hawkins & the branch for the course they had taken. Bro. [redacted] would not repent but justified the course he had taken as correct and therefore they had suspended him. After hearing all that they had said, Bro. ~~Hammond~~ Hawkins & I counseled the brethren to take the course ~~recommended~~ <taught> by the word of the Lord in such cases."[25] It is curious that the names and other material were removed from the published version of this narrative, which comes from the Cannon diaries. The originals are unavailable for clarification, so it is currently impossible to untangle the meaning.

Whatever the dust-up, the transgression may not have been sexual, although the gulf between the missionaries and the members on issues of modesty and sexuality was in constant tension. This is apparently why the Protestant missionaries denied most natives the right to become church members, and it may have been the reason the Mormons reserved the Melchizedek Priesthood to foreigners. On July 31 at Laie, Elder Farrer consulted with Elder Bigler about a church member who committed "the crime of Adultery." It was decided that since he had "confessed his wrong & [expressed] his desire to ... do better, we felt it was our duty to forgive him & let him keep his standing in the church."[26]

Three days later, on August 3, Hammond discussed the general propensity of the natives to engage in promiscuity:

> The sin of adultery is very common with them. Almost every week some of ... [them are] up before the Church for this crime. This is the greatest thing which they have to conte[n]d against. To day heard of one of our first [Aaronic Priesthood men having told a woman] ... that if they did sin a little that the Lord would forgive them. This he taught to the woman of his love. I feel my weakness more than ever and my inability to teach this people and make anything of them, without the

25. *JGQC*, 185.

26. Farrer journal, July 31, 1852.

> assistance of the Spiret of the Lord, both with me and them, but I do not feel discourage[d], but trust in The Lord.[27]

The Utah elders felt they should keep the members in good standing, if they could—particularly if the transgressors were high-status priesthood holders—as long as they had contrite spirits, which they generally did; but this was contrary to the excommunication that often resulted from the same transgression if committed on the continent.[28] It would not be surprising to find this same kind of familiarity adversely affecting the elders, since they often worked in remote areas without a companion and lived in a small hut or cottage for long periods of time with host families who might or might not wear much clothing and might be fond of *okolehao*, the alcoholic drink derived from the ti root. Hiram Clark's inability to maintain a distance from the native women while serving as mission president might suggest how difficult it was for the younger missionaries to maintain a strictly anthropological appreciation of cultural norms.

27. Hammond journal, Aug. 3, 1852. He worried about pushing too hard, saying the church members sometimes responded by becoming "cold and formal, not like they use[d] to be when they first came into the church ... They are a peculair people," he concluded.

28. Writing in his journal in Tahiti on Nov. 21, 1844, Addison Pratt complained of licentiousness as "the crying sin of these islands," a sentiment repeated by his companion, Benjamin Grouard, in his journal in May 1845. Mark Twain wryly observed in 1866 that if the Hawaiian government collected a $30 fine levied for each instance of adultery, their revenues should "exceed those of the United States." *Letters from the Sandwich Islands*, 203.

CHAPTER 9

Trouble in Paradise

This morning went out to see our horses, when Bro Bigler told me what Bro Lewis thought of me in regards to my leaveing Lahaina to come over here and get the language without his counsel. He said that he [Lewis] often spoke of it to him and condemned my course in the strongest terms, and said that if he had the power he would take the keys of the priesthood from me so that I should do no hurt to the cause, &c &c. This gave me pain to hear that I had not the confidence of my President, but the Lord judges betwixt him and me. I have tried to be governed by the spiret of the Lord and the counsel of my brethren on this Island.

—*Hammond journal, Sept. 8, 1852*

Many of the difficulties in the mission came from the missionaries, who were as susceptible to the relaxed atmosphere as the members and sometimes acted inappropriately or otherwise demonstrated the range of human emotions including arrogance, pride, and paternalism. For instance, when the members failed to provide James Hawkins with a horse to attend two church dedications on August 10–12 in the Kula area, he petulantly remained in Makawao and said he would not attend if he had to walk.[1] While he was sulking, the Hammonds, James Kipp, and David Rice arrived and Hammond wrote that they heard some "slander" that Marcus Baker had been "reporting ... about Br Hawkins and [Hammond's] wife [Mary Jane]. He [Baker] says that he is willing to see Br H[awkins] and myself together and clear it up." For the moment, however, there was not time because the missionaries were preparing for the

1. Keeler journal, Aug. 10–11, 1852.

August 10 event in Kula—all "except Br Hawkins," who still "waits for a horse from Kula."

Hammond went on to describe their arrival at Kula and the dedication of the first of the two meeting houses. In Cannon's description Hawkins finally arrived at "about noon" the next day. In Cannon's description of the dedication ceremonies on August 10, he gave his impression that the new meeting house was "quite a good looking <thatched> building about 30 feet wide <long> by about 18 wide" and said that "several tables [were] set [with] sweet potatotes, poi, fish, goat meat, pork, turkeys, fowls &c., and musk and watermelons abounded." Since Hawkins had not yet appeared, Keeler rode to Makawao to see what had happened to him.

After they had eaten, put away the tables, and were getting ready for the dedication ceremony, the Burnhams, Hammonds, Kipp, and Rice arrived without having seen Keeler, presumably because he had "taken the upper and they the lower road." After the new arrivals had finished their meal, they began their dedication meeting. "Bro. Hammond gave out the hymn," wrote Cannon, "after which I prayed and dedicated the house unto the Lord & was blessed exceedingly with the Spirit." The congregation sang another hymn, Hammond got up to speak (presumably in native), but soon faltered and had to concede the floor to Cannon, who read from Isaiah 60. Hammond then felt confident enough to continue speaking, which he did with greater success.

Keeler arrived from Makawao without Hawkins. Transportation may not have been the primary issue for him. Maybe Baker's accusation against him was the real sticking point. In any case, they finally conceded to Hawkins's demand for a horse the next day and he arrived; it was all the elders could talk about: how strange his behavior had been. In Honolulu at this time, President Lewis had received "a letter from ... Bro. Hawkins and another from Bro. Perkins stating that Sis Perkins was sick and asking council about taking her home [to Utah] and I counciled [him] to do so as soon as practicable." The president gave his approval. Lewis also recommended, "Bro Hawkins to go home if he could be spared from his field of labor," raising a question as to whether Hawkins's apparent request had anything to do with the accusation involving Mary Jane Hammond.

It is interesting that the missionaries on Maui were meeting in Makawao at this time (Aug. 13) and were being paired with native men: Uaua to go with Hawkins to an area not yet reached by Mormons ten miles from Makawao; Napela with Hammond to West Maui; and Kaleohano with Keeler to the northeast coast of East Maui; while Cannon would continue translating the Book of Mormon at Wailuku. "There was a strong desire expressed by the brethren to have a General Conference of the elders on the Islands," Cannon added. "It was motioned by Bro. Hammond and seconded by Bro. Hawkins that I should be appointed to write him <(Bro. Lewis)> a letter expressive of our feelings.[2]

Permission was given, and everything went well until the "blessing meeting" at the end of the conference, when a disagreement broke out, according to Hammond's journal:

> After br[e]akfast we had a meeting to bless one another for our several appointments ... Br Cannon was blest[,] Br Hawkins being mouth,[3] he [Cannon] was blest in the translating of the Book of Mormon &c &c. Next Br Hawkins was called and bles[s]ed, Br Cannon, being mouth ... Next, I was called, but wishing to hounor the old Elders who had come first, [I] declined in favour of Brother Keeler ... Brother Hawkins ... felt as if I had no right to call on him to be mouth, and felt as if I was a scheeming about it, and [he] felt very much aggreived ... for which I feel very sorry. He felt as if I was assuming authority that did not belong to me ... [Otherwise] we had a glorious time.[4]

Surprisingly given Brother Baker's accusation, "Sis. Hammond was blessed [by] Bro. Hawkins," which may have made Frank very uncomfortable. Hammond received a flattering blessing from Cannon, promising that Hammond would preach "the truth to the inhabitants of these Isles, that they should seek me [Hammond] for council, and

---

2. *JGQC*, 192–95.

3. They would all place a hand on the head of the person being blessed, and the one assigned to be "mouth" would pronounce the blessing.

4. Hammond journal, Aug. 15, 1852.

mighty should be the words which should flow from my lips, that I should be blessed in my family."[5] Afterward "Br Hawkins went along with me to see brother Baker about the story he had reported about him and my wife. Br Baker says he done wrong and is sorry for what he had done. [He] ... acknowledged that he had lied and that without any foundation." One can imagine that Baker may have heard or seen something he misinterpreted or exaggerated. On the other hand, he may have falsely said he lied to get off the hook and avoid an inflammatory situation. Without more information, it is impossible to know. One wonders if the heavily censored Cannon journal entry a month earlier (July 15 at Makawao), which involved Hawkins (and others whose names were deleted), had something to do with this explosive controversy. If so, one can understand why the editors censored the journal entry, and it would indicate that Cannon knew of the Baker accusation, though there is no evidence elsewhere in his journal that he was aware of it.

Hammond was otherwise occupied in trying to tame a horse, and the details of that experience, provided in his journal, show a different side to his personality. On August 6, he wrote, "In the afternoon I received a horse from Mr. Edmunds to br[e]ak for him, and have the use of him for 6 months to pay me for breakeing him. He is 4 years old and has been tried 2 or 3 times by natives to brake, but without success. He is very wild but a good horse. I had him in the yard for about 2 hours with a good whip. He is stub[b]orn." Hammond was obviously not a "horse whisperer" but a stern taskmaster. He documented here the beginning of a dangerous test of wills between the two, the rider proving as stubborn as the horse.

On August 17, Cannon, Hawkins, and Rice traveled to Wailuku while Hammond stayed behind at Waiehu to work with his animal. "I got a hard fall through his cutting up this morning. Fell upon my back and hurt it quite bad." After breaking his back eight years earlier—and dogged by back problems the rest of his life—one would think he would not have engaged in this kind of dangerous activity,

5. *JGQC*, 195–96.

but he wrote that he was "up [on] my horse" the next morning after breakfast. "After a while I succeed[ed] in getting the saddle on him[,] when of all the antics that ever was cut by a horse[,] I think, he cut and finaly got loose and ran off about 3 miles, but did not get the saddle off. I got on an[d] ro[de] him for the first time." The next day the pain in Hammond's back was so severe that he was unable to go to a meeting scheduled by Cannon at Wailuku.

On August 20, Hammond's rodeo-like adventures resumed with near-disastrous consequences. "After bre[a]kfast [I] saddled my horse ... He is not very bad when you are on his back, but he hates to be handled or touched. I rode him about 8 miles. He fell down once with me while under full speed [and] pitched end over end in a sand bank[,] but I was fortunate and did not get hurt. I feel to acknowledge the hand of the Lord in many ways of late[,] when if he had not preserved me I would most surely have been hurt with this horse, for I have ran some very narrow escapes." The next day, Hammond reported that he visited Edmunds, the horse's owner, who empathized with Hammond, saying that "if [the horse] gets killed accidentally, it would be [the owner's] loss not mine," an indication of the owner's low opinion of the horse.

The missionaries on O'ahu traveled to Maui to attend a late-August conference at the Napela house in Wailuku.[6] Three days later Hammond and four other missionaries set out for Keanae, about forty miles away, to dedicate a new meetinghouse. Farrer and Keeler both mentioned in their diaries that Hammond had difficulty with his horse.[7] It probably wasn't wise to ride a barely tamed animal over a trail that ran along ocean cliffs, but they arrived safely on September 1 and were joined by Hawkins and Kaleohano, who had been working in the Hana area about twenty miles farther on.

The dedication on September 4 followed a standard format, Cannon speaking first, followed by Hammond. Hawkins also spoke. Cannon mentioned that the chapel had been built by the members. To his eye, it "excels the Calvinistic Meeting House" in the village,

6. Farrer journal, Aug. 27, 1852.

7. Ibid., Aug. 31, 1852; Keeler journal, Aug. 31, 1852.

and he was so pleased he called it "the best [chapel] of any we have built."[8] Hammond mentioned it was "built after the native fas[h]ion & covered with lauhala [palm-like leaves]." Afterward, they sat down to a "sumptuous dinner" prepared by the members "in native style & ... consisting in part of Pork, Turkey, fowl, [and] fish." It was all "baked under ground," Hammond explained, "together with poi [crushed and fermented taro root], Kalo [taro], swe[e]t potatoes, melons, & bananas. After eating till all were satisfied we repaired to the water again—[and] a number of persons were baptized."

The next day during the "foreign elders" meeting, Hammond reported on a "misunderstanding" between Hawkins and himself, saying "it was all settled without trouble." It was "voted and carried that I should represent the branch at Keanae at the coming conference." Farrer indicated that all was not well and that there was more to this story than Hammond had alluded to, that Cannon became involved. "Some feelings existed between bro's Hammond, Hawkins, & Cannon, which appeared to have arisen through mis[u]nderstanding," he wrote, but nevertheless claimed the matter "was all amicably settled when they had an explanation."[9] Cannon reported that it took place on September 6, beginning at breakfast, and he described it at length:

> Bro. Hawkins made some remarks about the field that he had been appointed to preside over and said he felt it to be a large ~~field~~ <one> ... and he would like it if someone could take charge of Kula branch if they felt like it &c. &c. Bro. Hammond said that things had been going ~~so~~[,] too much so, and that there had not been regularity enough, that the way things had been going on was not calculated to do well, no one having a settled place, but first one preaching <at one time at a place> and then another following and preaching at that same place ... I [Cannon] asked how this could have been avoided ... and [said] that <at> our last Council Meeting ... he [Hammond] knew that we had taken measures to prevent confusion of this kind in future by setting off to each one his field of labor. There were several remarks and replies made backward and forward and considerable feeling manifested.

8. *JGQC*, 198.
9. Farrer journal, Sept. 6, 1852.

For Hammond, this seemed to bring to the surface several issues regarding President Lewis's laissez-faire approach to the mission and Cannon's presumption to criticize other missionaries in Lewis's absence.

"I thought," Cannon wrote, "that Bro. Hammond intended to cast reflections upon me as he alluded to me as having acted partially and ... insinuated that I wanted to help the others forward and to keep him back—and these feelings had caused him to make a remark some time <before> that 'he was only a passenger on the ship.'" Cannon suggested that since they "were in the house" of a native, they "had better put off our conversation until after breakfast and retire by ourselves lest they <(the people)> should think wrong and form incorrect conclusions."

They moved to the new meeting house, where Bigler "was chosen to preside" over the discussion. Cannon "arose and told my feelings in regard to the remarks of Bro. Hammond and disclaimed all thought of doing as he said I <had> done in regard to favoring some to the prejudice of others &c. &c. And I wished him to state in what respect I had done this and what his reasons were for making the remarks he had." At this,

> Bro. H[ammond] said that his feelings had been hurt and he had borne and forborne and did not design to give vent to his feelings [and so] he had curbed them ... and this had caused him to think about returning to-day [to Waiehu] lest this should happen, but the remarks of Bro. Hawkins had brought it out. One thing, he said, was that their had been remarks made that he had no right to stay and act upon this island [outside of Lahaina] without the consent [of President Lewis], although he (Hammond) [admitted that he] had received the Pres'. counsel [not to leave Lahaina]. (This remark had been made by Bro. K[eeler] some time ago and as I thought had been settled.) H[ammond] also had desired to go into Lahaina to preach. He had alluded to it to me several times to <try &> draw me out but he could not ... I had said that it needed wisdom and a good knowledge of the language to go to Lahaina. He had felt that he was treading on toes and therefore he had made the remark "that he was only a passenger on board the Ship." These things had grieved <him> because he thought there was a disposition to keep him back

> especially when he thought that he had made sacrifices as well as his brethren [and] that he had done all he could do.[10]

Cannon biographer Davis Bitton interpreted Cannon's remark that going to Lahaina would require "wisdom and a good knowledge of the language" to be "a put-down, implying that [Hammond] was deficient in these areas."[11] Cannon's journal makes it clear that he believed his knowledge of the scriptures, doctrine, and native language was superior to that of other missionaries and it earned him the right to take charge in many instances. When this presumption was brought to his attention by Hammond, Cannon was so shocked he was unable to speak, "as my feelings were so much wrought up ... I never, to my remembrance, in my life experienced such feelings." He and Hammond "had mingled together and I had unbosomed myself to him time and again," Cannon wrote, "and yet all this time he had these feelings against me and had hinted to me and I had been so dull that I did not understand." Cannon had been accused by Hawkins and Keeler of having favored the onetime whaler, and with good reason, he now thought, because he had always shown Hammond more attention than the others. For his part, Hammond said he had not meant to "hurt my feelings or to throw reflections upon me or my course in general." Still, Hammond seemed to see Cannon as his most immediate mission leader and feel conflicted over the contradictory instructions he had received from Cannon and Lewis. Hawkins, perhaps still upset about Baker's accusation, joined in the conversation and criticized Hammond for not having recognized Hawkins's "right to take the lead" in branches where he had had conversions. Cannon sighed and said he thought that, if nothing else, some good might come of this newfound "spirit of candor."[12]

The conflict with Cannon may have come about because Hammond was older, well-traveled, and relatively good in the language, while the younger, overly self-confident Cannon had seemed to

10. *JGQC*, 200–01.
11. Bitton, "George Q. Cannon in Hawai'i," 179.
12. *JGQC*, 201–02.

denigrate Hammond's abilities as a missionary. Hammond was an admirer and friend of Cannon and did not even mention this altercation in his journal. The next day, the elders had a hard time getting back as their horses struggled through the mud along the dangerous, rain-soaked cliff trail ("pali"). They arrived at Makawao around 5:00 p.m., and the next morning a letter from Bigler at Honolulu informed Hammond that President Lewis was still angry with him (see epigraph at start of chapter).

Hammond tried to concentrate on his work at Waiehu, where he had begun making shoes to raise funds. On September 16 he rode his spirited horse to Lahaina.

> Arrived there about 10 a.m. [and] found Bro & Sister Perkins there. Sister P is quite poorly and has been for some time past. They are on thire [their] way home again to the Mountains, on account of Sister Ps health ... After supper we went down to take a bath, when Brother Kipps wife desired to be baptized. So I baptized [her and] returned to the house and confermed her. She is a half white [native] and a very fine woman. I knew her when I was on the Islands before. Her name is Kua Moo. She has been very kind to me & Mrs H[ammond], & in fact [to] all the Elders ... Received word from Bro Lewis that he & Sister L[ewis] will leave Honolulu on Fri[day] the 17 inst for Maui to join us at our conference. I was very glad to hear that he was coming up[,] for we all wish very much to see him in our midts [midst].[13]

About midnight on September 23, Cannon, the Kipps, and the Lewises arrived at Wailuku where all the other Utah missionaries except Elder Woodbury had assembled.[14] Keeler wrote that "we war [were] all pleased to See them [President and Sister Lewis] ... for the purpose of counciling together and also [to] setle Some difficulty that had Existed between Bro Hammond & him for some time in concequence of bro Hammonds leaving Lahaina without his Council."[15] Lewis's feelings must have been common knowledge in the mission. Nevertheless, the next day passed without Lewis bringing up the

13. Hammond journal, Sept. 16, 1852

14. *JGQC*, 204.

15. Keeler journal, Sept. 23, 1852.

subject, and not until the following day, September 25, would Hammond take the initiative after the missionaries walked to a council meeting in the Iao Valley. He wrote:

> After we had rested a little Bro Lewis called the council to o[r]der by pray[e]r. Then the Brethren was called upon to speak thire [their] feelings[,] or rather to know what buisiness there was to council about. When I arose and suggested the propriety of first settling any feelings that may have existed in our midts [midst]. This seemed to meet the views of all the brethren. I then told them that I would like to know what Bro Lewiss feelings were towards me in relation to my leaveing Lahaina[,] as I did [it] without asking his advice. He said he had had feelings about it but he had buried them and did not wish to have them brought up again. But I had heard some things that he had said which grieved me and caused me to have feelings towards him. He told Bro Cannon to not let me come over on this side of the Island but to keep me in Lahaina, & Bro Bigler told me that he had heard Bro Lewis often speak in terms of disaproval of the course which I had taken & that if he had the power he would take the keys of the Priesthood away from me. This and some other things has caused me to feel very much depressed in my mind for some 3 weeks past. Bro Lewis did not remember having said what Bro Bigler said he had[,] but inasmuch as Bro Bigler said he did say so, he would not contradict it, but asked my pardon[,] for it was a very hasty and unwise remark.[16]

The only thing that Lewis himself recorded about this affair was that "all the brethren of the mission except Bro Woodbury[,] who had not yet arrived, met in private council, and settled a misunderstanding which existed among the brethren, when a good spirit seemed to pervade the breasts of all."[17] Cannon's only mention of this was that Lewis said he "buried" what negative feelings he had formerly harbored. "These feelings were against Bro. Hammond as he thought Bro. H. had disobeyed his Counsel."[18]

Hammond reviewed in his journal how the president had told

16. Hammond journal, Sept. 25, 1852.
17. Lewis journal, Sept. 24, 1852.
18. *JGQC*, 204–205.

him to "stay in Lahaina & work at my trade and get the language as best I could." The president himself "would go down to Oahu & get the language & then come back & preach to the folks in Lahaina," he had said, but the president never returned. Hammond found he was unable to learn the language in Lahaina and that "the way closed up so that I could not get any work" there, so when "Bro Kipp offer[e]d to take care of my family and let me have my whole time to persue my [language] studies," he accepted the offer and "went over to Keanae with Bro Keeler," fifty miles away. He "remained [there] 6 weeks and returned to Lahaina." In the meantime, he began reaching out to former acquaintances, proving instrumental in converting Burnham and Winchester, among others; and then having done so, it made sense to move his family to Makawao. He "wrote to Bro Lewis stating what I had done, but he never received it," he noted. Whether Hammond believed the mission president had not received the other eight or so letters he had sent to him is doubtful, as the island postal system was very reliable.

Hammond defended his actions in his journal in a progression of events that read like a legal brief, ending with the observation that the missionaries "all commended the course that I have taken and believed that I had been led by the spiret of the Lord, but had ought to have wrote to Bro Lewis before I left Lahaina." He liked that it had been "moved and seconded that all these difficultys be buried and forgotten." By doing so, "general confidence was restored among all the brethren." Unfortunately, if he really believed that this would be the end of the matter and that he could put it behind him, he was wrong.

CHAPTER 10

The Shoemaker Priest

Baldwin the Preist after the o[r]der of Baal was around among the people to day stirring them up to reject the truth[,] telling them we were deceivers after money, &c. He tried hard to get a couple of old men which he had turned out of his church sometime ago to go back again but they would not, but told him they were going to join the Church of Christ [Mormon]. They are well off for the things of this world and had been in the habit of paying him 200 dollars a year.

—Hammond journal, Nov. 19, 1852

On September 27, 1852, the Utah missionaries at Wailuku spent the day conversing together on the issues facing the mission. They decided that Patty Perkins, whose health was declining, should return to Lahaina and that her husband, William, and Elvira Woodbury should accompany her.[1] Elvira's health was bad enough that she was counseled to leave the mission altogether if she could find a way to do so.[2] Of the four women in the mission, only Mary Jane Hammond retained her good health.

Frank came close to serious injury as he continued to match wills with his high-spirited horse. "After brakfast" on September 30, "I went out after my horse [and] made an at[t]empt to get on to him bare backed[,] when he commenced rearing and plunging & jumping stiff legged. He finaly got me onto his ne[c]k, when he succeeded in getting me off[,] throwing me high in the air, striking [me] on my head and shoulder [and] hurting me quite bad, but not seriously. I

1. Farrer journal, Sept. 27, 1852.

2. Madsen, "Mormon Missionary Wives," 148.

feel very thankful that I got hurt no worse." It is amazing that he kept tempting fate with his horse.

On October 3, Mary Jane received a letter from her mother, Eliza, containing the news that Mary Jane's father, Caleb Dilworth, had died several months earlier on March 25. He was the Quaker husband the family had left behind in Pennsylvania when he refused their embrace of Mormonism. Frank wrote that "he left no will. Was willing to die as he could not be with his family." Perhaps that is why he left no will. Mary Jane was busy at the time, as was her husband, making preparations for the native-members conference on October 4.

The council meeting of "foreign elders" was held at the Rice and Hammond residence at Waiehu to finalize the program.[3] The elders "sustained" Lewis as mission president, and it was decided that Cannon would continue translating the Book of Mormon, preaching "from time to time when the spiret directed." Hammond was instructed to go to Lahaina and work "as the spiret of the Lord may Direct." There were only three members of the church in Lahaina at the time, which may explain why Hammond asked the other missionaries to pray for him. "The people," he said, "are stiff necked and not so well disposed to receive the truth as in many places." The remaining elders were sent back to their previous assignments, spread thin as they were, without any missionaries for the islands of Hawai'i or Kaua'i.[4]

During the afternoon meeting Hammond noted that once again "Bro Woodbury spoke in tounges," and "I gave part of the interpretation," thinking there was some of it he had missed.[5] President Lewis then stepped in and elaborated on the interpretation, saying that God was speaking through Elder Woodbury to let them know that "the Lord was well pleased with us, that his poeple were a remnant of Israel, that all opposition should be over-come, that temples should be built in these lands and that this poeple should be redeemed, and that the Elders were sent to <u>these</u> Islands through the prayers of [the]

3. Hammond gave the date as Oct. 4, but Cannon recorded it as Oct. 5. *JGQC*, 206.
4. Manuscript History of the Hawaiian Mission.
5. See also Keeler journal, Oct. 4, 1852; *JGQC*, 207.

fathers who have gone to the world of spirets, and that it was necessary to obey council &c."[6]

The next morning the large native conference convened to hear the missionaries preach on the second coming of Christ, the Holy Ghost, and the necessity of faith and priesthood administrations instead of relying on medical doctors. "There was also some good instruction given to the native brethren with regard to their manner of living," wrote Farrer, "recommending cleanliness in their persons & in their houses together with industry &c." The missionaries again mentioned tithing.[7]

The mission president organized an all-out offensive in Lahaina to help Hammond launch an effort there, backed by Cannon and Brother Uaua, and a few others for a short time. The missionaries left for Lahaina at 2:00 p.m. on October 20, traveling counter-clockwise around the island in a whaleboat, "the wind blowing in little squalls sometimes nearly turning the boat over." Except for Hammond, everyone became seasick; drawing on his previous vocation, he was "attending to the sail all the time," according to Cannon.[8] In Lahaina Hammond wrote, "Bro and Sister Kipp & Antoney [Silver were] glad to see us. Got a br[e]akfast after which we felt better. Antoney Silver ownes the house, a nice Adobia well furnished and a very pleasant situation. Antoney does not belong to the church, but is very favorable."

The next day Elder Woodbury received a letter from his wife informing him that she was boarding the "Schooner Sallay" in Honolulu, bound for San Francisco, accompanied by William and Patty Perkins. Edward Dennis had purchased a sixty-dollar ticket for her. On the second day after the missionaries arrived in Lahaina, they launched their offensive, James Kipp posting notices in Hawaiian advertising the first Mormon meeting ever to be held there in the native language. It took place on Sunday in the Silvers' yard, which was,

---

6. Lewis journal, Oct. 6, 1852; also Bigler journal, Oct. 7, 1852, qtd. in Manuscript History of the Hawaiian Mission; Farrer journal, Oct. 6, 1852. The "remnant of Israel" was understood to be Native Americans.

7. Farrer journal, Oct. 7, 1852.

8. *JGQC*, 210–11.

Hammond wrote, "well shaded with kiukui trees." He noticed that there were thirty whaleships in the harbor, and he liked to talk to the captains to learn how successful the whale hunts had been. Despite his aversion to the town's vices, he found he liked its comforts. By the next day, he and his wife were "living more comfortable than at any time since we have been upon the islands. The house is very clean and airy[,] just painted. Mrs Hammond is quite well. Employed in teaching Mr. Antoneys boys their lessons & sewing at the same time." Mary Jane would go on to establish a profitable elementary school.

They put their best foot forward on Sunday by having Cannon and native convert William Uaua speak. "There was not a very crowded attendance, very few coming" in the morning, Cannon explained, but "in [the] afternoon [when we] again held meeting[,] [we had a] rather better attendance—I preached and Bro. Hammond bore testimony."[9] Hammond's review of the proceedings was mixed:

> This day we held the first native meeting in this place. We held it under some trees in Antoneys yard near the Hospital. Bro. Cannon preached from Acts 2:37, 38. Had about 40 Natives to hear. They payed ver[y] good attention. After Elder Cannon, Bro Uaua, a native Preist bore his testimoney to what had been said. Closed with benidiction by Elder Cannon. [At] 3 o[']c[lock] p.m. met again. Had about 50 to hear. Bro C[annon] preached from Ephesians 4:5. Good attention but none offered themselves for baptism ... The people seem very shy of us here, having their minds poisend by the [Protestant] missionarys. I feel as if it requires a great portion of the Sperit of the Lord to open the way for the Gospel here in this place. There is no preaching here in English, although there is some 3 or 4 hundred sailors on shore of a Sunday. But the Bethel [Church] is shut up and they have refused to open for us to preach in it. But I hope to be able to preach some in English after a little while[,] either on boards of the ships or in the hospital, where there is a good many sick sailors, some from all nations of the earth. I feel my weakness very much and feel to call upon my heavenly Father for strength.[10]

9. *JGQC*, 211.

10. Hammond journal, Oct. 24, 1852.

The Bethel Church was an impressive stone building capable of holding eighteen hundred worshipers. The seaman's chapel seated about two hundred, an example of many small sanctuaries of this type in port cities, established by Protestant missionaries in hope of influencing sailors. The chapels were supplied with newspapers, Bibles, religious tracts, and sometimes a "seaman's chaplain."[11] There were also hospitals established by the US government to treat American sailors in foreign ports. Hammond would later preach at the Lahaina hospital on a regular basis and convert a few recuperating sailors.

When the other missionaries left Lahaina later in the week (Cannon and Keeler to Wailuku, the Lewises to Honolulu, and Woodbury to Moloka'i), Hammond felt "loansome ... for I do always rejoice in the company of my brethren." He continued to have the assistance of William Uaua, however, who spoke with him on the program at 9:00 a.m. the next Sunday in

> an old house with the roof of[f]. Had about 60 or 70 natives to hear me preach. I preached on the first principles. The congregation paid good attention whilst I was trying to set forth the way of life and salvation. After I was done Bro Uaua bore his testamoney to the truth of what had been spoken. He spoke well and at some length upon the manner in which the Gospel had been preached to them before by the other Missionarys. He is hard on them [Protestants] for not coming as the bible directs without money &c.
>
> In the afternoon at 3 o.c[lock] we met again. [I] Preached from 2 Tim[othy] 3:5. Had not as many as we had in the morning but they were quite as attentive. Bro Uaua followed again with good affect. He is a perfect horse in this language[,] having been bred a Lawyer. He is good in scriptures also, but says he has got all of his knowledge of them from us[,] for they were as good as sealed to him before ... Called for subjects for baptism but none offered themselves which makes me feel quite down[,] for I did expect that there would be a great many that would come in in this place ...
>
> This is one of [the] strongest holds of Calvinism that can be. [It] started upon the Islands under the direction of D[wight] Baldwin. He

11. Gibson, *Yankees in Paradise*, 276.

> has about 800 members well drilled and schooled in sectari[a]nism and has been buisy in filling the minds of the people [with] predijice [prejudice] against the truth[,] which I pray the Lord to reward him for. It is a hard thing to get many to join from that church[,] but from the catholic we have got a good many, but generaly of the lower class, as the upper class allmost all belong to the Calvin church. All the chiefs and great men of the nation are there and they feel they are safe and need no more teaching, but the poor and dispised come to hear us preach. Well[,] if the Lord is satisfied with them[,] I am, for it is ever so that the poor of this world are the ones to receive the Gospel, poor in this worlds goods but rich in faith.[12]

On the first Sunday in November, Jonathan Napela, who had been in Lahaina attending court, was available and attracted around eighty people at the morning service. Hammond also spoke. The two spoke again in the afternoon, after which six people responded to the call to be baptized, with about three hundred people gathering on the beach to watch the spectacle.

Five days later Hammond had a testy confrontation with Dwight Baldwin and his wife at their home.

> Went and called again on the Rev. Mr Baldwin[.] Asked him for his church to preach in but he would give me no direct answer, but said he did not want to [learn] anything about our religion. He knew enough already. He had had a good oppertuinity to know about it. I told him he was not honest then or esl [else] he would have embraced it. He and his wife bothe felt that they had indulged me to[o] much all ready in listening to my talk. He invited me to take tea with them provided I would not say anything about my relig[i]on. I thanked them and declined. He was very unreasonable [and] would not hear to reason at all. Said his relig[i]on was good enoug[h] for him and [he] did not want any new [one]. He said if I would raise the old Governer from the dead he would then believe. But I told him I was not sent to work miracles but to preach the Gospel. He condem[n]ed[,] or rather his wife [Charlotte] condem[n]ed[,] our course of takeing in sinners into the church, before we know whether they are good men or not &c &c.

12. Hammond journal, Oct. 31, 1852.

The home of Dwight Baldwin.

> I found that there was no use in prolon[g]ing the interview, so I got up and bore my testamenoney to him in humility, that Joseph Smith was a truth prophet, the book of mormon was true, [and] the preisthood had again been restored to the earth. I told him these things in the name of Jesus Christ, and by virtue of the preisthood invested in me. I left him and went and done unto him as the Scriptures direct.[13]

The next day Cannon mentioned a postscript to an August 31 letter from John Caine informing him that "the doctrine [of plural marriage had been] published to the world," Orson Pratt having spoken on the subject in a public sermon in Salt Lake City on August 29. "This is what I have been expecting and looking [toward] for some time; it is all right and I think it will be apt to bring things to a focus," Cannon wrote.[14] Carried by the American press, the sensational information spread rapidly throughout the mission.

At the next native services in Lahaina on November 14, Hammond admitted that he "had hard work to make myself understood,"

13. Hammond journal, Nov. 12, 1852; evidently he shook the dust from his shoes (Matt. 10:14; Mark 6:11; Luke 9:5, Acts 13:51).

14. *JGQC*, 215.

but Brother Uaua preached effectively in the morning and afternoon, and his explanation of baptism for the dead "seemed to please the people very much." Consequently, in the evening they baptized sixteen women and five men. "There was also a number of for[e]igners there to whom I spoke a few words [in English]. They appeared quite attentive and expressed a desire to hear more."

Brother Uaua remained in Lahaina for a few weeks assisting Hammond, and during this time he and his wife "lived down on the beach." Hammond spent much of his time "employed in translating some paragraphs respecting the Priesthood" from the Doctrine and Covenants, drawing on Uaua's help "corectt[ing] my translations." Like Cannon with Napela, Hammond was making wise use of Uaua's education and translating skill.

On November 20, Hammond made a revealing comment regarding his racial views, consistent with those of Brigham Young. He said he "attended [a] meetting this morning. Had a good time in teaching the Saints their duty to each other and to God, the object of mar[r[iage], &c., and not to marry with the Nigros &c." Four days later he reported that he "Saw a Negro Man yesterday by the name of Hitten. He was mad because I had baptized his wife without his consent. I told him if I done it it was not done knowingly nor intensionly, but he appeared to want to make trouble about it ... I came away and left him for he was a little drunk." A little while later, on January 13, Hammond reported that he excommunicated "the wife of a Negro named Mary for bad conduct, contempt of the church, authority &c.," likely a reference to Hitten's wife.

On Sunday, November 21, Napela and Uaua spoke in the morning service, and afterwards eight more converts were baptized. Hammond then decided the congregation had grown sufficiently large to organize it into a branch and ordain "two Teachers, and two Deacons." However, that evening "Bros Napela and Uaua came and desired to be baptized over again[,] as they had fallen into sin and they desired to repent and do so no more. Their sin was over being to[o] free with the woman. This is thire [their] most besetting sin." Hammond rebaptized them and noticed that they were "melted to tears while [I was] conferming them. May the Lord now preserve them from falling into sin again." On November 22, one day after hearing Napela's and Uaua's confessions, Hammond reported in his journal only that he "wrote a letter [to] Br George [Cannon]," without divulging the content. By November 24, Napela was back with Cannon, and although the missionary responded to Hammond three days later by mail, he did not mention the two men's transgressions and rebaptism, nor did he mention this very significant information in his journal.

On the last Sunday of that month, November 28, Brother Uaua gave Elder Hammond "a paper printed here in native called The Messenger, and in it was an article written by the Rev. Mr Baldwin setting forth the duties of a Minister of the gospel." Toward the end, Baldwin mentioned how "rum was brought here to distroy the people, then the Pope, and last of all the Mormon's." The Mormons were simply "the youngest child of the Devil," and even worse because they were "more cunning and smart and [have] less shame than any of the others." Hammond commented that Baldwin was "useing every exertion to put down the work of the Lord."

Hammond continued to push forward with his goal of eventually introducing every key Mormon belief and practice to the converts. The first Sunday in December he called on the members "to set apart the first day of ev[e]ry month for a fast day, to lay aside their food and water and their [tobacco] pipes on that day." This prompted some interesting observations in his journal:

> This is the hardest of all the rest, their pipes; they are very much attached to them. Some of them ... thought that our church allowed smoking, drinking, whoreing &c &c appearantly by their conduct after they came in[,] ... that it was a very comfortable church, nothing to pay their preacher and could do about as they were a mind to. Hence they [some missionaries] are afraid that if we do not allow them to smoke, that our church will not stand. This was caused by Bro. Napela's preaching the word of wisdom the other Sunday. He was not wise in doing [this] so soon but should have waited until the church had strenght and wisdom to understand the commandments of the Lord.

> But he done it with a good intention. There has very few come in [by baptism] since he preached it.[15]

The day Napela preached abstinence from smoking, Hammond received news by letter from his father that his brother, John Fletcher Hammond, had drowned two years earlier in a shipwreck off the Virginia coast. "Sad news. He was about 21 years old," Frank wrote. Despite their distance from each other, he had "loved him much." Trying to take the long view, he decided "not [to] grieve like one with no hope. Peace to his memory. There is now only 6 [children] of us left out of nine, and I [hope] that they may all embrace the gospel."[16] The last time Frank had seen his younger brother was in late June 1843 when he left on the *Thames*. On the day he learned of his brother's death, he wrote his father "a long letter setting forth the gospel to him. Also one to Bros S[amuel] Smith, E[dmund], [and] Sanford [Bartlett]." Neither his parents nor any of his siblings would ever join the Mormons.

Meanwhile, Cannon was working virtually every day on his translation of the Book of Mormon at the Napela house at Wailuku. On December 16 the Rev. Baldwin confided to his daughter in New England that "the Mormons have been making outrageous efforts at Lahaina for a few months past. Within a few days I have seen 4 or 5 foreign Mormon priests here, who came from Salt Lake. They have baptized about 30 here, who, our people say, are all vile characters—not a very hopeful beginning. They [Mormons] tell all sorts of lies—are brazen to the last degree & will doubtless deceive some."[17]

Hammond's journal entries for December 16–17 indicate that there was truth to Baldwin's assessment of at least some of the native converts. One of them, a man named Emiwale, had "come into the meeting last evening drunk with beer … He is rich and he thought we would put up with anything from him. He had, or rather they all

15. Hammond journal, Dec. 1, 1852.

16. Frank and Mary Jane would later name a son born at Lahaina in 1855 Fletcher Bartlett Hammond; Frank's second (plural) wife, Alice Howard, would bear a son named John Howard Hammond.

17. Dwight Baldwin to Abbey, Dec. 16, 1852.

had been members of the other church, and they thought we did not teach and act as they did." Then there was "the wife of Opunui," who "had the Devil in [her] big as [a] big rat." Emiwale was soon "cut off ... by the consent of the whole [branch]," and the wife of Opunui, who defended him, "went off mad."

On Sunday, December 19, about 200 natives attended the morning and afternoon services in Lahaina. After Cannon preached, eight people were baptized, attracting more bystanders who were curious about it being performed by full immersion. "We preached to the bystanders," he wrote, "but they did not care to hear, as they only came out to see us baptise, it being quite a novilty here, as the other sects baptise by sprinkling only." He said the approximately three hundred spectators "made me think of the multitudes that use[d] to go out to see John the Baptist baptise."

Hammond planned to travel to a missionary gathering at Makawao during the Christmas holidays, leaving the five-months pregnant Mary Jane and Frankey behind at Lahaina. He knew his wife "would be left rather loansome" and that "she felt very bad about it," but he departed anyway. However, after progressing two miles and thinking it over, he changed his mind and returned. Mary Jane "was very glad to see me back. She had been weeping hard. Mr. Antoney had told her that he would go and get some things and they would have a Christmas dinner too."[18]

"I am not sorry that I returned," he wrote on Christmas, "as I can be with the branch now on Sunday. Then if I should wish to go over the mountain on Monday, I can do so. To day is Christmas. We are all well and enjoying ourselves." In addition to dinner, including mince pies and cake, they had a "good time" reminiscing, their mood turning nostalgic as they thought of home. Mary Jane overexerted herself preparing the food, and Frank wrote that she was "very tired after her days work."

Problems soon arose in the mission because the missionaries were telling white converts they were expected to immigrate to Utah—to "gather to Zion," as it was called—but the invitation was not being

18. Cf. *JGQC*, 227.

extended with as much urgency to native converts. Some of the white converts who had married native or half-Hawaiian wives were counseled to leave them, Cannon assuring them that they would be justified in doing so if their wife resisted moving. This is documented in his journal entry for April 18, 1853, with his recommendation to Brother Rice that if "his wife had utterly refused to go with him to" Utah, he would be justified if he "forward[ed] her a bill of divorce."[19]

The missionaries were constantly trying to change the lifestyle of the natives. On January 25, 1853, Cannon talked at length at Wailuku about this, making clear his attitude regarding the proper place of wives. "I told them that the way they were now living was not <the> way that the~~y~~ Lord desired them [to] live—we had come to these lands to teach and instruct in relation to things both temporal & spiritual." They needed to "lay aside [their] present habits." Why? Because "you are degraded and low in the scale of creation[,] and in order that you may ascend[,] it is proper to attend to these things, to cleanse your bodies, your clothing, your houses, all that pertains to you, that you may be pure and holy." Their customs were "a trick of the devil," he said. "[T]here will be a remnant of the redskins saved [who would] ... become a white and delightsome people," while the others would be lost. "Regulate your families, teach your wives ... [that] it is not the wife's place to dictate to, and teach the husband[,] any more than it is your place to dictate to, and teach me."[20]

Making her own contribution to what she considered the civilization of the islands, Mary Jane Hammond opened a school on January 14 with "three scholars and a prospect of more." This was charitable in essence but also practical since she received "seventy five cents per scholar, per week."[21] The income was important for the survival of her family, while her contribution to the city's children, many of whom were half-white, helped the Hammonds gain respect among the foreign population.

19. Ibid., 263.
20. Ibid., 236–39.
21. On January 19 Hammond called it "a little English school."

The situation in the Silver home deteriorated two weeks later when the landlord clashed with Kipp's wife. Frank outlined it.

> Antoney [Silver] and Sister [Kua Moo] Kipp had a quarrel. They were both to blame. It resulted in Antoney's forbiding Sister Kipp's touching anything that belongs to him [and telling] her to leave the house. They both talked bad. Sister Kipp went out to her mother's at Ka[a]napali in the afternoon, and Bro. Kipp set sail for Oahu to see about a place to live and to work ... We are all aloan again in the house at night, as Antoney sleeps away. It leaves us in pos[s]ession of the house the great part of the time, and yet it is not like having a house of our own, for we [don't] know what day Antoney may get tired of us, and we have to look for other quarters.[22]

On February 3, Hammond was summoned to the local court as a juror, and four days later he "had an interview with F. D. Austin," an attorney who professed to believe in "free toleration for every man to worship god as he sees fit, but he cannot beleive Mormonism." Why had "many hundred years" passed away "since there was any mericals [miracles] wrought on the earth"[,] he wanted to know, "but now in these days there is a great mircal wrought": "an angel" seen by Joseph Smith, "a book [of scripture] received [by Joseph Smith], and &c &c. Too much for men to beleive." Hammond said he "reasoned with him on the necessity of haveing the same Gospel now days as the people had in the day of the Saviour &c.," to which Austin "made no objection but did not appear very an[x]ious to investigate" further. "He invited me to call again." On February 10, Hammond loaned him a book. He referred to Austin as "the king's attorney," which would be the equivalent of a district attorney. Eventually Hammond was invited by Austin to be a court translator, which gained Hammond another important source of income and began a longstanding friendship, which extended to his second mission to the islands in the mid-1860s.

A few weeks later, Hammond saw for the first time a house he

22. Hammond journal, Jan. 26, 27, 1853.

liked. Purchasing their own home would allow them to avoid the stress of living at the Silver home.

> In the afternoon went and saw Mr. Hoofmire[23] about buying his house ... It is a very nice little house, surrounded with a good fence, and a fine lot of pineapples, bananas, grapes, &c, growing in the yard, a fine well of water, and comfortable out houses. Has a lease of it from [the] King for 15 years. Asks $350, for the improvements, and they go not with the land, but belong to the one that makes them. I am quite anxious to get it for my family. It is so retired and pleasant. May the Lord grant that we may be able to raise the means to buy it for the church, as there is sufficient land to build a large Church on if needed.[24]

Since Frank did not have the funds to buy the house himself, he wrote that two days later, "I went round to see those who are sending their children to schoole, to ask them to advance money to buy a place for us to live in and keep schoole. They were all willing to help some, and manifested a good spiret towards us, for which I feel very thankful; but I am not sure of being able to raise enough to buy the place I want, which will cost $350." In fact, they quickly raised the money and purchased the house.

---

23. Hammond later remembered that he purchased the cottage "from the ex-Cons[u]l from Germany" (journal, June 3, 1891).

24. Hammond journal, Feb. 28, 1853.

CHAPTER 11

New Brethren

My eyes are nearly over come by stud[y]ing the native language [and] br Karren is nearly in dispair[;] he says it looks hard for a man to have plenty [of comfort] at home [in Utah] & then [live without purse or scrip and] cra[w]l after the natives to their little nasty camps for a little of their filthy food & then fail of giting it after all & then go to a white man for his supper after going with[out] breckfast & diner ... We realise our disgrase more than a babe could realise[,] ... for men think our calling mean[.] But we know their salvation depends on us ... We have books & are using our best judgement to git the language as fast as possible[,] [but] br B F Johnson is [oc]casianly sad & disheartened intirely.

—*Nathan Tanner journal, Apr. 8, 1853*

News reached Frank Hammond on February 21, 1853, that new elders had arrived from Utah. President Lewis wanted the missionaries to get to know each other, so he instructed those on Maui and Moloka'i to join the rest of them at Honolulu for a mission conference. On March 7, Cannon rode in to Lahaina with $20 from James Kipp and John Winchester toward his travel expenses. "Kipp also gives us an o[r]der on Bro. Burnham for some money when we get there," wrote Cannon. Later that day, Cannon and Hammond, joined by Hawkins and Keeler, sailed to O'ahu on the *Maria* and arrived in Honolulu at 7:00 a.m. the next day. All were seasick but Hammond.[1]

The nine men representing the third wave of missionaries had

1. *JGQC*, 251. "The voyage from Honolulu to Lahaina [can be] made by sail vessels usually in less than 24 hours; to Hilo [on the big island] in three or four days," according to *Commercial Relations*, 4:480.

disembarked in Honolulu on February 17. They were not exactly youngsters, and like the previous missionaries would struggle to learn the language. They were Elders Edgerton Snider, 27; twins Reddin A. and Reddick N. Allred, 31; James Lawson, 33; Benjamin Franklin Johnson, 35; Nathan Tanner, 38; Thomas Karren, 43; William McBride, 46; and Ephraim Green, 46. A week later Lewis called a blessing meeting with the new missionaries, which was "a day long to be remembered[,] particularly as Bro [Benjamin] Johnson was impressed by the spirit," President Lewis wrote, "to bless me[,] which he did and I received a great blessing under his hands."[2] Given what subsequently transpired, Johnson's presumption to give the mission president a dramatic blessing could be seen as the opening salvo on Johnson's part to curry favor with, and exercise power over, the mission president.

Some of the newer and older missionaries had reason to know each other. An early convert to Mormonism, Benjamin Johnson, like Lewis, had been a member of the Council of Fifty in Nauvoo and had been a friend, business manager, brother-in-law, and bodyguard for Joseph Smith. He arrived in Salt Lake City a year after Brigham Young, full of ambition, and established a harness and saddlery shop—the first in the region. In 1850 he was elected to the first of fourteen terms in the territorial legislature.[3] Karren knew some of the older missionaries because he had been in the Mormon Battalion.

The new missionaries brought with them a copy of Joseph Smith's revelation on plural marriage, Hammond reported. It recently had been "published to the world" and Hammond was "ready to back it up." The missionaries would do so, he said, "even unto death itself if called to it." Despite this melodramatic endorsement, some of the female members of the small Mormon community in Honolulu were upset by it. Hammond admitted that "Sister [Mary] Burnham is in great trouble about the new doctrin[e]." On the other hand, "the Brethren [have] all received it well as far as I know," he

2. Lewis journal, Feb. 24, 1853.

3. See Benjamin Franklin Johnson papers; Zimmerman, *I Knew the Prophets*, 5–8.

said. Elder Cannon received the doctrine with great enthusiasm, saying it "caused our hearts to burn within us and filled us with joy and thanksgiving, that our lots had been cast in this day and generation." But he confirmed that Sister Burnham, for one, "appears to be much troubled at this new (to her) doctrine." Her husband, Albion Burnham, and others such as David Rice, "&c. &c., believe it."[4]

Mormon leaders and many of the rank-and-file had secretly practiced polygamy at least since the early 1840s, while publicly denying it until apostle Orson Pratt issued the announcement in Utah on August 29, 1852, declaring it to be official doctrine and practice. News of the announcement created a sensation in the islands, as the Utah elders—then and in the future—had to constantly explain and defend it.

The more immediate concern of the missionaries in March 1853, however, was the in-house conflict they needed to resolve. Hammond called it "some difficulty among themselves [that they had] to settle" when they gathered on March 9. "A good deal of time was consumed and some feelings hurt," Cannon recorded in his version of the events, but he "believe[d] it resulted in good" because the elders had been allowed to air their complaints. Before getting too deeply into the discussion, they "thought [it] best to a[d]journ to a more secret place where the brethren could give free vent to their feelings[,] as there was danger of being over heard by outsiders," Cannon continued. When they did so, Johnson and Tanner let their feelings be known about "Bro. L[ewis]'s course of conduct ... in regard to his coming here and taking the presidency ... without any vote being taken whether we would accept him or not, &c. &c., and he confessed that he had blundered in this thing." They then made a motion to accept Lewis as mission president; the vote was unanimous; Karren and Tanner were chosen as counselors and they were unanimously sustained. "While speaking in relation to the choice of counselors, some latent feelings aroused in regard to the things [that transpired]

4. *JGQC*, 252–53.

Benjamin Franklin Johnson

Courtesy Daughters of Utah Pioneers.

Nathan Tanner

Courtesy Daughters of Utah Pioneers.

on the journey [to the islands] which <it> was thought had better be adjusted before proceeding any farther with the conference."[5]

The next day of the conference, Hammond explained, the feuding brethren were "will[ing] to throw away all their [bad] feelings," but at this meeting Lewis committed a major blunder:

> Pres. Lewis said he expected the conference to reject Bro. K[arren,] as he was not his choice, but ... Bro. MacBride was the man he wanted. This caused Bro. K[arren] to feel bad[,] and in fact all the conference ... Bro. K[arren] said he did not want to serve unless it was the will and mind of the Lord. Bro. L[ewis] acknowledge[d] he had commited an error and wished Bro. K[arren] to forgive him, which he did. The conference still upheld Bro K[arren] as counsellor.[6]

Cannon said nothing about the dispute regarding the counselors, writing only on March 10 that "having arranged all misunderstandings

---

5. Ibid.

6. Hammond journal, Mar. 10, 1853. Hammond consistently referred to Thomas Karren as Brother Kearnes.

to the satisfaction of all, we again proceeded with the business of the conference."[7]

The new elders were given companions and assigned to their fields of labor. Karren, Johnson, and Tanner were to stay on O'ahu with Lewis, Farrer, and Bigler, while Green and Woodbury traveled to Moloka'i and the rest went to various locations on the island of Maui: Hammond and McBride to Lahaina "to preach in English for a season"; Cannon and Snider to Wailuku; the Allred twins to work with native members in the Kula/Makawao area; and three elders, Hawkins, Keeler, and Lawson, to the Hana region. "All felt pleased with their appointments," explained Hammond, "except Bro. [Benjamin] Gonson who seemed to feel a little dissatisfied at first, but I think it was all allayed before we left." Johnson initially was assigned to work among the natives at some unnamed location, but he resisted the assignment and managed to have it changed to Honolulu.

Most of the "new Elders w[e]re [sent] to other Islands to git the language thare," according to Tanner, while "my self[,] B[enjamin] F Johnson & Thomas Karren was a pointed to preach to the foreners in this City if the[re] should be any Chan[c]e of an opening."[8] Since the number of whites in Honolulu was small, there was little reason to have four missionaries there, where they were not likely to learn the language.

Johnson chafed against being "treated unkindly," along with the president, at the mission meetings and personally "defend[ed] Prest. Lewis against abuse," according to his notes. He listened to part of the proceedings from his cot because he was sick but was able to tell the missionaries "the presidency's" predictions, presumably in reference to the First Presidency in Salt Lake City, regarding the Sandwich Islands and how Johnson would fill a central role in the missionaries' success there. This "seemed to inspire jealously," he wrote with feigned innocence. Nathan Tanner became critical of the assumption that Johnson would be the savior of the mission. "To all appearances I was in disgrace for having faith in the words of the Prophets to

7. *JGQC*, 253.
8. Tanner journal, 1852–55.

me," Johnson wrote. "Prejudice against me resulted in Br. Tanner being chosen first counsellor to Prest Lewis, and in assigning me to take alone, as my field of labor[,] the poorest and most hopeless." But while Johnson was recuperating from his sickness, he claimed that Tanner had a falling out with Lewis when "a difference commenced between them which increased to [a] dispute, or quarrel, and even to threatening words by Br. Tanner." As a result, the president supposedly began to see Johnson in a new light, with "new thoughts and feelings towards me," Johnson wrote. The president kept Johnson in Honolulu so he could oversee the mission's foreign interests, which pleased Johnson because the last thing he wanted to do was leave Honolulu and work among the natives.[9]

On March 11 the elders endorsed the idea of the Hammonds procuring a house in Lahaina where the missionaries could stay while waiting for inter-island transportation. The next day Frank "received a note (by Brother Woodbury who arrived yesterday) from Mrs. Hammond, requesting me to return as quick as possible, as she was afraid she might be sick befor[e] long," meaning she was about to give birth. Before he left Honolulu, Hammond borrowed fifty dollars from Brother Dennis as part of the payment on the house. Hammond agreed that the house would be useful not only to his family but also for all "the Elders[, that they] may have a place to stop and rest as they are going to and fro." Hammond collected an additional thirty dollars each toward the house from Brothers Burnham and Franklin. "I gave my note to them for this money," Hammond wrote, confirming that the funds were loans and not donations. The Hammonds quickly repaid these loans, and thus the house was theirs and not the mission's.

The friction with the Rev. Dwight Baldwin followed the missionaries to Honolulu. During the mission conference, Baldwin wrote to the Rev. Richard Armstrong, the king's Minister of Public Instruction:

> The mormons are making strenuous efforts to get a hold here, I presume they think their prospects brighter—for Hubbard and several

9. Johnson papers.

> of our ... beer sellers have turned out to one of their meetings, at least. The wife of the shoemaker priest has commenced taking scholars—has six now, I am told. Some of those who send [their children] ... abhor the mormons—but what can [t]he[y] do? [Judge Jones] said [he thought his daughter] must be under some instruction & he requested the teacher not to say anything about religion to [her]. But it is exceedingly uncomfortable to see children gathering round such a vile combination.[10]

Hammond attended a morning blessing meeting for the elders on March 12 that was conducted "according to [the ancient] o[r]der of pray[e]r, and I was glad to have an opportunity of learning the true o[r]der &c," he wrote.[11] Apparently Tanner blessed Hammond, and Ephraim Green indicated that "Bro. Luis anointed Bro. Jo[h]nson and blest him in the name of the Lord that he should due a mi[gh]ty work on these Lands and return in honor to his friends, in the vallys of the mountains. Bro. Jo[h]nson then blest Bro. Luis."[12] For whatever reason, the mission's oldest missionary (Lewis) and one of the new arrivals (Johnson) had formed a bond of mutual appreciation and commonality of intent.

Hammond set sail at around 5:00 p.m. that day on the *Maria*, a schooner, and not able to resist the opportunity to stir up controversy initiated a discussion with a clerical friend of Baldwin, the Rev. Alexander.[13]

> He would not say anything to me, so, I thought I would ask him for his opinion of Mormonism. He replied he thought of [it] as he did Mahomedanism, and he beleived it to be one of the frogs which John saw, &c.[14] I told him if he would listen a few moments to me I would show him what he was and then we would see which was the big[g]est

---

10. Dwight Baldwin to Richard Armstrong, Mar. 11, 1853.

11. The prayer circle they engaged in was part of the LDS endowment ceremony, performed in temple robes. See Quinn, "Latter-day Saint Prayer Circles," 79–105.

12. Diary of Ephraim Green, Mar. 11,, 1853.

13. William Paterson Alexander (1805–84) spent forty-one years on Maui; in about ten years from this date he would found the theological school at Wailuku. See Bartholomew, *Maui Remembers*, 18; also Missionary Album, 18–20.

14. See Rev. 16:13–14.

> frog. I then went on to show him wher[e] all the modern churches came from, that they had all decended from the Mother of Harlots[,] the [Catholic] church of Rome, and if the Mother was or is a Whore, what must the daughter be. He felt a little used up. I then told him that I knew that Mormonism was true. He said he had knowing to [known of] its orriganating in a lie and of course it could not be true. I had a long talk with him without much profit, except to prove to those who were present that we [Mormons] could substansiate our doctrin[e]s from the bible &c. He was down on me about the doctrin[e] of poligamy but I showed him that it was a doctrin[e] of the bible, and [that] the servants of the Lord beleived it in days of old. He said he would like to read a book setting forth our principles. I had none with me except the Deseret [News] extra, with all the big doctrin[e]s in [it][15] and I felt like letting him have it and see for himself what the doctrin[e] was and then let him help himself.[16]

Hammond landed at Lahaina about 9:00 p.m. on March 13, and the next day "Antonio Catalin brought his adopted son ... for us to board and schoole, for one year. He paid down one hundred dollars in advance," and later that day Hammond visited Mr. Hoffmire about finalizing the purchase of his house. "He will take three hundred dollars down and fifty at the end of the year," Hammond learned. In five days the money exchanged hands and "Mrs. H[ammond] feels highly elated about it." They moved into the house on March 22.

On March 16, Hammond wrote to Brigham Young claiming that the polygamy revelation had "not create[d] half the excitement which I had anticipated; the people appear as if some unseen hand had prepared them for it. The government officers were not at all surprised at it; but told us we would be narrowly watched, and if we were caught marrying two women to one man, they would be down heavy upon us; we told them that that was not what we were sent out for, but to preach the gospel and to live in subjection to the powers that be and to uphold them."[17]

---

15. This was the church's official announcement of polygamy.

16. Hammond Journal, Mar. 13, 1853.

17. Frank Hammond to Brigham Young, Mar. 16, 1853, extract included in the Manuscript History of the Hawaiian Mission.

President Lewis also wrote to Young that same day, noting that "Bro. Tanner is retained [in Honolulu] for the present to give the foreigners [whites] a try, and if nothing can be done, he will turn his attention to the native language." He did not say, however, that it was not just Tanner who was focusing on the relatively few whites in the city, but also himself, Bigler, Karren, and Johnson. He generalized about the natives:

> This people are naturally a kind hearted people, and could they have been left alone, they would have been better off, as they are but little better than slaves, all that they know has been taught them by the [Protestant] missionaries, which is little less than bigotry and superstition. The consequence is they are an ignorant, idle, bigoted, downtrodden race of beings, and if they are ever raised from their present degraded condition, other means besides preaching the Gospel to them will have to be employed; they must be taught habits of industry, before much good can be done among them; but how this can be effected with the whole force of the Government and the missionaries against us, is a problem which remains to be solved.[18]

Lewis thought that "all the brethren who have just arrived will, as a general thing, I think[,] obtain the language very quick; at any rate, they have advantages that those who came before have not had." The advantages were no doubt the help of companions and church members, whereas the first missionaries had nothing in the way of a church structure to rely on. Even so, the newer missionaries would not, in fact, learn the language as fast as the previous two waves of elders, and most did not learn it at all. The only ones from the new batch who would excel were the Allred twins, who would find accommodations in the home of Brother Kaleohano at Kula where very little English was spoken. In a letter, Reddin wrote:

> We attended closely to our study, and our teacher spared no pains and gave us all the aid and instruction that lay in his power. As to our fare [provisions], it was very different to what we had been accustomed

18. Philip Lewis to Brigham Young, Mar. 16, 1853, in Manuscript History of the Hawaiian Mission.

> to; yet we soon got used to it and could take our allowance of food as it came along. By continually striving with god in prayer and by diligence in study, I found that I was improving in the knowledge of the language. For a length of time I did not allow myself to take up a book in the English language and read in it … After continuing my studies for four months, I commenced to speak in public and from that time I traveled, generally taking with me one of the native Elders as a co-worker in the ministry, and many of them labored [in] earnest for the spread of the truth.[19]

As the Hammonds settled into their new home toward the end of March, Frank became interested in his garden where he could plant seeds harvested in the mountains. Elder Ephraim Green visited the house and wrote about what a "delightful" and "fine" yard the Hammonds had. Near the back door was a large breadfruit tree, and deeper into the garden were banana plants, locust trees, tutus, flower beds, ground cover, and even a few prickly pears on a full acre of land.[20]

When the Hawaiian legislature met in early April, three representatives from Maui who were Mormon converts, Brothers Kauai, Kauwahi, and Uaua, relayed to fellow legislators and others in Honolulu their experiences in their new faith, resulting in the kind of success the missionaries had experienced on Maui in 1851–52.[21] This occurred despite most of the O'ahu missionaries themselves, who were as yet unable to adjust to their circumstances. On April 4, Tanner wrote of the "degraded state" of the native people, complaining that the food was not fit for animals, that back home the "hogs would nearly blush at sum of it." He gave as an example the squid offered by a convert, Brother Kauwahi, which he found it hard to believe the Hawaiians considered "a chois dish … dryed heads gills fins guts & all."[22]

Frank decided not to attend the April church conference in Wailuku because Mary Jane was close to giving birth. Cannon

---

19. *Deseret News* 5:344; qtd. in Manuscript History of the Hawaiian Mission, Apr. 10, 1853.

20. Ephraim Green diary, Mar. 26, 1853.

21. See Farrer journal, Apr. 1–2, 1853.

22. Tanner journal, Apr. 4, 1853; also Apr. 8, this chapter's epigraph.

prepared for the conference by translating Joseph Smith's revelation on plural marriage (now D&C 132) and the recent address on polygamy by Orson Pratt. On April 7, Cannon wrote that he was "translating at the revelation this morning and did not go to meeting but stayed to finish it. I gave it to Napela to read and he was very much pleased with it and felt to praise the Lord for it—it was the first intimation that he had of it."[23] Later that day Cannon spoke for two hours on the subject and did so boldly in order to combat the negative treatment in the Hawaiian newspapers. He "forcibaly" impressed on them "the necessity of not medling with those things that at present ... were not for them," according to Woodbury.[24] Cannon read the full text of the revelation to the congregation of about 1,000 members, and in response "the people felt well and enjoyed the spirit," Woodbury concluded.[25] Green agreed that it "tuck [took] well with them" because it "agree[d] with thare former practices before the whites came among them."[26] That was a hurdle the missionaries probably had dreaded and were relieved to have behind them.

23. *JGQC*, 261.

24. There was a double standard here, since the Mormons in Utah were being strongly urged to take plural wives. However, bigamy and polygamy were illegal in the Sandwich Islands, while in the Utah Territory polygamists were being charged only with adultery in the absence of a specific statute against polygamy. Firmage and Mangrum, *Zion in the Courts*, 137

25. Woodbury diaries, Apr. 7, 1853, the day's entry matching closely Cannon's at *JGQC*, 162n42.

26. Green diary, Apr. 7, 1853. Newton, in "Nineteenth-Century Pakeha Mormons in New Zealand," 231, added that the missionaries in New Zealand allowed polygamy at first among the Maori, but "later actively discouraged" it.

CHAPTER 12

Dramatic Success on O'ahu

We then descended to the stream to the place of baptism which was just below some falls in the creek while there was a bank on each side of several feet. Such … was lined all round by people estimated, to number betwixt ten & fifteen hundred … Elder UaUa called on the multitude to keep good order while the ordinance was being performed … The Brethren then sung a hymn with good spirit. Prayer by Elder Uaua. Elder Uaua & myself then went down into the water & baptised 39 persons. Good order prevailed all the time[,] [and] this was a scene long to be remembered.

—*William Farrer journal, Apr. 24, 1853*

Mary Jane Hammond began keeping a journal on April 15, 1853, and her first entry recorded the "blessed event" that day of "suffering with child birth. Before 6 o.c[lock] pm was delivered of a fine son weighing 9 lbs. All the assistance was two native women but the lord was merciful unto me and he shall have the glory. So ends this eventful day."[1] The happy father noted that "we have Sister [Kua Moo] Kipp with us, and a native sister who has been here since morning … I believe they far excell our people in knowledge of" midwifery. He was fascinated with "their mode of treatment," which avoided internal medicine and was done through a process by which they applied a deep rub to affected parts of the body.[2] Frank "slept but little through

1. Mary Jane Hammond journal, Apr. 15, 1853.

2. The healing massage, *lomilomi*, associated with child birth and sickness, involved kneading the muscles with one's hands, knuckles, elbows, feet, sticks, and anything that could be used to reach the underlying tissue, accompanied by chanting and prayer. Practitioners were called to this vocation at about age five and raised as shamans. The Protestant clergy disapproved of their approach.

the night. Mrs. H[ammond] had a good deal of pain all night [and] slept but little" herself. They named their second son Samuel Smith Hammond after his grandfather.

Nathan Tanner disclosed how much the missionaries depended on the convert William Uaua and how ineffectual their own efforts were by comparison.

> We are encuredging br Uaua all that we can and instructing him what to do & he is doing the best he can torge [towards] inlighting the king & the chiefs. We have to make use of such tools as we have, tho we feal sumtimes as if we ware not dowing [doing] much yet ... We have been talking of going to sum other islands but as yet the Lord seams to check us hear [here] ... The metings are giting full & very interesting a speshely [especially] when Uaua speaks & he can speak to their understanding[;] he is a la[w]yer & has been colledg[e]-bred.[3]

The next day Tanner offered the following strange assessment of the elders' importance, suggesting that even though they could not communicate very well with the natives, their smiling faces added something to the tableau: "This morning there is a call for Uaua to preach in the after noon & baptise. [H]e baptized 3 yesterday. It seems to have an influence with the natives for us who cannot speak [the language] to be present, [as] our countanence makes an impression on them. May god inlighten them & bless & make our presance a [silent] s[e]rm[o]n of grate worth to them." Tanner had reconciled himself to the reality of a supporting role for now: "We are striving to inform the most intelligent natives [who are] scholars & ordaining them[,] for we can teach them & they can teach others[,] handerds of them[,] before we can learn the language." The next day the elders ordained Edward Dennis, Hosea Kauwahi, and William Uaua as elders, in keeping with the strategy Tanner had outlined. The importance of the ordination of native men to the Melchizedek Priesthood cannot be underestimated, although the missionaries still restricted most Hawaiians to the "lesser Aaronic Priesthood office of priest," even when placing a native man over a congregation.[4]

3. Tanner journal, Apr. 17, 1853.
4. Ibid., Apr. 18, 21, 1853; Farrer journal, Apr. 22, 1853.

On April 21 white convert David Rice arrived at Lahaina from Honolulu on his way to do missionary work on the island of Hawai'i, and he informed the Hammonds that King Kamehameha and his people had inquired about plural marriage. "They believe it quick as a general thing," he said, and so "the prospect is good at Honolulu at present among the natives. But rather dull among the whites. No meetings at present among them. Have had none since we were down there, about 4 weeks ago." Thus there was virtually no progress by the curiously concentrated missionary force in Honolulu consisting of Johnson, Karren, Lewis, and Tanner.

Rice's claim that Hawaiians were embracing Mormonism because of polygamy was wishful thinking. Britsch has acknowledged that the new doctrine was a problem for the missionaries, as much in Hawaii as elsewhere, regardless of whether the target audience was expatriates or natives. "Many newly converted members fell away because they could not stand the harassment to which they were subjected by their former associates and friends" over the issue of polygamy, Britsch has written.[5]

In the meantime, the newly minted native elders, Uaua and Kauwahi, worked with Elder Farrer who could speak the language, and together they made astounding progress on O'ahu. On April 24 they had a morning baptismal service near Honolulu (Waikahalulu) that turned into a dramatic public spectacle. It began in the morning when Kauwahi and Uaua spoke powerfully to a congregation of Hawaiians and were well received. Farrer and Kauwahi spoke in the afternoon session, and "we then gave out that we would repair to the water for baptism[,] a distance of about one mile[,] when the road was litterally crow[d]ed with people of all kinds going to witness the ceremony." When thirty-nine people requested baptism, Uaua queried them about their faith and asked them "to forsake their sins & observe the commandments of the Lord," which they agreed to do.

Farrer estimated that up to 1,500 people witnessed the baptisms.

5. Britsch, *Moramona*, 32.

Uaua "then called on the [onlookers] to take of[f] their hats while singing & prayer was attended to, which request was answered to by about all" within earshot, with the exception of a few sons of Protestant missionaries "who I suppose thought it would be humbling themselves to[o] much to pull of[f] their hats to the Mormons." Over all, however, "good order prevailed" and it was "a scene long to be remembered."[6] The following Sunday, President Lewis assisted in a baptismal service for forty-three people. It was again witnessed by a crowd of onlookers, mostly natives but also some white foreigners.[7]

The euphoric days in Honolulu contrast starkly with the situation Hammond found in Lahaina, where stagnation had set in. On April 24 he lamented that "the Branch is in a low state at present. Their faith is very weak ... They are truly babes yet in the Gospel, and have need to be taught the first principles over again. Out of about 60 members [there are] only about 25 that appear to have any life in them." Late that afternoon he excommunicated four women "for bad conduct, not [at]tending the meetings, and treating the teachers with disrespect, visiting beer shops &c &c." Mormonism on Maui continued to be the strongest in the Wailuku and Kula areas.

It did not help that Hammond was still having to defend himself against negative appraisals from his old acquaintance Dwight Baldwin, who on May 1 filed a mission station report describing Mormons, somewhat accurately, of having experienced a lack of success in the main port town. "When the Mormons first came to Lahaina, in the fall of 1851 perhaps, they made great efforts, among foreigners only, but never made one convert." After leaving Lahaina and working in Wailuku, Kula, Loolau, and elsewhere, they were able to convert intellectuals such as Napela, Uaua and Kaleohano. "One of them [Hammond] worked long at Lahaina & prepared a few for Mormonism. In three successive Sabbaths, the foreign priest [Hammond] who came to gather in the harvest, baptized 7, 20, & 3. Many of these, perhaps all, were among the vilest of our population. The

---

6. Farrer journal, Apr. 24, 1853. See also the Journal of Nathan Tanner for the same date.

7. Farrer journal, May 1, 1853.

three last baptized were persons we have excommunicated from our ch[urc]h for living, as we supposed, in licentious habits." Baldwin said the converts stayed with the Mormons only briefly, despite strenuous efforts by the missionaries, including promises of miracles. He continued:

> When they first came to Lahaina, they denied, that any such thing as polygamy existed at Salt Lake. Lately they justify it. One has said, that Jesus Christ had two wives, at least, perhaps many others; or if not, that he evidently lived with Martha and Mary, as wives, without ever being formally married to them. Another said[,] "As God had a Son, he, of course, had a wife, & many other children, doubtless, that he enjoyed the family relation the same as men did."
>
> All these & many other things were too much for our excommunicated persons. They came to an open rupture with the [Mormon] priests in their meetings[; they] first disputed, then ridiculed & forsook them. Whether they had already gone the length of their tether, or whether the three apostates brought them into discredit, is not clear. From that time, we hear little said of Mormanism in Lahaina. Except the 30 baptized, at first, I know not that any other[s] have joined them. I look upon them only as a sieve, to sift out the vilest dregs of the people, perhaps because God sees they are ripe for destruction.[8]

On May 15 he wrote to his daughter in New England informing her that "the Mormons are said to be making great inroads [in the] Hana district. Judge Lee wrote me last week, that they were [also] baptizing at Nuuanu stream, Oahu (by immersion) by fifties & by hundreds, mostly apostates from the [Protestant] ch[urc]h[e] s & from Catholics. But they are coming out with such absurdities & lies, that nothing but the lowest dregs will join them, I should think. They did baptise 30 in Lahaina some 5 or 6 months since, but, we are told, that all who joined them here have forsaken [them], or nearly all."[9] Baldwin was right about the number of people still attending the Lahaina branch; he also was correct in saying the Utah elders had claimed miraculous healing powers.

---

8. Baldwin, Report of Lahaina Station, May 1st, 1853.

9. Baldwin to Abbey, May 15, 1853.

The problem with having said that miracles were a sign of the true church was that the Utah missionaries' track record was mixed at best. In April 1853, Hammond repeatedly blessed a blind member in Lahaina for his sight to be restored, but it was not. The next month in Honolulu, Elder Farrer noted somewhat hesitantly that "we are called on two or three times nearly every day to administer to the sick & ... the sick are receiving benefit by it," but what benefit there was seemed to be as often fleeting as permanent.[10] Elder Tanner agreed that there was "considerable sickness" and that "the dev[i]l & all his imps" could not "hinder" their proselytizing. They performed an exorcism. Karren declared that "it puts me in mind of the days of the Saviour when the people th[o]ught if the[y] only Could touch the h[e]m of [Christ's] garment the[y] would be healed. This people has great Faith in administering to the Sick and the Lord will make Manifest his power in their Midst."[11]

Whether the healing claims of the missionaries were legitimate or not, the promise of healing contributed to their success on O'ahu in the spring of 1853. Historian George Ellsworth found that converts in Tahiti assumed that "baptism would bring healing" and that a blessing "with [consecrated] oil for the restoration of health" would result in a miraculous turns of events.[12] The Mormons in New Zealand, Peter Lineham observed, "were extremely active in anointing the sick with oil. [Elder] Cox's healing of Miriama Rotorama, who was thought to be dead, was ... important in encouraging Maori to respond to preaching in Waotu ... Exorcisms of demons were also not uncommon."[13]

Despite a passionate faith in the healing power, however, Hammond was deeply troubled by an incident that struck very close to home. On May 2 when his son Frankey developed a severe earache, "I anointed him and laid hands on [him] several times [and] finally he got better." Why he thought he needed to undertake the anointing

10. Farrer journal, May 2, 1853.

11. Ibid., May 4; Tanner journal, May 2; Karren journal, May 8; Manuscript History of the Hawaiian Mission, May 3, 8, 12.

12. See Ellsworth, "New Wine and Old Bottles," 22.

13. Lineham, "Mormon Message in Maori Culture," 218.

and blessing repeatedly is unclear. In any event, he was affected by his son's suffering. "It caused me some reflecttions on the cause of pains and aches in little children &c., why they should be subject to pains[,] seeing that they had never sinned; but [I] felt to praise the Lord for the power of the priest-hood which has the power to rebuke."

On May 12, Elder Johnson at Honolulu wrote confidently that "this morning as usual [we] administered to many sick who throng the house, and we witness the power of God greatly manifest. Some are healed who for months had been afflicted, some even for years; and they go forth joyfully into the waters of baptism."[14] These faith-healing convictions were about to be challenged by a smallpox epidemic that would arrive in Honolulu in late May with devastating results, starting on O'ahu and spreading to East Maui and the island of Hawai'i.

14. Johnson papers, May 12, 1853.

CHAPTER 13

Smallpox

In the afternoo[n] held a meeting at my house [with] very few present. Talk[ed] upon the necessity of having faith enough to have power over disea[s]es, and not to be afraid of the scourges which the Lord will pour out upon the nations. We have heard that the "Small Pox" is in Honolulu, the saints whished to Know if they should not go and get vaxinated, as all the people were doing so. I told them if their faith was weak and [they] dare not trust the Lord to go[,] but as for myself I should not go, and if I died all was well.

—*Frank Hammond, May 18, 1853*

"Heard Small pox is in Oahu," the February 15, 1853, entry in Hammond's journal reads. It had been rampant in California that winter and spring, so it was almost inevitable that it would find its way to the Sandwich Islands on the many ships going back and forth between the mainland and the islands. Six days later an alarmed Dwight Baldwin wrote to his daughter Abigail in New England that five days earlier the ship *Charles Mallory* had docked at O'ahu "with a case of small pox from California." Doctors were already overwhelmed at the possibility that the disease would break out on the island and wreak havoc among the natives, who unlike whites were especially vulnerable because they had no natural immunity to it.[1] "We vaccinated some

1. European Americans had a higher natural immunity to smallpox due to a historical connection with the virus (most children were exposed to some form of it and become immune; whereas adults who were not exposed as children were unable to withstand an infection) and cultural proximity to cows and sheep. Milk maids, for instance, were immune to smallpox, something that served as inspiration for Edward Jenner's experiments. See, e.g., Diamond, *Guns, Germs, and Steel.*

1000's, a few years ago," he continued, but it was apparently for other diseases and the vaccination did not include the "kine pox," the name at the time for cow pox, which was the antidote drawn from animals to give humans immunity.[2]

On March 1 the Rev. Alexander, who twelve days later would have a testy religious exchange with Hammond, wrote to ask Baldwin if he would collect mucous from "clean white children" whose arms had been infected with the cow virus, with which he would "vaccinate my little Lotty & Jenny."[3] In correspondence between Baldwin and the Minister of Public Instruction, Richard Armstrong, we learn that Baldwin was frantically vaccinating missionary children and vulnerable natives who worked near the docks in anticipation of an outbreak. "I have considerable confidence," the reverend wrote, "that even if the small pox is landed here [at Lahaina], it will not ravage extensively."[4]

When guides today take tourists through the Baldwin House in Lahaina, they credit him with protecting Maui from viral devastation. "Without Baldwin," Gail Bartholomew has written, "innumerable lives would have been lost in a disastrous smallpox epidemic in 1853."[5] There were eight physicians among the early Protestant missionaries to Hawaii in the 1820s–30s, who taught people to trust medical science even though the standards of the day were nominal, as acknowledged by descendant Garritt P. Judd IV, who nevertheless credits the pioneering physicians with paving the way for people to accept such concepts as trusting a remedy for smallpox in diseased cows. The missionary physicians had also "performed operations," although "without anaesthesia in the early days," and introduced "hygiene far in advance of the primitive medical lore of the native population."[6] In the 1850s there were also secular physicians in Lahaina, Honolulu, and Hilo.

---

2. Baldwin to Abbey, Feb. 21, 1853.

3. W. P. Alexander to Dwight Baldwin, Mar. 1, 1853. When given the vaccine, the patient developed a pustule on the arm, from which pus could be harvested to inoculate the next person. Care had to be taken not to transmit venereal diseases and other infections in the process.

4. Dwight Baldwin to Richard Armstrong, Jan–Jun 1853.

5. Bartholomew, *Maui Remembers*, 18.

6. Judd, *Hawaii: An Informal History*, 51.

Baldwin wrote to his daughter on May 15 the "sad" news "that three native women, at Oahu, have small pox. If [true], the whole population will soon be exposed."[7] That same day the Mormon missionaries "appointed Wednesday, as a day of fasting & prayer on account of the ... small pox [that] was said to exist in the City."[8] But instead of encouraging Mormons to get vaccinated, the elders told them to rely upon prayer, faith in God, and priesthood administrations. Hammond's foolish advice (see the epigraph at the beginning of this chapter) would not only endanger the native members but would also bring them into conflict with city authorities in Lahaina and elicit contempt from more sensible foreigners. Mary Jane Hammond wrote in her journal on May 18 of hearing about the smallpox cases in Honolulu, without commenting further about them.[9]

Four days later, Baldwin wrote another anxious message to Armstrong. He admitted that the smallpox probably "cant be stopped on one island," but that "it is of immense importance, that its spread be delayed as long as possible. Every week is a great gain, as it gives time for vaccinating." In Lahaina a certain proportion of the people had not yet "take[n] the trouble to be vaccinated, or to look after their children." He thought that "in the back districts of Maui, & in many portions of Hawaii ... the majority are not [yet] vaccinated." He begged Armstrong to "keep the disease confined to Oahu as long as possible," and offered a long list of suggestions as to how to accomplish that, including stopping traffic, with some exceptions, to other islands.[10]

On May 20 the Honolulu *Polynesian* newspaper carried an announcement indicating that many of the steps urged by Baldwin had been taken, including the appointment of health commissioners on each major island to deal with the threat. Those appointed for Maui were Sheriff Peter Treadway, Dr. J. R. Dow, and Dwight Baldwin.[11] Three days later, however, Finance Minister Gerritt Judd complained

7. Baldwin to Abbey, May 15, 1853..

8. Farrer journal, May 15, 1853.

9. Mary Jane Hammond journal, May 15, 1853.

10. Baldwin to Armstrong, Honolulu, with "Public Instruction, Misc.—Island of Maui, Jan–Jun 1853," copy obtained from Maui Historical Society.

11. *Polynesian*, May 21, 1853.

to Baldwin that the suggested travel restrictions were too extreme. "I dont think the case requires that our coasters [ships] should be laid up or natives be forbidden to go to and from Honolulu. If you get the small pox at Lahaina, report to us immediately, and show how wide awake & thorough you can be in destroying its contagion."[12] If we can read anything into the flippant tone, it appears that Judd, a medical missionary himself in the 1830s, was irritated by Baldwin's presumption to tell him what needed to be done. Undoubtedly the cabinet did not want quarantines to interfere with trade and commerce. In the end, Judd's negligence would cost thousands of native lives and his government position.

On May 25, Baldwin again wrote to Honolulu, probably to Armstrong and Judd, imploring them to impose a quarantine on O'ahu. They should "let no one come this way, or go from Oahu to other islands except such as have had kine pox. This seems to us the only probable way of limiting the disease to Oahu, or even delaying its spread." He ended by saying that "if these means are not sufficient, in the end, to limit the disease to Oahu, they may, at least, delay its spread[,] wh[ic]h will be [a] great gain."[13]

The Utah elders should have known that by giving blessings to infected native members, they would become carriers of the highly contagious disease, though they never acknowledged this in their journals or letters. Two of them, Thomas Karren and Nathan Tanner, decided to elude the quarantine and travel to the big island, Hawai'i, on May 31. Since their departure was attended by a large gathering of Mormons dockside who wanted to see them off,[14] it was clear the authorities at Honolulu were taking a permissive view of travel in and out of the city. Though their timing was poor, Karren and Tanner were finally going to attempt missionary work among the natives. Johnson remained in Honolulu, though not because of the quarantine.

On Maui on June 1, "half-white" convert George Raymond and

12. Judd to Baldwin, May 23, 1853.
13. Baldwin to Honolulu, May 25, 1853.
14. Lewis journal, May 30–31, June 1, 1853.

Hammond rode horses counterclockwise around the north coast of West Maui from Wailuku to the village of Hanakahau. They found that many people "were gone to [Lahaina to] get vaccinated for the small pox which is reported to be in Honolulu." The elders traveling to the big island, Karren and Tanner, stopped at Lahaina on June 4, accompanied by a young native elder named John Kahumoku. They were implementing the Tanner strategy of using a native convert to preach to natives. In fact, Hammond mentioned that Karren and Tanner "cannot speak much native, but Br. John Kahumoku can talk some English, and so they will be able to teach him and he teach the people." Kahumoku was a twenty-four-year-old attorney who was "as sma[r]t a native as I have seen for his years," Hammond said. Kahumoku had attended boarding school for seven years and then studied law. "He bids fair to do a great work in this Kingdom."

Karren and Tanner boasted about how many native baptisms there had been in Honolulu, without indicating much concern for the smallpox epidemic. They told the Hammonds the members in Honolulu were "all well generally" despite a few cases of the disease. For those who were infected, "the brethren [had] administerr[e]d to [them] ... and they got better." Since Karren and Tanner had been laying hands on those with smallpox, they were unwittingly traveling as angels of death; Frank and Mary Jane Hammond and their two boys had not been vaccinated.

On June 5, Hammond met with the Lahaina branch and preached from Matthew 11 about how Christ healed the lepers, the blind, the lame, and the deaf. The intent was to assure his listeners that the Lord and the elders would protect them, but the next day in O'ahu President Lewis succumbed to reason and was "vaccinated with matter taken from Bro. Uaua's arm. The Smallpox is raging. All ingress & egress forbidden to & from Honolulu by land," he wrote in his journal.[15] Before the plague subsided, more than 5,000 Hawaiians would be dead, most of them on O'ahu. Whether because of the shock of seeing so many infected people or under pressure from the government, all of the missionaries would eventually inoculate themselves.

15. Lewis journal, June 6, 1853. Emphasis in original.

It was not until June 6 that George Cannon first mentioned the smallpox epidemic, noting that he had "received several letters yesterday" from Bigler and Farrer that the "small pox is spreading" in Honolulu. John Winchester "arrived last night from Honolulu and started early this morning for Makawao," Cannon recorded. "All are well at Honolulu, the small pox is spreading and city is all excitement; Bro. H[ammond] says this is also the case at Lahaina." Happy to be informed but not too concerned, Cannon went back to translating the Book of Mormon.[16]

What Elder Winchester told the Hammonds at Lahaina as he passed through on his way to Makawao, was that the smallpox in Honolulu was "very bad" and the people "are in great fear."[17] He said "a number have died already and the town is filled with fear and dread. The work still continues to go ahead, but not as fast as it did." Even so, Winchester had been allowed to leave Honolulu and land at Lahaina, and he went on to meet with Cannon, Ephraim Green, and the native Mormons in Wailuku and elsewhere.[18]

When Winchester was traveling to his assignment on Maui, a terrified Elder Farrer back in Honolulu complained of having had a fever but was feeling "a little better today ... The small pox is spreading considerable & many are dying, & we are much exposed to it having been called to administer to several who had it before it broke out. May the God of Heaven preserve us from this direful disease."[19] Farrer and his fellow missionaries clearly understood that they could catch the infection from those who were sick. On June 10, when Hammond learned of the situation on East Maui and the island of Hawai'i, he said with little comprehension or compassion that "it is what we have told the people" to expect, that "scourges would follow this work &c." It was, he strongly believed, divine fulfillment of the promised apocalypse prior to the Second Coming and Millennium. His wife was worried that the virus might be more indifferent

16. *JGQC*, 286.

17. Mary Jane Hammond journal, June 7, 1853.

18. See Ephraim Green diary, June 7, 1853.

19. Farrer journal, May 7, 1853.

to their faith. "Mrs. H[ammond] is quite fearful for the children," he wrote. Mary Jane tried to reassure herself, writing in her journal that she knew "the Lord is all powerful," but she was apprehensive.[20]

The next day Frank wrote to apostle Parley Pratt to request "counsil about going home by the way of N[ew] Y[ork] &c." Mary Jane was against it—perhaps fearful of going around Cape Horn—but Frank was eager to introduce her to his relatives on Long Island. It had been ten years since he left home. He discussed the smallpox epidemic, saying it had been "brought here from the coast, either in some old clothes which were landed at Oahu, or spread from a person landed from a ship ... The whole country is in an uproar about it, except the saints and they are prepared in a m[e]asure for such things, for we have taught them that the scourges followed close upon the preaching of the Gospel." Hammond understood how the disease was spread but continued to hold to the idea that its unleashing was part of God's plan and the Mormons would be spared from it.

His conviction was rudely jarred the day he wrote the above letter to Pratt, because two letters arrived from O'ahu, addressed to Elder Cannon, explaining that the elders in Honolulu had been inoculated. The president "recommended ... all the Elders to do likewise. Bro. Farrer is unwell and they do not know but what he has taken the Small pox, as he with the others have been exposed." Interestingly, "the brethren had vaccinated themselves" rather than having a doctor do it, indicating a fundamental distrust of non-Mormon physicians.[21]

On June 11, Farrer, who in fact had contracted a mild form of the disease, again violated the Honolulu quarantine, as did many other Mormons.

> This morning Bro. Kauwahi furnished me a horse & I went to Nuanuu about 4½ miles to meet with the Brethren in that district & to administer the sacrament to them. Had a good time[;] about 50 or 60 members present. 5 baptised ... in the afternoon returned [to Honolulu] ... Today Bro. Kauwahi staid here to take charge of the [native] meeting in this place & held [a] meeting in the forenoon at

20. Mary Jane Hammond journal, June 10, 1853.

21. *JGQC*, 287–88.

> our meeting house & then told the people to meet in their different districts in the afternoon[,] as the small pox was so bad in the neighborhood of our meeting house that we did not think it wisdom to gather the people together there untill it is better. Elder Uaua went today to Ewa to open up the gospel in that place[,] a distance of about 10 miles from town[,] where he baptised 13 persons. Bro. Kapahi went to Kalihi to meet with the Brethren there, & Priests Isaaka, Kamahiai & Nuhi[, a] Teacher[,] went to Koolau to meet with the Brethren over there so that every one is busy in his calli[n]g.[22]

All of this activity was going on despite President Lewis's news that "some 15 persons [are] reported to have died in th[e] neighborhood" where the Mormon meetinghouse was located, and that they had stopped holding worship services in a central meeting house. The epidemic had spread to many small villages on O'ahu, likely aided in part by the peregrinations of families and Mormon missionaries. In fact, the Mormon native Isaaka, an Aaronic priest who left Honolulu to preach in Koolau, caught the highly contagious disease and died, probably after having helped spread it.

Back at Lahaina, Hammond grudgingly followed orders on June 12, reporting that he "attended [a native] meeting in the morning. A[d]vised them to get Evoccinated [vaccinated], according to the advice from Honolulu; and to keep out of the water." Hammond added tersely that two non-Mormons named Marston and Smith "called and spent the evening with us; conversation, Small pox." The two may have been government representatives, and it may have been about operating a school without supporting the vaccinations.

Although Cannon was advised to see that the elders, and probably the members, on Maui were vaccinated, there is no evidence that he went out of his way to show any urgency about it. From the missionaries' standpoint, it undermined their authority; they had told the native Mormons that they would be available to dispense miraculous healing priesthood blessings, and that they would be spared from the divinely directed "scourge." Probably in part as a consequence of having been visited by the non-Mormons, Hammond

22. Farrer journal, June 12, 1853.

> went and got little Tommy, the boy that we are schooling, [and had him] vaccinated for the Kine pox; also got some matter and vaccinated our two boys, but being unacquainted with the buisiness, did not get it done very well.—Had it not been for the counsel from the brethren at Honolulu, I should not ... have paid any attention to it; but trusted to the Lord entirely, for him to preserve us from pe[s]tulence, and famin[e], &c. Went and asked Dr. Dow to call and see the children. Said he would call in the evening.—Had some unplesant feelings in my family; happy is the man that can rule his own house in righteousness.[23]

It is likely that the unpleasant feelings had to do with whether to call in "gentile doctors." Hammond's concluding remark, which takes on the character of patriarchal grumbling, suggests that he lost the argument to his wife. Mary Jane wrote only that the next day "the Doctor came and vaccinated" the children.[24] Frank wrote:

> From reports from Oahu the Small pox is rageing there to some extent.~~—The brethren have been vaccinated and~~.[25] Some 15 have died, and a good many [are] sick with it. The course which the authorities take is calculated to spread it fast; they take every native they find with it and send him to the Hospital; and the natives are as [a]fraid as death of such a place; so as soon as they discover any thing the matter, the[y] leave directly for the country; for fear of the Hospital and the Doctors. But if they would ... just let it take its own course, it would not be near so hard on the natives. About 10 O.c[lock] the Doctor [Dow] came and vaccinated our two boys [with] the Kine pox.[26]

It is not clear why Hammond crossed out the line about the O'ahu elders being vaccinated, though he was clearly conflicted by the news.

23. Hammond journal, June 13, 1853.

24. Mary Jane Hammond journal, June 13–14, 1853.

25. Evidently this means that Bigler, Farrer, and Johnson were all vaccinated, although they did not mention it in their journals or correspondence. Given their faith-healing views, they may have felt uneasy admitting it.

26. Hammond journal, June 14, 1853.

CHAPTER 14

Violating the Quarantine

I saw Priest Baldwin in great consternation a run[n]ing about among the natives houses trying to prevent it [the disease from] spreading. But the Lord can and will do his own work without any hindrance from the Priests of Baal. He is able to save all who put thire trust in him and keep his commandments.

—Frank Hammond journal, June 23, 1853

The Rev. Dwight Baldwin wrote again to Richard Armstrong at Honolulu on June 13, 1853, and complained that although he and two others had been appointed "subcommissioners for Maui & the adjacent islands," Lana'i and Moloka'i, "unless native passengers can be stopped coming from Oahu here," the work of the subcommissioners would be undermined.[1] The Rev. Edward Bailey was getting people in the Wailuku area vaccinated and was begging for more vaccine.[2] For their part, the Mormon missionaries George Cannon and Ephraim Green, and the native members at Wailuku, were uncooperative. Green reported that

> the inhabitan[ts] of this place is very much alarmed about the small pox and thay are all giting vaxinated[,] but our [native] Brethren say it is a judgment from the Lord and thay feel to trust in him. This appears to be the faith of our Brethring in this place. I thank the Lord for giving them such faith in the gospel of his son. [The] Judge then impressed a fine on all that did not git vaxinated of five dollars[.]

1. Baldwin to Armstrong, June 13, 1853.

2. Edward Bailey to Dwight Baldwin. Bailey had been in the islands since 1837, mostly at the Lahaina-luna and Wailuku Female Seminaries.

> Thay then was oblige[d] to go and be vaxinated[,] for they had not the five dollars to pay [the fine]. I have seen them after thay ware vaxinated pick thare arm and then suck it with thare mouth to git the mat[t]er out.[3]

Cannon recorded nothing about these events in his journal, but in a June 14 letter to the First Presidency in Utah, he noted that "the small pox has commenced its ravages in Honolulu, and we hear that it is also on this island [Maui]." Everyone, both natives and whites, were troubled by the epidemic, "with the exception of the saints who believe that this is confirmatory of what we have told them in regard to the scourges; they desire to be resigned and exercise faith in the Lord that he will deliver them." He agreed that God alone "has the power to curb the destroyer."[4] Like the other missionaries far removed from the awful slaughter and disfigurement occurring on O'ahu, Cannon clung to his view that it was a divinely directed scourge prior to the Second Coming, while the missionaries who were closer to the center of the viral storm were now less likely to express that view.

On June 17, the Rev. W. P. Alexander wrote to minister Richard Armstrong in Honolulu that "pretty much the whole population of Lahaina have been vaccinated & officers are in progress around the island to make thorough work of it."[5] That day Mary Jane Hammond observed that "all the talk is small pox,"[6] while Frank huffed that "the vaccination of our little ones does not appear to take very well; and I do not know as I care but little about it."

In Honolulu the infected Farrer continued to illegally travel outside the city to visit Mormons in their native villages, baptizing and confirming converts and taking the sacrament with them. On the same day, June 20, that President Lewis noted he "administered" to a member who had "broken out with the small pox," Lewis recorded

3. Ephraim Green diary, June 13, 1853.

4. George Cannon to Brigham Young, Heber C. Kimball, and Willard Richards, June 14, 1853, in *JGQC*, 585.

5. William Alexander to Richard Armstrong, Jan–Jun 1853.

6. Mary Jane Hammond journal, June 17, 1853.

that "19 person[s were] reported to have died in the vicinity of the meeting house" the day before. The disease was "spreading very fast," and he spent the next five days administering healing ordinances to the diseased.[7]

In his sermons on East Maui, James Keeler—like Hammond, Green, and Cannon—connected the epidemic to the Second Coming. "I spoke to them on the judgments that was a comeing [to] the earth [and] also [reminded] them that I had provecied [prophesied] to them of the thing that [was] at their dores."[8] On June 23 at Lahaina Hammond wrote that, "I found the people were in great confusion, fearing and trembling for thire lives on account of the small pox[,] which has just broke out near the large Calvin church, right in the neighborhood where the Lord set me to labor to day."[9] "I saw Priest Baldwin in great consternation a run[n]ing about among the native houses trying to prevent its [smallpox] spreading. But the Lord can and will do his own work without any hindrance from the Priests of Baal. He is able to save all who put thire [their] trust in him and keep his commandments."

His lukewarm directive to the Lahaina Mormons to get vaccinated was largely ignored, forcing Dr. Dow to issue a threat on June 26, which Hammond conveyed to the morning branch meeting.

> Br. Maiola preached ... I followed, telling them what Doctor Dow told me as I was on my way to the church. He told me to tell all the members of our church that if they did not go and get vaccinated that [they] would all be put in the fort &c. I beleive it is a hatched up thing between him and Baldwin the Priest of Baal. Some of the brethren were for resisting the o[r]der. I told them to be cautious, and if they found that it was from the Governor, to be car[e]ful how they acted, for that was what they called us now, a set of rebels seeking to overthrow the government &c &c.[10]

In Honolulu few people were attending church, so the elders

7. Lewis journal, June 20–25, 1853.
8. Keeler journal, June 20, 1853.
9. Hammond journal, June 23, 1853, emphasis in original.
10. Ibid., June 26, 1853.

decided to cancel any further meetings for the time being.[11] Two days later Farrer and Johnson accompanied the mission president to the Honolulu smallpox hospital, about which Farrer wrote in graphic detail.

> The small pox has spread much in town [Honolulu] since I had left & many had died & among the rest some few of the brethren & Sisters were still sick. In the afternoon went along with elders L[ewis] & J[ohnson] to visit the sick Brethren & I shall not soon forget the scenes of misery & wretchedness my eyes beheld. The first man we visited was one of our priests & a faithful man by the name of Kamahiai. When I left he was well & hearty to all appearances but now he was so disfigured with the small pox that no traces of his countenance were discoverable & his throat was so stopped up that his voice was scarcely audible. We administered to him & several others. The last three were in a house w[h]ere some persons had died the day before of the small pox & they had got the simptoms very strong. We administered to them & recommended them to take some ginger tea & take a sweat, & I left them.[12]

When Hammond preached in the "lower part" of Lahaina on June 28, he noticed "quite a number of strangers out to hear the word. The people are dre[a]dfully frighten[e]d about the small pox. Many of them I fear will be swept away with it befor[e] it is done here. May the Lord guide it." Not that he wanted God to *stop* the epidemic, only that he wanted to see God's latter-day plan confined to the wicked as the chaff was separated from the wheat.

The next day at the afternoon Sunday service, Hammond read a letter from William Uaua claiming that, while possibly 1,000 had died, the Mormons on O'ahu had clearly found favor with God, many having been healed through priesthood blessings and only one death among them. "The other church with their priests," noted John Woodbury at Lahaina, "are filled with fear and dismay all the day long."[13] Uaua would temporarily leave the Mormon Church for a

11. Lewis journal, June 26, 1853.
12. Farrer journal, June 28, 1853.
13. Woodbury diaries, June 29, 1853.

time because of the smallpox catastrophe, but at this juncture he was unprepared to face the reality of the situation.

On June 30, Farrer wrote more negatively than Uaua about the development, writing to a brother in Utah that the epidemic was killing islanders "by scores & hundreds" and the situation was getting worse, as he had seen first-hand. However, of all the church members who had become infected, "scarcely one has died as yet that has been administered to. If we administer to them they will get well," he claimed, "but if the Doctors doctor them they will have to die."[14]

Just as the health commissioners on Maui were angry with Hammond for undermining their efforts, the authorities at Honolulu were upset with President Lewis for endangering people. Relations between the church and the community became so strained that on July 1, when Lewis was blessing an afflicted female convert, a man named Turner assaulted him and Farrer, accusing them of having thrown the "doctor's medicine out of Doors." The man "threatened us that if we went into his premises he would shoot us."[15] "Apparently raving mad," Lewis wrote, he lunged at the two missionaries "with his fists clenched," struck both of them with several blows, tore their coats, and took a bottle of Farrer's olive oil that had been consecrated for priesthood blessings. Farrer and Lewis ran into a store for protection, and the proprietor ordered Turner to leave the premises, which he did. Johnson subsequently went to the marshal, but while he and the officer were talking Turner came up and indicated that he had acted as the marshal had advised. Turner said he held the missionaries responsible for his mother-in-law's death.

In another letter updating his daughter on the epidemic, the Rev. Baldwin worried about what would happen on Lana'i because doctors had not yet made it there with vaccinations. He said the small outbreak on Maui had been contained, but it was another story on O'ahu. Fifteen hundred people had shown symptoms in the main city alone, and every day there were over a hundred new cases. "The Lord has spared wicked Lahaina such dreadful scenes as I had feared. But

14. Farrer to "Brother James," June 30, 1853.

15. Farrer journal, July 1, 1853. A Doctor Lathrop was present, according to Farrer.

wicked Honolulu has drank the cup, dregs and all," he wrote. Baldwin apparently believed the epidemic was, at least to some extent, a punishment for transgressions, although many O'ahu natives outside of Honolulu died as well.[16]

The day after he was assaulted, President Lewis wrote to the church's First Presidency expressing his hope that the mission would be able "to procure a printing press, as one seems much needed here." He said he "expect[ed] to start for Kauai in a few days, to remain for a season, where I can mingle more exclusively with the natives, and acquire more properly the use of the language." He did not say why he had delayed getting away from Honolulu for so long, and it may have been a coincidence, but moving out of the city had the advantage of escaping retribution from people he had advised not to get vaccinated. He would be violating the quarantine and possibly spreading the disease to Kaua'i, which at this point had been free of it.

Addressing the epidemic itself, Lewis added that "such scenes of wretchedness and misery, my eyes never before beheld." Those who followed counsel and relied on God's mercy had, he said, "almost universally been blessed," while those who had listened to the doctors and had been "induced to take medicine or bathe in cold water ... are now dead." However much he wanted to still view the course of events through a lens of faith, the injudiciousness of his council would become clear, if for no other reason than that "the doctors and priests are getting mad, and we were threatened and commanded not to go again among the sick. Br. Farrer and myself," he continued, were "about to lay our hands on a sister who had sent for us, when we were assaulted, knocked down, bruised considerably, and our clothes literally torn off."[17]

The Utah elders entered a complaint at the Honolulu police court against Charles Turner on July 5. The next day in court, Turner's attorney, a Mr. Bates, attempted to show, Lewis wrote, "malpractice

16. Baldwin to Abbey, July 1, 1853.

17. Lewis to First Presidency, Manuscript History of the Hawaiian Mission, incorrectly dated June 30, 1853. In his journal, Lewis indicates that the assault took place on July 1 and that he wrote to the First Presidency the next day.

on our part, for anointing with oil and laying [on] of hands according to the scriptures."[18] Benjamin Johnson stepped up to speak on behalf of the plaintiffs, shifting the focus back to the assault, falsely claiming he could judge the usefulness of cures because he was a medical doctor. The court was none the wiser, and he temporarily became a mission hero for such brash courtroom antics. Prior to his mission, he had studied law with his brother-in-law, Almon W. Babbitt, who had represented the LDS Church in Washington, D.C., and after his return to Utah he would obtain a license to practice law, but would not pursue that profession. In the end, as Lewis put it, all the court did was to fine Turner $12, after having beaten two men and torn their clothes nearly completely off of them, "and here the farce ended."[19]

18. Lewis journal, July 5, 1853; Farrer journal, July 5.

19. LeBaron, *Benjamin F. Johnson*; Lewis journal, July 6–7; Farrer journal, 6–7.

CHAPTER 15

Rationalizing Death

On arriving at the house we found that he [Br. Isaaka Kahoouluwaa] had just died [and] our hearts were made to grieve at this our loss. Bro. Isaaka was a good man & one that had always been on hand to assist in Bearing off our Father's Kingdom ... & on Wednesday last he was ordained to the office of elder[,] which office he was not permited to magnify here as he was taken sick on the evening of his ordination. But [he] has received that priesthood that will enable him to act among his country men [in the "spirit world"] who have died without a knowledge of the gospel, & will exalt him in the Kingdom of God.

—*William Farrer journal, July 13, 1853*

During the smallpox epidemic, George Cannon was focused on translating the Book of Mormon at Wailuku and seemed unaware of what was occurring in the outside world. At least, he said very little in his journal about the disease. Then on July 4, 1853, he noted that "the people are filled with fear on account of the small pox—there is no other topic of conversation scarcely at present ... [But] the saints," he wrote reassuringly, "do not appear to trouble themselves about it, believing that it is only as we said it would be—that the scourges were soon to be sent on the nations."[1] That was the familiar refrain among Mormon missionaries.

Five days later Elder Lewis, Albion Burnham, and Hosea Kauwahi violated the quarantine and sailed to Kaua'i. That same day Farrer tried to explain to some Mormon converts in Honolulu why so many of them were sick, despite having been administered to for

1. *JGQC*, 293.

their health. As he, Elder Johnson, and Edward Dennis went to visit Isaaka Kahoouluwaa and found him ill, they told the worried church members that this episode represented one of many obstacles the elders faced in the islands ("our difficulties here") and that as fellow Saints "they might expect such things." "The multitude that John saw on Mount Zion" in the New Testament Apocalypse (Rev. 14:1–16:7), Elder Farrer explained, "were those that had come up through great tribulation." He "exhorted the saints to faithfulness & to seek the spirit of the Lord that they might be enable[d] to stand fast to the end, & showing them the consequences of forsaking the truth after having embraced it."[2]

Farrer did not let his own infection stop him from traveling in and out of Honolulu with Kahoouluwaa before the Hawaiian came down with the disease. Farrer's rationalization, as he expressed it to the members, indicates that he sensed the potential for the native members to lose heart and bolt. On Maui, things were becoming more critical as well. At Kipahulu on July 11, Elders Keeler and Lawson prophesied that the disease "would spread & the hand of Man could not stop it. Therefore it was necessary for them to repent their siness [sins] that they Mite bee Saved in the kingdom of God." Two days later at Kawaipapa, the elders found the natives "very mutch Scaret [scared] about the small pox." But instead of calming their fears, "Bro Lawson spoke to them of their distruction in this Plase & that the seeds of death ware so[w]n among them & their days ware short on the earth &c."[3] The problem with these gloomy predictions was that vaccination was proving to be effective in stopping the disease from spreading.

On July 13, Farrer reported the death of Isaaka Kahoouluwaa, the native man who had just been ordained an elder and was given a priesthood administration for his recovery (see above epigraph). Farrer was the first to articulate the rationalization that would become most popular among the missionaries. "This morning," he wrote, "Bro. Johnson & myself started [from Honolulu] for the Nuanuu Valley

2. Farrer journal, July 10, 1853.

3. Keeler journal, July 11, 13, 1853. He added that he translated for Elder Lawson.

about 4½ miles to administer to some sick," and "on our way about 1½ miles from home we came near the house of Bro. Isaaka Kahooulu-waa. On nearing the house we heard the people mourning very much which indicated to us that Bro. I[saaka] was dead. On arriving at the house we found that he had just died [and] our hearts were made to grieve at this our loss ... [We] had expected him to be an useful instrument in preaching the gospel" on the islands. In Farrer's mind there was a reason the good brother had been taken from the earth. "He has recieved that priesthood that will enable him to act among his country men who have died without a knowledge of the gospel."[4]

Undaunted, the elders continued on to Nuanuu and "administered to several sick & gave them such advice as we deemed necessary as the small pox has begu[n] to prostrate the people in this settlement," Farrer wrote. "One of the brethren name[d] Nuhi died a few minutes after our arrival here," he admitted, adding that he himself had "found this evening that several pox had come out on my face & body but not enough to make it a matter of any serious consideration." Although perhaps noble in his stated lack of concern about himself, he was unaware of, or indifferent to, the threat he presented to the natives.

The compiler of the Manuscript History of the Hawaiian Mission in the late nineteenth century, Andrew Jenson, a member of the Church Historian's staff in Salt Lake City, acknowledged that "a number of Saints died in Honolulu with the small pox, [and] Elders Johnson and Farrer were busy administering to the sick." Jenson neglected to comment on the quality of the advice they were giving the members to avoid vaccinations or the fact that they were themselves spreading the disease.[5] There is something more comprehensive in Britsch's explanation that the missionaries "spent their time administering to the sick with holy oil and blessing them,

4. See also the Bigler journal, Nov. 16, 1853, for a similar articulation. The Mormon post-life residence between mortality and the final judgment is analogous to purgatory in Catholic theology. The explanation failed to take into consideration the deaths of native Mormon sisters.

5. Manuscript History of the Hawaiian Mission, July 13, 1853.

using more than two quarts of oil a day. But many good members of the Church died on Oahu."[6] What neither Jenson nor Britsch realized, or acknowledged, was that by traveling around the islands administering blessings to sick members, the elders were themselves infecting more people.

On July 19, Farrer reported that "Sister [Hakuole] Dennis has got the small pox but is doing tolerable well[;] her sister has had it & has got well. Bro. [Gustaf] Linn's little boy who lives with Bro. D[ennis] has also got it but not very bad."[7] Linn's son could have been Isaac, the "half-white" boy Frank and Mary Jane Hammond would later adopt and take with them when they left the mission in 1856.

A day after Farrer's report, Hammond responded to inform his colleague of what Doctor Dow had said, that he would see to it that any Mormon who did not take medical precautions would be incarcerated. The "native Mormons would not be vaccinated," the doctor had complained.[8] By his own admission, though, Hammond was depressed. On July 20 he preached at the Lahaina branch meeting and "did not have much of the spiret, therefore[e] did not edify myself, and I doubt much if the saints were much edified." He continued:

> I had a real spell of darkness. Seemed as if a thousand evil spirets were hovering round me driving away all light. I felt miserable. I sometimes feel as if [it] will be just as much as I shall be able to do to save myself. Therefore I feel to call on the Lord for help and strength to magnify the priesthood unto which I have been called[,] that it may not prove a condemnation to me at the last day! My heart trembles for fear that I may possibly yet be left to myself and greive the holy spiret and finaly get into darkness and deny the truth. But my prayer to the Lord is that he will take me away to himself before ever that shall come to pass.
>
> My dreames for the last month have all been about fighting myself or seeing others engaged in fighting. Some of them [are] causing me to feel frightful, and [I] wake up with fear and dread resting upon

6. Britsch, *Moramona*, 34. A blessing is administered with not more than one or two drops of olive oil.

7. Manuscript History of the Hawaiian Mission, July 19, 1853.

8. Hammond to Farrer, July 20, 1853.

me. My feelings are that the Lord is going to commence anew his work, & the Devil will also commence his.[9]

Hammond's deep depression was probably related to the epidemic, as he spoke the next day at a gathering of the Lahaina branch "on the necessity of being prepared to die, &c. Told them of the death of a native elder, [a] preist & many of the brethren & sisters at Honolulu with the smallpox. The native Elder was much beloved by all the church." There were other priesthood holders who had died, so Hammond was perhaps unintentionally minimizing the death toll when he said the native elder, Isaaka Kahoouluwaa, was "the first man out of this nation in this generation that has died with the Holy priesthood on him." It would appear that the deaths of so many, running counter to Hammond's treasured beliefs and expectations, had delivered a shock to his confidence.

On July 21, Keeler traveled from East Maui to Wailuku and had his own rude awakening. The five elders—both Allred twins, George Cannon, Ephraim Green, and Edgerton Snider—were all well, but the news he heard from O'ahu was that smallpox had taken "thousands of the Natives [and] there has been a quite a number of [our] brethren died for want of" what he called, but did not define, "proper care."[10] Two days later Farrer wrote in detail about the smallpox hospital he and Benjamin Johnson had visited in Honolulu. They saw "Sister Mahainaina near breathing her last. She was so far gone that she did not know us. She was an object of Pity & must have suffered a great deal. The skin had nearly all come of[f] her face & the smell that proceeded from her was almost intolerable." They saw people in various stages of infection and remarked that "the stench of the room was almost unendurable although the natives in attendance on the sick kept burning tar or something else ... to purify the room." On a lower floor, also filled with sick people, "lay two corps[es] ready to be carried of[f] to inter in a coffin." For Farrer, "Such scenes of wretchedness & suffering

9. Hammond journal, July 20, 1853.
10. Keeler journal, July 21, 1853.

as we here beheld I would be glad to never again [have] to witness, for it was truly appalling to the stoutest's heart."[11]

The next day, July 24, despite reports of this kind of horror, ten elders on Maui gathered at the Hammonds' house in Lahaina to celebrate "Pioneer Day," the church commemoration of the day Brigham Young entered the Salt Lake Valley six years earlier.[12] That afternoon they took a break to visit a citizens mass meeting where a minor confrontation occurred between Jonathan Napela and a member of Baldwin's church. Hammond described it as follows:

> Elder N[apela] got up to speak and as he went on to point out what people done in ancient days in such cases[,] how they sought the Lord by fasting & prayer &c[,] he recom[m]ended them to do the same now; but soon the devil made his appearance. One of Baldwin's members got up and called a vote to have <u>Napela</u> set down, when a general row ensued, but a few sensable men being there, they over ruled [the motion] and he was permited to go on; he preached a little to them & set down.
>
> When they im[m]ediately took a vote that none but residents should be allowed to speak in the meeting [and the vote] carried. So that cut off Bro. N[apela] from speaking any more[,] as he belongs to Wailuku.[13]

The anger was due to the fact that in advocating a faith-healing approach to the epidemic, Napela was implicitly rejecting the success of the scientific treatment. Cannon's view was that it amounted to "three hours spent in confusion and making various ... propositions," doing what they "might have been done in ten minutes ... [I]t was quite a contrast to our [Mormon] way of doing business with the priesthood presiding, [in this case] every one thinking that his plan and opinion was the best & wisest." Presumably, Cannon would have told everyone to go home and pray and be done with it.[14]

The Mormons reconvened at the Hammonds' home and enjoyed

11. Farrer journal, July 23, 1853.
12. *JGQC*, 297–98.
13. Hammond journal, July 25, 1853.
14. *JGQC*, 298–99.

the afternoon together eating, conversing, and singing. They held a meeting to discuss ways to utilize the Book of Mormon in their preaching and how to collect more funds for the Hawaiian translation of the Book of Mormon. Cannon said he would take responsibility for it and the next day wrote to Bigler, Farrer, Johnson, and Lewis about it. Yet, the epidemic still raged, and on July 29 Bigler discovered rows of empty houses in Honolulu, forcing him to conclude that "the occupants have either died or have fled to some other place, leaving everything behind them, [their] dogs, hogs, and fowls to take care of themselves."[15] That day Farrer and Uaua visited some members who were sick. "Bro. Hoomana died just as I got there." During the next week, Farrer learned of the death of another prominent member.[16]

While Hammond and Cannon were traveling on foot clockwise around West Maui on July 30 from Lahaina to Wailuku, Hammond made an intriguing admission in his journal and then crossed it out. At Honokahau he wrote that they "went and took a good bath in the cold mountain stream, ~~Bro. C[annon] and myself were a little fearful about going in, as we were vaccinated, but~~ which refreshed us much." Perhaps because he had previously offered pejorative comments about vaccinations in his journal, he felt embarrassed admitting that he had capitulated to it. Cannon recorded nothing about receiving an inoculation.

Dwight Baldwin's wife, Charlotte, wrote to their daughter on August 10 to say the "great suffering (at Honolulu) [was] painful to think of" but that, from her perspective, "the disease ha[d] dealt powerfully with the ... wicked part of Honolulu called the black sea, [which] I have been told is nearly desolated."[17] She could not resist the thought that the infection was God's plan to punish the wicked, the same as the Mormon view of it.

Other Protestants interpreted the epidemic in that way. In the

---

15. Bigler, "Extracts from Missionary Experiences," July 27, 29, 1853.

16. Farrer journal, July 30, Aug. 6, 1853.

17. Charlotte F. Baldwin, to Abbie, Aug. 10, 1853. The Black Sea neighborhood was referred to elsewhere as a slum. See Warren Goodale, "Honolulu in 1853," *Papers of the Hawaiian Historical Society* 10 (1897), 4.

Rev. Titus Coan's memoirs, he remembered that it had been "God's just punishment for natives [being] stiff-necked about the Gospel."[18] When he and fellow missionary Lorenzo Lyons arrived in Hawaii in 1835, they proclaimed that their preaching would be accompanied by divine destruction prior to the Second Coming of Christ. Therefore, when a tsunami struck the islands in 1837, he claimed it was God's purifying hand. Thousands of terror-stricken natives believed him and quickened their conversions. In fact, the post-tsunami period has been compared to the Great Awakening and Second Great Awakening of eighteenth- and nineteenth-century New York revivalism.[19] The Mormon missionaries were not alone in visualizing disasters as the start of a divine apocalypse.

In a letter to his parents on August 9, Farrer acknowledged that he and the other elders on O'ahu "were daily exposed ... by administering to those who were afflicted with [smallpox], many of whom were in a state of Putrifaction & the smell of them was almost intolerable ... We were called on to administer to some of the brethren who had it very bad. Bro Johnson & myself had the fever & symptoms ... which made us feel very bad for a day or two & I had a few pox break out on me but not enough to confine me to the house after the fever left."[20] The O'ahu elders were proud of the fact that none of them had become seriously ill, but none expressed awareness of the fact that they had been a medium for spreading the disease.

Farrer told his parents "our ranks will be thin[n]ed by the sickness" and already had been through the deaths of "several of our most active officeres & faithful members[,] which makes us somewhat shorn of help at present." "Shortly before he died," historian Scott Kenney found, Isaaka Kahoouluwaa was disillusioned with the healing promises the elders had made and "asked to be restored to his position in Reverend Smith's [Protestant] congregation if he survived. His wife declared she would leave Mormonism whether he lived or not. The widows of Opunui and Umu, and doubtless others,

18. See Furnas, *Anatomy of Paradise*, 139, 263.

19. See Daws, *Shoals of Time*, 97–102.

20. Farrer to parents, Aug. 9, 1853, LDS Archives.

also refused to have anything to do with the church after their husbands died." Even William Uaua briefly left.

There is little documentation in native journals and correspondence for this period, but the evidence that does exist points to a significant decrease in baptisms. Kenney found that "from April through July [1853] there had been 750 baptisms—188 a month," while the six-month period from August to February 1854 showed a drop to 18 per month, followed by 12 per month for the five-month period following that. A small increase of 20 baptisms per month was the average over the next year through July 1855, "barely a tenth of the number averaged by Uaua, Kauwahi, Paku, and Kahoouluwaa in the summer of 1853."[21]

In his journal for August 26, Farrer described the death toll among Mormons in his district. "In going round in the small branches on the outskirts of [Honolulu] & out in to the country I have heard of several of the Brethren & sisters that have died & some have died this week. Indeed there is scarecely a day but what some one of the Brethren & sisters is dying of this disease." He said his district, which had numbered about 400 Saints, had been reduced by a fourth to about 300, for "in one small yard near our meeting house there were 53 persons at the commencement of the disease[,] 32 of which died. In another small yard there were 11 taken sick & taken to the hospital[,] 10 of which died, & many such like cases have occured & many houses have been left without inhabitants."[22]

Britsch maintained that by October 1853 the "Saints had grown in number and were over three thousand strong" on all the islands, "despite the unfortunate deaths of almost 180 who had succumbed to smallpox."[23] His count may be right, but it seems likely, looking at other journal entries and similar documentation, that about 700 members died, which is more in line with the percentage Farrer cited. Whatever

21. Kenney, "Mormons and the Smallpox Epidemic of 1853," 13–14.

22. Farrer journal, Aug. 26, 1853. The neighbors Farrer mentions were probably non-Mormon; he seems to have left off counting Mormons, after saying that about 100 had died, to describe the general devastation.

23. Britsch, *Moramona*, 26.

the precise number, it was a blow to the church that resulted in fewer members because of the deaths and a good deal of out-migration as people expressed their disillusion by leaving the church. It was also a blow to the missionary psyche, in particular to Hammond's confidence in the healing power of priesthood holders and his belief that the native Mormons would be protected and preserved.

Peter Lineham mentioned a similar problem in New Zealand. "Religion and healing have always been associated in the Maori mind because of the traditional role of the tohunga [native healers] … In a community where the death rate was so high that most people expected the Maori race to die out, the [Mormon] elders' ministrations were virtually a trial of their doctrine … to ascertain who had divine authority … A bitter comment from [one] Maori [Mormon during that period was that] … 'you elders lay hands on the sick and they are not cured.'"[24]

24. Lineham , "The Mormon Message in Maori Culture," 218.

CHAPTER 16

The Gathering

We have been preaching that the hour of God's judgments were at hand, and the small pox has borne a faithful testimony to the fact. It is supposed that one half of the population of this city [Honolulu] have died since we came here, and is only abated for the want of subjects. It is spreading all over the islands, and its number has thrilled our hearts.[1] *There have died in this city from 50 to 60 in a day.*

—*Nathan Tanner to Bro Campbell, Sept. 9, 1853*

An important accomplishment in Hawaiian mission history occurred at 2:00 p.m. in Wailuku on July 22, 1853. George Cannon completed his first draft of the Hawaiian-language Book of Mormon, a process in which Jonathan Napela had played a crucial role. There would be additional drafts.

That same day, the missionaries throughout Maui, Cannon included, left for Lahaina at 4:00 and enjoyed an emotionally powerful meeting four days later when "the gift of prop[h]ecy & tongues was manifest[ed] in our midts," particularly on the part of Elder John Woodbury.[2] For the third time on his mission, Frank Hammond attempted to interpret Woodbury's tongue-speaking and admitted he had gotten, "only a little of it." Elder Woodbury completed the interpretation and sang hymns in tongues, but he gave no interpretation to his musical mumblings.

1. The word *thrilled* conveyed more pain than pleasure in the nineteenth century: "to pierce, penetrate; as something sharp; particularly, to cause a tingling sensation that runs through the system with a slight shivering," according to Noah Webster's 1828 dictionary.

2. Green diary, July 22, 1853; *JGQC*, 297.

Cannon too was caught up in the excitement and "had a vision of toungs," Hammond writing that "he [Cannon] saw as it were toungs in the room before his eyes." Interestingly enough, a Brother Keano spoke in tongues that day at a native gathering at Wailuku. Hammond "wonder[e]d why the [native] saints did not get the gift of tongues," and here it was happening for the first and only time. He decided that "the Lord knows best when & where to bestow his gifts." A month earlier at Wailuku, Cannon urged Elder Woodbury to speak in tongues, and not only did Cannon receive "the interpretation in part, ... Bro. Napela also received a part of the interpretation and was in vision."[3]

There was bad news from Hawai'i, Elder Karren reporting that the educated and talented young elder, John Kahumoku, had suddenly become ill, though not with the smallpox. The elders gave him a priesthood blessing, but shockingly, he died. Karren complained bitterly that "my self and Bro Tanner cried unto the Lord in his behalf but ... the heavens Apeared as Brass[,] our Prayers Seemed to [re] bound back upon us." He fell into the rationalization first suggested by Farrer that the native elders must have had "a Special Call; to go to the world of Spirits to preach to his people there." Karren praised Kahumoku lavishly, insisting that "a more faithful young man I never Knew. His Caracter was [un]impeachable." Not only that, but Kahumoku "was our Spokesman & Initerpreter." Now they had no one to help them communicate with the native people.[4] Farrer received a letter from Karren and Tanner on August 3 and agreed that "they will feel his loss most severely as they have not got the Native language ... & I believe have not any natives there who speak the English enough to communicate their ideas to them."[5]

Cannon received a letter from Elder Johnson on August 18 noting that they needed equipment to print the Book of Mormon, that the proper printing equipment "was not [to be found] on [the] Islands," and asking Cannon to influence Brigham Young to send a

3. *JGQC*, 290–91.

4. Karren journal, July 24, 26–27, 28, 1853.

5. Farrer journal, Aug. 3, 1853.

Thomas Karren

Courtesy Daughters of Utah Pioneers.

press. In fact, that same day Cannon received a letter from Young, addressed to both Cannon and President Lewis.[6] Davis Bitton noted that a close relationship developed between Cannon and Young, and Cannon and his "surrogate father" John Taylor, and this Bitton acknowledged presented the "potential ... for jealousy" on the part of the other missionaries, particularly Lewis, although Bitton charitably found "little inclination" on Cannon's part "to puff himself up or to boast of his 'inside track.'"[7]

The letter from Young dealt with the question of whether to urge native converts to immigrate to Utah. Everywhere else in the world, new members were directed, on their conversion, to "gather to Zion." Beginning with Joseph Smith's revelations in the early 1830s, Missouri had been designated as the place of the New Jerusalem where faithful members could gather prior to the Second Coming of Christ. If they were in Jackson County, Missouri, they were told, they would be protected from the destruction that would precede the apocalyptic cleansing prior to Jesus's arrival. Mormons were driven out of

6. *JGQC*, 308, 306–07.

7. Bitton, "George Q. Cannon in Hawai'i," 185.

Missouri in the late 1830s, so the focal point for gathering was moved to the new church headquarters in Illinois, then to Utah Territory.

What Young suggested was that, while "approving of the course that had been taken [in the islands] up to the present as far as he knew—in not preaching the gathering, &c. very strong," he would "suggest that, if possible you obtain a fitting island, or portion of an Island where the brethren can collect in peace & sustain themselves unmolested, [and] it might be much pleasanter for them, & they be better able to prepare themselves for gathering to this continent when the way shall open." Cannon "felt gratified at receiving this counsel and felt to obey it," agreeing that he had seen "the necessity more and more every day for something of this kind to be brought about."[8]

This had already been tried in the Society Islands. Historian George Ellsworth drew attention to a line in an 1850 letter by Protestant missionary William Howe in Tahiti that Mormons had selected Tupuai as a "Jerusalem" and were gathering converts there in "considerable numbers."[9] What role, if any, that experiment played in President Young's directive to the Sandwich Islands mission is unclear, but eight days after the missionaries received Young's letter, Hammond called on Doctor James Dow "for passes to go to Lanai to preach & to see after some members which we have over there," apparently in search of an island that was thinly populated enough for church members to appropriate. Hammond explained in his journal that it was "a small island laying to the west" about "9 miles from here."

His request resulted in a testy exchange with Dr. Dow:

> The Doctor gave me a pass, but seemed to want to have a slap at us on the plurality [of wives] system. What started him was my telling that I was going over to Lanai to peddle Mormonism, and perhaps he would think that [Mormonism was] quite as bad an infection as the Small pox. He said he did not know but [that it was] ... I then, at his request, showed some pro[o]fs in favour of the [polygamy] doctrin[e], but he could not receive them ... He said my brain was so "bedibbled" that I would believe anything no matter [how] absurd; I told him that

8. *JGQC*, 306–7; quoted in the Manuscript History of the Hawaiian Mission.
9. Ellsworth, "New Wine and Old Bottles," 26.

> I should pray the Lord to always keep me so "bedibbled" that I will be willing to believe all truth as fast as it shall be made known unto me. For the want of time we could not talk long with him[,] as our [time] for meeting had arrived; The Judge of the Poleice Court & Mr. Biglow[,] the acting U.S. Consul[,] was present, but kept close[d] mouths and looked on.[10]

That same day the Hammonds were visited by three missionaries passing through Lahaina from Hawai'i on their way to Honolulu (Thomas Karren, David Rice, and Nathan Tanner), saying they were going "to seek redress concerning the greiveences and indignities which they ha[d] received from the judge," incited by claims from the "Priest [Elias] Bond."[11] They also may have been looking for an excuse to get back to Honolulu. Hammond probably heard their explanation about why John Kahumaoku had died, writing approvingly of the idea that the native missionary had "gone to the spiret world, no doubt to do a far larger work than he could do here, for there is but a remnant, as it were of his people on the earth [and] a far greater share of them have gone behind the veil" and are "anxiously waiting for some one to come and open the Gospel door to them."[12]

The scene that greeted Karren and Tanner at Honolulu was grim. "The Distroyer has laid low his thousands and spread death and devastation through this land. Yet he has Sent his Angels to protect his Servants That are labouring on this island and has delivered them from all harm all dough [although] there is a bout 1 hundred of Our Native Brethren that has fallin, and gone into the Spirit world. And, Some of Our Best, and Many Usefull Elders; it has been a time of great Mo[u]rning among the people of this place."[13] It is hard to understand Karren's view of a "distroyer" God who would "send his angels" to protect the Utah elders, while allowing the native

10. Hammond journal, Aug. 25, 1853.

11. Originally from Maine, the Reverend Elias Bond arrived in the Islands in 1841 and labored on the big island for fifty-five years. He founded schools and started the Kohala Sugar Plantation to provide natives with employment. *Missionary Album*, 54–55.

12. In his later account, Benjamin Johnson repeated this as if it had been a miraculous revelation to him. *My Life's Review*, 157–58; also qtd. in Britsch, *Moramona*, 34.

13. Karren journal, Aug. 27, 1853.

Mormons to die. The fact that few whites of any faith died of smallpox seems to have escaped his notice.

Hammond was determined to visit Lana'i, but Lahaina officials were not allowing foreigners to go there because they might spread smallpox to the vulnerable natives. He found this difficult to understand, writing that "they are in great fear of the small pox going from here to there, and yet we have had none of it here worth mentioning." The success of the drive to inoculate people in Lahaina, and the havoc the disease was wreaking on East Maui—where the doctors had gotten a late start in inoculating the natives—did not add up in his mind to evidence of the vaccine's efficacy. He reported a prickly exchange with Baldwin, the "Priest of Baal," whom he visited in order to get "health passes to go to Lanai. He refused to give any. Said he had never given any, but I had seen one which he had given to Mr. [Judge] Ma[r]ston. But he said that was a different case ... We stood about 10 minutes and he never asked us to set down ... May the Lord reward him for all his works, speedily."

Meanwhile, according to Elder Bigler, Edward Dennis, the wealthy white member in Honolulu, donated to Elders Cannon, Johnson, Karren, and Lewis—the committee to raise funds for printing equipment—"one thousand dollars in gold that they may speedily purchase a printing press for the use of the mission. Brother Dennis has been a good brother [and] his house has been a home for us elders."[14]

Although the Mormon elders, at least at first, had willfully rejected the smallpox vaccination program, native people could understand the positive results the Rev. Baldwin and secular doctors had achieved with the inoculations on Maui, as well as the failure of government ministers Richard Armstrong and Gerrit Judd to protect the native population on O'ahu. In fact, people started gathering at public meetings in Honolulu through the summer of 1853 to express indignation and call for their resignations. On September 6 there was a similar protest meeting at Lahaina. Hammond was not there, but he knew how high the feelings were running. Karren wrote

14. Bigler, "Extracts from Missionary Experiences," Sept. 2, 1853.

in his journal that Judd lost his position as finance minister and was replaced by Elisha Hunt Allen, the former American Consul at Honolulu, while Armstrong weathered the storm and kept his position.[15]

Tanner wrote to a "Bro. Campbell" in Utah on September 9, and portions of his letter appeared in the *Deseret News.* He boasted about the number of conversions they had realized in Honolulu the previous April and May. "We have been preaching that the hour of God's judgments were at hand, and the small pox has borne a faithful testimony to the fact ... Some of our native saints have died, and some of our foreign elders have had a slight attack; but they have not been alarmed by it—continuing to administer" healing blessings (see above epigraph).[16]

Mormon publications in the 1830s and 1840s regularly featured news articles on tragic natural and man-made disasters under the premise, sometimes stated and sometimes assumed, that the "signs of the times" were being manifested, meaning that people were living through the divinely directed "scourges of the wicked" prior to the Second Coming.[17] All the Utah elders in Hawaii in 1853 viewed the smallpox epidemic in this light and looked forward to the time when the reigns of government would be in their hands. On September 21, 1853, Hammond preached that "the time would come when if a man or woman was caught" in adultery, they "would pay the penalty with the forf[e]it of his head &c."[18] The occasion of this sermon was the excommunication of four native branch members, one for "getting drunk" and three for adultery.

Hammond received a letter from Elder Tanner on September 22

15. Karren journal, Sept. 6–8, 1853; for more, see Daws, *Shoals of Time*, 141–46.

16. *Deseret News*, Dec. 15, 1853; qtd. in Manuscript History of the Hawaiian Mission, Sept. 9, 1853.

17. Official publications during this period were the *Evening and Morning Star*, *LDS Messenger and Advocate*, *Elders Journal*, *Times and Seasons*, and the Liverpool *Millennial Star*.

18. Hammond's scriptural text was Matt. 5:13–16, wherein Jesus says that "if the salt have lost its savour ... it is henceforth good for nothing, but to be cast out, and to be trodden under foot of men." In Mormon terms, this was an exposition of the doctrine of blood atonement, by which it was thought that some sins (adultery, apostasy, miscegenation, murder) were so serious they required a person's blood to be spilled in order for Jesus's atonement to take effect. See, e.g., Bagley, *Blood of the Prophets*, 50–51.

arguing that the mission needed a boat for travel to and from the islands, and two days later Cannon received a similar letter in which Tanner wrote that "we have a good deal of sailing to do and it is likely to increase." The only downside he could see was the possible burden on the poor, since the church members would have to finance the boat. Cannon liked the idea and thought it would benefit both the missionaries and the members.[19] Despite the directive that they proceed to establish a "gathering place" for native Mormons in Hawaii, Tanner's plan to secure a boat soon grew to involve not just a whaleboat or schooner but a brig or barque for transporting native converts to the Mormon settlement at San Bernardino, California. If the members, still recovering from the smallpox epidemic, could supply enough funds, Tanner was ready to bring every last church member to the mainland, and through the rest of his mission this would be his pet project.

19. *JGQC*, 314–15.

CHAPTER 17

The Haleakala Excursion

I should think that there was 5000 acres of good land to be seen at one sight from where I stood on the south rim of the [Lana'i] basin. A better tract of land in one body I have neve[r] seen on these lands ... I have never seen a place better calculated for the colonizeing of the saints on these islands than this is.

—Hammond, Sept. 26, 1853

After George Cannon finished the first draft of the Hawaiian Book of Mormon in July 1853 with help from Jonathan Napela, he and two more proofers, a man named Pelio and Jonathan's brother Kanahunahupu, helped him proof a second draft. They finished it two months later on September 27, one subsequent draft away from publication.[1]

Three days before Cannon and his two assistants finished their work, Hammond persuaded two members, Brother Kaai and his wife, to take him to Lana'i in a canoe, circumventing official notice. They left Lahaina at 7:00 a.m. and "had a ple[a]sant passage accross the chanell, which is about 9 miles wide," he wrote, cutting the actual distance in half. "When about mid way the prospect was very fine," he continued. "We could see the islands [of] Molokai, Maui, Kawealawe, a desolate Island, Molikini the same,[2] & Hawaii the mother of them all (so says the tradition) [which] lay away off to the south with the Mountains 'Mauna Kea' & 'Mauna Loa' stretching their lofty heads far above the clouds, making quite a grand sight."

1. *JGQC*, 314.

2. The two desolate islands are Kaho'olawe, later a bombing range for the US Navy, and Molikini, which today is almost completely submerged, only the southern half of the top rim of the volcano visible.

In the future Hammond would cross the Auau Channel in a whaleboat to let the wind augment the work of rowing. He would also avoid traveling during the day because the trade winds that came up every morning between Moloka'i and Maui churned up four-to-six-foot waves.[3] A midnight launch also was better because it was cooler at night. When there were few clouds in the sky (almost always), Maui and Lana'i could be seen silhouetted against the night sky and it was easy to find the way. Hammond wrote:

> We arrived at about 3 o.c. at Manele[,] a small village situate[d] on the beach at the back of an open arm of sea which forms an indppenent [independent] harbor for small craft only when the wind is from the South.[4] The people were glad to see me. Found two sisters here and they were exceeding kind to me; I felt a good deal fateigued, as I had to sit about in one position all the way over and it made my bones ache very much. One of the Sisters[,] Pooinene[,] she lurnileemied [massaged] me from head to foot and it helped me much. Her husband is a catholic.
>
> I went out just at dark to a bye place for secret prayer. I prayed the Lord to take the curse of[f] from that Island[,] and I dedicated it to the Lord and for the benifit of thes[e] Saints on these Islands. I also prayed that no Preist of Baal might be permited to land there from that time forth to distract the people[,] but that they might all turn to the Lord; there is about 700 inhabitants on the Island.[5]

Already he was dedicating the island for a gathering. Why he thought the island was cursed is unclear, although natives believed it had once been haunted by supernatural beings, and in the conquest of the island Kamehameha I slaughtered the inhabitants, leaving few remaining. Unfazed by its reputation, Hammond confidently preached the next day, Sunday September 25, to fifteen or twenty natives and baptized four of them. The following morning, accompanied by Brothers Kaai and Nakalo and their wives, he rode a horse

3. Hammond talks about this in his journal; it is still true, as I learned from the captain of the ferry that travels back and forth between Lahaina and Manele Bay.

4. In other words, the bay is protected because the persistent trade winds blow from the northeast.

5. Hammond journal, Sept. 24, 1853.

two miles to the top of a ridge and was entranced by what he saw on the other side. This was the crater of the old volcano that had formed the island. "I came to the top of the rise of a great basin," the Palawai Valley, "laying at the foot of the large Mountain on the east and run[n]ing off to the west." At the "top of a high ridge," he could see a "perfectly enclosed a large tract of good land" (see epigraph above). The only "fault with the place [is] that ... there is scarseity for water a part of the year, but resavoies [reservoirs/cisterns] could be prepared and so have a plenty of water for man and beast," he imagined.

Riding down into the valley, Hammond "stop[p]ed at an old house, and soon it was filled with natives anxious to see the face of a white man"; foreigners were not often seen on the island. He "talked a great deal to them setting forth our principles to them. They seemed to all believe what I taught." After they fixed him a chicken and sweet potato dinner, he walked up the mountainside for "a most buiteful prospect of the basin & of the sea, & sur[r]ounding country." The mountain ridge on the east side of the island facing Lahaina includes Lanaihale Peak at 3,370 feet.

Returning to Manele on Wednesday morning, Hammond organized a branch there with just nine members under the charge of a man, Hookuanui, whom he ordained a deacon and Kaai who was ordained a teacher. Then it was off again in the canoe for a six-hour trip back to Lahaina. Hammond commented that because Brother Kaai and his wife were "weakhanded," he had to do most of the paddling. When they arrived at the house, there were four missionaries waiting for him: Reddick and Reddin Allred, William McBride, and John Woodbury. He told them how perfect Lana'i would be as a gathering place. In the morning he excused himself to go to the Lahaina police court to earn some money. Out of curiosity, two months earlier he had observed the murder trial of a "Chinaman" and found that the court needed interpreters. Judge Marston offered him $241 per year to work full-time translating. "I am not my own man," he regretfully responded, explaining his ecclesiastical responsibilities, but said he would translate whenever he was free. This began an intermittent but profitable arrangement.

Reddin Allred and Reddick Allred

Courtesy Daughters of Utah Pioneers.

On October 2 the mission president and five elders arrived at Frank's and Mary Jane's house on their way to Wailuku for a mission conference. Their visit made "a good deal of work" for Mary Jane, who nevertheless said she greatly enjoyed their company and bragged about feeding them chicken, bread, cake, poi, and fish, a "very good supper" considering that she had only "one pot to cook in."[6] She accompanied the missionaries to Wailuku and stayed at the Napelas' house, as did Frank and the children. On October 5, Frank recorded, they were "in council all day" deciding what to present to the native conference two days later.[7] Their decisions included "that we

6. Mary Jane Hammond journal, Oct. 2, 1853.

7. See also Lewis journal, Oct. 5, 1853.

obtain a printing press, also that we seek out a location or locations for the colonizing of the saints upon these lands according to Pres. [Brigham] Youngs instructions. Resolved that we own a [sailing] vessel as soon as possible."

The question of whether to purchase a printing press "was the first thing taken into consideration, whether we ought to have the Book of Mormon printed by hiring or whether we should purchase a press of our own and publish it and other works necessary for the instruction of the Saints." Some of the elders were concerned that "if the press was bought, we would have <to> stay & take charge of it." Cannon "did not consider that my mission was fully filled until I saw the [native] Book of Mormon in press[,] if there was a prospect of it being done in a reasonable time," but he did not want to "deter them from doing what they thought wisdom demanded." In fact, only he knew how to run a press. The council decided to buy the printing machinery and work out the details later and assigned a three-man committee consisting of Cannon, Johnson, and Lewis to raise funds and finalize the purchase.[8]

Next they talked about purchasing a ship. They were interested enough in the Palawai Basin that Hammond described, in the center of Lana'i, to form a committee of five—Dennis, Hammond, Johnson, McBride, and Tanner—to "make a circuit of the islands"—the same as the printing press committee—"to accomplish the object[s] in view," meaning a determination of where the gathering place would be and to collect funds for a ship.[9]

The next day they decided that the first-wave missionaries would leave for home in six months, allowing them to begin making plans for their lives subsequent to being released at the mission conference in April 1854.[10] Four missionaries were assigned to the island of Hawai'i: Nathan Tanner as conference (district) leader, accompanied by Elders Thomas Karren, James Lawson, and Edgerton Snider. Then someone pointed out that none of them could speak the language,

8. *JGQC*, 357; also qtd. in Manuscript History of the Hawaiian Mission.

9. *JGQC*, 357–59.

10. Keeler journal, Oct. 6, 1853; Mary Jane Hammond journal, Oct. 7, 1853.

so three more elders were assigned to the area: James Keeler, Gustaf Linn, and David Rice, along with some native elders. William Farrer was named president of the new Kaua'i conference, assisted by William McBride and a white convert named Davis. Henry Bigler was requested to stay where he was and supervise the smallpox-devastated O'ahu conference, assisted by James Hawkins and John Winchester. John Woodbury, aided again by Ephraim Green, would be president of the small Moloka'i conference.

Surprisingly, Reddick Allred was appointed president of the Maui conference, to oversee Hammond, Jonathan Napela, and William Uaua. Hammond did not record what his reaction was, but it must have been something of a shock that he was not selected to preside. He seemed ideal for the position, given his greater experience in the area (having lived on the island for over five years), his proficiency in the language, and his house in Lahaina. Allred had been in the mission for eight months and had been speaking the native language haltingly in public for only a few weeks. He and Hammond were about the same age, Allred having turned thirty-one the previous February and Hammond following suit nine months later.

Although one might expect this selection reflected Lewis's longstanding animosity toward Hammond, actually it was Cannon who made this appointment. Cannon prefaced his decision by explaining that "it was thought best, as I was appointed to collect means for the press and travel thro' the different conferences and branches to effect this, that I be released from the duties of presiding over the Maui conference." He was not expecting to be asked to nominate a successor and "demurred saying, that I thought it was the place of the presidency to make such nominations, but they pressed it upon me." After praying for guidance, he felt inspired to nominate Allred "without fear <of giving offence> or division of feeling on the subject."

Twenty-two native elders and priests would be called on missions to accompany the "foreign elders." Early on the morning of Friday, October 7, prior to opening the conference of native members at 10:00 a.m., the Utah elders met once more to confirm their decisions of the past few days. Cannon conducted the meetings at which the missionaries explained to the native members the need for securing the printing press and for establishing a gathering place, both of which, Hammond claimed, were "heartily sustained by the saints." With equal enthusiasm he reported that "a representation of the branches ... showed an increase of 3 fold during the last 6 months ... about 1000 present."

Having dragged their feet for some time on ordaining only a handful of native brethren to the higher Melchizedek priesthood, Cannon noted with some satisfaction that "in [the] evening we ordained some twenty three elders," along with "twenty nine priests, sixteen teachers and twelve deacons." They "commenced collecting means for the press" by obtaining an admittedly small amount, but it was enough, Hammond thought, to show "their willingness." Although the Utah elders felt the natives had joyfully "sustained" these predetermined decisions, subsequent events would indicate that they were unhappy with the financial demands being placed on them, the frequent mission calls for lengthy periods of time to other islands, and the imposition of a gathering place on one island, which meant that everyone else would be uprooted from their ancestral villages and islands.

On Monday morning, the conference having concluded the previous day, the Utah missionaries appointed Farrer to write a synopsis of church history for the native elders; Hammond to translate items on church government from the Doctrine and Covenants (he had already started on it); and Woodbury to compile a selection of hymns. Cannon and Winchester would prepare the conference minutes for mailing to Utah.[11]

They had also decided to visit the Haleakala Crater at the top of the extinct volcano in the middle of East Maui "for recreation and geological observations under the direction of the [mission] Presidency," as Farrer put it.[12] Mary Jane Hammond chose not to join the men. She left Wailuku at noon on October 12 and traveled by foot "for Lahaina with a Native," carrying her infant son Samuel for

11. *JGQC*, 361–65.

12. Farrer journal, Oct. 8, 1853.

twenty-five miles while her four-year-old son Frankey walked beside them. She arrived home "tired and sleepy [and] very lonesome."[13]

The elders, excepting four who were sick, left the next day. Brother Kapono fed and housed them that night at Kula on the western slope of the volcano, and early the next morning the native brethren provided the missionaries with free horses, food, and guides. This was unusual because typically they were paid for tourist services. The elders and six or seven native guides rode on horseback, two donkeys laden with provisions, and made it as far as a cave just below the rim of the crater, where they spent the night. The native brethren fed them dinner and that night fixed a luau-style buried meal of goat's meat, potatoes, and kalo pie that was ready the next morning for breakfast.[14]

Reaching the rim of the crater at an elevation of over 10,000 feet, the Americans marveled at what they saw. Johnson wrote most eloquently that

> we stood upon the very rim of this most awful abyss, almost just beneath us. Here opened to our view a scene sublime, grand and wonderful. Before us was a chasm some thousands of feet deep and 30 miles in circumference, once, to all appearance, the mightiest volcano that ever shook the earth … And while standing at this great altitude the view stretches away over the mighty deep, taking in all the surrounding islands, which appear but as dots in the watery expanse. And never has any view so impressed me with the majestic greatness of Nature's God and the smallness of finite man.[15]

Hammond penned a detailed description of the inside of the crater. It was

> some 30 miles in ci[r]cumference, with 13 large cones down in the bottom of the Crater, some of them 250 ft. high; We decended down into the Crater … it was a soft bed of sinders where we ~~slide down~~

13. Mary Jane Hammond journal, Oct. 12, 1853.

14. Karren journal, Oct. 12, 13, 15, 1853. *Kalo* is Hawaiian for *taro*, a plant with a potato-like tuber.

15. Johnson papers, Oct. 14, 1853; see also *JGQC*, 366–69.

> ^decended^. I should judge the decent to be about 5000 ft. At the bottom we found a hard bed of sinders, looking as if they had but just come out of the furnace ... It was one of the grandest sights that my eyes ever beheld.[16]

Climbing back out was grueling with the hot sun beating on them, and when they reached the rim they discovered that Elder Hawkins was missing. It was too late to make their descent when they finally found him, so they were forced to spend the night in another cave near the rim, this time with little food. By 10:00 a.m. the following morning, however, they reached Kapono's cottage at Kula, where they were fed an ample breakfast. Both Hammond and Woodbury noted that there was discussion at the time of situating the gathering place at Kula due to its already large Mormon community, but they were unable to reach a consensus.[17]

16. Hammond journal, Oct. 14, 1853; see also *JGQC*, 368.
17. Woodbury diaries, Oct. 15, 1853.

CHAPTER 18

Removing from Babylon

I sometimes feel as if it was almost impossible to make any thing of this [Hawaiian] people so long as they are so mixed up with, and surrounded by their old friends in sectarianism, that it is a hard matter to root it out of them, [and] ... if it is necessary for the whites to come out from "Babulon" and be separate, how much more this people, who are, as it were only half awake and easy led back again to their old ways.

—*Hammond to Parley P. Pratt, Dec. 3, 1853*

The Utah elders reported that the Maui members supported their plan to purchase a press, while in fact there was real opposition. Elder Keeler found that, when he left Wailuku to visit Kula to obtain money for his passage to the island of Hawai'i,

> some of them had been finding fault about perchaceing [purchasing] the press &c. ... I got up & told them that it was for them & not for us that we ware tyring to exalt them from the low degredation into which they had fallen & that we could not doe it with out their help [and] neither could the Lord unless they ... give their means freely for the work of the Lord with all they had ... I also asked them if they could help us to some means to help us up from here as we had not any [means] to pay our passage to "Hawaii." Bro Kekoa gave me one dollar & that was all that I got from this branch of the church.[1]

That day Hammond and several other missionaries crossed the channel to Lana'i in a whaleboat and landed at Manele Bay "about

1. Keeler journal, Oct. 19, 1853.

sundown." Their purpose was to determine the island's suitability as a gathering place.[2] Conspicuously absent was President Lewis. The consensus among the missionaries was that it would be perfect if it had fresh water. "Our search for water was not concluded very flatteringly, for there is but very little water even for the present population," according to Hammond, who felt they could dig wells and construct cisterns to catch rain water. Cannon found the spot Hammond had discovered to be "a beautiful basin of about two miles width, shut out entirely and secluded from the view of the sea; it remined me of Deseret [Utah]. It was a splendid piece of land and seemed to be well adapted for a gathering place."[3] Apparently Tanner, who was still bent on transporting the islanders to the mainland, was the only committee member who opposed Lana'i.[4]

After the committee returned to Lahaina, Reddick Allred thought more about the water issue and decided they should look elsewhere, especially because they were trying to teach the natives cleanliness.[5] Below the surface was a struggle for mission leadership, especially between Johnson and Tanner as the latter "manifested much unkindness" toward his colleague, according to Johnson. It showed up in a nightmare Johnson had in which someone was trying to harm him and the assailant turned out to be Tanner. During a follow-up discussion in Honolulu, Tanner accused Johnson "of seeking to control the mission, which charge [Johnson] at once called upon Prest. Lewis and the council to investigate."

The accusation "proved only [Tanner's] dislike and jealousy of me," Johnson wrote. When the O'ahu missionaries met again on October 27, Johnson claimed that William McBride took his side, saying that God never intended for Tanner to be a counselor in the mission presidency, nor had Brigham Young wanted it. President Lewis, according to Johnson, tried to tamp down the disturbance and told "Br. N[athan Tanner he] had no cause for accusation and should make satisfaction."

2. Karren journal, Oct. 19, 1853; Farrer journal, Oct. 19, 1853.

3. *JGQC*, 372–73.

4. Johnson, *My Life's Review*, 167–69; also qtd. in Britsch, *Moramona*, 35–36.

5. Reddick Allred journal, Oct. 20, 1853.

"Finding he had failed, he arose and sought to smooth his offense, saying he did not wish to hurt Br. Johnson," to which Johnson replied that "although we may try[,] we can do each other no lasting harm, but we can easily hurt ourselves. Said [he] would forgive Br. N. the wrong he had done [him], and would be glad to know he had not hurt himself."[6]

During the last week of October, Hammond said goodbye to his whaling friend James Kipp and family, who were on their way to the Mormon settlement of San Bernardino in southern California.[7] Three days later Hammond noted that the port of Lahaina was exceptionally busy; it was winter in the northern whaling grounds:

> There is some 60 ships now in the harbour. There has been as high as 67. I never knew so many before to be here at one time. They leave a great deal of money on shore, but as to the wellfare of the [Hawaiian] nation I beleive they would be far better off if the ships should not touch here, for I think it tends to make the [native] men idle & the women licencious, and if the sailors were not to come among them I think it would be far better for the people, both temporaly & spiretualy. It is heart sick[e]ning to see the awful affects of the venereal deseaias [diseases] upon this people. They are litterally wasteing away under its influence. It is more easily discover[e]d in a seaport-town like this than back in the country.[8]

One of the reasons Lana'i looked appealing to him was because it was isolated from these influences and away from the Protestant missionaries.

On October 30 an important development occurred at Honolulu when William Uaua brought a member of the royal Privy Council, Levi Haalelea, to the home of Edward Dennis to visit with five of the missionaries. Haalelea was sympathetic to the Mormon message and even offered to help them secure a printing press. In addition, he owned land on Lana'i that he was willing to let the church have "on favorable terms," explained Farrer, "if we could find a peice suitable

---

6. Johnson Papers, Oct. 25–27, 1853. Farrer dismissed this as a mere "misunderstand[ing]" and said it ended in peace. Farrer journal, Oct. 26, 1853.

7. *JGQC*, Oct. 24, 1853.

8. Hammond journal, Oct. 27, 1853.

for a gathering place for the saints."[9] Two days later Cannon wrote in his journal that Haalelea had even said that if "any of his lands were suitable we could settle on them without any charge on his part, and that after [the colonists] got well started and liberated from the immediate embarrassments of settling &c., they ~~had~~ could then come to an equitable arrangement in regard to the rent &c."[10]

Still inclined to disregard the smallpox quarantine, four of the Utah elders and eight native missionaries left Lahaina the next day on a schooner bound for the big island. When they arrived at Upolu at the northern tip of the island, they were put in jail (quarantined) for fourteen days for medical observation, for which they refused to see any justification, complaining bitterly that it was "contrary to all Law and Justi[ce]" and a Protestant "opperation" to undermine their proselytizing. "The diviel [devil] is mad and is bound to hedge up our way if he can," Karren wrote. A few days later, four of them escaped "while the guards was a sleep,"[11] once again in violation of the quarantine.

Back in Honolulu, Cannon and Lewis were exploring options for securing a press in San Francisco. They met again with Haalelea, who offered to loan them $500 toward the purchase. They thought they could arrange the transaction through John Horner, a Mormon real estate developer in the Noe Valley area of San Francisco. "Our object," wrote Cannon, "was to get the Book of Mormon in press as quickly as possible" and to do the printing in Honolulu.[12]

Hammond, who sometimes resorted to practicing his cobbler skills to keep his family afloat, wrote on November 4 that he was "employed in shoemaking, to get a little money to get myself some clothes, as mine is getting rather shabby; it is not according to my will that I work at my trade; but the [native] branch is poor, and I do not feel to burden them any more than I can help." Mary Jane's school-teaching helped to finance the family as well, although they

9. Farrer journal, Oct. 30, 1853.

10. *JGQC*, 376–78.

11. Karren journal, Nov. 1, 5, 1853.

12. *JGQC*, 379–82.

admittedly relied in part on the generosity of the members who "furnished us with a good deal of poi."

In November the Hammonds received a note from Cannon at Honolulu informing them of "Sister Lewises intention of paying us a visit soon." She was unwell, and instead of sending her to live with her sister (Elder Woodbury's wife) in California or taking care of her himself, President Lewis decided to palm her off on the Hammonds. In fact, she had tuberculosis ("consumption").[13] The Hammonds felt put upon but were hospitable. "Eearly this morning Sis Lewis [and] Bro.s Tanner [and] Woodbury arived here from Oahu very sea sick and tiered [tired]," Mary Jane wrote. "Sis Lewis is going to live witth us for sometime[,] for she has no home of her own. I have a learge famiely to do for and [it] is very hard for me[,] but I trust in the Lord for help."[14]

Jane Lewis had no home of her own because her husband had decided to return to Kaua'i to live with natives in his attempt to learn the language. After he "received a letter from my wife saying that she was well received," on November 17 he left for Kaua'i with Farrer and McBride, leaving Johnson in charge in Honolulu.[15]

The same week, Nathan Tanner, Ephraim Green, and John Woodbury crossed the Pailolo channel from Maui to Moloka'i to investigate the Haalelea property there, and they concluded that it was "first rate" but had a more serious water deficit than Lana'i and therefore ruled it out as a gathering place.[16]

The Rev. Dwight Baldwin was still busy dealing with the smallpox epidemic. He wrote to his daughter informing her that he had ridden a mule to see the infected sites throughout East Maui and found that the "disease had raged, some time, in Hana, & Kipahulu, & had entered Kaupo ... Up to this day, 63 have died in Hana, 27 in Kipahulu, 15 in Kaupo, 2 in Kahikinui, & 2 in the region of Makawao." After his return, he said he "was obliged to go to Lanai."[17] Hammond believed

13. See Lyman, *San Bernardino*, 306.

14. Mary Jane Hammond journal, Nov. 7, 1853.

15. Lewis journal, Nov. 11, 16, 1853.

16. Green diary, Nov. 25, 1853. See also Woodbury diaries, Nov. 25, 1853.

17. Dwight Baldwin to Abigail, Nov. 18, 1853.

he traveled there to investigate what the Mormons were doing, but it appears more likely he wanted to vaccinate vulnerable natives.

Toward the end of the month, Cannon wrote a long letter to Brigham Young discussing the plan to buy a press and print the Book of Mormon translation in Honolulu. "It seemed to us necessary to bring every auxiliary, such as a press &c., to bear … to raise them [the natives] from their present degraded and deplorable condition to a situation where they can enjoy and appreciate (which they are incapable of at present,) the blessings the Lord has in store for His people."[18]

The Hammonds received a letter on the first of December from apostle Parley Pratt, answering Frank's question about "going home by the way of" Cape Horn, the southern tip of South America, and visiting relatives in New York. "Pratt stated that we had best come home and then go [to New York] if wisdom [dictated]," which pleased Mary Jane: "I do not want to go on account of my children traveling over the waters."[19] According to Frank, when Pratt "showed my letter to the [First] Presidency," the brethren advised "to not take my family round there. This is just what I wanted to know[,] the mind of the Presidency, &c, Now I am satisfied. It is as good as a revelation to me on the subject, & it pleases Mrs. H[ammond], as she did not like the idea at all of going that way home."

"It is quite satisfactory to me," he responded to Pratt, and "Mrs H[ammond] feels double glad," and even added that it was not only his wife's opinion "not to go that way home; neither was it mine, unless I should be councilled directly in the matter." He hinted at his true feelings, however, when he added that "if I should never see the face of my 'Kin' again, in the flesh, I will not go counter to the authorities of this Kingdom, for, I know that as soon as I do, that I am on the road to distruction."[20] He tried to sound sanguine but knew the real possibility existed of perhaps never seeing his family again; in fact, it would be sixteen years before he would return to Long Island.

18. Cannon to Young, Nov. 20, 1853; qtd. in *JGQC*, 593.

19. Mary Jane Hammond journal, Dec. 1, 1853.

20. Hammond to Pratt, Dec. 1, 1853.

On December 2, when Elder Tanner returned to Lahaina from Moloka'i, a letter arrived from Reddin Allred announcing that, according to Mary Jane's telling of it, "Sis Gaston is ready to come in to live with us whenever Mr. H[ammond] goes after her." Mrs. Hammond was ecstatic. "I am very glad," she wrote, "for I need some help very much, for my school takes up all my time [and] if she will help me I shall feel first rate for I do not have much help."[21] Jane Lewis was giving her little assistance, and Mary Jane believed Diana Gaston would. Mrs. Gaston's husband, Judson, had left for California without his family, never to be reconciled. In fact, what had happened to their baby is unclear; she did not bring the child with her to Lahaina.[22]

Frank picked up his pen three days later and added more to the letter he was drafting to Pratt (see above epigraph for a portion of the letter). "There is some of the [Hawaiian] saints here who have manifested as strong [a] faith as any I have heard among the white saints," he marveled.

> The last year has been one of severe visetations to them in the shape of a scourge from the "Smallpox" which has swept off its thousands; and yet so few are they who are left alive [and far] from repenting that it appears to me that they are still more hardened in wickedness and unless there is something put on foot for their immediate salvation, they will soon be numbered among the nations that were. I believe that our plan of colonizeing them [at a gathering place on the Islands] is the thing that will do it, if we can get it to work; by it we will be able to save a remnant of them.[23]

During the first week of December, President Lewis and Elder Farrer examined Levi Haalelea's property on Kaua'i, as well as the Fitcomb and Rhodes plantations. The president found the properties unsuitable.[24] At Lahaina, Frank Hammond noted that "Sister Lewis's things arrived to day from <u>O'ahu</u>," indicating that "she designs making

21. Mary Jane Hammond journal, Dec. 3, 1853.

22. Cannon heard from Gaston that he was doing well and would like to correspond. *JGQC*, 404.

23. Hammond to Parley P. Pratt, Dec. 4, 1853.

24. Farrer journal, Dec. 5–6, 1853; Lewis journal, Dec. 6, 9, 1853.

her home with us for the present." There was news from Honolulu that "the brethren had been talking of sending an Elder along with Bro. D[ennis]" to San Francisco to make arrangements for the missionaries of the first wave who would be traveling home soon, making advance purchases of wagons and teams for their trek to Utah.[25] Elder Johnson gave a more thorough account, writing that

> about the 1st of December 1853 Br. Dennis sold his property, obtaining a first payment [of] $7,000 in gold, $1000 of which he had promised as a loan toward buying the printing press and materials,[26] and besides the $500 promised by Halalia [Haalelea], we have obtained quite an additional sum ... Prest. Lewis, with Bro. McBride and others being on the island of Kauai, we wrote him upon the subject, with the suggestion that the money be at once remitted to Bro. John M. Horner of San Francixsco, and through his agency obtain from Boston the press and material at an early day.
>
> In answer to our letter Br. McBride came with instructions or suggestions from Prest. Lewis, that Br. McBride proceed with the means to San Francisco, and with Br. Horner's assistance, make the necessary arrangements. Also, that as Brs. Cannon, Bigler, Farrer, Hawkins[, Keeler,] and others had been for years upon the islands, and it being their privilege now to return home, it was suggested that Br. McBride labor [in northern California] through conference for the means necessary for their return.[27]

Hammond objected to this strategy, explaining that he wrote to Cannon on December 9, giving him "my thoughts about sending a man [McBride] to the coast to gether [gather] means for the [first-wave] elders out fit home; I did not feel to favour the plan, but [preferred] for them to get their out fit from the mission where they have spent their time &c." He apparently thought it reflected badly

25. The terms "out-fits" and "fit-outs" meant the ship fare and equipment, such as teams and wagons, necessary to get from Honolulu to San Francisco, from there to the Mormon San Bernardino settlement, and from there to Salt Lake City.

26. Note that this was to be a loan, not a gift. Unfortunately, it was never repaid, which may, at least in part, account for Dennis's subsequent apostasy.

27. Johnson Papers, Dec. 9, 1853.

on the mission and on them as missionaries if they had to impose on members 2,000 miles away for their "return."

The mission president asked Cannon to meet with him on Kaua'i. Cannon boarded a steamer from Honolulu the same day, December 10, and arrived the next morning at Nawiliwili, then continued two miles inland to Lihue, the home of Albion Burnham, a convert who worked at a sugar mill. In a meeting the next day with other missionaries and native elder J.W.H. Kauwahi and his wife, Cannon remarked that he "like[d] the appearance of this island very much, fruit is more abundant, timber more easily procured and plentiful and [there is] more arable land than [on] Maui for the same amount of distance. They were very picturesque the views we had to day in travelling." Elder Kauwahi was asked if he, along with Cannon and Farrer, would devote the time necessary to read the native translation of the Book of Mormon and guarantee its accuracy, and he agreed to do so.

A week later a conference was held for about 150 native Mormons on Kaua'i in the town of Lawai, where Cannon spoke about "the press and printing the Book of Mormon," followed by Kauwahi, who Cannon said "spoke with power—he is a mighty man and one capable of doing a vast amount of good if he will only walk aright. He comprehends principle as readily as any man I ever saw, either white or native, and is also the most gifted speaker among the natives and is very apt to teach."[28]

The first-wave missionaries agonized over how they were going to pay for their return home, given the fact that they were going to be raising funds among the native members to pay for the press.

> Looking at things naturally, it does not seem probable that if the brethren Bigler, Hawkins, Farrer and Keeler should be released at the spring [April 1854] conference, (as they expect to be), that they will be able to raise the necessary amount, some $200 or $300, to carry them on to the coast, as <all> the means that can be collected from <the [native] Saints> will be devoted to the press &c. If we intended to get through [to Utah] the next season, wisdom seems to dictate the

28. *JGQC*, 384, 386–89.

> necessity of all ~~getting~~ or at least a sufficient part, getting to the coast … as the opportunities would be better for raising the needful [revenue there]. We all saw the propriety of some such move being made, and we thought that Bro. McBride would be the most suitable man, as his health and the difficulties which lay in the way of his acquiring the language, made his absence less felt than one who had both good health and the use of the language; it was also Bro. Mc B's desire to labor among those of his own language."[29]

Most of the five missionaries liked the idea of being freed from having to raise money for their passage home and were willing to have McBride do it for them among Mormons in northern California, which he was anxious to do since he had not been able to learn the Hawaiian language.

In the day-to-day business of running the branch in Lahaina, Hammond alternately showed his talents, limitations, prejudices, broad-mindedness, and pettiness. For instance, from a journal entry on December 16, 1853, we learn that he "tride [tried] to dissaude [a native] Mormon woman from marrying a negro, but to no purpose." Later, though the black man claimed he had joined the Mormon church in Honolulu, Hammond refused to integrate the couple into the Lahaina branch. He was equally unhappy that Elder Tanner had not yet left the Hammonds, and had exhibited mostly idleness while lingering with them for eighteen days. Tanner made excuses, saying he wanted to take a steamboat to the big island and went to the docks, only to find out he had counted on the wrong vessel, that "she does not go there this trip." He also demonstrated what Hammond considered to be incompetence in sending "a lot of letters through [a] mistake to Wailuku that were put up for Honolulu. It will make them some 2 weeks later than they would have been."

On Thursday, December 22, there was an accident in the home involving the Hammonds' infant son. "Little S[amuel] scalded his right hand sever[e]ly by up setting Sis. Lewis['s] <u>tea pot</u> full of boiling <u>hot tea</u>." Mary Jane said it was "just school time and I had to carres[s Samuel

29. Ibid., 389–90.

for] one hour." The next day the boy's hand was "one great blister."[30] He was about eight months old, Frank wrote, and "suffered severely."

The next day on the island of Kaua'i, Elders Cannon, Farrer, and Kauwahi settled into "a house belonging to Samuela, Bro. Kauwahi's father-in-law," in the coastal village of Waimea. It was chosen as the place where the final revisions would be made to the Book of Mormon translation. Cannon was pleased with this arrangement. "They appear to be an agreeable family." He had two goals in mind, which were to correct any inaccuracies and guarantee that they had not skipped any words or sentences in the translation.[31]

When Christmas arrived, it was not very lavishly celebrated by any of the missionaries. Mary Jane Hammond did not mention it at all in her diary, and Frank noted only that Brother Winchester "gave Mrs. H[ammond] a $2.50 peice as a Christmas present."[32] The Allred twins came to Lahaina for New Years, and Mary Jane was delighted that because it was a school holiday she could spend December 30 "bakeing pies and cakes and washing."[33] Frank was pleased when Sheriff Treadway paid an advance of "$30 on next years schooling" for his child, enabling him to almost pay off the loan on the house.

Things were going better for the Hammonds than for the mission generally. Hammond learned that the native elder who was so revered but had died, Elder John Kahumoku, had been living a double life, "acting bad with women, going out nights[,] unknown to [Elder Tanner] &c." Keeler wrote to Farrer that things were generally "in a bad situation" on the big island. "Our Brother J W Kahumoku has taught them some bad principals by precept & examples[:] he had a girl in ev[e]ry branch where he stoped [and] he sleept with [them] when ever he pleased. There is a great number of the Brethre[n] &

30. Mary Jane Hammond journal, Dec. 22, 1853. Frank and Mary Jane both underlined the words "tea pot" and "hot tea" in their journal entries for that day, perhaps emphasizing the fact that the mission president's wife drank black tea in violation of the church's Word of Wisdom, though they also did so occasionally as well.

31. *JGQC*, 391–92. "I think that Bro. Kauwahi has made a very good choice of a wife," Cannon wrote approvingly.

32. American currency at the time included a gold quarter eagle worth $2.50.

33. Mary Jane Hammond journal, Dec. 29–30, 1853.

sisters that believe that was the cause of his death." Keeler went so far as to say he "believe[d] that it was a good thing [Kahumoku] was taken when he was."[34] In addition to the behavior of native elders, almost all of the third-wave missionaries had not learned the language, preventing the first-wave elders from extricating themselves and returning home. Nor had the latter even decided how they were going to fund their return trip across the ocean.

Hammond wrote to Cannon on December 9 reiterating his opposition to the "McBride Plan," which would rely on contributions from California Saints. The Hawaiians, Hammond argued, were the ones who had benefited from the missionaries' presence, so they should be the ones who footed the bill. "The trial ought to be made among the [native] saints and they be the ones to furnish us with means among whom our time and means have been spent," Cannon's summary of the letter read. Otherwise they would "be establishing a precedent" for the future that would not be ideal. "The Lord had sent us," Hammond continued, "and [we have] faith to believe that He would open our way." In fact, according to Cannon, Hammond wrote that he "would hate when they got home and t[old] about the Sandwich Island Mission <& its success &c.> and" had to admit that they were forced to "send to the coast or to the 'Poor Fund' to get them home."

If there was going to be a precedent, Hammond wanted it to be that subsequent missionaries would look to them, that the first wave of elders "would be brought up as an example which they ought to follow" in finding support among the native people. This, he said, should be done for the "honor of the mission."[35]

Cannon was shocked by this criticism and gave in to it, responding that if they raised "means enough among the saints to start the press and clear it from all liabilities," that alone would be "accomplishing all that we could expect" and would be a great step forward in the mission. "Yet," he wistfully added, "I know that if they [the native Mormons] would implicitly obey our counsel, they could do

34. Keeler to Farrer, Dec. 31, 1853.

35. *JGQC*, 394–95.

that, and fit us out too, and not be any poorer in the end."[36] Here Cannon in effect acknowledged that it would be asking a great deal of the relatively poor native Mormons to pay for the printing press, while at the same time asking them to pay for the first elders' "return" to Utah, both of which might be resented.

36. Ibid., 396. Farrer was persuaded to oppose the McBride plan by Hammond's letter. See Farrer journal, Dec. 31, 1853.

CHAPTER 19

President Lewis becomes a Tinsmith

On receiving payment for the property he [Brother Dennis] had sold, he came to my room with a sack containing $7000 in gold, and laying it upon my table said he wished to leave it in my charge and that I might use any amount of it that I needed, just as though it was my own; and to give to my friends if they are in need. After he left me I reflected that I had it in a safe place of deposit,—and what was I to do with it? The thought came to go into my sleeping room, crawl under my cot and slip it under the floor mat,—which I at once did.

—Benjamin F. Johnson, Jan. 20, 1854

As 1854 dawned Mary Jane Hammond was in a thoughtful mood. "This is a new years," she wrote. "I have seen 22 of them [and] I hope I may see a great many more." It would actually come close to being her last. She described their lavish New Year's Day feast as one of "cake[,] baked pork, a can of turkey souse[,][1] pies[,] tarrow [taro,] and other things." Judge Marston and another guest spent the evening with them, and three days later Frank sent a twenty-dollar house payment to Edward Dennis, leaving Mary Jane in a state of momentary contentment.

She was increasingly thrilled on January 5 when Diana Gaston arrived from Kalepolepo. "I was very glad to see her for I have had a great deal of work to do and she will stop here till Bro [Judson] Gaston sends means on to her." Frank may not have told his wife that Judson had written the previous month and "does not care much

1. "Souse" is pickled meat, especially the ears, feet, and head of the animal or bird.

about his wife. He wrote a very cold and noncommittal letter. I think it very strange conduct for a brother" in the church.

A few days later, Mary Jane explained that "Sis Lewis is still with us. Sis Gaston is a great help to me," a revealing juxtaposition. Frank started to write about a confrontation his wife had with the mission president's wife and then crossed it out: "~~Evening employed in settling family difficult matter~~." Less reluctant to divulge the seriousness of their disagreement, if not the content of the argument, Mary Jane wrote that "Sis Lewis is making a shirt for Mr Hammond. I have had my feelings hurt a great deal many times and as this ev[e]ning we had some words but it was for the best [as] we found each other out better than we ever did before[,] when there was a[n] understanding [and] it was all right. She is a very difficult woman to get along with[;] it would pushe the best of women."[2] This altercation would convince Jane Lewis that she needed to consider other accommodations.

The Hammonds had another long-term lodger who had similarly worn out his welcome: Nathan Tanner. On January 14, Frank "coppied some verses which Bro. Tanner made. The subject is on his leaving our home, or Lahaina, setting forth his gratitude for our kindness to him while at our house, &c." The next day, as Mary Jane noted, "the steamer came in last night. Bro Tanner [and] Sis Lewis expects to sail on her to Oahu."[3] In fact, on January 16 the two house guests departed for Honolulu, carrying with them $5.00 the Hammonds had given them for their journey. They had been with the Hammonds since November 7, making it a total of seventy days.[4] Tanner had done virtually no work during this period, proselytizing or otherwise, apparently afraid to venture on to his field of labor on the island of Hawai'i, where little or no English was spoken, and his chances of eating regularly would not be good. Nor did he want to return to Honolulu to contend with Benjamin Johnson.

By coincidence, January 16 was the mission president's birthday,

2. Mary Jane Hammond journal, Jan. 10, 1854.

3. Ibid., Jan. 15, 1854.

4. Tanner had been on Moloka'i for a short time during this period.

and he was feeling like leaving the remote location of Kaua'i, where he had not been able to make any progress in the language. When he received an appeal from Benjamin Johnson in Honolulu the next day, Johnson needing him to render a decision about a tinsmith shop that had been bequeathed to the mission, Lewis decided to abandon his rural village and sail to O'ahu.[5] Farrer's journal entry was more detailed:

> Bro's Lewis & Tanner ... received letters [from Johnson], requesting Prest. Lewis to go to Honolulu as soon as possible, requesting his councel &c that Bro. Dennis was wanting to leave for Sanbernardino & that he had offered to let the committee have his tools and a quantity of Tin & other stock at 60 per cent discount & to wait for his pay till they could pay him. As the Brethren at Honolulu thought this would be a source of Profit & advantage to the committee to enable them to free themselves from the liabilities of the press & also be a means to help roll forth the work ... they wanted Prest L[ewis] to go to see about it.[6]

The letter Lewis received from Johnson on January 17 may have also included the news that Lewis's wife was returning to Honolulu and would need to be cared for.

When the president arrived back in Honolulu, the McBride plan was abruptly canceled. Cannon was informed by Johnson that "Bro. Mac B[ride] had not sailed as expected, in consequence of letters from Bro. Lewis stating disuinion among the Elders in regard to his going." McBride had already "engaged his passage" and had to "forfeit his passage money."[7] Lewis, instead of resuming his work as mission president, effectively turned over the mission to Johnson and took over the tin shop owned by Edward Dennis. And not being in a mood to tolerate laggards, apparently—being displeased with the performance of his counselor, Nathan Tanner, who had also still not learned the language, "Prest. Lewis—a stern

5. Lewis journal, Jan. 16–17, 1854.
6. Farrer journal, Jan. 17, 1854.
7. *JGQC*, Jan. 24, 1853.

and upright man, refused him a home with us and told him to provide for himself," at least according to his nemesis Johnson. "I felt this to be a terrible blow to a man of so much pride and self esteem and it came as a shock and a grief to me," Johnson wrote, making himself the center of the story. "Realizing the indignity of his words, after Br. N[athan] had withdrawn I begged Prest. Lewis to reconsider and invite Br. N[athan] to our home, which he seemed unwilling to do. But at last my tearful intercession induced Prest. Lewis to invite Br. N[athan] to return, which he did at once, and all was [a]gain pleasant." Tanner's suit was so tattered that Johnson said he felt compelled to give him some new clothing. "With tears in his eyes as he received them, he said 'Br. Johnson, I thought you were my enemy, but I feel as if that now you are almost my only friend.'" All was not forgotten, however. Tanner felt ostracized and no longer "needed in the mission." With the president's permission, he concluded to return home as soon as he could raise enough money for his passage.

According to Lewis, Elder McBride left Honolulu for California on January 21, 1854, with "means to establish a printing press for the benefit of this [native] people." Over the next two days the president looked for a new home and took steps to enable himself to pay rent. "Conclude[d] a bargain with Bro Dennis to purchase his stock in trade for the benefit of the mission," Lewis wrote, "for which we the committee agree to give [Dennis] $500, payable by [us] on demand." He seemed happy to begin working in the tin shop.[8] With personal as well as mission considerations in mind, he settled into his new role of providing for his ailing wife and putting aside the futility of attempting to learn Hawaiian. Meanwhile, the ambitious Johnson had achieved two objectives: assuming the clerical reins of the mission and easing out his rival Tanner.

Since by the end of the month, the three men who were working on the final draft of the Hawaiian Book of Mormon—Cannon, Farrer, and Kauwahi—had carefully read through the manuscript twice,

8. Lewis journal, Jan. 23–24, 1854.

all that was left to do was to raise the money that was needed to purchase a press on which to publish it. Cannon began a fund-raising tour that would take him to all the major Hawaiian islands. On the same day, the Dennises and William Franklin set sail for San Francisco en route to San Bernardino.[9] Frank Hammond continued to serve as a translator for the Lahaina Police court, and as a result he was invited in early February to dine with some of the social elite in Lahaina. About eleven a.m., Hammond wrote,

> Judge Marston came in and said he had an invatation for me from Mr. [George] Chase, the U. S. Consul to come and dine with him. He, the Judge, bo[ar]ds with the Consul. I gladly [ac]cepted the invatation and got ready and went up, and the Judge introduced me to [the consul], and I took dinner with him and spent a very pleasant interview with him. Found him to be very much of a gentalman, and a very intelligent man, possessed of a vast fund of general information, and a very liberal minded man, and no bigot. I don't know when I spent a more agreeable afternoon. [The consul] had been reading a late number of the "Deseret News" and seemed much taken up with it, and offer[e]d to loan me his files of news papers to look over any time when ever I would call for them.[10] He pressed me very warmly to call again. May the Lord bless him for his kindness. I consider it quite a privelage to have his countanance [disposed] favorab[l]y towards us as a people.[11]

It was no secret that the mission had encountered problems with sexual transgression among the converts, but Hammond was beginning to worry about the scale of such sins and the fact that many native missionaries were guilty as well.

> News from [the island of] Hawaii is that the Native elders are conducting themselves rather badly on their mission. Bro's Pelio and [George] Raymond have been caught in adult[e]ry, and Bro. K. writes that he is afraid that others are also guilty. I feel sad to hear such news from the native elders, for without their help in the ministry we will

9. Farrer journal, Jan. 31, 1854; *JGQC*, 409; Lewis journal, Feb. 1–7, 1854.

10. Hammond greatly enjoyed reading these newspapers, some from New York City, close to his Long Island hometown of Patchogue.

11. Hammond journal, Feb. 7, 1854.

> be short handed in the field[,] as a very few of the last lot of elders have as yet got the language.[12]
>
> I am afraid that there has not been caution enough used in ordaining natives. I fear there is but a very few of them that will magnify the priesthood when put upon them.[13]

Mary Jane Hammond had her own worries. Having had her spirits lifted by the departure of Tanner and Jane Lewis, she now became lonely and depressed without them. She wrote of being tired and longed for "some associates that I could run and see sometimes here. I am sunrise to sunset engaged in my school and looking after my children. I sometimes think I will be an old woman before I am a full grown [adult]."[14] She must have been pleased when two days later Frank reported that he was able to pay "Mr. Hoffmyer the balance of his note of 50 dollars" to complete their payments on the home.

Hammond received a letter from Johnson on February 10 informing him that President Lewis "thought [it] best ... to have our Elders conference defered until the 24 of July next[,] and then make that do for this year." In addition to that, "Bro. Tanner was appointed [on] a mission to the [California] coast to collect means to purchase a vessel for the emigration of the saints of these lands to San Bernardino." News of the cancellation of the April conference was a surprise that upset several of the first-wave missionaries. "I expected to be liberated in April to start home," Farrer wrote. The delay was caused by trouble the third wave was having in learning the language.[15] Not wanting to be a passive observer in matters that greatly concerned him, Hammond enlisted John Winchester to join him and left on February 18 for Honolulu to communicate their displeasure to the president. After locating President Lewis's home, they found several of the elders there: Bigler, Cannon, Hawkins, and Tanner. Jane Lewis was still very ill. They "had much interesting conversation"

12. The "very few" would be the Allred twins.

13. Hammond journal, Feb. 8, 1854; see also Woodbury diaries, Feb. 12, 1854.

14. Mary Jane Hammond journal, Feb. 9, 1854.

15. Farrer journal, Feb. 15, 1854. On February 17 Farrer indicated that he wrote a letter to Lewis and Johnson "expressing his [negative] feelings" about this decision.

until around 1:00 a.m., some of it no doubt heated. The next night they "had a good little council meeting. All felt well, councilling on the subject of gathering the saints on these lands &c &c."

Cannon wrote in his journal that Tanner had become convinced "a vessel can be raised on the coast" with funds contributed by members in California. "In consequence of this arrangement the presidency counseled <us,> the brethren ~~us~~ who came first, to stay until the general conference which had been postponed to the 24th of July, with the promise that if they would stay they should be blessed and their way should be opened, and that every exertion would be made to assist them to get off [the islands]." Cannon approached the mission presidency the next day and questioned Tanner's plan to ship the native converts to California, which Hammond also strongly opposed. Cannon wrote that "I made some remarks and expressed my feelings freely, in a manner that I would not have done had I been apprised ... when I arrived that this plan [Tanner's] had been deemed wisdom and decided upon by the majority of the presidency here; as it was, I was not aware of this fact, it having been merely stated to me that such a project was in contemplation."[16]

Cannon and Hammond must have reminded Lewis, Tanner, and Johnson that Brigham Young had suggested a gathering place for the native saints in the islands rather than the mainland. Furthermore, the elders had been actively looking for such a location since the last mission conference. Hammond consulted with Elder Uaua to see what the landowner Haalelea might think of their settling on Kaua'i. Uaua said he would ask, and reported back that Haalelea was "willing that we should have the land." Meeting with Haalelea the next morning, the scales tipped from Kaua'i to Lana'i:

> The land committee called on Haalelea, in company with Bro. Cannon, to ascertain his mind about the land [on Kaua'i] on what terms he would let it on. He proposed to let us have the whole body of the

16. *JGQC*, 410–11. The next day Cannon wrote to Farrer on Kaua'i that the "presidency here ... feel it is the will of the Lord," which had caused him to feel that he had "no more to say, only to express my feelings that I would support it by my faith &c. feeling that it was all right." Cannon to Farrer, Feb. 21, 1854; *JGQC*, 595–96.

> land, some 4020 acres, at 25 cts per acre, per year. This was to[o] much for us. We dare not enter into such an agreement for fear that we could not raise [pay] the rent ... But he offers us the privelage of going on to Lanai and have the use of this land there for 4 years without charge. This is a very fair offer, and we think of making some experiments there if the Lord wills. Haalelea expressed a good deal of interest in our church, but he looks out well for his money interest; he is the greatest land holder, I think, in the Kingdom. He has loaned the financial commit[t]ee $500 on interest for one year. Bro. Mac Bride took $1500 with him to the coast towards purchasing the press.[17]

The missionaries met that night and talked about where the elders would be stationed "after the first five leave," and decided they would be "very short handed." Hammond wrote to Farrer to inform him of these developments, declaring that his "own feelings" were "strongly in favor of" identifying a local gathering place. Some of the talk at the mission gathering had been about how few converts remained active members, how many had been excommunicated ("70 cut off on the east end of Maui since conference"),[18] and about the behavior of the native missionaries. Hammond thought the devil had done his best "to draw away men from the truth." He said "the news from [the island of] Hawaii is that most of the native elders have been caught, tride[,] and found guilty of adult[e]ry and their liscencies [licenses] taken away and sent home to await conference ... The native help to all appearance thus far has not been of much account[,] only where they were under the im[m]ediate care of a white elder who was master of the language.[19]

Feeling desperate about this, Hammond told Farrer he had related his opinion to the other missionaries at Honolulu that the

---

17. Hammond journal, Feb. 23, 1854. The delegation included Cannon and two members of the land committee, Hammond and Johnson. Absent were Dennis (sailing to the mainland), Farrer (although Hammond mistakenly said otherwise), McBride (sailing to America), and Tanner.

18. Reading between the lines, the convert retention appears to have been the worst where the smallpox hit the hardest, indicating a possible lack of confidence in the elders' healing gifts.

19. Hammond to William Farrer, Feb. 24, 1854. Emphasis in original.

first-wave elders "had all better stay another year and help us out of our pilikia [fix]. But no doubt you feel that your time, like Bro Keeler, has come for you to leave these lands and return to the Vallies of the mountains, [and] I cannot find it in my heart to hoole or to ohumu at you for this, but nevertheless, I should be glad if you all would stay another year."

CHAPTER 20

Pressuring the Moloka'i Mormons

I told them that the first time I saw the natives of the lands, I loved them, and that I had not lost my affection for them yet[,] that is[,] as regarded their form of [dark] compl[ex]ion, but I could not say that I loved their dirty, filthy habits ... [I] told them to turn their dogs out of doors and clean their houses, and set [free] the beasts in their own places, and not live with and have them in their houses. I also told them that they never would have visits from angels so long as they live in their filthy state.

—*Frank Hammond, Mar. 23, 1854*

Jane Lewis continued to be a problem for the Hammonds even after her departure. On February 27, Mary Jane made a grim discovery: the mission president's wife had left a legacy of bedbugs. "They came from Sister Lewis['s] things for she was very much troubled with them. So that is the way I came [in contact] with them. I am very sorry but with carefull observing and scallding I think we will be read [rid] of them."[1]

In Honolulu, President Lewis and Benjamin Johnson were besieged by criticism from missionaries whose departure dates had been postponed. Farrer heard from Cannon, Bigler, Hammond, and Tanner "that one conference a year was sufficient" because it was difficult raising funds to travel to the conferences, but they had expected to leave in April, not July. Surprisingly, the president offered the option of leaving when originally scheduled, a month from then, if they could find their own way home. He said that Tanner attempted to "raise a vessel

1. Mary Jane Hammond journal, Feb. 27, 1854.

& forward [it] here" for their transport and "for a gathering on these lands" but that the project "did not appear very promising at present."[2]

There also were disciplinary issues to be dealt with. A native priesthood leader had committed adultery and confessed, describing "how very bad he felt at losing his [ministerial] license." Cannon responded to Jonathan Napela and George Raymond offering a way forward for the transgressor, likely Raymond himself.[3] That same month, Elder Hosea Kauwahi, who was well respected and happened to be a candidate for parliament, was arrested for bigamy, although he maintained he had divorced his first wife. Farrer thought Kauwahi's arrest was an act of "religious intolerance & a desire to break down Bro K[auwahi], as they were afraid he would be elected a[nd] they dreaded his influence both as a politician & preacher of the gospel." Farrer went to visit him at the jail in Kaua'i, but because the missionaries were unable to post bail, Kauwahi spent months in prison. It was disappointing for Cannon, who had hoped he and Kauwahi would be able to fundraise together.

Hammond received a letter from his family in New York about this time telling him that his brother Samuel had gotten married on November 17 and that his father, at seventy-five years of age, was "strong & active" enough to still be working at his trade. Hammond added that "they are all very anxious to see me home."

While Elder Cannon was fundraising on O'ahu, apparently without much success, he wrote to Brigham Young complaining about how unmotivated he found the Hawaiians to be. Stirring them from their "stupor and lethargy" was "slow and tedious." None of the missionaries seemed to have a high opinion of their longsuffering hosts or appreciate their hospitality. Cannon snorted that they were "like little children," quick to fall into temptation and "superstitious." Comments like these must have shaped Young's negative view of the Hawaiian people, leading to his decision in 1857–58 to close the mission for six years.[4]

2. Farrer journal, Mar. 3, 1854.
3. The name was redacted from *JGQC*, 314, 415–20.
4. Cannon to Young, Mar. 14, 1854, in *JGQC*, 597; Journal History, Mar. 15, 1854.

Nathan Tanner decided to follow McBride to the mainland in search of funds and readied himself for the trip. Cannon's fundraising tour of the islands brought him on March 16 to Lahaina, where he "found Bro. & Sis. Hammond and family all well" and discovered that "Sis Gaston was living with them."[5] Cannon and Hammond stayed up late talking about mission business, and in the morning, despite a headache, Hammond repaired Cannon's shoes. By letter from California, they learned that McBride had been unable to find a printing press for sale in San Francisco and was having people inquire at Boston for one that could be sent to Honolulu or San Bernardino. The leading Mormons in San Francisco, including Jefferson Hunt and John Horner, wanted to establish the press in California rather than at Honolulu, though the money for it had been raised in Hawaii.[6]

President Lewis and Karren mailed letters from Honolulu the next day to church leaders throughout the mission—and presumably to California—informing people that "Elder Nathan Tanner has been appointed, and is duly authorized to proceed to California, and there represent the affairs of this mission, and with the counsel and co-operation of the local authorities there, to take any measures that may be deemed necessary for the speediest <u>procural of a vessel of sufficient size to commence the immediate emmigraion of the Hawaiian Saints to Lower California</u> [San Bernardino]." The islanders were "exceedingly poor," the letter continued, and a change in their "location and circumstances" would be of "lasting benefit." They were "a remnant of ... the children of Abraham," the elders reminded readers.[7]

When Tanner boarded the barque *John Wesley* to begin his journey to the West Coast, news reached Hammond that the mission president was unhappy with him. Hammond had taken back issues of the *Deseret News* from the president's home—a lot more than his share, according to the president. "I did not take any more than was given to me by Bro. Johnson," Hammond said in his defense. Keeping up on the news had become of heightened interest to Hammond

5. Cannon to Young, Mar. 14, 1854, in *JGQC*, 420, 598–99, 420.

6. Bigler journal, Mar. 16, 1854.

7. Lewis and Karren to "All Whom This May Concern," Mar. 17, 1854, Manuscript History of the Hawaiian Mission; also qtd. in *JGQC*, 600.

since he and his wife had begun socializing with the island's elite. He noted on March 19 that non-Mormon whaleship "Capts. Snow and Murdock called to see me," and that Snow invited Hammond and Cannon to visit him aboard his ship.[8] Eight days later, while Hammond and Cannon were on the island of Moloka'i, another captain paid Mary Jane an afternoon visit. "He was glad to see us[,] being 28 months since we last saw him," she wrote.[9]

While Hammond was preoccupied with other matters one day, Cannon filled in for him at the police court as an interpreter. By chance, Cannon found two letters awaiting him at the post office from California. One was from McBride informing him of his safe arrival. The other was from James Kipp, letting Cannon know he had made it to San Bernardino and explaining that two former missionaries, Addison Pratt and Benjamin Grouard, had apostatized and joined the spiritualists, or "spirit rappers," and "intend[ed] to return to Tahiti." The spiritualists communicated with the dead through séances, during which the spirits allegedly answered questions by knocking on the table and wall.

"This surprised me much," Cannon wrote, "to hear of <such> men's downfall." Kipp himself would soon leave the church under the influence of Grouard and Pratt. He informed Cannon that apostle Amasa Lyman preferred that the printing press be placed in San Bernardino. It hardly made sense, Lyman thought, to send the press across the ocean only to print the Book of Mormon. McBride eventually convinced the leaders in California, including Horner and Hunt, to send it to the islands once it was obtained. The church leaders were also in favor of the first wave of missionaries coming home immediately rather than waiting another few months. The only problem was that Cannon was the only competent printer in the mission.[10]

In late March some of the native brethren rowed Cannon and Hammond across the water to Moloka'i in a whaleboat, where they joined Elders Reddin Allred, Green, Woodbury, and Brother Maiola

8. *JGQC*, 420–21.

9. Mary Jane Hammond journal, Mar. 24, 1854.

10. *JGQC*, 421n22–22. See also Garr, Cannon, and Cowan, *Encyclopedia of Latter-day Saint History*, 938.

at the picturesque coastal village of Waialua for a lengthy church conference. Native leaders from four branches were present, representing 165 recent converts. The branches "were all in flourishing condition," wrote Hammond. On the second day of the conference, Hammond chose to speak about the biblical Noah when, he declared, "the inhabitants of the earth [had] to obey the command of God and gather together" with Noah in the ark, and in the last days there will be another gathering place "which the Lord has appointed for the gathering of his people ... [to] be hid up while the indignation of the Lord pass[es] over.[11] He obviously wanted to prepare them for the radical proposition of leaving their islands and ancestral villages to move to a designated island gathering place such as Lana'i or the American west coast.

When Allred spoke, he took a different tack and urged the members "to observe the law of cleanliness, and commence to pattern after the whites in regard to that law, that they should strive to keep themselves free from lice, fleas &c., and to keep their heads combed and their faces clean, and their clothes whole." Hammond and Cannon both spoke again to reinforce the same message.

In the afternoon meeting the impoverished natives received a fundraising appeal from Cannon, who read a lengthy letter from Elder Napela encouraging the Saints who could do so to contribute a dollar each toward the printing press. Cannon assured them that "whoever cannot make every sacrifice [of] money, houses, lands, wives, children, and relatives of every kind, and even his own life, cannot be a disciple of" Christ, and he laid out the "consequence of disobedience."[12]

Hammond said Cannon also "gave an interesting sketch of the history of the aborigines of America, showing that they and the people of the 'Pacific Isles' were of the seed of Joseph" of Egypt, the son of the biblical patriarch Jacob. Hammond was thrilled by Cannon's sermon:

> I never heard the subject handled better in the native tongue. My heart was filled with joy and I had some butiful [beautiful] views of

11. Hammond journal, Mar. 23, 1854.
12. *JGQC*, 422.

> the subject, more so than I ever had before. Bro. C[annon] has a great command of this language, and is a powerful speaker when the Spiret of the Lord rest[s] upon him. The native saints almost worship him. He has succeeded in gaining the affections of all the saints, and a large circle of friends out side the church, many of them first class native. I feel to dread the time when he and the other old elders shall leave for home, which will be in July next.[13]

Hammond was probably more impressed with Cannon's words than the natives were on this occasion, since Cannon's assessment was that "the people did not seem to enjoy as much of it" as he had hoped.[14] Two days later he spoke again to make another strong fund-raising appeal and finished by saying, "I am thinking of leaving these lands soon, but I have not at present a dollar in my pocket, but I know that if you have received the truth in good and honest hearts that I will not return destitute." Hammond followed and pushed the issue further, admonishing the saints to give "liberaly to the Kingdom of God," telling them "that they would never be saved only on the principle of holding themselves in readiness to give all they have to ... God." He admitted that "it was hard work to preach" when often the hungry natives "did not have their minds on the subject," the bread and wine of the eucharist in front of them, waiting to be consumed.

After the sacrament there were more appeals for money, with little success. Nor could the missionaries even convince anyone to row them back to Lahaina. Things were clearly not going well. Cannon pushed again for a dollar contribution for the printing press, and an elderly man named Keliiholokauai was the only one who responded, which upset Cannon. "Your fathers brought the red skin upon them in consequence of disobedience to the very priesthood which you have now in your midst, [and] if you pay attention to it, it will exalt you, and through it this curse will be rolled off from you," he scolded.[15]

Hammond and Woodbury followed to further hammer home the need for money. "I told them that by their works their faith

13. Hammond journal, Mar. 24, 1854.

14. *JGQC*, 426.

15. *JGQC*, 426–28.

would be known," wrote Hammond, who praised Keliiholokauai and the family hosting them for having exhibited "more faith than all the rest put together." Hammond acknowledged that the conference tried the faith of those who had "the idea that this was a church that did not require money &c, so it comes rather hard to them but I felt that they will be blessed in what they have been taught, or else the weak will leave the church. Bro. W[oodbury] told them that if they wanted to [leave] to do it and then we could go home."

The Utah elders were perfectly willing to shock the native converts and even drive them from the church if that was the result. "During our conference here," Cannon admitted to Farrer, "we have talked pretty plain to the saints on the subject of putting themselves, their property and all they have ... in[to] the work, [and] how it will operate with them I know not, but my feelings are that the people ought to be taught and tried on these things." He advised Farrer to push the "officers and saints" further. It was time for the missionaries "to do what we have to do if we intend to return to the valley [Utah] this season."[16]

Cannon wrote to Hawai'i to encourage the elders there to take the same approach to fundraising, though he knew Elder Keeler had not wanted to ask for personal assistance at the same time they were soliciting donations for the printing press.[17] By contrast, Cannon's entire focus had become raising funds. He had carried the same message to Kaua'i and O'ahu and would soon carry it to Maui and Hawai'i. It probably added to the steady decline in membership since the 1853 smallpox epidemic. The members had consistently fed and housed the missionaries and funded the construction of churches and other local projects, and now they were being asked to give money for the elders' return, a printing press, and an ocean-going ship. Soon they also would hear that they would be required to move to a small, isolated island, despite their great love for their ancestral island and village.

---

16. Cannon to Farrer, Mar. 27, 1854; also qtd. in *JGQC*, 601.
17. *JGQC*, 429.

KAUA'I
NI'IHAU
O'AHU
MOLOKA'I
MAUI
LANA'I
KAHO'OLAWE
HAWAI'I
PACIFIC OCEAN
N
0 km
50
100

0 km
20
Princeville
Kilauea
Hanalei
WAIMEA CANYON
KAWAIKINI PEAK
Wailua
Lihue
Waimea
Nawiliwili
Lawai
KAUA'I
Koloa
NI'IHAU

O'AHU
KOOLAU DISTRICT
Laie
Punaluu
Waialua
WAIANAE RANGE
KOOLAU RANGE
Kaneohe
Nuuanu
Ewa
Honolulu
DIAMOND HEAD CRATER
0 km
20
N

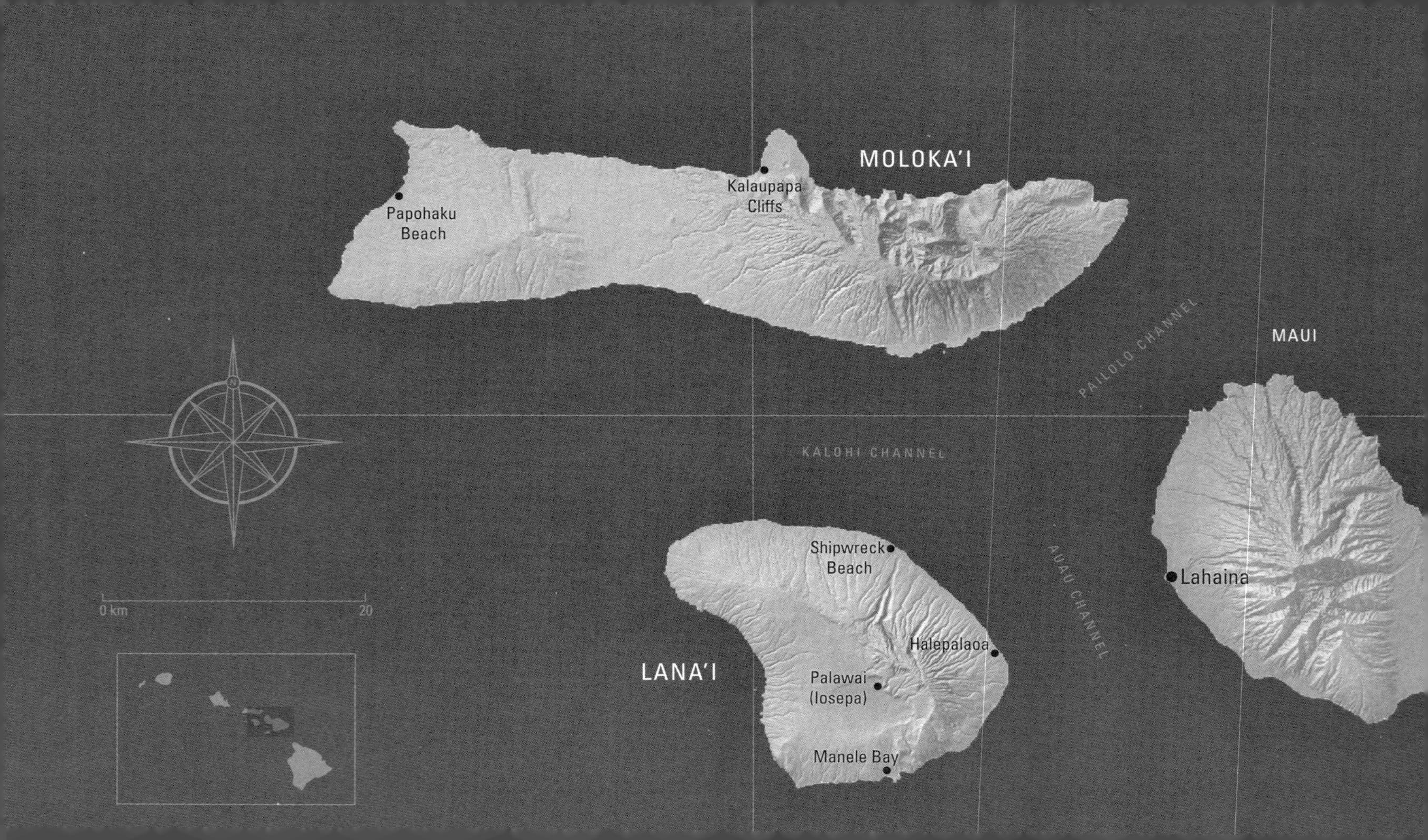

MOLOKA'I
Papohaku Beach
Kalaupapa Cliffs
PAILOLO CHANNEL
MAUI
KALOHI CHANNEL
Shipwreck Beach
AUAU CHANNEL
Lahaina
Halepalaoa
LANA'I
Palawai (Iosepa)
Manele Bay
0 km
20

MOLOKA'I
PAILOLO CHANNEL
MAUI
Kaanapali
Waiehu
Lahaina
Wailuku
AUAU CHANNEL
Makawao
Keanae
Wailua
Ukumehame
Maalaea
Kula
Kalepolepo
Waiakoa
LANA'I
Kawaipapa
Hana
HANAUAULA DISTRICT
HALEAKALA CRATER
Kipahulu
Uluplakua
Kaupo
KAHO'OLAWE
0 km
20

HAWAI'I
Upolu
Pololu
KOHALA DISTRICT
Waipio
Waimea
Hilo
KONA COAST
MAUNA LOA VOLCANO
KILAUEA VOLCANO
N
0 km
25
50

CHAPTER 21

Death's Door

She has had to work very hard during the last 2 or three years, and I fear she [Mary Jane] has broken her constitution. I have never seen a woman do more work than she has for the year past. Night and day has she labor[e]d to clear the little place where we live from debt. She, with my assistance[,] has succeeded, but I fear it has been done with to[o] great a sacrifice of health.

—*Hammond journal, Apr. 15, 1854*

Across the channel at Lahaina on March 25, 1854, Mary Jane Hammond gave vent to the loneliness and fatigue that consumed her. She let the school children go home early so she could rest during the afternoon as much as possible, given the fact that she still had her own children to tend. Little Samuel, for instance, was rarely content, and dealing with him had prematurely turned her hair "allmost w[h]ite," she wrote. "They say I am growing old fast ... If I was to go home, the folks there would not know me. No wonder, for I work like a slave."[1]

Her husband returned to Maui on March 29, accompanied by Reddin Allred, George Cannon, Ephraim Green, and John Woodbury, in time for the April native conference. Frank found a letter waiting for him from James Kipp, who was living at San Bernardino and was "well pleased with the place and people," he wrote, even though "the wages there are not equal to the prices of provisions." He reported that Elder Clark, who he thought had been a missionary in Tahiti, had committed suicide. He was apparently unaware that Clark had been the Hawaiian mission president prior to his own mission there.

1. Mary Jane Hammond journal, Mar. 25, 1854.

After reading a letter from Farrer that day, Hammond learned that the church on Kaua'i was struggling and that some of the members were about to leave Mormonism. "They came in under the impression that if they ... got into any difficulties, we would help them out &c., or rather that Bro. [Hosea] Kauwahi being a lawyer, that he would assist them." If anyone made the assumption at the time, they could not expect Elder Kauwahi to offer any legal assistance now because he had been jailed on a charge of polygamy. Cannon's fund-raising push also may have contributed to the decrease in enthusiasm among some of the members.

Benjamin Johnson wrote an essay about polygamy in April 1854, defending it against the scathing attacks that had appeared in the Honolulu newspapers. When the papers refused to print his lengthy response, he had it published as a twenty-six-page pamphlet in San Francisco, *Why the "Latter-day Saints" Marry a Plurality of Wives: A Glance at Scripture and Reason*. He may have used some of the $7,000 Edward Dennis secretly gave him to finance the printing. In any case, when the pamphlet arrived in Honolulu, he distributed four hundred copies throughout the islands and was pleased with the attention it attracted. "For many days there was general excitement throughout the city, and had a thunderbolt fallen at the feet of our enemies, it would not have made a greater sensation."[2] However, it probably did more harm than good in the long run to call attention to this controversial doctrine.

There was also still the issue of the gathering. Brigham Young told the missionaries again in an April 1 letter that they should look for a suitable location. "[I] rejoice at your prospects for having a printing press of your own, and at the probability of your being able to secure a quiet and measurably secluded nook for the Island brethren until the way opens more fully for their gathering [to California or Utah]."[3] He had not heard that the mission presidency was determined to ship the saints to California.

Hammond and the other elders struck out for Wailuku on April 3,

2. *My Life's Review*, 176–79; also LeBaron, *Benjamin F. Johnson*, 97–99.

3. Qtd. in *JGQC*, 605–06.

but two days later Hammond received an ominous letter from his wife that she was a little better "but still had pain in her breast," meaning her chest. There was also distressing news at Wailuku. At the morning conference session on April 7, the native elders reported on conditions in the different branches and revealed that "the increase for the last 6 months has not been much. Many have been cut-off from the branches on the east end of Maui," Hammond recorded. That is where the smallpox epidemic flourished; it may have affected the membership through both death and apostasy.

Many native missionaries from Maui had had their priesthood licenses revoked for sexual misbehavior while proselytizing on the island of Hawai'i, and this made other young men reluctant to consider mission calls. Nevertheless, the afternoon session of the conference saw six Maui brethren called to Hawai'i, two others to Kaua'i, and an additional pair to Lana'i. Two native missionaries were restored to their former status after having been disciplined for adultery. After the assignments, Elder Cannon stood "and spoke on the nature of the offices and gave them much good instruction on these things[,] that they must go forth fearing and trembling lest they should be overcome with temptation."[4]

Ironically, the elders heard another confession that very evening, this time a repeat performance from Jonathan Napela. Hammond explained his extreme frustration that a prominent native elder would fall into a repeating pattern of indiscretion and repentance:

> He confessed his falling again into the sin of adult[e]ry, [and] also of having been drunk once, and of his having partaken of the sacrament during his transgression. Soon after our last conference he fell into this trouble, and he said he had been in hell ever since, and dare not confess his sins to us. He seemed to be filled with repentance and deep contrition.
>
> We talked a long time with him, setting before him the laws of life and death ... We finally took a vote to restore him to our fello[w]ship, and he went away rejoiceing. Our hearts were all made heavy by this confession of Bro. Napelas. I sometimes feel that there is but a very

4. Ibid., 441.

> few [natives] in the church who are entirely clear of that sin. They never thought it any sin till after the gospel came unto them, and it is a hard thing for them to resist the tem[p]tations in that way.[5]

Not only was Napela forgiven, he was allowed to speak at the conference. Hammond and one of the Allreds spoke too, Hammond reporting that they had "received over one hundred dollars" in currency toward the printing press and a few gifts in kind: "two horses and three head of cattle." Hammond was pleased that they raised more funds at the conference "than all the others put together," this despite there being fewer members in attendance than at previous conferences.

The next day Mary Jane could hardly breathe and managed to write in her journal that she was "quite sick having chills and fever" and "suffered a great deal." It was probably pneumonia. Frank arrived home the next day at 2:00 p.m. to find her "in bed," having "given up" hope of a recovery any time soon. "I felt a good deal concerned about the pain in her breast," he wrote. It "caused her to suffer greatly." He "imediately anointed Mrs. H. and laid hands on her, and she was more comfortable all the afternoon."

To complicate the situation, one-year-old Samuel had diarrhea so severely, he was convulsing the next morning. Frank interpreted this to be demonic possession and performed an exorcism. "Bro. Rice being by[,] we ran to the cradle and laid our hands upon him, & I rebuked the foul spiret and commanded it to come out in the name of <u>Jesus Christ of Nazareth</u>. I never felt so strong in faith before in all my life. I felt as if I could whip a leigon of devils. The Lord heard our prayer and befor[e] we took our hands from off his body, he was restored to con[s]ciousness, and lay perfectly easey and quiet."

The next day everyone in the family was ill except Frankey. Even though Mary Jane's condition was the worst of all, she unselfishly

5. Hammond journal, Apr. 7, 1854, emphasis in original. Elder Woodbury explained that Napela had gone to Lahaina in November with some old friends and was drunk when he succumbed to temptation. Like the other missionaries, Woodbury saw in Napela, "a noble h[e]arted man" despite his flaws. Woodbury diaries, Apr. 7, 1854. At the end of Cannon's journal entry for this date, there is an ellipsis in the published version indicating that information was deleted. This was likely Cannon's mention of Napela's adultery. *JGQC*, 442.

focus on everyone else's needs. "S[amuel] is better[;] his ear aches and he has a sore mouth," she wrote. She made him some rose tea and cradled him while she stifled her own pain and did the washing and dinner. Her condition worsened on Sunday. "Very hard for me to breath last night," she wrote," and yet she "boiled nearly a gallon of molasses into Candy [and] we all injoyed our selves firstrate." Frank stayed home from church "to assist in getting breakfast &c as Mary J. is not yet able to do much about the house."

His journal is especially revealing as to how he viewed sickness. By Monday he "felt as if the hand of the destroyer was laid heavily upon my family, and he seems determined to afflict us all that he possibly can. I[t] greivs my heart to [see] little innocent children suffering under the effects of his grasp." His prayer was that "Satan shall be bound and have no more power to afflict the children of men. Prepare me O Father to obey thy every word; give me grace according to my day, and leave me not to myself, but guide me continually by thy holy spiret that I may not fall into sin and temptation." His belief that Satan caused sickness formed the basis of his further belief that God would intercede to end the suffering of those who deserved to be healed.

He otherwise had the notion that good people could get sick through over-exertion, and this is what he assumed about Mary Jane, that she had gotten sick from overwork. He administered to her several times over the next six days and regularly reported that she was "a little better" or "about the same." In actual fact, her condition was deteriorating. By April 18 she suffered from an even more severe pain in her lungs and was not eating. The next day Diana Gaston helped out by doing some washing. "How I wish the time had come for us to go home," Mary Jane wrote. Sick as she was, she still taught her school classes.

Four days later she was so ill, she finally "had to give up to day and lay down although it was against my will, I am getting quite thin. I think if Mother was to see me she would hardly know me for I am so old looking and poor." She had a fever the following morning. Frank gave her another priesthood blessing before leaving for meetings, and then it would be a little over two weeks before Mary Jane would make another journal entry.[6]

Frank was becoming more worried about his wife because he was beginning to think it must be her lack of faith that was responsible for the illness's persistence. "I administer[e]d to her, and in the name of Jesus Christ of Nazerath commanded the fever, chills and all diseases to leave her body, and told her that if she would have faith she should be whole from that moment. I felt much of the spiret while my hands were upon her. She was strengthe[ne]d much, and got up and went about the house, but her faith failed her and she went and lay down again, and before I went to our 9 o'clock meeting I laid hands on her again." That night he prayed mournfully for God to "hear our prayers in her behalf and raise her up to health again, and bless her with thy holy spiret, and the gift of faith even that she may be heal[e]d; for O Lord we have no where else to go but to thee."

The next day his sense of desperation increased as her condition worsened, and the long journal entry he made that morning was poetic and emotionally powerful.

> Mary Jane is no better. I administerd to her through the night while she had a violent fever; this morning I administerd to her again, but it is only momentary relief. I feel that nothing but the power of the Most High can heal her and I feel to call upon him mightily that he would heal my wife the companion of my bosom, and restore her to health.
>
> She is a most ami[a]ble woman, and has endured much suffering and affliction for the cause of truth in these days, and all with patience and resignation; and now it grieves my heart sick to see her laid upon a bed of suffering and affliction. Her principle trouble seems to be in her breast, a heavy pain there, and when she coughs it almost takes her breath, the pain being most intense. I have done all I could to doctor her up with such simple things as I knew to be good.
>
> I had a dream while I was over to Wailuku attending conference; and forgot to speak of it. It was like this. I dreamed that I was on boa[r]d of a vessel which was sloop rigged,[7] and I thought I took great

6. Mary Jane Hammond journal, Apr. 9, 11–13, 18–19, 22–23, 1854.

7. A sloop was a large ship but with fewer sails than a barque (notice Hammond's

pride in having her rigging, sails, spars &c &c all fixed in the best manner possible so that a little labor would manage her. I finally got her all [ready] to my mind[,] with the assistance of others[,] ... [and] put to sea all aloan having all things rigged so that I could steer, take in sail, make sail &c &c all myself and manage the craft myself, and felt quite elated with my success in having her so well rigged.

But after I had left the land and had got out to sea some distance, it all at once occurred to me that I was in a bad situation at last, for how thought I, am I to do when I get sleepy or tired or how should I do if I was to be taken sick having no one to assist me. Consequently I must perish and my little bark which I doted so much on[,] would be wrecked. These thoughts had the effect to cause me to change the course of my Bark and turn her head towards the land again, and I soon ... awoke. The dream left a very vivid impression upon my mind, which has not at all grown faint as yet although it is some three weeks or more ago since I dreamed it.

I don't know that I have the true interpratation of the dream; but I know that our place was just paid for about the same time[,] and we out of debt, and [we] began to feel a little independent; and that we had gained this situation through Mary Jane's ind[e]fatigable labors during the last year, teaching a school of some 14 or 15 scholars during the day, besides doing the cooking, washing, mending, ironing &c &c for our own family[,] 6 in number, and some times 14, when the elders ar[e] with us. Some times two and three of them are with us for weeks together.

I in the mean time have worked day and night at shoemaking and other ways to get our house and lot paid for; thus my little bark has been fitted up. And just as I thought I had her about right, behold Mary Jane is taken down sick; and it does appear to me that we have been very unwise, in the manner which we have taken to secure as we thought a home, but I fear it has cost a dear price, even the blessing of health which is one of the greatest gifts of God our Heavenly Father. So I fear it will be hard sailing my bark aloan. May the Lord help us to be more wise for the future, and preserve our health that we may live long on the earth to do his will. Amen.[8]

---

reference to his "little bark" in the next paragraph). Neither could be operated by a solitary sailor.

8. Hammond journal, Apr. 24, 1854.

He added that "Mary Jane gave up her school to day. She could hold out no longer. I beleive it would have been far better for her if she had given it up some time ago, but she was very ambitious to keep it up as long as possible in o[r]der to get something to go home with, but I fear she has been unwise about it."

Even considering how disinclined Frank was to be emotional, one can see in his extended *crí de coeur* a mounting sense of desperation for his wife's condition, even though he might say, if asked, that he was mainly concerned about her lack of faith since she had not been healed. In January he had blessed a native girl named Mariana Hina, baptized her for her health, and continued to administer to her repeatedly until February 8 when he wrote angrily that "the sick woman, which I baptized a few days ago, has lost her faith and gone to be doctored by a native doctor. She was in a fair way to get well, but her faith failed her. She could not believe the word of the Lord, and now I should not be su[r]prised if she died and that soon. O that the Lord would increase the faith of his saints in these lands, that they may be able to withstand the temptations of the Devil, amen." The girl left Mormonism altogether since Frank was unable to cure her of her high fever and headaches.

On the occasion of his wife's deteriorating health, Frank donned the sacred LDS temple clothing to provide an added spiritual dimension to his prayers. On April 26, "before I went to bed[,] I clothed myself in my 'Priestly garments' and prayed for Mary Jane, that she might be restored to health and raised up from her bed of affliction. I felt that my prayer was answer[e]d im[m]ediately. I administer[e]d to Mary Jane while clothed in my Priestly garments. O Lord help us to have that kind of faith which the brother of Jared had[,] even that our prayers may be answ[e]red, and that we may have faith to be healed when sick, by attending to the ordanances which thou has placed in thy church."

The next day Frank began to suffer with a headache, probably as a culmination of living on little sleep and taking care of Mary Jane. Despite his own discomfort, he tried everything he could think of to make his wife feel better, to no avail, and on May 2 sadly noted that "she grows weak very fast. The flesh is leaving her fast. I never saw her look so thin before. I continue to call on the Lord in her behalf, and anoint and lay hands on her frequently, and she always gets releif from it."

That morning at Waipio, Hawai'i, George Cannon wrote to Frank, apparently unaware of Mary Jane's life-threatening illness, asking him to look over the laws of the Hawaiian kingdom that he had access to as an interpreter for the court. At issue were any laws forbidding natives from emigrating "as Sailors ... only on the Captain giving bonds for their safe return, and also to keep the people from running off to the gold mines and suffer and perish." A judge, William Lee, had told two missionaries that the law was no longer in effect, but Cannon suspected that "for us to trust entirely to Judge Lee without consulting the written laws on the subject would be unwise, and if his opinion should be incorrect [it] would only make us [look] ridiculous if we should bring a vessel" to the islands to transport the native converts to California.[9] In fact, it turned out that Judge Lee was wrong, and the authorities would not have allowed Hawaiians to leave the Islands unless they were married to "whites."

As Mary Jane continued to experience extreme discomfort and fatigue, some non-Mormon friends in Lahaina tried to help, although Frank was distrustful of their reliance on gentile doctors.

> This afternoon I took a walk up to Mr. Chases [the U.S. Consul] to get some barley for Mary J[ane].[10] Mr. C[hase] is in a fe[e]ble state of health. He was very kind to me; expressed a good deal of sympathy for Mary J[ane].
>
> As I was on my way home I met Judge Marston and Dr. Helderbrand.[11] They had just come out of my house ... The Judge said if I had no objections he would like to have the D[octo]r return and look at Mary Jane. He said it should cost nothing &c. I told him that I had no objections. So we all returned to the house; and the Dr. made his examination on Mary J[ane]. He said she was in a rather critical

9. *JGQC*, 462.
10. He was using this for hot poultices.
11. Helderbrand is identified in Sterling, *Sites of Maui*, 26.

> situation and advised me by all means to apply immediately to a physician; that she had a severe attack of the ... dry cough, and that her liver was effected &c &c and said that she should be cupped [bled], and then take some calomel &c. &c.
>
> I told [him] our principles and faith did not allow us to employ [a] physician out of the church, and th[at] we beleived the Lord was able to heal his saints now as he did anciently &c; he [the doctor] said the day of miracles was past &c., the old story over and over; said it was in the days of ignorance that the Lord wrought thus among the people, and that now in these days of light we did not need such assistance &c.
>
> Mary J[ane] is satisfied with the Doct[or]s without giving them a trial. It was enough for her to hear me talk. I believe it strengthened her faith.[12]

In other words, he again insinuated that Mary Jane's real problem was that she lacked the proper faith to be healed.

The next day Frank described another dream, one in which "Mary Jane was dead indeed, and ... I was roving up and down through old castles looking for her spiret, mourning most pitifully. I awoke and found myself mourning greatly." She was slowly recovering in the dream, but even so, it was not fast enough for him to shake the idea that she had blocked the spiritual energy through her unbelief. On May 9 he prayed, "O Lord I ask the[e] ... that thou will raise her up speedily to health, forgive her sins if she has sinned in thy sight; also give her to enjoy much faith, even that she may be healed imideately, even so, Amen."

It was probably on May 10 (the date is struck out) that Mary Jane made another journal entry after a long abstinence from writing. It was a relatively long entry for her, and it described what had happened since she last wrote, hinting at a momentary division between her and Frank with regard to medical matters.

> I have been sick [and] have had many a dull feeling. I never was so home sick since I left home. My faith seemed to leave me. I had

12. Hammond journal, May 5, 1854.

a very bad cough and I felt somewhat frightened. When Mr Hammond would administer to me I would feel quite well for a short time then the evil spirits would tell me I would have to lay my body here and that I best have a doctor for I could not obtain faith enough to be healed.

So axcidently there was a doctor came to see Mr Hammond on business. The Judge [Marston] came with him [and said] ... it would be good for the doctor to examine me so he done so and pernounced me quite bad[,] much worse than I thought. I[t] was my liver affected and other complaints. In stead of feeling worse thinking I surely would die[,] I finely [finally] thought the doctor did not know anything, although he was counted a skillful doctor. But I was disgusted and feeling ashamed of my little faith. I wanted no more of him and thought I would trust in my God that made [me]. If he created me he surely can heal me and from that time I commenced to get better and felt to trust in my heavenly father and every day I grew better."[13]

There is much to consider here, especially when viewed against the backdrop of Frank's and Mary Jane's disagreement the previous year over getting vaccinated for smallpox. During her current illness, when she admittedly became "frightened" at its seriousness and the failure of her husband's administrations, she appears to have been trying to choose between Frank's religious approach and the advice of the local physician. She ultimately accepted Frank's explanation that evil spirits were what was encouraging her to rely on the medical profession instead of on God. As her condition worsened, she again considered turning to professional help, but that very willingness to consult medicine was interpreted by Frank as a lack of faith.

Medical science during this time was still in an infant state and sometimes practitioners did more harm than good. Dr. Hillebrand's diagnosis that Mary Jane suffered, at least in part, from a liver problem was probably wrong, as his suggestion was that she needed calomel, mercurous chloride, to cure the ailment. However, this may be what lay behind Frank's later giving her a too-healthy dose of the stuff, which was harmful but thankfully proved not to be fatal.

13. Mary Jane Hammond journal.

Frank's perspective is no longer shared by LDS Church leaders and members, who rarely hesitate to turn to medical doctors today—even gentile ones—when ill.[14] The episode provides a window into nineteenth-century Mormon thinking, though, when the tendency was to rely on God and people experienced cognitive dissonance when they were not cured by faith healing.

14. By contrast, nineteenth-century Mormons more closely mirrored the views of the Christian Scientists, the denomination that followed the founding of Mormonism by about fifty years and relied on faith and prayer alone to deal with illness, often with tragic results.

CHAPTER 22

Preaching at the Hospital

In the evening I called on Mr. [George] Chase[,] the U.S. Counsel [Consul]. Had a long talk with him and Doct. Hillderbrand [Hillebrand] on the formation of the earth[,] the origin, and destination of man, &c &c. Mr. Chase I found a confirmed infidel in his talk, having a great many theories which I would call far more absurd than to believe the bible account. He would not allow me to go to the bible at all for an[y] proff [proof], but from nature and analogy aloan [alone] would he reason.

—*Hammond journal, May 22, 1854*

A letter arrived from Benjamin Johnson on April 28, 1854, informing Frank Hammond that their fellow missionary Nathan Tanner was in San Francisco "fitting out a Schooner for the island trade. They think she will be here in time for the first five elders to return on her and so save paying their money into gentile hands for their passage." Johnson also explained that "if the First Presidency does not council directly about where the [church printing] press shall be located," apostle Amasa Lyman had said he would be happy to make "some suggestions." Lyman was in charge of the Mormon colony in San Bernardino.

Tanner's assumption was that the press would end up in San Bernardino and that he would begin in July to shuttle native church members from the islands to southern California. President Lewis agreed with Tanner's plans. As the president wrote to one missionary, "We have come to the conclusion that if the [native] saints gathered there [California], that will be the best place for [the press], and we have consequently written to the Presidency of the San Bernardino [settlement], that if they will f[inance] a vessel, that we will pledge ourselves to furnish the press."[1]

As the elders tried to keep abreast of developments, Hammond played a key role in the mission communication network, receiving and forwarding on mail. On May 2, Thomas Karren on Hawai'i included an interesting disclosure in a letter he was sending to Farrer on Kaua'i: "You know that I am not much of a corespondent and not very Akamai with the pen and as Bro Johnson and Bro Hammond is our General Corespondantes[,] the most that I have written is to them, knowing that all information goes from them" to everyone else.[2] In fact, Johnson had little else to do in the mission office but write letters to the other elders.

During the second week of May, four American missionaries and a few native elders traveled to the Kilauea and Mauna Loa volcanoes, active craters on the island of Hawaii, with a native guide. Elder Cannon was so overcome by the experience that he wrote a long and interesting description of it.

> A feeling of awe crept over me very naturally, and I felt how very insignificant man is, and how little he knows of the works and operations of his Maker. When we came to the edge of the [volcano] pit [where "the melted lava or matter was in constant motion, a perfect mass of liquid fire"], a sight met my eyes which I think I shall never forget, and which surpassed in sublimity and grandeur anything I had ever witnessed or imagined; language is too faint to convey any of my feelings; I could not repress my exclamations of delight and admiration, it so far exceeded anything that I had ever read or imagined. I felt amply repaid for all my toil since I left Maui until the present time, in beholding this awfully grand and stupendous work of the Creator.[3]

During the trip to the volcano, the missionaries spoke with a man who turned out to be the island's district attorney, and Elder

1. Lewis to Farrer, precise date uncertain.

2. Karren to "Bro Farrer," May 2, 1854.

3. *JGQC*, 472. The other elders included Karren, Keeler, Napela, and Reddick Allred.

Karren asked him about emigration, to which the attorney responded that "the penalties were heavy" for sponsoring any out-migration "in direct opposition to the laws." Cannon "scratched a few lines in pencil to Bros. Lewis & Johnson, Honolulu, to send by the vessel which leaves the bay this <evening> informing them of what we had learned and citing them to the law, where they would find it &c., and suggesting <to> them the propriety, if this should prove to be the case, of stopping <our> teaching the natives to prepare to leave." Cannon may have felt some relief to learn of the legal hurdles to emigration since he, like Hammond, had strongly disapproved of the Tanner plan to transport native members to California.

In Lahaina, Hammond was establishing a habit of visiting the sailors hospital. Early the previous January, he and Reddin Allred had preached to a few whites there. The next day Allred returned with Tanner and they discussed the subject of polygamy. Because of that fact, it was with some trepidation that Hammond returned to speak in the afternoon of Sunday, May 14, to about ten or twenty "anxious hearers." He chose to speak on the ancient apostasy from Christian primitivism, which he said the modern restoration through the prophet Joseph Smith had corrected. "I had a good flow of the spiret and felt well and spoke with freedom. The Lord took away all fear of men from my heart, and I was enabled to bear my testimony in power to the hearers, and they seemed to believe," was his suspicion. At least, he was "treated with great respect." If he also told them about his past as a whaler, that would have gained him additional respect.

The following Sunday he returned to discuss what he called the "first principles" of the gospel, while Elder David Rice broached for the second time to the hospital congregation the topic of polygamy. "Some of them told me[,] after the meeting was over[,] that they were much pleased with the doctrine, and would be glad to hear us preach if it was ten times a week." On June 1 he was asked about polygamy by a native member and decided to answer it, making it "the first time that I have ever preached on the subject," he said. His sanguine assessment was probably premature, and more likely people were just curious and silently critical. In any case, the missionaries seemed to be constantly on the defensive over polygamy. Most recently, for instance, Woodbury was grilled on the topic on the island of Moloka'i.[4]

Back at the Hammond house, Mary Jane continued to feel "quite feeble and weak" for nearly a month before she was able to teach school again. She felt "thankful ... that my life is spared" and that she could "continue my [other] dayly avocation" of sewing.[5] Frank was back to "shoemak[ing] a little" and found time to converse with his influential non-Mormon friends.

> In the afternoon I had an interview with [the king's attorney] Mr. J. Austin. He said there [were] two things which kept him from believing "Mormonism." "One was Joseph Smiths being a Prophet, and the [other was the] principle of Poligimy." Said he had rather be damned than to beleive and embrace such a doctrin[e]; I told him [he] would have the privelege of being damned all he wanted.
>
> It is his good name which causes him to reject the truth. He says there is none of the wise, rich and the noble that join our church, and he thought that sufficient reason for him to not embrace it; said the fact of the United States not taking hold of it, a nation standing high as they do in the world[,] was a bad sign &c &c. I told him the same arguments could be brought against ev[e]ry nation that had rejected the servants of God and his commandments in all ages of the world. He had read 3 nos. of the "Seer"[6] and said he would like to read more of them.[7]

That same evening Hammond visited the US consul, George Chase, with Dr. Hillebrand present, and they talked about the earth's creation. Frank learned that Chase was a skeptic (see epigraph above). Despite the fact that Hammond registered shock at such irreligious talk regarding science and religion, specifically the topic of evolution, he appears to have enjoyed engaging the other men and appreciated being listened to by individuals who were college-educated, as Chase and Hillebrand were.

4. Woodbury diaries, May 22, 1854.

5. Mary Jane Hammond journal, May 22, 1854.

6. *The Seer* was a monthly periodical published by Orson Pratt in Washington, DC, and Liverpool, England, between January 1853 and August 1854.

7. Hammond journal, May 22, 1854.

On May 26 Hammond composed a letter in English for a Chinese man named Ayoring, and it was the beginning of a profitable relationship with Chinese merchants in Lahaina. Ayoring offered to pay him $50 annually to write for him since the Asian was unable to read or write English. "I told him I would write a letter now and then," Hammond said. Two Chinese men visited the Hammonds and made a similar request, but according to Mary Jane, she and Frank had "not decided as yet" whether they would accept the offer.[8] In the end, however, the money was too good to turn down.

Another important communication that same day, May 26, took two months to reach Elder Cannon at Waipio on the island of Hawai'i. It was from Elder McBride in San Francisco reporting that they had "sent to Boston" for a printing press and another $1000 would be due on delivery. He also relayed information about President Hiram Clark's suicide, which "shocked" Cannon until he realized, as he thought about it, that it was "in consequence of" the mission president's "conduct on these islands" that he had "forfeited the spirit of the Lord and Satan has led him captive at his will."[9]

Hammond returned to preach at the hospital on May 28, accompanied by Mary Jane as the chorister even though she was still "quite weak" and still overcome if she engaged in the slightest exertion. Diana Gaston, who was still living with the Hammonds, was not energetic but kept Mary Jane company and helped out a little. "I do not know what I should of done if she had not been here," Mary Jane wrote. Diana was "no worker," Mary Jane confided to her journal, but "better than no one. Good to look after my children and she is very good to them."[10]

Hammond heard from Elder Tanner on June 10 that he was in San Francisco and would be in port with a sailing ship by July 24. The enterprise was being underwritten by a wealthy California Mormon, John Horner, who McBride said was "now worth as much or more than [Samuel] Brannan, the Apo[s]tate." The printing press would

8. Mary Jane Hammond journal, Apr. 6, 1854.

9. *JGQC*, 480–81.

10. Mary Jane Hammond journal May 29, 1853.

go to San Bernardino, Tanner explained. This dispatch was probably on Hammond's mind when he left Lahaina in a canoe less than two weeks later on the morning of June 20, with the intent of visiting native converts on Lana'i. He reached Manele at 3:00 p.m., borrowed a horse, and rode up to the valley to visit Brother Kaai. In doing so, he was impressed anew by the circumstances. "I found the saints injoy the spiret. Bro. Haole[,] their presiding Priest[,] is well liked."

The next day he "took a long walk to view the land towards the *lee* end of the Island. It is a far larger Island than I was aware of, [with] a great deal more tillable land than I had any idea of, a deep rich soil without a stone to be seen for miles. Also a much better prospect for water than I had thought when I was here before. There has been a dense population once inhabiting this Island, and I beleive there is a good opportunity here now for a settlement to do exceedingly well." He clearly believed this was the appropriate place for gathering together the native converts.

Back at Lahaina on Wednesday, June 21, Mary Jane wrote that "*last Monday* I took 2 *China* men to teach them English [and] they have learned fast." The next day she explained that the family was "very scarce of money[, and] it is pretty hard times for us now [since] the school children do not pay up for the scarcity of money[,] but my *China School* will be [a] sure 3$ a week." She was working harder than before her brush with death, but going forward, Frank would sometimes help teach the Chinese students.

On Lana'i on Sunday, Frank preached at three different meetings and then returned to Manele Bay to baptize four converts. Early the next morning, he became emotional when addressing the native Mormons. "I was so filled [with the spirit] that I could not talk for a time, but stood and wept like a child before them. They were all melted at the same time so that there was not a dry eye in the congregation. I got loose after a little and broke into prophesying and blessing them in the name of the Lord. I never was wrought upon and filled by the Spirit of God my Heavenly Father before. It was like living fire shot up in my bones."

He baptized four more natives on the "weather side of the island"

and then, about sunrise one morning, got in a canoe with some of the native men and traversed the channel in reverse direction, loaded with watermelons the native rowers wanted to sell in the port city. Because it was daytime, their passage was rough. "I bailed and paddled the most of the way over, yet the Lord was with me and [I was] preserved by his almighty power," Frank wrote, only hinting at how harrowing the trip must have been. The natives worried he could die if the boat capsized, but "I told them to not fear, the Lord would preserve me. They were glad afterwards that I was along," he suggested. He found when he arrived at home that George Cannon was there, having arrived about noon the previous day.

In the late afternoon on July 3, Frank, Mary Jane, and Frankey walked to George Chase's house to celebrate an early Fourth of July. The following day Frank rebaptized Marcus Baker. It was an act of forgiveness and reconciliation to put the previous year's unpleasantness behind them, when Baker made his explosive accusation about Mary Jane and James Hawkins. On July 5, knowing that the first wave of missionaries was preparing to depart, the Lahaina branch prepared a feast that Cannon said was as "excellent [a] dinner as I ever sat down to." They ate "chickens, pork, fish of several kinds, ban[a]nans, sweet potatoes, kalo, watermelons, pine apples, bread, butter, eggs, poi &c &c." The members contributed fifteen dollars to the elders' travel fund. "This is a small branch, and very few men in it. I don't think there is now more than 15 men in this branch. They have moved away, some gone a whaling &c." The next day James Lawson arrived from the big island, on his way with Cannon to the mission conference in Honolulu, where they would see the first-wave missionaries off for Utah. "It was with peculiar feelings that I took leave of the brethren and sisters, especially Bro. & S. Hammond and family," Cannon wrote as he left Lahaina, never to see it again.[11]

Coincident with Cannon's departure, Hammond heard from Henry Bigler on July 6 that Brigham Young thought the Hawaiian converts should gather on an island and "rest patient till the way shall

11. *JGQC*, 499, 501.

open up for their gathering to Zion [the mainland]."[12] Hammond was pleased to hear this.

> This is just as I have always thought it should be, for I never thought it wisdom to take this people right away and settle them in the midts [midst] of our people. They are not prepared for such a change, but [it is best] to colonize them here first on their own lands, and teach [them] how to work and how to live like foreigners &c &c. [and] then they will be better prepared to live among the whites.
>
> Therefore the vessel will not be needed yet a while for the native saints. Bro. Tanner was not sent by the voice of the conference to purchase the vessel, but by the [Mission] Presidency after our last fall conference. It was there voted to gather the saints on these lands first &c &c. Bro. Tanner[,] though[,] had his mind strongly [set] on a vessel at that time as a means of gathering the saints [to America] right away, although we had the first Presidency's counsel to gather them first here. So I should not be surprised at all if Bro. T. did not succeed in obtaining a vessel at present[,] for I don't beleive we need it yet.[13]

As Mary Jane's health improved, she began to take on more sewing for the missionaries, along with running her children's school and readying herself for the trip to Honolulu for the mission conference.[14] Frank kept busy outside his religious activities by making and repairing shoes; he even received a visit from the Rev. Alexander asking Hammond to make a pair for him. "He acted a little embarrassed, but I think he will see the day that he would like the privilege of making my shoes or blacking them either, if I keep in the Kingdom of God and he keeps out."

A week later on July 16, Hammond, Reddin Allred, and John Woodbury preached at the Lahaina hospital and Hammond once again bore his testimony "to the truth of polygamy. Told them if they were ever saved in a celestial glory, the[y] would have to be adopted in to the family of a poligamist &c &c." That same night Jonathan Napela came in from Wailuku to make another confession to adultery.

---

12. See also Farrer journal, July 8, 1854.
13. Hammond journal, July 6, 1854.
14. Mary Jane Hammond journal, July 7, 1854.

Apparently while traveling on a ship to Lahaina, he got drunk and fell sway to a woman on board—approximately the same story as before. As Woodbury explained it, when Napela "came to himself" he felt like "throwing himself into the Sea." After he made his confession, "we forgave him."[15] This was three months since Napela's last confession. Among other things, the gentle treatment Napela received was a double standard. Just two days earlier on July 14, the Allred brothers removed the priesthood license of Kenui, a native member, when he confessed to adultery.[16] The difference was Napela's importance to the mission, which cushioned him from loss of license. For some reason Hammond did not mention Napela's latest episode, though he had not hesitated to document this behavior in the past and would document it in the future.

The next day Hammond reaped the fruits of his preaching at the hospital, receiving a request for John Evans to be baptized. He performed the ordinance on the seashore, and afterward Evans walked to the Hammond home so Reddin Allred could perform Evans's conformation.

15. Woodbury diaries, July 15, 1854.
16. Reddin Allred journal, July 14, 1854.

CHAPTER 23

Bidding Farewell

The saints ... went by scores to the wharf to see us of[f] & give us a last farewell. We were also accompanied by all the elders & Sister Hammond[,] whose Kindness to the elders will long be remembered by all the elders who are returning [home] from the Islands ... At 2 P.M. the vessel moved from the ... wharf & sailed steadily out of the harbor while the elders & saints to whom we had given the parting hand & farewell stood waving the hat or hand, till lost in the distance. We had a fine view of the city & of the East & south East part of the Island of Oahu, & [this] brought to my mind ... the remembrance of our feelings on seeing the same on our arrival there [in 1850] ... We had not been long on board ... before we were sea sick & vomited.

—*William Farrer journal, July 29, 1854*

Late in the afternoon on July 17, 1854, Frank, Mary Jane, and Frankey Hammond left young Samuel S. with Diana Gaston and boarded the *Ka Moi*, along with the Allred brothers and John Woodbury, on their way to attend the mission conference at Honolulu. On the way Hammond "was up the latter part of the night talking Mormonism with the Capt. He is a fine man and I beleive he will make a Mormon some day. He did not charge us quite half price for our passage down." Arriving at Honolulu the next morning about 7:00 a.m. they found that the mission had rented a large home just opposite that of Philip and Jane Lewis for the meetings.

Hammond, the Allreds, Henry Bigler, George Cannon, and John Woodbury first traveled east over the mountains to attend a church conference at Kaneohe. On the second day there, according to

Hammond, they "took a license away from a Priest for being found in adult[e]ry, lying &c." This provided Hammond with an opportunity to speak his mind. "I spoke with some warmth on the subject [and] told them if it was me that had fallen into the sin, the sheding of my blood aloan [alone] could atoan [atone] for it, &c. Others spoke on the same subject. Bros Napela and Uaua spoke and spoke well too. I never heard Bro. Uaua speak better. He is a beautiful speaker." Here again, however, we see the extreme side of Hammond's theology in endorsing "blood atonement."

"One of the brethren confessed his sins—adultery &c. &c.," Cannon wrote, "and Bro. Hammond & I spoke on these subjects and on others, showing what the law of the lord would be in regard to these things" if they were in Utah.[1] There were several leading elders among the native leadership who had committed adultery without losing their ministerial licenses: M. K. Hawaii and Elders Kauwahi, Napela, and Uaua, while less important native brethren were swiftly thrown out or deprived of their priesthood licenses for the same behavior.

The harsh view Cannon and Hammond both had regarding punishment for adultery nevertheless mirrored that of the church leaders generally. On February 4, 1855, in the Salt Lake Tabernacle, First Presidency counselor Heber C. Kimball declared that "if He caught any man commiting Adultery with one of his daughters He would kill them both & so ought any righteous man." Nor would he allow Mormon girls to marry non-Mormons, he said. His colleague in the quorum of apostles, Wilford Woodruff, wrote the next day that there was "quite an excitement through the City to day among the Gentiles in Consequence of the preaching yesterday." Brigham Young spoke in the tabernacle two weeks later and supported his counselor, saying, "I would prefer to bury any wife or child I have than to have them live to dishonor my name & disgrace themselves by committing sin with the gentiles."[2]

Despite his earlier directive to find a gathering "nook" in the islands for natives, on July 19, Brigham Young wrote to the

1. *JGQC*, 505.

2. Kenney, *Wilford Woodruff's Journal*, 4:303.

missionaries that he had heard from Cannon about their "failure to secure a suitable temporary location for our native brethren, and of your subsequent operations for procuring a vessel for their conveyance to San Bernardino ... in all of which I frankly coincide & commend your wisdom and efforts." Yet he was not sure San Bernardino was the right place either. He had therefore "written to Bros. [Amasa] Lyman & [Charles] Rich to send a deligation to our missionaries on the Rio Virgin and ... its tributaries, or upon the Muddy [River], or both streams where the soil is good, climate similar to that of the Islands, [and] the aborigines [Indians] peaceable, and industrious[,] and where the Island brethren will be aloof from the contamination of settlements in California, be near us & among their lineal brethren the remnant of Jacob [the Indians], many of whom are now baptized and all of whom are said to be very industrious, friendly & peaceably disposed[,] this is the best arrangement that can be made for the present."[3]

The idea that the Mojave Desert was compatible in climate to the islands was mistaken because Hawaii is temperate and humid, compared to the dry heat of the oppressive Death Valley area. It would have been a disaster to send Hawaiians to what is now Nevada, less so if they had gone to San Bernardino but not that they would have felt very much at home there either. Young probably did not want to plant foreign converts on the coast where he already had a combustible mix of free spirits.

Hammond crossed the mountains back into Honolulu on foot to find most of the elders already assembled, but two were missing with only two days to go before the conference began. Keeler and Linn—coming from Hawai'i—had landed at Hana on Maui. Linn traveled on to Honolulu, but Keeler, who had not raised enough money to pay his fare to San Francisco, decided to do more fundraising on Maui where he was well known among the native members. The rest of the missionaries gathered in the rented house in Honolulu the day before

3. Brigham Young to "President Philip B. Lewis and the Elders & Brethren on the Sandwich Islands," July 19, 1854, qtd. in *JGQC*, 606–07. The Virgin River runs past what is now St. George and meets the Muddy River from the west and Colorado River from the south at what is now Lake Mead.

the conference. They expressed feelings about each other and the mission, making, Cannon wrote, "confession to one another for all our unwise speeches &c; a good spirit prevailed and I felt the spirit."[4]

Hammond had a good deal more to say about the meeting, which he too found to be cathartic.

> We held a council meeting preparitory to our conference (which comes off tomorrow) to tell each others feelings[,] inasmuch as there had been a good deal said about the different [projects since the October 1853] conference, such as purchasing the tin Shop, sending Br. Mac Bride to the coast to gather means for the press, return [to Utah] of the [first-wave] elders, preach[ing] the gospel &c &c. Also the sending of brother Tanner to purchas a vessell for the emigration of the native saints &c.
>
> I spoke my feelings in regard to the tin business pretty freely, saying that I regretted that it confined Prest. Lewis so closely that he had no time to attend to the spiritual concerns of the mission. I also enquired if it was likely to be as profitable as they had thought, who it belonged to, the mission or the committee! it was not very satisfactorily explained. However my feelings were all allayed. In fact I had no feelings, but I had said some things about it and I felt to confess my sins.
>
> The brethren all spoke their feelings on the subject. Bro. Johnson got his feelings a little grieved at what I said, but soon felt well again. I asked his pardon. [We] had a general time of confessing our faults. Bros. Hawkins, Cannon & Bigler had some griveances to make in relation to some remarks Bro. Lewis had made in relation to the elders going home, saying they might go as soon as they pleased, and not to write home that the Mission could not do without their labors &c &c. Bro. Lewis explained it, [including] the circumstances connected with it, and all was forgiven. A first rate feeling prevailed in our midts [midst] and we were all blessed with the spirit.[5]

Notice how willing Hammond was to believe that all their disagreements had been quickly resolved. He had forgiven everyone, so he assumed the sentiment was general. On the other hand, he had done his share of complaining about other people's decisions and assumed

4. *JGQC*, 507.
5. Hammond journal, July 23, 1854.

motivations, such as his criticism of the president running the tin shop while Hammond himself operated a cobbler shop, taught school, and was paid for translating at the police court.

There was a native meeting the next morning, at which Elders Cannon, Hammond, Napela, and Woodbury spoke. Levi Haalelea of the king's Privy Council and a high chief was "present and seemed much interested. He has been favorable to our cause for some time," Hammond wrote. The only distraction was the fact that Keeler and Linn had not yet arrived, and Hammond worried about this in several journal entries. In their absence it was decided to adjourn the conference until the next day so Hammond and Johnson could meet with Chief Haalelea about establishing a gathering place on Lana'i. "He received us as friends and treated us as such ... He seems to feel an interest in the prosperity of this work," Hammond reported.

The king's advisor proceeded to negotiate with the missionaries into the night, with Cannon now present. Since Brigham Young had not yet issued a firm ruling, the missionaries must have felt free to proceed as best they could to make their own determination about this all-important question. Hammond wrote that Haalelea advanced "the same offer as he did before,

> to let us have the use of all his land on that Island for the term of 4 years for nothing[,] or without expense; to make it [a] thourough experiment, and after it is decided that the land is good and we can live there and prosper[,] he will then expect us to either buy the land or lease it. He says how can he do anything against the interest of the church in which he beleives.
>
> He made answer thus to an inquiry [from us] if we had better not have writings [a contract] drawn, [and] he was sorry to have us distrust his word. We told him we were not afraid of him [changing his mind], but should he die his successor might not be like him. He then said he would give us an instrument of writing to make us sure.[6]

The next morning the foreign elders met again and sustained Lewis and Karren in their positions as mission president and counselor, after

6. Hammond journal, July 24, 1854. See also *JGQC*, 508–09. According to Cannon, Haalelea asked rhetorically, "Why should I do wrong to the church which I believe in?"

which "Bro. Lewis then nominated Bro. B. F. Johnson as his councillor pro tem[,] in the place of Bro. Tanner, gone to the coast." Johnson claimed in his journal that this made him first counselor, but Cannon, Farrer, and Woodbury stated in their journals that he was not to be a counselor but only a temporary substitute.[7] However, one could say that far from being a temporary replacement, Johnson was actually the *de facto* mission president. In any case, the question of titles and rank loomed high in the hierarchy of missionaries' priorities. In fact, Hammond's impression was that there had been considerable opposition to Johnson's temporary appointment.

> After it [Johnson's appointment] was moved and seconded, the President called upon the Elders for their feelings. A short and spirited discus[s]ion then ensude. The brethren thought it would be far better to have a man who had the language for councillor if such can be obtained[,] who can act well [in] other ways in that office. I expressed my feelings pretty freely on the subject. The vote [on Johnson's appointment] was then called for [and] carried unanimously. Bro. Green seconded the nomination.[8]

The Johnson motion was put by Lewis and seconded by Green, both non-native-language-speakers. But given the instinct the missionaries had to maintain harmony and follow the direction of their superiors, it is not surprising that they voted to sustain the president's appointment. It was then moved and seconded that Tanner and McBride, the two missionaries who had traveled to California to conduct mission business there, "be hounerbly [honorably] discharged from this mission," which "carried unanimously." It was "voted and carried that Br. Tanner act according to the direction of the Presidency in California."[9] Green wrote that Tanner "was left to act as curcumstances mite direct and in accordance with the authorit[i]es thare."[10]

7. Johnson papers, July 24, 1854, 174; cf. *JGQC*, 509; Farrer journal, July 25, 1854; Woodbury diaries, July 25, 1854.

8. Hammond journal, July 25, 1854.

9. See also *JGQC*, 509.

10. Green diary, July 25, 1854.

At the afternoon session, the missionaries discussed the status of the five first-wave elders, four of whom were present. They were "called upon to express their feelings in relation to going home. They all expressed a desire to return [to Utah], but felt to be in the hands of the conference to do as the spirit should dictate &c." It was moved by Hammond and seconded by someone else that "the 5 first elders be hounerably released from this mission, [which was] carried unanimously." President Lewis clarified that although Elders Bigler, Cannon, Farrer, and Hawkins were free to "return to the Valley as soon as circumstances would permit," Cannon was needed for the printing press.[11] It was decided to solicit the First Presidency in Salt Lake City by letter "to send [Cannon] back as soon as possible to aid in the work of the press &c &c" should that become necessary. The suggestion carried unanimously. Despite the talk of sending the press to San Bernardino, it would appear that the Utah elders in Honolulu assumed it would end up in the islands and that Cannon would return to operate it—which is apparently why Cannon did not take the Book of Mormon manuscript with him to the coast.

Hammond told the other missionaries that Haalelea would let them have his land for four or five years, and that the land was suitable for their needs, as far as Hammond could tell. His report was accepted and recommendation approved.[12] This was reaffirmed the next morning when the "question then arose whether we accept Lanai as a gathering place for the saints on these lands." The motion was moved and carried unanimously, as was another motion to disband the committee because its work was done.

Lewis wrote to Brigham Young the next week. In his letter, as Lanier Britsch has explained, Lewis sounded a bit unsure about what decision the missionaries had come to even though he "did his best to make the place sound attractive."[13] His uncertainty might have been based on his own personal reservations about Lana'i—or an island gathering place in general—beyond what he may have felt

11. Lewis journal, July 26, 1854.

12. Woodbury diaries, July 25; Green diary, July 25, 1854; *JGQC*, 511.

13. Philip Lewis to Brigham Young, Aug. 8, 1854; qtd. in Britsch, *Moramona*, 37.

comfortable discussing publicly at a mission conference. He had never visited Lana'i, and maybe the fact that Hammond was its advocate prejudiced Lewis against it.

When the meeting adjourned at 2:00 p.m., "Bro. Johnson & I went to see about getting passage" to the coast, Cannon wrote. "We can get on the steamboat in the 2nd cabin [steerage] for $50 a piece," he reported.[14] He liked steamships because he was less likely to become sea sick on them than on a sailing ship. Later that afternoon the president gave the elders their assignments for the following year. Woodbury was to assume leadership of the O'ahu conference; Benjamin Johnson would lead the small group of white converts on that same island. The island of Hawai'i would be divided into two conferences, Karren presiding over the Hilo area, assisted by Snider, and Reddick Allred taking charge of Kohala, assisted by Linn. Hammond was to run the Maui conference (including Lana'i), Lawson was given Moloka'i, and Reddin Allred Kaua'i. Marcus Baker was ordained an elder, and he and Jonathan Napela would work under Hammond on Maui and Lana'i. Kauwahi was assigned to work with Reddin Allred on Kaua'i.

When it came to Green's assignment, the mission president, intentionally or not, complicated Hammond's task of establishing the settlement on Lana'i by putting the project in Green's hands. This provoked considerable debate since Green could not speak the language. Hammond wrote that it was

> moved & seconded that Bro. Green labor on Lanai in the Maui conference and having charge of the farming interest relative to the gathering in conjun[c]tion with Brother F. A. Hammond (under the Presidency of the Mission).
>
> A long discussion ensued, in which nearly all the elders took part. The object was to have brother Green [given] honorable mention of in the minuetes ... Bro. Green has but a limited knowledge of the native language, so it was thought doubtful about his presiding entir[e]ly over the gathering opperations. So it was thought best for me to have

14. *JGQC*, 512.

> an appointment in that affair also. Question was finally called for and passed unanimously.[15]

Lewis wrote that he had initially intended Hammond to preside over just the *missionary activities* on Lana'i and Maui, with Baker and Napela under him. "Bro Green & Langi [would] oversee the farming operations relative to the gathering [but would] be associated with Bro. Hammond" in that activity.[16] In other words, Hammond and Green would share authority over the *farming activities*, which is how the other missionaries understood it. "Green in <u>conjunction</u> with Hammond under the Mission Presidency," is the way Farrer put it.[17] Hammond foresaw problems with the divided responsibility and he "had a little talke with Bro. Green. He is satisfied with his appointment. I received some special instructions in relation to the commencement of the gathering on Lanai."

With regard to the farming operation, Cannon was pleased to learn that Brother Van Houten had "offered the use of two plows, chains, yokes &c., also, in the event of a bargain falling thro' which was now pending, he would be able to help with some teams." Augustus Side "offered his services for one year at least, either his own labor or the produce of it, as should be thought wisdom. We accepted these offers gladly," Cannon noted, "feeling that there was a providence in it, as their services were very much needed."[18]

The main problem going forward was that President Lewis and Benjamin Johnson considered the matter of where to establish a gathering place to be still unresolved "and left to be settled by the mission presidency," which is curious in light of the fact that the missionaries had voted unanimously three times on two separate days that the colony would be planted on Lana'i, and that earlier Brigham Young had endorsed the idea of a gathering place somewhere in the islands.[19] It

15. Hammond journal, July 26, 1854.

16. Lewis journal, July 26, 1854.

17. Farrer Journal, July 26, 1854. For this date see also Woodbury diaries and Green diary.

18. *JGQC*, 513–14.

19. Johnson papers, July 26, 1854, 175.

is perhaps not surprising that Johnson would waffle on this, knowing that he and the president had not felt bound in the past by either the unanimous vote of the missionaries or directives from Brigham Young.

The missionaries spent the last evening of the conference pronouncing blessings on each other's heads, speaking in tongues, and bearing testimony to the truths of the gospel. As Hammond described the evening,

> Bro. Woodbury spoke in toungs [and] I interpreted. The interpretation was that the Lord was well pleased with the labors of the 5 first elders upon these lands, and their names should be had in everlasting rememberance among the children of Zion, and that we seek to houner [honor] and obey the council of those whom the Lord has placed to direct the affairs of this Kingdom, and that if we will uphold our [Mission] President & his councilors that all shall be well and prosperity shall attend our ev[e]ry move upon these lands, and all shall be well.[20]

Notice that Hammond got all of the interpretation this time, not just part of it. Either he was more fully inspired or he wanted to contribute to the sense of unity in the mission after so much criticism and strife. Not surprisingly, Johnson felt a similar impulse and "spoke in toungs [tongues]. Brother Lawson gave part of the interpretation, & Bro. Johnson got up and with spirit and power of God gave the rest, which was in effect that Bro. Lewis our President should have the confidence of the brethren to sustain him in bearing of[f] this Mission and for him to rejoice[,] for great should be his work on these lands &c &c."[21] Apparently some of the elders had attempted to interpret Johnson's mumblings and he overruled them to give his own version. Mary Jane Hammond said this explicitly: "Bro johnson spoke in toungs there was several had the interpretation but Bro johnson gave it himself[;] it was concerning Bro Lewis[,] that we must uphold him in his office."[22] His presumption to interpret his own spiritual utterance, contrary to the New Testament, might be

20. Hammond journal, July 27, 1854.

21. See also Farrer journal, July 27, 1854.

22. Mary Jane Hammond journal, July 27, 1854.

seen as coming from an overabundance of enthusiasm or an attempt to ingratiate himself with Lewis and bolster his authority and standing in the mission.

Whichever motivation was most prominent, Johnson did not leave it at that, for later that night he gave the president a congratulatory blessing, saying that Lewis would "grow in wisdom and the knowledge of God and be able to counsil his brethren in wisdom and righteousness and that he should have the full confidence of his brethren &c &c &c." With Cannon about to leave the mission, Johnson was stepping out from behind the curtain. Cannon understood what it meant to be the power behind the throne, having been the titular but not official mission leader himself, and he agreed with Johnson about the "importance of hearkening more diligently ... to the counsel of the presidency here. On this subject I felt much impressed," Cannon wrote, "also on the habit too prevalent among the elders, of canvassing each other's peculiarities and commenting on these things; it resulted in disunion and feelings among each other."[23]

The blessing meeting lasted until midnight. After one of the Allred brothers (Reddin) blessed Hammond, Cannon unexpectedly interrupted, saying he wanted, in Hammond's account,

> to add a few words of consolation to me ... [and] propheside in the name of Jesus Christ that many of my Father's house should be brought into the Kingdom of God and that ... they should look up to me for counsel and advice concerning their salvation. That I should do a mighty work on these lands; that I should have the gift of the native language to even become as fluent in it as my own tounge [tongue], that the native saints should seek knowledge and wisdom at my hands, and great should be the store of my knowledge and wisdom which the Lord shall bless me with, (to use his own words) you shall have the spirit and power of your office and calling to rest upon you, that you shall be able to preside with dignity over the Maui conference, and also over the affairs of the gathering on Lanai.[24]

When it was over, Hammond could not "write the ha[lf] of it

23. *JGQC*, 514.
24. Hammond journal, July 27, 1854.

... I know that it was by the spirit of prophecy and revelation that [Cannon] dictated it." Next Hammond blessed his wife, followed by several other elders, and their pronouncements were so grand that "greater blessings nev[e]r were placed upon the head of [a] woman on the earth. Bro. Karren poured out his soul in blessings and prophecies, [and] so did bro. Geo. Cannon ... All felt to unite in blessing her for her untiring labors to make the servants of God comfortable on these lands."[25]

An interesting aspect of Cannon's blessing was that he saw Lana'i as the unequivocal future gathering place and Hammond, not Green, as the one who would direct the settlement. Lewis and Johnson picked up on that and were quick to divert the attention away from the accolades Cannon was granting Hammond. They asked Cannon to give each of them—Lewis and Johnson—another blessing, which he did. "At the request of Bros. Lewis & Johnson he reblessed them," Hammond noted.

By July 28, Keeler still had not arrived, and Bigler, Cannon, Farrer, and Hawkins decided to leave without him at a cost of fifty dollars each, although they still lacked $20 toward their four tickets. Farrer wrote that "Bro. Keeler not having arrived it was thought best for us to go[,] as our way seemed open to get a passage though we had not sufficient means as yet to pay for it, yet our faith was strong that we would have [it] by the time the vessel was to leave at 1 oclock P.M."[26] Not only did they decide to leave their colleague behind, they booked passage without having enough money to pay for it.

The next day Lewis baptized James Whittet, his wife, and a native woman, and quickly ordained James an elder so the Whittets could accompany the departing missionaries to San Bernardino. At mid-morning the native members hosted a fundraising and leave-taking feast for the departing missionaries. Ironically, the missionaries were so emotionally moved that they could not eat. Cannon, for instance, wrote that "all my appetite had left me, the thoughts of leaving those with whom I had been associated in all circumstances for years

25. Hammond journal, July 27, 1854.

26. Farrer journal, July 29, 1854.

on the closest terms of brotherly intimacy, deprived me of all relish for food and I sat busily engaged in reviewing the past."[27] "Cannon spoke a few moments very affectionately to the saints," Hammond wrote. "All were heavy and grieved at the words he spoke about his going away, but cheered at the prospect of his return."[28] After Farrer and Hawkins spoke for a short time, Hammond noted that when "the saints were invited to hand in their freewill offering for the return of the elders, we received 66 dollars in all. I think full 25 of it was collected from Maui." Four Maui brethren—Maeuaua, Makahanohauo, Napela, and Uaua—each gave $5. Woodbury wrote that "sixty-six dollars was given," and "after paying their passage on board the Steamer Polyn[es]ian[,] whitch was fifty dollars each[,] they had some 20 dollars remaining."[29] Green put the amount of excess at around $100.[30]

Not knowing how much Elder Keeler had raised, the four elders took the excess funds with them. His absence "filled us with sadness, as we were all anxious to ... have him accompany us," Cannon wrote. He justified their abandonment of Keeler by adding that "Pres. Lewis and the brethren thought we had better go on this vessel."[31]

The parting was poignant. Hammond described the feelings he experienced from on shore, watching the missionaries board the ship and sail out of the harbor.

> The native brethren took the baggage and carried it down to the vessel. We all followed down to the w[h]arf to see the last of the brethren. We waited some 2 hours for the vessel to sail. I gave Bro. Cannon $10. Mary Jane gave Bro. Henry [Bigler] $2. I gave Bro. Hawkins $2.50 a[nd] Bro. Farrer $1.50. We felt like doing all we could, and had they not got enough for their passage from the saints, I had intended to give them more. I never felt so near to no men in all my life.

27. *JGQC*, 517–18.

28. It was forty-six years before he saw the islands again. He returned as an old man in 1900.

29. Woodbury diaries, July 29, 1854.

30. Green diary, July 29, 1854.

31. *JGQC*, 517, 18. Cannon was pleased that "the saints ... came forward and gave in their freewill offerings amounting about $66 and a colt [young male horse]" for which the mission president gave the departing missionaries $20. He also gave them an additional $17.50 from Brother Side.

> [At] 2 o'clock p.m. we bid them a last farewell and the noble Steamer left her morrings and stood majesticly out to sea. I thought my hearts deepest wells of affection were broken up. It seemed like parting with my own blood relations. I wept like a child. Br. Cannon seemed as near to me as an own brother. I never knew a [man] in whom I could place a greater confidence, and so with all those now tak[ing] their leave of these lands to join the saints in Zion ...
>
> Mary Jane was also deeply affected at parting with the brethren[,] especially Bro. George [Cannon], as he has been a great deal at our house since we have been on these lands. He seems like one of the family. We watched them till they were well out of the harbor, [and] then returned home with heavy hearts. I never felt it so hard to part with friends before. I have been closely associated with them for the last 3 years.[32]

Mary Jane expressed sentiments that were similar to her husband's. "I never sho[u]ld forget the parting of our brethren ... I felt almost as bad as I did when I left home. They were good men and done a good work on these Lands. They all was loved. It seemed somewhat Lonesome after they whent but I was glad to see them start for their homes."[33] Cannon wrote, "When the shores of Honolulu were receding in the distance ... a feeling of lon[e]liness crept over me at being so suddenly separated from the midst of so many of the brethren ... As I was bidding Bro. Hammond good bye, he slipped something into my pocket, which I afterwards found to be a $10 piece; I pray the Lord to bless him for his kindness." While he was happy to be heading home, Cannon felt that "the only drawback to my happiness is the absence of Bro. Keeler. I feel to sympathize with him, for I can imagine what his feelings must be when he arrives and finds us gone."[34]

32. Hammond journal, July 29, 1854.
33. Mary Jane Hammond journal, July 27, 1854.
34. *JGQC*, 519–20.

CHAPTER 24

The Ship Fiasco

In the mean time the captain [Thomas Moss] presented his bill, which amounted to eight hundred dollars. This extravagant bill produced quite an excitement in the minds of the owners of the brig. Bro. [Nathan] Tanner came on board of the vessel and tried his utmost endeavors to reason the case with the captain but all to no purpose ... A general quarrel ensued in which captain and owners participated to considerable extent. However the result was Bro. Tanner gave his note to the captain with a lease on the vessel for seven hundred dollars.

—*Silas S. Smith journal, July 11–Aug. 14, 1854*

While the missionaries were still in Honolulu, Hammond learned from a ship captain that a fourth wave of elders was soon to arrive in the islands, at least according to a captain who had been asked by missionaries in San Francisco "if he would wait 4 days [until] they would be ready and take passage with him; but he was loaded and could not wait. He also said there was another vessel soon to sail for these islands. So we have reason to look for them here in a few days," Hammond wrote.

Apostle Parley Pratt had recently arrived in northern California, having been called in April to supervise the church there. He was accompanied by twenty-three missionaries, some of whom were headed to Honolulu.[1] The four elders who had sailed from Honolulu to San Francisco in August 1854 met with their intended replacements and turned to apostle Pratt for advice on how to proceed because there was not enough money to go around. Pratt saw in this an opportunity

1. Grow, "Pratt and San Francisco Press," 102.

to ask George Q. Cannon to stay in California for six weeks to help Pratt write his autobiography, which Cannon agreed to do. Henry Bigler, William Farrer, and James Hawkins crossed "over the bay" to work in the agricultural fields "digging potatoes," Cannon wrote.[2]

Then ensued a controversy about whether they should leave as soon as possible for Utah or work through the winter and wait to travel the next year. Cannon recorded that on "about the 20th [of September], Bro[thers] Bigler, Hawkins and Farrer came over from the other side of the bay with the intention of going down to San Bernardino," but they were detained "in consequence of the counsel of Bro. Parly [Pratt], who thought it would be better for one or two of [them] to go and the [other two] to stay and endeavor to raise means & return in the Spring." It was anticipated that Cannon would need to return to the islands the next year, so he was given priority, with the suggestion from Pratt that Henry Bigler accompany him, leaving Farrer and Hawkins to stay and work. Bigler said he would just as soon stay and work, if it would be more helpful. "I realized full well that the real desires of his heart were to return home," Cannon admitted, yet he and the others agreed that if the onetime printer traveled quickly home without having to work, that would be an advantage for the mission. The other missionaries were urged to give Cannon the $100 they had brought with them from the islands, along with $50 Pratt contributed for the help with his autobiography. Furthermore, part of what Bigler, Farrer, and Hawkins "had earned while on the other side of the bay" also was given to Cannon, which rightly embarrassed him. "I felt under many obligations to the brethren for their liberality and kindness," he said.

Cannon left for San Pedro on the *Southerner* on September 23 and arrived at San Bernardino a week later. The next month he set out for Utah, and by late November he was in Provo, where he stayed overnight in the home of William Farrer's parents. Cannon elicited from Farrer's brother James a comment that Cannon was "so anxious

2. Pratt's book was published posthumously as the *Autobiography of Parley Parker Pratt*, ed. Parley P. Pratt Jr.

to see that patient Girl of [h]is" who had waited for him in Salt Lake City that Cannon could barely contain his excitement. The girl was nineteen-year-old Elizabeth Hoagland (Cannon was twenty-seven). Cannon admitted he "could not sleep all the night," thinking about her. He reached Salt Lake City on November 28 and married her less than two weeks later on December 10.[3] One wonders if this, at least in part, accounts for his extreme haste to get home, rather than purely an interest in being able to return to Hawaii in the spring. If so, it is interesting that he consigned his three companions to spend many more months of hard labor, raising money in California.

Back in the islands, Keeler left Wailuku for Lahaina on the morning of July 31 and learned by letter when he arrived in Lahaina that the other four missionaries had already sailed to California without him. "I ar[r]ived here about half past three oclock p.m. & to my great astonishment I learned that the Brethren had gone to the coast," he wrote.[4] Hurrying on to Honolulu, he found all the remaining elders there awaiting the arrival of the new wave of missionaries. Hammond wrote his impressions of this on August 1, saying how impressed he was with the president's tin shop and how indispensable it had proved to be in providing for the president and his wife, that "it has been a great blessing to the Mission in general. Had it not been for it I don't know how we could have been provided for during [the extended mission] conference, as it is very expensive living in Honolulu, and the branch is rather weak here, and do but very little towards supporting the Gospel in their midts." Hammond felt it was wrong for President Lewis to have to "work so hard, for he is an old man and should have his living from the church," but he "feels perfectly satisfide with his situation[,] and has enjoyed himself better since being in the Shop" than "any time previous." Continuing, Hammond wrote,

> I feel now that the mission is more united and is on a firmer foundation that at any time previous. More confidence in the head and in one another than I ever realised before on these lands. The fact has

3. *JGQC*, 527–31.
4. Keeler journal, July 31–Aug. 1, 1854. The letter to him was from Hammond.

> been there was not confidence enough in Bro. Lewis ... Some felt that he was not the man to stand at the head of the Mission. But bro. Geo. Cannon was always looked upon as head of the Mission, but that feeling is now done away and confidence placed where it belongs, in the head, and I pray the Lord to keep it so[,] even that the devil shall obtain no more advantage over us, but that our hearts may be cemented together like the heart of one man, even so, Amen.[5]

Despite the reassurance Hammond found in seeing the president take his place at the head of the mission in Cannon's absence, it was now possible for Benjamin F. Johnson to become the power behind the throne, even though he lacked the leadership skills necessary to step forward as a role model and lead the others in the open. On August 2, he and Hammond went together to visit Levi Haalelea, the member of the royal court, to see about the Lana'i property Haalelea owned. The minister said they would discuss "what the price shall be" after the colony was established and its suitability had been determined. Until then, he said, he was committed to giving them access to the land "for nothing." Not only that, he said, if they should "want any of the govt. land [on Lana'i] adjoining his[,] he [would] present the bill to the Privy Council." Hammond noted that the king's advisor "treated us very kindly."

That day Keeler arrived and claimed he had been prevented from arriving sooner because of the ferry schedules. Knowing he had been left behind, he wrote that he had "concluded it was all right" and "did not feel to complain[,] for the Lord knows what is for the best."[6] Hammond observed that his colleague was "not very tenacious about going home at present." This was probably because he did not yet have the funds to fit himself out to travel from California to Utah once he arrived on the coast. The president wrote only that "Bro Keeler arrived from Hawaii in good health & spirits."[7]

As the days passed and the fourth wave of elders failed to arrive, the Hammonds decided to split up for the time being so Mary Jane

5. Hammond journal, Aug. 1, 1854.
6. Keeler journal, Aug. 2, 1854.
7. Lewis journal, Aug. 1, 1854. Lewis got the date of Keeler's arrival wrong.

could check on their son Sam who had been left with Diana Gaston in Lahaina. She and Frankey left on August 3 on the *Ka Moi,* while Frank stayed to wait for the new elders. The next week Mary Jane resumed teaching school.

Hammond made himself useful at the office by first spending two days helping Elder Johnson by copying the minutes of the last conference. On August 8 he "had a warm talk with Br. Johnson about binding Book of Mormon." The substance of the disagreement has been lost, but the bitter tone is clear. Even so, Hammond continued with clerical work, mentioning that on August 9 he was "employed in copying a letter from President P. B. Lewis to President [Brigham] Young & council, written by Bro. Johnson." The surprising disclosure in that comment was that Johnson was ghostwriting Lewis's letters to the church president. While Hammond continued to wait for the new missionaries, he filled in one day for Jane Lewis by doing the cooking, just as Mary Jane had done two weeks earlier when Jane was helping a native woman named Whitit prepare to emigrate. This time Jane seemed to be bedridden by her illness.[8]

On August 12, Keeler was asked to return to regular missionary service even though he had been in the islands for four years and had been released from his mission. He asked the presidency for "a blessing & also an understanding [as to] what they wanted," according to Keeler. They responded by asking him to take over the leadership of the big island in place of Karren, with the expectation that his status would be reviewed at the April conference. That meant he would be kept in the mission at least eight months longer. Karren was pleased with this development because he was not excited about having to work on the big island. Keeler said he didn't mind, at least after the presidency "gave me a blessing and set me apart for that purpose[e]," which made him feel "well pleased ... After this Broth[er]s Van Houten, R. N. Allred & my self left on board of the schooner Paalua for [the island of]

8. Mary Jane Hammond journal, July 27, 1854.

Hawaii by the way of Lahaina at five oclock p.m."[9] He may have felt differently about re-immersing himself into missionary work if he had known that $20 that had been left behind for him, or that the other missionaries took $100 with them, $25 of which should have gone to him, or that Johnson had hidden a cache of gold coins under the mat in his bedroom. Apparently no one told him any of this. Rather than provide him with the funds to return home, Lewis, Johnson, and Karren gave him only a flowery blessing and sent him back to Hawai'i.

"Bro. Lewis received a letter from Bro. Tanner" in San Francisco stating that a brig had been purchased and that they "had her now hove down repairing."[10] Tanner informed the president that he intended to "sail for these Islands in Sept. next." This was not happy news for Hammond when he heard about it from the president. "I had thought it was all over with, and that Bro. T. was on his way home." About two weeks later, Hammond had a dream about Tanner coming back and "assum[ing] his place in the mission. A something of a bad impression remains on my mind on account of the dream" and in the dream the other missionaries all demonstrated "a delicacy in asking him why he returned."

The problem with Tanner's 271-ton brig *Rosalind* was that it was not seaworthy. His prediction that it would cost $200 to repair was underestimated; he hired Thomas Moss to supervise the repairs and assigned the fourth-wave missionaries to do the labor. However, the missionaries were put off by Moss's coarse language and insulting manner, nor were they ever paid for work. Tanner tried to make the ship viable, enlisting the help of wealthy bay area Mormons such as John M. Horner, but to no avail.[11]

---

9. Keeler journal, Aug. 12, 1854.

10. "Hove-down" meant tipped on its side to inspect and clean. "Hove" was the past-tense of "heave" (to lift), a common nautical term seen in "heave ho" (run something up a line) and "heave to" (lean into). Joe Silvia, "Whaling Terms for Landlubbers," www.newbedfordguide.com).

11. Amasa Lyman and Charles Rich to Brigham Young, June 1854; Woodbury diaries, May 3, 1854; John M. Horner to Brigham Young, July 21, 1854. Horner had passed through the Hawaiian islands with San Brannan on the ship *Brooklyn* in 1846.

Silas Smith, one of the missionaries waiting for his departure to Hawaii, mentioned seeing the ship on July 11 and commented sarcastically that it was designed in the "old English style" and you would think it was "built at or near the time that the American Pilgrims landed on Plymouth Rock," based on its "dilapidated state." Parley Pratt instructed the missionaries to move onto the *Rosalind* while they worked. Silas wrote that Nathan and Parley

> came on board and requested us to furnish some means to assist them in making the last payment on the old boat, promising that if the vessel did not succeed according to their expectations the money should be refunded. Our company furnished them with seven hundred dollars ... Bro. Pratt counseled us to go to work as many of us could ... and assist in preparing the Brig and those who could not work on the Brig to cross the Bay to San Jose valley and obtain employment to raise the necessary means to pay our passage to the Islands.

Smith picked up his pen again two days later, giving his entry a dateline of "July 13, Brig Rosalind, San Francisco Bay," and he wrote to say that

> this morning several of the Elders (myself included) went to work on the vessel under the direction of Thomas Moss an apostate Mormon. At 10 o'clock the steam ship Polynesian sailed for Honolulu. Previous to her sailing the captain offered to take us to the islands for thirty dollars each passage.
>
> I continued working on the vessel till the 14th of August, during which time I received several insults from the captain who was superintending the work. The circumstances that we were placed in at the time compelled us to submit to things that were not very pleasant. Soon after we commenced work it became apparent to every one that the man who had been put on board as captain was not in anywise qualified to act in the capacity of a captain. On one occasion while conversing with Bro. Pratt I took the liberty to express my opinion about Captain Moss. Bro. Pratt replied that he thought the captain understood his business. However in a short time Bros. Pratt and Tanner came to the conclusion that they would settle up with all the hands that had been to work on the vessel commencing with the

> Captain. Bro. Pratt called on me for a bill of the work done by the Elders. I accordingly presented him with a bill of service that had been rendered by our company amounting to $200. This being at the rate of two dollars per day. He accepted the bill but had not the necessary means to pay the demands[12] ... By this time our bill of work [$200] became a secondary consideration. We all left the Brig with the exception of Bro. H. P. Richards. He remained on board to keep the vessel from being plundered of its valuable stores. The most of the brethren crossed the bay to San Jose Valley.[13]

Silas Smith left the bay area for a week to visit some "friends who were then residing in Sonoma County," traveling to Petaluma on a steamship. On his arrival back on September 1, he was surprised to find that "the Brig was no nearer sailing than it was previous to my leaving the city, and that the owners had advertised her for sale." At that point he and eight other elders decided to abandon the project and head for Honolulu the next week on the schooner *Vaquera*.

Missionary Eli Bell confirmed the general facts of Silas's story. A month earlier, July 12, "brother Pratt & Tanner came on board the vessel, to hold a meeting with us to see how much money we could lend them to help pay for the vessel. So we let them have some thing between 5 or 6 hundred dolers, which they promist to return if the vessel should fail." The *Rosalind* was "a bad looking prospect ... as the rig[gi]n[g] &c ar[e] verey much torne and shackeld."

Bell said he worked from dawn to dark on the brig for a week and a half, then went to Pratt and complained that he was not suited for that kind of work. Pratt "counciled me to go over the bay & work, preach, which ever I could do the best at, to get means to go [to the islands] with, so I concluded to go [to the San Jose area]." He and some others crossed the bay in Horner's steamer named the *Union* and worked for an east-bay farmer for $3 per day. When Bell returned to San Francisco on August 13, he found that "the old Brig was about to prove a final failure," so he resumed his farm work until September 8 when he left

12. See epigraph at the beginning of this chapter.
13. Silas Smith journal, July 11–Aug. 14, 1854. See also *JGQC*, 524n6.

with eight other elders on a clipper ship named the *Restless*, headed for the Sandwich Islands. Bell was even able to loan "brother Silas Smith the $9.50" that Smith needed for steerage-class passage. They "left the remainder of o[u]r company" behind "as they have not means to go with [us] on this vessel."[14]

14. Eli Bell diaries, July 11–Sept. 27, 1854.

CHAPTER 25

Moses to His People

I had felt that when Bro. Cannon &c left us that the work would fall back for a season[,] on account of the scarsity of help, but I beleive there was never a time when the faith of the [native] saints was stronger than now. They begin to realize the greatness of the blessing which the first Elders brought to them, and begin to also stir about to fill their vacancies with native Elders. I can see that the saints about here [Kula] have increased in faith a great deal since I met with them before.

—Frank Hammond, Aug. 17, 1854

Unwilling to wait any longer for the new elders to arrive, Frank Hammond left Honolulu with James Lawson on the *Kamoi* on August 12, 1854. They arrived at Lahaina the next day in time to attend a native branch meeting at 4:00 p.m. "Spoke in relation to what I had seen and heard at our late conference. Translated Bro. [Brigham] Youngs counsel to ... [seek] a location for the gathering together of the native saints on these lands, where they can be taught the principles of life and salvation with far greater facility than where they are now, scatter[e]d as they are from Dan to Beersheba."

Three days later Hammond traveled to Wailuku, Waiehu, and Kula to inform the members of his appointment as Maui conference president and of the selection of Lana'i as the gathering place. This was the beginning of his passionate attempt to persuade the natives to move to that island. On August 17 he noted that the Kula brethren

> were all prepared for the word of the Lord; for them to get ready, a few of them, and proceed to Lanai and commence farming there, as pioneers for the church, building houses, digging wells, making roads,

> &c &c. Bros Kalehono & Kalawaia bore testimony to what had been preached; after this I called upon the branch to furnish 10 men, who were not afraid of work ... to get ready in the course of a few days, with all the different seeds they can obtain suited for planting, to go over on to Lanai; I then proceeded to cho[o]se those who were thought [to be] the most suitable for that mission; All that were called upon consented directly, and seemed to rejoice in having the privlege.
>
> I never enjoyed the meeting with the saints at Kula nei better.[1] They all seemed to be alive to the importance of the subject and rejoiced in the prospect of soon being able to gather out from the cursed inf[l]uence that now sur[r]ounds them on ev[e]ry hand ...I obtained 11 men, one plough, 2 yoke of oxen[,] and one cart for the Lanai experiment. None of the brethren felt in the least like holding back either their property or themselves. They are to be at Lanai next week ready to commence opperations.[2]

Hammond knew the Lana'i settlement would have to be carried out mostly by native brethren, and for the first time he referred to them as "pioneers," a term freighted with meaning for Mormons in the 1850s. He traveled on to Wailuku that afternoon and recruited ten more pioneers. "They all consented except one Bro., & he was sick. The branch voted to sustain them with their faith & prayers, and to send food to them as they shall need." The following day Hammond met Elder Napela and his family on the road to Lahaina, and the two spoke for about an hour. "At my suggestion he concluded not to go to Hilo [Hawai'i] to attend court[,] as he expects he will stay and assist me in taking care of the branches in this conference."

Four days later, Hammond, weighed down by his daunting responsibilities, penned the following anxious observations.

> Employed in shoemaking, to obtain a little means for the support of my family. The [native] branch at this place [Lahaina] is very slack in rendering any assistance towards supporting me or my family. I feel that I have a large field to labor in and have need to be in it all the time ... There is near 1700 members in this conference[,] with some

1. *Kula nei* means "this beloved Kula" (literally "this Kula" but implying affection).
2. Hammond journal, Aug. 17, 1854.

> 15 branches scattered over a large space of very rough and broken country. On this Island, Maui, I have some 200 miles to travel in visiting the different branches, and some 10 to 15 miles to travel by sea to reach Lanai, the Island where we are about to make a commencement in farming relative to our gathering.[3]

At Hammond's urging, on August 24 Ephraim Green, Benjamin Johnson, and Thomas Karren arrived at Lahaina to help select the settlement site on Lana'i, followed two days later by the "Kula company" of pioneers. Johnson explained that "as Prest. Lewis feels compelled to remain with our [tin] business in Honolulu he lays it upon me, with Br. Karren, to go to Lahaina and[,] with Br. Hammond[,] go to Lanai,—select a place, and organize a commencement for the gathering of our native brethren, at once, with Br. E. Green to go with us, and open up and super-intend the farming works."[4] At sunrise on August 28, the four left Lahaina in a "poor old leaky whale boat" that Hammond steered. "The brethren were a little sea sick [but we] had a tolerable good passage over and landed at Manele about 1 o'clock p.m.; all feel very tired and burnt much by the sun."

The next day the four Utah elders walked up to the valley early in the morning. There were already twenty-one Maui pioneers on the island, along with about fifty native Mormons from Lana'i awaiting instructions.[5] Hammond noted that "Bro. Green is well pleased with the looks of the land. Thinks it the best place on the Islands for a settlement of the saints." They talked over Green's role in the "spiritual affairs" of the branch. "Concluded to let Elder [Kanaluimehupu] continue his labors and preside over the natives; but I gave Bro. Green charge of the Island as his field, and for him to see that all things go straight[,] both temporal & spiritual." This turned out to be an impossible assignment for the language-challenged Green, but he accepted it nonetheless.

Hammond was not pleased with Johnson's attitude. He concluded that the member of the mission presidency was "not very well

3. Hammond journal, Aug. 21, 1854.
4. Johnson papers, Aug. 22–28, 1854, 175.
5. See Britsch, *Moramona*, 37.

in body nor mind." They had come prepared to dress in white ceremonial temple clothing and dedicate the land for colonization, but Johnson wanted to do so on the beach, which the others thought was too exposed a location for such a sacred rite. Then Johnson declined to participate anywhere else, and he assumed it was his place to take control of everything, "to lead and for us to follow," Hammond wrote, when in fact "he was appointed by Prest. Lewis in company with Br. Karren to come over here and assist Br. Green and I in selecting a spot for farming &c &c."

The party traversed the island the next day to the western shore, took a bath, and ate lunch. "Bro. Karren spoke to Bro. Johnson about praying according to [the secret temple] order, as we brought our temple clothes with us for that purpose," but Johnson continued to sulk, saying he would keep watch "but would not go himself to pray." So Green, Hammond, and Karren dressed in their robes and "called on the Lord to open up the way before us and to point out the spot for us to commence on[,] and that Br. J[ohnson] might have the spirit to rest upon him to point it out, and that perfect union might be in our mid[st] continualy.[6]

The next morning, August 31, Hammond became emotional as he talked to the native pioneers about what lay ahead.

> I preached to the people on the nature of the work we are now commencing, that it was the thing that would save this people, and that it is the stepping stone to their greatness; I could not talk [without pause] for sometimes my heart was so filled in contemplating this people and what they are designed to be as a covenant people of the Lord. When I first came into the house my heart was filled to overflowing, and when I stood up to pray I was so overcome that I could hardly talk so as to pray audibly. The whole congregation was filled with the like spirit, and wept tears of gratitude to our Heavenly Father ...
>
> [Brother Karren] blessed them and prop[h]ecied in the name of Jesus Christ that if they would be faithful and give heed to the counsel of those who are called to lead them, that they should never know want upon this Island, but be able to feed their brethren on the other

6. Hammond journal, Aug. 30, 1854.

> Isles when famine should overtake them, and they should come to them begging for food, and it should be their blessing to be able to supply the wants of their poor brethren. Br. Johnson also blessed them and prophecied many things on their heads.[7] All said they never enjoyed such a meeting before on these lands.[8]

Later that morning they selected the precise location of the settlement through a bit of grandstanding on the part of the elders, according to Hammond. Green saw it as his choice to make even though the spot he landed on was the approximate location Hammond had recommended before him.[9] Johnson, according to his later account, announced his decision dramatically, like Brigham Young looking over the Salt Lake Valley and exclaiming that it was the right place. He purportedly declared that the settlement would be named Joseph, centered in the Valley of Ephraim, and prophesied that "salvation should begin to go forth" from that spot "to the children of Joseph upon these lands." In retrospective references, he told of leaving seeds and tools, although there is no evidence for that.[10] Nor did Green or Hammond refer to the site as Joseph or Ephraim until a week later, and the native Mormons never took to these designations. Whatever the chronology or terminology, the most revealing aspect of the colony at its start was that the missionaries oversaw all the ceremonies without giving the native men any kind of role, even in selecting or naming the site.

After eating lunch that day, the four elders hiked back to Manele Bay and Hammond, Johnson, and Karren left in the same whaleboat. Green walked back up and began spading dirt, signaling the onset of the construction.[11] The next morning, across the strait at Lahaina, Hammond wrote to the elders on the islands of Hawai'i, Kaua'i, and Moloka'i that they needed "more pioneers [to] come as soon as possible with seeds and trees of all good kinds to plant on Lanai." He

7. Hammond would have had to translate for Johnson and Karren.

8. Hammond journal, Aug. 31, 1854.

9. Green diary, Aug. 31, 1854.

10. Johnson papers, 175–76; cf. Britsch, "Lanai Colony," 72.

11. Green diary, Sept. 1, 1854.

suggested quotas, asking Reddick Allred for fifteen volunteers, Lawson for five, and others for ten to be "supported from their respective conferences until a crop can be raised." Since Marcus Baker was unemployed, Hammond asked him to help transport oxen to the island, and "he was ready and willing to do as I should counsel."

Hammond also purchased six dollars worth of tools from B. F. Bowls & Co. "They were very willing to credit me for anything I wanted," Hammond commented. The value of his connection to the Maui business community proved inestimable. In a diary postscript, he added another important piece of information. "Bro. [Gustaf] Linn arrived this morning on his way to Hawaii. He left his son Isaac with us to school till next April, for which he give us $40 in advance." About six years old and half-white, he would eventually be adopted by the Hammonds and taken with them when they left the mission in 1856. They never mentioned who the native mother was.

Baker and Hammond left Lahaina at 11:00 on September 2 to deliver seeds and stock to the colony. The lack of regular transportation for freight between the two islands was an impediment for the colony. Borrowing a leaky whaleboat again, the same one as he had used a few days earlier, Hammond was frustrated to be confronted with "a head wind all the way" and a current that "set us well to the leeward so that we had hard work to fetch Kaohai, 9 miles from Manele;[12] going in over the reef we barely escaped being turned over. It was low tide and the sea was rough ... [W]e had a box of choice seeds from Austr[a]lia in the boat. Had they got wet in salt water it would have spoiled them."

The next morning Hammond spoke to seventy or so assembled natives at the Palawai site. After some congregational singing, he dedicated a meetinghouse. "I was so filled with the spirit that I could not give vent to my feelings," he wrote. "I dedicated it unto the Lord and asked him to accept it at our hands as our first offering to him on this Island." Quoting the words of his dedication directly, he said, "From here let thy word go forth to the people. Bless this land that it may yield

12. The island was divided into thirteen regions, Kaohai being the region just north of Manele Harbor. Continuing north are Pawili and Palawai, the equivalent of counties.

forth her strength &c." He repeated that he had never been "so filled before while praying[;] the house seemed filled [with] fire. Ev[e]ry soul felt to rejoice." The regional name of Palawai was adapted by the native Mormons to refer thereafter to the Palawai village in preference to the City of Joseph or even the native equivalent of Iosepa.

As it turned out, however, even with the nod to tradition, Hawaiians were reluctant to leave their villages and islands to settle elsewhere. Hammond thought he saw some thawing, albeit glacial, in their general resistance and wrote optimistically that some of them had "lost all their love for their places of birth, and their minds were now all center[e]d here on this little Island; I believe this is the feeling [of] all those from other islands, yet under other circumstances they are the greatest people I ever saw to remain on the spot where they were born. But the Lord has prepared them for his work, and they are will[ing] to do whatever he commands." Some of the members overcame the attachment to their home village and island, but most found it impossible to do so.

Hammond's journal for September 2 contains a long entry that ended with a prayer. In it he laid out his vision for the gathering, his role in it, and his feelings of inadequacy: "O Lord help thou thy servant to be able to teach them those principles which will be calculated to exalt them in the scale of being. I feel my weakness when I see the responsibility gathering upon me, but thou hast promised to uphold me and to give me wisdom." He

> went to bed feeling a great weight of responsibility resting upon me concerning the gathering of this people onto this Island. Bro. Green cannot say or teach much in the language [and] hence the burden of it falls upon me, and as I feel it resting upon me it makes me feel my weakness greatly, and I know I cannot bear off this work except aided continually by the spirit of God. O Lord forsake not thy servant, but be near him to guide him all the day long, give him mighty faith[,] that he may be a Moses to this people.[13]

With four of the first-wave missionaries gone from the islands,

13. Hammond journal, Sept. 2, 1854.

and the native-speaking elders who remained (the Allred brothers, Keeler, and Woodbury) assigned to other islands, Hammond realized that if the farming operation on Lana'i was going to succeed, it would be up to him. In that role, he saw himself as a Moses leading the Hawaiians out of their residences across the archipelago and into a future full of promise on Lana'i.

CHAPTER 26

Getting Oxen to Lanaʻi

This [island] has always been consider[e]d a forsaken land[,] and no white man dare to make a settlement here, but the Lord will take it and make it the head of the nation, and it shall no longer be termed baren or forsaken, and from here shall go forth the word of the Lord with an invitation to all to come here and be saved from the famin[e], pestilence, and sword &c &c. which is about to fall on the ungodly; but if you will obey with all your hearts the commandments of the Lord you shall here find safety from all those calamities.

—*Hammond to Lanaʻi pioneers, Sept. 3, 1854*

Apparently steeped in the communitarian revelations issued by Joseph Smith in the early 1830s,[1] Frank Hammond immediately began pushing the settlers on Lanaʻi to adopt a utopian system. Smith and counselor Sidney Rigdon had attempted to establish church-run collectives in Kirtland, Ohio, and in Jackson, Caldwell, and Daviess Counties in Missouri, but so many complaints and problems were encountered that they quietly shelved the program in 1838.[2] Hammond was determined to establish the egalitarian system on Lanaʻi, and that turned out to be one of the leading causes of the colony's failure.

He was disappointed to discover at Palawai on September 2, 1854, "a feeling among the saints, or at least some of them, to eat in families and not unite together. I told them that that was not pleasing unto the Lord, but for all to share alike so that the poor can rejoice too;

1. See Doctrine and Covenants 42, 51, 56, 70, 72, 82, 84, 85, 104.

2. See Arrington, *Great Basin Kingdom*; Bushman, *Joseph Smith*, 182–83; Hammond, *Quest for the New Jerusalem*, vols. 3–6.

they then all consented for me to show them how to do [it], which I did."[3] The next day there were meetings all day, and he continued to proclaim the communal ideal.

> Arose early this morning and attended meeting. I felt a strange feelling come over me. I could not account for it, but my anxiety was intense concerning how I should teach the people, the [Kula and Wailuku] pioneers and [Lana'i] residents, to commence their labors on this Island. But when I got on my feet and commenced to speak the spirit of teaching rested mightily upon me, and by the spirit of God and the power of the holy priest-hood I taught them how to commence this great work.
>
> I said to them that their calling was just the same as though they had been called to take a mission preaching; and said I, you must not allow yourselves to be covetous and get greedy and want to go and plant great fields for your own selves and families, but [rather] to feel that you are in the hands of the Lord and tha[t] he will provide for his saints. On you Pioneers, rests a great responsibility to set the examples to all others who may come after you.[4]

Hammond told the pioneers that the members who remained at home on the other islands would be destroyed in an imminent apocalypse, which produced in members like Kimo Pelia a "fear and trembling because of the mighty things which he had just heard from the mouth of the servant of [the] Lord[,] spoken by the spirit of God." Pelia said he felt so bad he might faint, and confessed that, on seeing the island they were to inherit, he had felt proud to be a part of the colonizing effort and experienced some covetousness. He "forgot [that] the object of his call to this land [was] to prepare an asyleum for the oppressed." He was ready to repent and work toward fulfillment of the promise, he said. The meeting lasted until 10:00 as others poured

3. Eating together as villages instead of as families was among the most unpopular features of the Utah and Arizona communes of the late 1870s. See the "1876 Journal of Frank Hammond," 65–120.

4. Hammond journal, Sept. 3, 1854. He promised them if they would receive the spirit of cooperation and charity, they would be "blessed in basket and store" and their crops would "not suffer with drou[g]h[t]." If they sought personal security, they would become "divided and weak" and be "scatter[e]d to the four winds."

out their hearts and confessed their sins. Hammond told them they should not let their work become an idol either. They should work when instructed to, in concert with others, and not on their own.

On September 4, Hammond gathered the pioneers together again and appointed elders Pelia and Kaolanui and deacon Leiula captains of three farming companies made up of men from Wailuku, Kula, and Lana'i. After kneeling down and praying for a blessing on the endeavor, "the Pioneers[,] ... with Bro. Green at their head[,] took their tools and started out to commence clearing the land for planting." It was considered fortuitous that the land was still wet from the previous day's rain. "The Lord is preparing the way before us," Hammond optimistically declared.

Back in Lahaina the next morning, Hammond woke early and began a flurry of letter writing to the mission presidency and the other missionaries asking for more pioneers, although not yet more than fifty, he estimated, because of the need to provide for them until they had harvested crops. He wrote in Hawaiian to Elders Napela at Wailuku and Kaleohano at Kula "concerning the "oxen, ploughs, carts, food &c to take to Lanai." Letters went out in English to a Mr. Townsend at Makawao for "seed corn, beans, onions, &c." Hammond asked him to "credit us for 6 months." He wrote to Mr. James Robinson at Waiehu "for boats to aid in transporting cattle to Lanai." Marcus Baker was sent into the island's interior to carry the letters to their recipients.

One week later Mary Jane revealed that the Hammonds were themselves considering moving to Lana'i, something she confessed she was looking forward to because the climate at Lahaina had been hard on her. "I should like to live at <u>Lanai</u> where the climate is somewhat cooler." She was concerned about giving up her school since "that is our support" but thought "the Lord can provide some other way for the support for his saints if we will put our trust in him and rely on his words." She admitted two days later that "my school is not very large. I only have 8 scholars now and I hope I may soon be read [rid] of them all. I have taught nearly two years next March."[5] The

5. Mary Jane Hammond journal, Sep. 12, 14, 1854.

loss of income could make things difficult for the family, but they assumed they would be able to blend in with the other pioneers at a common table.

The Utah missionaries responded positively to Hammond's appeal for pioneers,[6] including Lawson on Moloka'i, who said he could send a few men if the branch did not have to support them with food, which would be difficult for the indigent members on Moloka'i. Ironically, when Hammond approached "the brethren" in his own branch in Lahaina, "most of them had some excuse to make, so no one was appointed to go from [Lahaina] at present." In another unexpected turn, despite his opposition to Tanner's plan to buy a ship, Hammond decided they did need a way to transport people, food and Lana'i-grown produce to and from Lana'i, and could make use of a large ship. On September 18 he "took a walk down to Messrs. Reeds & Nortons to look at a schooner" they had just launched, "a handy little craft, but they ask to[o] much for her; they ask some 2500 dollars." The next day he "wrote a short letter to Bro. Lewis [for] council concerning the purchase of a small vessel which I looked at yesterday."

When Napela failed to procure the oxen needed for Lana'i, Hammond was upset. He decided that if he was going to get to the bottom of it, he would need to travel to Wailuku and speak to Napela directly. He found that the native leader had assumed it would not be possible to transport oxen on flat-bottom scows or lighters of the kind that were used to supply whaleships and that they would need to arrange for transport on a large commercial ship. To that end, he had begun raising funds, although he had only raised $2.75 so far. Hammond felt "grieved" because he thought that if Napela had acted according to instructions, they already would have cattle/oxen on the island, "where they are very much needed."[7]

While Hammond thought of how to correct the native leader "without being to[o] severe on him, for I do not want to hurt his feelings," he nevertheless addressed him at a Wailuku meeting on needing

6. For example, see Woodbury diaries, Sept. 17, 1854.

7. Oxen (castrated bulls) were much larger and more powerful than cows and were employed to pull wagons and plows. Uncastrated bulls were too dangerous to handle.

to do "just as [we] are told." Taking the hint, "Bro. Napela got up and said that he had done wrong, and that he was out of his place, and he was sorry for it ... He said the whole [hole] which he had just fallen in[to] he would not be caught in again, and that he was thankful for the teachings which he had just heard. He was humble and manifested a good spirit, and thus the Lord assisted me to teach the very things which were needful and in such a way that Bro. N. could be taught and edifide also."

Napela was a respected lawyer, judge, and commercial farmer, and Hammond in effect humiliated him in public before all the Wailuku native members and he was unwilling to leave it at that. He rode over to Kula and at a native meeting related the story of Napela's disobedience, bringing home the message that nothing less than unquestioning obedience to priesthood superiors would be acceptable. The congregation included some Napela relatives and employees. In any case, Hammond "called on [Elder] Kal[aheo]" the next day, September 21, and asked him to have the cattle in Lahaina on Monday next, to keep food ready for the pioneers, and to procure "timbers for a large meeting house on Lanai." He then rode down to Waiehu and arranged with Brother James Robinson to have "the privelege of his and Bro. Rice's boats to help me about the cattle." Back at Wailuku about four p.m., he went to Brother Napela's, "Got something to eat and then attended [a] meeting down by the stream ... I called for ten men to assist me about taking the cattle over to Lanai &c."

Early the next morning, Hammond found a letter in Lahaina from Ephraim Green wondering why no food had arrived from Wailuku and asking "what is detaining [them] about the cattle." The oxen were "very much" needed, he pleaded. And food was growing scarce on Lana'i. Green had just "told the brethr[en] that thay mite go afishing and see if thay could pick sun fish[,] for they had worked hard all the week on salt and potatoes."[8] Feeding the growing number of workers was a challenge.

On September 23 Hammond went on board the whale barque

8. Green diary, Sept. 22, 1854.

Lafayette and took dinner with Captain Charles Allen, who "gave me some rope to tie cattle's feet with." Allen, an old friend who had been studying Mormonism at sea, had accepted everything about the church except polygamy. That afternoon he "took tea" with the Hammonds. Over the next two days some of the *Lafayette*'s mates, or lesser officers, similarly came ashore to talk with the Hammonds about Mormonism. They related how Captain Allen had become "sick during his last cruise, [and] came near dieing," which may have been the motivation for his recent interest in religion.

Hammond heard from Elder Johnson of the mission staff that there was "good news concerning the prospect of purchasing of Govt. land on Lanai," suggesting that they could do well by using the land for "raising tobacco," at least if no one had a problem with "the prop[r]iety" of it. Three days earlier Lewis had noted in his journal that "Bro Johnson wrote to Bro Hammond upon the subject of raising tobacco on Lanai &c."[9] Johnson thought it would be so profitable it would support the colony. Apparently he and Lewis were unconcerned that tobacco was prohibited by the Mormon Word of Wisdom.

On September 25 Hammond "called and saw [merchant] Mr. B. F. Bolles about obtaining his scow to take the cattle over to Lanai in. He consented to let me have [it] for $5 per day. I think it will take us two days." The next day a native brother "arrived from Wailuku with one yoke of cattle [two oxen] from Br. Napela for the Lanai farm," and the following day the men from Kula arrived "with the balance of the cattle. They left them out of town till we should be ready to take them on board the scow."

Getting the eight oxen into the scow, which would be towed by whaleboats across the channel to Lana'i, was a daunting undertaking. It began on the afternoon of September 28 at four o'clock p.m. when

> the cattle were brought in, and in front of Mr. Bobles's Store we commenced to tie [their feet] to put [them] on board of the Scow. I had one man, Br. Keapu from Waihee, who was of great service to me in throwing down and tieing the cattle. Many stood by looking on, & if

9. Lewis journal, Sept. 20, 1854.

> we made a mistake they would laugh and mock us and ridicule us all they could, but the Lord assisted us and we got along well; at sundown we had them (4 yoke) all tied and stowed away on board of the Scow, ready to put to sea.
>
> I then left Bro. Baker to complete the readiness and I went to my house for my supper and things to take along with me. I had worked so hard that my garments, shirt, and vest were as wet as if I had been in the sea. I took a good bath and changed my clothes, after which I felt better. Got my supper, prayed with my family, blessed them and took my leave for Lanai with a Scow load of cattle, something that had never been done before on these lands.[10]

Probably Hammond employed a block and tackle on a swinging beam to lift the oxen into the scow. Since this took place in front of a store, we can assume it was on the Lahaina wharf where such devices would have been available, if not on the scow itself. The oxen were laid on their sides to prevent them from moving about and capsizing the vessel. The launch time was when it was optimum for crossing the Auau Channel, nine o'clock p.m. Hammond wrote that he

> left the harbor of Lahaina with 3 whale boats & crews and 3 women, myself, and Bro. Baker being [the only] whites, or foreigners. After we had got clear of the harbor I called all hands to come close to my boat, & we would pray and commit ourselves into the hands of [the] Lord. I prayed calling on the Lord to take charge of us and protect us and the cattle till we should land safe on the island of Lanai, a distance of about 12 miles across a bad channel, where the sea and wind is very high at times, [and] also [where the rip tides][11] are very bad; we sailed and rowed gentely along, making about 1 mile an hour. The sea was unusually smooth, [and] the wind fair a good deal of the time, but very light. The brethren were tired before we started[,] so it was very hard on them to row all night, but they stood it manfuly. The Lord was near us. I almost fancied that angels were near us guiding us over the deep.
>
> Friday Sep[tember] 29th [18]54. About 1 o'clock this morning we had got into the wake of the tide rips[,] where the sea was rough[,]

10. Hammond journal, Sept. 28, 1854.
11. Hammond called them "tide rips."

> and we discovered that the cattle had all shifted to the Stabbard [starboard] side of the Scow, and caused her to heel some 4 inches or more, and on the we[a]ther side at that.[12] But I knew that the rough sea would not last long, so we did not stop to trim ship. We soon got over the worst of it [to] where the sea was smoother; Bro. Baker was on the Scow and he said he was afraid she would roll over sometimes.
>
> At day-light we were about 4 or 5 miles from Lanai (the nearest point); I had wanted to land at Menele[,] close to our settlement, but I found that we could not fetch there[,] so we bore away for Kahalepalao,[13] a fine place to land on the weather side of the island, next to [opposite] Lahaina. We had the wind ahead, but we[,] by hard pulling[,] landed at Kahalepalaoa about 8 o'clock A.M.[,] making 11 hours on the passage; at 9 o.c. we had the cattle all on the beach, only one of them that appeared to be much injured. He was hurt in one of his forefeet and shoulder, but I think he will soon get over it. O how rejoiced the poor creatures were to get onto the land again. They[,] as well [as] we, had had a most miserable night of it.
>
> I felt to praise and magnify the name of our God, who had protected us across the deep and landed us safe on Lanai, notwithstanding all the prophesying of the wicked to the contrary. Many said we would never reach Lanai, but the tide would take us to sea and we would be lost &c &c. White men and natives joined in such talk, but it did not move me. I knew there was a God in heaven and that he was at the Helm, so I had no fear but what he would give us wisdom how to conduct the businesses safely.[14]

The oxen were more severely traumatized than Hammond had initially thought. Most of them soon recovered, but at least one was permanently disabled from having the circulation to its legs minimized for so long. After unloading the scow, the men rested that day and night while Baker walked over the mountain to inform Green that they had landed off course and the oxen were waiting on the beach. At about 4:00 a.m., Hammond and the whaleboat crews began

---

12. The side facing the wind.

13. This stretch of beach is about ten miles north of Manele Bay, near today's better-known Lopa Beach. Whitton, *Hawaiian Islands*, 434.

14. Hammond journal, Sept. 28, 29, 1854.

towing the scow back to Lahaina. "We had a light breeze of wind in our favor most of the way over; [and] about 10 o'clock A.M. we arrived at Lahaina, to the no small astonishment of those who had said so much to discourage our enterprise. I told all the brethren who had been engaged with me in this work to meet me at my house. They did so … I took down all their names, and blessed them in the name of the Lord, and taught [them] to always be ready to go whenever and wherever the Lord should say. They wept like little children while I spoke to them."

CHAPTER 27

Nine New Elders

I found not as good a spirit amongst the pioneers as I left them with. They had all been into transgression again, and had fallen into the very same snare as before. That was, they had gone to making themselves [individual] farms directly in opposition to what had been commanded. Bro. Green's not understanding their language, makes it very dificult for him to keep them straight.

—*Frank Hammond journal, Oct. 2, 1854*

On September 27, the first nine elders representing the fourth wave of missionaries arrived at Honolulu, bringing word from apostle Parley P. Pratt that as soon as the new men got "worked in to the harness & to talking the language," the second-wave elders were authorized to "begin to leave for home." In fact, John Woodbury was told that as soon as the mission felt it could spare him, he should also feel "at liberty to come home." Woodbury assumed that since the new elders were young, they would learn the language quickly, so he had reason to feel he would be on his way very soon.[1] Indeed, many of the missionaries were teenagers: Joseph F. Smith (the church founder's nephew) was fifteen, George Speirs and John Young (Brigham's nephew) were both seventeen, Eli Bell nineteen, Ward Pack twenty, and Silas Sanford Smith twenty-four. There were three elders who were thirty-two years old: William Cluff, Simpson Molen, and Silas S. Smith's first cousin by the same name (except for the middle initial), Silas Smith.

1. Woodbury diaries, Sept. 27, 1854.

"My lot fell to Maui and Lana'i," Silas reported on September 29, "where I was to labor under the direction of Br. [Thomas] Karren who was acting as counselor to Pres. Lewis." The elders at the mission home told Silas not to expect to "be able to get the native language" because of his age and to consider his calling to be "to assist in the temporal affairs at the gathering place on Lana'i. To this I made no reply but thought that time would prove whether I could learn a language that others could or not."[2] In fact, from that day on, he was determined to disprove the naysayers; and he eventually defied their expectations as an exception to the rule. For Hammond's part, he could not believe that the mission president would appoint Elder Karren to supervise the Lana'i farming operation.

The former whaler left for Lana'i early on October 2, Mary Jane poignantly mentioning that she was "up by dailight this morning baking some cakes for Mr. H[ammond]" to take with him. "How lonesome it is when he is absent for when he is at home all is right. He is all I have to comfort me in a foreign land and amongst strangers but when he is gone all is [a] dreary mess but I try to be as contented as I can be for I know we did not come here to live together but we must bear with all trials[,] let [them] be what they may."[3]

Arriving at Palawai in mid-afternoon, Frank discovered that Elder Green was upset with the pioneers for ignoring the decision to live communally. "I found Bro. Green well in body; but not as well in spirit as I could wish. He has been left to go hungry som[e]times long back [when he was on Moloka'i] and he feels hard towards the [native] saints, but I tell him to have charity for them[,] for they are weak and ignorant, and very like children." The pioneers had equally hard feelings for Green since, among other things, he had eliminated their practice, going back to their Protestant days, of holding religious meetings every morning. The morning hours could be better spent working, he had told them. Thus Hammond "found them all in a perfect snarl."

2. Silas Smith journal, Sept. 29, 1854.

3. Mary Jane Hammond journal, Oct. 2, 1854.

He told the natives that their refusal to go along with Green was like what happened with "Isreal of old" under Moses when the people lost the spirit of the Lord. The pioneers tended to work all night on their private garden plots and lack the energy they needed the next day to work in the church plots. They said they were sure God "would not be offended at them," but according to Hammond they "robbed the Lord" and fell for the "trick of the devil" who wanted to "break up the work on that Island." He raised these issues with them at another long meeting that lasted well into the evening—one that resolved nothing. Unfortunately, word of the conflict spread across the channel to the Maui branches in Kula and Wailuku, and Hammond began receiving letters from Kaleohano, Napela, Pelio, and others, asking "about the difficulty" at Lana'i.

Hammond spent one morning trying to persuade the pioneers to accept his collectivist approach to colony life, and they begrudgingly recommitted themselves to it.

> Arose early and had meeting. It held [lasted] till 10 o'clock ... Bros. Pelio and Wahine repented before the church of their sins. Wahine was very stubborn and hard hearted, and slow to repent. All the pioneers repented of what they had done in going again to plant for themselves, before the Lord should tell them [to]. They gave up all to the church, so it makes upwards of 30 acres planted. Bro. Pelio had been the first to commence [a private garden]. He was the first [to do so] before. I told him that that was the cause of the saints murmering against him, for he had been the first to transgress and had set the example. He repented with a good spirit.[4]

About this time, as reported by Woodbury, the mission presidency gave out the assignments to the new missionaries. "Silas Smith [was] to go to Maui[,] Bro. Karren to go & preside over the Temporal affairs on Lanai[,] ... Joseph [F.] Smith to Stop on Molokai [or] Maui at Napelas[,] as he liked, ... John R. Young to Stop on this Island [O'ahu], Sim[p]son M. Molen to go to Kauai [and] ... Brs. Silas S. Smith, Ward Pack, George Spears, Eli Bell & Wm. Cluff to accompany

4. Hammond journal, Oct. 3, 1854.

Bro. Snider to Hawaii." Before long, however, Lewis changed his mind, as he often did, and "decided he wanted Bro J[ohn] Young to stay in town [Honolulu] & peddle books a while ... Those bound for Maui & Hawaii set Sail on this evening on board a Schooner."[5]

When he returned to Lahaina, Hammond received a copy of apostle Pratt's letter. It was difficult for Mary Jane to receive the news that if Woodbury could be spared he should be released, while "Lewis & Hammond had better stay a while yet." She had been anticipating a release at the April conference, so the news "was very hard but I reconcile my self in thinking that I am on the Lord['s] erand and let his will be done but I cryed quite a good deal."[6]

The new elders brought additional news about the failure of the ocean-vessel project. Johnson's summary of what he heard constituted a garbled story about the ship being repaired and the former owners stealing it, "sailing in the night, and leaving bankrupt those whose money or labor was invested, and making trouble and loss for Br. P[arley] P. Pratt and other brethren living in California. And so," Johnson claimed, "Br. Tanner's long cherished hobby, of a vessel to emigrate the native saints—like all other air-castles built outside the legitimate channel—fell to pieces, involving loss to others and no honor to himself." Seeing that some elders were being allowed to return home, Johnson began complaining to anyone who would listen that he was suffering ill health and might be forced to leave. President Lewis, he claimed, "suggested that I return home—but how can I shirk the fast-increasing responsibilities now upon me!"[7] What those responsibilities may have been is unclear, except that he was laying the groundwork for his departure as a suffering hero rather than as someone who lacked commitment to real missionary work among the natives and, like Tanner, had been more ambitious than long-suffering.

5. Woodbury diaries, Oct. 30, 1854. Keeping the teenager Young in Honolulu to sell books was an odd assignment, but he was soon allowed to work with Woodbury outside Honolulu, where he rapidly learned the language.

6. Mary Jane Hammond journal, Oct. 4, 1854.

7. Johnson papers, 176–77.

Mormon historian Lanier Britsch interpreted the ship fisaco as "rather tragic" but gave a different account of its failure. Before leaving Honolulu, Britsch said, Tanner raised over $1000 to purchase the vessel and paid $6,000 for it after arriving in California. When the boat was made seaworthy, "the former owner, who had supervised the whole operation, took the missionary crew out on a shakedown [trial] cruise, and in fact it turned out to be a near disaster" because of the incompatibility of captain and crew. Pratt could see that the partnership would not survive a trip across the ocean and decided to sell the ship back to its previous owner at a loss. "As a result the new elders were forced to go to work to earn funds [and] pay for their passage to Hawaii. Because of this they were delayed two months."[8]

There is no corroborating evidence that the former owner stole the ship, and in fact the purchase price may have been as low as $2,600 rather than $6,000. Eli Bell and Silas Smith said nothing about a trial run, or "shake-down cruise," either, but did place the responsibility for the captain's incompetence on apostle Pratt for having employed him. By contrast, in a letter Reddin Allred received from Pratt, the apostle accused Tanner of having acted "in a way that brought [Tanner] under censure, in relation to the vessel, by 'selling' the vessel and put[t]ing the money to his own use, and then said that he had not received one dime." The missionary had thereby "lost his integrity and lied in the name of the lord," according to the letter's summary by Allred, who added that he hoped the apostle was wrong in his assessment.[9]

Unless Pratt was trying to shift blame for the project to someone else, then perhaps Tanner did pocket some of the funds raised in the islands and in northern California, to be applied to his own trip home. If so, this would put him in league with Johnson, who was still holding on to the gold coins he had been given. In any event, perceptive native Hawaiians, hearing that the money they had donated had been lost, were understandably unhappy.

On October 4 Hammond presided over his first island-wide

8. Britsch, *Moramona*, 215n2.

9. Reddin Allred journal, June 24, 1855.

semi-annual conference in Wailuku as the conference president. At the moment, he was not only the president but the only foreign elder on Maui. Two days before the meeting, he left the Napela house and

> went out for secret prayer in the place where I use to go with Br. Geo. [Cannon] and the other brethren [to the beautiful Iao Valley]. I felt very loanly. The very rocks and weeds I felt to love that were near the spot where we use[d] to meet and pray. I felt to call mightily on the Lord for wisdom to bear off the burden that is now laid upon me. I never felt my weakness so sensibly in all my life. I felt as though I should sink under the load of responsibility which was placed upon me. O My Father, I cri[e]d, do not leave me now, but grant me Thy Holy Spirit to guide my ev[e]ry step, that I may not go wrong.[10]

Early the next morning, before the conference sessions began, Hammond "wrote a letter to brother Geo. Cannon in answer to his of Aug. 8" to tell him "how much I missed [him], and how keen my feelings were at parting. Also how much Mary Jane grieved after those Elders [left] who she had been associated with so long on these lands." He related how forlorn he felt, arriving at Wailuku nei, and "instead of finding him and the other Elders here to council with, none but my native brethren" were there.

Previously the Utah elders had always met before the native meetings to decide important matters. This time Hammond "held a council meeting with the native Elders, to council and consult together about what measures to take at our conference." He reported that "it was agreed to send some 8 or ten missionarys to the Island of Hawaii agreeable to the request of Elders Ja[me]s Keeler & R[eddick] N. Allred; also agreed to send more Pioneers to Lanai. Some 20 odd were chosen, from Koulau [Keanae and Wailua], Hana, Kipuhulu, Kaupo, Honuaula and Hamakua." For the first time, native leaders were making these important decisions.

At noon the large native meeting began with Hammond speaking "for a short time." He said he felt like his "soul was filled with joy and light and intelligence [that] flowed forth from my lips by

10. Hammond journal, Oct. 5, 1854.

the power of the Spirit of the Most High, and we were melted to oneness. Many wept for joy because of the manifest goodness of the Lord unto us." Reports were made, and everything was said to be in a "good healthy condition, except a few branches on East Maui." That afternoon seven brethren were called to serve six-month missions to the various branches in the conference. Pioneers were chosen, twenty of whom were from East Maui. Elders Kaleo, Kaui, and Namakeina were assigned to send food to Lana'i. "Elders Paulo and Keilihune were appointed trav[e]lling presiding Elders and to ride constantly around east Maui, to teach, strengthen and instruct the saints in that qua[r]ter. They to[o] have the privelege of choosing their own partners [as] traveling companions." For the next six months native elders would be playing supervisory roles previously carried out by Utah elders.

The next day, when Silas Smith arrived in Wailuku, Hammond was astonished to think that Smith was a relative of the prophet and that three relatives of the martyred church founders were now in the Hawaiian mission. "I throwed my arms around Bro. Silas and embraced [him] as I would my own Father. My heart was filled to overflowing to meet with one of the Smith family so far away from Zion." To Hammond, the presence of the Smith family signaled that "the Lord has a great work to do on these lands ... May the Lord God bless them one and all with a speedy knowledge of this native language," he offered as a silent prayer in his journal.[11]

There was a conference in Honolulu at the same time, at which Elder Woodbury blessed "the land" in Lana'i "to bring forth in abundance" and to provide a sanctuary against the evil "influences which surround you."[12] At the Sunday morning meeting in Wailuku, Hammond took up the same theme and delivered an emotional appeal in an apocalyptic sermon. "It is by the principle of obidience that we are saved," he warned.

Who were the persons that were saved in the days of Noah? Were

11. Hammond journal, Oct. 8, 1854.

12. Woodbury diaries, Oct. 8, 1854.

they not those who obeyed the word of the Lord and went to with all their might to build an ark? ...

The Lord has said there is a great famin[e] coming on the earth, also great pestilence, sword, blood shed and great earthquaks; and he has commanded you to gather together on Lanai; in o[r]der to escape those calamities which surely will fall on all the ungodly and disobedient. Therefor you must lay to with all your energies to speedily effect your escape to Lanai; and in o[r]der to [do] this you must open your hearts and hands to contribute liberally to the support of your brethren who have gone and are going as pioneers to that land to put in crops for the salvation of the church, that is, for all who have faith to obey the word of the Lord.[13]

For the women, he advised them to sell their "silks and satins ... and [to] buy food and send [it] to the pioneers, that your children may not cry for food in days to come and you have none to give them; ... and let me say unto all unbelievers and scoffers, that the day of vengence is near at hand." Confident now in his ability to speak impulsively as prompted by the Holy Ghost, he considered the sermon to be his best effort yet, saying he was "neve[r] more filled with the spirit [than] at this time. The congregation," he wrote, "sat as if they were chained to their seats; and the unbelievers trembled before the Lord and the mighty power which the[y] saw manifested. It seemed to me that the saints turned white, being so filled with the spirit. The Lord was near." He was followed by Elder Napela and others who added their own confirmation to what Hammond had said, and as they did so "the house and all who were in it seemed clothed with fire."

The immediate response, beyond acclamation, was that the members "gave in liberally towards helping foreward the cause on Lanai." Several members donated the use of a boat, a cart, cattle, or lumber. Hammond explained that these commodities "were not given entir[e]ly to the church, but for the church to have the use of them" to build up the colony. At the end of the conference, the native saints wanted to hear from Silas Smith, so he arose and spoke

13. Hammond journal, Oct. 8, 1854.

briefly, saying he was "a stranger in their midts unacquainted with their langauge and customs," Hammond translating for him. Despite the distance between them, "he had come as a Messanger of Salvation to them, and he wanted them to pray for him that he may soon get the language and be able to teach them the principles of life and salvation. [He] said he knew Joseph Smith the prophet of the Lord when he was alive, and he knew him to be a man of God &c &c." The next day Smith left with Kekoa for Kula so he could mix with the natives and learn the language. Hammond "felt for him," knowing full well what lay ahead.

CHAPTER 28

Jurisdiction over "Zion Two"

On this account I think Bro. Karren has been appointed to Lanai; Bro Johnson feeling that I was not in favor of planting tobacco there ... I am not in favor of planting tobacco and setting the saints to work among a weed, the curse of which is short[e]ning many of their days.

—*Hammond journal, Oct. 10, 1854*

Back at Lahaina on October 10, Frank Hammond found a letter from President Lewis detailing the new elders' assignments. "In view of the arduous duties which you are at present called to perform, and the heavy tax upon your time," the president informed him, "it is deemed wisdom to releive you in a measure from some of the responsibilities which now rest upon you. We have therefore, after mature reflection, appointed Bro. Karren to preside over the temporal affairs of Lanai." Lewis clarified that Hammond would still oversee the spiritual matters there, as before.

Hammond was startled because his assumption was that he would continue for another six months in his calling until the elders convened their spring conference. It worried him to think that a linguistically unqualified elder would be relied on to bear such a heavy responsibility. Nevertheless, he prayed that "Bro. Karren may have the power of God and of his calling to rest upon him mightily, and that the work of gathering may prosper and this people begin to see the hand of God in all things tending to raise and exalt them in the scale of being."

Knowing that Johnson was more or less running the mission,

Hammond suspected that the change of responsibility was to get him out of the way so Johnson could push through his plan to have the native Mormons grow tobacco. "I have my own feelings in regard to this appointment of Bro. Karren," Hammond's journal reads. Not that he could say his feelings were "dictated by the spirit of the Lord, but I will write them[,] and time will tell if they are wrong." Johnson had suggested that the elders write down their thoughts about tobacco, and Hammond obliged in doing his part, writing that he hoped they would not resent him for being honest and give him a "whip[p]ing" for it. He summarized his thoughts in his journal, meditating on how the elders had "done all we could to get [the members] to obey the word of Wisdom," so why would they "set them to work raising the weed," which was the very thing they had been warned against? "Many other crops can be raised there by which money can be made fast, and I cannot think for a moment that the Lord requires us to make use of such means for the salvation of his people on these lands, but that he is able and ready to bring forth his work and accomplish the gathering of this people without having to resort to such means, as growing a weed which the Lord has said is not fit for the use of man &c. and I know it to be a curse to the land wherever it is growed; [it] tends to impoverish it quickly."

Hammond will later mention his own use of tobacco at a young age, implying that he must have quit when he became a Mormon in 1847, or at least by the time he began his Hawaiian mission, as his opinion of Johnson's scheme makes clear. One of his objections to Karren's appointment was that it was so capricious, contradicting what the missionaries had endorsed at the previous conference, when Green had been ratified by unanimous consent to run the temporal affairs on Lana'i. "I doubt the authority or rather the prop[r]iety of altering the decrees of an appointment of the conference," Hammond declared. If the president could act arbitrarily "in one case, he … [could in] any, therefore I see no need of calling a conference together." Despite his anger, he struggled with the possibility that he "may be wrong in this. If so I desire to be taught, for true principles is what I desire to learn." More than a superficial self-reminder to be humble, Hammond was in some anguish over the possibility that his attitude, leading to his strong criticisms of the mission presidency, might be in step with Satan's handiwork.

> I can see that the Devil would fain try me in this appointment of Bro. Karren, and make me beleive that the gathering will not go ahead without my aid &c &c. But my prayer is to God my Heavenly Father that I may be ready to acknowledge the hand of God in all things, and to believe in his power to bring forth his own work by just whom he pleases to choose. Therefore O' Lord wilt thou keep me thy servant from allowing the devil any advantage over me in any way, but to be able to decern his plots which he may lay to catch my feet ... [And] help me to give reverence to those whose place it is to lead in the affairs of this Mission, even so, Amen.[1]

He concluded by noting that he "wrote a short letter to Bro. Cannon," probably alerting him to this development and seeking his advice.

He wrote to Parley P. Pratt as well. After describing the farming operation on Lana'i, he mentioned that tobacco is a "profitable crop to grow here, the climet and soil being as admirably adapted to its growth and flavour, [that it is] not to be excelled, they say, by the best Spanish tobacco." Then he slyly added that "some of the brethren are in favor of trying" to raise tobacco "as it grows quick and can be brought into market directly and bring us money to pay for the land on Lanai." He told Pratt that the native saints referred to Lana'i as "Zion 2nd," and he assured the apostle "that all who have faith enough to gather there according to our counsel, and remain there so, will also according to counsel gather away to the coast [of California] whenever they are called for." He then let Pratt know that "Mary Jane was almost sick" because of Pratt's counsel that Hammond and a few others "stay awhile yet as they have their families with them." He hastened to add, however, that she wanted to "abide her time and fulfill her miss[ion] here honorably. She feels as I do, that the word of our [church] pres[iden]t is the word of the Lord to us, and our only way of salvation is to obey it."[2]

1. Hammond journal, Oct. 10, 1854.
2. Frank Hammond to Parley P. Pratt, Oct. 12, 1854.

In the early evening of October 13, Karren arrived at Lahaina with news that the printing press was in Honolulu and the government wanted them to "pay duty on it." Hammond brought up the recent touchy subjects with Karren, including the tobacco scheme and Karren's position of authority on Lana'i. At two o'clock in the morning, after probably getting very little sleep, they boarded a whaleboat together, accompanied by one of the greenhorn elders, Joseph F. Smith, and made their way to Lana'i, landing at Manele Bay at about 7:00 a.m. At Palawai later that day, they had an emotional discussion about the authority structure on the island. Hammond brought the president's letter with him and "in the evening read Bro. Lewes's letter to Bro. Green," who Hammond said

> felt hurt, thinking that Bro. Karren's appointment was calculated to supe[r]scede his in the temporal affairs here. He was huhe loa,[3] and felt grieved at his heart, thinking that Prest. Lewis was dissatisfide with his work here. But he is mistaken in the spirit of the Letter. We were all gri[e]ved [and] Bro. Karren felt like death. I felt that the Presidency had lost confidence in [me], yet I had thought I had done all I could to help forward the work. And I cannot understand the [limits] of the temporal bounds and the spiritual bounds. I cannot separate them.[4]

Hammond decided to separate himself from the group so he could think this through. "I wrestled mightily in prayer for strength to walk in the path which the Lord shall give me from time to time." He wanted to be "humble before my brethren" and "wept" to think of his "weakness before [God]." With that, he found he could go "back to the house comforted, feeling that it is good to be chastened of the Lord. All went to sleep feeling better, but I shall never forget the feelings I have had," he concluded, "since I first received Bro. Lewis's letter concerning my release from temporal duties on Lanai."

In his journal Green passed over this episode without mentioning that he was upset, writing only that he suspected Karren

---

3. If the term was *huhu wela loa*, it meant offended and angry. See Pukui and Elbert, *Hawaiian Dictionary*, s.v. *huhu*.

4. Hammond journal, Oct. 14, 1854.

had manipulated the president to send Karren to Lana'i so he could "make his fit out for the vall[e]y this spring."[5] Karren needed to raise enough money to reach Utah, and according to Green, he thought he would be able to raise it from the proceeds of the Lana'i farm. That morning Hammond spoke to the pioneers, summarizing his comments in his diary:

> I told them not to consider themselves under the foreigners, but to strive to become acquainted with all arts and s[ci]ences as fast as possible, so that they may not be dependent on [foreigners] for anything. I told them to all try and do as much work as Bro. Green, and not think that the white man was different from them in his organization, but to be ambitious and try and excell the white man. I told them if they would obey the counsel of the servants of God now in their midts, they would soon be able to compete with the Gentile whites in the arts and sciences.[6]

After the meeting, Hammond attempted to better organize the farming operation, making a number of assignments, and then he, Green, and Karren "had some more talk about Bro. Karren's appointment to preside over Lanai in temporal matters." Karren admitted "he could not see how he was going to be able to releive me from labors which I have been engaged in, but thought I had better continue as heretofore, and he would write to Bros. Lewis and Johnson to [have them] give a little more deffinet explanation of the diffirence between temporal and spiritual matters." Karren insisted, however, that they "acknowledge him in his office," which Hammond said he had "always [been] ready to do ... and hope I ever shall be." It is possible that no one in this drama had any ulterior motives; that President Lewis felt Karren could do more good on Lana'i than in Honolulu, and that, since he was a member of the mission presidency, he would need to be formally in charge on Lana'i. In any event, however, the effect on the ground simply added an additional layer of bureaucracy that did not improve the chances for success.

5. Ephraim Green diary, Oct. 14, 1854.
6. Hammond journal, Oct. 15, 1854.

After breakfast on October 16, everyone went to see the first touch of the plough on the farm acreage. Hammond admitted that three of the oxen had been "left to shift for themselves by the natives" and were not yet capable of pulling a plow. However, the missionaries blessed the oxen by laying their hands on them and uttering a blessing of sorts that was intended to "rebuk[e] the devil and to bring them up the mountain onto the farm ... The Lord blessed their administration," Hammond reported, "and in a day or two they had the cattle all up to the farm. They will all soon be able to work." This did not turn out to be the case.

About noon that day, Green, Hammond, and Joseph F. Smith journeyed to Lahaina on rough seas on a trip that lasted into the evening and highlighted the transportation problem. Two days later, probably due to a strong trade wind blowing late in the afternoon, Hammond noted that "a boat capsized loaded with food for Lanai." Thankfully, he said, most of the food was rescued; but Green said otherwise, writing that they "lost the food and swam ashore themselves."[7]

Two days later Hammond noted sardonically that Elder Johnson was talking about "taking leave for home, or a change of climate. He is a delicate man." Apparently Johnson admitted that he had sent Karren "to Lanai to buy up Turkies, hens, &c. &c. to prepair for obtaining something to go home with." This was met with concealed scorn by Reddin Allred, who in a letter to a former missionary in San Bernardino mentioned that the printing press had arrived and that Johnson was arranging for Brother Kauwahi to help with its operation. The well-educated Kauwahi, who had some ability in English, would have been a good choice for an office staff member. Allred added sarcastically that Karren had grown "tired of Honolulu" and was seeing what he could do in Lana'i.[8]

In other matters, Frank spoke at length with Mary Jane on October 22 about the doctrine of polygamy, which resulted in "many downcast moments." He prayed for divine intercession: "O Lord

7. Ephraim Green diary, Oct. 18, 1854.

8. Allred to Farrer, Oct. 21, 1854.

enlighten her mind and comfort her heart by day and by night." This tantalizingly brief entry indicates that she had qualms about the practice, and this fact was noticed by Hammond's clerical adversary, the Reverend Dwight Baldwin, who wrote in his May 1855 station report that

> there is a Mormon priest at Lahaina who is a shoemaker by trade ... [who] does not practice according to his preaching; for he preaches the taking of multiplicity of wives, while he says he has taken but one himself; for he says, his wife prefers, that he sh[oul]d not marry another. He speaks of polygamy as a Christian duty, but [has] acknowledged that some good [Mormon] wives of the present generation found it a hard doctrine to submit to. A more perfect generation may come when it will be very easy."[9]

Frank probably told one of his non-Mormon friends in Lahaina that his wife was opposed to polygamy, and the friend passed it on to Baldwin. Frank would not take a plural wife until 1864, the delay probably due to Mary Jane's persistent objection.

According to John Woodbury, Lewis and Johnson decided "not to set up the press for the present," knowing that without experienced pressmen and an editorial office, or even yet a reliable supply of paper, it would be difficult to maintain a credible publishing schedule. Their only operating funds were a $19.50 donation from the Honolulu branch. That afternoon there was a meeting of the white members who heard Johnson preach "for near two hours on the origen of the Bible [and] the set[t]ing up of the Gospel[,] first principles &c. He had a great flow of the Spirit."[10] Apparently his health was not poor enough to prevent him from delivering long sermons.

The arrival of the press was succeeded by delivery of a supply of paper, to which the customs agents threatened to add an import fee that would make it difficult for the mission to receive it. Not knowing what to do under the circumstances, the Hawaiian elders wrote to Parley P. Pratt, who advised them to turn the press around and send it

9. Report of Lahaina Station, May 1855, Dwight Baldwin.
10. Woodbury diaries, Oct. 27, 29, 1854.

and the paper back to San Francisco, where he would begin publishing a newspaper. He followed up with a letter to Brigham Young on February 15, 1855, requesting that George Q. Cannon be sent to California to print the Hawaiian Book of Mormon there. "I see no way to dispense with him, as he understands both languages, is a practical printer, & has the Book of Mormon in Manuscript in the Island Language," Pratt explained. "We can commence the publication of a 'paper' as soon as he comes."[11] Even though Cannon had not yet been told specifically to prepare for Hawaii, the native converts expected him to accompany the press, to be set up in the islands.

Commuting back and forth between Lana'i and Maui, Hammond found himself in Kula on October 27, and while there he blessed Silas Smith that he would "get the language as soon as any man had ever." He also blessed future church president Joseph F. Smith to be able to accomplish "a great work ... that he should not be one whit behind the foremost of his brethren in acquiring a knowledge of the native language." He blessed him "that his mind should expand, his intellectual powers should enlarge and a mighty man in council should he be, and the Spirit of his Father Hyram the Martyer should rest upon him." It was an emotional moment that Hammond characterized as "a melting time" for him.

Hammond continued on to Makawao to procure corn and wheat seed and beans from local merchants. In Wailuku he spent the night at the Napelas' house. He borrowed a horse the next morning and was back at Lahaina about noon, his brutal schedule during this period involving "making grain bags for Lanai to take seed wheat &c over in" and "work[ing] a little on the shoe bench." Besides that, he "bought some rope and sent [it] round by the boat to Kealia [Maalaea Bay] to tie the feet of the mules, Jack Asses &c with, which we wish to take to Lanai." He crisscrossed Maui to buy materials at Makawao, probably with his own funds or purchased on credit in his own name. He reached Kahi[ki]nui,[12] where he said he paused long enough to write letters in Hawaiian to other branches. Then he was on his way to

11. *JGQC*, 532.

12. Kahikinui was the southeastern district of East Maui.

Hana to exhort them to use "all dilligence in striving to obtain money for the press, also to assist in the work on Lanai," especially encouraging those who had been called as pioneers. At a testimony meeting at Wailuku on November 2, he said that "Bro[ther]s Napela, Kaihuman, Hoopuiaina, Kalihune, Opunui and Kainai all ... expressed great love and sympathy for me, seeing I was laboring so hard for their salvation ... I exhorted the brethren and sisters to be diligen[t] in aiding to pay the debt contracted on the press."

The native saints were asked to pay the import duty on the printing press, even though it was being returned to the mainland. According to a November 2 letter from Johnson to Keeler, the press had been damaged and needed repairs.[13] Cannon confirmed that when the press arrived in San Francisco in the summer of 1855, "the ribs were [still] badly damaged."[14]

13. Keeler journal, Nov. 2, 1854.

14. See Whittaker, "Placing the Keystone," 511.

CHAPTER 29

Problematic Authority

I am very lone some. I have not been out side of the yard since last July[,] the last of the month[,] and I am very tired. O how I should like to see, if only jack the dog from home[,] he would be company for me. When will the time come for us to leave these Islands.

—*Mary Jane Hammond, Nov. 18, 1854*

In early November Frank Hammond went to visit Prince Lot, one of the sons of King Kamehameha III, about the possibility of leasing the Kouhai section of Lana'i. The prince split his time between Honolulu and Lahaina. The land, he said, belonged to his sister, who was under the guardianship of the king, but he promised to "write im[m]ediately to his Father and ascertain his mind on the subject, and let me know." Hammond was impressed by the prince, who said he was happy to see the Mormons undertake their project at Lana'i and thought "good would come of it." He was fluent in English and handsome "but quite dark complexion[ed]." In making this observation, Frank demonstrated the typical white American reaction to the royal's skin color. Prince Lot and his brother, crown prince Alexander Liholiho, "were in the United States with Gerrit Judd in 1850 [and] were mistaken for negroes more than once" and treated in a humiliating way.[1]

Hammond became better acquainted with the prince over the next few months, and in December King Kamehameha III died and Lot's brother Alexander became Kamehameha IV. In nine years

1. Daws, *Shoal of Time*, 150.

Prince Lot Kapuaiwa

Courtesy Hawaii State Archives.

Alexander died and left the throne to Prince Lot, and thus when Hammond returned on his second mission in the mid-1860s, his old acquaintance had become King Kamehameha V. The brothers' terms were characterized by opposition to annexation by the United States because they feared the dark-skinned native Hawaiians would be treated like American negroes.

The day after visiting Prince Lot, Hammond traveled across the strait and found that Green was still obsessing about Karren's appointment. Consequently, Karren and Green were

> not enjoying themselves very well; Bro. Green feels that the Presidency did not regard his feelings at all in sending up Bro. Karren to preside over the Temporal affairs of Lanai &c. &c. I had a talk with him, and told him that it was his duty to acknowledge Bro. Karren as the head, and be in subjection to him all the time &c &c. He said he knew it, and he should do it after this.
>
> Bro. Karren had written a letter to Bro.'s Lewis and Johnson, requesting them to release him, on account of Bro. Green and myself not feeling well in his being here. I told Bro. K. that if [he] sent that letter he would be doing me injustice, for I had no feelings about his being here at all. So he concluded not to send it, but wrote another.

> Bro. Green was reconciled also and asked Bro. K.'s forgiv[e]ness, if he had hurt his feelings. So all is now right with them. Bro. Green is a good man and he means to do right all the day long, [and] so does Bro. Karren. I love the[m] both, and feel to pray for their prosperity.[2]

That day, as Frank acted as a peacemaker on Lana'i, Jane Lewis—terminally ill with tuberculosis—was preparing to leave Honolulu for San Francisco on board the schooner *Restless*.[3] Her mission president husband was shifting the burden of her care to a California relative, probably her sister Elvira Woodbury, and sadly he would never see his wife again.

On Maui, Mary Jane Hammond could not shake the depression that had come over her, no doubt due to Frank's hectic schedule, although there were other factors as well. On November 5 she exploded, writing in her journal that "Mr. Hammond has gone to and fro, he has no stoping place any more[,] as it were, here and there." They had a young boy living with them, Isaac Linn, and they were experiencing difficulties "break[ing] him in to our ways ... Mr. Hammond is over to Lanai" and "has just asked a Native woman and man to come to live with us which makes 10 in [our] family and there is not one of them I can depend upon." Diana Gaston was still in the house and had proved to be "nothing but an expense" in Mary Jane's eyes. "She has nothing but to depend on me for clothing and everything else. I am getting very tired of it and [everyone else] depend[ing] on my school for every thing. I feel like stoping it and then perhaps our family will stop" growing. She longed for the day when they could go back home to see her loved ones. "I feel old, and a great deal is resting on me. I am trying to get the yard in order so it will sell well, and planting beans and corn and all that I can."[4]

Frank received a letter from his brother Sanford Bartlett Hammond on Long Island, who sent him requested family genealogical information. This may have caused some homesickness for Frank as well. He explained that his brother's letter was "filled with sentiments

2. Hammond journal, Nov. 4, 1854.
3. Lewis journal, Nov. 4, 1854.
4. Mary Jane Hammond journal, Nov. 5, 1854.

of love and affection, begging me to come home as soon as possible." This moved Frank deeply, causing him to hope that he "may yet enjoy that privelege." Not in the near future, however, because he was so busy he could not imagine when it would be possible. He had stopped translating for the Lahaina court because he lacked the time, and even making and repairing shoes was an activity he had to put off for the time being. Mary Jane's school was virtually the only source of income for the family and frequent guests, and this may be why she finally had a break with Diana Gaston and started thinking about selling their house to raise means to travel to Utah.

When Frank arrived back in Lahaina on November 7, he received a letter from Reddin Allred saying he had been unable to recruit pioneers on Kaua'i. That meant the work force was coming solely from Hawai'i, Maui, Moloka'i, and O'ahu, and only the Maui branches were supplying food. Hammond probably felt like he was trying to keep his head above water; every time he approached the surface something came along to push him under. He counted "80 odd sail in the [Lahaina] harbor" and recently had seen "over a hundred in Honolulu, [including] 5 Men of War," due to it being winter in the northern whaling grounds. Lahaina was crawling with pleasure-seeking whalers, and Frank wrote indignantly that his "heart was made sick at the scenes which are now ex[h]ibited in the streets. I think the place is well nigh fitted for bur[n]ing."

Now that the mission president was alone, he and his counselors were looking for a housekeeper, a job Diana Gaston volunteered for, to Mary Jane's great pleasure. Perhaps Diana had heard something from Mary Jane that spurred her interest in moving. In all likelihood she would not have heard Frank's opinion, since he was busy, as always, "run[ning] round town hunting up articles which Bro[ther]s Karren & Green sent for." When Frank retired to bed one evening the second week of November, he had a toothache. "Mary Jane laid hands on me, but I did not get releif," he wrote. It was the second documented incident involving Mary Jane performing a healing blessing on him.

In mid-November seven more of the fourth-wave missionaries

arrived at Honolulu from California: William King, Joseph A. Peck, Henry P. Richards, Washington Rogers, Smith Thurston, John A. West, and Orson K. Whitney. There were still three others, John T. Caine, Sixtus E. Johnson, and Edward Partridge Jr., who had not yet raised enough money to finance their trip. Nor had the three first-wave missionaries, Henry Bigler, William Farrer, and James Hawkins, raised enough to move on to Utah.[5]

Around that same time, Hammond began looking around Lahaina for whaleboats for the Lana'i supply system, purchasing one for $93 and another for $75. For the former, he "gave my note for the same[,] payable in six months, at one per cent interest." He assumed the crops at Lana'i would "be ripe by then and we shall have something to pay with." That evening he called on his friend Sheriff Treadway, who owed Mary Jane $13.50 for schooling his child. In addition to collecting the money, Frank was able to borrow $46.88 from him, "for which I gave him my note on hand on demand. He is a real friend to me." This enabled him to pay for the second boat.

Mary Jane stopped writing in her journal after her November 5 entry, but began again two weeks later, explaining that they had taken in another native boy who now "wanted to go home." Frank consented, so "off he whent." Mary Jane was busy at the time "making a temple suit [white robe] for Brother Joseph [F.] Smith," which she had very nearly completed. She added that "Diana [Gaston] expects to go to Honolulu next Wedne[sda]y and I will be all alone." She was certainly happy to see the woman leave, but it made her feel lonely. "I must be patient and wait and be a wise woman and not get in such a hurry[,] but wait for the Lords time."[6]

On the morning of November 19, Frank spoke at length to the Wailuku branch and convinced them to donate money and horses. They also took out subscriptions to make payments of a certain amount in installments. George Raymond was chosen to "take charge of one of the [new whale] boats with 4 men," with which they would

5. Woodbury diaries, Nov. 13, 1854.

6. Mary Jane Hammond journal, Nov. 19, 1854.

"carry food paiai[7] to Lahaina." There he would sell it and "make money as fast as he can for the church." In return for that, the branch would "fill the boat with food" of all kinds.

The demands Hammond was making on the Maui Mormons were beginning to weigh on them. After a meeting of the Kula branch two days later, even though "Bro. Kekoa is doing all he can to help forward the work," Hammond was disappointed to find that "some of the brethren who offered carts, boats, &c. &c. at our last conference for the good of the church, have backed out from their word, and the work is b[l]ackened by it some. They will be sorry some day for their lack of faith." On a positive note, two of the new arrivals, Elders Thurston and Rogers, were "young men" who would prosper linguistically in East Maui, Hammond predicted. The fourth-wave missionaries who had just arrived ranged in age from twenty to twenty-five.

Hammond temporarily returned to shoe-making to earn enough to buy a barrel of roman cement[8] needed for the Lana'i cistern. "I feel very tired and sore, as I have not worked on my bench for some time," he observed. Instead of making shoes to save money for his family's return to Utah, he was spending his own money to buy materials for the Lana'i operation. This may have contributed to his criticism of the native brethren for being stingy with their horses when he and some pioneers needed to ride to Wailuku on November 27. It prompted him to wryly note that Hawaiians were "about as quick to loan their wives" as their horses. On a serious note, he believed they regularly mistreated animals and thereby showed themselves to be uncivilized. "A merciful man is merciful unto his beast," he wrote, quoting Proverbs 12:10. Watching them mistreat their dogs and pigs, another observer wondered if they "enjoyed torturing them" and found that their abuse and neglect of horses "sickened, and still does sicken, outsiders."[9]

7. Paiai is a semi-dry, paste-like form of poi.

8. There were two forms of cement mix available, the roman type from marlstone and portland mix (imported from the Isle of Portland, Dorset, England) from limestone. Both were mixed with sand and water.

9. Furnas, *Anatomy of Paradise*, 55–63, 100–01.

Hammond felt heavily the responsibility to meet with the church members in all the villages of Maui, but he was equally consumed with providing for the pioneers on Lana'i. He had to keep putting off his visit to the remote areas of Maui in order to service the Lana'i farm. "I have been trying since last Aug. to find time to take [a] trip or tour [of the island] but have been so busy in gathering together means for the advancement of the gathering interest on Lanai, that I have not had a moment's business time to devote to any other object. I hope by the middle of next month to have accomplished a trip round the entire Island." He accompanied Diana Gaston to the ship that would take her to Honolulu, mentioning how "heavy" she felt "in leaving the [Hammond] children." He wrote that she "shed many tears over them," but added that "the brethren need her to assist them at Oahu." "She has been nearly a year in my family, and the children had become very much attached to her. She is a young and inexperienced girl, and I pray the Lord to guide her and shield her from all evil."

That night, Hammond returned across the channel to Lana'i in one of the two new boats. At Palawai the next day, he discovered to his chagrin that Karren had excommunicated one of the pioneers. The problem was that since Karren did not speak the language, he had been unable to follow the relevant testimony in the case. "As Bro. Karren was sent up to preside over the temporal affairs of Lanai, I told him I thought he had steped over his bounds. He said he did not give it a thought before, but said he would not do it again, but [would] suspend [such hearings] till I should arrive." The ambiguous division of authority on Lana'i between Hammond, Green, and Karren, and between temporal and spiritual affairs, created confusion—and while spiritual problems mounted, so did temporal ones. Hammond noted that Karren and Green "feel rather cast down at present, as the worms have done a good deal of damage to the sweet-potatoes and beans, [and] also the ir[i]sh potatoes." All the months of planning appeared to have been in vain in the face of such challenges.

CHAPTER 30

Mad Dash for Home

Bro. [Parley P.] Parley has also writen to Bro. Luis [Lewis] to not set up the press in this cuntry[,] for Bro. Brigham [Young] has counceld that it should be taken to Sanbardeno [San Bernardino] and print the Book of Mormon thare. Bro. Johnson and Karren saild on the sixteenth of this month [for San Francisco] and Bro. Reddick [Allred] is now in Lahaina wa[i]ting for Bro. Red[d]in [Allred] to come from Kauai'i and thay are both goin [home] as soon as thay can get ready to go. Bro. Lawson is also at liberty to go as soon as they can make his fit out[,] [and] our Conference is put off till the 23 of July[,] then Bro. Hammon[d], Woodbury and myself will be at liberty to goe.

—*Ephraim Green diary, Jan. 21, 1855*

Mary Jane Hammond quickly realized how much help Diana Gaston had been to her and wished that she could have her back. Frank wrote to President Philip Lewis and Benjamin Johnson on December 3, 1854, asking them to "let Sister Gaston return here, as Mary Jane cannot do well without her." The next day he lamented that "Mary Jane is not very well. She haves it very hard now since Siter Gaston has gone. F. A. Jun[ior] is still bad with his cough." The new elders Thurston and Rogers were still there, sick with the "Lahaina Fever," as Frank called it,[1] and Mary Jane, who was ill, had to be schoolteacher, cook, housekeeper, babysitter, and nurse.

In two days, the Hammonds received a copy of the Pratt letter granting John Woodbury permission to return to Salt Lake City in the spring, as well as "all other elders who's health is poor and who are

1. He frequently referred to this sickness, apparently a malady that newcomers frequently caught, like Montezuma's Revenge in Mexico City, both mildly derrogatory.

suffering from climate or living." As a result of these instructions, President Lewis directed that Reddick Allred, Johnson, Karren, and Keeler "go home in March to be in time to go [to Utah] with Bro. [Parley] Pratt's company from [Santa] Clara [California], who start in May." The result was that third-wave elders Tanner, Karren, Johnson, Lawson, McBride, the Allred twins, and Snider would be allowed to leave the mission before second-wave elders like Woodbury and the Hammonds.

It was not long before Hammond realized the problem with the missionaries in Lahaina was butterflies as much as infection. The thought of heading alone into the back country, into a culture and language they were unfamiliar with, made them cringe. This was nothing new, of course, as evidenced by the fact that the elders who were being allowed to leave the mission (Karren, Johnson, Lawson, McBride, Tanner, and Snider) had arrived more recently than second-wave elders like Francis Hammond. When Frank realized that the elders staying at his house were experiencing anxiety, he invited them to accompany him to Wailuku, along with Joseph F. Smith and Silas Smith.

While at Wailuku on December 7, Hammond was shocked by another Napela confession.

> While our breakfast was being made ready, Bro. [Jonathan] Napela related to me how he had fallen again in to the sin of durnkness [drunkenness] and adultry while into Lahaina a few weeks ago attending court. About that time I had a dream concerning him in which I saw him drunk & cover[e]d with filth from head to foot, and thus the Lord showed me how he was into transgression. He said he was made drunk by a set of white men, who desired to see him leave the church. He said he had been in great torment ever since the day he fell. He said if he had lost wife, houses, or lands, that would have been small [compared] to what he had suffered. As I was going to Makawao and Kula and could not [stay for] their fast meeting I told him to wait and I would be back tomorrow afternoon and meet with them at their officer's meeting.[2]

2. Hammond journal, Dec. 7, 1854. Back the next day after dinner, they "had a long talk with Bro. Napela. Taught him the effects of his sin &c &c. He repented truly, and we forgave him." In gratitude, Napela "gave me a large grey horse to ride and use as my own till he is well broke in."

At Kula Hammond assigned new missionary Rogers to "go home with [native] Elder Kuahauli to Kaupo, and Bro. Thurston to remain at Kula for the present," then he and Silas Smith rode south to the Kealia supply and transfer station to find that the shipment of potatoes they had expected for Lana'i had not yet arrived. An irritated Hammond observed that "the brethren are very slow at Kula about getting food down to the beach.[3] In consequence of which, the pioneers go hungry often. They are a very slow people. One smart white man can do as much as ten ordinary Kanakas [natives]."

The next day a letter from Elder Karren arrived at Wailuku, addressed to Silas Smith, asking him to come immediately to Lana'i to help construct cisterns. Smith took a whaleboat on December 10 and arrived to find Baker, Green, and Karren doing well except for "the scarcity of water [which] is the only obstacle to overcome in making a settlement in the valley." Natives were having to travel two to three miles for culinary water, which Hammond knew would have a "tendency to retard the gathering of the native saints to the island." Over the next several days, Smith constructed two underground cisterns with walls of stone and plaster holding 340 and 680 barrels of water each.[4]

Hammond traveled as far as Lahaina, where he learned by letter from Lewis and Johnson that Diana Gaston would not be returning to the Hammond home. Then he was off again the same day for another tour of the island. In Kula he learned that native men "took advantage of the [new] brethren's not knowing the language and got them [Joseph F. Smith and Silas Smith] to assist in ordaining" many native brethren. This gave rise to more disparaging remarks about the Hawaiian people. "I am sorry to have to have so many ordained to the priesthood; for it is only a few that magnify their offices ... This

3. Kula was known as the "potato district" of Maui, where irish potatoes thrived at higher elevations and were then carried down to Maalaea Bay for transportation to Lahaina. Kuykendall, *Hawaiian Kingdom*, 1:313.

4. Silas Smith journal, Dec. 7, 10, 1854. The capacity, about 10,000 and 20,000 gallons of water respectively, would be equal to that of a home swimming pool. Most small-town water towers hold about fifty times that amount.

people are very much like children. They don't know what is good for themselves. They are all very anxious to obtain the priesthood."

He nevertheless recruited native members Kalauaia and Pake to assist on a clockwise horseback tour of East Maui beginning December 14. Elder Thurston accompanied them as far as Keanae and was left there so he could learn the language. They were surprised to encounter in that area some incipient opposition to the gathering place. Hammond "told them they could not be saved while living in the midts of Babulon, but they must leave as Lot did and make their escape to the place or places which God shall designate, and that they could not be saved while living on their old homesteads." John Piluai thought otherwise, telling them "they could be saved here as well as on Lanai, and that there was no need of gathering &c. I told them this teaching was from the devil and not to beleive it &c."

On December 17 the last of the fourth-wave elders, John T. Caine, Sixtus E. Johnson, and Edward Partridge Jr., arrived at Honolulu from San Francisco.[5] Their ship docked two days after King Kamehameha III died, so they encountered a city in mourning, the shops closed, and crowds at the palace waiting to greet the new king. Elder William Cluff, who was in O'ahu at the time but not in Honolulu, wrote that "never in my life did I hear or witness such a lonely and melancholy condition as that produced by the lamentations of the Hawaiian people at the death of one of their kings."[6] On East Maui, hearing of the king's death, Hammond observed that he had been "a good sort of fellow, but not much [of a] force." He commented on how "very fond" the king had been of "women and wine," as did Woodbury, who thought he had died of alcoholism.[7] The elaborate funeral, beginning with a long procession on a pili grass-covered boulevard, was held on January 6, but for Hammond and other Americans, mission life continued on as normal.

It was raining on December 21 as Hammond and native member

5. Lewis journal, Dec. 17, 1854.

6. "Death of the King!" *Polynesian*, Dec. 16, 1854, 2; William Cluff, qtd. in David Cluff Sr., *Cluff Family Journal*, Mar. 20, 1901, 120.

7. Woodbury diaries, Dec. 16, 1854.

Pake rode to Kaupo to investigate what had happened to Elder Rogers, who had left the branch around midnight the evening before and had not been seen since. Hammond wanted to get home for Christmas and hoped for the best. As he searched for the missionary, the elders from Lana'i and Moloka'i—Green, Karren, Lawson, and Silas Smith—were arriving at Lahaina to spend Christmas with his family.[8] Frank eventually found Rogers in Wailuku. Disoriented and paranoid, Rogers claimed that his companion at Kaupo, Elder Kauhauli, had gotten a "Big Head" and was "trying to ride over him." Hammond stayed to sort things out through Christmas Eve.

On Christmas Day he found a mule to ride to Lahaina. He offered to let Rogers and Joseph F. Smith walk along beside him, but they declined, knowing how far it was. Frank arrived at around seven o'clock that evening and found the house filled with the smells of Christmas; Mary Jane "and the little ones were overjoyed to see me." Her health was better, although the "little boys are still bad with the Hooping cough," he wrote. The guests were doing well. Elder Green wrote in his diary about how wonderful it was when "this morning ... Sister Hammon[d] presented us with chicken fried in bu[t]er and uther trimmings ... After breckfast was over we had a candy pulling. We puld and eat till we ware satisfied."[9]

During the country's transitional period in Honolulu, the adopted son of the deceased king assumed the throne to much fanfare. Meanwhile, President Lewis heard from Elder Parley P. Pratt concerning the printing press, "that it would ultimately go to California and be used in printing for that country as well as these Islands."[10] However, only the native Book of Mormon and one pamphlet introducing it would ever be printed for the benefit of Hawaiians, while everything else the workhorse printing press produced was in English for the benefit of the Mormons in California.

Anxious to see what the conditions were in Lana'i, Hammond and Green left Lahaina the next morning so they could reach Palawai

8. Green diary, Dec. 23, 1854.
9. Green diary, Dec. 25, 1854.
10. Lewis journal, Dec. 29, 1854; also Woodbury diaries, Jan. 4, 1855.

by mid-afternoon. They found that Karren had gone to Honolulu to make money for his return to Utah. In his journal, Johnson explained that Karren had been told "he should be at liberty to return home with me as soon as the way should open." The mission presidency assigned Johnson's nephew Sixtus Johnson to take over Karren's place in "labor[ing] with Br. Green." President Lewis sold the tin shop and paid "$600 to Halalia [Haalelea] on the press with its freight charges." Before the month was out, they received word from Pratt confirming that they were to "ship the Press and material to San Francisco." Johnson added that ultimately Brother Side paid for Karren's passage to the mainland and that Johnson's own passage was paid by Lewis with proceeds from the sale of the tin shop.[11]

Hammond was pleased to see that the Palawai village "now contains some 15 houses[,] all set in two rows on two streets run[n]ing south and north ... There is about 15 acres of wheat sowed. Some of it is up a finger length or more." Worms had damaged some of the crop "but not so as to hurt it a great deal as yet." In the end, only about five of twenty acres of sweet potatoes could be rescued, but there were no worms at all in the watermelons and "near half an acre of corn" had been harvested in their "ro[a]sting ears."

The year 1854 came to a close with Hammond on Lana'i and his family across the channel at Lahaina. Green's cottage proved to be an uncomfortable place to celebrate New Year's Eve and New Year's Day. "It rained nearly all night. I slept but little," Hammond complained. "The house leaked and I slept on a wet bed and took cold." He offered up a prayer for 1855: "Grant unto me O Lord thy holy Spiret in a double portion this year, that I may do a mighty work in thy name this year, and be the instrument in thy hands of doing much good to this people ... Preserve me from the grasp of Satan."

About noon on January 3, pressing his luck in some rough weather at the worst time of day, Hammond and some native brethren left Menele for Lahaina.

About 1 o.c[lock] we were abre[a]st [of] Koohai with the wind in the

11. Johnson Papers, 178–80.

> qua[r]ter and a heavy wind [at] sea. I never saw half so much sea at no time before in this channel. The wind blew heavy and I had to Steer all the passage over, as none of the natives could do it. They were also a little frightened, but we put our trust in the Lord[,] knowing he could rule the wind and the waves. We landed at Lahaina 20 minutes before 3 o'clock p.m., making the shortest passage I ever made from Lanai. Whites and natives were astonished at our coming over in such a storm.[12]

Reading entries like this one can grow tiresome, realizing that from Hammond's perspective, it was always the native brethren who were frightened and incapable of steering the whaleboats during these problematic crossings, never the fearless and intrepid former whaler. But in fact, his native brethren and sisters were more at home in the ocean than he was, crossing back and forth between Maui and Lana'i on a daily basis without him. They never lost their lives, nor their courage, during those crossings. Hammond's predecessor, George Q. Cannon, had in fact marveled that "the sea has no terrors for the Sandwich Islanders. They can swim in the water for hours without being at all fatigued."[13] The natives who traveled with Hammond in canoes and whaleboats during storms may have been fearful that something would happen to him, rather than being concerned about their own survival. Frequently he indicated that they tried to persuade him not to go with them for fear of his safety.

The state funeral and lavish coronation of Kamehameha IV took place in mid-January, events that John Woodbury described in detail in his diary.[14] For Hammond, the capital city was a world away as he struggled to keep up with his responsibilities. He recorded shock at seeing Reddick Allred arrive in Lahaina from the big island looking "thin and haggard and much wore down. His lungs is still bad. He is now on his way to Oahu to get ready for home." Allred had reason to leave, but he also seemed particularly eager to go, maybe because he had learned the language and felt it was unfair for the

12. Hammond journal, Jan. 3, 1854.
13. Cannon, *My First Mission*, 47–48.
14. Woodbury diary, Jan. 7, 1855.

other third-wave missionaries to leave before him. Green wrote: "I was sor[r]y to hear of his [Reddick's] ill he[a]lth for he is a useful man and this mishan [mission] will miss him[,] as it will leave his field [the big island] destitute of Elders thats got the language."[15]

Hammond received a letter from Silas Smith confirming that Washington Rogers was apparently suffering from mental illness. "Bro. Rogers has gone to Kaupo again; and seemed to be a little deranged and vis[i]onary. I fear he is out of his mind, for he acts really strange. M[a]y the Lord stre[n]gthen him from the grasp of Satan," Hammond wrote. One can see how blurry the lines were in those days between mental illness and devil possession. In more bad news, Hammond learned that Brigham Young had given his imprimatur to putting the Hawaiian Mission printing press in California. Hammond deduced that, "in consequence of this [directive], Bro[ther]s Johnson and Karren will sail next week for the coast, as there is no business to detain them longer here, and their health is very poor." It had been assumed that Johnson and Karren would help Cannon operate the press at Honolulu.

Hammond could see that if the Allred brothers and Lawson were "priveleged to sail for the coast as soon as they can obtain the means," then "the Molokai conference will come under the jurisdiction of the Presidency of Maui" as before. Hammond did not relish the idea because it would only add to his already heavy load. He also had learned that "our conference is put off until the 24th of July next, expecting that Bro. Cannon will be back by that time ... After these brethren [Allred, Johnson, Karren, Keeler, and Lawson] have obtained their outfits and sailed[,] then the rest of the old elders [Hammond, Lewis, Woodbury] can commence their out-fits[,] as the way may open up so as to be ready to sail im[m]ediately after conference next July."

Hammond met with Silas Smith and Washington Rogers at Wailuku on January 13 and learned of Rogers's paranoid behavior. Hammond wrote that "he has been back to Kaupo and again run away in the night, he says for fear of their killing him. He is laboring under some derangment of the mind which I cannot account for. He

15. Green diary, Jan. 14, 1855.

has laid out two nights, and he now looks as if he had passed through a severe fit of sickness. He thinks that Bro.'s Kuahaui, Kauuahoa, and Kauuahi were all plan[n]ing how they should take away his life. So he must be out of his mind."

If that were not enough, the opposition to Lana'i had spread to the stalwart village of Wailuku, where Hammond "called on 4 of the brethren to go in the boat [to Lana'i] with Maiola, [and] also for ten brethren to take sufficient food for one month and go to Lanai and help plant the crops now while the season is right," and some "made excuses and did not want to go, which gave me [the] oppertunity to teach them the principle of obeying council at all times in o[r]der to be saved." Seeing himself in the role of a Book of Mormon character, he wrote that the members shrank before him "and they did fear and quake for they knew it was by the power of God that I spoke." He proceeded to organize the Lana'i relief effort, telling them that they were also to "collect a lot of Pai Kalo [thick poi wrapped in leaves] and send [it] to Lahaina for the benifit of the elders who are returning [to Utah].[16]

As they prepared for their departure, Johnson and Karren gave farewell addresses to the Honolulu members. As described by Woodbury, "They each Spoke a few minutes in English espressing there [their] feelings & leaving their parting blessing with the Saints. I enterprited [interpreted] to the native Saints." In other words, the two elders who were about to retire from mission service were still unable to even speak simple Hawaiian. The members gave Johnson thirteen dollars for his journey home in two days. During the intervening day, Johnson and Woodbury visited the Kalua family and blessed their baby, naming it Marayann, and Johnson collected five dollars from the family in return for the blessing. It seems that he was soliciting funds but Karren was not. When Johnson returned home to Utah, presumably taking with him Brother Dennis's huge monetary gift, he portrayed himself as

16. Hammond journal, Jan. 14, 1855. George Q. Cannon called *pai kalo* warm poi "packed in the leaves of a shrub called ki" and allowed to turn "maggoty." "Some people eat maggotty cheese," he added for comparison. Cannon, "My First Mission," *Millennial Star*, Apr. 24, 1882, 258.

poor, both then and throughout his life, even though he owned property, acquired more property, and appeared to be wealthy.[17]

Silas Smith had some observations about Johnson's and Karren's departure that were probably influenced by Green and Hammond since Smith had only been in the mission three months. He pointed out that although "these brethren [Johnson and Karren] had been on the islands some two years,"

> they were neither of them successful in getting a knowledge of the native language. consequently their means of doing much good on their mission was quite limited. Bro. B. F. Johnson resided in Honolulu and acted as counselor to Pres. Lewis at the same time he presided over the foreign [English-speaking] branch of the church in Honolulu. This branch consisted of some six or eight members, therefore his labors were not very extensive. Bro. Karren traveled among the natives more or less accompanied by a native elder who could speak a little English. During his stay on the islands he baptized near two hundred natives but as he was not able to converse with them he could not give them much instruction pertaining to the laws and regulations of the church. Consequently they were no better after they were baptized than they were before.[18]

President Lewis recorded that within two weeks, another missionary who had been given permission to leave appeared in Honolulu. "Bro. Lawson arrived from Molokai, and being successful in obtaining means to take him to California on the 5th of Feb he embarked on the Bark Francis Palmer ... for San Francisco." Where he had obtained his "means" is unclear. Lewis explained that his sick wife Jane would leave California because some individuals "in Bro Pratts Company" said they would be "able to assist her" to Salt Lake City, "and Bro McBride had kindly offered to procure her a passage.[19] She got no farther than San Bernardino.

17. Woodbury diaries, Jan. 14–15, 1855; see LeBaron, *Benjamin F. Johnson*, 105–95.
18. Silas Smith journal, Jan. 11, 1855.
19. Lewis journal, Jan.–Feb. 1855.

CHAPTER 31

Keeler Left Behind Again

Here the tide and sea, which was very rough indeed, set us close into land. We took in sail and pulled hard for a long time before we could tell whether we gained ahead or not. The wind by this time had increased to a living gale and the sea [was] so high and irregular that I feared much [that] the boat would swamp or go ashore with us. The sea would roll up and brake over into the boat so often that it was difficult keeping her free.

—Hammond journal, Mar. 2, 1855

On January 18, 1855, Frank Hammond, Silas Smith, and a Brother Kanakanui set out on horseback on a tour beginning in Kula and going clockwise "round the east end of Maui nei by the way of Kaupo." Lunch that day was not very appetizing.

> About noon we arrived at Bro. Naheloea's [in] Ulupalekua.[1] He[re] we got a little dinner[,] such as they had on hand, which was a very little very salt[y] fish and some very nasty looking sweet potatoes[,] well mixed with dirt and water, and by way of sauce we had four or five little dirty sore eyed dogs scratching the fleas off them and licking the dishes and picking up the crumbs if any fell[,] which was not the case[,] for we had tight work to make out enough. But notwithstanding all the dirt &c, we were glad to get it and felt thankful too, for we were hungry, and a hungry stomach does not stand for trifles.
>
> The brother of the house was not at home, and his wife was living in with an old woman who did not belong to the church, hence the

1. Ulupalakua is twelve miles south of Kula.

> dirt and dogs, and I dare not scold them for fear of offending the old woman; the saints usually know better than to do so.[2]

They continued traveling twenty miles east of Ulupalakua across lava beds to the southeast coast, Hammond writing a letter along the way to Jonathan Napela "to call out ten more pioneers from that place for Lanai, for four weeks with food for that time, and go quick and help to put in a crop now while the ground is in good o[r]der." They reached Manuu on January 19 and there encouraged 160 or so saints to contribute toward the return of James Keeler and Reddick Allred to the United States. "The[y] gave in about five dollars in cash, and a few goats, 1 hog, 1 Turkey &c. &c." He asked for volunteers to go to Lana'i and three offered to go. "I scolded the officers a good deal for their lack of faith in this thing," he wrote. Later that day, after the application of considerable pressure, four more men offered to go to Lana'i.

By sundown on January 22, they reached Kipahulu, and two days later were close to the Hana harbor. "[We] went down and took a bath and changed our garments after which we felt better," Hammond wrote. "We often get lice on us while traveling among the natives, both head and body lice. I always endeavor to teach them how to live and keep themselves free from vermine, but they are slow to hear and obey the things which are calculated to raise them up and exalt them in the presence of their Maker." He frequently complained about how uncomfortable it was living among the natives, especially that he could not sleep in the huts because of the fleas.

Mary Jane Hammond described in her journal her own trials due to feelings of loneliness and the domestic challenges she faced, Frank contributing little to their income.

> I think we shall have more rain but I hope not for it will hinder Mr H[ammond] in his calculation for he thought he should be at home the 6 of Feb for I feel his [absence] much[,] the two children being sick. I feel quite bad. The food is very high in price[;] poi is 31½ c[en]ts a bundle[,] coal 37½[,] so it is quite hard on me. I have to live a[s] cheep as I can[,] bread [is] 24 c[en]ts a small loaf[,] so I do not

2. Hammond journal, Jan. 18, 1855.

> think of touching a mouthful of bread[.] If I can get it for the children I shall be glad. So I eat poi and pia cakes fried[3] but I am thankful for that. Frankey is a little better today. I made him [illegible] and rose tea and I think it will help him[.] Has a bad cold and it makes his whooping cough worse.[4]

Two days later near Hana, at the small branch at Kauaipapa, Hammond received $6 along with some chickens as contributions toward Keeler's and Allred's journey home. Keeler, who was on the island of Hawai'i, soon heard from Allred that "Brother Hammond was a going round the Island & he would doe what he could for us &c." Hammond was indeed unselfishly raising a collection for the other missionaries: a total of $22.50 that he passed on to Allred.[5]

Green had decided to give the pioneers more free time to work on their own private plots, which they seemed to enjoy more than working on the collective farms. On January 26 he wrote that he had "given them two days in a week to work fer themselves [and] they are very buisey on them days. I think they plant more them two days than they due in the uther fore [four]. I wish thay would plant the vally all over[;] it mat[t]ers not to me what days thay due the planting in [but] only so it is dun and the potatoes are in the ground growing."[6]

The next day the brethren brought Green "fresh meat and chickens and potatoes," but instead of appreciating their generosity he bitterly criticized them. "It is the highth of thare ambition" to lounge and eat what they can. "If thay can git plenty of potatoes and salt and on[c]e in a while a mouthful of meat," he said, "thay are contented and hapy as the king on his th[r]one. Thay live a misrable life in lazyness. Thay are filthy in thare habits." As an example, Green noted that "meny of them when they git a nue [new] shurt thay will put it on and never take it of[f] again till it is worn out. I have a time tr[y]ing to turn th[e]m to work and live more like civilized being[s]

3. Haupia custard was made from coconut milk and arrowroot starch (pia). It would have been nice for dessert but insubstantial as a meal.

4. Mary Jane Hammond journal, Jan. 23, 1855.

5. Keeler journal, Jan. 25, 1855.

6. Green diary, Jan. 26, 1855.

but this is a hard mat[t]er. I have not bin able to make twenty of them due [the] work tha[t] one white man would due in a day."[7] Given these extremely negative attitudes, it is easy to see how crucial it was that Mormons considered the Hawaiians to be part of the House of Israel. What is remarkable, though, is Green's blindness to the fact that he was contributing to a loss of personal incentive through the collectivist structure.

Hammond continued his own criticism of native Mormons, this time directing his thoughts toward the members at Keanae who resisted becoming pioneers. In his mind they were "a picuneish set." The word *picayunish* signified something trivial or cheap.[8] "Yet a few of them are good saints," he marveled,

> and are doing the best they know. I never scolded no set of saints as I did them ... This is a large branch yet their faith is weak and I cannot get as much means [donations] from them as from some small branches of a Dozen members.
>
> When we were done with this matter of collecting money then I called upon some of the officers to go to Lanai. Some few consented to go but many who's faith was weak made many excuses. I had hard work to get them to consent, but finaly suceeded in getting enough ... This is one of the hardest branches in all this conference to labor in.[9]

Hammond, Smith, and Kanakanui left Keanae early in the morning on January 29 and were exhausted by the time they reached Kula at sunset, learning by mail that Lawson had left Moloka'i intending to travel home, which put the Moloka'i conference back under the jurisdiction of the conference presidency. The members in Kula expressed newly formed reservations about Lana'i. "The saints were pos[s]essed of quite a different spirit from what they had when I left them," Hammond disclosed. The reason being that a Wailuku brother named Kauna, who had spent time as a whaler and knew some English, told people he had overheard missionaries in Lahaina say they would harvest the crops in Lana'i, "put the money in their

7. Green diary, Jan. 27, 1855.

8. See *Webster's New Universal Unabridged Dictionary*.

9. Hammond journal, Jan. 27, 1855.

pockets, and put off for home." Hammond could not believe the members would be "so easily led away after the lies and machinations of Satan ... I feel very much cast down in both body and mind; but my strength is in the Lord."

Taking the most committed brethren from the Maui branches to Lana'i no doubt weakened the congregations and made them more susceptible to rumors. Nor did it help that so many Utah elders—especially those on Lana'i—did not speak the language. On January 30 several of the elders met in Wailuku. Hammond and Silas Smith rode in from Kula and Reddick Allred and Joseph F. Smith arrived from the Ulupalakua/Honuaula area, Hammond writing that "Bro. Joseph spoke for the first time in native this morning. He baptized 12 while there." Barely sixteen years old, he had been in the mission only about three months. Hammond arrived in Lahaina on February 1, five days earlier than Mary Jane had expected, and she was overjoyed to see him. He was relieved to find that his family's health had improved.

On that same day, Green had a change of heart about the pioneers. If they were not the most reliable of laborers, he decided, then at least their spirituality and commitment were superior to other people's. "I met with them and I can safely say that I [have] never see[n] a more devoted assembly of people in my life," he gushed. They sat on the floor "spe[a]king or praying ... [and] it seam[e]d that the spirit ran from one to the uther till it went through the whole intire congregation." Green, who would not have understood much that was said, left the meeting when he became tired of sitting, but the natives stayed until after dark.[10]

Hammond went back up to Wailuku to collect $45 for Allred and Keeler, and two days later he was back in Lahaina putting two barrels of roman cement into a whaleboat and taking them to Lana'i for the construction of cisterns that would collect rain water. While there, he asked the pioneers to donate to the two missionaries whose time in the islands was up. In response they "cheerfully gave in some 25 dollars in cash, and some fifty or more in property." Green claimed

10. Green diary, Feb. 1, 1855.

"thare was nearly one hundred dollars subscribed [promised]." Four days after that, Hammond reduced the colonists' work schedule: I "regulated their work days, giving the pioneers 3 days for themselves and 3 for the church out of the week. They seemed highly pleased with the alteration."

Reddin Allred arrived in Honolulu from Kaua'i on February 9 with news that Brother Kauwahi had been found guilty and not only fined fifty dollars but sentenced to six months in prison. Allred thought the judge had "kanived [connived] ... to crush Bro. Kauwahi & distroy his influence, he being a Mormon & also one of the Smartest & most influential natives on the Hawaiian Islands."[11] Reddin's brother, Reddick, boarded the *Ka Moí* for Honolulu with the money Hammond had collected for him and Keeler to return to the continent. When Hammond returned to Kula to check on the state of things, he found the "branch ... in a low state ... Many are binging in drunkness, on sweetpotato Rum."

As the time approached for Mary Jane to deliver her third child, she grew more depressed. She spoke of the gloomy weather. It was "quite rainy," she wrote, "so we could not have [a] meeting in the Lanai [covered porch]," and she disliked having it "in the house ... with the[ir] dirt. I have to put up with a great many things that is trying to the patience but I hope soon to be released from it."[12] This would be the last entry in the journal she had begun keeping the day her second child was born; she stopped right before the third child came into the world. Green noted that the pioneers were gathering timber in the mountains of Lana'i for a house for the Hammonds. Mary Jane believed that it would be cooler there than at Lahaina, after she had her baby.[13]

Even though Woodbury had been told he could leave the mission in April, he was suddenly being pressured to remain because of his mastery of the language. Apostle Pratt communicated, through Woodbury's wife Elvira, the urgency of him staying because the Lord

11. Woodbury diaries, Feb. 9, 1855.

12. Mary Jane Hammond journal, Feb. 11–12, 1855.

13. Green diary, Feb. 12, 1855.

had more work for him to do. From Elder Pratt's perspective, so many of the elders were unexpectedly leaving the mission due to poor health that it was imperative to have a few of the older missionaries remain.[14] Woodbury agreed to linger for another half a year, which must have been difficult for him, especially as he watched third-wave elders leave: the Allreds, Johnson, Karren, Lawson, Tanner, and McBride.

Hammond returned home and worked in his garden and at his shoe bench for ten days while his wife neared childbirth. Despite her approaching date, she was up and "about baking some mince pies &c &c. ... [doing] her own house work." Feeling particularly sorry for her, Frank regretted that "she has had [so] many things to encounter coming to these lands." For a long time he had been pushing the members of the Lahaina branch to construct a meetinghouse, and now that he was preparing to leave, Elder Kaleohano, who was actually from Kula and had been assigned to preside over the Lahaina branch, organized the men to begin getting "materials ready for the meeting house." It was decided to build a structure fifty by twenty feet and to place it in the Hammonds' yard. Frank "concluded ... [to] not sell the yard but to let the Mission keep it and allow me what they are a mind to for it, as they need such a place in Lahaina."

The next day Reddick Allred boarded the *Norfolk* steamer for San Francisco, apparently without giving Keeler his portion of the money. Keeler was once more a no-show, and for some reason Reddin Allred also stayed behind. Keeler had wanted to make it to the harbor in time to sail but was once again stuck "waiting very impatiently for a Craft of some kind to take us a way," again from the northern tip of the island of Hawai'i. When no transportation came, he resigned himself to another few days "living on potatoes," sometimes sweet, sometimes sour.[15]

The church's whaleboat captained by Brother Maiola was about to depart from Lahaina to Lana'i, and Hammond decided he could wait no longer for the birth of the baby and rode across the channel, insisting on steering. The native men on board became the rowers

14. Woodbury diaries, Feb. 19, 1855.

15. Keeler journal, Feb. 26–27, 1855 ("some times sweat and some times Sowered").

when the weather turned rough. It took place at the worst time of day for the Auau Channel. Hammond once again portrayed himself in heroic terms and the others as shrinking violets.

> The boat [was] heavily freighted with irish potatoes, pae kalo, &c &c. [and the] wind [was blowing] from the South West ... We took in sail and pulled hard for a long time ... The sea would roll up and br[e]ake over into the boat so often that it was difficult keeping her free ... [It was] raining sometimes and the clouds [were] as black as night. I never saw them look worse; I had steered the boat from Lahaina and was quite tired by this time but I could not give up the helm for fear the boat would be swamped. So I kept to it and encouraged the crew to pull with all their might, which they did; one old man (pioneer) got frightened and wanted to know if it was not good to return: "e pono paha e hoihoi kakou,"[16] he said. I told him not to be afraid but to pray and we would be preserved. The whole crew were in much fear and consternation, but by the power of God we were preserved and about sun down we landed at Menele. We all felt to praise the God of Jacob who had wrought our salvation this day. I felt very thankful to reach the land in saf[e]ty.[17]

Although Hammond highlights his steering of the ship, the hazards involved in a daytime crossing of the strait were real. If they were blown very far north, the shoreline there was nicknamed Shipwreck Beach because of its reputation for being "particularly hazardous to ships." At that stretch of the channel, Moloka'i and Maui "create a venturi-like funnel that incites the winds to increase in speed, generating churning seas, propelling flotsam, jetsam, and ill-fated vessels onto the reef."[18] The problem for Hammond that day was a kona wind, which at least landed them at Menele Bay and not on Shipwreck Beach, whereas a trade wind would have directed them farther north.

They found that the new cistern had been completed and that "the old one [had been] repaired so that it now appears to be tight." The wheat and corn looked good. The bean harvest was light, due

16. "It is perhaps time for us to return."

17. Hammond journal, Mar. 2, 1855.

18. Black, *Lana'i*, 15–17.

to bad seeds, and the "sweet [potatoes] and Irish potatoes look fine, but very few if any will be ripe in time for this spring season." It rained so hard at Palawai that "the house leaked, and the rain run in till the house mats were all in a perfect muck. Had our fire in the house which smoked us till we were almost ready for bacon." Hammond thought he "could not endure the hardships which I am called to suffer on these lands" except for the "continual flow of the Spirit of God."

The next day he preached to about sixty pioneers[19] and gave the men instructions on "how to look out for their wives and daughters while the ships were in that they go not to Lahaina and follow prostitution, as is the common practice of the femal[e]s of these Islands." "With all of Man's wisdom," he said, the Protestant missionaries had "not been able to put a stop to these old practices of the people." He warned them against planting tobacco and encouraged all who could to "quit using it altogether." Hammond was able to take such a firm stand because Johnson had left the mission.

Hammond returned to Lahaina and wrote to Silas Sanford Smith and Henry Richards, who were on Hawai'i, asking them to "send down all the pioneers that they can find to come and aid in putting in crops now on Lanai, as the proper season has now arrived for planting." Later that day Hammond heard from Woodbury on O'ahu that President Lewis was upset that Hammond was making these kinds of requests for personnel without consulting him. "He said that if you wanted men from the other conferences, aside from the Maui conference, then it was your place to call on Him or tell him your wants, so that will be your proper course." Hammond's reaction was that he was

> a little surprised at this, for I had verily thought that it was my place to call on the different Presidents of the different conferences for their portion of pioneers. This is the way I understood the spirit of our last elders conference, but it appears I have been mistaken and have erred, for I have written from time to time to the different Presidents and

19. See Green diary, Mar. 4, 1855.

> they have accordingly responded to the call and sent pioneers, and I verily thought it was all right.
>
> When Bro. Karren was appointed to that field on Lanai he done the same what time he was there[,] showing that he thought it was right. But I desire to ever be found in the path of my duty, and ever have the prosperity of Zion a[t] heart.[20]

He decided he should speak to the president directly, so the next day he and Silas Smith rode the steamer *Kalama* to Honolulu. Before they left the Lahaina wharf, however, they heard that two schooners were available for sale at $1,800 each, something Hammond decided to discuss with the president. Arriving at the president's house the next morning, they found him "hard at work" in the tin shop despite its having been sold. The president was "glad to see me," Hammond thought, although this may not have been strictly the case. Lewis's account of the visit was that it was all business, at least at first. Hammond "arrived from Maui on business relative to the procuring a vessel for the benifit of the Mission, our having been offered them on advantageous terms. They report the settlement on Lanai in a favorable condition the crops growing finely, and a fair prospect of raising considerable means from the sale of produce ove[r] and above all liabilities, and the native Saints seemed to have great faith in the operation."[21]

The perspective Silas Smith offered was that they discussed schooners in the morning and "in the evening we laid the object of our mission before the president, which met with his approbation."[22] Hammond mentioned that the president complained about having insufficient funds to purchase a ship and thought there would be little inclination on the part of the native members to contribute the necessary funds. "Bro. L. thinks there is a poor show for much money doing here." On another topic, Hammond and Smith found Diana Gaston "well and in good spirits," which pleased him. He also noticed that two Man of War ships were in the harbor, one of which was the US Navy

20. Hammond journal, Mar. 7, 1855.

21. Lewis journal, Mar. 9, 1855.

22. Silas Smith journal, Feb. 8–Mar. 9, 1855.

sloop *Decator* that Hammond had sailed on in 1842. Seeing the ship in the harbor must have brought back vivid memories for him.[23]

He learned that Parley Pratt had summoned George Cannon "to come out and take charge of the press at San Francisco to print the Book of Mormon &c &c., in the native language." Hammond and the president spoke briefly about the leadership confusion on Lana'i, with Frank saying only that things were not "altogether as I had supposed" they would be. "Bro. Lewis felt well towards me," he claimed, even pretending that it had always been so.

On Sunday, Hammond was the featured preacher at the native worship service. He had "a full house of attentive listeners, mostly saints," who heard his report on the Lana'i gathering. Afterward Reddin Allred bore testimony to the importance of the project at Lana'i. He "then took a vote to know if the saints would contribute towards buying a small schooner for the use of the Mission in gathering the people to Lanai," and the vote was "carried unanimously." At an afternoon meeting, Allred asked the congregation to bring their donations to the front. "We receiv[e]d 31 dollars in cash and 34 dollars subscribed [promised] to be paid as soon as obtained[,] making $65.50. This is a much larger sum than we expected to receive." The service was memorable for another reason too, at least for Silas Smith, who reported that he was speaking the language well enough to tentatively venture his first sermon to a native congregation.[24]

Later in the day, the missionaries gathered together to hear a more detailed report and let Hammond advance his argument that a schooner was needed for "carr[y]ing our produce to market, gathering the saints to Lanai, &c." The reaction was positive "and it was agreed that I should go ahead and do all I can to obtain the money from the native saints," he summarized. "All the ... brethren manifested a willingness to do all they possibly can to help the object forward." A similar need had arisen in the Society Islands because the various branches were so far removed, they could only keep in contact if they had a ship. "This was solved," Maria Ellsworth wrote, "by building a

23. For his trip from Rio de Janeiro to Richmond, Virginia, see chapter 1.

24. Silas Smith journal, Mar. 11, 1855.

[schooner] the missionaries christened Ravaai (the Fisherman)." In that instance, Elders Jonathan Crosby, Benjamin Grouard, and Addison Pratt did most of the work. In any case, the ship was launched in the middle of May 1851, with ex-whaler Grouard serving as its captain. When the missionaries were forced to close the mission in 1852, the ship was "sold in order to help pay to transport the missionaries' families to the United States."[25]

There was another surprise that Sunday when two elders, Peck and Snider, arrived at the president's home and reported that they were sick. "Bro. Snider," Hammond wrote, "is bound home as soon as he can make an out-fit. Bro. Lewis has counseled Br. Peck to go to Lanai and see if his health will not improve."[26] If Frank believed or suspected that these elders were feigning illness, he kept these feelings to himself. "I am sorry to see so many of my brethren failing in their health. O my Father wilt thou [hold] back the hand of the destroyer from them that they may have power to fulfil their Missions on these lands[,] even so amen."

The next day Hammond got up early and, at Lewis's request, wrote to the native leaders on the big island for funds for the schooner and "for them to forward all the pioneers they can to Lanai and get them there by the first of April or sooner if practicable." That day, Keeler finally arrived at Lahaina from Hawai'i to find that Reddick Allred had left Honolulu for California three weeks earlier. "I was quite disapointed to hear of his leaving as he had promised to wait for me at Honolulu until I came down therefore my feelings was wrought up conciderable for he had writen to me to come down through his field [on Hawaii] & get what I could & he would goe down through Maui & get what he could there for us."[27] Apparently it had become a game of every elder for himself—or at least, no one could dawdle and expect anyone to wait for him. Again he had been deprived of travel money raised for him.

---

25. Ellsworth, "First Mormon Missionary Women," 37, 43, 45.

26. See also Lewis journal, Mar. 11, 1855.

27. Keeler journal, Mar. 12, 1855.

CHAPTER 32

A Star-Crossed Sloop

Bro. Charles [Baumann] came in to see me this evening & brought me some milk & fish & we spent the evening in agreable conversation & I told him my errand to him from Bro. Lewis concerning his sloop[,] to whitch his feelings with one accord responded[,] & he is going to town [Honolulu] tomorrow & will go & see Bro. Lewis about the matter. His sloop is some 36 feet long, 11 wide & 5½ deep & will soon be ready for running if he can get the sails, riging &c[,] whitch are lacking. He wishes us to assist him ... & then go in partnership with him in the vessel.

—*John Woodbury journal, Apr. 12, 1855*

In a gesture to improve their relationship, Hammond asked President Lewis to give him a priesthood blessing and Lewis then asked him for one in return with "all the brethren assisting." Frank added that they "had a good time together and felt unwilling to part." The blessings, often lasting for hours, had become a standard means for the missionaries to express affection for each other and give encouragement. The president also blessed Silas Smith. Then at 9:00 a.m. on March 14, Hammond and Smith left Honolulu on the *Ka Moi*, the same day the printing press was shipped from Honolulu to San Francisco.[1]

They landed in Lahaina at about midnight, and Frank learned that Mary Jane had closed her school. James Keeler was there visiting on his way to Honolulu. He would leave three days later on the steamer Hammond and Smith had arrived on, although Keeler still lacked the necessary funds to get him to the coast. He had "no faith in

1. Woodbury diaries, Mar. 14, 1855.

waiting any longer for means from the native saints; he has been here a long time," Hammond wrote, "and served faithfully in the ministrey, and I now pray the Lord to give him a safe and speedy passage home." It turned out to be safe, but anything but speedy.

Hammond had other things on his mind at that time. While Brother Maiola delayed in arriving with the supply boat, the California seed potatoes Hammond had procured were rotting on the beach. Green was equally unhappy with how things were progressing. The Hawaiians on Lana'i had "litle or no disposition to work more than to sup[po]rt themselves from hand to mouth," he wrote. "This makes the thing rol[l] rather slow." Green told them he found it unacceptable that they worked only two or three hours a day. "They are a stout able bod[i]ed race of men and have ben brought up in idleness [and] therefore it is hard to make them understand the importance of the benefit that thay would [de]rive from thare labers in so duing."

From a structural standpoint, however, Hammond and Green had enlisted volunteers in a commercial enterprise, the profits of which would go to the church. Nothing would be paid to the workers, who had to come up with their own means of support while they worked. If the point was to create a colony that would exist like any other Hawaiian town, with mostly subsistence farming, they were meeting that standard. If the main objective was to produce funds for Church projects they had no voice in and could not directly profit from, then they either detected the bait-and-switch or saw no reason for urgency.

Hammond was forced to make shoes again to provide for his family's needs in Lahaina. While he was doing so, he asked Silas Smith to tour the island to prepare the members for the April conference. After working at his shoe bench until around 3:00 on March 20, Hammond wandered down to the wharf and found a boat there selling seeds, beans, and wheat from Oregon and potatoes from California, all of which were needed on Lana'i. He committed to the products and had the crew take the cargo and himself to Manele Bay. Even though they left after sundown, they encountered high waves and rain and ended up with some of the produce becoming wet. "It was" Hammond wrote, "so dark we could not see well so we run on to a sharp rock and stove a small hole through the boat, but we all landed safe[,] for which I felt to praise the Lord."

Elder Green was pleased with the food shipment. They wanted to "procure the best ... of every kind of gra[i]n and frutes" for planting, he said, to "obtain the best price[s] in [the] market," again indicating that the farmland was not primarily intended to produce food for the colony.[2] Hammond returned to Maui, and four days later he was in Hana requesting pioneers to work on the Lana'i farm and contributions for the mission sloop. He was surprised to find Elder Snider, who had been given permission to return home to Utah because of his health, "at work now for himself getting good wages. He is resetting a set of sugar pots at Makawao on Wood's plantation." He was able to do hard labor when it came to earning his fare home, but not for missionary work.

Some of the missionaries were experiencing self-doubt and others were going through a momentary crisis of faith. Joseph Peck arrived at the Hammonds' home with a note from one of the missionaries in O'ahu, John Caine, asking Hammond to look after Peck because he was "not very strong in the faith, and needs some one to be a Father to him and counsel him and strengthen him up." Like other missionaries who had their eye on a return ticket home, Peck complained that his health was not good, but after Hammond observed him for a day he concluded that the young man was well enough to begin working. Choosing to be optimistic regarding him, Frank wrote that he was "desirous of doing right and to fulfill his miss[ion] here on these lands with honour to himself and the great cause which he espoused." That diagnosis turned out to be too optimistic.

When Captain Maiola finally appeared with the supply boat on March 26, he was carrying several pioneers who were returning to Maui so they could take care of personal business at their homes in Kula and Wailuku. Hammond was unhappy with this development and felt that they were shrinking their responsibilities. "It is

2. Green diary, Mar. 22, 1855.

a hard matter to keep them from trav[e]ling about. They are like children[;] a very small triff[l]ing thing will cause them to up and leave their work for weeks, whereas if they would remain at their work they would earn more by far than the thing is worth for which they leave."

Hammond himself was staying close to home because the birth of their third son was imminent. On March 30 he called in two midwives, Kahimiholo and Maluihi. "About 12 o'clock [mid]night … I had a beautiful little Son born unto me," he wrote with pride. "There was only about 2 or 3 hard pains preceeding the birth, but a great many little ones. I think one cause of it was [Mary Jane] has never allowed herself to ware [wear] tight dresses while she was pregnant. I laid hands on her and blessed her about dark and prophecied upon her head that she should have a good time and safe delivery. The child weighed 6 lbs, a very round and favor[e]d boy, healthy and strong[,] for which I feel to praise my Heavenly Father." He added that he got "no sleep during the night" and that the midwives, despite their help with the birth, "know but very little about civilize[d] manners." He sent them home. They decided to name their child Fletcher Bartlett after two of Frank's uncles, John Fletcher and Sandford Bartlett Hammond. He sagely added that, since he was responsible for the housework that day, he was reminded that "a woman's work taking care of a large family is great," going so far as to hope he would always "appreciate a woman's labors and not expect to[o] much from them."

He was unable to attend the pre-April conference meetings due to Mary Jane's condition, writing that "the housekeeping [still] falls upon me." He heard from Green that the pioneers were leaving the island to attend the church conference, leaving "the work … far behind." He asked Hammond to visit Palawai after the conference to see if he could instill some discipline, and for "Mary Jane to come over as soon as wisdom will permit of it." The reason Green wanted Mary Jane there, he confided to his diary, was because she was such a good cook, seamstress, and housekeeper. "Sister H[ammond] will soon be he[re] to keep our hous[e] and prepare our food," he hoped, even though he knew he might be "making too much calculation on the cumfert that we shall take in this change of our situation."[3] Frank, on the other hand, assumed that when they settled down on Lana'i, his wife would do less work and rest. Hammond was having interesting dreams at the time, where he was enjoying the perks of being "chosen Captain of a Ship" who could "select my officers," a fantasy firmly fixed in his psyche from his whaling days.

Soon he left Lahaina for the April conference at Wailuku, and unlike the last one, this time there were quite a few Utah elders present, although none of them could speak the language very effectively. The initial speakers were Hammond and three leading native elders, Hawaii, Kaleohano, and Napela. Hammond was pleased with how "Bro. Silas Smith dismissed the meeting in native," showing himself to be "progressing in the language." He would "soon be able to take hold of the work in good earnest," Hammond predicted. There was not yet an outpouring of the spirit on the first day of the conference, he observed. He and two others stayed that night at Brother Keilihune's house in the Iao Valley and were "treat[ed] ... first rate."

At the session the next morning, April 6, there were representatives from forty-two branches. Hammond presided over an English-speaking meeting at the Napela home in between sessions, where he gave assignments to Utah and native missionaries. Washington Rogers, despite his paranoid feelings regarding the members there, was sent back to Kaupo, accompanied by Napela. Hammond assigned a Brother Poo to go to Moloka'i to preside there.

As the conference came to a close on April 8, Hammond called on Joseph F. Smith to address the large native congregation, and he marveled that the young missionary "spoke ... by the spirit[,] causing the saints to rejoice exceedingly. He has only been here six months," and "the Lord has been with him in getting hold of the language. He spoke very feelingly and I was rejoiced much to hear his voice in the native language, for I have [had] no assistance except native[s] since last July, and now as the brethren begin to speak the language and take hold of the work it makes me rejoice." It had been a difficult period

3. Green diary, Apr. 4, 1855.

Joseph Fielding Smith

Courtesy Daughters of Utah Pioneers.

for the young Smith orphan, given that he was fifteen years old and had not even yet received mail from home. When he later heard from a cousin, apostle George A. Smith—after six months in the mission—it lifted his spirits. In reply, he wrote that "it was the first Letter that I had resieved from the valleys of the mountains. You must exkuse all the mistakes. As you well know, I am a new beginner."[4]

After Joseph's address, Hammond spoke for more than an hour about "the gathering out from Babulon," portraying himself in his diary in much the same way as when he crossed the channel, his performance at the speaker's stand being equally heroic: a divinely influenced communication leaving the congregation in rapture. "I never had more of the spirit on that subject," he said about this occasion. "The whole assembly (and a crowded house we had) set as if they were chained fast[,] so filled were they with the spirit of the Lord and a desire to hear his word. My mind was enlight[e]ned and [I] had clear and extended views of the nature of the fall of the Great Whore of all the earth, Babulon ... [The] saints were greatly blessed,

4. Kenney, "Before the Beard," 25. It is unfortunate that Joseph F. Smith's journal for the early part of his mission was destroyed in a fire at Palawai in early June 1856, while he was working on the big island. See Ricks, *My Candid Opinion*.

many wept for joy[,] and their countanances shined with the spirit of the Lord. I shall long remember the feeling I enjoyed during that short hour." The native elders who followed him spoke with "great spirit and good effect" too, he wrote. It must have been an inspiring session for those in attendance.

Hammond returned to Lahaina to find a letter from President Lewis informing him that the ship the mission was buying a share of was "about ready to be launched," having been completed by Brother Charles Baumann, a German who was offering half interest in it for an advance of $400. Hammond responded enthusiastically, and Woodbury, who had been to the northeast shore of O'ahu to see the sloop, wrote excitedly about the investment.[5] Although Hammond would later observe that Baumann was "neither a carpenter nor a sailor," at this juncture he was pleased with the development.

On April 16, Hammond visited Sheriff P. H. Treadway and discussed Mormonism with him. "Mr. Treadway made Mrs. Hammond a present of a bottle of <u>Port</u> wine," Frank wrote. "I pray the Lord to reward him for all his kindness unto us." The next morning Frank found himself "feeling quite unwell. I drank a glass of wine last night, and I believe that to be the cause of it. I rested very poorly during the night." It is unknown whether Mary Jane indulged as well.

Three days later Hammond received a letter from John Winchester describing the boat, and Hammond expressed satisfaction with it, as described, and the terms of purchase. "She is valued, when complete, at 1600 dollars, and Bro. Baumann will sell one half of her to the Mission for 800 dollars, 400 down and the balance when the Craft shall earn it," Winchester had explained. With an advance of $400 for parts, Bauman could have the ship ready within six weeks. Based upon what he had been told, Hammond thought "that this is [by] far the best offer that we have yet had" and that "the hand of the Lord [must be] in it."

Winchester's assurance that the sloop would be seaworthy probably indicated how unfamiliar Winchester was with the finer points

5. Lewis journal, Apr. 11, 1855.

of ship construction, though he evidently had been an aboard-ship carpenter. Lewis apparently accepted Baumann's own appraisal uncritically that the finished ship would be worth $1600. When Hammond finally saw the ship, he was surprised to find how glaring the ship's defects were. About this time Lewis's long-standing reservations about Hammond again surfaced. The president complained about Hammond not having sent elders to Hawai'i, for instance, although Lewis's letter suggesting this arrived too late for Hammond to act on it at the conference. Lewis wrote that he "order[ed] [Hammond] to send ...all the money given in for the vessel forthwith and to collect the balance subscribed for that purpose as soon as possible."[6]

John Caine transcribed a letter for Hammond that had arrived from Brigham Young suggesting that the missionaries should "be wise ... in teaching those poor natives" the path "back to rectitude" and to do so gently "by precept and example." Caine included his own note asking Hammond what he thought of the ship, but Hammond could not adequately judge its merits, having never seen it. He was in the process of moving his family across the Auau Channel to Lana'i, though he was doing so at the worst possible time of day, perhaps because Mary Jane would have been fearful of making the voyage at night.

> Mrs. Hammond done a large washing and packed up her things all ready to get into the boat by ½ 10 o'clock [A].M. At which time we set sail for Lanai with 3 boats well loaded with our furniture &c. &c. We were b[l]est with a good passage and landed at Manele about 5 o'clock P.M. Bro. Evans,[7] Mrs. H[ammond], and the children were all sea sick. We found a good share of the pioneers and Kamaainas [locals] on the beach waiting to assist us up the mountain with our baggage. Bros. Keolanui and Leiula had their horses ready for me and Mrs. H[ammond]. I took F[rancis] A. Jr. and S[amuel] S. on my horse and, Bro. Leiula took little Fletcher B. in his arms and thus we commenced our ascent up to the settlement[,] about 3 miles distance. We arrived without any accident at our new home about dark. Bros. Green and

6. Lewis journal, Apr. 21, 1855.

7. This was the sailor Hammond had converted at the Lahaina hospital.

> [David] Rice[8] were glad to see us ... We all feel very tired. The children and Mrs. H. enjoy the bracing air here very much.[9]

It did not take long, however, to wonder about the wisdom of the move. The next day Hammond noticed that "the children feel rather poorly. I think the climate is the cause of it, as it is quite cool here. The trade winds brake [break] over here strong."

8. Rice was helping Green with the farming operation.

9. Hammond journal, Apr. 23, 1855.

CHAPTER 33

Hammond Takes Charge

[I] addressed the saints on the law of tithing and consecration. I was filled to overflowing with the spirit. Bro. Keelepulu made some objections to the principles of uniting our labors in temporal matters, on the ground that there would be some lazy ones, and in consequence thereof the industrious ones would be kept back &c &c. I explained to him how the Lord desired us to do in all things, [and] he was satisfide. A few of the elders spoke and all upheld the doctrin[e] which I taught.

—*Hammond journal, May 5, 1855*

Brother Poo recruited eight pioneers on Moloka'i, and they arrived at the gathering place on Lana'i on April 28 as the first pioneers from their island. At about two o'clock the next morning, Edgerton Snider and Joseph Peck arrived. Snider had been working on a plantation at Makawao, and Hammond had talked him into helping with the Lana'i farming operation. Peck had apparently come for his health. Hammond was getting his family settled and taking care of administrative duties. He called six native missionaries from Lana'i on missions, in keeping with President Lewis's complaint that the big island was understaffed, making them the first missionaries ever called from Lana'i to other islands. In another action—that was seldom mentioned but probably common—he called two native women on missions to wash and iron the elders' clothing. Being spared this activity, Mary Jane was able to get some rest after childbirth, in anticipation of their journey to Utah. While this was happening on Lana'i, missionaries and foreign members on O'ahu were busy that same week inspecting the ship the mission was considering buying.[1]

Hammond was disappointed to learn that the Utah missionaries were not attending church meetings regularly, probably because they could not understand enough of the native language for it to be profitable for them. Hammond immediately took over supervision of the farming operation, shuttling aside Green and ignoring the assignment Green was given to manage the temporal affairs of the colony. Furthermore, although Hammond was backed up in this by some of the overly zealous pioneers, the collectivist directives he implemented contributed to the demise of the entire project. "Bros. Kailihune, Kaleohano, Pelio &c. said they were ready to commence living up to the law of consecration," Hammond wrote. He "taught the[m] many things on that subject, and told them to be car[e]ful how they enter into that doctrin[e], for it requires strong faith to abide it &c. &c." Those who wanted to cooperate with Hammond agreed to labor the entire week for the church, undergo rebaptism, observe a fast, and at the following Sabbath meeting take the sacrament in a new covenant of commitment.

Hammond received letters that week from George Q. Cannon, Silas Smith, and Philip Lewis, Cannon saying he might return to the mission with his family before he started setting up the printing press in San Francisco. Silas Smith wrote of "an excit[e]ment in Lahaina on account of Bros. Snider & Peck getting drunk there before they" left. "I am sorry to hear such reports of the elders of this church," Hammond noted. "May they speedily repent." In the mission president's letter, Lewis repeated his chastisement of Hammond for not having sent missionaries to Hawai'i, something Hammond again refused to take responsibility for since the president had not given him direction prior to the conference.

Hammond's effort to attract more pioneers to Lana'i was bearing fruit as the church's two boats, captained by Leiula and Maiola, brought twenty new pioneers across the channel on May 4. However,

1. Lewis journal, Apr. 29, 1855.

at an early morning meeting the next day, people criticized the collectivism Hammond was still trying to implement as part of his millennialist utopia. Hammond responded by saying they needed to repent and be rebaptized. And so it was: "After Breakfast Bro. Green and I accompanied all the native saints to the sea, where they were all rebaptised and confermed and reordained." In Utah the so-called Mormon Reformation was underway at this time, where similar acts of communitarianism and recommitment were underway after the smallest aspects of each church member's life was scrutinized by the bishops, so this was not entirely Hammond's own innovation.[2]

There was resistance in both Utah and Hawaii. "I had hard work to make some of them understand" that the Law of Consecration required that "their time only is to be devoted to the church[,] [not their wealth]," he documented himself having said, apparently now willing to compromise to make the system more palatable. He said that "Bro. Keelepulu was very stub[b]orn and set in his way to resist the doctrin[e]," but that it did not matter because "more than two thirds of the saints voted for it." He "administer[e]d the sacrament to near 200 saints. Many of the [native] brethren spoke in behalf of uniting in their labors to obtain out fits for the mountains of [Utah]," something Hammond seemed in harmony with. Although the majority of the pioneers said they were willing to go along with Hammond's vision for the island, by his own count sixty or more people had held out, in accord with Brother Keelepulu. It was a significant enough number of dissatisfied workers that it posed a threat to Hammond's leadership and "the gathering."

The next day, Hammond was heavily involved in the farm work; in the evening he "held meeting" until 10:00 p.m., organizing farmers into squads of ten each with a captain in charge of each unit. An eleventh person was attached to each group as a cook rather than a farm worker. "I had a good time in teaching them how to act in their respective tens," Hammond declared. He admitted there was "opposition from Ke[e]lepulu and a brother from Molokai, but all served to teach and instruct the saints in things pertaining to their duty."

2. See Peterson, "Mormon Reformation."

At about the same time on O'ahu, "Bro. Baumann came in to make arrangements to purchase the necessary articles to finish our vessel," Lewis wrote to Hammond. The money Hammond had "collected on Maui" was not yet at hand, so Lewis had to make a partial advance of "$60 to purchase su[ch] things as [Baumann] needed at this time."[3] Hammond, in fact, intended to collect more donations on Maui and had not found the time.

Hammond continued to face resistance to his communal imposition, writing:

> I spoke at some length on the principles of uniting in temporal things, being organized into tens and eat together and act as families and eat with knives & forks, &c &c. I answer[e]d some questions that a brother from Molokai and Kakalaau from Oahu asked. I was blessed very much with the spirit of the Lord, and I never felt the need of it more in all my life. I find that the devil is here and he is striving with all his power to block the work and keep us from organizing the people so as to instruct them according to the principles of righteousness. [Brother] Keelepulu is [i]n the back ground. [He] did not attend meeting. I fear he will fall unless he humbles himself and repents of his stubor[n]ness. I have a load now to bear off that takes my whole time to [do], and that too striving with all my might to do this people good, but I am grieved at the hardness of their hearts, and how slow they are to understand the ways of the Lord. They must certainly be the decendants of Israel, for they act just as [the Israelites] use[d] to.[4]

Although Hammond was passionately committed to the gathering of the Hawaiian Saints to "Zion 2," he could not resist encouraging some of the more zealous brethren to gather to "Zion 1," or Utah, as intimated above. On May 9 he "called on all those who desired to go with me home to commenceing getting ready and listen constantly to my advice. Many seemed to rejoice in this. I told them to give in their names to Bro. Kaleihano[,] all who desired to go," he wrote. In reality, though, opposition to his collectivist program was increasing and had

3. Lewis journal, May 7, 1855. The president was already calling the ship "our vessel."
4. Hammond journal, May 8, 1855.

spread beyond Lana'i. He called the workers together and "taught them the advantages of uniting together &c. [and] called on those who wished to work for themselves the balance of the week [it was Thursday] to manifest it." Apparently most people were reluctant to challenge Hammond directly, because "Bro. Hakalaau from Oahu was the only one present who voted for it, and one other Br. went with him." Even so, Hammond had heard that "Bro. Makahamahau and Co. ... wrote a letter to Honaaula [Maui] telling the saints to not come here[,] for if the[y] did they would be pilikia (in trouble)[,] [or] so I have understood."

That day Hammond "had a little talk with Bros. Snider and Peck about their conduct in Lahaina. They did not manifest so much humility as I would like to see, but they are good boys and I desire to see them do well," he concluded. The next day "Bro's. Snider and Peck set out for Lahaina about sun rise on their way to Honolulu. Bro. Peck is on his way home on account of ill health." Snider was also leaning in that direction.

Then Hammond received a shocking letter from Lewis, telling him he had gone too far with his collectivism on Lana'i. "Pres. Lewis counsels to teach the natives the law of tithing and not to take but one tenth of their time. This is in answer to mine [Hammond's letter] concerning consecration of their time &c, but as I did but write a few words on it I fear he has misunderstood me." The truth is that the president understood clearly what Hammond was doing and had overruled him.[5]

Probably too embarrassed to acknowledge this new protocol, Hammond essentially told the pioneers that the amount of time they would devote to the church's plots was up to them. In response, as he recorded on May 13, "Makahanohana and company from [Maui] wo[r]k[ed] two days for the church, [the] Oahu company 3 days out of the week. The [Lana'i] residents work[ed] 2 days, but the majority are willing to devote their whole time to the church." He wrote to Lewis, trying to explain and perhaps justify what he had asked of the

5. See also Lewis journal, May 10, 1855.

pioneers. While waiting for a response, he began applying the brakes to the ones who wanted to continue to offer six-day commitments, telling them they should give "half the time only for the church." How confusing it must have been for the native workers to hear him promote what he had said a week ago was heresy. He neglected to disclose the source of this new directive, nor that what Brother Keelepulu and other disgruntled soldiers in the army of pioneers had said was now the gospel truth. In allowing a 50 percent commitment, Hammond was still ignoring President Lewis's insistence on a 10 percent offering and putting off making—or perhaps hoping not to have to make—a confession about having been overly demanding.

On May 17 at Honolulu, Keeler did something remarkable and, one could argue, foolish: "This morning at ten o clock a.m. Bro. Joseph A. Peck left and went on bo[a]rd a vessel bound for California. I loaned Bro. Snider fifty dollars for Joseph A. Peck to pay his passage home."[6] The $50 could have paid for Keeler's own passage home, and surely he, rather than Peck, had earned the right to leave. Lewis wrote that "Bro Jos[eph] Peck sailed for San francisco on his way to the Valley on account of ill health. [I] sent [with him] to Bro [Parley P.] Pratt the manuscript of the Book of Mormon." How interesting to trust the immature elder, who had thus far proven unreliable, with such a valuable manuscript. Silas Smith's view of the situation was that "during the time [Peck was] in the islands his health was poor. He seemed to have no desire to obtain the native language[,] consequently he learned but a few words during the time he remained on the islands." Lewis mentioned that on the same day as Peck's departure, the president "wrote to B[r]o[ther] Hammond giving counsel &c &c &c.," meaning in regard to the Law of Consecration.

Many of the pioneers were losing confidence in the gathering on Lana'i. As they became disaffected, they spread their dissatisfaction to their home villages. Two of the men, Kalaelo and Keluli, asked to be released from their callings because, they said, they were too weak in the faith to continue. If so, they were not alone. "This is a place to

6. Keeler journal, May 17, 1855.

sift the saints," Hammond smugly concluded. He could not yet see his utopian commune as the problem. He was upset to learn from the president's letter that Snider and Peck—probably angry at Hammond for his criticism of their behavior at Lahaina—had bad-mouthed Lana'i. They reported that "the natives are not getting enough to eat and that very little produce will be raised for market this season." Lewis thought that, in light of this, Hammond "had better return to Maui and collect all the money" he could for the ship. That remained "paramount to every other object at present," he emphasized.

It was true that the pioneers were short on food, Hammond wrote in his diary, but not any more so than in Maui, "for I hear that food is very scarce there." The reality was that food was scarce on Maui in the villages where Mormons were sending food to Lana'i. As far as Hammond was concerned, the pioneers had "generaly manifested a good spirit and feel happy and contented." He disregarded the president's request to immediately return to Maui and instead asked the pioneers if they would return home and raise money for the ship and bring it to him. He wrote to President Lewis about Peck's and Snider's "conduct at Lahaina, how they got drunk &c., according to Bro. Silas's letter to me,"[7] perhaps getting even after their negative assessment of the Lana'i operation.

In a bind because of Lewis's directive to limit labor to a tithe (10 percent of their time), Hammond had to rein in the more zealous pioneers, such as Kailihune and Pelio, when they argued so forcefully against the less ardent brethren that they hurt their feelings. A growing number of pioneers was thinking about returning home, if only temporarily. When Hammond heard from President Lewis again, the letter contained another directive to go immediately to Maui and not put off any longer the raising of funds which were so badly needed. Giving in to the widespread desire of the pioneers to return to their native villages, Hammond called on them to go home and "return [to Lana'i] when called upon." He probably imagined he could thereby

7. There were allegations of more serious infractions that Hammond kept to himself, which will be discussed later.

put pioneers in place to help raise some money, weed out the less committed volunteers, start over on new terms at a later date, and avoid losing face. On May 29 he recorded a dream in which he was "trying to lead a jackass along, but had great difficulty in doing it," partly because of "all [the] old dry trees" along the bank of the stream he was following until "a mighty torrent of water rose up out of the ground and swept ... all [the] trash away and a very few little green trees were [all that was] left."

As he condemned the pioneers who had wanted to leave Lana'i, Hammond forgot that he had coaxed many of them to work for only about one month, to help get the spring crops planted. Now that it had been done, the temporary laborers were anxious to return home. What could he do to stop this migration? He decided to join them and cross the channel to Lahaina, thereby at least fulfilling the president's request to raise money. What he found among the native members was a surprising degree of enthusiasm for raising money for the mission sloop.[8]

In his May 1855 station report, the Rev. Dwight Baldwin made some interesting observations concerning these various activities.

> For many reasons, the Mormons can never make much advance, with their peculiar system, unless they can form an independent community by themselves. Their customs run counter to the laws of every Christian nation, & therefore, in order to carry out their principles, they must have a secluded spot or independent location, in whi[ic]h they can manage both ch[urc]h & state. There is no doubt, that they have searched for such a place on these islands. Whether they have pitched upon the spot I cannot say; but numbers of their priests have been over to Lanai, & they have hired a land there, of one of the chiefs [Haalalea]. A few foreigners & perhaps natives have gone to live there; they have planted Irish potatoes wh[ic]h the <u>peelua</u> [worm] has eaten up. I know not, that they have built even a grass hut; but they have begun to talk about the City of Joseph in the valley of Ephraim.[9]

Hammond began touring Maui, preaching first to the Wailuku

8. Green diary, May 30, 1855.
9. "Report of Lahaina Station," May 1855.

branch on June 3. Unyielding in his version of the narrative of what had transpired on Lana'i, he told the congregation that "Bro's. Kaelepulu and Hoopiiaina [had] repented of their conduct on Lanai in opposing the o[r]der which I desired to organise there that was to unite in the work." He omitted the part about retreating from a stricter order than the mission president had allowed. Instead, he said that as far as he could tell the mission work "generaly on all the islands is in a cold state as far as I can learn," and in fact he was right about that.

When he returned to Lahaina two days later, he was worried about the food situation at Palawai where his family still resided. He soon had two ominous dreams that

> tend to show me that there is trouble ahead for the church on these lands, and I feel to pray God my Heavenly Father that he will guide our little "bark" safely over all contending billows. I never knew the church in so cold a state as it is at the present. From all qua[r]ters the news comes in of the coldness of the saints and their great indifference towards attending meetings, and also of contributing ... their means for the return of [the] elders[,] purchasing of the vessel &c &c. A very little money having been obtained in the other conferences, the most of it has been raised in this [Maui] conference, oweing no doubt to the saints having had more teaching here than on the other Islands.
>
> In view of this I feel pained to see the old elders all leaving the field so fast, for it keeps the Mission continualy weakened, ... for alth'o we have many native edlers [elders] yet I am sorry to say that there is only a very few inde[e]d of them who ar[e] worthy to be entrusted with the watch care of branches, hence the great need of foreign elders in their midts. Had all the old elders, who obtained the language, remained until now I am satisfide that it would have been far better for the Church.[10]

Hammond recognized that the lack of native-speaking Utah elders was part of the problem, but he did not see that the incessant fundraising, the reluctance of the natives to leave their ancestral

10. Hammond journal, June 8, 1855.

island and village, his insistence on radical collectivism on Lana'i, and the heavy burden on Maui branches to feed the pioneers there were factors that contributed to what he considered to be the general decline of the mission.

CHAPTER 34

The Faltering Lanai Experiment

> *Gave out corn and wheat to the pioneers. They are pilikia [troubled] indeed while they are cro[p]ping [farming]. I have burst into tears many a time while looking at them, knowing how much they are suffering for the Gospel sake. It sometimes appears as if the Devil would get the advantage and we not be suffer[e]d to plant a stake of Zion here.*
>
> —*Hammond journal, June 16, 1855*

Silas Smith wrote in his journal at Wailuku on June 2, 1855, that Hammond "wished me to repair immediately to Lanai and superintend the affairs of that place. I accordingly made the necessary preparations and on the 5th of June I went to Lahaina and on my arrival ... I found a company of Saints from [the island of] Hawaii; they were on their way to Lanai." The next day was Smith's birthday, and it was memorable. Crossing the channel at the worst time of day through choppy waters, he squeezed into a whaleboat with twenty-two natives and an abundance of furniture, writing that it was "crowded ... uncomfortable and ... unpleasant."[1] Blown off course to the north, they had to climb over the mountain to reach Palawai. They arrived exhausted at about 6:00 p.m.

Four days later Smith witnessed a hearing held by Hammond to try Elder M. K. Hawaii for his membership due to adultery. Hawaii was an important native leader whom Hammond had previously described as being one of the church's best orators. Being charged with

1. Silas Smith journal, June 2–6, 1855. Unfortunately, his journal ends on June 13.

"the sin of adultry" was by now a more-or-less routine disciplinary action, but in this case Hammond called for a public confession and indication of contrition, the accused having initially denied the charge. Even though it was decided to withdraw Hawaii's membership, he was predictably "forgiven and restored to fellowship" in the same meeting with the same kind of favoritism the other leading elders (Kauwahi, Napela, and Uaua, etc.) had received.

Hammond spoke of the need to keep watch on Maui when the farmers returned home, to "stren[g]then up the branches and strive to counteract an[y] bad influence that may arise from some disaffected ones returning from Lanai and circulating evil reports." He appointed Jonathan Napela and George Raymond to the task and asked Joseph F. Smith and H. K. Kaleohano to assist them. The four left for Lahaina the same day in a supply boat carrying seeds from the recent wheat harvest to sell on Maui. Hammond was determined to make a commercial success of the Lana'i farming operation and was using: volunteer native labor; food to feed the volunteers/pioneers donated mainly by the branches on Maui; superior seeds and roots; and markets principally at Lahaina. He was initially unwilling to allow the Lana'i pioneers and their families access to the produce they themselves were growing, except to the extent that the food they produced ended up for sale at their local markets in Wailuku and elsewhere. This exploitation, disguised as utopian communalism, undermined the spirit of the gathering.

Unable to delay any longer, Hammond too crossed the channel to Lahaina a day later to fundraise for the mission's sailing ship. He concluded his effort by giving $195 to a Captain King to deliver to Lewis in Honolulu. Then he returned to Lana'i on one of the supply boats (the next day the boat traveled back to Lahaina with "a good lot of green corn to sell"). Yet the food situation was dire enough on Lana'i that Hammond was forced to allow the pioneers to dip into the produce they had farmed, which was otherwise intended for sale.[2]

On O'ahu, John Woodbury learned from President Lewis,

2. See epigraph at the beginning of this chapter.

who had heard from Brigham Young and Parley Pratt, that George Cannon had been appointed to superintend the printing press in California and that Pratt would return to Utah the next month. The elders who had left the islands recently with alleged health issues had all seemingly improved when they arrived on the coast. Elders Johnson and Karren were already only a few days from Salt Lake City; Reddick Allred and Tanner had already arrived. Progress was being made on the mission sailing vessel. Lewis agreed to advance Bauman another $93 on the promise that Baumann would deliver the ship in three weeks.[3]

Hammond pitched in and worked alongside the farmers on Lana'i for a few days, then left again on June 22 for a tour of the Maui branches. This time he was "glad to have an opportunity to leave Lanai, for I do not enjoy myself here." He was depressed, he confided, his "spirits ... bound and I feel that it is not on the account of the native brethren." He worried about what would become of the church farm after he left and about his relationship with Ephraim Green, which had deteriorated due to the ambiguous authority structure on the island. Mary Jane was unhappy to see him leave and was similarly "depressed." She felt "very much like returning home." She was one of the few women at Palawai, and it was hard for her to relax after having taught school, hosted dignitaries, and assisted the missionaries as she had done for most of her mission. On Lana'i she could not even raise money toward the family's return to Utah.

That Sunday morning, just as the Lahaina native branch meeting was commencing, Hammond was "surprised to see the Elders from Hawaii make their appearance," looking forlorn and "nearly out of close [clothes]," as Green explained. They had decided to travel to Maui to work for a month to pay for more clothing, prior to the church conference scheduled to be held on Lana'i.[4] In the afternoon, Hammond conducted a worship service at the hospital and baptized Charles Atkins, a well-educated Irish patient who had lived

3. Lewis journal, June 20, 1855.

4. Green diary, June 25, 1855. There were eight foreign missionaries (Bell, King, Linn, Pack, Richards, Silas S. Smith, Spiers, and West) and several native elders.

in America. In the evening he preached again at the native meeting, followed by the missionaries from Hawai'i. Hammond found, to his delight, that the elders were making "good progress in the language. They all can talk some."

On Tuesday, Hammond saw the Napelas in Wailuku. After "taking some refreshment" at their house, "we persued our way up the [Iao] Valley to Br. Kailehume's" at about 10:00 p.m. and "took a good cool bath in the stream and felt much refreshed." They were now staying with the Kailehumes when in the area instead of the Napelas, perhaps because, as Hammond wrote in his journal:

> Bro. Joseph [F. Smith] tells me that Bro. Napela was drunk and whoreing while he was at Oahu a short time ago. Br. Joseph had a dream to this effect, and he told it to Napela[,] [who] acknowledge[d] directly that it was too true, for he had indeed fallen again into transgression. I am pained and grieved to the heart to hear this, for this is the 4th [fifth] time he has been found in the like, and I fear much he will never overcome this passion of his for women and wine, alth'o he is a good man naturaly[,] and was he away from the [bad] influences which surrounds him he would be a good and exemplary man.[5]

Hammond took three destitute elders (Bell, Pack, and Spiers) to Makawao and introduced them to a merchant named Townsend, who agreed to employee them, as he was already employing Snider to help him raise enough money for his trip home. After getting drunk with Joseph Peck in Lana'i, Snider had "lost the spirit of his mission," as Hammond put it, and Hammond sought him out with a message from the mission president to attend the conference so he could be tried for his membership. He "consented and said he would be there," although he probably had little intention of doing so. Bell said that when the time came, they left him behind "under pretexts that he could not leave his work to go to conference."[6]

In Kula, Hammond found that the members were struggling under the burden of the gathering on Lana'i, and the returning pioneers had

5. Hammond journal, June 27, 1855.

6. Bell diaries, July 15, 1855.

not given stellar reports of the progress at Palawai. "Had a hard time in dealing with those who have lately returned from Lanai on account of the stories which they have reported since they returned here," Hammond wrote. He instructed them at length, telling them not to find "fault with the officers." Eventually "they got up and repented of their wrong," and on a more salutary note "Bro. Joseph [F. Smith] spoke a little while" and was "improving very fast in the native language," Hammond was pleased to discover. Members also donated an additional $3.75 for the mission ship. This surprised him, Hammond said, because "Kula had always been slack about contributing of their means." It is a curious comment in light of his previous adulation because of their generosity. The more committed Kula brethren had gone to Lana'i as pioneers, and those who remained probably were less so, and they had come to resent the constant demands for money and food for Lana'i.

There was more bad news from the other islands. Brother Poo had been to Moloka'i and said "the saints are not very strong over there since the return of those last Pioneers. They were the cause of some confusion in regard to Lanai." A despondent Hammond offered a poignant prayer: "Oh my Father forsake me not. Leave me not to myself but gently guide by the light of thy Holy Spirit into all truth. Help me to constantly keep in mind my covenants which I have made before thee. Deliver me from the spirit of apostacy, from ambition or a desire to become some great one in thy Kingdom, but help me to be as a little child, passive at all times in thy hands, filled with charity for my brethren and preferring them before myself at all times." Two days later at Wailuku he

> spoke a few moments upon the subject of gathering &c. &c. Then called upon all those who had sinned to confess and repent of the same[,] as we were about to partake of the Sacrament. One sister confessed and repented of the sin of adult[e]ry, one brother for getting drunk on beer, one for Striking a man who at[t]empted to Strike him in a quarrel. Bro. J H Napela repented before the Church of his have [having] been drunk and Whoreing also; they were all sever[e]ly chastized and taught on these different subjects, after which they were forgiven. I feel that the spirit of the Lord does not

> [strive] with the saints as much as it did. I fear there is many of them living in transgression.[7]

The remedy, he harshly concluded, was for God to "put forth thy hand and assist thy servants to prune thy vineyard on these lands."

He returned to Lana'i on July 12 and discovered, to his pleasure, that the pioneers had "worked on the road two days, and it is so improved that the Cart can now go quite comfortable up and down to the beach." Four days later, the time for conference approaching, William Cluff and Edward Partridge arrived after a particularly "rough time" sailing over in a whaleboat. Conditions were such that they had had to throw supplies overboard to prevent the boat from sinking.[8] On the evening of July 18 nine more Utah elders arrived at Manele Bay after an eight hour passage across the channel. King and West crossed the channel from Waihee-Waihee on the north side of Maui the next day, along with thirty passengers. It was a "rough passage." They were joined by native saints who were traveling to the conference from Maui.

The following evening Hammond held a meeting for white elders only, in preparation for the "special conference" for native leaders that began around noon the next day. He was confirmed as conference president and spoke for about an hour, followed by Cluff, Joseph F. Smith, and three native elders. About 4:00 p.m., President Lewis and the Honolulu elders arrived after a difficult climb up from the beach over the northeastern mountains. It was the first time Lewis had set foot on the island, and he did not intend to stay long.[9]

7. Hammond journal, July 8, 1855.

8. Green diaries, July 16, 1855.

9. Lewis journal, July 19, 1855. Henry Bigler "arrived in Salt Lake City" that same day, almost a year since he had left Honolulu. His father, who was there to meet him, had grown older, "his voice ha[ving] changed," and his family had moved to Farmington. "I went home with Father[,] where we arrived at sundown and [I was] made welcome by all ... I have been absent five years nine months and eleven days," he wrote. See Bigler, "Extracts from Missionary Experiences," July 20, 1855.

CHAPTER 35

The 1855 Conference

The native brethren had a poor time in their meetings to day. They went to work and organised a conference and draftend out some resulutions to present to our [white] conference. They all agreed to petition us to not send any of them on missions for one year. 3 of the brethren, [Kaleoo]kailihune, Kimo Pelio, and [Elder] Pahile, said they would do as the Lord should direct through his [Utah] servants. For this independence of theirs the [native] conference thought best that they [Kailihune, Pelio, and Pahile] should be cut off from the church. They entertained false spirits and had a most disagreeable time.

—*Hammond journal, July 23, 1855*

Hammond spent the evening of July 21 in Palawai talking with President Lewis. The next morning, at the Sunday worship service, Hammond gave "a few introductory remarks and then called upon the Presidents of the different branches for their representations." His summary indicated that things were stagnant. "The work has not increased as regards numbers since last Apr[il] Conference," he summarized. At the afternoon meeting, he was followed by Jonathan Napela and then Joseph F. Smith, the sixteen-year-old future church president who continued to impress his seniors. For instance, John Woodbury was "astonished at the fluency with which [Joseph F.] Spoke in the Native language[;] the Natives say he will soon be as good as George Cannon in the language."[1]

As usual, the Utah elders met prior to the native conference to make important decisions, although this time they excluded the

1. Woodbury diaries, July 22, 1855.

native missionaries so they could proceed uninterrupted in English. They began with a Sunday evening prayer meeting, described by Woodbury as one in which "the Spirit of prophesy rested upon those who Spoke." Early the next morning, Allred, Hammond, Kaleohano, and Woodbury spoke to the native Mormons "upon temporal subjects." Then, as Woodbury put it, a meeting "appointed for the native saints [took place] while the [Utah] elders of the mission wer[e] in council, to consult the business of the conference [for the general membership] which is to commence on the morrow."

President Lewis took charge of the business meeting, in which he made a surprise announcement that he intended to return home; he was resigning from office "in favor of Bro. Silas Smith" as mission president. "We then set off the elders to their dif[f]erent fields," Green wrote, and "counseled concerning what business we should want to bring before the [native] conference."[2] While this was going on, the native leaders in their conference, reacting indignantly to the division by race, suggested that they should no longer let the foreign elders determine everything for them (see above epigraph). Hammond reacted badly to the news of this short-lived revolt, as did Woodbury, who thought the spirit of independence manifested in the native brethren was evidence that they had "lost the Spirit of the Lord. I mention this to Shew how they are like children & if left to themselves will soon run astray ... They Kneed to be watched over ... & led along in the Straight & narrow way," he believed.[3]

To the contrary, it was the Americans' paternalism that had angered the Hawaiians in the first place. Oblivious to this, Hammond "rose early" the next "morning and opened our native conference" with a scolding. "I told them they were all to blame for the course they took yesterday," which he found misguided and a sure way to lose "the spirit of God." He berated them so severely Woodbury called it a verbal "whipping." The remarks were probably counter-productive in the end, in that they resulted in more bad reports to home branches about how things were proceeding on Lana'i.

2. Green diary, July 22, 1855.

3. Woodbury diaries, July 23, 1855.

One of the items of business in the whites-only meeting had been the suggestion that "the hand of fellowship [be] withdrawn from E[lder] Snider for unchristian-like conduct."[4] Reddin Allred described this trial and provided important detail.

> Bro. Kaluau was called in as a witness: He said, Bros. Snider and J[oseph] A. Peck came into Lahaina with a man that did not belong to the church, and put up at a house near by his place, [and] at the house where they put up, ther[e] was some women living, that was noted for looseness of character. He [Kaluau] ... went and tried to prevail on [the elders] to go home with him, but they would not—said that he did not see them drink, but he knew that they were drunk—Snider was the drunkest. Sister Kahinuholo was then called on to give her testimony. She testified ... that they or Snider in particular was very familiar with the women ... and when she spoke to him (Snider) about being drunk, he swore and said that he did not care, and told her to clear out.[5]

Peck was found guilty of the same offense, but since he had already left for Utah, no action was taken aside from sending a letter to the First Presidency about his behavior.[6] It seems it was not the consumption of alcohol that was the major offense, but his sexual transgression and failure to appear at the trial. If he had appeared and asked for forgiveness, it is possible he would have been treated the same as the native leadership, although Utah elders were no doubt held to a higher standard.

At a morning meeting of the English-speaking missionaries on July 24, Lewis nominated Silas Smith to succeed him as mission president. After Smith was unanimously sustained, he presented for consideration John T. Caine and Silas Sanford Smith as his counselors. They received unanimous approval, although both Smiths were only minimally proficient in the language and Caine could not speak it at all. Of course, with second-wave elders about to return home

4. This was written upside down at the top of the next journal page. Actually Hammond got the date wrong, noting that it was July 23, when this trial really occurred the next day.

5. Reddin A. Allred journal, July 24, 1855.

6. Green diary, July 24, 1855.

and fourth-wave missionaries already gone (other than the young Joseph F. Smith), there were not many alternatives. The presidency proceeded to make assignments to other leadership positions in the conferences throughout the islands.[7] Of particular interest to Hammond was that Joseph F. Smith would replace him in charge of the Maui conference. The youngster was being given an assignment that today would be equivalent to serving as a stake president and mission zone leader both at the same time.

In addition to that surprising announcement, "Bro[ther]s Lewis, Woodbury, R[eddin] A. Allred, Linn, Green, and I were released to return home as soon as we can obtain our out fits," Hammond wrote, adding that he did not see "the prospect for my out fit home [as being] very flattering at present." He felt sadness as he gave his thoughts on preparing to leave and the problematic state of affairs on the islands. "Here ended my labors of 4 years upon these lands[,] and how well I have performed the duties assigned me I will leave for others to decide," he began, owning his "many weeknesses" and particular "incompetency to fill the station to which I was called by the Spirit of the Lord." Despite his faults, however, he felt he had done his best with "the little wisdom which my Heavenly Father had given to me." He believed the new presidency would succeed and that the "degraded children of Jacob shall be redeemed from all their ingnorance and superstition and corruption, and be exalted with all the children of Israel in the presence of their God."[8]

At the native meeting the next morning, Hammond became emotional in referring to his pending departure. "I spoke on the present prospects of the old Elders soon leaving here for Zion as we have all been released from our labors as missionaries upon these lands. I was overcome in my feelings and I wept like a child before the saints, who were all filled with sorrow and also shed tears of pure affection and manifested deep feelings toward me. I never witnessed a more melting time." That evening there was another mission meeting, this one to decide the future of Lana'i. They voted to keep the

7. Woodbury diaries, July 24, 1855.

8. Lewis journal, July 24, 1855..

property if they could and appointed Hammond "a commitee of one to wait on [Levi] Haalelea and try and secure the land through lease or otherwise." This action contradicted the ambiguity that existed, with relatively few of the native brethren staying there and its future uncertain. According to Woodbury they addressed that in their meeting, including what the official stand should be in relation to the pioneers who had left—or even toward those who had stayed.[9] It was decided "that all the native brethren who have arrived here from the different Islands and cannot support themselves" should in fact return home "and seek their own food until they shall be called upon by the Presidency to return." This would "only leave some 15 of the old pioneers" at Palawai who "have some food in the ground by which they can be sustained."

Lewis reported on Charles Baumann's progress with the ship, which would be "left in the hands of the [new] Presidency to make such farther arrangements as they see proper." Hammond made a motion that the mission should establish a school at Lana'i and teach English to the children. John Caine seconded the measure and suggested Ward Pack as headmaster.[10] Someone—probably Hammond—proposed that a few native brethren be allowed to go to Utah rather than stay on Lana'i. When a few families were told to "gather together means for their out-fits for Zion," the news "was received with aclimations of joy," Hammond wrote.[11]

Ephraim Green said the assignments were actually made by Brigham Young, but if that were the case, it would contradict Young's directive to establish an outpost in the islands themselves, at least for now. Despite Hammond's report of how happy the chosen families were, he wrote on September 7 of trying to persuade a reluctant Jonathan Napela to get "ready to gather up to Zion, as I have heard that he was not so much in favor of it." Hammond also received a letter

---

9. Woodbury diaries, July 25, 1855. See also Green diary, July 25, 1855.

10. No action was taken after the meeting. In fact the same idea was advanced again a year later by Elder Kaleohano as if it were a new idea. Spurrier, "Kaleohano", 294.

11. H. K. Kaleohano, Hosea Kauwahi, Elder Keolanui, Jonathan Napela, and George Raymond.

from Brother Keolanui stating that he too could not leave, that he was "willing to go home with us but his wife is not."

At the native meeting on July 26, Hammond made an emotional appeal for funds to help him get his large family home. "I never had my feelings so wrought up betwixt grief and joy as they has been since I received and made known my release from my labors on these lands as a missionar[y]. The saints manifest a deep feeling of lasting respect towards me and my family," he was pleased to find. Although no money was forthcoming, "Bro Kimo Pelio gave in a Cow towards my return."

Later that morning the Utah elders met with native members about the ongoing question of "how much of the time of the pioneers who shall remain at the gathering place shall be devoted to the Church. After discussing the question at some length, hearing also the mind of the native brethren (who were present) on the subject[,] it was resolved that two days out of each week should be the time that all shall work for the church[,] and they [otherwise] support themselves all the time. This shall remain until there is a plenty of food, and the gathering place permanantly established." This meant that for the present, the pioneers would continue to support themselves and not expect to be fed from the produce they grew on church plots, nor would they share in the profits derived from the sale of the crops.

The next afternoon saw missionaries and foreign members segregated once again into separate meetings for white foreigners and native people, the latter presided over by Napela. At the meeting of English-speaking foreigners,

> the old elders were called upon to speak their feelings. Bro. Lewis, Allred, Green, & Woodbury spoke with much feeling. Bro. Woodbury spoke in tongues. I [Hammond] had the interpretation, but I fear I quenched the Spirit and was not able to give the whole of it. The Lord made known unto us his will and mind concerning his work upon these lands. Words of consolation and comfort were made known unto Pres. Lewis and those who have been associated with him upon these lands, [and] also to the present president, Bro. S[ilas] Smith[,] instructing the elders to uphold and sustain the head

> at all times. I also spoke some of my feelings, but I did not feel that liberty which I could desire.[12]

After this whites-only session adjourned, three of the Utah elders spoke at the native meeting to convey to the native members what had been decided regarding mission business. Hammond gave what he characterized as "a short farewell address, in which I felt a deep and abiding interest in the salvation of this people." That evening the Utahns huddled together on their own for a hurried blessing meeting. Hammond bid the departing missionaries "a reluctant farewell" and regretted that his "spirits [were] cramped down from some cause or other." The weather was "unfavorable," so the departing missionaries slept in one of the whaleboats that night and crossed to Lahaina in the morning. By the next day, they were on their way to Honolulu on a schooner and arrived there on July 31.[13]

Back in Palawai, Hammond could not shake his depression, which was felt by others as well. The English-language sessions continued to be held in tandem with the native conference sessions. At the Tuesday-morning English meeting, Hammond was one of the speakers.

> I said I had been cast down in my feelings during our conference. What the cause was I did not know, but [I] felt an unaccountable depression. The brethren all one by one testifide to the same things. All had felt similar feelings. Adjourned for one hour.
>
> Met again according to adjournment. Time employed in searching to find out the cause of our all feeling so heavy and so little interest manifest in our conference affairs. It was finaly thought that the cause originated in [the departed missionaries] being in too great a hurry to get through with the [conference] business.[14]

Leading the unseemly hasty departure was President Lewis, who left Hammond and the new presidency to prepare the conference report and implement decisions.[15] He announced his resignation his

12. Hammond journal, July 26, 1855.
13. Lewis journal, July 26, 1855. See also Green diary, July 29–31, 1855.
14. Hammond journal, July 31, 1855.
15. Lewis journal, July 26, 1855.

first full day on the island, then left in the middle of the conference. Add to that the strange new policy of segregating the natives from the foreigners, and no wonder the remaining missionaries were left feeling disoriented and unhappy.

CHAPTER 36

Struggling to Get Fitted Out

The principle of the word of Wisdom was then discussed at great length. Quite a strong feeling seemed to prevail [in] the minds of the brethren to observe it, but to not pass any vote on it. I was surprised to learn that so many of the new brethren [from Utah] were in the habit of using tobacco. The majority of the eighteen have used it more or less ever since they left their homes. I spoke my feelings on the subject pretty freely. They were in favor of observi[n]g it strictly while on these lands as missionaries.

—*Hammond journal, July 28, 1855*

At the final conference session for the foreign elders the morning of July 28, one of the subjects discussed was tobacco use, as Hammond's comment above demonstrates. Smoking was seen as something to avoid but not yet as a moral issue, in contrast to the way the LDS Church views it now as a gauge of one's faith. In fact, one of the elders using tobacco at this time was future church president Joseph F. Smith.[1]

That afternoon Hammond went back to working the land with the remaining pioneers, threshing and grinding wheat, and the next morning met with the white members while the native Saints again met separately in a session presided over by "half-white" elder George Raymond. Hammond pointedly explained "some of the difficulties [the members] would necessarily encounter under their new organization, and exhorted them one and all to strictly obey the Word of Wisdom." After that, Silas Smith spoke, bore testimony, and according to Hammond told people that "he was prepared to enter into it

1. See Kenney, "Before the Beard."

and he took from his pocket what tobacco he had and throwed it on the table," then "exhorted the brethren one and all to do the same. They all followed his example to a man," Hammond wrote, "which caused me to rejoice exceedingly. I do attach great importance to the word of wisdom." The problem with Hammond's zealousness on this occasion was that he had, in essence, called out the new mission president, which may have created the same kind of bad feelings he had struggled to shake in his interactions with the previous president. He had worked with Silas for months, would have known of his tobacco use, and did not want the mission president to be a tobacco user.

That afternoon Hammond met with the native saints to bid them farewell. "I was so filled [with emotion] I could not retain my feelings," he recorded about the moment he bore testimony of his belief in Mormonism. He then begged for help for his "family in our return to Zion," saying it was important to give support to "the true servants of God." In response, "they gave in quite liberally of their substance ... a cow, ... a horse, ... turkey[s], chicken &c &c." Native leaders such as Jonathan Napela, Kaleohano, and George Raymond bore testimony of the impact of Hammond's labors among the people. "These things gave me great joy," Hammond wrote. "All [of us] seemed to be filled with heaviness at the thought of parting."

Before leaving, he needed to revise and condense the conference minutes and help set apart the missionaries for their new assignments. After the missionaries "blest my wife and family," he reminded them to "always maintain their dignity before the native saints, and all men, for just in proportion to the amount of respect you pay to yourselves just so will the world and the saints respect you." He endorsed the separation of members by language because they could teach people so much more in their own tongue than in "a mixed congregation on Sundays and other days." He had not yet decided how "to obtain my out-fit for home," and he had other unfinished business on his itinerary. He wanted to inspect the Baumann sloop and possibly sail it for a few months. He requested that the elders "pray much for me while I go to see Haalelea on the business of securing the land of Palawai for the gathering of the native Saints."

Most of the missionaries left for their fields of labor, but Hammond lingered for a few days before crossing over to Maui with John Caine, Silas Smith, and Orson Whitney to board the *Ka Moi* for Honolulu. Just before they sailed, Hammond noted that "about 3 o'clock p.m. the ship [*Ka Moi*] came in from Kahului [Maui] bound for Honolulu," and "E. Snider was on board. He came on board and accompanied Br. Caine and I up to the house." They would have told him he had been disfellowshipped, and about sundown that night he sailed for Honolulu on the *Ka Moi* with Hammond, Silas Smith, Caine, and Whitney. If they had sailed a day or two earlier, they would have been able to traverse O'ahu to the east side in time to witness the ceremonial launching of the *Lanai*, as the mission was christening the ship. Woodbury attended and found "quite a crowd of people assembled" to watch as "she slided off into the water stream" at Kahana Bay at 2:30 on August 8. Actually, the men in the crowd had to "assist in pushing her off. They laboured under some disadvantages[,] not haveing mashinary &c.[,] as [found] at docks where Ships are built," but soon enough they prevailed and were pleased to see the sloop afloat, steadied by ropes. Everyone then sat down to a feast.[2]

Hammond's priority was to meet with Levi Haalelea and his agent William Harper Pease about the land on Lana'i. To that end, he met with these men at the Lewis house, where Lewis was still making preparations to leave but was not yet quite ready to go. In two days Woodbury arrived to report on the launching of the *Lanai*. Although she did not yet have masts ("launched but not spar[r]ed. Now waiting to have some blacksmithing done"), she looked seaworthy. On August 13, Hammond had another meeting with Haalelea, this time at his office. It "did not go well," he summarized. He found the Hawaiian suddenly "offish" and not inclined to "treat us with that courtisey that he has heretofore. I fear we will not be able to do much with him; I believe he is influenced by his Agent, Mr. Pease, and he is no friend of ours." Hammond must have assumed Haalelea had not been briefed about the uncertain state of the colony and that his reserve was strategic.

2. Woodbury diaries, Aug. 8, 1855.

With the negotiations ongoing, life went on for the other missionaries. Woodbury set sail for San Francisco on the schooner *Willimantic*'s $50 fare, evidently having been more successful raising donations on O'ahu than Allred, Green, and Keeler had been in earning money for their tickets as carpenters. He was accompanied by a group of Australian converts. Lewis blessed him, assisted by Allred and Hammond, after which Woodbury "shook hands with Bro. Lewis & others who I did not expect to See again." As he carried his luggage onboard, he was accompanied by "a goodly number of the Saints" who walked with him. He was touched by this gesture of friendship. "I had been labouring upon these lands & now I was bid[d]ing them fare well, once more to return to my family & to the bosom of the church," he wrote from his berth.[3] On the wharf, as Hammond watched the ship disappear, he felt "aloan as the old brethren are now all gone except Bro. Lewis[,] and he expects to go in about 2 months." He failed to mention that James Keeler was still trying to find a way to get home.

Hammond and Caine went to see Pease one more time on August 14 and learned he had done nothing since they last talked to him. During the delay, Hammond thought about checking on the progress on the mission sloop. "Took a walk with brother Caine to look for some horses among the brethren to ride to Koulau to see the vessel, which I understand is launched," he noted. They were unable to secure the horses immediately, so Caine and Smith inexplicably—without the experienced mariner Hammond—went to "make such arrangements as wisdom may dictate with regard to … [the] command" of the sloop. Caine returned to Honolulu a few days later but offered "no flattering news of [Hammond] run[n]ing the vessel." Since Hammond had indicated earlier in his journal that he wanted to "sail the sloop for a few months" in order to make money for his family's return to Utah, he surely would have mentioned this to Caine and others, and it appears that Baumann initially insisted on piloting it.

As days stretched into weeks, Caine and Hammond received a

3. Ibid., Aug. 13.

proposal from Pease they considered unacceptable and made a counter-offer. Toward the end of August Haalelea responded that he would allow them to lease his land for fifteen years beginning in January 1856, and that, as Hammond explained, it would cost the mission next to nothing, only "175 dollars per year, [although] all the improvements [would] go with the land when the lease expires." Hammond made a quick calculation and realized that "there is enough taxes collected from tenants to pay one hundred dollars per year." He translated the document into Hawaiian and made a copy for Pease. The Americans then visited Prince Lot. According to Hammond, they "had a very plesant interview" and the prince "expressed himself very favorably disposed towards us and our opperations on Lanai." He said the government would collaborate with funds for an English-language school if they would like. "Said he would use his influence in favor of our having the marriage license granted unto us again" as well.

A few days later Hammond and Smith were in Lahaina, having sailed back on the *Ka Moi*, and found that the "talk about town is that we have about given up our operations on Lanai." There was a good "deal of gossip ... abroad concerning it." This was of particular concern to Hammond because he had made arrangements to purchase seeds and shoots from merchants, who had promised to help market the resulting products. Of course, it was true that the colony was floundering, so there was not much the two missionaries could say to stem the tide of rumor.

Keeler was finally ready to leave the mission. He, Reddin Allred, and Ephraim Green secured passage from Honolulu to San Francisco for $25 each, which was less than what Keeler had been cheated out of more than once in his attempts to get home. Lewis had planned on joining them but was sick the day they left the harbor on August 30.[4] Meanwhile, Hammond and Silas Smith returned to Lana'i so the Hammonds could begin "getting ready to move back to Lahaina" for their final preparations. On the following Sunday, believing it to be "the last time I shall meet with the saints on Lana'i for a season," Hammond

4. Keeler journal, Aug. 28, 30, 1855. See also Green, same date. On September 2, Lewis wrote that he had been "confined the past week by sickness."

gave a "farewell address and bennidection." He "spoke a few words to the officers, then to [the] members, then to the wives and husbands, and then to [the] children.[5] It was a very ple[a]sant time, a time long to be remember[e]d by me and many saints. They all felt as though their father was about to leave them, so they expressed themselves."

The Hammonds "took an affectionate farewell" the next morning and "set out for the beach" on horses, assisted by natives who transported their belongings to Manele Bay by cart. The party set sail at the midday hour. As a result, the journey lasted nine hours. "Our boat leaked bad," Frank wrote, and the children became seasick. Eventually even Frank succumbed. "I finaly got sick" too, he admitted. That "made it very bad for us all, but I kept about and managed to make myself useful." They were glad to make it home safely and to be able to get "some supper ready and [have] a good bath and [be] ready for bed by 11 o'clock."

A week later Hammond was caught off guard when he received a nasty letter from the mission president on Lana'i accusing him of having stolen mission kitchenware. One wonders if the real source of his ire was the fact that Hammond recently embarrassed him in front of the other missionaries concerning his tobacco use. Hammond carefully explained the issue and his position relative to it.

> He [Silas Smith] finds fault with me for bring some tin pans away [from Lana'i] which Bro. Lewis gave to me, some that he had made and sent up before conference, but as the Mission did not seem willing to allow him anything for them he told me to take them and dispose of them if I was a mind to[,] to aid me in getting away home. Also told me to take the big coffee Mill too. Bro. Silas talks rather hard about it and throws out some insinuations which are ca[l]culated to hurt and wound my feelings; I am sorry that he does not understand me nor my motives no better; He [talks] ... as though I had now lost all interest in the Mission since I was released. Also says that Bro. Lewis had no right to transfer those things to me, any more than ... to go [into] the

5. This is one of the few (if any) times when Hammond mentions the presence of native children in these meetings. They were noticed by the Utah missionaries even less than the native sisters.

> Taber[na]cle] and take the sacrament plates and convert them to private use, conveying almost the idea that we had robbed the house of the Lord of a doz[en] Tin plates.
>
> I however do not feel very much conscience smitten about it, for the Miss[ion] is at the least some $100 or more dollars in our debt now for things furnished for the farm at Palawai, and a good share of it money taken from Mary Jane's School money; had we not taken this course but converted all our means to our own use we could now have had means sufficient to take us to SanBarnardino. So I feel a little hurt to be treated so after doing all we could to advance the cause of the Mission ... May the Lord aid me ... to do right at all times, and be kept from the snares of Satan.[6]

Hammond apparently, mistakenly, believed that if he devoted his time to completing negotiations with the Hawaiian officials, the mission would help him and his family with the financial aide they needed for their return to Utah. He now knew that this would not be the case, despite the fact that he had raised money to help other elders return home and for the mission projects such as the printing press, the sloop, and the farm. The immediate effect of Smith's chastisement was that Hammond was unable to sleep well. "The letter I received from Bro. Silas Smith troubled me a good deal. I dreamed about it nearly all night." He responded by letter the next day, and about two weeks later he indignantly "sent a lot of tin pans" back to Lana'i.

He was spending most of his time now laboring at his shoe bench. When he heard from Caine at Honolulu on September 14 that, although the terms of the contract with Haalelea had been agreed to, the Hawaiian had not signed the lease, he responded negatively. "I don't know as I care much if he nev[e]r does," he wrote with exasperation, Haalelea's generosity looking more like a ruse every day. Hammond wondered if they had obtained "any great barg[a]in" at all since "the Government are [equally] willing to sell or lease us lands."

Hammond took advantage of an opportunity to raise additional funds when a church member, Albion Burnham, asked if his pregnant

6. Hammond journal, Sept. 8, 1855.

wife, Mary, could stay with the Hammonds through her delivery. Albion needed to continue working near Honolulu and promised to pay room and board for his wife. "May the Lord prosper him in all his labors to obtain means for our journey home," Hammond wrote with approval in his diary. This turned out to be a financial liability rather than a windfall.

When Allred, Green, and Keeler reached San Francisco on September 16, they learned from Elvira Woodbury that Jane Lewis had recently died.[7] That evening her husband received that same news by letter. "This sad event was not unexpected by me as I had anticipated it from dreams and other manifestations of the spirit," Philip Lewis noted the next day. He nevertheless felt "sad and lonely having no bosom companion nor even a child to solace me in the hour of affliction, but her pure spirit is at rest from all its suffering and I am resigned to the will of Heaven." While getting ready to leave for San Francisco, Lewis wrote a quick note to Hammond informing him of Jane's death. A few days later he added that he was "packing my things and collecting my debts ready for departure."[8] This was the former mission president's last entry in his journal.[9]

Lewis' parting letter gave rise to deep sympathy from Hammond concerning the man who had been a onetime nemesis:

> I feel to sympathize with Bro. Lewis in his berev[e]ment. He will return home sad and lonely[;] no wife or little one to cheer him while he winds his way homeward. He left [Utah] with a wife and one fine little boy. He buried his boy at Los Angelos, and now his wife has been snatched from him just as his Miss[ion] was filled on these lands and [he was] about to join her and seek again the society of the saints in Zion. May the Lord bless and console him in this his day of adversity.[10]

---

7. Keeler journal, Sept. 16, 1855. They had sailed on the *Connecticut Yankee*.

8. Lewis journal, Sept. 16–17, 22, 24, 1855.

9. See *Life History of Philip Bessom Lewis*. He reached San Bernardino in mid-November and arrived in Salt Lake City in the spring of 1856. The next year he married Mary Scott; they moved to St. George and then Kanab, Utah. When she died in 1875, Philip married Emily Lewis (no relation). He died at Kanab on November 13, 1877, at the age of seventy.

10. Hammond journal, Sept. 28, 1855.

"How widely different my lot has been thus far since I left my mountain home," Hammond realized. He had been "blessed with health and an increase of two fine boys to my family, and [we] are all alive and well." Mary Jane opened her school once again on October 8, without as much enthusiasm as previously but happy to be earning money for their return to Utah. Frank marveled at his wife's talents. "She teaches school, cooks, makes shirts, and does her own washing," he enumerated.

He was reminded of other benefits that awaited them in the United States when on October 23 he received a letter from his Long Island family. They enclosed "a lock of silvery hair from the head of my dear old Father, who is now 64 years old. He sent me an account of my Fore-Fathers on both sides as far back as he could gain any information. Grand Mother Terry is still alive. Mary C. has lost her little boy." Mary Caroline was Frank's older sister, born in 1821. Despite the sad news and the reminder that he had not seen them in years, "I was very happy to hear again from my parents and friends. They all greatly desire to see me. Father does not like the doctrine of 'plurality' [of wives]. Still he does not oppose me in my new faith (as he calls it). They have built a new house [in Patchogue] on the site of the old one."

Five days later when Frank wrote back, he took the occasion to defend polygamy. His father had influenced him more than any other person in matters of religion, and he was determined to convert him to Mormonism on his return home.

CHAPTER 37

Sailing the Lanai

Wind from the South & West all night and we appear[ed] to be sailing fast through the water, and we flattered ourselves that we would be up to Hana by daylight or before, but Judge of our surprise and second disappointment when we discover[e]d ourselves to be only up to where ... our Rudder [had become detached]. After toiling hard all night at our oars, all our hands blister[e]d, and we felt more dead than alive ... we held on beating until noon, [but] ... could not steer her (so as to keep the sails full), so we ... c[a]me to anchor about dark. I believe we were as nigh used up as men can well be and live th[r]ough it. I Know the hand of the Lord was near us or we should have never reached Port.

—*Hammond journal, Dec. 12, 1855*

Hammond was anxious to see what could be done with the *Lanai*, the mission sloop he had heard so much about but had not seen. On October 23 "Bro. Kaleo arrived from Oahu and stated that the Sloop sailed a few days ago with Bro. [John] Caine on board for Lahaina, but had to put back on account of head winds. She sailed again for here on yester-day." The next morning "the Sloop 'Lanai[,]' Cap[tain] Bauman[n][,] [and a hired crew] arrived from Honolulu." Hammond also "received a letter from Bro. Caine asking me to advise and counsel with Bro. Bauman in regard to how the Sloop shall be employed, &c. &c. That is in case Bro. Silas Smith should not be here." Hammond must have had mixed feelings as he went to examine the ship. In his diary he proclaimed it to be "as uggly looking as anything I ever saw afloat."

On the other hand, Baumann "has done well considering he is neither a sailor nor carpenter," he granted. In fact, Baumann had been "most indefatigable in his labor. Has been some 3 years in building her. He built he[r] of timber from the Oahu Mountains. He had little or nothing to commence with and labored under many disadvantages, and is deserving of much credit for his enterprising spirit." Hammond estimated that the ship had a 21-ton displacement, making it the size of a small yacht.[1]

Hammond "tried to get employment for the Sloop from the merchants, but their arrangements were all made for the season. So I counseled with Bro. S[ilas] S. Smith[,] and as Bro. Bauman desired it we thought it would be well for me to go with him to [Kalepolepo] and Kula and assist in obtaining a load of potatoes on credit from the saints." First, however, he suggested a test run there and back. Kalepolepo is on the east shore of Maalaea Bay near present-day Kihei. Seeing her handle, his well-informed judgment was that "the Lanai sails well, but is very crank. Needs a deal of balace [ballast]." In nautical terms, a crank ship was unstable, "liable to lurch" and even capsize.

The return trip to Kalepolepo was successful, and at about midnight on October 25, the *Lanai* set sail with 239 barrels of potatoes, reaching Lahaina as the sun came up. Hammond made an unsuccessful attempt to sell the potatoes. He then stayed behind, due to feeling unwell, as Baumann continued on to Honolulu. Since Hammond had been formally released from his mission in late July, he was surprised to receive a letter from President Silas Smith on October 30, delivered by Elders King and Pack, requesting that he take charge of the sloop. He wrote a reflective entry in his diary:

> This is my birth day. I am 33 years old to day. 8 years next month since I obeyed the Gospel, 4 years last August since I landed here as a Missionary, [and] 12 years last June since I left my Father's house on a whaling voyage ... [On the] 16th of this month I will have been married 7 years. We have now three boys, the oldest 5 years old and the youngest 6 months old ... Mrs. Hammond is as busy as she can be with her school, taking in sewing, cooking for 9 [who are] steady in the family besides comers and goers. She works too hard, but the idea of going home keeps up her faith and strength. She has earned 26

1. For comparison, the *Santa María* was 108 tons, *HMS Bounty* 220, and *HMS Beagle* 235.

dollars with her needle since we left Lanai. Her ambition is too great for her strength.[2]

A few days later, Frank observed that he had "felt more the spirit of going home to day and yesterday than at any time heretofore. I do hope we may be able to get away in January next." They wanted to arrive in Utah in the spring so they could plant crops and harvest them for the subsequent winter, but leaving in January was contingent upon whether "we can raise money enough to pay our passage." He was engaged in sorting through his papers and deciding what to pack. He had "recieved some 800 letters, most of them Island correspondence, some 200 of them in the native language." It indicated how important he had been in the mission communication network.[3] While he recuperated from his illness and packed, Mary Burnham gave birth to a son on November 7.

Six days later Baumann arrived back from Honolulu, "willing that I should sail the vessel" instead of him, "but I don't know what to do about it. I desire to do right in all things." Sensing that Baumann had met his match in trying to handle the little sloop, Hammond went on board and sailed her back to Kalepolepo, where he ran into the three Elder Smiths—mission president Silas, Silas Sanford, and Joseph F. After "a short conference it was concluded that I should sail the Sloop for the time being." Later that night Hammond and the crew, including Baumann, departed for Kaupo on the southern coast of East Maui. The fact that Hammond had delayed accepting the offer to be the captain indicates he knew he was taking a risk and delaying his departure from the mission. It was a badly constructed ship and the worst time of the year, the winter season being when the islands are battered by strong southwesterly Kona winds.

Sailing counterclockwise around East Maui on the morning of November 16, they "beat all day against a heavy sea and wind, all night continued the same." Early the next morning they "anchored

2. Hammond journal, Nov. 1, 1855.

3. Some forty years later in the Four Corners area, he wrote in his journal that he had been "reading and sorting over old letters and burning up a great lot" (Bluff, Utah, Nov. 22, 1894)—disheartening news to historians and archivists.

at Wailua" and "lay all day here, a heavy sea rolling in so that we could not get off any potatoes. A miserable harbor this. About midnight we got under way and stood out to sea, intending to beat up to Hana, if we could, heavy wind and sea with a strong current against us all night."

They never made it to Hana, and it was not until the afternoon of November 18 that they were able to anchor only off Kipahulu, where there was "a tolerable good harbor ... but no good landing place. I went on shore and walked about 3 miles to Bro. [Kalaeaula's], where I remained all night. The saints were much rejoiced to see me again." After breakfast the next morning he returned to the *Lanai* and "lay here all day waiting for the natives to dig their potatoes."

On November 21 Hammond and crew finished loading "about 30 barrels of sweet potatoes and a few barrels of corn," and "about 1 o'clock p.m. we left Kipahulu and returned to Manuu. Had a gale of wind from the East. Lay all night at Manuu waiting for passengers." The next morning "about 10 o'clock A.M. we left Manuu and sailed with a heavy wind and sea to Honuaulu." Hammond "went on shore and met with the brethren" in the local branch. "Bro. Kekaula [went] up to the potatoes reigon [Kula,] early in the morning [to] have potatoes brought down for us."

Two days later they "took in about 50 barrels of Irish potatoes" and at "Sundown set sail for Lahaina," arriving about sunrise the next morning. Hammond "spent the day in run[n]ing round town looking up freight &c. About Sundown we sailed for Honolulu. Had a very plesant passage down." Pleasant passages would not be the rule, sailing the *Lanai*.

Landing at Honolulu on Sunday, November 25, he "went up and met with the native saints" and at 3:00 p.m. "preached to the foreign saints." Two days later, having sold all their cargo, they "commenced to get ready for sea" and "discharged all the old crew except one man." Hammond noted that it "took near all our means to pay expenses." Then they had considerable trouble getting out of the harbor on November 29. "Took in some Salt Lumber and fish. Got ready to sail and found our Rudder unhung, unshipped it[,] repaired it[,] and shipped it again and got underway, at dark. Run ashore on the edge of the channel; pulled her off and was blessed in getting out of the harbor." The *Lanai* was hard to maneuver in the first place, and the rudder problem was a bad omen.

Baumann stayed at Honolulu and David Rice took his place on board. "He is going [on] a trip or two with me. He is poor again, having lost over a hundred dollars by Bro. Winchester, who run away with Diana Gaston last Monday week." Winchester and Gaston had boarded a ship for New London, Connecticut, with a Captain Kiblin. "Winchester had conducted himself very improperly for some time back, had taken to drinking very hard &c &c," which made Hammond think "the wheat is being sifted, while the chaff is blowing away." Winchester had abandoned his half-native wife, Louisa, and Diana Gaston was presumably still married to Judson Gaston, who had nevertheless left her for California. Many of Hammond's converts were not panning out well.

When the *Lanai* reached Lahaina on December 2, brothers Pelio and Keolanui were waiting to come aboard. They had volunteered to help without pay, treating it "as though they were on a Mission." With their assistance, the crew sailed from Honolulu to Honuaula, where they obtained some oil and other provisions. They then tried once more to sail for Kipahulu, but the winds were too strong and the sea so out of control that they were once again forced "to put back, and anchor ... near Honuaula."

They tried again the next day. Comically, they left some passengers on shore who decided to walk rather than to take their chances with the ship. In addition to the other problems, "most of my help have been sea sick," Hammond moaned, "and it has mad[e] it very hard on me." They loaded forty-five barrels of potatoes at Honuaula, then sailed for Lahaina, arriving on December 7, where they "discharged our cargo on board [a] French Ship, bought an anchor & chain and got ready for sea by dark, weather very Squally and bad." They left about 8 p.m. on the night of December 9, setting off again for Kipahulu. It was early the next morning that a long and dangerous ordeal began.

> Daylight this morning we found ourselves about 15 miles below ... Kaupo. Tacked Ship and stood in shore, made a few short tacks, and about 7 o'clock A.M. it commenced to rain and the wind to freshen, and about 8 o.c., Ship close with the Rocks[,] our Rudder carried away just above the upper band and floated off on its own hook. Just at this time the winds shifted and came down off the Rocks[,] which made our vessel luff up,[4] and we came near going ashore, as we had no command over her. We got our main sail down and two large Steering oars out astern[,] with which we managed to get her before the wind, and we could with all hands manage to steer her with the Jibs and a little of the head of the Main sail up. We run back to Honuaula, but for fear of not being able to get a Rudder made there, we concluded to Keep on to Lahaina. Had very light winds from the east and a Strong current from the West all night.[5]

It was a bad decision to try to reach Lahaina rudderless. Two days later they found themselves "10 miles off Kahoolawe," an uninhabited island to the southwest of East Maui, "having been set astern by the current all night. We were sorely disappointed to find that we were so far from Port ... The wind continued from [the] west to the South, [so we] "steer[ed] for Hana, East point of east Maui. Wind light all day. Saw one Ship bound in to Lahaina, but too far off to hail." The next day's journal entry (see epigraph) describes how they could not make Hana and had to return to Honuaula/Wailea, where their ordeal finally ended.

It took them three days to have a new rudder made. Hammond disembarked and borrowed a horse, which he rode halfway up the Haleakala Crater to Lincoln Torbert's cattle ranch.

> I found Mr. Torbert very willing to assi[s]t us all in his power as far as materials, but [said he] could not help make it. But as Bro. Rice [a carpenter] is along, he consented to make it. There being no blacksmith here[,] I had to ride to Waikapu (about 20 miles) where I arrived a little before dark, and got J[ohn] Crowder to go right to work making the [iron] Straps and Pindles, I lending a hand to blow and strike.

4. A ship would luff up if it "turned too close to the wind" and began to shake. See *Webster's New Universal Unabridged Dictionary*.

5. Hammond journal, Dec. 10, 1855.

> [The next day] ... at dark I arrived at Honuaula, having packed the iorn [iron] on horse back, making it very fateiguing to me to ride. Bro. R[ice] has the Rudder ready for the iorns.
>
> [On Saturday] after a deal of trouble we succeeded in hanging our rudder, having made a good job of it, [a] far better one than the other. We were till about 3 P.M. getting our Rudder [hung] ... [and] got under way ... to [Maalaea Bay]. Took in 20 bar[re]ls of potatoes, Bannanas, fowls, Watermelons &c. One boat load of potatoes sunk. Lost bags and all. About 12 o.c. P.M. we sailed for Lahaina, light winds all night.[6]

They were sailing with one crew member less than when they arrived, the man's wife having come to see him and the two having walked up to Kula. Since he did not return, it indicates that he had probably had enough of the madcap enterprise.

All the while Mary Jane was managing the makeshift mission guest home at Lahaina. An appreciative Simpson Molen described her as "indeed a good woman as well as very industrious. She keeps one boarder besides all the Elders that happen to come along, which is not seldom, does all her own sewing and washing and cooking, takes care of three small children, teaches a school of 10 scholars and takes in sewing for other folks to the amount of 2 or 3 dollars a week."[7] Frank stopped in for a brief stay-over, even then spending most of the day preparing to sail again for Honolulu despite cloudy skies. They found their way and anchored in the harbor, and the next day "employed [themselves] in discharging cargo, selling produce &c."

For the next five days while he suffered from dysentery, Hammond and his crew were "employed in heaving down an[d] cleaning ship." Christmas was approaching, but it was not a topic Frank dwelt on in his diary. He was still taking onboard "lumber &c" for the east coast of O'ahu, a village called Punaluu, five miles south of today's Laie. Unfortunately the lumber proved to be "too long to go in the hold, in consequence of which the vessel could not sail to any advantage to the windward [and] ... drifted off towards Molokai." After two

6. Hammond journal, Dec. 13, 1855.
7. Molen journal, Dec. 14, 1855.

days of fighting the drift, they cut up the lumber and placed it below deck, thus "alter[ing] the trim of the ship."

It was not until early on December 30 that "we squared away for the Harbor and after [pitching] one or two bo[a]rds in[to] the mouth of the channel we came safe to anchor in Punalu." Since it was Sunday, Hammond "tried to get a meeting of the saints" in the village "but did not succeed. They are nearly dead here." They "discharged 2,000 f[ee]t of lumber" the next day and towed it "about 3 miles to Kahaula, [which made them] feel very tired, being in the water a good deal of the day." When they re-entered the ship, they were pleased to be able to bring vegetables with them. It was now two days into the new year. Night fell, and they "got under way with a very light breeze from the mountain and stood out to sea ... I have made bar[e]ly my expenses on this trip," Hammond lamented. "The lumber, most of it[,] went to pay Bro. Bauman's debt." In addition to that, he had hurt his foot.

They arrived back at Honolulu on January 4 and unloaded their freight. When they sailed for Lahaina, John Caine and Albion Burnham joined them, the latter wanting to see his new baby. Coming to anchor about daylight on January 10, they found that the Hammonds' infant Fletcher

> had met with a serious accident a few days ago while playing with a stick of wood in his mouth. S[amuel] S. came up and fell over on to him from behind throwing the babe forward on to his face[,] run[n]ing the stick into his throat; Mary Jane pulled it out[,] when a stream of blood followed as large as the stick. She administer[e]d to him and he soon began to recover. The day before I landed he had a high fever and spasms, and it was with great faith and prayer that his Mother was able to hold on to him and drive back the power of the distroyer. Thanks unto God for all his blessings unto his saints.[8]

This was the third time Mary Jane was documented administering to a sick person.

The *Lanai* left Lahaina for Honuaula that evening and experienced

8. Hammond journal, Jan. 10, 1856.

"rough weather all night." They approached shore to land a passenger at Honuaula, at which "Bro. Kekaula came on board and told me he had 70 bar[re]ls [of] potatoes ready for us." Despite rough weather, they loaded them and once more attempted to circle East Maui, thereby experiencing yet another close call. "About 2. p.m. we were off Kaupo," Hammond later wrote in his diary, "With a kona (South Gale) increasing. Could not make any harbor on this side of the Island, so we scudd[ed] away for Hana. Off Hana at dark in jibbing over we carried away our [binnacle],[9] and I had a miraculous escape from being thrown over board in the maine sheet [rope to the main sail]. We ran by the harbor (being too dark to go in) and layed to all night under our jib."

They had no life preservers, and there are few beaches along the eastern coast, mostly big waves beating against jagged lava rocks, so if Hammond had gone overboard he probably would have perished. He explained that on Saturday the twelfth, the

> gale continued near all day. Towards night we made sail and stood down for Hana, to be ready to go in early in the morning.
>
> [On Sunday the] tide took [us] far off to sea and to the leeward, so we beat all day and just got in before dark and anchored at Hana. I went on shore and visited the saints. I slept on shore. The Gale was severe here. Met and preached to the saints.
>
> [The next day they] tried to sell some Salt &c [but] could not [and] about 1 o'clock P.M. sailed for Kipahulu. We here got Bro. Kaheki to assist [us] to Lahaina. I have had only 2 men besides myself on boa[r]d through all our bad weather, which has made it excep[t]i[o]n[al]ly hard on me. I feel almost worn out. Just at dark we anchored at Kipahulu.[10]

When they got to Lahaina on January 17, he "found that we were likely to have some passengers so I sent one boat load of our wood on shore, also sold 7 or 8 bar[re]ls of potatoes. A little after dark we sailed for Honolulu. Bros. S[ilas] Smith, J. T. Caine, and Burnham

9. "The case in which the compass and a light are kept on board ship for use by the steersman." *Webster's New Universal Unabridged Dictionary*.

10. Hammond journal, January 12–14, 1856.

passengers, and about 20 natives passengers on deck." Over the next two days, Hammond was busy marketing the cargo, transporting people, and delivering letters and messages. Hammond learned that Burnham, by abandoning his work to see his new baby, had lost his job and was now unable to pay the Hammonds for room and board for his wife and children.

On Sunday, Hammond "attended [the] native meeting" in Honolulu and "preached a long discourse on the cause of the present low state of the church on these lands," unfortunately without recording what he thought the cause of the lack of enthusiasm was. In the evening he attended two foreign meetings and preached in English. His foot badly infected, when he walked into town the next day the pain was so great he was forced to stop, and when he got to the ship and "commenced to poultice it,"[11] it would be the beginning of a week laid up in bed, the *Lanai* grounded. "Foot very painful, attended with much fever and a general prostration of the whole system," he wrote. Two days later "the Swelling on my foot broke, or rather Br. Caine cut it open with a razor." On Sunday Hammond attended a meeting of foreign members in Honolulu and preached to them, and in doing so paid a price because his "foot pained [him so] much" he had to poultice it "again through the night."

Brother Rice, Hammond explained, had "consented to go with me on board the Sloop for this trip," and they arrived in Lahaina just before sundown on January 30. "My family were very glad to see me. Mary J[ane] has been unwell a good deal of the time, and having many cares to see to tends to wear her down." When she saw his infected foot and run-down condition, she no doubt felt more depressed. Nor was Frank ready to rest. The next day he unwisely sailed to Kalepolepo for a load of wood for J. J. Halstead, and when they were back to Lahaina that afternoon his foot was so bad he could barely make it home. "I concluded to not go down to Oahu," he conceded, and let Rice take over. The sloop "sailed about noon, leaking very bad. My foot growing worse." Two days later his foot was "greatly inflamed and

11. A poultice is a "soft, hot, moist mass, as of flour, mustard, meal, bran, flaxseed, or similar substances, applied to sores, inflamed parts of the body, etc." *Webster's.*

swollen." In addition to the pain, the forced idleness was frustrating. "When I can, I read to pass away the time. I find it very bad to be laid up now when we are so much in need of means to get away with."

Swallowing his pride, if not his suspicion of doctors, Hammond summoned Dr. Hutchinson on February 7 to lance his foot, which he admitted helped tremendously. No sooner had "a large quantity of black blood and matter r[u]n out" than he felt "much releived." His foot gradually improved as he avoided using it and got some rest. Rice arrived a week later. The sloop, he said, had come "near sinking with them going down," and the crew had been forced to make repairs during its "long stay at O'ahu." Hammond rode a horse to town the next day and "saw Mr. Gillman and Hoffmeyer" while Rice took the sloop to Honuaula for "potatoes and Beef ... She sailed about dark." Not surprisingly, Hammond found that his foot was "worse on account of my riding and hopping about on it."

The *Lanai* returned on Tuesday, February 19, and Hammond had progressed to the point that he could "touch [his foot] to the floor a little," so he rode into town the next day. The pain resumed so forcefully, however, that he knew it was still too early to join the crew. As he convalesced, he revealed in his journal how the situation with Sister Burnham and her children had been and how it had worn on Mary Jane. The *Ka Moi* was in the harbor, and "Sister Burnham commenced getting ready to take passage on her for Honolulu ... It will be a great relief to Mrs. H[ammond] when Sist[er] B. leaves," he wrote, "as she and her little ones have only been as boarders with us for 5 months and more, which has caused a deal of hardness for Mary J[ane], besides a great deal of unpleasant feelings—the children causing much disturbance—but we are all the time learning lessons."

When Sister Burnham and her new baby and other children left for Honolulu, Frank learned how precarious the Burnhams' finances were, with "a dull prospect for Bro. B." raising enough money to get "away from these lands for some time yet to come." In the wake of the Burnhams' departure, though, the Hammonds felt "very much at home again with only our own family in the house. Mrs. H. enjoys it greatly, for she has been sorely tried for the last few months." It was similar to when Jane Lewis and Nathan Tanner had stayed indefinitely, then finally left after enjoying the Hammonds' hospitality for much longer than they should have. Frank wrote a lengthy letter to George Q. Cannon on February 24, which Cannon summarized in the *Western Standard* newspaper he had begun publishing on the mission printing press. It was an honest report. "Sandwich Islands," the dateline read. "Elder F. A. Hammond writes, that he hopes to be able to leave the Islands for this place, on his way to Utah, about the middle of May [1856]. He informs us that the prospects on Lanai—the island on which the Saints had gathered—were rather dull, the worms having commenced their ravages on this seasons' crops."[12]

Hammond's foot improved to the point that he "took [his] Cane and hobbled down town." It was there that he received some disturbing news by mail.

> Rec[eived]d a letter from Br. Caine with two letters enclosed. They were from Bro's. Kipp and Franklin, San Berna[r]dino, written to Br. Burnham ... Br. Kipp is evidently on the back ground [backsliding]. He writes to Br. B. to beware how he comes to that place [San Bernardino], and to not be so liberal in giving away his means to the support of the elders. Complains bitterly of the return[ing] elders for not calling to see him. Says he has been two years striving to get means to return here [to the Sandwich Islands] &c.[13]

Frank noted on February 29 that Mary Jane was "not very well." The next day he did something foolish and nearly lethal in an attempt to help her: "gave her too much Calomel, and it begins to salavate her. But no doubt it will do her good in the end, for her system has been afflicted for a long time with a complication of deseses [diseases] and I hope this dose will purge them all out. I administer[e]d to her and asked the Lord to rebuke all evil effects from the medicen." Calomel, mercury chloride, was used as a cathartic for intestinal worms and other ailments and was toxic. Realizing it was an overdose, Frank was now trying to counter its effects with prayer.

12. *Western Standard*, May 7, 1856, in Journal History.
13. Hammond journal, Feb. 25, 1856.

The next day he spent his time comforting his wife as her "mouth begins to get sore" and she was "entirely prostrated." The following day he called on Dr. Dow "and got some Alum for a wash for M[ary] J[ane]'s mouth, which is very sore indeed. I never saw a person salavate so easily before ... Mrs. H. suffers very much with her mouth. The Babe [Fletcher] also is unwell, and I with my lame foot." With everyone else in the family sick or lame, they had to rely on their foster child Issac Linn, whom Frank referred to as "a stupid little half white boy some 8 years old." His comment showed his exasperation, as well as probably some ethnic prejudice, because there is no evidence the boy was slow-witted. While both Frank and Mary Jane were incapacitated, they had to close the school.

> Mary Jane is no better. She suffers greatly with her mouth. She has eat[en] nothing except a little chicken broth since last Friday ... I know of nothing to do for Mary J., only to keep her bowels open and let the mercury work off. Her mouth is too sore at present to admit of taking any thing as an antidote, if there was any to take.[14]

The next day "Mary Jane [was] no better ... I never saw a worse mouth produced by mercury."

This was a low point for the family, and in the midst of it Hammond heard from Orson Whitney that "Bro. Lewis says times is hard at San Bernardino, and many apostate spirits [are] there. About all the brethren who went from here [Hawaii] are on the back ground." Then David Rice arrived with a horror story of a strong "gale of wind" in Honolulu that had forced the sloop into a reef, although the ship was spared irreparable damage. The crew was able to sell the lumber they were transporting, "but expenses have eat[en] up all the profits." Hammond considered these facts and thought about how, instead of raising funds to get his family to Utah, this venture was becoming a drag on his finances, and he realized it was more than "discouraging to me where our out fit is coming from." If he continued on his current path, he would not have enough to purchase the oxen and wagon he would need to buy in California. He was helping the mission with

14. Ibid., Mar. 4.

a problem they might not have had if they had consulted him from the beginning about the badly constructed sloop.

At this point, on an impulse he did what he should have done seven months earlier. When the whaleboat *George* came into harbor, Hammond inquired about its schedule and purchased tickets to San Francisco. Then he went into town and made it known that he was selling his house. Remarkably the very next day, they

> sold our place for 200 dollars and paid [110] for our passage to San Francisco. Isaac Linn[,] Bro. Linn's little boy[,] I get to [take] along for 10 dollars. The Lord has made bare his arm in our behalf, and raised up friends to us on every hand. Some forgave the debts, others gave us clothes, such as we stood very much in need of. P[eter] H. Treadway, Cha[rle]s Lake[,] G. Hoffmeyer[,] and B. F. Bolles[,] and G. D. Gillman all rendered us great assistance in getting away, and may the Lord reward them an hundred fold.[15]

The ability to sell their house so quickly is testimony to the good relations Frank and Mary Jane had established with the non-Mormons in Lahaina. On the other hand, selling for $200 what they had purchased in March 1853 for $350 must have been disappointing. No matter. Over four and a half years after arriving in the Islands, they were overjoyed to finally be on their way home.

15. Hammond journal, Mar. 12, 1856.

CHAPTER 38

Apostasy at San Bernardino

The saints, as a general thing, here are cold and a great many are disaffected. Br. [Charles C.] Rich has all he can do to get done what he desires. This is a regular catch-all of a place, and all kinds of Spirits congregate here, and Self is the great principle that seems to actuate the Mass.

—Hammond journal, May 13, 1856

As the Hammonds were preparing to take inexpensive passage on the whaleship *George*, an official arrived from Honolulu and seized the ship on March 13, 1856, for unpaid debts. The ship was ordered to Honolulu immediately to have "the right of property ... tested." The agent fortunately refunded the Hammonds' money, and Frank and Mary Jane "concluded to go on board and proceed to Honolulu[,] and if the George is detained there[,] take the next best oppertunity for the coast." Frank's diary is silent about the emotion he must have felt in leaving the island and city that had been his home for upward of eight years: "About 4 P.M. we bid adiue to the saints at Lahaina and our many kind friends and set out for Honolulu. Bros Silas and Silas S[anford] Smith arrived from Lanai, just in time to see us off." The mission president gave Frank $10 in exchange for his shoemaking tools.

Elder Sixtus Johnson mentioned, from his assignment on Lana'i, that the Hammonds left "on a whale ship in Company with Brother John S Eldrig and James Grayham," the two missionaries who were on their way home from Australia, having survived a shipwreck and two months on a remote island near Tahiti. Among the rest of the passengers and crew who were rescued, thirty were Latter-day

Saints.[1] Their urgency to continue on without pause may have been a factor in Hammond deciding to proceed at once as far as the *George* would take them.

They arrived at Honolulu on March 17. The next day, "finding no prospect of the Barqe George being released," Hammond secured passage for $190 on the *Tawny Major* under Captain Lawton and had to spend most of their remaining funds to do so, although a few native members at Honolulu were generous when, on March 20, the "Sisters came in to bid us aduie and ga[ve] Mrs. H[ammond] 10 dollars. Bro. Kauwahi also gave me 10 more towards paying Isaac's passage. So the Lord blessed us on ev[e]ry hand." They had breakfast with Albion Burnham, who "feels very bad because he is not able to pay us anything on his famil[y's] board," referring to his wife and children having lived with the Hammonds for many months in Lahaina.

At two o'clock that afternoon they left their friends and made their way in a steam tender across the reef to board the *Tawny Major,* where almost immediately they found themselves the object of curiosity from people who wanted to know about polygamy. "They will talk about nothing else," Frank complained. "There is some 20 cabin passengers, and 8 or 10 Steerage passengers," all eager to hear the details of Mormon domestic arrangements. While usually he got along well with ship captains, Frank could not make headway with Captain Lawton.

> We feel very indignant at the manner in which we are treated on board this vessel. The Capt. is an unprincipled man, and seems to care only for the money. I pay 190 dollars for a nasty little room about 6ft x 4, but I was promised another room at the time I was bargaining for our passage. Mrs. H. will not go to the first Table any more on account of the non-attention of the Capt. On the part of the passengers we are treated with great respect. Mr. Ja[me]s Luzetta, Fairbanks Burges, W. Howes first Mate and some others are very kind to us. I feel to ask the Lord to send us a fair wind, that we may be speedily released from our present unple[a]sant situation. The care of the little ones devolving up[on] me makes it rather hard times for me. My foot is also some lame yet.[2]

1. Sixtus Johnson diaries, Mar. 14, 1856.
2. Hammond journal, Mar. 26, 1856.

As he did almost every day, the experienced mariner made note on March 28 of the ship's location and conditions: "Wind veered more to the Eastward during the night, so that we were enabled to head N[orth] by E[ast] Lat[itude] 24.20 to day, a heavy sea from the north. Ship rolling and plunging about badly. She is loaded very deep." Two days later he "felt some desire to preach to my fellow passengers, but they are such a rough set that I had but little encourag[e]ment to ask permission." What was more, the cabin was so small that he preferred to "sleep on deck" rather than in the "small narrow berth with two of my little boys."

He noted wryly on April 1, without elaborating, that there were attempts "to make april fools." Five days later his thoughts returned to Hawaii. "My brethren of the Sandwich Islands Mission are assembled in conference to day; may the Spirit of the Lord be in their midst." That evening he consented to talk to the passengers about polygamy, but lectured them on the supposed morality and discipline of it, declaring that the Mormons held adultery to be a capital offense: "He who should defile his neighbor's wife must die," he announced. This elicited surprise and contempt. All but one "united in saying that it was a hard law," and Hammond assumed it was because they were personally guilty of transgression. "They know it would condemn <u>them one and all</u>." The way Hammond saw it, he could "find no one on board who is willing to converse about eternity or eternal things a moment. They will turn my words into obscene jest and low vulgar blackguard whenever I at[t]empt to introduce truth." He had, of course, startled them with his talk of capital punishment and may have confused their sense of injustice at the severity of the punishment with sympathy for the crime.

A few days later "we made the Fare Lanes [Farallon Islands], some long high Rocks about 20 miles from the mouth of the passage into San Francisco Harbor." He could not help exclaiming: "O how happy I feel to have the privilege of once more beholding the land of Joseph, and when I shall have the privilege of beholding the seed of Joseph enjoying the land of their inheritance, I shall be thrice happy." At about 5:00 p.m. on Saturday, April 12, they "came to anchor near [the office of] G[abriel] B. Post & Co's [on Cunningham's] wharf." Hammond could barely contain his excitement and went immediately in search of George Q. Cannon's office on Montgomery Street, finding Cannon "overjoyed to see me," and likewise for Hammond to see his "old friend and Brother. He went with me down to the vessel and accompanied me and the family up to his residence on Valle[j]o St, at Sister Sergents, form[er]ly Sister Lincolns. Mrs. H[ammond] was overjoyed to meet with Bro. & Sister Cannon. They have a fine little son, some two months old."

Hammond soon encountered other old friends and met Cannon's typesetter Joseph Bull and printer Matthew Wilke, skilled Latter-day Saints who had accompanied Cannon from Utah. They had "lived on bread and water sometimes, but the saints see their determination to keep the commandments of the Lord, regardless of consequences, and so they now begin to lend their aid and assistance." Hammond had heard by letter in October that Cannon was working on the Hawaiian Book of Mormon. Cannon had promised to begin a semi-monthly periodical in Hawaiian too, but as he now understood his assignment, as it was explained to him by apostle Parley P. Pratt, it was "to publish the Book of Mormon in the Hawaiian language, and to assist Elder Pratt in the publication of a paper [in English]." Even that expectation was modified when Cannon arrived in San Francisco and had to hunt down Pratt, who was on his way home to Utah and was staying with a church member at a ranch in the San Jose area. Cannon explained that Pratt "set me apart to preside, in his place, over northern California and Oregon, and we separated, he to go home [to Utah], and I to return to San Francisco.[3]

The brick building where the editorial office and press were located was owned by Samuel Brannan and managed by Brannan's brother. Soon enough Cannon would begin binding 2,000 copies of the Book of Mormon his staff had printed over the space of seven months. In December 1855, they had also produced a pamphlet that announced the Book of Mormon, an eight-page tract, *He Olelo*

3. Cannon, *My First Mission*, 62–63.

Hoolaha, meaning an announcement, with a short history of how the Book of Mormon came to be, a sketch of the life of Joseph Smith, and a declaration that the Book of Mormon had been printed in translation. Fifteen hundred copies of the pamphlet were prepared and mailed to the missionaries in Honolulu. John R. Young reported on March 15 that "the Saints appear to be delighted with it."[4]

The pamphlet set forth the view of the Book of Mormon that Native Americans, and by extension Polynesians, according to Cannon's interpretation, were among the lost tribes of Israel. They had the honor, he wrote, to be "the first dark-skinned people to have this Book in your own language." The Book of Mormon would soon be translated into several other Polynesian languages: Maori, Samoan, and Tahitian, followed later by editions in Tongan, Rarotongan, and Fijian. In a sense, Cannon was right about the honor of being first to have their own translation, among native people, since to this day there has not been a complete edition of the Book of Mormon in any North American Indian language (Apache, Cherokee, Navajo, etc.). Although it has been translated into one indigenous language in Central America, the Guatemalan Q'eqchi, and one idiom from South America, Bolivian Aymara, we can see the greater degree to which Polynesians took to Mormonism than Native Americans. In Central and South Americans the interest would come mostly from those of mixed race. In any case, Cannon cited the promise that converts would lose their curse of skin pigment and gradually turn white, and if in fact the Hawaiians were pleased with this message, it indicates how firm the racial views were at the time by those who were disadvantaged by them as well as by the privileged whites.[5]

Cannon and his assistants completed the print run of about 2,000 copies of *Ka Buke a Moramona* about the time Hammond arrived, so he must have been treated to a view of the signatures stacked up

4. Whittaker, "Placing the Keystone"; George Cannon to Brigham Young, July 27, 1855, and Brigham Young to L. D. Young, Mar. 15, 1856, qtd. in *JGQC*, 532–39, 611–12.

5. *JGQC*, 518–29. Whittaker appends "Placing the Keystone" with a translation of the pamphlet.

in the print shop. The paper needed to be folded and bound, which Cannon would find a "harder challenge than getting it printed," as were the marketing and distribution.[6] He threw his energy instead into publishing a weekly newspaper, the *Western Standard*, for Mormons in northern California, beginning February 23 and continuing for a year and a half. Three months into the publishing schedule, the paper had only attracted 146 subscribers, so they reached out beyond the Bay Area. By the end of its run, it had attracted a subscriber base of 800 in Utah alone.[7]

The second day the Hammonds were in San Francisco was a Sunday, and they walked with others to the home of a Sister Evans, where Hammond was "called upon to speak, but my feelings overcome me to such an extent that I could not free my mind, so after giveing a short synopsis of the work on the Islands, I gave way." They were invited for lunch to the home of Father Morey, who Hammond was surprised to learn was "carried away with Spiritualism." The Hammonds attended two more LDS worship meetings in the afternoon, followed by tea with a Brother Ephalet, the Cannons, and two other church members. It was "a most Happy time. An excellent supper prepared by Mrs. Ephalet. She does not belong to the Church, but she is a fine woman."

Hammond was curious enough about spiritualism to attend a lecture at the American Theater with Cannon and Wilke on April 15. He was unimpressed.

> It was the most sens[e]less affair I ever listened to, and yet they say the Lecturer is the best Medium on the earth. If that be true the Devil help the poor ones. He spoke in the Clarivoince state, fell senseless to the floor once, another spirit then took possession of him[,] and he spoke a short while longer. I though[t] it would do very well for a man who was drunk or a sleep, but a most miserable affair for a man awake. A large respectable aud[i]ence was present, but they could

6. Only 700 copies were ever bound, 200 in California and 500 in Hawaii, while the loose signatures were shipped to Hawaii and lost in a fire while in storage in 1868. Crawley, *Descriptive Bibliography*, 3:268–69.

7. See Bitton, *George Q. Cannon*, 75–77; Ekins, *Defending Zion*.

> with difficulty be restrained from hissing him from the Stage. I should have felt very much taken in if we had paid for our tickets, but this was not the case. Bro. Cannon procured us free tickets on the account of the Editorship which he holds.[8]

Despite the negative review, Hammond "attended another Lectur[e] on Spiritism" the next day, although it too was judged to be "a total failure."

He was asked again to preach on April 20 and spoke "at some length on the principle of gathering. Also gave a short sketch of my Mission to the Islands and called upon the saints to assist me home," which elicited a total of seven dollars. Four days later Hammond ran into church member Jefferson Hunt, a member of the California State Assembly representing San Bernardino, who "kindly offer[e]d to see the Capt. of the Steamboat about our passage."[9] Hammond said it was "the first time since I came into the church that I have been the object of charity." Hunt was on his way back to the colony and would travel with them. After he "engaged our passage for San Pedro" with the ship's captain, a man named Haley, the Hammonds boarded the *Sea Bird* at 4:00 p.m. and reached San Pedro, just outside of Los Angeles, on April 27.

They stayed over night and secured their baggage the next morning. In the early evening they climbed aboard Hunt's wagon, underway for San Bernardino, and on arriving five days later were "warmly welcomed by the Saints." They accepted Hunt's invitation to stay with him for a time. Hammond found San Bernardino to be among the "most delightful place[s] as I ever saw. Every thing looks smiling. Fruit of almost a[ll] kinds looks well and crops look extremely fine." Two days later at the local election, he discovered that just below the surface appearances, all was not well. Some of the ex-Mormons and non-Mormons were part of an opposition party that was putting forth candidates for public office. Half of the dissidents were

8. Hammond journal, Apr. 15, 1856.

9. Hunt would soon move to Utah and found Huntsville, near Ogden, where the Hammonds would live for some twenty years beginning in the 1860s.

former missionaries to Hawaii or Tahiti: Woodville M. Andrews, John Dixon, and Benjamin Grouard. They were supported by Edward Dennis and James Kipp. While it was not the only reason for their alienation from the church, their dissension originated in the practice of the colony's leaders handpicking the town's candidates, something Mormon leaders had always done. Dennis, Kipp, Grouard, Sherwood, and others protested by putting themselves forward in the election, for which they were swiftly excommunicated.[10]

Grouard's odyssey is interesting. An ex-whaler, he and another former whaler, Addison Pratt, and Noah Rogers had been the first LDS missionaries to the Society Islands. Beginning in 1843, Grouard served for nine years while his wife waited for him in Nauvoo, Illinois, and he meanwhile married a young native woman, Tearo, who gave him a daughter. When Tearo died, Grouard married Nahina, who bore him three sons,[11] and he then married a fourth wife, Louisa Maria Hardy, in 1853, while visiting Utah. Far from being disciplined for this complicated marital history, he was encouraged in it. Eventually he moved some of his wives a short distance west of San Bernardino and joined other protesters who started a separate settlement to farm on public lands, engaged in spiritualism as an alternative to Mormonism, and became completely alienated from their previous roots.[12]

The Hammonds moved their bedding into the home of a Brother Tyler to live in temporary accommodations for a time, beginning May 7. Not long ago their landlord had shared the same space with Hawaiian missionary Ephraim Green, who was in San Diego working in a coal mine he had established. Tyler offered the house "rent free with a privilege to use the Garden [produce] as fast as it is fit for use." They felt well-cared for, especially after learning that in Utah people were "in short allowance of provisions ... Many of their Cattle have perished during the winter, frozen to death. There was never Such a

10. Lyman, "Rise and Decline of Mormon San Bernardino," 60–61.

11. Perrin, "Seasons of Faith," 205.

12. Lyman, *San Bernardino*, 285, 299.

winter Known there before." Frank decided it would not be so bad to remain for a while as they continued to raise money for the trip.

The next day Sister Kua Moo Kipp did the Hammonds' washing. An appreciative Hammond editorialized that "she would be a good woman if she had a good man." Hammond "had a talk with Kipp and Dennis" and discovered the degree to which "they are led away by Spiritualism." Two days later he spoke with Sherwood, who "thinks he has been badly treated by the heads of the Church. Also thinks the present admi[in]stration [under Brigham Young] is not after the o[r]der that Br. Joseph [Smith] established. Poor man, he has sowed to the wind and must reap the whirlwind." The colony clerk, Richard Hopkins, loaned Frank a milk cow and the sisters donated butter and milk. On May 15 the older boys, Frankey Hammond and Isaac Linn, began attending school. Everything seemed to be going well.

Frank was asked to speak Sunday morning, May 18, by apostle Charles C. Rich. The newly returned missionary gave a summary of his experiences in Hawaii, and afterward he "slipped out a few moments and ran over and heard the Spiritualist[s] hold forth. Sparks and Grouard were the speakers. They are bitter in denouncing the leaders of the Church. They are led captive by the Devil. Grouard is a smart smothe tounge[d] fellow well calculated to lead away the unwarry." A few days later when the opposition candidates tried "to excite the community in relation to the Indians. I fear there is trouble brewing," Hammond wrote, "and the saints may soon have to leave their fair pos[s]essions here and flee again to the mountains." Three days later he "had a talk with Br. Tyler in the evening. He is in the dark, does not know that this work [Mormonism] is true. I Pity him." At a meeting the next day, Apostle Rich "said it would be well for the saints to keep away from the apostates who are trying to bring destruction upon this people." Over the next several weeks, Hammond avoided the dissidents and dedicated himself to making shoes in a local shop. He found plenty of work but few colonists who could pay him cash for his labor.

Toward the end of June, Hammond reported that the conflict

between the opposing camps of Mormons and ex-Mormons had become violent.

> Last Monday and Tuesday there was a fight on each day. A man by the name of Chapman ... of the opposition party, was down to the [El] Monte [village] a few days ago, and told some awful lies about the people of this place. Monday a young man by the name of Nelson, asked him about the stories which he had circulated &c. Chapman was crusty and independent about it, when Nelson pitched into him and gave him a good pounding, and then went and paid his fine.
>
> The other man who got whipped was named R. Matthews, he also is of the opposition. That party will perhaps be a little more car[e]ful how and where they use the language they have been in the habit of concerning the church authorit[i]es.[13]

There appears to have been an attempt—whether coordinated or not—to physically intimidate the "opposition" Mormon dissenters, and Frank apparently had no problem with this..

Hammond learned from Cannon's *Western Standard* that Silas Sanford Smith was in San Francisco and by letter he learned that a foreign (white) convert from Hawaii had apostatized at San Bernardino and returned to Hawaii. "He gives the saints here a hard name," Hammond was told, and "says Mormonism is all a humbug, the speaking in tongues all false &c &c. May the Lord reward him according to all his deeds," Hammond wrote in disgust. A letter from Caine countered that the mission was "healthy." Curiously, Gustaf Linn wrote that he was pleased the Hammonds had taken his boy to America. It appears that Frank had not asked permission in advance to take the boy to Utah.

Hammond described an overnight visit with Dennis, the Honolulu convert who was now a church critic:

> Yesterday I and my family rode up to Dennis's place about 8 miles from town. Stayed all night and rode home this evening with C[harles] Hill. I can see that all the Brethren from the Islands who are now here have received the spirit of apostasy. They can not speak

13. Hammond journal, June 28, 1856.

> well of an individual in the place. They are all Anti Mormon. In am not sorry that I went to see them, as I had an oppertunity to see into their ways and practices. They lead miserable lives, and far from being happy in my opinion they are about all Spiritualists. Their wives (native) manifest far the best spirit. Would to God they had better men for their husbands.[14]

A contrary finding was noted by French travelers Jules Remy and Julius Brenchley, who discovered that the Hawaiian women with white apostate husbands were equally unhappy, although they probably did not express their true feelings to Hammond.

> Hakuole Dennis ... lamented ever leaving the climate, lifestyle, and people of her home islands, tearfully striking her breast for having done so. She explained she came out of love for her Mormon convert husband, who emigrated to California through obedience to direction from the missionaries he had befriended. However, both he and his wife had abandoned the Latter-day Saints faith, and she hoped they could raise sufficient funds within the year to return to Hawaii.
>
> Part of her discontent stemmed from the "dreariness" of the land and climate compared to her former home ... Undoubtedly her greatest problem was her perception that she had not been fully accepted. She had no visitors, even though she had gone to the trouble of learning English ... She also exhibited some deeply hurt feelings involving her supposition that the white sisters regarded the simple island ways as "savage," further expressing the opinion that they regarded her "as if she was a negress."[15]

Hammond heard from his brother-in-law at Fort Las Vegas that the William Bringhurst family was anxious to help the Hammonds with their immigration, although not yet as they were "short of breadstuffs again this year." Bringhurst promised to send a wagon as soon as he could. Unfortunately, his "animals are poor &c." At about the same time, there was encouraging news from the recent April general conference regarding a new wave of missionaries that had been called to Hawaii. The *Western Standard* reported that twelve

14. Ibid., July 20, 1856.
15. Qtd. in Lyman, *San Bernardino*, 297–99.

new missionaries were already "on their way" and had "taken the North route [to San Francisco] via Carson Valley," meaning by way of Virginia City and Sacramento. What the missionaries would find when they arrived in Honolulu in October, however, would be anything but good. Silas Smith wrote to Brigham Young in July that "despite all our exertions to strengthen, build up and increase the Church on these Islands, there is a very manifest falling away, both in numbers, and in the faith and good works of those who pretend to hold on to the work."[16]

Hammond decided to keep his head down and concentrate on making shoes and horse harnesses. Unaccustomed to the heat, he complained of the weather from June through August, and his foot bothered him. Through much of the summer, Mary Jane's health was poor, including trouble with a tooth she had someone pull for her on August 9. Instead of coming free, the tooth "broke off and caused her much pain." She was only twenty-five years of age, but she had already broken or lost several teeth, as had Frank. On August 29 he "had to leave my work to day in consequence of a great pain in my face caused by cold in the Stump of an old tooth, upon which I had a false tooth fast[e]ned before I left home in [18]51. I was almost crazy some of the time."

On August 26 Edgerton Snider arrived and indicated that he had regained his fellowship in the church in San Francisco. He had earned enough money there to begin making his way toward Utah. "Bro. S[nider] says Bro. Caine is looked for from the Islands" as well, having gotten "into trouble about the Sloop." Although Hammond does not say what happened, it must not have been good for the *Lanai*. There was a second letter from Las Vegas, with an enclosure from Mary Jane's sister Ann telling her their sisters Lavina and Rebecca were now plural wives in the Mormon Carson Valley (Nevada) settlement, their husbands, Charles and Levi, having recently married other women. This probably would not have been welcome information to Mary Jane, who probably had kept Frank from taking a plural

16. Smith to Young, July 3, 1856. Britsch adds that "during the next year matters became even worse," that there was "mass apostasy." *Moramona*, 44–45.

wife. There was also good news. "Bro. Wm says 'cheer up,'" Frank told Mary Jane, "'for we shall go home [to Utah] in the due time of the Lord.' [William] will be here in Dec. next with cattle to trade for mules. He tells me to prepare some harness[es], and he will bring a Wagon."

As the fall arrived, Ephraim Green abandoned his work at the coal mine in San Diego and set his sights on Utah, stopping in San Bernardino along with a mining partner.[17] In San Francisco that same month, Cannon finished binding 200 copies of the Book of Mormon and sent 180 of them to Honolulu.[18] For the mission, as also for the Hammond family, it was a time of progress as well as hardship.

17. Green diary, Sept. 1–2, 1856.

18. Cannon to Young, Sept. 27, 1856, qtd. in *JGQC*, 540–41.

CHAPTER 39

Return to Utah

We found the saints verry backward and they were greatly affected by the report of John Hydes leaving the Church. The [Honolulu weekly] '[Ka] Hae Hawaii' came out with a long defamatory Editorial against the Mormons, however we succeeded in dispelling some of their fears, in regard to the matter.

—Joseph F. Smith diary, Nov. 15, 1856

A terrible ordeal for the Hammond family began on August 31, 1856, when "Isaac [Linn] was taken sick to day with a fever. It seems a hard matter for us to all be well at the same time." Whether he meant it literally or metaphorically, he calculated that "the distroyer has not been entirely clear of our house since last May." Two days later the child they had all but adopted had become "worse [with] a high fever [and was] sick at the Stomach and [had] a bad head ache." In early September the boy was "still very sick. I administer to him from time to time and Mrs. H[ammon]d nurses him like a baby." The next day "Isaac was out of his head." There is not another journal entry until September 14 when Frank confirmed that Isaac had been "verey sick all the week, a high fever, and some part of the time flighty." The local "Doct[or] Mcintyer has been tending on him since last Thursday."

It was at such an inopportune time that "Bros. Green and Park arrived from San Diego" with "talk of going to the [Salt] Lake this fall ... [and] kindly offer[ed] to take us along with him." Hammond could see that, among other things, "there would be too many in one wagon."[1] More pressing at the moment, the condition of the Linn child

1. Green left for Utah on October 12.

continued to deteriorate. Running out of options, Frank decided to immerse him in water in a healing baptism, feeling that this would be a comfort to his soul as well as his body, one of the common remedies for sickness in the church at that time.[2] Accompanied by a Brother Hemings, Frank took Isaac to the river on Monday, September 15, and baptized him "for the restoration of his health," then brought him home and confirmed him a member of the church in case that would offer any help. "He seemed to revive … and we now hope he will recover." It is possible that the cold water brought down the fever. Momentarily at least, the boy's appetite was returning, which gave the Hammonds reason to hope for the best. Still, "I would his Father was here to see how we attend to him," Frank confided.

The next eight days were agonizing, as Isaac suffered from something along the lines of appendicitis, "his bowels much inflamed, and it appears to be increaseing." Frank explained that his "wife sent for me today [because] she thought he was dieing." She "put mustard plaster on his bowels," then sent for Frank again when she thought she detected "signs of mortification." On Sunday, Frank could only report that "Isaac still lives but our hopes are faint for him." On the morning of Tuesday the 30th, "his Spirit took its flight for another world. He got easey for a few hours before he died, so that we could hardly tell when he breathed his last." They had a coffin made the next day and buried him. Four days later Hammond expressed grief as the family felt "the loss of Isaac very much."

The bound copies of the Book of Mormon arrived in Honolulu in October,[3] and Cannon informed Brigham Young that it had cost $110 to bind 200 books in sheep skin, a third of them in red because it was "an attractive color among the natives." He had priced the red-leather edition at $1.25 and the rest at $1.00. He rightly worried about whether the missionaries would be successful in selling them because of the "scarcity of money and the languishing state of some of the branches." Nor was there an allowance for members who had contributed heavily to its publication, which must have been an

2. See *JGQC*, 235.
3. Ricks, *My Candid Opinion*, 57.

irritation.[4] Word was also trickling back that the leader of the new group of missionaries, John Hyde, had decided during his voyage to the islands that he no longer believed the teachings of the church, so that when he arrived on October 5, instead of proselytizing and joining the missionaries for the conference on Maui, he began publishing and lecturing against the church. Soon he was accompanied by Protestant clergymen, happy to translate his message into the native language.[5] It must have caused Hammond to grate his teeth to imagine the Protestant ministers "gloating themselves over it," and in his diary he included a mild curse: "May the Lord reward him."[6]

As fault lines became exposed in Hawaii, in Utah there was an attempt to stiffen the spine of the membership; news of the so-called Utah Reformation reached San Bernardino in early November. "I understand that the first Presidency are going thro' the settlements in the [Salt Lake] Valley and ... [re]baptizing those who are worthy," Hammond wrote. He found the *Deseret News* to be a good source of "instructions" on the matter, from which he concluded that "the time seems to have nearly come when the Sinners in Zion shall tremble. Prest. Young set the 6th of Oct. for all the women who desired to be released from their husbands to come and he would set them free. This offer was made to all the women in the Territory. A scarcity of bread, this winter, is again anticipated. Still the faithful Saints do not tremble because of the calamities which are fast overtaking the wicked."

At the end of October, John Caine passed through southern California on his way to Utah and was able to purchase "an out-fit home" with help from "the Saints here," who were "very kind to him." Frank

4. George Cannon to Brigham Young, Oct. 1, 1855, qtd. in *JGQC*, 540.

5. Ricks, *My Candid Opinion*, 58; Britsch, *Moramona*, 45. Hyde decided that rather than walk away from Mormonism, its "moral depravity and religious ruin ... demand[ed] more serious attention." *The Polynesian*, Oct. 14 [18], 1856. On October 20 he gave an evening lecture to a "crowded" Bethel Chapel attended by "many of the elite of Honolulu." A rebuttal from Utah missionary Edward Partridge Jr. pointed out that "not more than six weeks since [Hyde had] lectured in favor of polygamy ...Thus he proves himself to be a liar, hypocrite, and deceiver of his fellow men." Ibid., Oct. 25.

6. *Western Standard*, Dec. 7, 1856. Hyde published his views in *Mormonism: Its Leaders and Designs*. A young missionary, Brigham's nephew John R. Young, debated Hyde in Honolulu. See *Memoirs of John R. Young*, 82–86.

offered his own silent blessing, "May he have a speedy passage home to his family," with a note that he too "desire[d] greatly to return to the Valley with my wife and little ones. May the Lord keep me from every evil and preserve me and mine to see that day." He must have envied Caine and the preference members gave to an unmarried missionary returning home, compounded by the fact that Hammond knew he had never learned the language and had done little missionary work, none outside Honolulu.

Caine brought with him news that the mission had sold the *Lanai* for $200, which was much less than its outstanding debts. One can imagine Hammond groaning to remember how Baumann had valued it at $1,600. He learned that David Rice had contracted an infection onboard, while serving as the ship's captain, and was recuperating. "Bro. Burnham and family [are] about as usual ... [but] Bro. [John] Evens has about apostatized," he was told. And "Bro [John] E. B. Winchester was driven in a gale of wind to china" with Diana Gaston. Winchester wanted to return to his home in Connecticut, backtracking by sea, supposedly intent on eventually continuing on to Utah from there. Feeling sorrow for the course of some of his converts, Hammond concluded that "the way of the transgressors is hard."

In late November, he was "appointed in connection with others to labor as a home missionary here this winter. I feel to do all that lays in my power to aid in the work of the Lord," he said. His assignment became more difficult when several "disaffected Saints" arrived later in the week from Cedar City, Utah, and elsewhere. The reformation was driving them out of Utah to San Bernardino, with its reputation as a safe haven for free-thinkers. Apostle Amasa Lyman "instructed the Teachers and all others to not" accept these refugees as church members until they had proven themselves over the course of a year.[7]

In Hawaii, meanwhile, the trend was in concert with the exiles from Cedar City, as Jonathan Napela started drinking again and stopped attending meetings, and Hosea Kauwahi not only left

7. See Walker, Turley, and Leonard, *Massacre at Mountain Meadows*, 25; Bagley, *Blood of the Prophets*, 116.

but joined John Hyde in proselyting against the church, authoring his own pamphlet critical of its teachings.[8] William Uaua left the fold, and Joseph F. Smith learned from George Speirs on Moloka'i that one could "hardly call [the members] saints ... [They] have all been drinking potatoe rum ... One of the Elders, of which there [are only] five or six good for nothing ones here! would not listen to us. Disfilowshiped him &c ... My private opinion is that there is not one here that is good for anything!"[9]

In the wake of this kind of news, when the reformation was officially introduced to San Bernardino on December 9, Hammond accepted it wholeheartedly and preached it from the pulpit. "Tues. night I attended meeting at Bro. Ben[jamin] Mathews. A good many out. Bros. Thomas, Mathews, Sullivan and I preached. All spoke on the necessity of a reformation among the people." Six days later he observed that "the Presidency of the Stake and high council, Bishops, and a few others were rebaptised to day. I should have been with them but I did not hear of the appointment." The next day he wrote approvingly of how "people are waking up to the business of the reformation," later reporting that

> I and my wife were rebaptised, by Wm. Cox. A good number were present and the same ordinance was administer[e]d to the most of them. I pray God my Heavenly Father that this may be the last time that I may ever be baptized for a remission of my Sins. In the evening we met at the School house and attended to the ordinance of confermation. Bro. Wm. Cox confermed me. Bro. Amasa Lyman assisted. Our geneoligy [vital statistics] was taken anew, so as to be able to give a correct report as to the condition of this branch. Bro. Lyman gave us some excellent instructions.[10]

While the Hammonds were away from Utah, their farm in the

8. According to William Cluff, Kauwahi later felt contrite and, with tears in his eyes, said "he did not leave Mormonism because ... it was wrong, but because of his own sins." He declined to re-affiliate with the church, however. Ricks, *My Candid Opinion*, 74n24; William Cluff to Joseph F. Smith, May 23, 1857; Whittaker, "Placing the Keystone."

9. George Speirs to Joseph F. Smith, Dec. 8, 1856, qtd. in Ricks, *My Candid Opinion*, 81n43.

10. Hammond journal, Dec. 17, 1856.

Salt Lake Valley had been cared for by Mary Jane's brother-in-law David Brinton, the husband of her sister Harriet. On December 20, Frank "received a good long letter" from David reporting that "5 cows of mine died or were lost last Winter, leaving me now some 12 head[,] young and old," and that Frank's share of the harvest was forty bushels. David had donated the forty bushels in Frank's name toward tithing. The farm needed repairs, but Frank should not "wait any longer for fear of not having anything to eat when I get home," David reported, because there had been success with "some corn, wheat, meat &c" and David would "devide with us." Frank and Mary Jane may have left San Bernardino earlier had they known that.

After being re-baptized, Frank helped initiate other people into the reformation, "conferming some 80, who were [re]baptized," and judged that "a good feeling now pervades those who [have] renew[ed] their covenants." On Christmas Day he bought his wife "a pair of $4 ear rings and presented [them] to her. Bro. G. Crosby invited us out to take dinner at his house—we had a verey fine time." In the waning days of December, sixteen more church members were rebaptized, and on December 31 the Hammonds received a special New Year's Eve gift when the Bringhursts arrived from Las Vegas with cattle to sell and a wagon for Frank, along "with their 4 little ones." Incredibly they also had a baby that was "born on the way," on the trail "between here and the Vegus." Ann was expecting and due to give birth, and yet they still had traveled across the desert to help the Hammonds get outfitted for their trip to Utah.

Hammond heard Lyman make a request in a sermon delivered on January 11, 1857, in which the apostle asked members to assist the Hammonds in putting together their "outfit," but it resulted in little help. Frank was left "feeling [so] tired" that he "did not go out to any meeting in the evening." He confessed that "since I came to this place I again indulged in my old habit of using Tobacco, and I now find it a hard matter to desist. May the Lord help me to obey his every word." He acknowledged in later journals, however, that he was not able to break the habit for forty years, even when he was a mission president in Hawaii, a bishop in Huntsville, and a stake president in southern

Utah.[11] Nevertheless, he criticized the other members in mid-January for no longer talking about the reformation. "I feel that the mass of the people here are in the dark as pertaining to the things of God," he wrote. Historian Leo Lyman confirms that in terms of acknowledgment of church authority, "approximately half of the Latter-day Saints [at San Bernardino, 1856–57,] proved committed enough to heed the orders of their ecclesiastical leaders, and the other half did not."[12]

There was a positive turn of events in the Hammonds' sojourn when Frank was able to buy "a span of Mules" for $115, aided by a $60 loan from his brother-in-law. Gustaf Linn wrote to say he "wishes me to take his Son Charles with me to the Valley." Apparently the father had come to terms with his other son's death and trusted Frank and Mary Jane to see that Charles made it to the mountains, something the apostate Edward Dennis family, with whom the youngster was staying, would not do. But When Hammond visited Dennis, he found the ex-Mormon to be "not willing for Charles Lynn to go with me to Utah agreeable to his Father's request."

It was another two months before the Hammonds were able to begin their long-anticipated journey. Bringhurst "loaned us a pair of mules and his little Wagon" so they could leave with the apostles Lyman and Rich and "some fifty men to escort them over to the Mohave River." Mary Jane was almost eight months pregnant. On May 18, soon after they had crossed over into Utah Territory and reached "Cottonwood Springs, Santa Clara River, Frank reported that

> this morning at about ½ 6 a.m. my wife gave birth to a fine little girl. She had a good time and trav[e]led all day with the Co[mpany]. The Lord has greatly blest us in all things. We name the babe Mary Mosell. We have had a long and tedious passage across the Deserts. I never was more we[a]ry of a land trip.
>
> The Indians have been kind to us. The feed and water we found good. 17 Wagons composed our company. I came [on] the old route

11. The First Presidency wanted him to resign his position as president of the San Juan Stake in 1896, but the members voted to retain him if he would promise to stop using tobacco. He said he would and apparently kept his word. Hammond journal, Feb. 22–23, 28, 1896.

12. Lyman, "Rise and Decline of Mormon San Bernardino," 68.

> with Bro. Rich. Part of the Co[mpany] went the Kingston road with Bro. Lyman. That is the best road. Bro. Rich lost a little girl at the Mountain Meadows.[13]

They camped at the idyllic Mountain Meadows, less than four months before the all-Mormon Iron County militia and Indian allies besieged approximately 120 Arkansas emigrants and treacherously massacred them. It happened in a context of paranoia and fanaticism that was rampant at the time due to the reformation and deteriorating relations between the LDS Church and the federal government. The tension was so acute, US President James Buchanan ordered 2,500 US soldiers to the territory to subdue what was described as a state of rebellion when the church leaders refused to cooperate with federally appointed territorial officials. The mass murder left no one—man, woman, or child—alive if the murderers thought they were old enough to relate what happened, although in fact some of the spared young children did tell tales. The reverberations from this and other events in this troubled year would soon impact the Hammonds.

For now, at 4:00 in the afternoon of June 8, they safely arrived in good spirits at their farm south of Salt Lake City in the Big Cotton Wood area.[14] "We were most joyfully recieved by our friends," Frank wrote. He could barely contain his pleasure. "O how thankful we feel to once more see the faces we love and again mingle in the society of the Mountain Saints." Two days later they rode into the city to see Mary Jane's mother and other relatives. "Enjoyed a day of uninterrupted pleasure. It was a heaven on earth indeed." The next day Hammond visited Brigham Young, who "bade me welcome back to Zion." Hammond was amazed to see how Utah had changed. "The Vallies are becoming full of Settlements. G.S.L. City is a wonder to see how fast it had grown up. I feel almost a stranger at home." They had been gone six years.

On Sunday, June 14, when they attended church, there was "a deal of news from the States. Papers were read from the Stand, showing

13. Hammond, May 18, 1857.

14. Hammond mistakenly recorded the date as June 18.

what the [American] people think of the Saints." Still, they would not learn for another month that US troops were on their way to the territory. In the meantime, Hammond felt adventurous enough for him and his brother-in-law to explore the Weber Valley north of Salt Lake City, "to look out [for a] site for a farm &c. I was well pleased. Think of going out the[re] to open a farm—40 miles from the City. Wood, water and good land [are] plenty." When he heard that apostle Parley P. Pratt may have been "shot in Arkansaw on his way to the Valley," he was distressed and "hope[d] it [wa]s not correct," but it was. Hammond had known Pratt since 1848 and admired him. The apostle was shot in mid-May by the legal husband of one of his plural wives.

The end of Hammond's last entry on June 26 observed with satisfaction that the "crops never looked better in the Valley," followed by a gap in the journal record of nearly eight years. As Frank began making daily entries again in his ninth surviving Hawaiian Mission journal book, he was preparing to serve a second mission to the islands in 1864. But in the fall of 1857, he was signing up with the Mormon militia bivouacked in the Wasatch Mountains to resist the US Army in what was called the Utah War. It was thankfully resolved through negotiation, Brigham Young stepping aside as governor and allowing Alfred Cumming to take his place. Hammond and the other insurgents were allowed to return home after a year-long confrontation in which there was the extensive destruction of US Army supplies but few casualties and no full-blown battles.[15]

15. For more on the Utah War, see Moorman and Sessions, *Camp Floyd and the Mormons*; MacKinnon, *At Sword's Point*, 2 vols.

CHAPTER 40

Closing the Mission

Everything seems dead or dieing. The elders say they have to labor with their hands to support themselves and keep themselves in clothing[,] and all testify they do not believe there are more than one or two natives in the whole mission but had more faith in their old [Hawaiian] religion than they had in the truth [of Mormonism], and would pray sooner to their old Gods than to the God of Heaven, except two or three hundred Saints in the Island of Lania [Lana'i], the gathering place.

—*Henry Bigler, Honolulu branch, Sept. 13, 1857*

Surprisingly, at the general conference in Salt Lake City in April 1857, just before the Hammonds left San Bernardino for Utah, a handful of previous missionaries to the Sandwich Islands was called to serve again. These men had only been at home for a short period of time, and were just beginning to adjust to life in Utah, when Henry Bigler, James Farrer, Ephraim Green, James Keeler and John Woodbury left Salt Lake City on May 18 for Hawaii. They traveled by way of the northern Nevada route along the Humboldt River to Virginia City and on to San Francisco.[1] The day of their departure, Mary Jane Hammond, three hundred miles to the south, gave birth to her first daughter. Had the Hammonds arrived back in Salt Lake City sooner, it is almost certain that Frank also would have been called to join the others on their return trip to Hawaii.

That the mission was in crisis is evident from the negative

1. See Woodbury diaries, May 13, 18, 1857. Green was called again even though he was relatively old and could not speak the native language.

reports the missionaries who were still there gave. For instance, the teenager Joseph F. Smith wrote to a cousin that "when you hear of the purity, splendor and magnificence, the advancement, civilization, educational proficiencies &c, of this people, you may deside," after hearing the reality of the situation, that "it is all a hoaks [hoax], there is no trouth in it." He and his new companion, Thomas A. Dowell, crossed from Maui to Moloka'i at the end of April to proselytize there and found that none of the members would feed them. Everywhere they encountered only lapsed native Mormons, and "on asking for the [branch] president, we were informed he [too] had left the Church." Not only that, the meeting house had been converted into a carpenter shop, "full of rub[b]ish, boards, Tools &c." When they tracked down the branch president and asked why he had allowed this to happen, he told them everyone else had left, so he did to. "The rest was leaving, and his mind changed &c. I gave him a good preaching to warning him, of his perrilous situation, his forfiture of all blessings &c, but it seemed wors[e] than throwing words away to talk with him." Smith and Dowell were forced to find work milking cows for a foreign dairyman, and soon Joseph F. moved for the last part of his mission to Lana'i, where he did no more proselytizing among the natives.[2]

The returning missionaries arrived in San Francisco on July 12, where they reunited with George Q. Cannon. He assigned four of them to labor in northern California under his direction while they raised money for their fare to Honolulu. It was decided to send Henry Bigler ahead to the islands on the *John Laud* on August 22, probably because he was the oldest, but also because it was hoped he would arrive in time for the October mission conference planned for Honolulu. Since Cannon was only able to advance him enough for passage in steerage, which was the notoriously unsanitary lower deck where people lived in a common open space without bathroom facilities, he arrived in Hawaii with an ear infection that left him permanently deaf in his right ear.[3]

2. Ricks, *My Candid Opinion*, 94.
3. Bishop, *Henry William Bigler*, 102–03.

It had been almost three years since he had last been in Hawaii, and when he attended a native meeting in Honolulu on September 13 he was shocked to find only two dozen or so in attendance. "Everything seems dead or dieing," he wrote, and most people had returned to their former churches. The only stalwarts were the "two or three hundred Saints in the Island of Lania, the gathering place" (see epigraph). Joseph F. Smith similarly found, perhaps because the gathering had "gleaned out most of the faithful and diligent brethren," that there were not enough committed members left on the other islands to maintain the integrity of the home branches.[4]

When Woodbury arrived on the *Yankee* a few weeks later, he found the fourth-wave missionaries—coming to the end of their terms—pessimistic and only interested in earning money to go home. His "old native acquaintance[s] here seem glad to see me & I am glad to see them again, but [I am] sorry to find them so dilitory & not liveing their religion." A recurring complaint was that the missionaries had spirited off the printing press to California. The complaints grew loud enough that Cannon conceded to send it back to the islands, resulting in Bigler and Woodbury anticipating its arrival and making preparations in Honolulu to house it.[5] Farrer, Green, and Keeler were going to sail with it. However, the printing press was not all the members were upset about. The other projects they had contributed to, such as what Bigler called the "ship speculations"—which could have been a reference to either the Tanner vessel fiasco or the failed mission sloop *Lanai* (or both)[6]—were also complaints. Nor had things gone well on Lana'i. At the October conference in Honolulu, it was "moved and carried that a committee be appointed by the Presidency of the Mission to go & look at the different Islands & try & Select a more Sutiable place than Lanai has proved to be, for the temporary gathering of the native Saints."

At the mission conference, Edward Partridge reported on how "dilatory" some of the branches on Maui had become. According to

4. Bigler, "Extracts," Aug. 22–Sept. 13, 1857; Smith, *Life of Joseph F. Smith*, 183.
5. Woodbury diaries, Sept. 24, 27, 1857; Bigler, "Extracts," Oct. 4, 1857.
6. Bigler, "Extracts," Oct. 4, 1857.

Eli Bell and Sixtus Johnson, the branches on the big island did well as long as they had foreign elders among them, but the members fell away as soon as the missionaries left. The total membership count for all the islands was 3,192,[7] compared to about the same number, 3,008, four years earlier. The membership had spiked at 4,198 in mid-1855 and fallen off again, and—aside from those on Lana'i—even many of the active members had become more lukewarm since then.

Mission president Silas Smith announced his retirement, as well as the release of all twelve remaining fourth-wave missionaries at Brigham Young's request. Henry Bigler was named Smith's replacement, which was unanimously sustained. He nominated James Keeler and John Woodbury as his counselors, although Keeler had not yet arrived and would never do so. President Smith stated that most, but not all, of the mission's debt had been paid. The remaining ten fifth-wave missionaries were given assignments on the major islands outside O'ahu, while the new presidency planned to work that island.

When Cannon's plan to freight the printing press back to Honolulu was mentioned, the missionaries made dismissive comments. They knew the cost involved in operating such a press was prohibitive. It could, however, become "a great weapon in defence of the truth," Woodbury ventured, if they could find a way to finance it. But since most of the members who purchased a Book of Mormon were paying for it in installments, one could see the burden it would be to support a newspaper and other publications. According to Woodbury, Elder Partridge reported that in regard to the Hawaiian Book of Mormon, "some 114 have been disposed of, but the money as yet has not all been collected." There were still sixty-six copies left, of those Cannon had previously sent, that had not been "sold or disposed of."[8]

Woodbury thought the elders should "go to work with their hands to accomplish the various mission objectives," and true to his word, he opened a school in Honolulu to teach English to Chinese merchants. On October 21 he registered disappointment that the *Tawney*

7. Woodbury diaries, Oct. 5–6, 21, 1857.

8. Ibid., Oct. 4, 1857.

Major had arrived without any new missionaries (Farrer, Green, and Keeler), without the press, and without any direction from Cannon. Ten days later, Bigler and Woodbury met with lapsed members in the Honolulu area, and some of them, Woodbury reported, "said they had left the church & gone to the Calvins [Protestants] because Kauwahi, Uaua, and others (who they said were wise men) had feel [fallen] into Sin & left the church, & they thought if it had been the true church, these men would not have left it."[9]

Writing in his journal in Carson Valley on September 9, Keeler mentioned that he, Farrer, and Green had turned around and were headed back to Utah. They had received word from Salt Lake City that all missionaries throughout the world were to return immediately to Utah, that the United States had declared war on Utah. Keeler and the other two missionaries had been given additional "orders to get a [ton] of [gun] powder" and bring it to Utah. When the Utah War was announced, everyone was expected to return to defend the heavenly kingdom against the approaching army.[10]

While other missionaries hurried to San Bernardino, Cannon remained in San Francisco long enough to sell the printing press and "transfer the whole [unbound] edition" of the Book of Mormon "to the S[andwich] I[sland] Mission." The expense of transportation for the unbound galleys, combined with the lack of success in selling bound copies of the Book of Mormon, "prevented Cannon from repaying Edward Dennis the [$1,000] he had loaned [Cannon] to purchase the press," as the editor of the published Cannon journals explained. It was a violation of the contract with Dennis and probably contributed to his leaving the church.[11]

The news of the impending conflict in Utah had traveled quickly to California, but it was not until the *Yankee* arrived at Honolulu on November 20 that the mission first learned of the American "intentions to abuse the Latter-Day Saints & trample upon their rights,"

9. Ibid., Oct. 31, 1857.

10. Keeler journal, Sept. 9, 1857. Keeler would later serve a second mission to Hawaii, 1876–78, as Green would, 1865–68.

11. *JGQC*, 541.

as Woodbury put it. Letters delivered to the mission presidency contained information about Cannon disposing of the press and an explanation that the sixth-wave missionaries (Keeler, Farrer, and Green) were returning to Utah. Mormons in San Bernardino—those at least who would "follow counsel," whereas many would not—and the northern California gold fields would also soon be leaving.

The mission presidency wrote to fifth-wave missionaries on the other islands explaining the "sudden change of affairs in the Mission," saying their "counsel at presant to the Elders is to ... not Say mutch about it." Their authority for this was a letter from Brigham Young, received on November 20, advising that since "the majority of the Saints on those Islands have either been dead or dyeing—Spiritually. It would appear that they have occasionally Spasmodically re-suscitated for a moment, only to Sink lower than they were before ... I think it is best for all of the Elders (with one or two exceptions) to come home."[12]

The attendance at church that Sunday in late November in Honolulu was high since the members expected to see old missionary acquaintances arrive from San Francisco. When Woodbury translated and read President Young's letter, "this Seemed to wake them up and their eyes ... bunged out with astonishment." Brother Keilhune, one of the faithful, responded that "he was not Sorry to hear of the Lord calling away his Servants[,] for it was only fulfilling what the elders had often told them," that the missionaries would be taken from them if the people "did not do better."

Bigler and Woodbury clarified to the presidents of the conferences that they should "lay aside traviling & preaching except as you have opertunity to do so without interfering with your duties or labours to obtain means for the accomplishment of the objects now before us[,] viz., raising means to pay debts & liabilities & then Something to pay passage from the Islands." The *Yankee* would return to California between December 5 and 8, a reasonable deadline to work toward, they suggested. If the gathering place was going to be "kept up at Lanai (as likely it will)," they continued (raising the possibility that Lana'i might

12. Woodbury diaries, Nov. 20, 1857.

not be retained), "the Brethren Say it will be necessary to have a new Mission boat to run between there & Lahaina." It was further suggested that the conference presidents read the Brigham Young missive to the native members, meaning that the shock just experienced by the Honolulu Mormons would be repeated all over the mission as the Utah elders translated and read to all the native Mormons in all the branches Brigham Young's harsh, dismissive message.

Twelve crates of unbound copies of the Book of Mormon had arrived on the *Yankee* with enough loose signatures for around 1,000 finished copies. After they had "landed them, got them to the customshouse and then to the [meeting] house," they estimated for the purpose of paying import duties that 200 copies had been damaged. Woodbury was perplexed that Cannon had sent no explanation or "instructions relitive to the books." Woodbury and two others met with Prince Lot in late November to get permission for three native men (Kalili, Keilihune, and Makahaiwale) to emigrate with them but were unsuccessful. Woodbury also met with the royal attendant Levi Haalelea about the payment due on the Lana'i colony and was told not to worry, "that when the five years wer[e] up we could [still] either rent the land or give it up[,] just as we felt to do, & it would be all right." In December, Bigler and Woodbury wrote to Brigham Young describing "the church debt whitch is yet due, $140," and the difficulty in raising money for their passage to the coast, since "the work here is at a very low ebb." The Saints at Lana'i were "among the best and the most ready to obey counsel," they wrote, "and enjoy a more lively and better spirit than at any other branch on these Islands."[13]

In summing up the situation at the end of the year, Bigler and Woodbury wrote about a number of factors they felt had led to the mission's precipitous decline, including opposition from Protestant ministers and the Hawaiian government, the assumed "degraded" nature of the people, and failure of the mission to obtain a suitable sailing vessel. One might add to these factors the resentment the native Mormons felt over the printing press and the distance of Lana'i from their

13. Ibid., Nov. 23–25, 29.

ancestral homes. Bigler and Woodbury considered the negative effect of "apostates and dissenters," in particular Kauwahi and Uaua. One could add to that short list the activities of former missionary John Hyde and the negative stories being spread about San Bernardino by ex-Hawaiians Edward Dennis, Brother S. Guess, Charles Hill, and James Kipp.

Other factors included a distaste for the constant fund-raising, the official announcement of polygamy, the impotency of healing administrations in the face of the smallpox epidemic, the failure of so many of the missionaries to learn the language, and the superficial instructions given to new converts. Woodbury described how one day he rode into a village on the north coast of O'ahu, preached to several natives on horseback, got off his horse and baptized some of them, and then rode on, baptizing more in two separate villages. How effective could these "conversions" have been with no existing branch infrastructure to integrate members?

Eight missionaries from the fourth wave had left the mission, or were about to, by the time Bigler and Woodbury wrote on December 3 to Brigham Young, a copy of the letter appearing in Woodbury's journal. After explaining the instructions they had sent to the missionaries, Bigler ventured to Young in a postscript that "from the Spirit of your letter" it might be "justifiable" for him and Woodbury to travel "home with the elders."[14] They were too timid to come right out and ask permission but clearly wanted it. For the time being, they continued to act in their offices, fielding questions and making decisions for the missionaries as they prepared to leave.

Alma Smith at Palawai wanted to know what to do about the "disposal of five work oxen and a cart" that had been donated by members, over which the mission had exercised "controll ... since the commencement of the Lanai Settlement." Smith suggested that the proceeds from their sale might be used "to buy a boat (which is mutch kneeded)" and "for paying church debts &c." Implicit in his letter was the implication that large-scale commercial farming would be terminated or

14. Ibid., Dec. 3, 1857; Britsch, *Moramona*, 45.

that the settlement was being closed down altogether. Paradoxically, the idea that a substantial vessel was needed for Lahaina–Lana'i traffic was still assumed. Woodbury responded on December 14 that, indeed, the oxen should be sold. Besides paying debts and making it possible to purchase a boat, the money could be used to bind the Book of Mormon, he ventured, "and then we could accommodate with books the Saints who donated money for the purchaseing of the printing press." Like Cannon, Bigler and Woodbury were feeling guilty about the broken promises regarding the press, although there is no evidence they distributed free copies of the native Book of Mormon to those who had helped buy the press it was printed on.[15]

On April 18, 1858, a letter from Brigham Young (dated February 4) arrived in Honolulu. "I was pleased to learn," he wrote, "that so many of the elders had sailed" for home, and he explained that the federal troops on their way to do battle in Utah had "gone into winter quarters at the ruins of Fort's Bridger and Supply, (which were vacated and burnt by us last fall) and we are taking active measures to be in readiness for any movements they may choose to make when spring opens." He left open the question of Bigler and Woodbury staying or leaving, but they chose to read between the lines that they had permission to depart, and they did so as soon as they could, arriving back in Salt Lake City in October 1858.[16] Beforehand, they had tried several times to obtain a more definitive contract with Haalelea to resolve the imminent lease payment of $175, for which the church had no means with which to pay. Haalelea offered to sell 10,000 acres to the settlers for $300, but they had to decline for the same reason.[17]

The last native conference held in the mission before the mission president's departure was on April 25, 1858. Another conference held six months later, after the Americans had left, reported a total membership of only 632, and the conference took the drastic step of excommunicating all native Mormons living on Moloka'i. The report of the proceedings were the last that would be forwarded to Salt Lake

15. Woodbury diaries, Dec. 9, 14, 1857.
16. Bigler, "Extracts," Apr. 22, 1858; Young to Bigler and Woodbury, Feb. 4, 1858.
17. Woodbury diaries, Dec. 3, 1857.

City. By late summer 1858, after the Utah War was resolved, missionaries were quickly sent back to Canada, Europe, and the eastern states, but not to the Sandwich Islands, indicating a change of sentiment regarding native people. Instead of being called to Hawaii, George Q. Cannon was sent to Europe to supervise the British Mission. Some of the resulting confusion in Hawaii was because President Bigler had left without appointing a native elder to succeed him. This led to "contention regarding who was the leading Church authority ... Elder Kailehune of Lanai claim[ing]" that title. He was president at the Lana'i gathering place, so he argued that he was "superior to all other [conference] presidents," a claim they did not necessarily accept.

Assistant LDS Church Historian Andrew Jenson visited the Islands in 1895 and found that things had become "less orderly" after 1858. "Contentions had arisen among the Hawaiian elders that were difficult to settle." In addition, "money that had been collected throughout the islands for the purpose of purchasing the Palawai lands was used by President Kailehune for his own purposes. Although he was excommunicated, the money, over three hundred dollars, was not recovered."[18] This could have been avoided by the presence of one supervising Utah elder fluent in the language or the designation of a native presidency.

The problem was ethnic prejudice. The Utahns regarded native elders as below them in status and unable to take over when they departed. Neither Brigham Young nor the mission presidency even considered the possibility that native elders could supervise the seventy-five or so native branches on six islands. The frequently repeated mantra that the islanders were divinely favored descendants of Abraham was contradicted by this dismissive attitude. Into the vacuum created when the missionaries left the islands came the colorful opportunist Walter Murray Gibson on July 4, 1861. Until then, for the space of three years, there would be no official church representation in Hawaii.

18. Britsch, "Lanai Colony," 80.

CHAPTER 41

The Walter Murray Gibson Fiasco

I view him [the Hawaiian] and treat him as an interesting yet feeble younger brother, a subject of an oceanic empire ... Who or what shall I fear where I am King ... I am King; not of oceanica, not of Malaysia, not of Hawaii nei, not of Lanai, but of Palawai on this day of grace. But this is but the baby of my Kingdom. Oh smiling Palawai, thou infant hope of my glorious kingdom.

—*Walter Murray Gibson diary, Jan. 31, 1862*

"Most of what [Walter Murray] Gibson told people about himself" may or may not have been true, Gavan Daws wrote, because the stories usually involved "no other witnesses." What is known with certainty is that the adventurer was born in England in 1822 and his parents moved to Montreal when he was at a young age. His schooling in French proved to be an asset, and in fact he became very fluent in many languages, including (much later) native Hawaiian.[1] After his family moved to New York City, he was apparently hired to drive a carriage to South Carolina, where he stayed to teach school, got married, and fathered three children. When his wife died in 1844 he left his children with their grandparents and returned to New York City.

Within a few years, he purchased a schooner and sailed in 1851 to the Spice Islands (Indonesia), where Dutch colonial authorities seized his ship, arrested him, and charged him with attempting to foment a rebellion among the natives. He escaped from prison,

1. Daws, Dream of Islands, 132; Adler and Kamins, *Fantastic Life*, 3–4.

Walter Murray Gibson

Courtesy Hawaii State Archives.

according to his telling, and boarded a ship that was about to sail to the United States. When he arrived in America, he gained some respectability by lecturing about the Spice Islands to the American Geographical and Statistical Society, and by writing a romantic account of his experiences in Asia.[2]

When the Utah War became a burning national issue in 1857–58, he took an interest in the controversy, proposing that the Mormons could be moved to the Pacific islands or somewhere in the Indian Ocean, and he began to talk excitedly about it in his lectures. When President James Buchanan rebuffed the idea, Gibson reclaimed his children and traveled to Utah to suggest the idea to Brigham Young in late October 1859. Young was uninterested but took an interest in Gibson, telling the visitor that if he joined the church, Young would send him on a mission to the Pacific. Gibson took the challenge and was baptized, along with his daughter Talula, on January, 15, 1860. Three months later Young called Gibson on a mission to New York City and took Talula into his own home, to be cared for by his polygamous wives, while her father was away. While he was in New York

2. Gibson, *Prison of Weltevreden*.

City Gibson wrote articles about Mormonism, Joseph Smith, and Brigham Young for an encyclopedia. Having been told that he should feel free to return in the fall if he desired to,[3] Gibson made his way back west. Before long, Young invited him to give lectures in the Tabernacle, and at a dinner in the Lion House "presented him with an engraved and handsome watch."[4]

Then came the call to the Pacific islands on November 18, with three certificates signed by the First Presidency. One of them "was addressed to the Malay potentates and peoples," another a good will message to the "Tycoon of the Islands of Japan," and the third an elder's certificate declaring him to be on a "mission to preach the Gospel and administer its ordinances," requesting people to "give heed to his teachings and councils as a man of God, and to assist him in his travels." Taking his daughter and leaving his two sons with the Mormons, Gibson left Salt Lake City on November 21 and took the southern route to California. After reaching San Francisco, the two remained eight months while Gibson delivered public lectures and reported on them to Brigham Young. He and Talula stayed with Dwight Eveleth, a Mormon, but Gibson never publicly announced in his lectures or to the newspapers that he was a Mormon. Brigham Young wrote urging him to venture farther west and south, to visit Mormons in the Sandwich and Society islands, to which Gibson responded positively.[5]

He and Talula left San Francisco on June 15 on the bark *Yankee* and arrived at Honolulu on June 20.[6] He immediately contacted the *Pacific Commercial Advertiser* to announce his presence. The newspaper responded by sending a reporter to a lecture he gave on July 12 on Malaysia, explaining that the audience "went away delighted and instructed." Bailey mentioned that Gibson and his daughter were studying "the new and throaty Hawaiian language" in the morning

---

3. Barrett, "Walter Murray Gibson," 147.

4. Bailey, *Hawaii's Royal Prime Minister*, 50, 89, 93, 105, 107–09; Jenson, "Walter Murray Gibson," 10–11;

5. Adler and Kamins, *Fantastic Life*, 46–48; see Barrett, "Walter Murray Gibson," 49–50; CHL CR 1234, 1 outgoing FE–Gi, Gibson Reel 37 (baptismal record, missionary certificate, and draft letter to rule of Japan); *Deseret News*, Nov. 18, 1860.

6. *Deseret News*, Nov. 18, 21, 1860.

and had begun "meet[ing] with the Mormons of Hawaii, quietly at first. He told them he had come to take charge of the church in the islands and would do a great work for them, but for the time being they were to tell no one about this."[7]

He attended the October 1861 conference at Wailuku that drew about 1,000 native members and quickly won them over. "Not only did the Hawaiians accept him as the Lord's anointed, sent out from the seat of authority in far away Utah, but they welcomed him with joy and praise. Henceforth he was known to Hawaiian natives as 'Kipikona.'"[8] Andrew Jenson wrote that "it stands to reason that the unsuspecting natives, after being left alone so long, would receive any elder from the headquarters of The Church with open arms, and with almost unlimited confidence." Gibson reported on his activities to Brigham Young, sought his advice, and was surprisingly clear about his ambitions. On November 1, 1861, he wrote that he would "do all the good I can for the Saints on the Hawaiian Islands, with the little money they have contributed, and then I will sail for the Malay Islands." In another letter two months later he gave Young his opinion that the native Saints "must remain ... within the range of their own tropic and fruity latitudes" and not be gathered to Utah, adding that "it is the desire of my heart to establish a centre stake for all Oceanicans ... I rejoice in the hope that the fruits of my labour here will enable me to push on next season to Japan, or Malaysia in company with a few intelligent Hawaiian Saints. They will be invaluable aids in advancing the gospel in Oceanica."[9]

Gibson bound some of the loose sheets of the Book of Mormon and elicited some bad publicity when he neglected to pay the binder. Apparently he sold forty-one copies for $1.00 each. Like those who had come before him, he soon adopted a condescending attitude toward the native people. His diary entry on November 5, 1861,

7. Bailey, *Hawaii's Royal Prime Minister*, 110, 115, 120; Adler and Kamins cite an interview with Sister Kapo, widow of Elder J.W.H. Kauwahi.

8. Jenson, "Walter Murray Gibson," 12–13. "Kipikona" signifies a "rebel storm." Pukui and Elbert, *Hawaiian Dictionary*.

9. Ibid.; Adler and Kamins, *Fantastic Life*, 66.

contains his opinion that "the people are poor; in pocket, in brain, in everything. They are material for a very little kingdom," although one he wanted to make "glorious" by establishing "a port and a commerce; a state of civilization. I would make millions of fruits" and "fill this lovely crater with corn and wine and oil and babies and love and health and brotherly rejoicing and sisters' kisses and memory of me evermore." Influential people began to comment favorably upon his philanthropy (*The Polynesian*) and social reform (*Sacramento Union*), whereby he had transformed a slum where "about forty families [were] living in small, ruinous and unhealthy houses" on Lana'i. He said that when he arrived, the people were languishing in "crowded" conditions and had "no agriculture, no industry, no water, [and were] without ambition or hope." He said he revived them to a state of health and happiness.[10]

Bailey contends that Gibson's kingdom was, in fact, "expanding and prospering," and that while the "departed Utah elders had left the native branches to flounder without authoritative leadership," Gibson "inspired new confidence, and in less than three years had rebuilt Mormonism into a vital and dramatic force." Both Brigham Young and Joseph F. Smith—from afar—were pleased with what he was accomplishing, but Britsch reminds us that they "did not have the full picture of what Gibson was doing." It would be strange if they had received accurate reports since the church Gibson established on Lana'i bore slight resemblance to the church in Utah, although the First Presidency never made an effort to check on his activities.

According to Andrew Jenson, Gibson called off all church meetings and "prevailed upon [the members] to turn over to him" all real estate, in return for which he promised he would procure land for them for a gathering place. He had everything "deeded over to him ... and unto his heirs and assigns, and not, as he had promised them, in behalf of The Church." They sold the meetinghouses on other islands, so that when Elder Smith visited they had no place to meet.

10. JGQC, 545; Daws, *Dream of Islands*, 133; Bailey, *Hawaii's Royal Prime Minister*, 123–24; Barrett, "Walter Murray Gibson," 151–52.

Gibson charged fees for ordinances and offices. He ordained twelve apostles and charged them each $150.00 for the privilege, as well as for another native Mormon to be the church's archbishop. "With the money thus obtained, and other means received by contribution from the natives," explained Bailey, "he purchased half the island of Lanai."[11]

Barret points out that Mormon "contemporaries of Gibson expressed little or no concern about his acquisition of real property" on Lana'i, whereas "important Mormons eventually came to believe that Gibson had managed to gain title to LDS Church lands, failing to realize that the Utah elders had not completed any fee-simple land transactions before their departure in 1858." The land Gibson purchased was Haalelea's, although he probably led native members to believe he was purchasing the land on behalf of the church. Barrett continues:

> Gibson may have felt that he was simply following the example of his religious mentors in Great Salt Lake City when he placed Lanai lands in his own name. Since the days of Joseph Smith, Mormon leaders had held church property in their own names. While serving as "trustee" for church property, both Joseph Smith and Brigham Young had also acquired large tracts of personal property ... Brigham Young, who was busy demonstrating his own business acumen in Utah, said that neither he nor his associates cared how much property Walter Gibson acquired.[12]

Andrew Jenson learned that Gibson "surround[ed] his own person and residence with such a halo or sacredness, in the minds of the natives, that they always entered his house on their hands and knees." A giant rock became the repository of relics, which "if any person touched it he would be struck dead," Gibson told them. He liked to wear a flowing white robe, and he "set apart his daughter as a high priestess."[13] Finally a group of native elders drafted a long letter to

---

11. Bailey, *Hawaii's Royal Prime Minister*, 126–27, 133–34; Barrett, "Walter Murray Gibson, 154; Britsch, *Unto the Islands of the Sea*, 120; Jenson, "Walter Murray Gibson," 88.

12. Barrett, "Walter Murray Gibson," 152–53, citing the *Deseret News*, June 1, 1864; *Millennial Star*, Apr. 12, 1864.

13. Jenson, "Walter Murray Gibson," 89–90.

Brigham Young in Hawaiian describing the conditions, and the letter was translated and read by Young in the presence of several of the apostles. Galvanized by what he read, Young immediately dispatched apostles Ezra Taft Benson and Lorenzo Snow to travel to the islands and investigate, accompanied by former Hawaiian missionaries Benjamin and William Cluff, Alma L. Smith, Joseph F. Smith, and John R. Young. They left on March 2, 1864.[14]

All the while Gibson was busy lobbying various church dignitaries through correspondence, writing to apostle George A. Smith on March 13 that he had done "the best I could, according to my light." He complained that Hawaiians were "lazy and filthy, and objects of white men's contempt. I felt that they needed some improved organization of their daily life, more than preaching to." He claimed that his native Mormons had improved to the point that they could now "live their religion like first class white men." Even so, he added, there were "a lot of pestersome old sore heads" who had "not contributed "one grain of value in any form whatever" to the church who were grumbling about the changes he had instituted.[15]

When the Utah delegation arrived on Lana'i on April 2, they met with Gibson, and William Cluff said their meeting was "quite formal, and on [Gibson's] part, cold and distant. He had no intimation of our coming until our messenger arrived that morning." The delegation spent several days prior to the April 6 conference collecting information, learning that Gibson "had represented to the Saints that his jurisdiction and authority in Polynesia was equal with President Brigham Young in America." Every day he was "drilling [the men] daily in military tactics." When asked about this, he said without hesitation that he intended to conquer "all the islands in the Pacific Ocean. Then organize one great Polynesian empire."[16]

A dramatic confrontation took place in Palawai on April 6, at

14. Bailey, *Hawaii's Royal Prime Minister*, 129–30; Staker, *Waiting for World's End*, 278–79.

15. Gibson to George A. Smith, Mar. 13, 1864. There is a note at the top of the letter indicating that Smith received it on Apr. 20, long after the high-level delegation had departed.

16. Jenson, "Walter Murray Gibson," 90–92; Cluff, "Fall of Walter Murray Gibson," 470–71.

an event that was well attended by native Mormons. Gibson tried to take charge by appealing directly to the people in their language, reminding them that he was their protector and father and that the delegation from Utah—these "strangers" he called them—had given no "notice" they were coming. At this juncture Benson asked Joseph F. Smith to respond to Gibson in the native language. Smith said,

> I am pleased after an absence of over seven years, to return and meet with you again ... We have been referred to here as strangers. It is true we came to these lands and traveled among this people without purse or scrip, as Christ and His Apostles did, and commanded all His co-laborers to do. Did we not travel on foot, and preach the Gospel to this people for eight years? Visiting you in your homes, administering to the sick, eating such food as you eat, depriving ourselves of the comforts and blessings of home and friends for the Gospel and your sakes ... Did we set a price on the offices of the Priesthood we conferred on you? Did we exact tribute from you to purchase lands for us and our heirs? Now, when you contrast the labors of Pukuniahi [George Q. Cannon] and associates and us who came after them, with our friend here who assumed to be your leader and boasts of what he has done, you may say whether we are strangers among the Hawaiian people.[17]

Cluff was disappointed that, even though "Elder Smith enjoyed a great flow of the Holy Spirit and spoke with much power, yet we could see that Gibson had a great influence over many of them."

At a priesthood meeting that night the letter to Young from the eight native brethren was read. In response, Gibson produced one of the documents from the First Presidency authorizing him to preach. Snow inspected it and announced that it authorized Gibson to preach, but not to "preside over the Hawaiian Mission of the Church. You have assumed that authority." Gibson, brandishing the document, declared, "Here is my authority, which I received direct from President Brigham Young. I don't hold myself accountable to these men."

17. Cluff, "Fall of Walter M. Gibson," 471–72. "Pukuniahi" meant "gun-burning fire," according to Professor Kali Fermantez, "The Right Place at the Right Time," devotional speech, BYU–Hawaii, Oct. 1, 2013.

Joseph F. Smith reported that

> Brother Benson and Snow required him to sign the land over to the Church as it was deeded to him and his heirs. This he flatly refused to do informing them he should take his own course, that he was not sent here by the Church, had received no counsel from Brigham Young, had acted upon his own responsibility in what he had done, and he was not behold[en] to the Church. He also told them he should ask no counsel of them, but would pursue his own course for the future ... He declared he should use his influence to keep the natives in his power, and persuade more to come there if he could, that they should receive no benefit from the land they had bought only as they would become subject to him. It is useless to say more.[18]

At this point Apostle Benson, his words translated into native, summarized the case against Gibson: "We have thoroughly investigated the charges preferred against Brother Gibson by several of your native Elders, and found them substantially true ... For all these unlawful acts we disapprove of his course and say he is not the president of this mission. And we ask you Saints to sustain us in this decision." The Utah delegation was shocked when the native brethren overwhelmingly voted down apostle Benson's motion. A "majority of those present" were loyal to Gibson, Cluff wrote. Jenson portrayed it even more dramatically: "When this was put to vote all but one of the native elders voted against the motion." The apostles "gave notice that on their leaving for home they would appoint an Elder to preside over the Hawaiian Mission, and that all who desired to retain their fellowship and standing in the Church should leave Palawai and return to their former homes on the several islands, where these Elders—Joseph F. Smith, Alma L. Smith and W. W. Cluff—would visit them in the near future, and set the branches of the Church in order and preach the Gospel to them in the spirit thereof."

The next day, April 8, the Utah delegation went back to Lahaina and held a council meeting that evening, during which they

18. Joseph F. Smith to George Q. Cannon, May 1864, qtd. in Britsch, *Unto the Islands of the Sea*, 122–23.

excommunicated Gibson for false teachings, defrauding the native members, "introduc[ing] pagan superstitions, and encourag[ing] ... hula dancing." They decided to disfellowship any who remained on Lana'i. Meanwhile Gibson, anticipating what was to come, had already written to Brigham Young saying he retained "love and regard for your person, although you have dealt precipitately and harshly with me.—My daughter remembers tenderly your interesting family. I think and feel that though my spirit has not responded to your call, and we are now in different channels, that yet my course will never," he emphasized, "lead me into an attitude that will be hostile to you, or the work you direct." In June Gibson surrendered to John R. Young the remaining copies of the bound Book of Mormon in his possession.[19]

In a short period of time, Gibson became "high and influential in the Hawaiian government," Bailey noted, and in that capacity he was "known to display the watch ... Brigham Young had given him. And he always treated visiting Mormon missionaries with great respect and kindness."[20] Jenson agreed that when Gibson came to power in the kingdom, "he befriended the elders from Utah and the Saints generally."[21] Apostles Benson and Snow left Hawaii with Joseph F. Smith in charge, Alma Smith and William Cluff acting as his assistants, and they departed from Honolulu on April 18. When Brigham Young received their report at a meeting in the Tabernacle in June, including the fact that Gibson had been excommunicated, Young "stated briefly ... that the [main] charge against Walter M. Gibson ... [had been] his persistent refusal to be dictated to by the Priesthood."[22]

The native members attempted to recover their land on Lana'i, but the Utah apostles and ex-missionaries showed little interest in that pursuit, first because Joseph F. Smith "did not believe that Lanai was worth fighting for. His feelings about the matter had apparently not changed since 1857. Second, he was convinced that the costs of the

---

19. Cluff, "Fall of Walter M. Gibson," 472-73; Bailey, *Hawaii's Royal Prime Minister*, 143; Adler and Kamins, *Fantastic Life*, 74, 75; *JGQC*, 545.

20. Bailey, *Hawaii's Royal Prime Minister*, 294n14.

21. Jenson, "Walter Murray Gibson," 94–95.

22. Cluff, "Fall of Walter M. Gibson," 473; Adler and Kamins, Fantastic Life, 75–76.

court battle would be greater than the value of the land." Six months after Gibson's excommunication, most of the former members had gravitated back to the official church, with only fourteen individuals reportedly still living under his direction on Lana'i. In October the fourteen holdouts requested and were granted excommunication.

Gibson turned his Lana'i lands into pastures for sheep and cattle and later left for a life in politics in Honolulu, founding a newspaper that continues to this day and winning election to the Hawaiian legislature. When King Kalakaua reorganized his government on May 20, 1882, he appointed Gibson prime minister and foreign affairs minister. In office, Gibson talked about his dream of conquering Samoa, and in 1887 was found complicit in a plot against the Hawaiian government and forced to resign his cabinet position. This was just before the overthrow of the monarchy by pro-American businessmen. In the wake of that action, Gibson went into exile in San Francisco and died of tuberculosis on January 21, 1888.[23]

When Joseph F. Smith was later serving as second counselor to LDS President John Taylor, and went on the run to escape prosecution for polygamy, he chose Hawaii as a place of hiding. On April 38, 1887, prior to Gibson's resignation, he wrote to Frank Hammond in Bluff, Utah, where Hammond was president of the San Juan Stake, and perceptively described the would-be king of the Polynesians.

> W. M. Gibson, is as ambitious for power as ever, he has the enmity of nearly the whole foreign population of Hawaii nei. The independent papers goad and thorne him after the Spirit and fashion of the S[alt] L[ake] Tribune. In politics he is shrude [shrewd], cunning, selfish, cold and intriguing, and more than a match for his opponents. In financial matters he is keen and grasping personally, and extravagant with public funds. He is full of wild schemes and adventures. His ambition is to found a polenycian Empire, with Hawaii at the head, himself dictator. He holds with a firm grip the reins of government and possesses the confidence of the King whom he flatters and fondles as you would a pup[p]et or a toy. He is kind to us [Mormons] and willing to shew us

23. Britsch, *Unto the Islands of the Sea*, 123; Barrett, "Walter Murray Gibson," 27, 157–58.

> many favors, but stoutly refuses to grant permission to our people to emigrate [to Utah] from here, as his aim and ambition is increase and power ... It is the opinion of the inteligent public that he and the government will soon go down with a crash, to ruin.[24]

In the Sandwich Islands much earlier, a young Joseph F. wrote to Brigham Young on July 5, 1864, suggesting they look for a new gathering place in the islands. Britsch notes that Young still "was reluctant to believe that much should be done in Hawaii. His letters to Joseph F. reveal that he was disturbed with the unfaithfulness of the Hawaiians and wanted to see some indication of repentance before he committed more Church resources."[25] And Young's feelings were mirrored in those of many Hawaiian Mormons, who wanted to see an indication of commitment from their religious leaders before they contributed more of their funds, their time, and their hearts to the church.

24. Smith to Hammond, July 5, 1864.

25. Britsch, *Unto the Islands of the Sea*, 125.

CHAPTER 42

A Triumphant Return

Brother Francis A. Hammond, who is familiar with the Islands and the people, has been appointed a mission to those lands. He will establish a tannery there, and as fast as practicable, commence the cultivation of cotton and sugar-cane, and other productions. An effort will be made to gather the people, and to teach them to labor and to exert themselves for their own support and development and exaltation, temporally and spiritually. Brother Hammond will probably take [the] stage from this place and proceed by the quickest conveyance to the Islands. If we carry out the contemplated mission, his family and some few others will follow.

—*Brigham Young to Daniel H. Wells, Oct. 19, 1864*

Joseph F. Smith wrote to inform George A. Smith on July 14, 1864, of how he and the other four Utah missionaries were faring. William Cluff had just left Honolulu to "make a tour" around Kaua'i, Alma Smith and John R. Young were doing the same on Hawai'i, while Benjamin Cluff was "upon the back side of this island [O'ahu] studying the language." They would soon meet at a native conference scheduled for Maui. Joseph F. confessed to an ambivalence for the culture, a sentiment that had not changed since his first mission in the 1850s. The "food, such as it is," he wrote, was so "cheap, ... the people are always idle excepting a very small portion of their time." They "soon weary of anything, that requires more of them than they are accustomed to do for themselves." They were simplistic, "their wants are small," he wrote. It was "doubtful" whether the church could ever sustain a gathering place for them, on the islands, at least not if it had to rely on "the labour of the Native Saints."

This was not just his view, he offered, but the "settled" opinion of other "foreigners" in the islands, encapsulated in the saying, the "Natives Won't Work!" They "bear a close relationship to our Utah Indians in that respect," he thought. They needed more than "preaching" and "moral example & influence ... Something must be done ... to do away with their present ["immoral"] habits and customs and change the whole course of their lives." He said the Hawaiian government and the collective "wisdom of the Nation" had tried and failed to rescue the people from their "barbarism," and they remained on a course for the "speedy extinction of the Race." He pessimistically declared: "How far it may be possible to compel the civilization of a people, whose whole inclinations have tended to barbarism is not clear, but it is evident that no inducement can be strong enough to persuade them into it."[1]

Walter Murray Gibson's "learned opinion," Smith maintained, was that the Hawaiians and American Indians had not "descended from the same Race," and this prompted him to observe that the "course adopted by Capt. Gibson with regards to the gathering and instructing them in labour, was just what is needed." Gibson's "cupidity led him," however, to great "extravagance," and it "became apparent to many of them that his object was solely to acquire wealth, at their expence, [and] ... they were diserting him 30 at a time." Joseph F. was "not in favour of diserting the Mission," but surprisingly enough, he thought "two elders [for the entire mission] would fare better, have more influence & do more good than more." Brigham Young had given him the opportunity to remain as mission president, but he had no desire to do so.

Smith did, however, preside over the conference at Wailuku, Maui, during the first three days of October 1864, where only about 200 native members showed up—illustrating the dramatic decline from the glorious days in the early 1850s. He told them he wanted to "inaugurate a reformation" among them, and he and the Utah elders then

1. Joseph F. Smith to George A. Smith, July 14, 1864. In other words, Joseph F. Smith did not believe the people were naturally lethargic or dim-witted but needed some motivating force.

proceeded to re-baptize 113 members. Elder Kaleohano "addressed the meeting, rejoicing in the restoration of the link with Church headquarters and with the authority of the prophet." Smith told them that he, William Cluff, and John R. Young would leave the mission but that Benjamin Cluff and Alma Smith would remain to guide them.[2]

Not waiting to hear further from Joseph F. Smith, while the Wailuku conference was being held Brigham Young concluded that the mission should be re-established and called Francis A. Hammond and brother-in-law George Nebeker to serve as co-presidents. Nebeker, who had never been to the Pacific, had two wives who were sisters of Mary Jane Hammond: thirty-five-year-old Elizabeth and thirty-year-old Maria Louisa. Why Young designated him a co-president is unknown. It may have been assumed that Hammond would stay long enough to train Nebeker and then leave him, which is what happened, but it appears that initially Hammond expected he would stay much longer than he in fact did. Their main assignment was to find a new gathering place. How ironic for Hammond, considering that he was the one who had played the primary role in establishing the first gathering place. His selection as mission president was poetically just, given his adverse treatment by Presidents Lewis and Silas Smith. Picking up his journal writing again, he documented this second assignment in the ninth and last of his surviving Hawaiian books.

Hammond and his family had spent roughly six and a half years in Utah, beginning in June 1857. During the interlude he moved his family to Ogden and went into partnership with Bishop Chauncey West, who had served a brief mission to Asia in the 1850s. He and West manufactured leather shoes, saddles, and harnesses in a profitable enterprise, while Hammond also served as a justice of the peace and for roughly five years was a counselor to West in the Ogden bishopric. Hammond also was elected to the Ogden City Council. On July 25, 1859, Mary Jane's fourth son, George Albert, was born, and another son arrived two years later on August 11, 1861, William

2. Britsch, *Unto the Islands of the Sea*, 125–26; Spurrier, "Kaleohano," 295.

Edmund. This brought the number of sons to five: Frank Jr., Samuel, Fletcher, George, and William, and one daughter, Mary Moselle. On December 28, 1863, a second daughter, Lizzie Fontella, was born.

The biggest change to the family came when Frank became a polygamist on July 10, 1864, in a ceremony officiated by apostle Heber C. Kimball in Salt Lake City, uniting forty-one-year-old Frank with nineteen-year-old Alice Howard, an English emigrant. First wives were usually present to signify their approval, but whether Mary Jane was there is not clear. She was now thirty-two years old, had lost a number of teeth, and over the years had given birth to seven children. Now she was going to share her husband with this nubile teenager from England. Most likely the fact that Mary Jane's sisters were already polygamists, combined with the heightened pressure on church officials to become polygamists, exerted enormous influence on her to embrace what she had opposed. If Frank was keeping journals between 1857 and 1864, they have not survived.

Alice Howard grew up in Southport, England, as an orphan after her father drowned at sea in 1858 and her mother died four years later. A year after her mother's death, she and four of her siblings immigrated to Utah, leaving another five siblings behind. Why some stayed is unknown, although the youngest émigré, six-year-old Richard, would eventually leave the church and migrate back to England. The youngsters, including Alice's twenty-year-old sister Hannah, eleven-year-old sister Elinor (a variation of Eleanor), and nine-year-old brother Hyrum, departed from Liverpool on the packet ship *Cynosure* on May 30, along with 770 other Mormon passengers. The group had been organized by George Q. Cannon and was led by David M. Stuart.[3]

In New York the company that included the Howard children was placed under the direction of Peter Nebeker, a brother of George Nebeker. It thus was in the midst of the American Civil War (the Battle of Gettysburg was underway) that the company wended its course toward Florence, Nebraska, and from there to Salt Lake City, arriving in late September 1863. Alice worked first as a maid in

3. See Sonne, *Ships, Saints and Mariners*, 57.

Cannon's home and then at the residence of Ogden's stake president, Lorin Farr. Less than a year after she arrived, she married Frank. Her younger sister Elinor later became a plural wife of William Halls, one of Frank Hammond's best friends in Huntsville.

Cannon, now an apostle, arrived back in Salt Lake City on October 10, 1864, a few months after Hammond's plural marriage and about a month before Hammond was called to Hawaii. Given the critical role he played in the mission's history, he must have been consulted about the appointment, and he may have been the one who suggested that Hammond be the mission president. In any case, Brigham Young wrote a long letter on October 19 to his counselor Daniel H. Wells and son Brigham Jr. in the mission office in England, explaining that in

> a letter from Joseph F. Smith, recently written from the Sandwich Islands, we learn that a friendly chief [Levi Haalelea]—he who owned the land on which the natives gathered, and where Gibson had been operating—has offered the brethren a good tract of land, suitable for a plantation and settlement, on the island of Hawaii, consisting of 15,000 acres, for $3,000. I have written to brother Joseph F. that, if the land be as good and as suitable for a plantation and settlement as represented, to close for it [buy it], and draw on me for the amount.[4]

Hammond and Nebeker took the new northern route that had been surveyed in 1859 by James Hervey Simpson of the Army Topographical Corps and was about 300 miles shorter than the previous trail. It was used by nearly all the wagon trains carrying freight and immigrants to Carson City and Sacramento, including the Pony Express and similar mail carriers and even a stage coach line, as well as those who strung the Pacific telegraph.[5] On November 10, 1864, Hammond began his ninth Hawaiian Mission journal by writing that he and Nebeker "left Salt Lake City in the over-land stage for the S[andwich] I[slands] on a mission, first having been called and set

4. See epigraph at the beginning of this chapter, and notice that Young does not mention Hammond's "co-president." The letter appears in the Journal History, Oct. 19, 1864, 2; and is quoted in the *Millennial Star*, Dec. 17, 1864, 815.

5. See Petersen, *Route for the Overland Stage*.

apart by Prest. B. Young[6] and carrying letters of instruction to obtain a land or lands thro[ugh] purchase or lease suitable for growing cotton, Sugar, rice, tobaco, [and] to establish a Tannery &c. &c and enter into any buisiness that saints can enter into lawfuly."

The mention of tobacco is especially interesting since in the 1850s Hammond had so strongly opposed it. He evidently was using tobacco again, but then so was Brigham Young and some other leaders. Continuing his account, Hammond explained that they were "six days and a half traveling time to Sacramento," where they took a steamboat to San Francisco and remained "about 3 weeks waiting for a passage to the Islands. Visited my old friends Bro. J[ohn]. M. Horner and others." They also met with Joseph F. Smith, William Cluff, John R. Young, and the widowed Mary Burnham and her children, all of whom were heading to the Salt Lake Valley. On December 8 they sailed to Honolulu, arriving on the 23rd. "Had a plesant passage," he reported, but "Bro. N[ebeker] was sick most of the way." Once in Honolulu, they found Alma Smith and Benjamin Cluff, who had been left "in charge of the Mission." They stayed with Charles Wings, a white convert.

Brigham Young wrote another letter to his counselor and son in Liverpool on November 18, in which he made some additional comments with regard to the Hawaiian mission: "Elders Francis A. Hammond and George Nebeker started by stage on Thursday Nov. 10, on their missions to the Sandwich Islands, to accomplish what I explained in my last letter to you. Elders Joseph F. Smith, William W. Cluff and John R. Young, with two native Saints and a few other persons, [are] ... in San Francisco [and] ... will not leave ... until the Elders from here [Hammond and Nebeker] reach there, and they have the privilege ... of returning to the islands with the brethren if they choose."[7] As noted, they chose not to.

6. They were set apart on November 10 by Brigham Young, John Taylor, and George A. Smith. Journal History, Nov. 10, 1864.

7. Ibid., Nov. 18, 1864.

CHAPTER 43

The Laie Plantation

This place called Laie, is situated on the Island of Oahu, about thirty-five miles from the city of Honolulu, on the north side of the island, where we always have the refreshing, cool sea breeze. It is a beautiful place. Our dwelling-house is situated on a very pleasant elevation, about a quarter of a mile from, and overlooking the deep blue sea.

—Alma Smith to Millennial Star, Feb. 21, 1865

Two days after he arrived in the islands, Hammond attended Sunday meetings in Honolulu. "I was enabled to speak [the language] much better than I anticipated," he wrote. "The Saints were rejoiced to see me back again. I saw many of them shed tears of joy, and indeed I was effected also to tears. I feel that the Lord is about to commence again his work on these lands." The next day he realized that since he had left nearly eight years earlier, "Honolulu has improved very little ... The[re] is a great falling off in the midst of the native population. They do [not] seem to be doing as well as formily [formerly]." Apparently he was referring to the continued decline in the native population due to foreign diseases, perhaps a reminder of the 1853 Honolulu smallpox epidemic, although he had not witnessed it first hand. He then mentioned his old acquaintance Prince Lot, who had become King Kamehameha V the year before. "The present King is a bold man with a good education and altogether the smartest King that has ever set on the Hawaiian throne. May he be a defender of the rights of God's people."[1]

1. For information about Prince Lot, see Kuykendall, *Hawaiian Kingdom*, 2:33, 124–25, 239–41.

The next day was spent enquiring about options for purchasing land for a new gathering place. Before long, Hammond had learned of several available locations they could either purchase or lease. One possibility was on the island of Kaua'i, where "the King has lands for sale, so has the princess, so has the executors of Haalealea; we have seemingly arrived at just the right time to effect a purch[ase], but lands are very much higher than they were when I left here." The two missionaries who had been left in Hawaii were making progress in learning the language and would help establish the new gathering place. Alma Smith was becoming fluent, and Benjamin Cluff had acquired a "tolerable knowledge" of Hawaiian. Hammond considered them to be "good and faithful elders [who] have done much good for the natives."

Within a day of being on shore, Hammond met with his former acquaintance the king, who directed him to see William Jarrett, clerk for Robert Crichton Wyllie, foreign minister. Hammond had also known Jarrett since his first stay in Lahaina twenty years earlier.[2] The next morning Wyllie prepared letters of introduction for Hammond to acquaint him with the landowners on Kaua'i, and that afternoon Hammond, Cluff, Nebeker, and Smith took the schooner *Excel* to Kaua'i, an island Hammond had never set foot on before.

Coming ashore at Nawiliwili on the next-to-last day of the year, the Jarrett and Allen letters gave the missionaries entrée to the elite of the island and first-rate treatment. The sheriff, Thomas Marshall, "took us up to his house, or rather at Mr. Widimans, where he is boarding[,] and mad[e] us welcome to his table." Mr. Marshall then "took me in his carriage round to see the sugar plantation of Lahuie." Over the next few days the men examined plantations in the Hanalei, Kilauea, and Princeville areas along the north coast, visiting Wyllie's own sugar plantation at Hanalei, where they were provided free food and lodging.

2. Wyllie was a Scottish surgeon and bachelor who had become wealthy in South America before serving as Hawaiian foreign minister from 1845 to his death in mid-October 1865. He was "one of the three or four most important figures in the history of the Hawaiian Kingdom." Judd, *Hawaii*, 72.

Returning toward Nawiliwili, they looked at the lands owned by Charles Fitcomb, who fed them and put them up for the night. "[He] has been on these Islands some forty years," with "a family of children by a native which he has never married and says he never will." They inspected three of Fitcomb's cultivated areas and were so impressed they made him an offer of $12,000 for all three. Although he was interested, he counter-offered at $15,000. When Hammond agreed to increase his bid by $1000, Fitcomb "took a fright and withdrew his offer" altogether. That night they were nevertheless treated to a luau by the owner of a neighboring plantation, a Mr. Krull, with whom they had stayed earlier. Two hundred people "of all ages and sizes" attended. After the feast they were treated to an exhibition of hula dancing performed by two native girls. The dance so shocked Hammond that he called it the "most disgusting sight that I ever saw."[3] Afterward they witnessed horseracing, which was more to Hammond's liking, and he praised the level of expertise as "very creditable."

Next they traveled ten miles north to the Wailua Valley on January 8 to visit one of the most stunningly scenic areas in the entire Hawaiian archipelago. A German couple led them to the 80-foot Wailua Falls where other travelers had seen young men dive from the top to impress girls. The next day the sight-seers visited a water-powered mill at Kaloa where sugar was processed. The day after that, wanting to be sure they had not overlooked any good prospects, Hammond rode alone along the southern coast but found nothing "suitable to our wants." Back in Kaloa, the four elders met again with Mr. Fitcomb but could not reach an agreement. "About sundown we went on board of the 'Kalama'" for Honolulu, followed in short order by Fitcomb, who evidently wanted to sell his land. Hammond spent the next day "run[n]ing about town making calls on those who could give me any information about lands." He and his brother-in-law went to see James W. Austin, the attorney Hammond had become acquainted with in the 1850s, and hired him to help with the land

3. Prince Lot, a bachelor, disliked puritanism and revived some ancient Hawaiian practices such as the hula. He also altered the constitution to give himself more power. Judd, *Hawaii*, 89–90.

negotiations. "Told Mr. Austin that we would still stand by our offer of $12000 for his [Fitcomb's] lands[,] stock[,] [and] improvements of all kinds." Unfortunately, when Fitcomb arrived he repeated to Austin his original bid of $15,000 and said he would accept nothing less, resulting in Hammond and Nebeker withdrawing their offer and ceasing negotiations. The two talked things over and Hammond suggested that it would be "best for [Nebeker] to return to Utah for our families, while I stop here and make a purchase of land as soon as possible and then commence to put in a crop. We have no fears but what we can buy all the lands we want." Nebeker set sail the next day.

Hammond saw Nebeker off and then began looking for land on O'ahu. Traveling in a counterclockwise direction from Honolulu, he found a plantation on the northeast coast that impressed him, and he spent all day on January 20 enquiring about it. The landowner, Thomas T. Dougherty, owned 6,000 acres near the ancient village of Laie, also the name of the plantation.[4] To Hammond's delight, Dougherty said he was willing to sell it "with all the improvements," as indicated by the following journal entries, documenting Hammond's historically important negotiation and purchase.

> Sun. 22nd. Arrived at Laie. We are now about 55 miles from Honolulu. There is a large branch of the church here.
>
> Monday 23th. Rode over the farming land on Laie. Also had stock drove into caroll [corral] so that I could see it. Counted about 250 head.
>
> Tues. 24th. Rode up and over the mountainous part of the land to examine the timber. Had a very hard trip. About 1 o.c[lock] p.m. left the good land of Laie and returned to Mr. Lane's.
>
> Wed. 25th [19]65. Rode into Honolulu [and] arrived a little before sundown very tired, and a little sick with a bad cold.
>
> Thursday, January 26th, 1865. Called on Mr. T[homas] T. Dougherty and offer[ed] him 12000 dollars for Laie[,] with all the stock, houses and improvements thereon. He would not take less than 14000 dollars. I finaly[,] after a little consideration[,] consented to give it.
>
> I agreed to send him a draft for 3000 dollars in ten weeks from date and pay 5000 dollars more by the 1st of July [18]65, 6000 in two

4. The general region was known as the Laie Ahupuaa.

George Nebeker
Courtesy Daughters of Utah Pioneers.

> years from date[,] bearing at 12 per cent per annunm, giving a mortgage on the place for security. I take pos[s]ession im[m]ediately. Bros. A[lma] L. Smith & B[enjamin] Cluff takes charge and [will] put in crops while I return for my family. I agree to not Kill or sell any of the stock until the first payment is made. Then[,] if [we] pay 5000 dollars, the deed is made out and deliv[re]d to Bro. Nebeker & I. Every body says I have made a good barg[a]in.[5]

The next day Hammond's connection to Austin and other acquaintances proved fortuitous, as the attorney helped him draft the Laie purchase and "told Mr. Dougherty that my word could be relyid on, [and] so also did Mr. Walker of the firm of Aldrich, Walker & co. I could not have effected such a trade if I had not had friends here." Now Cluff and Smith could immediately take possession of the land and begin planting a crop before Hammond even had to make the down payment.

While waiting for the next ship to sail to California, Hammond went to foreign secretary Robert Wyllie and obtained "his likeness

5. Hammond journal, Jan. 22–25, 1865.

and the late King's—Kamehameha the 4th—also Queen Ema's, his wife, to be presented to President [Brigham] Young." On Sunday, January 29, Hammond spoke to the native Mormons about "the nature of my present Mission to these lands, it being a temporal mission connected with the spiritual also. I refer[e]d them to the consistent course that the elders from Utah had always manifested in their labors here," which was an exaggeration, depending on what aspect of the missionaries' labors he meant. The next day, prior to leaving for San Francisco, he called on Secretary Wyllie to renew his passport—one he had received seventeen years earlier. "He wished me all success in my contemplated enterprise, [and] sent his kind regards to Prest. Young. Said he would be glad to see 200 Mormons [come] to the Islands and settle." Hammond saw Austin, giving him the inventory of the Laie plantation and relaying the information that the Aldrich, Walker & Co. shipping agents and merchants had agreed to "furnish to Bros. Smith & Cluff whatever they may need in my absence to carry on the place."

That afternoon Hammond sailed on the barque *Eldridge* for San Francisco and described in detail the ship, its captain, fellow passengers, and nautical locations. When they began running into rough weather, the narrative became dramatic. His informed entries about the storm and how the sailors reacted are a pleasure to read.

> Saturday, February 4th, 1865. Commenced with fresh gales from the W[est] N[orth] West. It blowed fresh during the night. Had to shorten sail. We are now running under double reefed topsails. Had our fore topsail split, sent it down[,] and bent another. Sea running high, and sometimes Shipping a good deal of water ...
>
> Sunday, February 5th, 1865. The wind blew a strong gale all night. About 10 o.c. p.m. yesterday, we split [our] foresail. Had to clue it up and let it hang until morning. Then bent another. It blew so hard and the sail being so old and poor that we soon had to clue it up for fear of having it blowed away. The sea is now running high and very irregular. Shipping a good deal of water on deck. About 8 o.c. p.m. shipped a heavy sea over our weather bulwarks[,] striking a hatch house over the mainehatch. Stove in the weather side of house, causing some damage

> and a great deal of fright, especially to those gentelman occupying the house at the time ...
>
> Monday, February 6th, 1865. The gale still increasing. Had our jib blowed away during the night. Run all night under short sail. Passengers very sick and uncomfortable ...
>
> Messrs. Catrall, Mr. Garrity, Allen, and the first mate of our ship, Mr. Bean, were occupying the hatch house last night at the time when it was struck by the sea, and by all accounts it was a most laughable scene, to see them all crowding to see who should be first out of the house, not refusing to creep between each others legs, or breach over each others heads in their great haste to leave those diggings.
>
> Tuesday, February 7th, 1865. Gale continued through the night, and this morning finds us still contending with this oncommon [uncommon] north gale (in this latitude). We are making little progress. The sea is so rough that we cannot carry but very little sail. We are about 800 miles from San Francisco ...
>
> We have a chief steward, assistant Steward[,] and a half white boy who are all the time engaged in waiting on the passengers ...
>
> Wednesday, February 8th, 1865. Gale continued through the night, with squalls of rain falling in torrents for an hour or so at a time. It is becoming very disagreeable, and very trying to one's patience. To day the wind seems to be more fitful as though the gale was drawing to a close. Still blowing too hard to admit of carrying more than double reefed top-sails.
>
> Our Captain has been up for three nights in succession. Sometimes all hands have been on deck securing sails to keep them from being blowed away. A good deal of water has passed down into the cabin during the gale, filling some of the state rooms knee deep in water, [and] causing some of the lady passeng[er]s to pray heartily.[6]

Hammond does not say whether he lent a bos'n hand to the sails when the crew needed help, but where he says that all hands were on deck, he probably implies that he did. The storm began to abate

6. Hammond journal, Feb. 4–8, 1865. A double-reefed topsail is one that has the sheet drawn up partway to reduce the surface area exposed to the wind. The main hatch house is where the crew eats and sleeps, and other hatch houses were for equipment. To stave (past tense "stove") is to bash or crush something. A jib is the triangular sail in front of the foremast. A state room is a private cabin.

the next day, and on February 18 they entered the bay—through the opening that was already called the Golden Gate—and sailed into the wonderful San Francisco harbor.

> Crossed the bar at 11½ & took pilot on board. Arr[i]ved at San Francisco at 1 P.M. Anchor[e]d of[f] from Wharf. Took a boat and went ashore to Telegraph office. Sent dispatch to Prest. [Brigham] Young concerning my arrival and purchase at the Islands. Called on [forty-year-old brother-in-law] Br. J[ohn] Dilworth. Found himself and family all well. From there proceeded to Bro. [Dwight] Eveleth['s]. Himself and family in good health. I spent the night here. Learned from Bro. E[veleth] that Bro. Nebeker[,] who was somewhat unwell[,] had left here on 15th, ins't. for G[reat] S[alt] L[ake] City.[7]

Hammond traveled to Oakland two days later with fruit trees he had brought from the islands for John Horner, the Mormon who was developing the San Jose and Noe Valley areas. Back in San Francisco, Hammond found a message waiting for him at the telegraph office from Brigham Young requesting more information about Laie. That day Alma Smith—2,000 miles away—drafted a letter to the church newspaper in Liverpool, the *Millennial Star*, explaining the land purchase and indicating that Hammond and Nebeker "had gone to Utah, to make arrangements for a permanent stay on the Islands." The letter was published in the newspaper four months later.[8] In it, Smith described the beauty of the setting and explained that up to thirty natives were already working the land by "fencing, ploughing, planting, &c." Adopting the condescending view that was typical for Utah missionaries in the 1850s and 1860s, he unfortunately editorialized that "some of them understand different kinds of work, but most of them, like the cattle on the place, are ignorant and unbroken. A person would require the wisdom of Solomon, and the patience of Job, to accomplish anything; but, as patience and perseverance will sometimes accomplish a

7. Ibid., Feb. 18, 1865. John Taylor Dilworth (1825–1905) was Mary Jane Hammond's older (and only) brother. He became estranged from the Mormon Church and returned to the family's homeland in Chester County, northwest of Philadelphia.

8. *Millennial Star*, June 10, 1865, 360–61; epigraph at beginning of this chapter.

great deal, we do not mean to get discouraged, but to persevere in well doing, believing that all will work out right in the end."

Hammond "waited on Mr. Aldrich" the next day, the man connected with Brooks & Co. "in the Hawai[i]an Packet line. Mr. Aldrich very readily consented to assist me by writing to his partners at Honolulu to pay over to Mr. Austin or Dougherty the $5000 at the expiration of the ten weeks as spoken of in the article of agreement. I wrote to Mr. Austin our agent to this effect [and] also to Bro[s] Alma Smith & B[enjamin] Cluff."[9]

That afternoon Hammond took the *Crysalise* shallow-draft steamboat to Freeport, ten miles south of Sacramento, a stop on the Sacramento River. From there he boarded a train at 1:00 a.m. to Laytrobe [Labrobe], at the foot of the Sierra Nevada mountains, for a stagecoach that took him twenty miles to Placerville. By the time he reached Salt Lake City he had taken five distinctly different modes of transportation: tall ship, riverboat, train, sleigh, and stagecoach. Continuing his travel narrative, he left Placerville and took a stagecoach north, during which he and his fellow travelers "were all [day] and night till 11 p.m. getting [100 miles to the] Strawberry Valley Station, [including] some 60 miles of the worst road for mud I ever traveled. We remained there until daylight. Had a good supper. They keep a good house here, and charge moderate."

On Sunday morning Hammond set out by sleigh, "nicely fitted up with six horses & bells to match," on a sixty-mile trek through the high mountains to the terminal for another stagecoach line, this one bringing him to Virginia City. After spending a restful night in the National Hotel in the famous boom town, he embarked on the penultimate journey, 600 miles in the direction of Salt Lake City, in a "spring[-suspended] conco[r]d Waggon covered with canvass[,] drawn with six horses."[10] The trail more or less followed the

9. The main reason for Hammond's trip to Salt Lake City was to obtain $5,000 for William A. Aldrich, whose firm (Aldrich, Walker & Co.) was connected to the Charles Walcott Brooks & Co. fleet in San Francisco. Aldrich is best known today for having co-founded the First Hawaiian Bank in 1858, and in fact, his import firm will close in 1866. Brooks, on the other hand, will be named US Consul to Japan in 1870.

10. These stage coaches were built by the Abbott and Downing Company in Concord, Massachusetts, and thus the name.

present-day Nevada Route 50 as far as Austin, Nevada, and then continued farther east and north to Ruby Valley, about 30 miles southeast of present-day Elko. All along the way, the horses and drivers were changed frequently, meaning that the passengers had to tough it out for days and nights at a time, catching what sleep they could in the swaying stagecoach. Hammond indicated that during one stretch he rode "on the boot"[11] with a driver named Baker, "who had been a sailor and was once upon the Sandwich Islands."

Indian attacks had fallen off in the Great Basin, but it was still a threat. In May 1860 a group of Paiutes—unhappy that the stage and mail stations dominated the few water sources and best available grazing ground—had razed the stations, driven off livestock, and killed sixteen Pony Express employees. Then in March 1863, Goshute Indians attacked and killed a stagecoach driver and wounded a passenger, and later burned a station to the ground, killed two stockmen, and stole the horses.[12]

On February 28 Brigham Young wrote to Daniel Wells and Brigham Jr. in England, informing them of the arrival of Nebeker in Utah and Hammond's purchase of Laie plantation:

> The brethren who are acquainted with the place, say 'it is the best place on that island,' [and] brother Hammond thinks it a good bargain. Brother Nebeker and he take the place on their own responsibility—such being my wish, if it were taken at all—and agree to refund the money, which I advance them to help them to make the first payment. Brother Hammond telegraphs that he expected to have 100 acres of cotton planted by the 1st of March, and brother Alma. A. Smith and Benjamin Cluff were left in charge, until he and brother Nebeker returned. There were seventy of the native Saints already living on the land; they will form a nucleus for the gathering. How long the brethren will be suffered to remain there, to pursue their operations in peace, is a question; but they may be undisturbed sufficiently long, to give them an opportunity to save a small remnant

11. The boot was the driver's seat, and more specifically the leather-lined storage box the driver sat on. It was used for storing mail and purses.

12. See Anderson, *Stagecoach*, 33, 56–57.

> of those who belong to the Church, or of their children, from that extinction which seems to be impending over the [native] nation, and from which the Saints cannot escape by gathering to the continent—the laws of that kingdom prohibiting emigration in effect.[13]

As speculative and pessimistic as the prediction was, it followed the thinking of other religious leaders such as the Rev. Henry T. Cheever, who—apparently not tongue-in-cheek—wrote about "the mysterious providence of God [to see] the whole native race expire just as it is Christianized."[14]

The real estate agreement put the Laie Plantation in the names of Hammond and Nebeker and made them responsible for the mortgage payments. If the agricultural endeavor did not pan out, they were financially responsible, and if it earned a profit, they would not benefit. It was a good deal for the church but not for Hammond and Nebeker; for them it was a financial and psychological burden. Young believed that the Second Coming was imminent and only those who gathered to the intermountain West would be saved. Since the Hawaiian government would not allow native Mormon converts to immigrate to Utah, he apparently assumed God would spare at least a "small remnant of those who belong to the Church, or their children," who gathered to Laie. This was the same doctrine Hammond had preached to the native Mormons regarding Palawai, Lana'i, in the 1850s.

About 7:00 p.m. on February 28, the large Concord stagecoach pulled by six horses arrived at Austin, from where Hammond continued in a lighter coach through a stretch that involved "coming to and leaving a Station about ev[e]ry 15 miles[,] where we change horses, and about ev[e]ry 40 miles change drivers." The Wells Fargo Company would brag that summer that it carried four dignitaries—US Speaker of the House Schyler Colfax and three newspapermen—from the Midwest to San Francisco in record time, cutting a third off the normal travel time between Salt Lake City and Austin, Nevada.

13. Journal History, Feb. 28, 1865; published in the *Millennial Star*, Apr. 29, 1865, 270–71.

14. Cheever, *Island World of the Pacific*, 214.

According to historian Andy Anderson, the participants found it a "memorable experience ... but not one they wished to repeat. The jolting, dust, and lack of sleep were constant."[15]

Hammond knew he was making good time, but this early in the year he saw they "could have come on a Sleigh from Austin ... clear through to Salt Lake City." The stage reached Fort Crittenden (formerly Camp Floyd) early in the morning on March 4, and the passengers heard that soldiers from Camp Douglas at Salt Lake City were planning to stage a downtown parade in celebration of Abraham Lincoln's reelection as US president. Leaving the fort at 7:00 a.m., they "made all possible speed in o[r]der to get [there] in time" but were too late. Hammond heard it was "a grand affair," and he went directly to Brigham Young's office instead to report on his activities. Young "received me very Kindly [and] envited me to dine with him. I accepted the invitation." Afterward he "called on Bro. Riters where I remained all night." Levi Riter was married to Mary Jane Hammond's older sister Rebecca.

15. Anderson, *Stagecoach*, 62–63.

CHAPTER 44

An All-Night Struggle

Had a very interesting talk [last night] with my family lasting till near morning. My [first] wife Mary Jane goes with me on my Mission [to Hawaii]. My [second] wife Alice will make a home in Bro. L[orin] Farr's family [in Ogden] for the present.

—*Hammond journal, Mar. 20, 1865*

On the morning of March 5, Hammond "took passage with Bro. Merrick" for Ogden, and seeing that his family was doing well spent the next day settling business affairs prior to moving to the islands, presumably for a multi-year stay. The following day Frank, Mary Jane, Fontella, and Frank Jr. took the family carriage to Salt Lake City to visit Mary Jane's relatives. While there Frank and George Nebeker reported to Brigham Young on the progress of the mission. Young said he would loan them $5,000 for the first payment on the mortgage for Laie at an interest rate of 10 percent. "We then commenced trying to get exchange on San Francisco for that amount, to save the risk of taking the money through," meaning that if they could locate a business that had offices both in Salt Lake City and San Francisco, they could arrange payment by telegraph and avoid having to carry all that cash through some very wild country.

The *Deseret News* reported that while Hammond and Nebeker were meeting with Young, a riverboat port was at that moment being established on the Colorado River by Anson Call to add to "Elders Hammond's and Nebeker's operations on the Sandwich Islands, from whence sugar and long-staple cotton can be brought by water to within some 500 miles of this city." The reporter speculated that "pending the completion of the railroad across the Continent, ... it will greatly aid Utah in attaining results beneficial to true, sound and enlightened progress."[1] In other words, Young was making no secret of the plan to bring sugar and cotton from Laie to Utah Territory. In fact, this would be done for a few years, sugar arriving from Laie to the coast and transported up the Colorado River on steamships, presumably to Call's Landing, about thirty miles east of Las Vegas Springs.[2]

Young advised Hammond on March 9 to "select some mechanics[,] a few men who has some capital[,] and a few Elders who have the native language" to accompany him. As Hammond advertised the need, he found there were a "great many [who] would be glad to go if they were called," although very few who were qualified in any way. For instance, George Cannon was back from England but would soon be called as Young's private secretary.[3] Of the men who said they were available, only James Lawson and William Wright had experience in Hawaii. According to Hamond family lore, Frank discussed with Young and other leaders which wife he should take. According to the stories, he was encouraged to take his younger wife Alice on what would have been a kind of Hawaiian honeymoon, since he had only recently married her.

A few days later, Hammond told Young that they had been "unable as yet to affect an exchange for the $5000 in San Francisco. The banks & merchants are all out of funds in that city." The next day, Hammond wrote, "Prest. Young told me I had better get ready and start back im[m]ediately to the islands and take the money with me." He obeyed but knew it was a dangerous proposition. Traveling back to Ogden in the family buggy on March 17 with Mary Jane and Fontella, he took time out of his preparations to preach on Sunday. "Had a very full house. The people seem very much interested in the far off Isl[e]s of the sea." He also "had a very interesting interview with

1. *Deseret News* Mar. 8, 1865, 180.

2. Chase, "Hawaiian Mission Crisis of 1874," 61.

3. Bitton, *George Q. Cannon*, 140.

Bro. Lorin Farr, President of the Weber Stake of Zion," who "gave me some most excellent advice [and] ... proved a father to me and mine." That probably meant they talked about which wife Hammond should take with him to Hawaii. Alice had lived and worked in the Farr household before marrying Frank. In addition, Farr "kindly loaned me three hundred dollars in gold to defray my expenses back to the islands," Hammond wrote. He would soon be due additional funds from business partner Chauncey West, but that money was not yet available.

The next day Hammond "had a very interesting talk with my family lasting till near morning." The conclusion was that his "wife Mary Jane [would go] with me on my Mission. My wife Alice will make a home in Bro. L[orin] Farr's family for the present." Since the discussion lasted "till near morning," one can assume there was a disagreement and that Frank argued long and hard that Alice should accompany him. It would have been much more practical, since Alice had no children and Mary Jane had many. Taking them all to Hawaii (removing them from their schools) would have been an expensive proposition. It is true that Mary Jane was familiar with the native people and customs, but she had hated her many years on Maui. One is left with the conclusion that the idea of Frank and Alice living together without her for years (George Nebeker stayed in Hawaii for eight years) overcame whatever reservations she had about returning there. That, at least, is one story the Hammond family tells.

The next morning, with very little sleep, Frank set out at 11:00 for Salt Lake City, leaving Mary Jane to come later with the other missionaries, their wives, and children. Frank "took a very affectionate farewell of my family and on horse back set out, ... Prest. Farr & Bishop West accompanying me as far as the Weber Bridge." He "arrived at the City about 6 o.c[lock]. p.m." and "called at the office," where he "found that Brooks Co. had telegraphed that their next packet for the Islands would sail about the first days of April." This was probably too soon for him to reach the coast, but worth trying. That he met once again with Brigham Young indicates the importance Young placed on Hammond's assignment. That evening Frank took Mary Jane's mother and niece, Lizzie Riter, to the Salt Lake Theater to see *Uncle Tom's Cabin*. He was pleased with it. It was a "great success for the firstnight," he wrote. "The house was full, the scenery and playing good." Probably it was the melodramatic adaptation of Harriet Beecher Stowe's book by playwright George L. Aiken, which historians have said was as influential as the book.[4]

On Friday, Hammond obtained the $5,000 from Young and secured it in what he called his "valice," along with the $300 loaned him by President Farr. Hammond family accounts say Frank constructed a leather carrying case with coin slots in panels to keep the many coins from jingling. Well, family stories are sometimes accurate and sometimes not. In this instance, Lydia Alice Hammond Fielding, the daughter of Alice's sole son, John Howard Hammond, wrote that Frank had "$20,000 in gold[,] all in $20 gold pieces," and stored it "on the deck of the ship, no one but the captain knowing what it contained."[5] This legend inflates the amount of money and possibly conflates Frank's steamboat ride from Sacramento to San Francisco with his Pacific Ocean voyage to Hawaii, after he paid his debt with the coins on the mainland.

To mention just one other apocryphal account, in the 1993 biography of Frank Hammond by Nathan Adamson (also a descendant of Alice), West Hammond is quoted as saying Young gave Frank "a thick belt to go around his body to hold his trousers up," which he used for storing the "$25 and $50 gold coins," something Frank continued to wear "on a freighter" from San Francisco to Honolulu. The real irony of these two inaccurate tales is the assumption that there was greater danger at sea than on land, when in fact the overland trip by stagecoach, railroad, and steamboat was much more perilous, not to mention that it is the experience that Frank Hammond actually documented in his journals.

He begins by mentioning an ominous departure from Salt Lake

4. Robbins, "Uncle Tom's Cabin."

5. "Biographical Sketch of Francis Asbury Hammond," an unpublished family history I obtained from Aunt Fern Ellis of Mancos, Colorado. Her mother, Effie, was Lydia's sister, and Aunt Fern told me exactly the same story in the mid-1990s. I did not know it was false because at the point I had not yet read Frank Hammond's journals.

City at 10:00 a.m. on Saturday, March 25, "in the midst of a dreadful snow storm." He emphasizes his nervousness by writing as an aside, "M[a]y God protect me and prosper me on my journey." He was relieved to discover that he would have two US Army officers as "traveling companions," a Major Bull and his clerk, Bull being a "pay master [who] has been out as far as fort Bridger paying off troops. He is a jolly companion to travel with." It must have been reassuring to have men in the stagecoach with him who could defend themselves, but could even they be trusted had they known how much cash he was carrying?

Interestingly enough, Hammond reported that when the stage "arrived at Porter Rockwell's, where we took lunch, Porter then got on board and accompanied us to fort Crittenden, where we arrived just at dark." It must have been pre-arranged because Rockwell sometimes served as a bodyguard for Brigham Young. The reference to Rockwell's was to his Hot Springs Brewery Hotel just south of the Salt Lake Valley in Lehi.[6] The Hammonds knew him fairly well. When Frank Jr. ("Frankey" in Hawaii) traveled to Arizona in 1876 and stopped at Porter's hotel, he referred to the celebrated gunslinger in his journal simply as "Port."

One of the entries in the LDS Journal History for March 25 is a letter written that day by George Q. Cannon to Daniel H. Wells and Brigham Young Jr. in Liverpool. Cannon told them that

> Bro F. A. Hammond started by stage for the islands again to-day. He will be followed by his family and brother Nebeker, and some other missionaries and their families, as soon after [April] Conference as they can travel. They have bought a fine plantation on the Islands, and calculate to raise cotton, sugar, rice and other saleable productions [he does not mention tobacco], using native Saints' labor as far as practicable, and endeavoring to teach them industrious habits as fast as possible, so that they may be redeemed from the degradation in which they are involved.[7]

The way the leaders described the plantation, it always sounded less

6. See Schindler, *Orrin Porter Rockwell*.

7. Journal History, Mar. 25, 1865; *Millennial Star*, May 20, 1865, 318.

like a millennial place of safety and more like a way of turning native saints into manual laborers so they could supply raw products to Utah mills and factories, like the commercial farming operation envisioned for the first gathering place in the 1850s on Lana'i.

Hammond carried with him a letter from Brigham Young to King Kamehameha V. In it, Young mentioned Hammond but not Nebeker and said he would be pursuing temporal and cultural, as well as spiritual, objectives:

> The departure of Francis A. Hammond, Esq., a resident of this Territory and a gentleman with whom I have been long acquainted, for your Majesty's dominions, affords me an opportunity of writing of which I gladly avail myself, as I am desirous of making explanation to your Majesty in relation to the expected operations of Mr. Hammond and his colleagues in the midst of your Majesty's subjects. Mr. Hammond and his friends, (who will follow him in a few weeks with their families) go from this Territory with the intention of locating upon lands in your Majesty's Kingdom. They will go there as religious teachers; but while this is their calling they will not confine their labors to spiritual matters only.
>
> According to the precepts of our religion, the spiritual and temporal are so intimately blended, that we view no salvation, or system of salvation, as being complete which does not provide means for the welfare and preservation of the body as well as the salvation of the spirit. The spirit and the body are both the products of our Heavenly Father and God, and they are both the objects of his solicitude and care, as is fully proved by the pains which the Lord took to teach our Father Adam in the beginning upon temporal subjects. Mr. Hammond and other friends who will labor in conjunction with him, will therefore endeavor to teach [with one object in mind throughout] your Majesty's Kingdom, and that ob[j]e[c]t is: the benefit of your Majesty's subjects; and we fully believe that with proper management and the encouragement and protection which the Constitution and laws of your Majesty's Kingdom extends to other settlers, this can be done and the people be taught the arts of industry and self-preservation and be benefited morally and physically without involving a pecuniary outlay that will not be in the end amply remunerative.

King Kamehameha V

Courtesy Hawaii State Archives.

> Sire: As the King and Father of your people, it will be a cause of heart felt pleasure to myself and friends to have your Majesty's sanction and approbation of this enterprise upon which they are about to enter for the amelioration of your Majesty's subjects. Should this effort—which is, I think, wisely limited to a small field to commence with—be likely to prove successful, operations will be gradually with your Majesty's approval—extended to wider fields.

Young explained that Mormons viewed Hawaiians as of Israelite descent, connected by race to indigenous mainland Native Americans. It was a delicate subject, fraught with difficulty given the dark-skinned king's sensitivity to racial slurs he had been introduced to in America.

Sire; A few word[s] in relation to our views may not be inappropriate, and may explain and account for our motives in taking these steps and the interest we feel in the successful accomplishment of this plan.

Doubtless your Majesty has heard that the Church of Jesus Christ of Latter Day Saints believe in a book, which is known by the name of the Book of Mormon—a record that has been divinely revealed, and which purports to be an abridged history of the people which formerly inhabited the American Continent—And that we believe in the book as we do in the Bible, the Scriptures of the Old and New Testaments. Because of our belief in this record we have been derisively called 'Mormons.' Yet it is our belief in that Book, and its teachings and promises, which has prompted us to view the aborigines of this continent as we do, and to deal with them as we have—treating them with such uniform kindness and consideration in all our intercourse with them for the years that we have been surrounded by them, that they look upon us as fathers. This record teaches us that the aborigines of this continent are [of] Isreral [Israel,] de[s]cendants of that Joseph that was sold into Egypt and that their ancestors were a highly enlightened people, blessed of God, and enjoying His favor but that, subsequently through transgressing His laws and sinning against the great light and knowledge which they possessed, his anger was kindled against them and he punished them with a heavy punishment. Nevertheless, He had promised their fathers, by a covenant, that they should be held in remembrance by Him and that [they would be recipients of] His favor and blessings, when they should become a mighty people in the land of their fathers.

Sire: We have not a doubt in our minds but that your Majesty and the people of your Majesty's nation, over whom, in the providence of the Almighty, you have been called to rule, are a branch of this same great family. You are the House of Israel and heirs to all the promises made to the chosen seed; the Book of Mormon, (which is another witness of God's dealings with the children of men corroborative of the Old and New Testaments[,]) is your book; for the promises and covenants of the Almighty which it contains, are applicable to your Majesty's nation as to the nations of this continent.

This being our belief, accounts for the interest which we feel as a people in your Majesty's nation; it may also serve to explain the hopes we indulge in, respecting the results of our labors. We believe there is

> nothing to prevent your Majesty's people working out a glorious destiny for themselves, if they will avail themselves of the opportunites which are presented to them. They are capable, and Heaven will help them if they will only exert the powers with which the Great Creator has endowed them and seek to help themselves.

This racial doctrine provided the rationale for the Mormon missionary program directed at Polynesians since at least the late 1840s or early 1850s. Notice that Young avoided telling the king that the "heavy punishment" God had inflicted upon his ancestors was the "curse of a black/dark skin." Even so, Young could not help himself from going further and referring to the "low condition" of the Hawaiian people compared to the "refined" manners of the missionaries, who would teach them how to improve their "morals."

> It will be a pleasure to my friends, in their comparatively limited sphere, to cooperate with your Majesty in advancing the well-being and development of your people. Their aim will be to gather the people at a suitable place or places, and inculcate in them good morals and how they can best be elevated from their present low condition to a state of enlightenment that will make them suitable associates for the most refined. They will take special pains to impress upon them the absolute necessity there exists for them to observe such laws as will stop their decrease and enable them to perpetuate their race. There is no reason why they should perish and their lands become the property of the stranger. The same God watches over and cares unto them all. My friends will endeavor to open schools for their benefit, teach them trades and the arts of industry by which they may learn to know and appreciate the value of the favored country which providence has assigned them as a habitation.[8]

Young then made some complimentary references to the king's character, probably contributed by Hammond, who greatly respected him. "The sentiments which are attributed to your Majesty, and which have thus far, I understand, characterized your Majesty's public policy and reign, augurs much for the success of the design which

8. Brigham Young to Kamehameha V, Mar. 24, 1865.

our missionaries have in view in going to your Majesty's Kingdom." It pleased Young to know that the ruler's personality "comports with the dignity and character of a truly good King" which would only reap benefits "in the elevation of your people."

The letter concluded with an assurance that the Mormons would be obedient and loyal subjects. "I have advised my friends to be guided by your Majesty's political affairs, and whenever they shall be advised of your Majesty's wishes on these points, they will be happy to carry them into effect." He assured Kamehameha V that the settlers would "sustain the power of the throne and ... recognize and uphold your Majesty's Kingly authority to the fullest possible extent. I trust my friends will be obedient to your Majesty's wishes in all these things. If there is anything which your Majesty should wish to communicate with me respecting them and their operations in your Majesty's Kingdom, I shall be happy to receive it at any time." He closed with the line, "Praying the Lord to Preserve your life and to give your Majesty a long and prosperous reign. I subscribe myself, with sentiments of high consideration, Your Majesty's servant in the Lord, Brigham Young."

When Hammond arrived at the Fish Springs Station about one p.m. on March 27, he "got dinner [really lunch], and telegraphed back to Prest. Young of my progress. Trave[e]led on all day and all night without any accident." The next morning when the stage arrived at the Schell Creek Station, probably under orders to do so, Frank "telegraphed again to President young that all was well ... Traveled on all night and no accident." Understandably he was nervous.

There was disappointing news at the Ruby Valley station when Hammond learned that Major Bull and his clerk would be making a "call at a military post" and not be continuing on immediately. At Austin, "where we take the large Coach and six horses from here to Vergeinia City," he was worried when they "took on board severall passengers, some of whom I can't say I liked the appearance of very well," although they traveled without incident. "One lady and two children [also] on board, and one very talkative Yankee." The pro-Union man would have been excited because the defeat of Robert E.

Lee's Confederate Army of Virginia was imminent. The news about these dramatic closing events of the American Civil War would have been carried by telegraph to stations along the stage line.

When they reached Virginia City about 2:00 p.m. on April 1, Hammond was finally able to put up at a hotel. He "took a warm bath, called at the Telegraphed office[,] and dispatched a telegram to Pres. Young of my safe arrival &c." At that point, when he discovered the dates in his journal were off by two days, he stopped writing for two days to correct for the discrepancy rather than change the dates on the older entries, which meant he failed to describe the rest of his dangerous journey by coach, horse-drawn sleigh over the Sierras, rail for the last part of the stretch to Sacramento, and by steamboat to San Francisco. He simply noted that on April 1 he arrived "all safe but very tired. Called at Bro. J[oh]n F. Dilworth's and spent the night." He must have been exhausted.

The next day he "telegraphed to President Young that I had arrived safe and all was well." The day after, he "called on Mress. Brooks & co. and paid over to them the $5000 that Mr. Aldrich paid for us at the islands, or was to have paid. Saw Mr. Aldrich. He was pleased to see me and informed me that ... the money [had been] duly paid over to our Agent Mr. Austin [in Honolulu]." Although he still carried the $300 in coins loaned him by President Farr, he must have been relieved to be free of the $5000, as Aldrich probably was to see that the payment had come through.

On April 4 when the stunning news arrived "that Richmond [was] taken and [Robert E.] Lees army [is] in great dange[r] of anialation," Hammond was preoccupied with the state of things in San Francisco and human nature in general, for he next wrote: "They have lately passed what they call a Sunday law here prohibiting theatrical performances on Sundays. Consequently the seekers after pleasure now rush into the low dens of vice found in the dance cellars on pacific Streets and other places. It is a hard matter to legislate men into heaven, or to force them to be moral and virtuous, when they are corrupt as they can well be and all they desire is to roll in their filth and abominations."

Although the news from the East was not all-consuming for

Hammond, it powerfully affected the residents of San Francisco. Hammond's comments the next day reflected the general lack of emotional connection Mormons felt with regard to national events.

> Great rejoicing to day over the downfall of the "Rebel Capital." A large mass meeting called to meet this evening in the City Hall. Fire works & &c. the o[r]der of the day. Politics is all the rage at the present. All seem to feel that it is of the greatest importance that they should talk loud and long in favor of the present [Lincoln] administration. A man that doe[s] not do it is im[m]ediately proscripted, and he is in bad od[o]r im[m]ediately. But God sees and understands all of their ways, and he can work and none can hindre. He has an account to settle with this nation, and they need not flatter themselves that their trouble is over. It is not so.[9]

Hammond's view—as it was the view of other Mormon leaders—was that the terrible American Civil War had been God's punishment for the way the nation had treated the Mormons. One has to keep in mind that seven years earlier, Hammond was camped out with fellow Mormon soldiers preparing to fight the US Army on its way to establish federal control over the theocratic Great Basin kingdom.

9. Hammond journal, Apr. 5, 1865.

CHAPTER 45

Missionaries and Families Arrive

I held meeting with the native saints. I preached on temporal salvation. Bro. [Jonathan] Napela followed on the same subject. Bro. Kaleohano also spoke a short time. The saints who have been led by Capt. [Walter Murray] Gibson, into many things that was calculated to weaken their faith, feel a little sore and some of them are quite cautious how they embark in any new enterprise.

—Hammond journal, May 14, 1865

Hammond telegraphed Brigham Young that he was preparing to board the *Onward* for Honolulu and waited for the reply the next day thanking him for "the package of fruit," the apparent code phrase they had agreed on to signal that the $5,000 had safely arrived in San Francisco. Young reported that Hammond's "family are all well" and that the April "conference [was] progressing finely." With that in mind, Hammond sailed at 2:00 p.m. on April 8, 1854, on a "free ticket" presumably provided by Aldrich, Brooks, & Company.

He found the *Onward* to be "a good sea boat" that sailed swiftly, and the trip was pleasant. The captain, who had formerly commanded a whaling ship, met with Hammond's approval. He talked to him and two passengers about religion, and even after finding that "they have no hearts to receive the principles of the gospel," he nevertheless praised Captain Denuison Hempstead for being "as fine a Capt. as need walk a quarter deck."

A day after entering the port of Honolulu on Sunday, April 23, Hammond and the attorney James Austin met with Thomas Dougherty, who confirmed receipt of the $5,000 and turned over "full possession" of the property. At that, Hammond "sent a note to Bros. A[lma] Smith and [Benjamin] Cluff for ... them to come in and take us out to Laie." The ships arriving from the continent were bringing with them news of the cessation of the American Civil War, which stimulated the three hundred Americans or more in Honolulu to celebrate by marching to the "house of the Amarican Minister, Mr. [James] McBride, where speeches were made ... interspersed by songs." The ambassador read a letter from US Secretary of State William Henry Seward confirming the news. The crowd enjoyed a "handsom[e] colation of food [that] was set out for the compnay. In the evening there was a ball at the City hall." The celebrations continued for a week, with special services at the Fort Street Church (sponsored by the American Seamen's Friend Society) involving "speeches, prayers, singing, [and] shouting." Hammond recorded all of this as an onlooker, without feeling at all a part of the expatriate community.

Instead he visited the Hawaiian attorney general Charles C. Harris to deliver the letter from Brigham Young. Alma Smith arrived and stayed a few days while Hammond completed his diplomatic chores, so that when they were finally able to leave on April 29 it was raining and the roads were muddy. Even so, they reached their destination that evening, so that the next day Hammond was able to attend Sunday service with around 100 native people, most of whom were members. As he preached for an hour, he was "greatly blest in speaking to them. I did not think I would be able to speak more than a few moments on account of my deficiency in the native language, but the good Spirit of the Lord assisted me greatly."

On Tuesday, Hammond was pleased to find, touring the plantation, that the "late pl[a]nting of corn and cotton look well" even though "the first planting has been distroyed by the wind and worms." He was encouraged to hear that four key native men were going to move to the plantation. "They are four of about the best brethren that we have in the church," he said of Jonathan Napela, H. K. Kaleohano, and two others. H. K. and his wife, Kaahanui, according to a biographical essay, would soon construct "one of the few frame houses owned by Hawaiian families" on the island.[1]

Two days later Hammond made note of the pressures he felt. He "call[ed] upon the Lord for his spirit to guide me in all my labors upon this land, for I feel that [it] is a great responsibility resting upon me." He wrote to Daniel H. Wells in England describing his mission. "Brother Nebeker," he explained, "remained [in Utah] to take charge of a small company to be selected and sent out in May ... I expect to leave here in a few days for San Francisco, to meet the company en route for this place." He anticipated that the company would include Mary Jane and her children. Describing the agricultural effort at Laie, he said they had "some 40 acres fenced, about 20 planted in corn and cotton—it looks well. I think sugar will be our main crop as the land is well adapted to sugar culture." He ended predicting that "if we are permitted to dwell here in peace, in a few years we can make a grand garden of this place. Our enterprise is well received by both king and people, as far as extending a hearty welcome to us is concerned. I pray we may have power to do all for this poor degraded people."[2]

On May 10 the news reached O'ahu that President Lincoln had been assassinated and "Sec[retary] Seward was also attacked in his own house and badly wounded." Hammond and Cluff had traveled to Honolulu, where they found, while they stayed with Charles Wings (or Wing), a former American whose wife was native, that "the Americans [were] wearing mourning, some of them with [black] crepe on the Hat and left arm." It was not the Mormon missionaries in Honolulu who mourned Lincoln's death, but "the Americans." Hammond and Smith felt no urge to wear black armbands. They had other matters on their minds, especially after Hammond "heard that the King was not very well pleased with Presidents Young's letter. I am very anxious to see him, and explain fully the object of our Mission here." Before he did that, however, they "held [a] meeting

1. Spurrier, "Kaleohano," 296.

2. Frank Hammond to Daniel H. Wells, May 7, 1865; *Millennial Star*, Aug. 19, 1865, 527.

with the native saints" on Sunday in which Hammond "preached on temporal salvation. Bro. Napela followed on the same subject. Bro. Kaleohano also spoke a short time." Recording his only comment about Walter Murray Gibson, Hammond wrote that "the saints who have been [mis]led by Capt. Gibson ... feel a little sore and some of them are quite cautious how they embark in any new enterprise." He is curiously silent about his emotions in seeing two of the most prominent Maui brethren again for the first time in years. Evidently they were among those who expressed resentment that the church had abandoned them and burdened them with Gibson, and Hammond had no sympathy for their legitimate feelings.

"I will not be able to see the King before I leave again for San Francisco," Hammond was told at the palace, because the king's "health [was] poor & he will not see any one." Two days later when he visited the foreign minister, he heard from Secretary Robert Wyllie that the king, upset by Young's letter, had given it to the Privy Council and ordered them to draft a response. Wyllie "assured" Hammond "that the answer was not such as he [Wyllie] would have made," implying that it would be harsh. The task, he said, had been given to "C[harles] C. Harris (King's Attor[n]ey Gen[eral]." Hammond "called upon Harris," who showed Hammond "the letter he was preparing in answer to Prest. Youngs," which Hammond explained "does not acknowledge us as relig[i]ous Teachers, but we can come and labor in all temporal pursuits, and find protection from the government." Frank never said what it was in Young's letter that upset the king.

One problem, of course, was Young's line about the missionaries wanting to teach Hawaiians "good morals and how they can best be elevated from their present low condition to a state of enlightenment that will make them suitable associates for the most refined." Beyond that, researcher Jeffrey S. Stover, who has thoroughly examined the issue, found that the Hawaiian hierarchy thought the Latter-day Saints wanted "a foothold from which to take over the islands" and Laie was assumed to fill that role. The king and advisors had learned that Mormons, during the Utah War, had looked at abandoning the Great Basin and moving to Vancouver Island or the Sandwich Islands. They became suspicious when the church separated its members from the general populace and established the Lana'i colony. In a report Robert Wyllie submitted to the legislature on March 31, 1858, he mentioned the supposed threat of a Mormon invasion three times, and Gibson's subsequent imperialistic megalomaniacal activities had done nothing to temper that suspicion.

In addition, while President Young was requesting permission to establish a settlement on O'ahu, everybody already knew that the deal had been completed due to a story that had appeared in the *Pacific Commercial Advertiser* on February 4, nine days after Hammond and Dougherty had signed the contract. The story revealed that the Mormons intended to make Laie "a cotton plantation," that Brigham Young had authorized the purchase, and that Mormon "farmers, artisans, machinists and an engineer" were being recruited to move there. According to Stover, this only "confirm[ed] the government's alarm about a Mormon invasion." Nor was it reassuring that Young had written to the king about the need to merge "temporal and spiritual" realms, seemingly confirming a political as well as spiritual aspiration in the kingdom. The king's advisers knew that converts placed "obedience to their prophet above obedience" to the king, assurances to the contrary notwithstanding. "Consequently," Stover explained, the Hawaiians feared that "Brigham Young might at anytime claim divine revelation that the Mormons should renounce their allegiance to the King and claim their rightful 'inheritance,' ... overthrowing the sovereignty of the Hawaiian Kingdom."[3]

Finding that he had done what he could in Honolulu, Hammond departed for San Francisco on May 18 on the clipper ship *D. C. Murray* with "thirty two cabin passengers, ... ten Steerage passengers," and "some 8 hundred tons of Sugar & Molasses on board." He intended to meet his family and other missionaries and return with them to the islands. Having made this trip four times in as many months,

3. Stover, "Wars and Rumors of Wars," 50–52, 55. The king's letter, copied by his secretary, was printed in the *Honolulu Advertiser*, July 23, 1865.

he found it tiresome. He had hoped to talk to passengers about religion but found "few" who had "any desire to hear anything about salvation," which for Hammond meant that he had little to stave off boredom. Two days out he prayed for God to "preserve me from temptation while I travel in the midst of wickedness, that I fall not into sin and transgress his holy laws and commandments. I feel my weakness more forcibly than ever before." The temptations he faced were that "some are playing cards, some are reading novels, some are drinking Whiskey, & thus is the time passed by my fellow passengers." He eventually found solace reading the Hawaiian Book of Mormon, apparently a bound copy, which he found to be better than any other book he had read in translation. "The Lord bless the translator (Bro. Geo. Q. Cannon)," he wrote.

On June 7 the ship anchored off North Point in San Francisco, just a few blocks from Fisherman's Wharf, concluding a twenty-three-day journey. He found a letter from Nebeker saying the missionaries had departed from Salt Lake City the same day Hammond had left Honolulu. That meant they would arrive shortly. Four of them, Eli Bell, Ephraim Green, James Lawson, and William Wright, had been in the Sandwich Islands before and were bringing their wives and children with them. All told there were eight other couples with them, Alma Smith's and Benjamin Johnson's wives, a single man (Philip Pugsley), and thirteen children.

Nebeker had decided to bring Mary Jane's sister Maria Louisa, rather than his other wife, Elizabeth, another Dilworth sister who was five years older than Maria Louisa. The latter would stay five years out of the eight George would serve as mission president. Historian Carol Cornwall Madsen wrote that in order to accompany her husband, Maria Louisa had to sell her home, farm, cattle, and almost everything she owned except for "a change of clothing for my child and myself," according to her account.[4]

To Hammond's surprise and shock, the letter also revealed that

4. Madsen, "Mormon Missionary Wives," 146, 166n47; Manuscript History of the Hawaiian Mission, July 7, 1865. Some of the property came from a previous marriage to the deceased John C. Leonard.

Maria Louisa Dilworth Nebeker

Courtesy Daughters of Utah Pioneers.

"my family are not coming. Mrs. Hammond['s] health and that of the children would not admit of it." It is hard to imagine how discouraging that would have been. Below the succinct transmission of information was the fact that Mary Jane, a strong-willed woman, had refused to go to Hawaii with her children. Sickness or no sickness, most wives in that age would not have had the temerity to refuse to join their husbands on missions, especially when the other elders' wives were joining them abroad—one of whom was Mary Jane's younger sister. Mary Jane's decision to remain in Utah—whether for health (little Fontella was not a healthy child and died in 1867)[5] or unhappy memories—left Frank without any family in the mission.

He tried to keep his head up despite the unexpected setback, but the news would affect his plans and result in an abbreviated stay this time around. He notified Brigham Young of his arrival, and in his reply the next day Young told him George Nebeker's company had

5. Frank gives this date in his last Hawaiian mission journal, but LDS Church genealogical records list Lizzie Fontella's death as 1866.

reached Carson City and "hired their passage out [over the Sierras] to Latrobe." This gave Hammond some time to catch up on correspondence. He wrote to Mary Jane, George Cannon, and Brigham Young. "I feel to thank the Lord and his servants that my Wife and our large family of children are not coming, for I can see, [it is] a hard Mission for families to be connected with," he confided to his journal, resigning himself to the fact that they would not be joining him.[6] He did not indicate whether he also wrote to his second wife, Alice.

The missionaries arrived by steamboat on Monday, June 19, and "put up at the International Hotel ... very much fatigued from the effects of the journey."[7] While they recuperated, Hammond spoke to one of the riverboat captains and a booking agent about whether they thought it possible to ship Hawaiian sugar and cotton up the Colorado River by shallow-draft steamboat, which apparently was the First Presidency's plan. The missionaries and their families left San Francisco on Thursday afternoon on the ship Hammond had just arrived on, Frank doing what he could to help them when they all quickly became seasick. In two weeks East Maui came into sight, and Hammond wrote that they could see "Hale a Kala [Haleakala crater] about 70 miles distant" while sailing "along in sight of Maui & Molokai all day." By 9:00 p.m. they were able to "anchor off Di[a]mond Head. Pilot came on boa[r]d, [and] Mr. Brooks, Capt. Bennett & I took a boat and went on shore. I went up to Bro. [Charles] Wings. Found Bro. Alma Smith there. All well at Laie."

Hammond decided to transport the large company to the other side of the island on the schooner *Emiline* at a cost of $100. It anchored off Laie at 11:00 the next morning, and it took seven hours to transport everyone and their luggage ashore in five trips by way of a smaller boat. "Night found us all under shelter on the land of Laie. The natives were very kind in assisting us with our baggage to the house." A few days later the missionaries and their families attended

6. There is a hint here that Mary Jane had not wanted to drag seven children to Hawaii. Frank probably originally invited Alice because she could travel unencumbered.

7. The International Hotel, built in 1854, was an elegant five-story structure on Jackson Street with 250 rooms.

a native Sunday service at which Hammond spoke in Hawaiian on "the necessity of uniting the temporal with the spiritual in o[r]der for a complete salvation. Bros. Kaloa & Kahumaunu followed, and spoke with much spirit. The saints all seemed to feel well, as also the out siders" in attendance. In the afternoon there was an English-language service. It was during that meeting, without the native people present, that Laie was formally "dedicated ... for a gathering place for [the Lord's] people on these lands."

Hammond's journal entries end here, and what follows was written after he completed his mission to the islands and returned home.

> I now write from memory. I remained on the land at Laie several weeks, assisting the brethren in locating on the land and counseling in the affairs of the Mission. The brethren sent down there to opperate on the Mission did not see much money in the sugar business, and soon began to feel a desire to return to Utah.
>
> I soon received a letter from President Young releasing me to return home whenever I should see proper. Accordingly about the last of Aug[ust] 1865 I left Honolulu on my return home.
>
> 23 days passage brought me to San Francisco. I think I returned on the Barque 'd. c. Murry,' Capt. Bennitt. Spent a few days in San Francisco and then took passage by overland stage for home. Arrived in Salt Lake on Oct. 6, 1865.
>
> I found my family all well. My wife, Mary Jane, and children had spent the Summer in Salt Lake City[,] she teaching school. My wife Alice had remained at President Lorin Farrs [in Ogden].

It seems the reason Hammond did not remain long in Hawaii was that he had no family with him, and it may be why President Young left it to him to decide whether to stay. There are at least two family stories that have been handed down among Frank's descendants. One of them claims that Mary Jane actually went to Hawaii and left Alice to take care of Mary Jane's seven children in Huntsville, where they all nearly starved to death.[8] "The Howard side of the family has never forgotten this injustice!" my Aunt Fern Ellis told

8. Interview with Fern Ellis, summer 1995, Mancos, Colorado. The Hammonds did not move to Huntsville until after the second Hawaiian mission.

me, with fire in her eyes. Another story contends that the church "advised him to take his young wife [Alice] with him. He went ahead [to Hawaii] intending to send for her later, but when he was gone, Mary Jane[,] the older wife, took matters into her own hands, borrowed money and followed her husband, leaving the young wife to [go to] work ... to get money for her sustenance."[9]

These stories are false, but they share a sense of indignation that Mary Jane was obstructing Alice from traveling with Frank, which supposedly was what Frank and Alice and the church authorities all wanted. The fact that these two family stories are skewed toward Alice and against Mary Jane shows a lingering sense of how emotionally charged the struggle over this issue was in the spring of 1865.

9. Lydia Alice Hammond Fielding, "History of Alice Howard Hammond," unpublished.

Afterword

About six months after Hammond left the islands, Alma Smith wrote to the editor of the *Deseret News* about Laie.

> I think we will, the coming spring, get in upwards of 50 acres of cotton, beside[s] some corn, and probably about six or seven acres of rice. There has been an acre of cane planted as an experiment. I am confident that this land will produce good cane, and that, with sufficient capital, a successful sugar plantation could be established upon it. A frame meeting-house is now in course of erection by the foreign and native brethren, conjointly, for the accommodation of the native Saints. Sister Randall is teaching two schools, one for the foreign, the other for the native children. We hold two meetings every Sabbath, one for the foreigners, the other for natives. Our meetings are well attended, and a good spirit pervades them. Occasionally new converts apply for baptism.[1]

President George Nebeker wrote to Brigham Young later in the year that the Kaua'i and O'ahu branches were doing well, although "the Saints on Maui, Molokai, and Lanai were apathetic, and the Church was reportedly dead on the Big Island," according to Britsch's summary of the letter.[2] It is not relevant here to detail the subsequent history of the mission, but a few generalizations are in order. Cotton production was discontinued after several years because worms destroyed the crop. Sugarcane became the primary crop for some time, a mule-powered

1. Alma Smith to *Deseret News*, Feb. 15, 1899; *Millennial Star*, June 23, 1866, 398.
2. Nebeker to Young, Oct. 14, 1866, qtd. in Britsch, *Moramona*, 80.

factory to extract the juice was built, and the arduous cane-field and factory labor was carried out primarily by native Mormons.[3] Furnas noted that even though the church was able to get the natives at Laie to work, no one, least of all the Hawaiians, "care[d] for long hours of slogging with a cane knife through a choking, sun-baked thicket of cane."[4] Other plantations imported Chinese and Japanese workers to do this.

According to Britsch, the Utah families who arrived at Laie in 1865 "were part of President Young's plan to show the Hawaiians how proper Saints lived and conducted their lives. He expected the Utah Saints to take sufficient funds with them to be able to live at a standard well above that of the Hawaiians, for he did not want his missionaries living like native Hawaiians, or depending on them for sustenance."[5] While this may have been the plan, it was not adhered to; few Mormons could afford to live in colonial splendor for the sake of appearances. Increasingly the church reverted to sending single men as missionaries, including my great-grandfather Samuel Smith Hammond, born at Lahaina in April 1853.[6] Gradually the missionaries were also sent out to other islands to travel, as they had before, without means and to live with native Mormons. In fact, six months after the missionaries arrived in July 1865, Alma Smith and Eli Bell were sent to Kaua'i to proselytize and were told to rely on natives for food and lodging.[7]

Although the number of Mormons expanded after the reestablishment of the mission in 1865, it remained fairly small throughout the nineteenth century. From the nadir of 1,000 members, cited by Andrew Jenson for the 1860s, by 1872 there were 2,627 native Mormons, Britsch claims. By the end of the decade, the numbers had surpassed 4,000, only then reaching the level prior to the Utah War, representing a tenth of the total population of native Hawaiians.[8]

3. See Gibson, *Yankees in Paradise*, 255.

4. Furnas, *Anatomy of Paradise*, 161.

5. Britsch, *Moramona*, 75.

6. There was one single man among the missionaries who arrived in 1865, Philip Pugsley.

7. Smith to *Deseret News*, Feb. 15, 1866.

8. This was coincidentally at the low point in the number of indigenous people

By 1894 the church had nearly 5,000 Hawaiian members.[9] An interesting development was that most members avoided Laie, the number there plateauing at 275 in the 1870s and representing only one out of every fifteen Mormons in Hawaii.[10] Britsch acknowledges that the plantation "did not grow rapidly over the years, for most local Saints preferred to live in or near their ancestral villages, but the missionaries never stopped preaching about the importance of gathering." It was a futile exercise, as Frank Hammond had discovered in the 1850s.

Despite his weakness for "wine and women," as Hammond had put it, no one among the native population proved to be more important to establishing Mormonism than Jonathan Hawaii Napela. After he overcame his resentment of how the church had closed the mission—and over the Gibson debacle—he and his wife, Kitty, became the first Hawaiian Mormons to visit Utah. In 1866 they attended general conference and were initiated into the sacred temple ceremonies, and Jonathan was ordained a Seventy. Back in Laie, he was appointed supervisor of the mule-powered sugar mill.[11]

Tragically in 1872, Kitty Napela contracted leprosy and was committed to the Leper Colony isolated at Kalaupapa on Moloka'i, and because Jonathan could not tolerate their separation, he moved in with her in May 1873 and soon contracted Hansen's disease himself. Henry P. Richards visited them in October 1878 and said Jonathan was so disfigured he was hardly recognizable. Ten months later he died, and Kitty passed away two years later.[12] In 1997 a statue of Jonathan Napela and George Cannon was dedicated by church president Gordon B. Hinckley on the BYU–Hawaii campus.[13]

---

in the islands. See Sumner La Croix, "Economic History of Hawai'i," *Economic History Association*, online at eh.net.

9. Britsch, *Unto the Islands of the Sea*, 135.

10. Britsch, *Moramona*, 87, 89.

11. Britsch, *Unto the Islands of the Sea*, 122, 131, 135; Chase, "Hawaiian Mission Crisis," 60–61.

12. See Chase and Bell, "Faith, Hope, and Hansen's Disease." My wife and I took the scary mule ride down the sheer cliff face to Kalaupapa in 2006. It is a beautiful location where a few elderly lepers still live, although we did not see them.

13. Underwood, *Pioneers in the Pacific*, 1.

In the mid-1870s a new Hawaiian monarch, David Kalakaua, allowed native Mormons to migrate to Utah. A few of them took advantage of the opportunity, and they struggled economically and socially in the Salt Lake City area. Seeing their difficulty, the church created a search committee to find a spot where it was thought they could flourish, and the committee's recommendation was a ranch in Skull Valley, seventy-five miles southwest of Salt Lake City on the far side of the Stansbury Mountains near present-day Dugway. It was a desolate location, as the name of the valley indicated, but the Hawaiians made the best of it and called it Iosepa, which was Hawaiian for Joseph, in honor of Joseph Smith.[14] The first fifty settlers arrived in late August 1889.

Exactly one year later, the First Presidency—Wilford Woodruff, George Q. Cannon, and Joseph F. Smith—dedicated the town as a gathering place for Mormon Hawaiians and other Polynesian saints.[15] Despite a push to populate the area, the town only contained 228 individuals at its apex in 1915, and when plans for a Hawaiian temple at Laie were announced that same year the settlers quickly, with the church's blessing, moved back to Hawaii. By the summer of 1917, the town was empty.[16] Despite the mission's troubled beginnings, Hawaii was the first site for an LDS temple outside the continental United States, preceding the Canadian temple in Alberta by four years. Its construction stimulated conversion in Hawaii so that by 1926 the membership surpassed 14,000.[17]

At the conclusion of his ninth Hawaiian journal, Hammond described his family's history for a couple of years after his second mission. "President Young sent me back to Ogden City to remain under the Jurisdiction of B[ishop] West & President Farr [and then] ... concluded to send me to Huntsville" to serve as branch president.

14. This was also the name of the gathering place on Lana'i, although the Hawaiians continued to refer to it as Palawai.

15. See Staker, *Waiting for World's End*, 385–86.

16. See Panek, "Life At Iosepa," 179.

17. Britsch, *Unto the Islands of the Sea*, 159. Another dramatic membership spike occurred after World War II.

He moved his entire family there, and Mary Jane was unhappy to be moved so far away from Ogden to the primitive environment of a mountain valley east of the city. Frank accepted the call but also was ambivalent about their surroundings and economic situation:

> My circumstances was very much reduced. We had a yoke of cattle, one old wagon, one poney, and one little bob tail cow. C[hauncey] W. West paid me some means on the notes I held of his for my interest in the Tannery and property I sold to him in Ogden. This enabled me to buy 20 acres of land, two houses, and two lots in Huntsville. [The] houses were Log Cabins with dirt roofs.
>
> There were about 25 families in Huntsville at that date. A small log cabin for a school house was the amount of public building. A very rough and roudy set of young men in the place. Very little refin[e]ment among young or old. It was a great trial indeed to my first wife[,] who had been raised in good society. It was all she could do to endure this hardship and trial, but she submitted to it with as much grace as possible, and she and the rest of the family went to work to make ourselves as comfortable as possible.

At this point in the journal, a leaf that would have been pages 204–05 has been torn or cut out, leaving just a half-inch stub of the sheet remaining. Who did this we do not know, but it eliminated what probably was Frank's discussion of Mary Jane coming to terms with her husband's marriage to a second wife, Alice Howard. The family was, for the first time, living together—Frank, Mary Jane, Alice, and Mary Jane's seven children—all in two small log cabins. His first task was to complete an attractive two-story frame structure that came to be known as "Mary Jane's house," while Alice, and eventually her two children, John and Mary Alice, would continue to live in a cabin until Alice's death on January 28, 1873, two weeks after giving birth to her third child, Hannah. Since Alice is not otherwise discussed in the rest of the journal, one can imagine that she was mentioned in the portion that was excised.

After the missing sheet in his journal, Hammond continued to discuss Huntsville, and as he had a tendency to do, he found a silver lining in a dark cloud.

I thank the Lord for casting my lot up here away from the temptations that abound in Ogden City & other places.

I was appointed post master soon after our settlement here and retained it for some eight years. My wife [Mary Jane] done most of the business. The summer of 1866 we raised some grain and potatoes and had hay for a few head of Stock.

My boys was a great help to me in making a new home, and my wives[18] assisted all they could. My wife Mary Jane taught School after we enlarged the School House.[19] Wm Lish & David McKay[20] was call[e]d to act as my counselors in the affairs of the Branch, and the Lord did bless us exceedingly, and a better state of society began soon to appear in our midst.

On the 28th of January 1867 our little Daughter Lizz[i]e Fontella died. She was take[n] [ill] Sunday night, and Monday about 2 o.c[lock] p.m. she died.

This spring [1866] we commenced to build a rock meetinghouse. Finished it in September, when Prest. [Brigham] Young & party was here on their way from Bear Lake & held meeting in it.

Had a fair harvest. Summer spent in farming and Canyon work. The Branch is growing in numbers and an increase of good society.[21]

For continuation of this see old pocket book diary commencing January 2st 1867 at Huntsville.[22]

In the 1850s Hammond had frequently mentioned his intention to one day visit his family in New York and convert them to Mormonism. His mother, Charity Edwards Hammond, died in April 1867, followed by his younger brother Sanford Bartlett in March 1869. He either had not found time or funds to travel east, or had not received permission from Brigham Young to do so, but in May 1869 the transcontinental railroad was completed, and President Young called 500

18. This oblique reference to "my wives' is the only reference to Alice in these concluding remarks.

19. Today there is an attractive monument next to the Huntsville elementary school recognizing Mary Jane as the first school teacher in Utah.

20. The Scottish emigrant David McKay was the father of future LDS President David O. McKay, a boy Hammond confirmed at age eight.

21. When the branch became a ward, Hammond was named bishop.

22. The "old pocket book diary" has not been located.

men, including Hammond, to proselytize in the eastern states. This finally enabled him to be reunited with what was left of his family on Long Island; a father, brother, two sisters, and other relatives he had not seen for twenty-six years. They greeted him warmly, but, to his chagrin, were not interested in his religion. He would later spend several weeks with them in the winter of 1889–90 while testifying about Utah-Colorado Indian affairs in Washington, D. C. His father passed away in 1875.

There is a gap in Hammond journals until 1883 (journal number 10) when he was called by the First Presidency to visit the LDS congregations of southern Arizona. At Smithfield (now Pima), Arizona, on December 30, 1883, he wrote: "2 o.c[lock] p.m. attended meeting ... I was very much overcome with my feelings as I saw many faces that I had been familiar with many years ago. I saw Bros. James Keeler, Reuben Mc Bride, [and the] Wife of Reddin Allred[,] who had larbored with me on the S[an]dwich Islands 25 [30] years ago."

Shortly afterward he was called by LDS President John Taylor to preside over the San Juan Stake in the Four Corners area. The stake comprised southeastern Utah, southwestern Colorado, and northwestern New Mexico. The church wanted to secure the area (at least the Utah portion) against non-LDS cattle and mining interests, as well as to provide a haven for fugitive Mormon polygamists and/or some of their wives and children.[23] Hammond moved his large extended family by wagon from Huntsville and made his residence in the town of Bluff, Utah, for nearly the rest of his life. There are thirty four extensive Hammond journals documenting this frontier pioneer experience. Bluff was far more remote and primitive than Huntsville, but this time Mary Jane was not alive to complain.

In the intervening years, 1866 to 1883, Frank had lost both his wives to child birth, Alice in 1873 and Mary Jane in 1877, and in addition to that, his oldest son, Frank Jr., died at age twenty-five in Arizona, probably of pneumonia. His sons George Albert, nineteen, and William Edmund, seventeen, also passed away in January and

23. For more on this, see Peterson, *Look to the Mountains*.

February 1879.[24] He touched on this heartache when he spoke at a quarterly stake conference in Bluff and "related some of his experience in the loss of two wives and three young sons, young men grown, [and] how the Lord [had] tried him to the center of his heart, and taught him to put his whole trust in the Lord."

After Mary Jane's death, Frank hired a Danish immigrant woman, Martha Marcussen (1850–1935), to take care of his surviving children—Mary Jane's ten and Alice's three. She had been a plural wife, her husband recently had died, and she was without children. Frank married the twenty-seven-year-old widow on her birthday, April 5, 1881, in what was considered a marriage until death, not a temple sealing for eternity, since she was sealed to her previous husband for the afterlife. Even so, they loved each other and spent the rest of their lives together, although without having children (she apparently was infertile).

He continued to defend polygamy publicly as a bishop and stake president, even though apparently he had soured on it. He never took another plural wife, nor did any of his children become involved in polygamy. Although the San Juan area was a haven for polygamists fleeing prosecution, when the 1890 Manifesto signaled the beginning of the end of polygamy, he said in a sermon on June 1, 1891, that plural marriage had been "the caus[e] of much sorrow and trouble to Ancient & Moderen Isreral [Israel]."

Frank's second son, Samuel Smith (the one born at Lahaina in April 1853), served a mission to Hawaii in the early 1890s. His wife, Elnora, and four children,[25] stayed behind in Mancos, Colorado, in what they described as a cabin with a leaky roof. He wrote to his father in the summer of 1891 that he "visited the house where I was born and drank out of the old well. The house is in a sad state of

24. He would lose two more children at young ages, his daughters Eliza Dilworth in 1888 and Hannah in 1894, both of them in their twenties.

25. One of them was Samuel Smith Jr. (1882–1946), my grandfather, who died when I was five years old. I knew "Elnora" ("Granma Hammond"), who died in 1960 when she was in her nineties. A Danish immigrant convert, she had a wonderful sense of humor. In her memoirs she quipped that "it always rained in our Mancos cabin for several hours after it stopped raining outside."

neglect, once one of the prettiest little cottages and grounds on the Island," now owned by "a Chinaman."[26] In a May 1892 letter, he described "2 nice Mango trees" his father had planted in front of the house, and there were "CoCoa nuts standing around the Old pond."[27] Two months later he elaborated in a letter from East Maui that "while at Keanae I saw & talked with an old man that you baptized & confirmed. You are Known all over the Is[land]."[28]

Frank died violently in a buggy accident on November 26, 1900. Ten months prior to that, he wrote in his journal about the smallpox epidemic that was sweeping the country and the recurring controversy about vaccination. Unfortunately, he did not say whether his negative view of this medical procedure had changed since the 1850s. In any case, he lived a full life that had lasted longer than one might expect, given the vagaries of circumstances and twists of fate he had endured. His time in the Four Corners area proved to be as unpredictable, challenging, and suspenseful as his Hawaiian missions. I am, at the time of this writing, working on a second volume about Frank's life using his thirty-four later journals as the primary source, with a working title "Desert Sojourn: The San Juan Mission of Francis A. Hammond, 1885–1900."

One interesting aspect of the change in venue is that the contrast in landscape and culture could not be more extreme. Hawaii was defined by its lushness, enjoyment of life, and exotic traditions. The Four Corners area was characterized by ruggedness, sparseness, and threats to life—a primitiveness that would have been a challenge to a man half Frank's age. Additionally, key players in his life—his first two wives and four children—had passed away, and two other children would die in the San Juan country while he was alive. Despite these traumatic losses, however, he had many other children and grandchildren, and he continued his total dedication to them and the church he had embraced in 1847. With that note, the adventure continues.

26. Samuel Smith Hammond Sr. to Frank Hammond, June 5, 1891.

27. Ibid., Aug. 20, 1891.

28. Ibid., July 12, 1892. Sam's youngest child, Genevieve (1900–80) also served a mission to Hawaii, and she was at Laie for the dedication of the Hawaiian temple in 1919.

Bibliography

BOOKS AND PAMPHLETS

Adamson, Nathan W., Jr. *Francis Asbury Hammond: Pioneer and Missionary.* Salt Lake City: David H. Allred and West Hammond, 1993.

Adler, Jacob, and Gwynn Barrett, eds. *The Diaries of Walter Murray Gibson: 1886, 1887.* Honolulu: University Press of Hawaii, 1973.

Adler, Jacob, and Robert M. Kamins. *The Fantastic Life of Walter Murray Gibson: Hawaii's Minister of Everything.* Honolulu: University of Hawaii Press, 1986.

Anderson, Andy. *Stagecoach: Wells Fargo and the Rise of the American Financial Services Industry.* New York: Simon and Schuster, 2002.

Arrington, Leonard J. *Great Basin Kingdom: An Economic History of the Latter-day Saints.* Salt Lake City: University of Utah Press, 1993.

Autobiography of Parley Parker Pratt, ed. Parley P. Pratt Jr. New York: Russell Brothers, 1874.

Bagley, Will. *Blood of the Prophets: Brigham Young and the Massacre at Mountain Meadows.* Norman: University of Oklahoma Press, 2002.

———, ed. *A Road from El Dorado: The 1848 Trail Journal of Ephraim Green.* Salt Lake City: Prairie Dog Press, 1991.

———. *Scoundrel's Tale: The Samuel Brannan Papers.* Logan: Utah State University Press, 1999.

Bailey, Paul. *Hawaii's Royal Prime Minister: The Life and Times of Walter Murray Gibson.* New York: Hastings House, 1980.

Bartholomew, Gail. *Maui Remembers: A Local History.* Honolulu: Mutual Publishing, 1994.

Bell, Kuulei, and Lance D. Chase, "Faith, Hope, and Hansen's Disease: The Saints at Kalaupapa." In Underwood, *Voyages of Faith.*

Bergreen, Laurence. *Over the Edge of the World: Magellan's Terrifying Circumnavigation of the Globe.* New York: Perennial/HarperCollins, 2004.

Bingham, Hiram. *A Residence of Twenty-one Years in the Sandwich Islands: Or the Civil, Religious, and Political History of These Islands*, 3rd ed. rev. Canandaigua, NY: H. D. Goodwin, 1855.

Bishop, M. Guy. *Henry William Bigler: Soldier, Gold Miner, Missionary, Chronicler, 1815–1900*. Logan: Utah State University Press, 1998.

Bitton, Davis. *George Q. Cannon: A Biography*. Salt Lake City: Deseret Book, 1999.

———. "George Q. Cannon in Hawai'i, 1850–54: Relationship Challenges of a Young Missionary." In Underwood, *Pioneers in the Pacific*.

Black, Duane. *Lana'i: The Elusive Hawaiian Island—The One That Captain Cook Missed.* New York: Vantage Press, 2001.

Bliss, Edwin Munsell, et al., eds. *Encyclopedia of Missions.* NY: Funk & Wagnalls, 1904.

Britsch, R. Lanier. *Moramona: The Mormons in Hawaii.* Laie: BYU Institute for Polynesian Studies, 1989.

———. *Unto the Islands of the Sea: A History of the Latter-day Saints in the Pacific.* Salt Lake City: Deseret Book, 1986.

Bushman, Richard L. *Joseph Smith, Rough Stone Rolling: A Cultural Biography of Mormonism's Founder*. New York: Knopf, 2005.

Cahill, Thomas. *Sailing the Wine-Dark Sea: Why the Greeks Matter*. New York: Doubleday, 2003.

Cannon, George Q. *He Olelo Hoolaha*. San Francisco: By the author, 1855.

———. *My First Mission*. Salt Lake City: Juvenile Instructor Office, 1879; 2nd. ed., 1882.

———. *Writings from the "Western Standard."* Liverpool: By the author, 1864.

Carter, Kate B., comp. *Heart Throbs of the West,* vol. 8. Salt Lake City: Daughters of Utah Pioneers, 1947.

———. "Journal of Louisa Barnes Pratt." In Carter, *Heart Throbs of the West*.

Cheesman, Paul R., and Millie F. Cheesman. *Early America and the Polynesians*. Provo: Promised Land Publications, 1975.

Cheever, Henry T. *Life in the Sandwich Islands: Or the Heart of the Pacific as it Was and Is*. New York: A. S. Barnes, 1851.

———. *The Island World of the Pacific*. New York: Harper and Bros., 1851.

Clement, Russell T., comp. *Mormons in the Pacific: A Bibliography*. Laie: BYU-Hawaii Institute for Polynesian Studies, 1981.

Cluff Family Journal. Provo: David Cluff Sr. family, 1899.

Coan, Titus. *Life in Hawaii: An Autobiographic Sketch of Mission Life and Labors, 1835–1881*. New York: Anson D. F. Randolph & Co., 1882.

Columbia Encyclopedia, ed. Paul Lagasse. NY: Columbia University, 2000.

Commercial Relations of the United States with Foreign Countries, vol. 4. Washington, D.C.: US State Dept., 1857.

Cook, James. *A Voyage to the Pacific Ocean: Undertaken ... in the Years 1776–1780,* 3 vols. London: W. and A. Strahan, 1784.

Crawley, Peter. *Descriptive Bibliography of the Mormon Church,* vol. 3. Provo: BYU Religious Studies Center, 2012.

Creighton, Margaret S. *Rites and Passages: The Experience of American Whaling, 1830–1870.* New York: Cambridge University Press, 1995.

Dana, Richard Henry. *Two Years before the Mast.* Herefordshire, Eng.: Wordsworth American Library, 1996.

Daws, Gavan. *A Dream of Islands: Voyages of Self-Discovery in the South Seas.* New York: W. W. Norton, 1980.

———. *Shoals of Time: A History of the Hawaiian Islands.* Honolulu: University of Hawaii Press, 1968.

Diamond, Jared. *Guns, Germs, and Steel: The Fates of Human Societies.* New York: W.W. Norton, 1997.

Dodge, Ernest. *Islands and Empires: Western Impact on the Pacific and East Asia.* Minneapolis: University of Minnesota Press, 1976.

Ekins, Roger R. *Defending Zion: George Q. Cannon and the California Mormon Newspaper Wars of 1856–1857.* Kingdom of the West Series, vol. 5. Spokane: Arthur H. Clark Co., 2002.

Ellsworth, S. George, ed. *The History of Louisa Barnes Pratt: Being the Autobiography of a Mormon Missionary Widow and Pioneer.* Logan: Utah State University Press, 1998.

———, ed. *The Journals of Addison Pratt: Being a Narrative of Yankee Whaling in the Eighteen Twenties.* Salt Lake City: University of Utah Press, 1990.

Fermantez, Kali. "The Right Place at the Right Time." *BYU Hawaii,* online at byuh.edu.

Firmage, Edwin Brown, and Richard Collin Mangrum. *Zion in the Courts: A Legal History of the Church of Jesus Christ of Latter-day Saints, 1830–1900.* Urbana: University of Illinois Press, 1988.

Furnas, Joseph Chamberlain. *Anatomy of Paradise: Hawaii and the Islands of the South Seas.* New York: William Sloane Associates, 1948.

Fustel de Coulanges, Numa Denis. *The Ancient City: A Study on the Religion, Laws, and Institutions of Greece and Rome.* Garden City, NY: Doubleday, 1956.

Garner, Stanton, ed. *The Captain's Best Mate: The Journal of Mary Chipman Lawrence of the Whaler* Addison, *1856–1860.* Hanover, NH: University Press of New England, 1966.

Garr, Arnold K., et al., eds. *Encyclopedia of Latter-day Saint History*. Salt Lake City: Deseret Book, 2000.

Gibson, Arrell Morgan. *Yankees in Paradise: The Pacific Basin Frontier*. Albuquerque: University of New Mexico Press, 1993.

Gibson, Walter Murray. *The Prison of Weltevreden: And a Glance at the East Indian Archipelago*. New York: J. C. Riker, 1855.

Hammond, Francis A."Life Sketch of Francis Asbury Hammond." In Jenson, *Latter-day Saint Biographical Encyclopedia*.

Hammond, John J. *The Quest for the New Jerusalem: A Mormon Generational Saga*, 8 vols. Bloomington, IN: Xlibris/Scotts Valley, CA: CreateSpace, 2011–13.

Holliday, J. S. *The World Rushed In: The California Gold Rush Experience*. New York: Simon and Schuster, 1981.

Howard, Leon. *Herman Melville: A Biography*. Berkeley: University of California Press, 1951.

Howe, Daniel Walker. *What Hath God Wrought: The Transformation of America, 1815–1848*. New York: Oxford University Press, 2007.

Hyde, John, Jr. *Mormonism: Its Leaders and Designs*, 2nd ed. New York: W. P. Fetridge, 1857.

Jenson, Andrew. *Latter-day Saint Biographical Encyclopedia*. 4 vols. Salt Lake City: Andrew Jenson History Company, 1901–36.

Johnson, Benjamin F. "Autobiography, 1852–53." In *Fragments of Experience*, ed. George Q. Cannon. Salt Lake City: Juvenile Instructor Office, 1882.

———. *My Life's Review*. Independence, MO: Zion's Printing and Publishing, 1947.

———. *Why the 'Latter-day Saints' Marry a Plurality of Wives: A Glance at Scripture and Reason, in Answer to an Attack through the Polynesian*. San Francisco: Excelsior Printing Office, 1854.

Judd, Gerrit P., IV. *Dr. Judd, Hawaii's Friend: A Biography of Gerrit Parmele Judd, 1803–1873*. Honolulu: University of Hawaii Press, 1960.

———. *Hawaii: An Informal History*. New York: Collier Books, 1961.

Kenney, Scott G., ed. *Wilford Woodruff's Journal*, 9 vols. Midvale, UT: Signature Books, 1984.

Kuykendall, Ralph S. *The Hawaiian Kingdom*, 3 vols. Honolulu: University of Hawaii Press, 1947–67.

Landon, Michael N., ed. *The Journals of George Q. Cannon: To California in '49*. Salt Lake City: Deseret Book, 1999.

LeBaron, E. Dale. *Benjamin F. Johnson: Friend to the Prophet*. Provo: Grandin Press, 1997.

Lyman, Edward Leo. *Candid Insights of a Mormon Apostle: The Diaries of Abraham H. Cannon, 1889–1895*. Salt Lake City: Signature Books and Smith–Pettit Foundation, 2010.

———. *San Bernardino: The Rise and Fall of a California Community*. Salt Lake City: Signature Books, 1996.

MacKinnon, William P., ed. *At Sword's Point: A Documentary History of the Utah War to 1858*. Kingdom in the West Series, vol. 10. Norman, OK: Arthur H. Clark, 2008.

Madsen, Carol Cornwall. "Mormon Missionary Wives in Polynesia." In. *Proclamation to the People*.

Malo, David. *Hawaiian Antiquities (Moolelo Hawaii)*. Trans. Nathaniel B. Emerson. Honolulu: Hawaiian Gazette, Ltd., 1903.

Mauss, Armand L. *All Abraham's Children: Changing Mormon Conceptions of Race and Lineage*. Champaign: University of Illinois, 2003.

Memoirs of John R. Young, Utah Pioneer, 1847: Written by Himself. Salt Lake City: Deseret News, 1920.

Messadié, Gerald. A *History of the Devil*. New York: Kodansha USA, 1997.

Michener, James A., and Arthur Grove Day. *Rascals in Paradise*. New York: Random House, 1957.

Missionary Album: Portraits and Biographical Sketches of the American Protestant Missionaries to the Hawaiian Islands. Honolulu: Hawaiian Mission Children's Society, 1969.

Moorman, Donald R., with Gene A. Sessions. *Camp Floyd and the Mormons: The Utah War*. Salt Lake City: University of Utah Press, 1992.

Morris, Robert J. "Same-Sex Friendships in Hawaiian Lore: Constructing the Canon." In *Oceanic Homosexualities*.

Murray, Stephen O. *Oceanic Homosexualities*. New York: Garland Publishing, 1992.

Neilson, Reid L. *Strangers in a Strange Land: The Rise and Demise of the Early LDS Japan Mission, 1901–24*, diss. in Religious Studies, University of North Carolina–Chapel Hill, 2006.

Neilson, Reid L., and Laurie F. Maffly-Kipp, eds. *Proclamation to the People: Nineteenth-century Mormonism and the Pacific Basin Frontier*. Salt Lake City: University of Utah Press, 2008.

Newton, Marjorie. "Nineteenth-Century Pakeha Mormons in New Zealand." In Neilson, *Proclamation to the People*.

———, *Southern Cross Saints: The Mormons in Australia*. Laie: BYU Institute for Polynesian Studies, 1991.

Olmstead, Francis Allyn. *Incidents of a Whaling Voyage: To Which Are Added Observations on the Scenery, Manners and Customs, and Missionary Stations of the Sandwich and Society Islands*. Rutland, VT: Charles E. Tuttle, 1969.

Orton, Chad M., ed. *The Journals of George Q. Cannon: Hawaiian Mission, 1850–1854*. Salt Lake City: Deseret Book, 2014.

Owens, Kenneth N. *Gold Rush Saints: California Mormons and the Great Rush for Riches*. Kingdom of the West Series, vol. 7. Spokane: Arthur H. Clark, 2004.

Paine, Thomas. *The Age of Reason: Being an Investigation of True and Fabulous Theology*. London: Barrois, 1794.

Parry, Donald W., et al. *Revelation, Reason, and Faith: Essays in Honor of Truman G. Madsen*. Provo: FARMS, 2002.

Perrin, Kathleen C. "Seasons of Faith: An Overview of the History of the Church in French Polynesia." In Underwood, *Pioneers of the Pacific*.

Petersen, Jesse G. *A Route for the Overland Stage: James H. Simpson's 1859 Trail across the Great Basin*. Logan: Utah State University Press, 2008.

Petersen, Mark E. *Polynesians Came from America! An Address Delivered at the 132nd Annual Conference of the Church of Jesus Christ of Latter-day Saints*. Salt Lake City: Deseret Book, 1962.

Peterson, Charles S. *Look to the Mountains: Southeastern Utah and the La Sal National Forest*. Provo: Brigham Young University Press, 1975.

Pukui, Mary Kawena, and Samuel H. Elbert. *Hawaiian Dictionary*. Honolulu: University of Hawaii Press, 1986.

Quinn, D. Michael. The *Mormon Hierarchy: Origins of Power*. Salt Lake City: Signature Books, 1994.

Reeve, W. Paul. *Religion of a Different Color: Race and the Mormon Struggle for Whiteness*. New York: Oxford University Press, 2015.

Ricketts, Norma Baldwin. *The Mormon Battalion: United States Army of the West, 1846–1848*. Logan: Utah State University Press, 1996.

Ricks, Nathaniel R. *"My Candid Opinion:" The Sandwich Islands Diaries of Joseph F. Smith 1856–1857*. Salt Lake City: Smith-Pettit Foundation, 2011.

Robbins, Hollis. "Uncle Tom's Cabin and the Matter of Influence." *History Now*, online at www.gilderlehrman.org.

Robertson-Lorant, Laurie. *Melville: A Biography*. Amherst: University of Massachusetts Press, 1996.

Rogers, Jedediah S. *The Council of Fifty: A Documentary History*. Salt Lake City: Signature Books, 2014.

Rose, Roger G. *Hawaii: The Royal Isles*. Seattle: University of Washington Press, 1983.

Schindler, Harold. *Orrin Porter Rockwell: Man of God, Son of Thunder*. Salt Lake City: University of Utah Press, 1966.

Smith, Bradford. *Yankees in Paradise: The New England Impact on Hawaii*. Philadelphia: J. B. Lippincott, 1956.

Smith, Joseph. *History of the Church of Jesus Christ of Latter-day Saints*, 7 vols. Salt Lake City: Deseret Book, 1946.

Smith, Joseph Fielding. *Life of Joseph F. Smith, Sixth President of the Church of Jesus Christ of Latter-day Saints*, 2nd ed. Salt Lake City: Deseret Book, 1969.

Sonne, Conway B. *Ships, Saints and Mariners: A Maritime Encyclopedia of Mormon Migration, 1830–1890*. Salt Lake City: University of Utah Press, 1987.

Spurrier, Joseph H. "Kaleohano: Hawaiian Ali'i, Early LDS Convert." In Underwood, *Voyages of Faith*.

Staker, Susan, ed. *Waiting for World's End: The Diaries of Wilford Woodruff*. Salt Lake City: Signature Books, 1993.

Sterling, Elspeth P., comp. *Sites of Maui*. Honolulu: Bishop Museum Press, 1998.

Stevenson, Russell W. *For the Cause of Righteousness: A Global History of Blacks and Mormonism, 1830-2013*. Draper, UT: Greg Kofford Books, 2014.

Stewart, John J. *Mormonism and the Negro*. Salt Lake City: Community Press, 1960.

Stover, Jeffrey S. "Wars and Rumors of Wars." In Underwood, *Voyages of Faith*.

Taggart, Stephen G. *Mormonism's Negro Policy*. Salt Lake City: University of Utah Press: 1970.

"Thames Keel and Shipbuilding Exhibit," *Mystic Seaport: The Museum of America and the Sea*, www.mysticseaport.org.

Thomas, Nicholas. *Cook: The Extraordinary Voyages of Captain James Cook*. New York: Walker Books, 2003.

Turley, Richard E. "Gathering Latter-day Saint History in the Pacific." In Underwood, *Pioneers in the Pacific*.

Twain, Mark. *Letters from the Sandwich Islands: Written for the Sacramento Union by Mark Twain*. Stanford: Stanford University Press, 1938.

———. *Mark Twain's Letters from Hawaii*. A. Grove Day, ed. Honolulu: University of Hawaii Press, 1989.

———. *Mark Twain's Letters,* comp. Albert Bigelow Paine, 6 vols. NY: Harper & Brothers, 1917.

Underwood, Grant, ed. *Pioneers in the Pacific: Memory, History, and Cultural Identity among the Latter-day Saints.* Provo: BYU Religious Studies Center, 2005.

———. *Voyages of Faith: Explorations in Mormon Pacific History*. Provo: Brigham Young University Press, 2000.

United States Commission of Fish and Fisheries: Report of the Commissioner for 1875–1876. Washington: Government Printing Office, 1878.

Voltaire, *Candide* (NY: Modern Library, 1918); online at "eBooks and Texts," *Internet Archive: Digital Library*, archive.org.

"Voyages of Thames II (Ship)," American Offshore Whaling Voyages, *National Maritime Museum Digital Library*, mdl.org.

Walker, Ronald W., Richard E. Turley Jr., and Glen M. Leonard. *Massacre at Mountain Meadows: An American Tragedy*. New York: Oxford University Press, 2008.

Wallace III, William Kauaiwiulaokalani. *The Church of Jesus Christ of Latter-day Saints in the Hawaiian Islands for 1850–1900: An Abridgement,* available online at *La'ie Community Association*.

Webster's New Universal Unabridged Dictionary. NY: Barnes & Noble, 2003.

Whitney, Orson F. *History of Utah,* 4 vols. Salt Lake City: George Q. Cannon and Sons, 1904.

Whittaker, David J. "Placing the Keystone: George Q. Cannon's Mission of Translation and Printing the Book of Mormon in the Hawaiian Language." In Parry, *Revelation, Reason, and Faith.*

Whitton, Kevin. *Hawaiian Islands.* Chico, CA: Avalon Travel, 2014.

Zimmerman, Dean R. *I Knew the Prophets: An Analysis of the Letter of Benjamin F. Johnson to George F. Gibbs.* Bountiful, UT: Horizon, 1976.

MANUSCRIPTS

Allred, Reddick Newton. Journal, typescript. MS 70009, Daughters of Utah Pioneers Museum, Salt Lake City.

Allred, Reddin Alexander. Journals, typescript. Daughters of Utah Pioneers Museum; holograph MS 15967, LDS Church History Library, Salt Lake City.

———. To William Farrer, Oct. 21, 1854; Jan. 2, 1855. MS 4552, LDS Church History Library.

Baldwin, Dwight D. Journal. Hawaii Mission Children's Society, Honolulu.

———, and Charlotte Baldwin. Reports, correspondence, and diaries, 1840s–60s. Hawaii Mission Children's Society Library, Honolulu.

Bell, Eli. Diaries, 1854–64. MS 4040 1–4, LDS Church History Library.

Bigler, Henry William. Autobiography, ca. 1898, LDS Church History Library.

———. "Extracts From Missionary Experiences," typescript. MSS SC 3095, L. Tom Perry Special Collections, Harold B. Lee Library, Brigham Young University.

———. Journal, Feb. 1846–Oct. 1899. MS 1853, LDS Church History Library.

———. To William Farrer, Mar.–May 1853; Feb. 28, 1854; to Farrer and George Q. Cannon, Feb. 13, 1854; Apr. –June 1854. MS 4552, LDS Church History Library.

Cannon, George Q. To William Farrer, Mar.–Apr. 1854; to Henry Bigler and William Farrer, June 23, 1851. MS 4552, LDS Church History Library.

Cluff, William W. To William Farrer, Oct. 11, 1855. MS 4552, LDS Church History Library.

Farrer, William. "Biographical Sketch, Hawaiian Mission Report, and Diary," typescript. Perry Special Collections.

———. Journal, Oct. 1849–Aug. 1854. MSS 1521, Perry Special Collections.

———. To "Brother James," June 30, 1853; to "parents," Aug. 9, 1853; to "Brother Horns," Aug. 12, 1853. MS 4552, LDS Church History Library.

Gibson, Walter Murray. "Captain Walter M. Gibson," document excerpts, ca. 1870. MS 3691, LDS Church History Library.

———. Collection, five folders. MS 4015, LDS Church History Library, originals at Hawaii State Archives.

———. Diaries, 1886–1887. MSS SC 47, Perry Special Collections.

———. Diary Excerpts, Sept 4, 1861–May 23, 1862. Typescript of document found on Lanai. MS 4075, LDS Church History Library.

———. Papers, 1860–1867. 2 folders. LDS Church History Library.

Green, Ephraim. Diary, 1852–1856. Box 8670.1, Perry Special Collections.

———. To William Farrer, Mar. 5, 1854. MS 4552, LDS Church History Library.

Grouard, Benjamin Franklin. Journal, June 1843–Sept. 1846. MS 1388, LDS Church History Library.

Hammond, Alice Howard. "History of Alice Howard Hammond," typescript. MSS 18, Perry Special Collections.
Hammond, Francis Asbury. Hawaiian Mission Journals, 1852–1857, 1864–1865, 9 vols. MS 20124, LDS Church History Library.
———. Papers, 1851–1901. MSS 18, Perry Special Collections.
———. To David M. Edwards, June 14, 1889, photocopy. MS 2139, LDS Church History Library; original at Suffolk County Historical Society in New York.
———. To Parley P. Pratt. Dec. 1853, Oct. 1854, June 1855. Parley Parker Pratt Collection, MS 2248, LDS Church History Library.
Hammond, Mary Jane Dilworth. Journal. In Francis Asbury Hammond Papers, MSS 18, Perry Special Collections.
Hawkins, James. To William Farrer, Mar. 25, 1854. MS 4552, LDS Church History Library.
Jenson, Andrew. Index to missionaries from Zion who have labored in the Hawaiian Mission, 1850–1900. LDS Church History Library.
———, comp. Manuscript History of the Hawaiian Mission of the Church of Jesus Christ of Latter-day Saints. 6 vols. LR 3695–2, LDS Church History Library.
Johnson, Benjamin Franklin. Journals, Oct. 1852–June 1891, 4 vols. MS 1289, LDS Church History Library.
———. Papers, 1852–1911. MS 1289, LDS Church History Library.
———. To William Farrer, Apr. 23, May 21, 1854. MS 4552, LDS Church History Library.
Johnson, Sixtus Ellis. Journal, May 1854–Apr. 1858, 3 vols. MS 1491, LDS Church History Library.
Journal History of the Church of Jesus Christ of Latter-day Saints. Digital scans, 1830–1923. CR 100 137, LDS Church History Library.
Karren, Thomas. Journals, May 1853–Oct. 1854. MS 8387, LDS Church History Library.
———. To William Farrer, May 2, 1854. MS 4552, LDS Church History Library.
Keeler, James. Autobiography, comp. Laura Ann Keeler Thurber. MSS 436, Perry Special Collections.
———. Journals, Sept. 1850–Jan. 1890. MSS 834, Perry Special Collections.
———. To Henry Bigler, Sept. 8, 1853. LDS Church History Library.

Lewis, Philip B. Journal, 1851–1873. MSSH 104, Archives and Special Collections, Joseph F. Smith Library, BYU–Hawaii; typescript by Glade Tew in Perry Special Collections.

———. "Life History of Philip Bessom Lewis (My Father)." MSS Film 920, no. 91, Perry Special Collections.

———. To William Farrer, Mar. 26, 1853. MS 4552, LDS Church History Library.

Molen, Simpson Montgomery. Journal, 1854–1857, 1877–1879, 4 vols. MS 14408, LDS Church History Library.

Pratt, Addison. Autobiography and Journals, 1843–1852. MS 8226, LDS Church History Library.

———. Family papers. MSS 228b, Special Collections and Archives, Merrill–Cazier Library, Utah State University, Logan.

Pratt, Louisa Barnes. Journal, 1850–1880, 3 vols. MS 8227, LDS Church History Library.

Pratt, Parley Parker. Papers, 1837–1857. MSS 7, Perry Special Collections.

———. Correspondence, 1842–1855. MS 897, LDS Church History Library.

———. Journal photocopy, Mar. 1851–Oct. 1852. MS 2616-1, LDS Church History Library. The original is at Perry Special Collections.

Smith, George G. "Journal of a voyage in the ship Thames of Sag Harbor, commencing July 7th 1843, Jeremiah H. Hedges Commander." Sag Harbor Whaling and Historical Museum, Long Island.

Smith, Joseph F. Autobiographical sketch, diaries, 1838–1848, 1856–1909, 28 vols. MS 1325, LDS Church History Library.

———. To Elias Smith, Apr. 14, 1857. LDS Church History Library.

Smith, Silas. Journal, May 1854–June 1855, MS 18803, LDS Church History Library.

Smith, Silas Sanford. Journal, 1854–1906. MS 13320, LDS Church History Library.

Tanner, Nathan. Journal, Aug. 1852–Apr. 1855, 5 vols. MS 1521, LDS Church History Library.

———. To William Farrer, Feb. 21, 1854, MS 4552, LDS Church History Library.

Woodbury, John Stillman. Diaries, Mar. 1851–Dec. 1877. MSS 168, Perry Special Collections.

———. To William Farrer, Jan. 5, 1854. MS 4552, LDS Church History Library.

Woodbury, Susan Camilla. "History of John Stillman Woodbury," Perry Special Collections.

Young, Brigham. To King Kamehameha V, Mar. 24, 1865; and reply, May 10; photocopies. Miscellaneous Foreign File, Hawaii State Archives, Honolulu; copies also in Brigham Young Correspondence, MSS SC 1869, Perry Special Collections.

PERIODICALS

Barrett, Gwynn. "Walter Murray Gibson: The Shepherd Saint of Lanai Revisited." *Utah Historical Quarterly* 40, no. 2 (1972): 142–62.

Britsch, R. Lanier. "Another Visit with Walter Murray Gibson." *Utah Historical Quarterly* 46, no. 1 (1978): 65–78.

———. "The Lanai Colony: A Hawaiian Extension of the Mormon Colonial Idea." *Hawaiian Journal of History* 12 (1978): 68–83.

Cluff, William W. "The Fall of Walter M. Gibson." *Juvenile Instructor*, Aug. 1901, 470–73.

Douglas, Norman. "The Sons of Lehi and the Seed of Cain: Racial Myths in Mormon Scripture and Their Relevance to the Pacific Islands." *Journal of Religious History* 8:1 (June 1974): 90–104.

Ellsworth, Maria S. "The First Mormon Missionary Women in the Pacific, 1850–1852." *Mormon Pacific Historical Society* 11, no. 1 (1990): 123–40.

Ellsworth, S. George. "New Wine in Old Bottles: The Latter-day Saint Conversion Experience in French Polynesia, 1843–1852." *Mormon Pacific Historical Society* 2, no. 1 (1981): 1–10.

Everett, Amelia D. "The Ship Brooklyn." *California Historical Society Quarterly* 37 (Sept. 1958): 229–40.

The Friend, Honolulu, 1842–84 (monthly, originally as *Temperance Advocate and Seaman's Friend*), ed. Samuel C. Damon. Available at Maui Historical Society archives, Wailuku.

Goodale, Warren. "Honolulu in 1853." *Papers of the Hawaiian Historical Society* 10 (1897): 1–9.

Grow, Matthew J. "A Providential Means of Agitating Mormonism: Parley P. Pratt and the San Francisco Press in the 1850s." *Journal of Mormon Studies* 29, no. 2 (Fall 2003): 158–85.

Hammond, Francis Asbury. "In Early Days: My Introduction to Mormonism," *Juvenile Instructor*, June 1, 1894, 353–55; June 15, 1894, 364–69; July 1, 1894, 395–98; Aug. 1, 1894, 463–64; Aug. 15, 1894, 517–21.

Hammond, John J. "The 1876 Journal of Frank Hammond Jr.: 'Travailing' to the Little Colorado," *Journal of Mormon History* 33, no. 1 (Spring 2007): 65–120.

Hansen, Lorin. K. "Voyage of the Brooklyn." *Dialogue: A Journal of Mormon Thought* 21, no. 3 (Fall 1988): 47–72.

Jenson, Andrew. "Walter Murray Gibson: A Sketch of His Life and Adventures." *The Improvement Era,* Nov. 1900, 5–13; Dec. 1900, 86–95.

Journal of Discourses, Liverpool, Eng., 1855–86, ed. Franklin D. Richards.

Kenney, Scott G. "Before the Beard: Trials of the Young Joseph F. Smith." *Sunstone*, Nov. 2001, 20–42.

———. "Mormons and the Smallpox Epidemic of 1853." *Hawaiian Journal of History* 31 (1997): 1–26.

Lineham, Peter. "The Mormon Message in the Context of Maori Culture." *Journal of Mormon History* 17 (1991): 62–93.

Loveland, Jerry King. "Hagoth and the Polynesian Tradition." *BYU Studies* 17, no. 1 (Autumn 1976): 59–73.

Lyman, Edward Leo. "The Rise and Decline of Mormon San Bernardino." *BYU Studies* 29, no. 4 (1989): 43–63.

Madsen, Carol Cornwall. "Mormon Missionary Wives in Polynesia." *Journal of Mormon History* 13 (1986): 61–85.

Maffly-Kipp, Laurie F. "Looking West: Mormonism in the Pacific World." *Journal of Mormon History* 26, no. 1 (Spring 2000): 40–63.

Messenger and Advocate, Kirtland, Ohio, 1834—1837, various editors.

Millennial Star, Manchester, Eng., 1840–42, ed. Parley P. Pratt; Liverpool, 1843–65, various editors.

Newell, Linda King. "A Gift Given, A Gift Taken: Washing, Anointing, and Blessing the Sick among Mormon Women." *Sunstone,* Sept.–Oct. 1981, 16–25.

Panek, Tracey E. "Life at Iosepa, Utah's Polynesian Colony." *Utah Historical Quarterly* 60, no. 2 (1992): 64–72.

Peterson, Paul H. "The Mormon Reformation of 1856–1857: The Rhetoric and the Reality." *Journal of Mormon History* 15 (1989): 59–87.

The Polynesian, Honolulu, 1844–1860, ed. James Jackson Jarves; 1861–1864, ed. Abraham Fornander.

The Seer, Washington DC, 1853-1854, ed. Orson Pratt.

Quinn, D. Michael. "Latter-day Saint Prayer Circles." *BYU Studies* 19, no. 1 (1979): 79–105.

Shaffer, Donald Robert. "Hiram Clark and the First LDS Hawaiian Mission: A Reappraisal." *Journal of Mormon History* 17 (1991): 94–109.

Times and Seasons, 1839–1846, Nauvoo, Illinois, monthly/bi-monthly, various editors.

Index

agriculture, *see* farming
alcoholic drinks, 64, 75, 354; *okolehao*, 97; rum, 38. *See also* wine; Word of Wisdom
Allred, Reddick, arrival in Hawaii, 124; conference president, 180, 247; leaves Hawaii, 364; photo, 178; released from mission, 306; success with language, 131, 311–12
Allred, Reddin A., arrival in Hawaii, 124; conference president, 247; photo, 178; released from mission, 355; success with language, 131
American Board of Commissioners for Foreign Missions, xi–xii, 40
American Seamen's Friend Society, 16n36, 458
architecture, *see* building styles

Baker, Marcus, 87; ordained elder, 247; slanders Mary Jane Hammond, 98–101
Baldwin, Charlotte, 114, 163
Baldwin, Dwight, comments on FAH's monogamy, 295; comments on Lana'i colony, 343; contentious meeting with, 73–74, 114; FAH description of, 114; first interaction with missionaries, 72; low opinion of Mormons, 118, 128–29, 177; medical background, 72n14; photos, 74, 115; Protestant pioneer, 113; vaccinates against smallpox, 142, 189; writes of smallpox epidemic, 141, 143, 150, 154, 188
baptisms, decrease in, 165, 352, 394; description of, 136–37; FAH baptized, 20; for health, xi, 139, 226, 397; immersion, 69–70, 91, 93–94, 103, 119, 134, 140; increase in, 181, 210, 221, 470; mass baptisms, 64, 69, 77, 81, 88–89, 95, 116, 119, 136–38, 148; of excommunicated Protestants, 138; of foreigners, 77, 83, 87, 106; performed by natives, 92, 95; rebaptism, 68, 93, 116, 237, 400–01, 429; vicarious (doctrine), 116. *See also* converts
Bell, Eli, arrival in Hawaii, 280; assigned to big island, 282
Benson, Ezra T., sent to investigate Walter Gibson, 421
Bigler, Henry W., assigned to O'ahu, 72; called as gold missionary, 47; called on mission to Hawaii, 48; called on second mission to Hawaii, 405; conference president, 180; documents discovery of gold, 21; named mission president, 408; photo, 28; struggles to learn language, 77
Bingham, Hiram, arrival in Hawaii, 40; influence on government, 43; outrage at Hawaiian culture, 40–41
Blackwell, Hiram, called on mission to Hawaii, 48; leaves mission, 54; predicts downfall of mission, 69
boats, 275, 334, 365, 411–13; canoes,

32n5, 33, 38, 175, 177, 236–37, 311; longboats, 3, 9–10; scows/tenders, 8–9, 18, 32, 274, 276–79, 440–41, 445, 448, 455; steamboats, 48, 193, 261, 384, 389, 432, 441, 448, 455, 464; whaleboats (hung on side of whaleships), 3–6, 11–15, 94–95, 111, 176, 184, 209, 265, 267–68, 276–78, 292, 302, 307, 311, 319, 321–22, 346, 351, 358. *See also* mission sailing vessels

Book of Mormon (Hawaiian), bound copies, 386, 395, 418; delay in printing, 295; description of bound books, 397; difficulty in selling, 397; FAH assessment of, 462; manuscript sent to California, 341; pamphlet announcing, 386–87; proofed, 175, 192; revised, 194, 200; translation (Cannon and Napela), 89, 118, 146, 157, 163, 167; unbound copies, 388n6, 409, 411; unique among North American Indian languages, 387; Walter Gibson surrenders copies, 424. *See also* printing press

Brannan, Samuel, meets FAH, 19; possibly confirms FAH, 20; role in gold rush, 21

Brinton, David, 26, 401

building styles, 113, 310, 323; adobe, 111; brick, 386; frame, 73, 115, 122, 275, 320, 459, 467; log cabin, 25, 471; native, 15, 51, 65, 71, 99, 103; stone, 25, 36, 113, 472

Burnham, Albion, baptized, 78; ordained, 82

Burnham, Mary, baptized, 91; boards with FAH, 367; trouble accepting polygamy, 125–26

Caine, John T., arrival in Hawaii, 308; counselor in mission presidency, 354; returns to Utah, 398; struggles with language, 354, 399

California Trail, Humboldt route, 22, 394, 405, 409; Simpson's route, 431, 441–42, 452–53; Southern route, 27–29, 48, 191n25, 201, 255–56, 367n9, 398, 401–03, 417. *See also* transportation

Cannon, George Q., 48, 55, 64–65, 76, 88–89, 168, 237, 246, 252, 255, 414, 431; accepts polygamy, 125, 133; assigned to Kula (Maui), 72; baptizes hundreds, 69; charismatic preacher, 70, 78; clashes with FAH, 104–05; close to Brigham Young, 169, 189; description of volcanoes, 232; helps Parley P. Pratt write autobiography, 255; journals censored, xiv, 96, 101; language ability, xiv, 52–53, 61–64, 74–75, 80–81, 84–86, 99, 103, 105, 210–11, 352; marries, 256; meets and boards with Jonathan Napela, 63, 80–81; mission leader, 52, 83–84, 86, 91, 105, 221, 250, 406; photo, 49; prints Hawaiian Book of Mormon, 325, 348, 386, 409; publishes *Western Standard*, 388; recommends proselytizing among Hawaiians, 50, 55–56, 210, 387; statue of, 469; translates Book of Mormon into Hawaiian, 89, 118, 146, 157, 163, 167, 175, 194, 200; visits King Kamehameha III, 77

Catholicism, 29, 42–44, 114, 130, 138, 159n4, 176

cattle, 38, 75, 79, 89, 141n1, 142, 222, 273–74, 287, 357, 361, 374, 390–91, 395, 401, 406, 425, 462, 471, 473. *See also* oxen

chapels, LDS, 66, 81, 98–99, 102–03, 268, 275, 321, 406, 419, 467; non-LDS, 1n1, 14–16, 50–51, 111, 113, 152, 398n5

chickens, 32, 177–78, 237, 309, 317, 361, 381

children, vii, 210, 403, 430, 435, 447, 465, 467, 471, 473, 475; accompany parents on missions, 26n23, 27, 178, 334–35, 462, 464; develop immunity

to disease, 141n1, 142; expenses, 316–17; experience pain, 140, 223; FAH delivers sermon to, 364–65; tended by nannies, 304, 474; vaccinated, 149
Christmas, *see* holidays
church, *see* Latter-day Saint Church
church discipline, 221, 239; all natives on Moloka'i excommunicated, 413; blood atonement, 173, 241, 385; double standard for notables, 97, 239, 241, 347; for moral transgressions, 96, 173, 207, 221, 241, 346, 354; for various reasons, 78, 116, 137–38, 304, 390, 423; for Word of Wisdom, 119, 173, 354; investigation of Walter Gibson, 421–25; missionaries excommunicated, 201, 204, 349; native president excommunicated, 414; public confession, 347
Clark, Hiram, accused of moral impropriety, 52n19, 97; allocates missionaries, 50; called as mission president, 48; expands mission to Marquesas Islands, 53; experiences difficulties with missionaries, 53–54; indecision of, 50; leaves mission and commits suicide, 54, 219, 235; predicts downfall of mission, 69
clothing, clean and neat, 120, 210, 336; fashionable, 93, 42; muumuus, 45n18; sewing, 79, 92; shabby condition of, 187, 200, 348; shortage of, 348, 382; temple undergarments, 277. *See also* temple, LDS, clothing; shoes
Cluff, Benjamin, 441, 458–59; ability with language, 421, 434; left in charge of mission, 427, 429, 432, 437–38, 442; sent to investigate Walter Gibson, 421
Cluff, William, arrival in Hawaii, 280; assigned to big island, 282; assistant mission president, 424; sent to investigate Walter Gibson, 421
cobbler, *see* shoes
colony, *see* gathering place
Conde, Daniel, opposition to missionaries, 63, 80
conferences, 123, 178–79, 192, 219, 240, 244, 284, 286, 331, 352–53, 413, 428; authorities meet privately before, 285, 351–52; consult native elders, 285; FAH presides over, 284; hosted by Jonathan Napela, 102; native leaders want larger voice in, 353; resolutions, 179, 356; segregated meetings, 352, 357, 359–61; with Walter Gibson, 418
Congregationalists, 40, 63
consumption, *see* sickness
conversion, 9, 20, 66, 69–70, 78, 136, 236–37. *See also* baptisms; converts
converts, 56, 77, 82–83, 118–19, 132, 137, 139, 201, 387, 461; struggles to keep, 76, 78–80, 138, 154, 204, 220, 373, 392, 399–400, 412. *See also* baptisms; Gaston, Diana; Gibson, Walter Murray; Kahumoku, John W.; Kauwahi, J.W.H.; Napela, Jonathan H.; Uaua, William H.
corn, 273, 296, 300, 310, 322, 346–47, 372, 401, 419, 458–59, 467
Council of Fifty, members of, 27, 124; summary, 27n27

Dennis, Edward, baptized, 92; critic of Mormonism, 392, 409; donates toward printing press, 172, 191; loan never repaid, 191, 409; married to native wife, 92; ordained an elder, 135; spiritualist, 391
Dennis, Hakuole, 92, 160, 393
dental hygiene, 301, 394, 430,
Dilworth, Caleb, death, 110, rejects Mormonism and loses family, 24
Dilworth, Eliza, 110; leaves husband and goes to Nauvoo, 24
Dilworth, Mary Jane, *see* Hammond, Mary Jane Dilworth
disease, *see* sickness
Dixon, John, called on mission to

Hawaii, 48; leaves mission, 54; plans to leave Hawaii, 52
dogs, 31–32, 163, 206, 298, 315–16; treatment of, 10, 303
dreams, 15, 53, 306, 331, 343, 349, 366–67; conflicts reflected in, 185; factor in FAH conversion, 20; FAH nightmares, 87–88, 95, 160–61, 224–25, 228, 259, 344; presage conversions, 78n6

education, 356, 364, 391, 400, 408, 415, 453, 467; Central Maui Female Seminary, 64n66; Hawaiians, 43, 116, 406, 443; Mormons, 2, 16, 63–64, 81, 145; Protestants, 17, 40, 45, 63, 72, 129n13, 171n11, 234. *See also* Hammond, Mary Jane, teaching school; Lahaina-luna Seminary
Edwards, Charity Elizabeth, *see* Hammond, Charity Elizabeth Edwards
Evans, John, baptized, 239; nearly apostatizes, 399
excommunication, *see* church discipline

faith, crisis of, 329; in lieu of medicine, 141, 154–55, 162, 222, 226, 229–30; lack of causes sickness, 224, 228; necessity of, 111; of natives, 190
farming, 459, 467; cash crops, 302, 318–19, 323, 329, 347, 357, 449; communal effort, 263–64, 271–72, 281–82, 328, 336–41; harvesting, 36, 273, 310, 322–23, 360, 372, 401, 468, 472; irrigating, 177, 185, 236, 303, 307, 319, 322–23, 419; planting, 264, 267–68, 273, 310, 313, 316–17, 323, 343, 437, 440, 442; tobacco, 276, 289–92, 323; worms, 304, 310, 343, 380, 458, 467. *See also* cattle; chicken; corn; goats; kalo/taro; oxen; pigs; potatoes; rice; sugar cane; wheat
Farrer, William, assigned to O'ahu, 72; called on mission to Hawaii, 48; called on second mission, 405; called to write church history synopsis, 181; contracts smallpox, 147, 159; photo, 49; plans to leave Hawaii, 52; president of Kaua'i conference, 180; success with language, 136
fasting, 117, 143, 162, 306, 337
financial demands on natives, 181, 184, 195–96, 210–12, 220, 264, 284, 297, 302–03, 319, 325, 328, 343–45, 350, 397, 407–08, 413
food, ix, 32, 275, 309, 316–17, 342, 347, 422, 427; bananas, 15, 31–32, 103, 122, 132, 237; banquet/luau, 39, 99, 103, 177, 182, 197, 237, 251, 362, 435; breakfast, 111, 123, 182; coconut, 32, 317n3; cooking, 15, 75, 92–93, 119, 178, 194, 223, 323, 330–31, 338; fish, 99, 103, 178, 237, 275, 315, 327, 372; melons, 8, 99, 103, 237, 310, 375; pies, 7–8, 119, 182, 194, 197, 321; poi, 15, 99, 103, 178, 188, 237, 303n7, 313, 316–17; tea, 32n5, 153, 193–94, 223, 317; turkey, 99, 103, 197, 316, 361; white views of, 32–33, 123, 132, 313n16, 315. *See also* farming

Gaston, Diana, 240, 258, 301, 324; baptized, 91; boards with FAH, 190, 197–98, 208, 223, 235; burden on Hammonds, 300; elopes, 373, 399; helps Mary Jane Hammond, 235, 305; leaves Hammonds, 301–02, 304–05, 307
Gaston, Judson, baptized, 87, 91, 94–95, 190, 197
gathering place, 169, 269, 272, 356; Brigham Young on, 203, 220, 237, 241–42, 263; commercial aspect of, 247–48, 273, 328–29, 347, 364, 413, 450, 458–59; donations for, 287, 302; founding pioneers, 264–66, 272–73, 285–86, 316, 319, 323, 342, 351; government official offers land, 186, 204, 244, 246, 257, 276, 298,

361–64, 366, 411, 413, 420, 431; Laie, 440, 458, 461, 467; Lana'i, 176, 179, 246, 263–67, 273–74, 316, 337, 342, 356, 364; leaders of, 174, 185, 203, 231, 247, 265–67, 270, 281, 289, 293, 299, 337; location debated, 183, 185, 203–04, 407, 410–11, 426, 429, 434; private vs. common good, 271–73, 282, 287, 317, 320, 328–29, 337–42, 345, 347, 357; promoted, 190, 210, 272, 308, 323, 389, 443, 450, 461, 464; resistance from native members, 269, 271, 281–82, 303, 308, 313, 319, 338–39, 341, 344, 407, 469

Gibson, Talula, 416–17, 420, 424

Gibson, Walter M., accepted by Hawaiians, 418, 422; ambitious, 418, 421, 461; baptized, 416; binds copies of Book of Mormon, 418; biographical information, 415–16, 424–25; called on mission, 417, 419, 422; charges money for priesthood offices, 420; excommunicated, 424; followers rejoin Mormonism, 425; government official, 424–25; language fluency, 415; lecturer, 416–17; lobbies church leaders, 421; meets Brigham Young, 416; mission to New York, 416; opposes church leaders, 423; photo, 416; purchases half of Lana'i, 419–20; rituals, 419–20; stay in San Francisco, 417; view of Hawaiians, 419; view of race, 428; writes articles about Mormons, 417

gift of tongues, xi, 85, 95, 110, 392; among converts, 168; among missionaries, 50, 84, 95, 167–68, 249, 357

goats, 9–10, 15, 38n25, 99, 182, 316

gossip, 98, 100–01, 250, 364

Green, Ephraim, arrival in Hawaii, 124; called on second mission to Hawaii, 405; called to oversee gathering, 247, 265–66, 299; clashes with Thomas Karren, 299–300; leaves Hawaii, 364; released from mission, 355; struggles with language, 247, 265, 405n1

Grouard, Benjamin F., biographical sketch, 390; involvement with spiritualism, 209, 390; leaves for Society Islands, 4; married to native islanders, 22n12

Haalalea, Levi, offers to rent/sell land, 186, 204, 244, 246, 257, 276, 361–64, 366, 411, 413, 420, 431

Hakipuu, congregation organized, 77; half of membership leaves, 80n10

Haleakala, 217, 374, 464; visit to, 181–83

Hammond, Alice Howard (second wife), 118n16, 430, 445–48, 464–66, 471, 472–74

Hammond, Charity Elizabeth Edwards (mother), 1–2, 472

Hammond, Fletcher B. (son), 330, 334, 376, 381, 430

Hammond, Francis A. (Frank),

—early life (1822–1840)

attends school during winter, 2; named after a bishop, 1; runs away, 2; sees family for last time, 3; tall, 2n5

—whaling (1840–44)

back injury, 13; duties as bos'n, 9; leaves sweetheart behind, 7; promoted to steward, 3

—Hawaii (1844–47)

attends Protestant church, 14; founding member of Temperance Society, 16; hears of Mormons, 15–16; religious outlook, 16–17; shoemaker, 15; views on Hawaiians, 9, 17

—California (1847–48)

arrives in San Francisco, 18; baptized, 20; goes to gold fields, 21; leaves for Utah, 21; opens cobbler shop, 19; views on religion, 19

—Utah (1848–51)

arrives in Great Salt Lake City, 22; buys house, 25; description of early forts, 22; introduced to polygamy,

24; marries, 25; moves, 26; meets Parley P. Pratt, 22; travel from California, 22; unimpressed, 22
—first mission to Hawaii (1851–56) ability with language, 85, 88, 92, 99, 105, 107, 115–16, 181, 250; accused of stealing mission property, 365–66; adopts Isaac Linn, 268; anoints and blesses son, 139; arrives in Lahaina, 66; boards with locals, 75, 84; brashness, 274–75; buys house, 122, 130, 202; clashes with missionaries, 81, 94, 100, 103–07, 208, 266, 292, 299, 304, 323, 337, 340, 367–68; concern for wife, 226; conference president in Maui, 180, 247, 284, 351, 355; connections to foreign population, 74, 87, 177, 201, 227, 234–35, 268; contentious meetings with Dwight Baldwin, 72–74, 114, 137; dedicates Lana'i for gathering, 176; demands on, 289, 296, 301, 304, 312; depression, 160–61, 358; gives prophetic blessings, 222–23, 227, 229, 251, 330; interprets glossolalia, 95, 110, 249, 357; keeps journal, vii, xiv, xii–xiii, 87; leaves mission for San Francisco, 383–84; misses George Q. Cannon, 285; mission, 26–27, 29–30, 66, 72, 84, 87, 110, 232, 268, 343–44, 348, 355, 361, 383; nightmares, 87–88, 160–61, 225, 228, 259, 344; preaches, 121, 233–36, 238; preaches faith over medicine, 141, 147, 149; reaction to first wave departure, 252–53; rebaptizes missionaries, 68; receives prophetic blessings, 95, 100, 250, 296, 301, 327; relationship with parents, 78, 118, 147, 189, 300, 368; relationship with wife, 119, 289, 294, 305; sailing, 111, 176–77, 237, 311, 322; sees God as source of smallpox, 147; shoemaking, 71, 106; struggles with horses, 101–2, 109–10; suggests calling single missionaries, 71; takes boarders, 188, 268, 367; view of Hawaiians, 97n27; views on race, 116, 193, 293, 355
—return to Utah (1856–64) appointed home missionary, 399; business partner with Chauncey West, 429; buys wife earrings, 401; city councilman, 429; encounters dissidents in San Bernardino, 389–402; investigates spiritualism, 388–89; involvement in Utah War, 404; Linn child dies, 396–97; marries plural wife Alice Howard, 430; preaches Reformation, 398, 400, 402; reaches California, 386; regains tobacco habit, 401; seeks farm, 404; shoemaking, 391, 394; visits Brigham Young in Salt Lake City, 403; visits George Q. Cannon in San Francisco, 386
—second mission to Hawaii (1864–65) arrives in Honolulu, 457, 464; arrives in Salt Lake City, 442–44, 465; arrives in San Francisco, 440, 462; becomes mission president, 429, 446; buys Laie site, 429, 435–37, 443, 445, 455, 458; carries letter from Brigham Young to King Kamehameha V, 450–54, 459–61; comments on Walter Gibson, 460; danger in carrying gold, 448–49, 454; family stays behind, 446–47, 462–63, 465–66; first visit to Kaua'i, 434; preaches, 438, 457; preparations, 445; reacts to world news, 455–56, 458–59; reads Book of Mormon to avoid temptation, 462; reports mission to Brigham Young, 445; resumes journal, 429; telegraphs Brigham Young in code, 457; tobacco habit, 432; travels overland to Virginia City, 431–32, 447–49, 454–55; views of mission, 447, 449; views on members, 307,

433; visits friends in California, 432; visits Wailua Valley, 435
—later years (1865–1900)
branch president, 472; called to visit Arizona, 473; journals, xii, 471, 473; marries Martha Marcussen, 474; president of San Juan Stake, 473; sent to Huntsville, 470, 472; visits family in East, 472–73; visits missionary acquaintances, 473
Hammond, Francis, Jr. (son "Frankey"), 26, 68, 76, 119, 139, 181–82, 222–23, 237, 240, 258, 316–17, 334, 349, 430, 445, 449, 473
Hammond, George A. (son), 429, 473
Hammond, John F. (brother), also named after bishop, 1n2; death, 118
Hammond, Lizzie Fontella (daughter), 430, 463
Hammond, Martha Marcussen (third wife), 474
Hammond, Mary Jane Dilworth (first wife)
—Hawaii
begins keeping journal, xii, 134; blesses FAH, 95; clashes with Jane Lewis, 198; demands on, 190, 219, 236, 238, 251, 300, 305, 316, 368; disagrees with FAH, 229, 295, 447; domestic skills, 89, 225, 234, 302, 316–17, 330, 368; gives birth, 26, 134, 320, 330, 429–30, 402, 429; gives Henry Bigler two dollars, 252; helps FAH, 79, 225, 273; hosts guests, 178, 188, 197–98, 225, 240, 253, 301, 309, 375; misses Diana Gaston, 305; moods, 89, 182, 202, 219, 281, 300, 302, 316, 348; nurses sick family members, 223–24, 305, 396; photo, 23; preparing food, 178, 194, 197, 281, 321, 370; receives blessing, 251; receives gift of port wine, 333; sick, 222–27, 234; slandered, 96, 98–101, 103, 237; sympathetic to doctors, 146–47, 149, 227–29; teaches natives to sew, 92; teaches school, 112, 120, 130, 187, 190, 202, 226, 234, 236, 258, 273, 327, 368; temporarily boards native boy, 302; tries to learn Hawaiian, 92–93; wants to leave, 253, 283, 291
—Utah
considers returning to Hawaii, 446–47, 465–66; death, 473; pregnant during return trip, 402; rebaptized during Reformation, 400; sketch of youth, 24–25; teacher, 472; unhappy in Huntsville, 471; welcomed home, 403
Hammond, Mary Moselle (daughter), 402, 430
Hammond, Samuel (father), 1–2, 207, 368
Hammond, Samuel, Jr. (brother), 207
Hammond, Samuel S. (son), xin5, 134–35, 181–82, 193–94, 207, 219, 222, 240, 430, 468, 474–75
Hammond, William E. (son), birth, 429; death, 473
Hanks, Knowlton, buried at sea, 5; leaves for Society Islands, 4
Hawaii, *see* Sandwich Islands
Hawaii, M. K., tried for membership, 346–47
Hawai'i ("big island"), maps, 213, 217–18
Hawaiian government, authority recognized, 454; Brigham Young writes to, 450; control of marriage licenses, 364; creation of monarchy, 43; expansion, 43; failure over smallpox, 143–44, 172; limited democracy, 43; Mormon converts in, 132; Mormons appeal for redress, 171; official meets missionaries, 186, 244; official offers land to Mormons, 186, 204, 244, 246, 257, 276, 361–64, 366; Protestants within, 79; public schools, 45; restricts emigration, 227, 233, 411, 443, 469; suspicious of Mormons, 411, 460–61; tries

to shut down Mormon meetings, 74; Walter Gibson's role in, 424–25
Hawaiian landscape, flora, 32, 38, 88, 91, 112, 132, 440, 475; volcanoes, 36, 175n2, 177, 181–82, 215 (map), 217–18 (maps), 232, 374, 419, 464; waterfalls, 50, 134, 435
Hawaiian language, ability to learn based on age, 86, 105–06, 124, 131, 281, 303; difficulty learning, 51–52, 77, 79, 84–86, 135, 306–07, 313–14, 319, 344, 405n1
Hawaiian Mission, closed for seven years, 207, 410, 412–14; communication between elders, 232, 371; decline in conversions, 394, 405–08, 411–13; inception, 5, 26–27, 29–30, 48; meetings of, 126, 178, 243, 249, 357, 407–08; native elders assist Utahns, 100, 132, 136, 180–81, 187, 331, 336, 353; native elders falter, 201–02, 204, 221–22; not initially directed toward natives, 24, 50, 55; presidents (Clark, Lewis, Smith, Hammond, Nebeker) 48, 54, 83–84, 198–99, 35–54, 408, 427, 429, 431, 464–65; reopened, 421, 424, 432, 462; wives, 26, 68, 79, 92–94, 109, 336, 429, 447, 462–63. *See also* baptisms; gathering place; Gibson, Walter M.; mission sailing vessels; missionaries, LDS; printing press; smallpox
Hawaiian Missionary Society, 43, 45
Hawaiian people, foreign influence, 38, 44; *kapus* (taboos), 35, 37, 41; literacy, 45; Mormons attempt to change, 120, 316–18, 334, 428, 440, 449–50, 453, 460, 468, 470; native religion, 36, 39–40, 134n2; reception of Mormons, 16, 51, 80, 117–18, 133, 136, 154, 210–11, 244, 356, 459; said to be of ancient Israel, 24, 56, 110, 208, 210, 355, 387, 451–52; sailing skills, 32–33, 311, 322; sexuality, 37, 40–41, 96, 186, 194, 201, 221–22, 428; views on war, 37; white views on, 38, 40–41, 52, 120, 132, 190, 206–07, 210–11, 316–17, 328, 427–28, 440, 453. *See also* converts
Hawkins, James, 91, 94, 123, 127, 180, 191–92, 202, 246, 251–52; called on mission, 48; clashes with FAH, 100, 103; interprets tongues, 50; learns language, 86, 90; on big island, 30, 50–51, 53, 55, 64, 84; rumors about, 237; struggles of, 79–80, 83, 96, 98–105, 183, 237, 243, 255, 302
Hedges, Jeremiah, 5, rumor of death, 10; sent home sick, 6
holiday celebrations, April Fools Day, 385; Christmas, 7, 51, 119, 194, 309, 375, 401; Fourth of July, 237; New Year's Day, 7–8, 194, 197, 310, 376, 401; Pioneer Day, 162
Honolulu, description, 48, 50; focus on foreigners, 136; initial meeting of missionaries, 50; lack of missionary success, 136; mission conference, 123, 240, 286; shrinking branch, 407, 433
Horner, John, develops land in California, 187, 440; underwrites mission ship, 135
hospitality, 9, 178, 182, 197, 237, 251, 321, 348, 375, 379–80, 435
houses, *see* building styles
Howard, Alice, *see* Hammond, Alice Howard
hula, criticized, 41, 423–24, 435; described, 31, 32n6; photo, 34
hygiene, 142, 406, 471; animals in houses, 31, 206; bathing, 50, 69, 106, 155, 163, 266, 277, 316, 320, 349, 365, 455; cleanliness urged, 111, 120, 185, 206, 210; bedbugs, 206; fleas, 38n25, 210, 315–16; leaky roofs, 25, 310, 323, 419, 474; lice, 31, 210, 316; washing clothes, 194, 223, 225, 334, 336, 368, 375, 391. *See also* dental hygiene
hymns, 50, 70, 99, 134, 167, 181, 235; native hymns, 31

Iao Valley, 88, 91, 107, 285, 331, 349
irrigation, *see* farming, irrigating

Johnson, Benjamin F., arrival in Hawaii, 124; assumes (clerical) control of mission, 124, 127–28, 185, 245, 249–50, 257, 266, 290; clashes with missionaries, 185, 266; false claim to be a doctor, 156; ghostwrites mission president's letters, 258; photo, 126; reluctance to work among natives, 127–28, 247; speaks in tongues, 249; wants to leave, 283, 294, 306; writes pamphlet on polygamy, 220
Johnson, Sixtus E., 302, 308, 310, 383–84, 407–08

Kaahumanu, queen mother, 38–39
Kahoouluwaa, Isaaka, 148, 165; death, 157–59, 161; disillusionment with Mormonism, 164; ordained elder, 157
Kahumoku, John W., death, 168; double life, 194–95; interpreter, 168; success as missionary, 145; to preach in spirit world, 171
Kailehune, Elder, claims office of mission president, 414; excommunicated, 414
Kaleohano, H. K., 74–75, 137, 337, 356n10; branch leader at Kula, 131, 273, 282, 321, 347; conversion, 67; missionary, 94, 100, 102; moves to Laie plantation, 457–60; speaker, 331, 353, 361, 429
kalo/taro, 32, 38, 103, 182, 197, 237, 313, 322
Kamehameha III, death, 308; visit of George Q. Cannon, 77
Kamehameha IV, 437–38; coronation, 311
Kamehameha V, Brigham Young letter to, 450; FAH respect for, 453; photos of, 299, 451
Karren, Thomas, arrival in Hawaii, 124, called on second mission to Hawaii, 405; clashes with Ephraim Green, 299–300, 304; conference president, 247; counselor in mission presidency, 125; photo, 169; released from mission, 306; struggles with language, 145, 179, 289, 304, 313–14; supervises farming, 282, 289, 293, 299
Kaua'i, conference, 192; description of, 192; map of, 214; possible gathering site, 203–04, 434; struggles of converts, 220, 301
Kauwahi, J.W.H., assists with Book of Mormon translation, 192, 194, 200–01; baptized, 66; becomes critic, 399–400, 409, 412; generous, 384; given favored treatment, 241, 347, 356; legislator, 132; meets missionaries, 64; ordained elder, 135; prison time for bigamy, 207, 220, 320; proselytizing success, 136, 147, 165, 247; to assist with printing, 294; violates the quarantine, 157
Keanae, branch organized, 67; conflicts, 83, 93, 317–18; converts leave Mormonism, 76
Keeler, James, assigned to Keanae, 72; called as gold missionary, 47; called to Hawaii, 48; leader on big island, 258; leaves Hawaii, 364; left behind, 252, 256–57, 321, 326; named counselor in presidency, 408; never arrives for second mission, 408; photo, 49; released from mission, 306
Kimball, Heber C., officiates in FAH marriage, 25; officiates in FAH plural marriage, 430
King, William, 302, 348n4, 351, 370
Kipp, James, boards FAH, 75; companion to FAH, 74; leaves Hawaii, 186; married to half–Hawaiian, 75; ordained, 82; spiritualism, 391
Kipp, Kua Moo, 391; baptized, 106; clashes with Antonio Silver, 121; midwife for Mary Jane Hammond, 134
Kula, area for growing irish potatoes,

67, 307n3, 370, 372; at foot of Haleakala Crater, 182; "beloved," 264n1; disillusionment in, 318, 320; early converts from, 67, 98, 137, 263–64; few foreigners live in, 131, 288, 307; George Q. Cannon confronts Protestant minister in, 65; residents help settle Palawai, 265, 272–73, 276;

Lahaina, branch organized, 116; busy port, 9, 112, 186, 301, 328; climate, 273, 320; concerted missionary effort, 111; first meeting conducted in Hawaiian, 111; meetinghouse, 321; moral character in, 84, 110, 154–55, 186, 301, 323; seaman's hospital, 14, 112–13, 233, 235, 238–39, 334n7, 348
Lahaina Bethel Church, 14, 16, 51, 72, 112–13
Lahaina-luna seminary (Protestant), 43, 63–64, 81, 150n2
Laie, Brigham Young letter regarding purchase, 442–43; FAH and George Nebeker financially responsible, 443; gathering site purchased, 436–37; members later avoid, 469; site described by Alma Smith, 440, 467; take possession of gathering site, 458; temple, 470; Utah families to be model, 468
Lanai (ship), 333–34, 369–79, 394, 399, 407. *See also* mission sailing vessels
Lana'i (island), apathy among members, 467; construction on gathering site begins, 267; curse on, 176; FAH dedicates for gathering, 176; first baptisms, 176; government official offers to rent/sell land, 186, 204, 244, 246, 257, 276, 361–64, 366, 411, 413, 420, 431; land blessed, 286; leaders give up on, 424; map, 216; settlement site selected, 265–66; strength of members, 407, 411; sustained as gathering place, 246, 251; Walter Gibson purchases half of, 420. *See also* gathering
language, *see* Hawaiian language
Latter-day Saint Church, membership growth, 63, 67, 69, 77, 81, 90–92, 132–33, 136, 165–66, 181, 209–10, 408, 413, 467–70. *See also* baptisms; chapels; Hawaiian Mission
Lawson, James, arrival in Hawaii, 124; conference president, 247; interprets glossolalia, 249; leaves Hawaii, 314; struggles with language, 179
Lewis, Jane, boards with FAH, 188, 197–98; death, 367; drinks tea, 194n30; goes to O'ahu with husband, 72; leaves bedbugs in FAH house, 206; leaves Hawaii, 300; leaves on mission, 27; returns to O'ahu, 200; tuberculosis, 188
Lewis, Philip, 27, 29, 66, 72, assaulted, 154–55; blesses missionaries, 327; clashes with missionaries, 81, 87, 94, 106–7, 128, 199–200, 208, 323, 337, 340; donates to Society Islands Mission, 5; focuses on white foreigners, 74, 131; member of Council of Fifty, 27; ordained mission president, 29; photo, 74; preaches on theological mysteries, 71; questionable leadership style, 69, 83, 86, 110, 125–26, 249, 258, 290; resigns as mission president, 353, 355; resists gathering place, 246; sees need for printing press, 155; son dies en route to Hawaii, 29; struggles with language, 84, 86, 188; tinsmith, 199, 243, 256, 310, 324
Liholiho, Prince Alexander, 38–39, 41, 74–75n21; meets with George Q. Cannon, 77
Linn, Gustaf, baptized, 95; leaves son with FAH, 268, 392; married to native wife, 268; mission, 179–80, 242, 247, 348, 355; requests that FAH take another son to Utah, 402
Linn, Isaac, 160, 300, 381; adopted by FAH, 268; boards with FAH, 268;

death, 397; goes to California with FAH, 382, 391–92; severe illness, 396–97
London Missionary Society, 2–3n7, 45

Maikai, Ioane W. E., shows interest in Mormonism, 66, 76
Makawao, 76, 87, 94, 98, 100–01, 119, 127, 273, 349; branch organized, 87–88, 90; Hammond stays in, 108
Manele, branch organized, 177; branch presided over by native, 236; described, 176; difficult crossing to, 236–37, 265, 268, 277–78, 315, 322, 328–29, 334, 351, 365
Marcussen, Martha, *see* Hammond, Martha Marcussen
Maui, core of missionary successes, 66–67, 77, 132–33, 136; maps of, 213, 217; members lack direction, 347, 408, 467; native conference, 219; praised, 52, 315. *See also* Haleakala; Iao Valley; Kula; Lahaina; Makawao; Wailuku
McBride, William, arrival in Hawaii, 124; role in gathering donations, 179, 191–93, 195, 199; travels to California to buy printing press, 200, 204
McBride plan, *see* McBride, William
medicine, as rival to faith, 111, 227–30, 141, 147, 154–56, 162; FAH falls back on, 149, 152, 163, 379; home remedies, 224, 378, 380–81; native practices, 134, 176, 226, 330. *See also* sickness
meetinghouses, *see* chapels
membership, *see* Latter-day Saint Church, membership growth
mental disturbances, depression, 160–61, 300, 358; hallucinations, 90, 168; megalomania, 415, 420–21, 425–26; paranoia, 308–09, 312, 331. *See also* suicide
midwifery, 134, 330
miscegenation, Mormon views on, 59, 116, 193
mission sailing vessels, *Ravaai*, 325–26; *Rosalind*, 173–74, 179, 202, 208, 235, 238, 259–61, 283–84, 362, 394, 399, 407; two whale boats, 302–04, 328–29, 346, 375, 377–78. *See also* *Lanai* (ship)
missionaries, LDS, first wave, 48, 55, 68, 179, 202, 204–06, 246, 251–52, 255, 312, 355, 357, 364, 367; second wave, 66, 79, 280, 305–06, 358; third wave, 123–24, 131, 195, 202, 313–14, 364, 405; fourth wave, 254, 257–59, 280, 301–03, 308, 354–55, 407–08, 412; fifth wave, 393–94, 398, 408–10; sixth wave, 405, 407–09, 412–14
missionary wives, 26n23, 89, 92–93, 95, 109, 119, 291, 390, 464. *See also* Hammond, Mary Jane Dilworth; women
Molen, Simpson, 280, 282, 375
Moloka'i, all native Mormons excommunicated, 413; considered for gathering place, 188; leper colony on, 469; map, 216; mission activity, 52, 94–95, 127, 180, 234, 309, 318; native conference held on, 209–10; "pioneers" from, 301, 336; poverty, 274; saints weak, 39, 281, 350, 400, 406, 467
Mormon Battalion, members of, 19, 21, 124; purpose of, 18
Mormon Church, *see* Latter-day Saint Church
Mormon Reformation, FAH preaches, 400, 402; Hawaiian version, 428–29; influence on Hawaii, 338; news of reaches San Bernardino, 398; reaches California, 386; rebaptisms, 400–01
Morris, Thomas, assigned to Honolulu, 50; called on mission, 48; leaves mission, 54
music, *see* hymns

Napela, Jonathan H., assists with translation, 89, 167; baptized and ordained, 63, 81, 91, 469; contracts leprosy, 469; double standard regarding, 239, 241; endowed in Utah temple, 469; hosts conference, 102; importance to mission, 80–81, 92, 94; interprets gift of tongues; 168; letter to Brigham Young, 92; moral transgressions, 116, 221, 238, 306, 349–50, 469; moves to Laie, 458; photo, 82; publicly humiliated by FAH, 274–75; rebaptized, 93, 116; statue of, 469; stops attending church, 399; struggles with alcohol, 64, 221, 306, 349–50, 399, 469; works with FAH, 247, 264

Napela, Kitty, contracts leprosy, 469; death, 469; endowed, 469; meets missionaries, 63; visits Utah, 469

Native Americans, 24, 391, 428, 473; assist emigrants, 402; attack wagon trains, 22, 27, 55, 403, 442; "cursed with dark skin," 57–58, 62; no Book of Mormon translations for, 387; Protestant missionaries to, xi–xii; said to be of Israelite origin, 111n6, 387; said to be related to Hawaiians, 57, 62, 242, 451

native Hawaiian wives, 22n12, 38, 69, 119–20, 134, 336, 393. *See also* Hawaiian people; women

Nebeker, George, co–mission president, 429; FAH's brother-in-law, 429, 462; financially responsible for Laie site, 443; leaves for mission, 431; photo, 437

Nebeker, Maria Louisa Dilworth, 429, 462–63

nudity, prevalence in Hawaii, 31, 33, 40–42, 69, 97

O'ahu, conversions, 66, 136; death of king, 308; fund-raising on, 207, 363; map, 215; mission headquarters, 50; mission ship, 333, 336–37, 339, 362, 379; missionaries, 132; missionary assignments, 72, 127, 247, 282; northeast coast, 412, 436; "pioneers" from, 301; villages, 64, 66, 77, 84, 148, 375, 427. *See also* Honolulu; smallpox

oxen, 22, 26, 264, 268, 271–78, 294, 381, 412–13. *See also* cattle

Pack, Ward, 54n28, 280, 282, 348n4, 349, 356, 370

Palawai, church services at, 268, 352, 358; communal eating, 271, 281, 365–66; criticized, 349–50; farm workers, 344; fire at, 332n4; housing, 323; leadership in, 330, 415, 421–23; place of refuge, 443; real estate negotiations, 361; settlement scaled back, 356, 412, 414; valley, 177, 179, 268n12, 346; village, 269, 310, 470n14; women, 348

Partridge, Edward, Jr., arrival in Hawaii, 302, 308, 351, 398n5, 407–08

Peck, Joseph A., 302, 336; disfellowshipped in absentia, 354; may have feigned illness, 326, 329, moral transgressions, 337, 340, 342, 349, 354; struggles with faith, 329; struggles with language, 341

Perkins, Martha ("Patty"), 26, 29; arrives in Hawaii, 79; returns to California, 111; sickness, 99, 106, 109; visits Moloka'i, 94–95

Perkins, William, arrives in Hawaii, 79; delayed in journey to Hawaii, 29; leaves for mission to Hawaii with wife, 26; returns to California, 111

pigs, 31–32, 99, 103, 197, 237, 316, 323; treatment of, 303

plural wives, 118n16, 138, 207, 294–95, 394–95, 398, 430–31, 462, 474. *See also* polygamy

polygamy, factor in mission downturn, 384, 412; FAH marries plural wife, 430; FAH opinion of, 24, 130,

294, 385, 474; FAH writes Brigham Young about, 130; George Q. Cannon translates revelation on, 132; King Kamehameha inquires about, 136; missionaries hear of public announcement, 115, 124; natives struggle with, 136; pamphlet on, 220; preached, 133, 233–34, 238, 474; prevents converts, 234; source of sorrow, 124, 136, 412, 474; women struggle with, 124, 394

potatoes, irish, 304, 307n3, 322–23, 343, 370, 372; sweet, 8, 32, 103, 177, 182, 237, 304, 310, 315, 372

Pratt, Addison, 24, 85, 86n30, 95, 97n28, 326, 390; involvement with spiritualism, 209; leaves for Society Islands, 4, mission in Tahiti, 26n23; travels with FAH to Utah, 22

Pratt, Louisa Barnes, 24n15, 95

Pratt, Parley P., appointed president of Pacific Mission, 26; author of Voice of Warning, 20; death, 404; George Q. Cannon helps write autobiography, 255; meets FAH, 22; photo, 28; recommends printing in California, 296; supervises gold missionaries, 48, 254; tells of biblical origins of Polynesians, 24; writes to FAH about trip to East, 189

prayer, "ancient order of," 129; at an altar, 50; by native shamans, 39, 134n2, 405; by Protestants, 65; earnest, 292, 310, 350; for answers to questions, 20; for guidance, 80, 180, 294–95; for health, 228, 380; for prosperity, 300; for protection, 277, 322; for revenge, 39, 114, 172, 392, 398; hats removed for, 137; in nature, 88, 176, 285; in a ritual circle, 129n11; in temple clothing, 226, 266, 302; sometimes ineffective, 168; to preserve journals, vii; to resist temptation, 223, 400, 462; using sailing metaphors, 344

Presbyterians, 17n39, 40

priesthood, Aaronic, 81–82, 90–91, 96, 135, 148; honoring/magnifying, 160, 202, 307–08; Melchizedek, 82, 96, 135, 181; obedience to, 162, 211, 249, 274–75, 424, 461; perquisites, 97, 241, 306n2; scriptural passage relating to, 116. *See also* priesthood blessings; priesthood ordinations

priesthood blessings, 222–23, 227, 229, 296, 301, 330; by women, 95, 301; for babies, 313; for callings (setting apart), 29, 48, 88, 98, 107, 258, 361, 386, 420, 431–32; for comfort, 100–01, 124, 129, 236, 249–51, 259, 327; for health, 95, 111, 139–40, 143, 148, 153, 162, 223–24; for oxen, 294; promises fulfilled, 25, 48; promises unfulfilled, 139, 157–58, 164, 166, 168, 226, 230, 412; using consecrated oil, 26, 95, 139, 154–56, 159–60

priesthood ordinations, 81–82, 90–91, 116, 177, 247, 307, 469; for Hawaiians, 135, 158, 181, 286; good into next life, 157–59, 161, 168; licenses, 204, 207, 221, 239, 241, 417, 422; offered for a price, 420, 422; preference for non-Hawaiians, 82–83, 90–91, 96, 202, 307; withheld from blacks, 57–62

printing press, arrival of, 293; conflicts about, 258; correspondence with Brigham Young about, 189, 312; damage to, 297; debate on location, 208–09, 231, 235–36, 246, 296, 309; donations for, 172, 181, 184, 192, 195, 201, 210–11, 222, 295, 297; government offer to assist, 186–87; natives opposed to, 184, 411; need for, 168; pressmen, 294, 325, 348, 386; resolution to purchase, 179; returned to Hawaii, 407

prophecy, 58–59, 90, 115, 127–28, 152, 158, 234, 236, 250–51, 266–67, 288, 330, 353, 429, 461

Protestants, early missionaries, 40–43, 45; efforts with sailors, 113; envy Mormons, 77; establish schools, 45; oppose Mormons, 79, 112, 411; reluctance to baptize Hawaiians, 42, 96; see smallpox as God's curse, 155, 163–64; threaten Mormon converts, 63, 65; welcome Mormons, 16, 51
Punaluu, congregation organized, 77, 215, 375

race, American ideas about, 63n59, 443; conversion to Mormonism reverses curse, 211, 387; intermarriage forbidden, 116, 193; Mormons ideas about, 56–63, 120, 355, 414, 428, 449, 451–53; reluctance to give priesthood to natives, 82–83, 307–08
rice, 432, 449, 467
Rice, David, 98–99, 101, 110, 120; accepts polygamy doctrine, 125, 233; baptized, 83–84, 87–89; helps with mission farm, 275, 335n8; helps with mission ship, 373–74, 378–79, 381, 399; ordained elder, 90; performs exorcism, 222; proselytizes, 136, 171, 180
Rich, Charles C., FAH reports to, 77; oversees San Bernardino, 75, 383, 391; suggests Sandwich Islands mission, 48, 52n19
Richards, Henry P., 261, 302, 323, 348n4, 469
Riter, Levi, 88, 394, 444; FAH's brother-in-law, 22
Riter, Rebecca Dilworth; discusses polygamy with FAH, 24; photo, 23
Rogers, Noah, 4–5, 86, 390,
Rogers, Washington, arrival in Hawaii, 302–03, 305; mental illness, 307–09, 312–13, 331

sailing, 3–4, 9–10, 13, 123n1, 247, 277–78, 315, 322, 438–39; dreams of, 15, 224–25. *See also* boats; *Lanai* (ship); mission sailing vessels; ship terminology; ships; whaling
Sandwich Islands, ix, 9, 33–44, 50n8, 51, 64, 97n28, 133n24, 182, 311, map, 213. *See also* Hawaiian government; Hawaiian landscape; Hawaiian language; Hawaiian people
seasickness, 76, 111, 123, 188, 240, 247, 265, 334, 373, 432, 439, 464; FAH, 365
second coming, gathering to precede, 169, 443; preached in Hawaii, 111; signs, 287; smallpox epidemic sign of, 146, 151–52, 164, 173
sermons, 42, 51–52, 152, 238, 295, 325, 348–49, 412; by George Q. Cannon, 210–11; by FAH, 88, 160–61, 233, 236, 266, 286–87, 323, 343–44, 378, 474; by Joseph F. Smith, 331, 351–52, 422; by Philip Lewis, 69–71; by Protestants, 45, 63–66; by William H. Uaua, 113–14.
sexuality, *see* church discipline, for moral transgressions; Hawaiian people, sexuality
ship terminology, 438; barque, 2, 224n7; binnacle, 377n9; boatswain, 3; double-reefed topsail, 439n6; gam, 5; heave, 259n10; jib, 439n7; luff, 374n4; main hatch house, 439n7; sloop, 224n7; square-rigged/latin-rigged masts, 2; state room, 439n7; stave, 439n7; steerage, 406; trim, 278, 376. *See also* sailing
ships, 123n1, 144, 186, 260–62, 430, 461–62; *Brooklyn*, 22; clippers, 262, 461; packets, 430, 441, 447; shipwrecks, 118, 294, 322, 383; sloops, 3, 224n7, 324–25, 327, 333; steamers, 29, 192–93, 198, 247, 252–53, 260–61, 321, 324, 327, 382, 389, 446, 457; *Thames*, 3–5, 7–11, 13–15; warships, 42, 324; whaleships, 1–19, 69, 112, 209, 274, 383. *See also* boats; mission sailing vessels; ship terminology; whaling

shoes, 25, 71–72, 75, 106, 187, 225, 234, 264, 295–96, 303, 321, 328, 366; cobbler apprenticeship for FAH, 1–2, 15; custom, 238, 391; repair of; 208, 301; saddles similar in construction, 394, 429; shaking dust from (ritually), 115n13; tools for making, 383.

sickness, 321, 326, 394, 396–97; caused by lack of faith, 224, 226, 228–29; caused by Satan, 223, 312; causes disillusionment, 146, 148, 152, 166; demonic possession, 139, 222; ear infection, 406; from foreigners, 33, 44, 172–73; Lahaina Fever, 305–06, 326, 329, 348; leprosy, 469; Mormon approach to, 143, 155; Mormon distrust of non–Mormon doctors, 147, 149, 227–28; tuberculosis, 188; whooping cough, 222, 224, 228–29, 305, 309, 317. *See also* dental hygiene; mental disturbances; priesthood blessings, for health; smallpox

Silver, Antonio, children schooled by Mary Jane Hammond, 112; conflict with Kua Moo Kipp, 121; hosts Mormon meeting, 111; interest in Mormonism, 75; visits with FAH, 111

smallpox, 172, 475; inoculation described, 142; foreigner/native immunity, 141; massive deaths, 141, 161, 165, 171, 173; missionaries impede vaccinations, 150, 172; missionaries unknowing carriers, 144, 148, 159–60, 164; Protestant view, 155, 163–64; quarantines imposed, 144, 147, 151, 157–58, 172, 175, 187; said to be God's plan, 147, 150–53, 158, 171, 173; vaccinations enforced, 145, 152, 160, 163; victim described, 161

Smith, Alma L., assistant mission president, 424; sent to investigate Walter Gibson, 421; success with language, 434

Smith, George G., 7; diary onboard *Thames*, 4; duties, 6; mentions FAH discharge, 14

Smith, Joseph, teachings of, 56–57, 271; visit to Missouri in 1831, 57

Smith, Joseph F., arrival in Hawaii, 280; blessed by FAH, 296; conference president, 355; early success, 319; mission president, 424; negative report, 406, 427; photo, 332; sent to investigate Walter Gibson, 421; sermon, 422; success with language, 331, 350, 352; writes FAH, 425–26

Smith, Silas, 283, 288, 408; accuses FAH of stealing utensils, 365–66; arrival in Hawaii, 280; assigned to Maui, 282; blessed by other missionaries, 296, 327; connection to Joseph Smith, 286; named mission president, 353–54; oversees Lana'i colony, 346; success with language, 281, 325, 331

Smith, Silas S., 348n4, 371, 383, 392; arrival in Hawaii, 280; assigned to big island, 282, 323; counselor in mission presidency, 354; cousin of Silas Smith, 280; helps with *Rosalind*, 254

Snider, Edgerton, arrival in Hawaii, 124; disfellowshipped, 354, 362; loses spirit of mission, 349; rejoins Mormonism, 394; struggles with language, 179

Society Islands Mission, 4–5, 26n23, 27n26, 29, 86n30, 95, 170, 325–26, 390, 417; Protestant counterpart, 45–46

Speirs, George, arrival in Hawaii, 280; assigned to big island, 282; gives report on Moloka'i, 400

spirit world, 53, 209; evil spirits, 160, 229, 352; post-mortal, 110–11, 157, 159, 168, 171, 228; pre-mortal, 60–61

spiritualism, 209, 388–91, 393

spirituality, congregation appears to shine/turn white, 62, 287, 332–33; a feeling of "fire in the bones," 20, 236,

269, 287; "filled with joy," 210–11, 236, 266, 268, 285–86, 336, 361; a good "flow of the spirit," 70, 78, 233, 295, 319, 323, 422; "hearts burned within us," 125, 210–11, 253; singing in tongues, 167; visions, 90, 168; weeping, 70, 236, 266, 279, 285–86. *See also* gift of tongues
sugar cane, 38, 427, 432, 449, 459, 465, 467–68; mills, 192, 435, 469, ; plantations, 171n11, 329, 434; transportation, 445–46, 461, 464
suicide, 54, 219, 235

Tanner, Nathan, 198, 200, 208; arrival in Hawaii, 124; assigned to purchase ship, 173–74, 202, 284; clashes with Benjamin F. Johnson, 185; conference leader, 179; counselor in mission presidency, 125; photo, 126; struggles with language, 135, 145, 179, 198
tapa cloth, 31, 32n7, 34
tattoos, 54
temples, LDS, 27; at Laie, 470, 475n28; clothing, 226, 266, 302; endowment, 26, 469; entrance to, 61; marriage, 25n20, 474; prayer circle, 129, 226, 266; prophecy concerning, 110
temples, native, 36, 39
Thames, see ships, *Thames*
theater, 455; American Theater (San Francisco), 388–89; Salt Lake Theater, 448; *Uncle Tom's Cabin*, 448
Thurston, Smith, 302–03, 305, 307–08
tin shop, 199–200, 243–44, 256, 310, 324; tinsmiths, 27, 92, 197
tithing, slowly introduced, 91, 111, 336, 340, 342, 401
tobacco, agricultural crop, 276, 289–92, 323, 432, 449; smoking (pipes), 38, 117, 360–61, 365, 401–02
transportation, 98–99, 268, 294, 351; buggy, 446, 475; concord wagon, 441–43, horseback, 48, 101–02, 106, 109–10, 144–45, 147, 296, 303, 306n2, 308, 315, 334, 365, 374–75, 412; pack train (mules), 18, 21; sleigh, 441, 444, 455; stagecoach, 427, 431–32, 441–44, 448–49, 454–55, 465, 447; train, 441, 448, 472; wagon and ox team, 22, 26, 29, 191n25, 274n7, 381–82. *See also* California Trail; boats; ships

Uaua, William H., assists FAH in Lahaina, 112–13; baptized and ordained, 81; importance to mission, 135, 148; leaves Mormonism, 165, 400, 409, 412; moral transgressions, 116; ordained, 91, 135; performs baptisms, 95; rebaptized, 116; skill in preaching, 113, 115
United Order, *see* farming, communal effort; gathering place, private vs. common good
Utah War, Brigham Young letter on, 413; causes recall of missionaries, 409–10, 414; diplomatic impact in Hawaii, 460–61; FAH involvement in, 404; impact on LDS demographics, 468; Walter M. Gibson interest in, 416

vaccinations, *see* smallpox

Waiehu, 83–84, 88, 101, 104, 106, 110, 263, 275; FAH moves family to, 87
Wailua, Kaua'i, 214, 435; Maui, 67, 74, 76–77, 79, 217, 285, 371–72
Wailuku, 62, 168, 178, 181, 217; apostasy at, 220–21; Book of Mormon translated at, 87, 89, 100, 118, 157, 167; FAH speaks at, 88, 274–75, 302, 350–51; George Q. Cannon speaks at, 120; healings at, 93; highest concentration of Mormons, 137; Jonathan Napela's residence at, 63, 67, 80–81, 306, 349; Joseph F.

Smith speaks at, 319; mass baptisms at, 81; mentally ill elder at, 309, 312; mission conferences, 91, 106, 109, 132–33, 178–79, 284–85, 331, 418, 428; "nei" (beloved), 285; "pioneers" from, 264, 272–73, 276, 313; residents vaccinated, 150
West, Chauncey W., 429, 447, 470–71
West, John A., 302, 348, 351
whaling, accidents, 10, 12; Christmas on whaleship, 7; competition among ships, 6; danger, 6; description of killing/harvesting, 6–8, 10–11; overhunting, 5; process of chasing, 5, 8–9, 12; right versus sperm, 5; use of contents of whale's head, 7
wheat, 296, 310, 322, 328, 346–47, 360, 373, 401
White, John, employed by FAH, 19, 25
Whitney, Orson K., arrival in Hawaii, 302, 362, 381
Whittle, Thomas, 51–54; called to Hawaii, 48; chosen as assistant to president, 50; killed in Utah, 55
Winchester, John, 76, 108, 123, 146, 180–81, 194, 202, 333; baptized, 78; called as branch president, 87–88; married to Hawaiian wife, 14; ordained, 82; runs away with Diana Gaston, 373, 399
Winchester, Louisa, 14, 78, 373; house of, 76, 88,
wine, 7, 43, 211, 308, 333, 349, 419, 469
women, administer healing blessings, 301, 376; convert to Mormonism, 67, 116, 118–19, 137; keep house, 301, 330, 336; nurse the sick, 193–94, 397; raise children, 202, 210, 305, 316–17, 365n5; serve as teachers, 25, 120, 223, 467, 472; sew, 79, 89, 92–93, 112, 234, 238, 302, 370, 375; show hospitality, 251, 321, 348, 375, 379–80; socialize, 208–09, 470; subservience to men, 120, 241, 385. *See also* Kaahumanu, queen mother; midwifery; missionary wives; native Hawaiian wives; plural wives
Woodbury, Elvira, 26, 92, 94, 320–21; arrives in Hawaii, 79, delayed in journey to Hawaii, 29; Jane Lewis's sister, 300, 367; returns to California, 111; sickness, 109; teaches natives, 79
Woodbury, John S., 26; assigned to Lahaina, 72; authorized to leave Hawaii, 305, 355, 363; begins mission, 26; called on second mission, 405; compiles hymns, 181; conference president, 180, 247; departure delayed, 320; mission changed to Sandwich Islands, 29; named counselor in presidency, 408; opens English school, 408; photo, 28; speaks in tongues, 95, 110, 167–68, 249, 357
Word of Wisdom, 194, 276, 290, 333, 337, 401; difficulty for Hawaiians, 64, 117–18, 137, 173, 350, 399–400; FAH thoughts on, 290, 323; Jonathan Napela preaches on, 117; nearly forces FAH to resign position, 402n11; status of tobacco, 360–61, 432. *See also* food, tea; tobacco; wine
Wyllie, Robert Crichton, assists FAH, 434, 437–38, 460–61; importance in Hawaii, 434n2

Young, Brigham, ambivalence about Hawaiian mission, 426; angry at San Bernardino colonists, 27; approves of Laie purchase, 442–43; approves press for California, 312; calls FAH as president, 429; calls missionaries home, 21, 56, 409–10; calls missionaries to gold fields, 47; calls Walter Murray Gibson, 416, 421; close to George Q. Cannon, 169, 207; communicates with FAH in code, 457; counsel on gathering, 203, 220, 237, 241–42, 248–49, 263; creates alternative gathering, 170, 220; letter to

Kamehameha V, 450; photo, 28; racial views, 56
Young, John R., 387, 427, 429, 432; arrival in Hawaii, 280; assigned to Kaua'i, 282; debates John Hyde, 398n6; sent to investigate Walter Gibson, 421, 424; success with language, 283

ABOUT THE AUTHOR

JOHN J. HAMMOND holds B.S. and M.A. degrees from Brigham Young University and a Ph.D. from SUNY (State University of New York) at Buffalo. Having taught political science and philosophy at Kent State University in Ohio for thirty-five years, he retired in 2007; for the past sixteen years he has enjoyed what he refers to as a second career in Mormon history. He is the author of a multi-volume series, *Quest for the New Jerusalem: A Mormon Generational Saga*, and a forthcoming companion to the current biography, *Desert Sojourn: The San Juan Mission of Francis A. Hammond, 1885–1900*.

"The story of Francis Hammond provides a fascinating lens into the world of the nineteenth-century Pacific. As a crossroad for commerce, empire-building and evangelism, Hawaii represented a small but vital piece of the Mormon aspiration to bring the gospel to all lands, and Hammond's life work, so precisely detailed in this biography, greatly enriches our understanding of the earliest years of this venture, both its successes and failures. This is an honest and indispensable contribution to the history of Mormon missionary work." —LAURIE F. MAFFLY-KIPP, Archer Alexander Distinguished Professor in the Humanities, Washington University at St. Louis; co-editor with Reid Neilson of *Proclamation to the People: Nineteenth-century Mormonism and the Pacific Basin Frontier*

"This engagingly written examination of Francis Asbury Hammond's life provides an intimate, personal perspective on the first decades of the LDS Hawaiian Mission. It is grounded in solid scholarship and an array of primary sources, and considerably broadens our understanding of the mission's successes, failures, and challenges. It is an important addition to the growing literature on Mormonism in Oceania." –J. MATTHEW KESTER, University Archivist and Associate Professor of History, Brigham Young University–Hawaii; author, *Remembering Iosepa: History, Place, and Religion in the American West*

"John J. Hammond has produced a delightfully candid account of his ancestor Frank Hammond's mission to Hawaii. Family histories are too often triumphant and congratulatory. Hammond's story is anything but, as he casts a critical eye over both the religious and cultural colonization of a people and the ethnocentrism that allowed for it. Brutally honest in recounting the fraught nature of these nineteenth-century cross-cultural encounters, Hammond's work is informed and fresh." —GINA MAREE COLVIN, Lecturer in Cultural Studies, University of Canterbury; co-author with Joanna Brooks of *Decolonizing Mormonism*

"*Island Adventures* is a fascinating examination of the whaler-turned-evangelist's survival, with George Q. Cannon and Joseph F. Smith, of the tragedies and triumphs of their Hawaiian outreach. The adventures are myriad, involving shipwrecks, a smallpox epidemic, threats from outsiders, and tension from within the mission brotherhood itself. At the heart of the story is Frank's conversion to Mormonism and adaptation to Hawaiian customs. In placing the smallest details within a larger context, the author has made a significant contribution to Mormon studies." —NATHANIEL R. RICKS, recipient of the 2008 Mormon History Association Best Thesis Award; editor of *My Candid Opinion: The Sandwich Islands Diaries of Joseph F. Smith*

"John Hammond offers new insights into the mid-nineteenth-century Mormon missionary struggle to establish an Anglo-American church among indigenous Hawaiians. His views are gleaned in particular from the full and honest journals of his missionary ancestor, Francis Hammond. From that pioneering diarist's record, the charismatic experiences, cultural connections, conflicts (internal and external), compromises, successes, and failures of the first turbulent Hawaiian mission are interpreted anew. The descendant–scholar has achieved empathy and critique in equal measure." —IAN G. BARBER, Associate Professor, Department of Anthropology and Archaeology, University of Otago; author of "Matakite, Mormon Conversions, and Māori–Israelite Identity Work in Colonial New Zealand" in the *Journal of Mormon History*